This volume is the first part of a project designed to meet the long-felt need for a new edition of the Chester Mystery Cycle, one of the four extant cycles which evidence the literary and dramatic qualities of the medieval Corpus Christi plays. The present volume presents Text and significant Variant Readings based upon completely new transcriptions of the eight manuscripts which attest the Cycle, and makes available for the first time full descriptions of the manuscripts and a comparative assessment of their value as individual texts. A second volume, the 'Commentary', will follow in due course.

The Society's device on the front of the jacket is a reproduction of the Alfred Jewel which was found near Athelney in Somerset in 1693 and is now preserved in the Ashmolean Museum, Oxford.

THE
CHESTER MYSTERY
CYCLE

VOLUME I · TEXT

EARLY ENGLISH TEXT SOCIETY

S.S. 3

1974

The Cappers playe:

Incipit pagina quinta de Moyses & de lege sibi data:/

Deus ad Moysen /

Moyses my servant leeffe and deare
and all my people that binne heare
yee wotten in Egipte when yee weare
   out of thraldome I you brought
I will you have noe god but mee
noe false gode none make yee
my name in vayne name not yee
   for that liketh mee nought
I will you hould your holydaye
and worshippe yt eke alwaye
father and mother all ye maye
   and slea not man nor wheere
fformication yee shall flee
noe meanes goods steale yee
noe false witnes for to beare
your neighbours wyffe desyre you nought
servantes nor goode that hee hath bought
love now alsoe in deede not thought
   nor nothinge that is his
I now wrongefully to have his thinge
agaynst this love and his likinge
In all these keepe my byddinge
   that yee doe not amisse /

Moyses

Good lorde that art ever soe good
I will fulfill thy mylde moode
thy commandemente for I stood
   to here thee none full styll
fowrty dayes now fasted have I
that I might thee the more worthye
to lerne this token truly
   nowe wyll I worke thy will

Tunc Moyses in monte dicat populo:/

Good folke dread yee nought
to prove you with god hath this wrought
take theese wordes in your thought
   none knowne yee what yt binne
By this sight nowe yee may see
that god is pleasied of poste
therfore love this token trulye doe yee
   therof that yee ne blynne

Lector

Lordinges this commandemente
was the first lawe that ever god sent
in poyntes shall hime take intent
   that most esserte ys in

Deus

Moyses my servaunte life so dere'
and all the people that be here
you wott in Egypte when you were
out of thralldome I you broughte .

I wyll you honour no God saue me
ne Mawmentrye none make yee
my name in vayne myn not yee
for that me lykes noughte .

I will you hold yo[r] holy daye'
and worshipp also by all waye'
father and mother all that you maye
and slaye no man ne where

Fornication you shall flee'
no mens goodes steale yee
ne in no place abyde ne bee,
false wytnes for to beare

Your neightboures wyves covettes noughte
servant ne good that he hath boughte
Oxe ne Asse in deede ne thoughte .
nor any thinge that is his

Ne wrongefullie to haue his thinge
agayne his will and his lykinge
in all these doe my byddinge
that you doe not amisse

Tunc princeps Sinagoga (statuet e[n] in loco et quasi pro populo
loquitur ad d[eu]m e[t] Moysen

princeps Sinagoga .

Ah good Lord much of mighte
thou comes w[i]th so great lighte
we bene so afrayde of this sighte
no man dar speak ne talke

God is so grym w[i]th vs to deale   Tunc Moyses (stant super
but Moyses mas[ter] w[i]th vs thou mele   montem loquatur ad popu-
els we dyen many and feele   lum
so afrayde bene all wee

Moyses .

Gods folke drede you noughte'
to prove you w[i]th, God hath this wronght
to make you afrayd in deede and thonghte .
aye for to avoyde synne'

By ~ this sight you may now see'
that he is perves of postye'
therfore his teachinge looke none yee
thereof that yon not blyn .

II. British Museum MS. Harley 2124, f. 23[v]

THE CHESTER
MYSTERY CYCLE

EDITED BY

R. M. LUMIANSKY

AND

DAVID MILLS

Published for
THE EARLY ENGLISH TEXT SOCIETY
by the
OXFORD UNIVERSITY PRESS
LONDON NEW YORK TORONTO
1974

ISBN 0 19 722403 2

Printed in Great Britain
at the University Press, Oxford
by Vivian Ridler
Printer to the University

CONTENTS

PREFACE   vii

INTRODUCTION   ix

BIBLIOGRAPHY   xli

TEXT (The titles here given for the plays are editorial choices.
For the titles as they appear in H, see Textual Notes)

    I. The Fall of Lucifer—The Tanners   1

    II. Adam and Eve; Cain and Abel—The Drapers   13

    III. Noah's Flood—The Waterleaders and Drawers of Dee   42

    IV. Abraham, Lot, and Melchysedeck; Abraham and Isaac—
        The Barbers   56

    V. Moses and the Law; Balaack and Balaam—The Cappers   79

    VI. The Annunciation and the Nativity—The Wrights   97

    VII. The Shepherds—The Painters   125

    VIII. The Three Kings—The Vintners   156

    IX. The Offerings of the Three Kings—The Mercers   175

    X. The Slaughter of the Innocents—The Goldsmiths   185

    XI. The Purification; Christ and the Doctors—The Blacksmiths   204

    XII. The Temptation; the Woman Taken in Adultery—The
        Butchers   217

    XIII. The Blind Chelidonian; the Raising of Lazarus—The Glovers   230

    XIV. Christ at the House of Simon the Leper; Christ and the
        Money-lenders; Judas' Plot—The Corvisors   251

    XV. The Last Supper; the Betrayal of Christ—The Bakers   268

    XVI. The Trial and Flagellation—The Fletchers, Bowyers,
        Coopers, and Stringers   284

   XVIA. The Passion—The Ironmongers   303

    XVII. The Harrowing of Hell—The Cooks   325

  XVIII. The Resurrection—The Skinners   339

    XIX. Christ on the Road to Emmaus; Doubting Thomas—The
        Saddlers   356

xx. The Ascension—The Tailors 369
xxi. Pentecost—The Fishmongers 378
xxii. The Prophets of Antichrist—The Clothworkers 396
xxiii. Antichrist—The Dyers 408
xxiv. The Last Judgement—The Websters 438

APPENDICES:

ıA 'The Raven-and-Dove Scene' from Play III in H 464
ıB Play V in H 466
ıC The Final Section of Play XVIA in H 481
ıD The Final Scene of Play XVIII in H and R 486
ııA Manuscript M, The Manchester Fragment of 'The Resurrection' (Play XVIII) 490
ııB Manuscript P, The Peniarth 'Antichrist' (Play XXIII) 491
ııC Manuscript C, The Chester 'Trial and Flagellation' (Play XVI) 517

TEXTUAL NOTES 533

PLATES
1. MS. Huntington 2, f. 27ᵛ *frontispiece*
11. British Museum, MS. Harley 2124, f. 23ᵛ *facing frontispiece*

PREFACE

THE purpose of this volume is to present an accurate and somewhat regularized version of what we consider the best extant text
of the Chester Mystery Cycle, together with the significant Variant
Readings from the other four extant cyclic manuscripts, and the
full texts of the one small fragment and two complete single-play
manuscripts. Our definitions of 'best' and 'significant' and the
explanation of our editorial treatment of the material are set out
in the Introduction. The volume also contains descriptions of the
eight manuscripts, and Textual Notes.

A second volume, presenting analyses of the Text and ancillary
material helpful for a full understanding of the Text, is in prepara-
tion. It will include the explanatory notes and glossary; a checklist
of relevant manuscripts; an edition of the Banns using a hitherto
unpublished version of Rogers's *Breviary*; and discussions of
such matters as history, sources, and manuscript relationships for
the Cycle. We also intend to bring out in the future facsimiles
of the other Cycle-manuscripts similar to that for Bodley 175
(see Bibliography), and a modern English version of the Cycle
based on this volume.

In preparing the present volume we first made new transcriptions of all the manuscripts from photographs and microfilms,
which we then compared with earlier editions. The proof-read
final typescript was checked directly against each of the manuscripts. We divided the work more or less equally between us,
with each of us checking every segment of the other's work.
Although we have tried to ensure that the material in this volume
is accurate, it is possible that some errors remain. If such errors
become apparent in the course of our work on Volume II, we will
include a list of them in that volume.

Our work with the manuscripts has taken us, sometimes singly
and sometimes together, for visits of varying lengths of time, to the
Bodleian Library, the Chester City Archives, the Henry E.
Huntington Library, the Manchester Public Libraries, the National
Library of Wales, and the Students' Room of the British Museum.
We are indebted to the officials of these institutions for permission

to use their manuscripts and for the courtesies which they have shown to us. We are, also, indebted to the Huntington Library and to the Trustees of the British Museum for permission to reproduce parts of their manuscripts as plates. We are further grateful to the Curators of the Bodleian Library and the Librarian and staff of the Harold Cohen Library of the University of Liverpool for allowing the Bodley manuscript to be placed on loan at Liverpool. We are particularly indebted to the Coopers' Guild of Chester for permission to use their copy of the 'Trial and Flagellation' (Play XVI). We have received assistance on details in the description of the manuscripts which is acknowledged at the appropriate points in the Introduction. Unfortunately, because of a shortage of staff and facilities the British Museum was unable to provide such verification. For help with the several French passages in the Cycle, we wish to express appreciation to Professor Ruth J. Dean and Professor William Roach of the University of Pennsylvania, and to Dr. G. S. Burgess and Dr. J. Linskill of the University of Liverpool.

In addition, we wish to express our appreciation of other assistance given to us in our work on this volume. R. M. Lumiansky received a grant-in-aid from the University of Pennsylvania for the purchase of photographs of the manuscripts, research leave for a semester from that University, and a Fellowship from the John Simon Guggenheim Memorial Foundation. David Mills received research grants and a travel grant from the University of Liverpool, a grant from the American Philosophical Society to enable him to visit the Henry E. Huntington Library, and a subsistence grant from the Huntington Library. He has also received assistance from the Department of English Language at the University of Liverpool in the purchase of microfilm and towards the cost of postage. We wish to acknowledge the expert typing assistance given by Mrs. Doris Skalaroff and by Mrs. Joy Mills. We are especially grateful to Dr. P. O. E. Gradon for generous assistance with many problems connected with this volume.

Finally, we should like to dedicate this volume to our wives, Janet and Joy.

THE EDITORS

INTRODUCTION

I. THE MANUSCRIPTS

EIGHT manuscripts which present some or most of the Chester
Mystery Cycle are known. They are, in chronological order:

1. M   Manchester Fragment; MS. 822. 11c2   15th century (?)
2. P   Peniarth 399   *c.* 1500 (?)
3. Hm Huntington 2   1591
4. A   Additional 10305   1592
5. C   Chester Coopers' Guild   1599
6. R   Harley 2013   1600
7. B   Bodley 175   1604
8. H   Harley 2124   1607

Descriptions of these manuscripts follow below. (See also Textual
Notes in this volume.) Among the eight manuscripts, Hm, A, R,
B, and H are the five cyclic versions; M is a brief fragment of
Play XVIII ('The Resurrection'); P presents the whole of Play
XXIII ('Antichrist'); and C presents the whole of Play XVI
('The Trial and Flagellation').

M: This manuscript is in the Manchester Central Library, St.
Peter's Square, Manchester. Bound with it are communications
from F. J. Furnivall and W. W. Greg. A postcard from Furnivall,
dated 26/4/–83, contains his identification of the manuscript for C.
W. Sutton, then Chief Librarian of Manchester, who had sent it to
him, as a part of Play XVIII. Here is the earliest reference to M.
The earliest public notice of M is apparently that in *The Academy*
for 5 May 1883, referring to it as 'part of an old book-cover'. The
manuscript had seemingly been found in the binding of a book,
but the Library has no information about the date or circumstances
of the discovery. The volume in which M is bound bears a
catalogue stamp of 7 April 1924; the present calf binding dates
from 18 August 1959. In 1935 Greg suggested that M may be the
lost parchment fragment described in the 1808 Catalogue of
Harley manuscripts as once partially covering Harley 1950.[1]
    The manuscript is a single leaf of vellum, roughly trimmed at
the top and sides and torn across the bottom, leaving the right side
slightly longer than the left. Its size is $7\frac{1}{16}$–$7\frac{5}{16}$ inches in length by

[1] *Chester Play Studies*, pp. 87–8.

$6\frac{1}{5}$–$6\frac{3}{5}$ inches in width. The verso layout shows that the scribe would have required about two inches to complete the lost eight lines, so that the total length would have been about nine inches.

Lines 1–8 are in Italian script, with the remainder of the text in imitation of black-letter type; probably all is by one scribe now unknown. Red ink was used for the Play-heading and for the A of *And* at 41. The speeches of Pilate and Cayphas are divided by a red-ink line. *Heare Beegy* is in capitals with large decorated initial letters; *Per* (1) and *Yee* (9) are also in capitals with large decorated initials. No rulings are visible. Stanzas are separated by a single-line space, and a somewhat larger gap separates the French from the English after line 8. Every fourth line is indented by about 1–$1\frac{1}{2}$ inches, and line 10 is indented by $\frac{3}{10}$ inch. All lines have initial capitals except 30 and 34. Speech-headings are centred and have initial capitals. The leaf is not numbered.

The manuscript is in very poor condition. It is heavily stained at the right side; towards the bottom of the page the stain extends inward and becomes heavier, progressively obscuring the text toward the bottom right corner. On 1ᵛ there is apparently a crease along the length of line 22; the area below the crease is stained and worn, with particularly heavy staining at the edges. Many words have been worn away, with the result that a number of readings are faint and some are visible only on an infra-red photograph. Previous editors recorded more readings than we could see, which may indicate a continuing deterioration of the manuscript. Opinions about dating vary from the fifteenth to the early seventeenth century; supporters of a later date regard the black-letter script as a late imitation. The manuscript seems to have been carefully written. The form of the title and the absence of a play-number and a Guild-ascription suggest that the manuscript may have been copied for the content of the Play and was not intended as a guild- or acting-text. Possibly the large space between *the* and *Pagent* in the Play-heading occurs because the manuscript being copied read *the XVIIIᵗʰ Pagent*.

P: This manuscript is in the National Library of Wales, Aberystwyth.[1] Although designated Hg by E. K. Chambers (*Mediaeval Stage*, ii. 407), it was given the symbol P by W. W. Greg in his

---

[1] We are indebted to the National Library of Wales for providing many details of this description.

edition of 1935.[1] The manuscript was owned by Robert Vaughan of Hengwrt (d. 1667) and is apparently referred to in a catalogue of his library that he compiled some time after 1658: 'A treatise dialogwise in English between Antixt, Enoc and Elyas, and many more. MS.' In the catalogue of the Hengwrt manuscripts published by Aneurin Owen in 1843 but compiled in or before 1824, the manuscript is given the number 229. The Hengwrt-Peniarth manuscripts were bought in reversion by Sir John Williams, Bart., in 1904 and presented by him to the National Library of Wales in 1909. Inside the front cover, this manuscript has a bookplate bearing Sir John Williams' name and the date 1909.

The twentieth-century binding by the National Library is brown morocco leather. It contains eleven paper folios at the start and ten at the end, with the ten folios containing the Play in the middle. The vellum wrapper described by Greg has not been preserved. There is one set of old sewing holes. Folio x contains a label in the hand of Richard Llwyd, who catalogued the Hengwrt library in 1806, to which has been added the number 229 by Aneurin Owen. Folio xi contains a letter of 1869 by W. M. Wood to F. J. Furnivall identifying the Play.

The Play is written on parchment. According to the National Library, measurements are c. 280 by c. 175 mm. (approximately 11 inches by $6\frac{9}{10}$ inches), and gatherings are 1^4, 2^6. The manuscript has been cropped at the top and sides, partially removing some letters. At some time it was also folded lengthwise down the centre.

P is written in one hand and usually assigned on palaeographic evidence to the end of the fifteenth century. The writing is Secretary hand with some Anglicana features. It is written in pale brown ink, with headings, speech-headings, and stage-directions underlined in red. Initial letters of lines are stroked with red. Speech-headings are centred and quatrain-division is marked usually by a paragraph-sign to the left; there are no rulings or indentations. There are no running titles or catchwords, and no decorations. The pages have been numbered on recto 1, 3, 5, etc. through 19; the final verso is numbered 20. This pagination is in the hand of Dr. J. Gwenogvryn Evans who examined the Peniarth Library at the end of the nineteenth century and compiled a report on the Welsh manuscripts in the collection for the Historical Manuscripts Commission.

[1] All references are to the description of P in W. W. Greg's *The Play of Antichrist from the Chester Cycle* (Oxford, 1935), pp. xx–xxii.

In sixteenth-century hands there are undeciphered marks on folio 7ʳ that possibly represent a person's name, and on folio 10ᵛ *yowrek*. The text has also been touched up in black ink, where faded, at some points and there are occasional conjectured readings and additional directions in the margin, all assigned to sixteenth-century hands. The whole manuscript has also been re-inked by a modern restorer whom Greg confidently asserts to have been F. J. Furnivall. On occasion this restorer makes the original illegible, and it seems that he referred to MS. A or Wright's edition and sometimes attempted to reconstruct forms evidenced by A which P apparently did not possess. In the Textual Notes we have not attempted to distinguish these hands.

The leaves of the manuscript are markedly rubbed, but there is little other notable damage.

It is difficult to assess the purpose for which the manuscript was written, although it has been claimed to be a producer's copy or acting text.

Hm: This manuscript is in the Henry E. Huntington Library and Art Gallery, San Marino, California 91108. It was formerly designated *D* because it was owned by the Duke of Devonshire. Because of its present home, *Hm* for *Huntington manuscript* now seems more appropriate.

The manuscript was written mostly by a single scribe. On the final page appears 'By me Edward Gregorie scholler at Bunburye the yeare of our lord god 1591'.[1] We do not know who Edward Gregorie was—he is not included in the Oxford and Cambridge lists as a scholar. Bunbury, however, is a village in Cheshire some 11 miles south-east of Chester. In three passages, each probably by a different hand, the writing shifts from that of the main scribe: V. 160–71, VI. 83–108, and XXII. 288. On the final page of the manuscript the name of Richard Gregorie occurs, but the writing is not similar to that in any one of the three passages. Who Richard Gregorie was, we do not know. Plays II–XXIV are in English Secretary hand; to these were added a copy of the Banns and of Play I in a nineteenth-century hand; these late folios are discussed in Textual Notes.

The Huntington Library acquired the manuscript as a part of

[1] F. M. Salter's view that Gregorie was not the scribe—*RES*, xv (1939), 443—seems unconvincing.

the Kemble–Devonshire collection of plays. In 1912 the ninth Duke of Devonshire sent the collection from Chatsworth, Derbyshire, to Sotheby's for sale. In early 1914 a prospectus was issued in London with the title *Chatsworth Library Kemble–Devonshire Collection of English Plays and Play-bills*. Our manuscript is listed in this prospectus. Henry E. Huntington, through the agency of George D. Smith, bought the whole collection in 1914; consequently, no auction was held.

The sixth Duke of Devonshire had purchased a collection of plays in 1821 from John Kemble, and had subsequently added to that collection with the advice of J. P. Collier. Neither the catalogue of the 'Kemble Plays' made a few years before the sale to Henry E. Huntington and still at Chatsworth, nor the *Catalogue of the Chatsworth Library* made by Sir James Lacaita and printed privately in 1879 includes mention of a manuscript of the Chester Cycle. There is, however, at Chatsworth a catalogue of the 'Kemble Plays' compiled by Percy Simpson in 1906 which includes the following item:

CHESTER PLAYS   24 Scriptural Dramas
formerly represented at Chester   (Manuscript)   1600

Obviously, Simpson listed the date as *1600* rather than *1591* because the first of the nineteenth-century folios, copied from Harley 2013 (R), has *1600* beside its folio-heading. Simpson's entry makes clear that our manuscript was a part of the 'Kemble Plays' before Henry E. Huntington bought it. Further, J. P. Collier had used the manuscript in the Duke of Devonshire's library in 1836, fifteen years after the purchase of the 'Kemble Plays' by the sixth Duke. The binding of the manuscript has been dated '*c.* 1832' and matches that of the other Kemble–Devonshire volumes. On the spine of this binding one finds 'PLAYS/VOL. 10' with the Devonshire crest stamped below. Thus we can be confident that our manuscript was a part of the collection which the sixth Duke purchased from John Kemble, or that it was added to the collection within the next decade.

The earlier history of the manuscript is uncertain. On 41ʳ the name 'John Egerton esq' appears in a seventeenth-century hand. The Egertons were an important Cheshire family,[1] and the first

¹ Concerning this family, see James Croston, *County Families of Lancashire and Cheshire* (1887), chapter II.

three Earls of Bridgewater were named John Egerton. Their dates are 1579–1649, 1622–86, and 1646–1701. It is possible that our manuscript was in the possession of this family.

A curious event occurred in the more recent history of the manuscript. In the Introduction to the first volume (1892) of the EETS edition of the Cycle, Hermann Deimling reported that neither Lady Louisa Egerton nor the housekeeper at Devonshire House could find this manuscript for his use. But, in a note on the first page of the Introduction to the edition, Furnivall stated that the manuscript 'is still in the Duke's hands'. Perhaps the manuscript was not found for Deimling because it had been bound as volume 10 of the 'Kemble Plays' and thus was not immediately identifiable as an early manuscript.

The manuscript consists of 145 early paper folios, preceded by 12 nineteenth-century paper folios. The folios measure $11\frac{1}{2}$ inches by $7\frac{3}{4}$ inches. None of the folios is damaged. A series of sewing-holes is visible about half an inch from the paper-fold for the binding. Throughout the ink is black. The early folios are watermarked throughout by a pot similar to Briquet 12793 (1583) and 12794 (1591) and to Heawood 3576.[1] Some of the nineteenth-century leaves are watermarked 'J. Green 1829'. There are thirteen quires: 1^{12} (nineteenth-century), 1^{12} (leaves 1–5), 2^{14}, 3–12^{12}, 13^{4}. No signatures occur, and catchwords are not used. Each play begins on a fresh page.

Full horizontal rulings usually separate speeches and stage directions, and shorter rulings are frequently placed under fourth lines. No decorations or folio-headings appear. Speech-headings are centred. Each fourth line is indented about half an inch, and each first line of the four-line groupings begins with a capital. The handwriting is clear; difficult readings seldom occur.

The pages of the manuscript show signs of considerable use. Presumably the manuscript was prepared as a reading-text rather than as a central record for the city archives or as an acting-text.[2]

A: This manuscript is in the British Museum. Formerly it was

---

[1] C. M. Briquet, *Les Filigranes* (1907); E. Heawood, *Watermarks* (1950).

[2] For important parts of our description of Hm we are indebted to H. C. Schulz, former Curator of Manuscripts at the Huntington Library; to T. S. Wragg, Librarian and Keeper, Devonshire Collections, Chatsworth Settlement; and to Jean F. Preston, the present Curator of Manuscripts at the Huntington Library.

designated *W* because Thomas Wright was its first editor, but *A*
for *Additional* seems to us a more appropriate designation. The
name of George Bellin as scribe and the date 1592 occur at the end
of each play. Bellin served for nearly thirty years as scribe of the
Coopers' Guild in Chester; he also did similar work for the Ironmongers and for the Cappers and Pinners.[1] The manuscript contains only the plays; neither the Proclamation nor the Banns is
included.

The British Museum bought the manuscript for £16. 1s. 6d.
on Friday, 12 February 1836, the third day of Part 11 of the sale
by R. H. Evans of Richard Heber's enormous library.[2] The third
front flyleaf of the bound manuscript has the note 'Purchased Feb.
1836. Heber's Sale. Lot 497'. When and how Heber acquired the
manuscript does not seem to have been recorded. On the second
front flyleaf, however, are pasted two bookplates with coats of
arms. The upper is inscribed 'William Cowper of Colne, Esqr.
1728', and the lower 'Thomas Cowper Esqr. Overlegh'. Colne is
in Lancashire and Overlegh in Cheshire. Why these bookplates
are here is not clear, but the Cowper family was important in
Cheshire history and this William was a collector of Cheshire
antiquities, as well as mayor of Chester.[3] Thus we may speculate
that William gained possession of the manuscript in Chester, that
it passed to his nephew Thomas after his death in 1767, and that
Richard Heber, who started collecting at an early age, acquired it
after Thomas's death in 1788 and kept the bookplates with the
manuscript.

The manuscript consists of 168 paper folios, 11 inches by 7
inches. It is damaged at both the beginning and the end. No
folios seem lost at the beginning, although the possibility exists
that originally the Banns may have preceded the plays. Two folios
containing the last 96 lines of XXIV are missing at the end; the
corners of numerous leaves are also damaged, seemingly by

---

[1] See F. M. Salter, 'The Banns of the Chester Plays', *RES*, xv (1939), 436,
n. 2. He may be the George Bellin, ironmonger, who was clerk to Holy Trinity
Church, Chester, and died in July 1624.

[2] *Bibliotheca Heberiana: Catalogue of the Library of the late Richard Heber
Esq.* The copy of this catalogue in the British Museum includes sale-prices
written beside each item. Greg mistakenly gave the price as £16. 16s. 0d.
(*Bibliographical and Textual Problems*, p. 34).

[3] See George Ormerod, *History of Chester*, second edition revised by Thomas
Helsby (1882), i. 375–6, and *DNB*, 'Thomas Cowper, 1701–1767'.

crumbling of the paper. The extent to which readings of the text are missing is indicated in Variant Readings. The damaged leaves have been very skilfully strengthened and repaired. Since the *Bibliotheca Heberiana*, in its description of the manuscript, mentions the damage but not the repair, the assumption is that the latter was done by the British Museum. The edges of the leaves have been cropped; as a result rulings were at times cut away. The third and inner front flyleaf, which has the inner back flyleaf as conjugate, bears the watermark 'SE & CO 1818'. The first front flyleaf, of heavier paper, has '10,305' stamped upon it. The second front flyleaf is the same paper as the first; thus the Cowper bookplates were presumably pasted to it when the manuscript was bound. The binding is black leather and board, with 'Chester Pageants', 'Brit. Mus.', and 'Additional MS. 10,305' stamped in gold on the spine. The Museum's record shows that the present binding was done in 1912.

Two watermarks appear in the manuscript. The first is a pot with one handle, and the second a pot with two handles.[1] Neither of the two watermarks matches examples in Briquet or Heawood. No signatures appear. The quiring in the manuscript seems to be 1^8, $2-3^6$, $4-6^8$, 7^6, 8^{12}, 9^6, 10^8, 11^4, 12^{12}, $13-14^6$, 15^{12}, 16^8, 17^{10}, $18-19^{12}$, 20^{10}.

Double rulings occur at each side of the text. Double-rulings—at times triple—occur at the foot of the text, and multiple rulings—usually six—separate opening Guild-ascriptions and Play-headings from the text. Speech-headings are centred; they and stage directions are set off by triple rulings, usually with elaborate finials. Speech-headings, stage directions, and Latin texts are usually red. Guild-ascriptions are used as folio-headings on both recto and verso. No indication of division into stanzas, or into quatrains within stanzas, is given. Catchwords do not occur. In general, only the first letter of the first word in opening lines of speeches is capitalized. Each play begins on a fresh page and is numbered to the left of the Guild-ascriptions in Arabic numerals. The number for II has been lost through damage to the manu-

---

[1] The first occurs on folios : , 3, 5, 7, 9, 11, 19, 26, 29, 30, 32, 33, 34, 35, 36, 37, 43, 45, 46, 47, 48, 49, 54, 56, 58, 60, 61, 62, 64, 65, 69, 70, 71, 74, 75, 76, 77, 81, 82, 83, 87, 88, 89, 92, 94, 95, 148, 153, 155, 159, 160, 161, 163, 165, 166, 167, and 168. The second occurs on folios 99, 100, 101, 102, 105, 106, 113, 114, 116, 118, 121, 122, 123, 125, 129, 130, 132, 134, 136, 138, 141, 142, 143, and 145. The folio-numbering here is that of the later series; see Textual Notes.

script, those for VII and XVII are omitted, and there is no number against XVIA.

Bellin's handwriting in this manuscript is not particularly difficult to read, although a reader gains the impression that the manuscript was copied out rather hastily and at times carelessly. His purpose would seem to have been to provide a reading-version rather than an acting-text.

C: This manuscript is owned by the Coopers' Company of the city of Chester and contains Play XVI, 'The Trial and Flagellation'. The manuscript was discovered by F. M. Salter who designated it C.[1] The Coopers were one of the guilds responsible for the presentation of this Play and one assumes that this copy has remained in their possession since 1599. It is bound in an Apprentice Book—'the Booke of the Inrowlmente, bought by the consent of the Fletchers, Bowyers, Coopers and Stringers of the Cittie of Chester, written the xiiithe day of January in the yeare of our lorde God anno domini 1597', as the entry at the start of the book reads. The list of enrolments runs from 29th January 1597 to 13th January 1776, although some pages are blank and some are out of chronological order. The book has a leather cover, and the whole was bound in October 1962; a modern ink inscription on the leather cover is also embossed on the modern binding and reads *Apprentice Book 1597 and Passion Play 1597 (and* is omitted on the modern binding). The contents of the book show at least three gatherings and the whole has apparently been repaired on occasion. After the 36th leaf there is a vellum sheet which forms a cover for the section of the book containing the Play, the last section of the book. A similar vellum page is at the end of the play-section, before the leather binding. Within this section are twelve leaves: the first and last each contains a sentence neatly written out at the top and copied repeatedly in the rest of the page by a less expert hand, and the penultimate page is blank. The Play occupies the remaining nine leaves. It is possible that the Play was copied independently and bound in with the book at a later date. After *Finis* there is the following paragraph which accurately dates this copy of the Play:

This booke was written the 22th day of August, 1599, in the one and fortie yeare of the Reigne of our Soveraigne Ladye Elizabeth.

[1] *Chester Play Studies* (1935), pp. 1–73.

Mr. Thomas Lynaker, Cowper, and Thomas Thropp, aldermen of the said Companye; and Richard Powell, Fletcher, and Thomas Waylshe, Cowper,[1] stewards of the saide Companye. Mr Richarde Rathborne, mayor, and Mr. John Brewerwood and Mr. Lewyes Robertes, sheriffes, of the Citie of Chester. 1599.

[1] *Cowper* inserted above line.

The leaves are $11\frac{1}{2}$ by $7\frac{3}{5}$ inches. They are of paper and bear no watermarks in the play-section. They form a single gathering.

The scribe was George Bellin, who also wrote manuscripts A and R. The layout is that of A and R, but there are no running titles, no page-numbers, and only one example of a catchword—*Cayphas* at the foot of 1[r]. Red ink is used for the Guild-ascription, Play-heading, speech-headings, and stage directions. Bellin usually places a red-ink asterisk on either side of each speech-heading, sometimes begins stage directions with a similar asterisk, and makes sporadic use of black asterisks at the end of lines. A double red-ink line marks the left margin, a single black-line the right except on 1[r], where the line is double. A widely-separated double red-ink line with poppy head, from margin to margin, marks the top of the page, and a less widely separated black-ink line with poppy head, from margin to margin, marks the bottom. The Guild-ascription and Play-heading are separated from the text by an elaborate four-line design from margin to margin. Double black lines with poppy heads extending from the left margin approximately $\frac{3}{4}$ of the width of the text mark the speech divisions. The speech-divisions are further marked by line spaces above and below the ruled divisions, and a similar line space separates the speech-headings from the following speeches. The speech-headings are centred. There are no line indentations or stanza-divisions marked.

The manuscript is in excellent condition. It has been carefully set out, neatly written, and has an attractive appearance. It would seem to have been a copy specially prepared for the archives of the performing guilds.

R: This manuscript is in the British Museum as a part of the Randle Holme collection formed in the seventeenth century by four generations of Chester antiquaries, Randle Holme I–IV. Their dates are I, 1571–1655; II, 1601(?)–59; III, 1627–99; IV, ?–1707. After 1707 the collection was bought by Francis Gastrell,

Bishop of Chester, acting for Robert Harley, first Earl of Oxford. In 1753 it was sold to the British Museum; this material now forms volumes 1920–2180 of the Harley manuscripts.[1] The manuscript of the Cycle has at various times been designated *h*, *K*, and *R*: *h* because it is a Harley manuscript and to distinguish it from Harley 2124 (H); *K* arbitrarily to avoid confusion with *H*; and *R* for Randle Holme. *R* seems most appropriate. In addition to the plays, the manuscript includes the Proclamation and the Banns.

There are 205 paper folios, 11½ by 7½ inches. The Proclamation is written vertically upward in a different hand from the remainder upon a small unnumbered leaf immediately preceding folio 1. The Banns cover folios 1–3, and the first play begins on folio 4. The manuscript is bound in tan leather with the coat of arms of the Earl of Oxford on front and back in gold; on the spine 'Chester Playes 1600 E. Coll. R. Holme Mus. Brit. Bibl. Harl. 2013 Plut. XXII. D' is stamped. The British Museum has no record of the date of binding. The manuscript is undamaged and generally in good condition. Nine sewing-holes can be observed.

Five watermarks appear in the manuscript: a coat of arms, a pot with one handle, a pot with two handles, a pot with one handle and a crescent above, and a vase.[2] Only the fourth is closely similar to watermarks in Briquet and Heawood: Briquet 12803 (1526) and Heawood 3583 (1621). No signatures appear. The quiring in the manuscript seems to be 1^3, 2^{14}, 3^{16}, $4-8^{12}$, 9^{14}, 10^{10}, 11^{22}, $12-15^{12}$, 16^{10}, 17^9. Between folios 106 and 107 a leaf has been cut out; the stub is clearly visible. Presumably this leaf was carelessly skipped by the scribe and later cut out. Each play begins on a fresh page.

The manuscript, except for the Proclamation, is written in a single hand, and the writing is generally clear. The name 'George Bellin' occurs at the end of III, XI, XII, XIII, XIV, XVIA, XIX, and XXI; 'George Billings'—presumably a variant of 'Bellin'—occurs at the end of IV. Thus, this manuscript was prepared by

[1] See J. P. Earwaker, *The Four Randle Holmes* (1892), reprinted from the *Journal of the Chester Archaeological and Historic Society*, 1891. See also the sketches of the four Holmes in *DNB*.

[2] The first is on the flyleaf. The second occurs on folios 1, 2, 5, 8, 9, 10, 14, 15, 17, and 18. The third occurs on folios 22–4, 26–9, 31–3, 37, 42, 94, 117–24, 126, 127, 130, 193, 194, 195, 199–202, and 204. The fourth occurs on folios 46, 47, 50, 53, 55–7, 61, 63, 64, 66, 67, 70, 71, 76, 77, 81, 83, 84, 85, 88–91, 141, 143, 150, 152–7, 159, 161, 162, 165, 167–71, 173, 174, 177, 183, 185, 186, and 188. The fifth occurs on folios 95, 96, 97, 101–5, 110, 111, and 112.

the same scribe who prepared A and C. It is difficult to understand why Greg, in comparing A and R, found little resemblance between the two and toyed with the suggestion that both are copies, by different scribes, of an original Bellin-manuscript.[1] Certainly the handwriting in R is smaller, neater, and clearer than that in A; further, R is as a whole more carefully prepared than A. But the formation of the letters seems almost identical in both. It is not hard to believe that the passage of eight years could account for any differences. It is true, however, that A is more decorated as a result of its more frequent use of red ink for speech-headings, stage directions, and Latin texts, of multiple rather than single rulings in many instances, and of larger and more elaborate finials.

Double rulings occur at each side of R's text and at the foot. Multiple rulings set off Guild-ascriptions and Play-headings from the text. Speech-headings are centred. Guild-ascriptions are used as folio-headings, usually on both recto and verso. For the most part, a single ruling occurs after each fourth line, and the first line of each quatrain begins with a capital. There is no indentation. Catchwords are regularly used. Each play is numbered in the margin to the left of the Guild-ascription or Play-heading in Arabic numerals. The numbers for II, III, XV, are omitted, and there is no number against XVIA; XXII is erroneously numbered 21.

We do not know why Bellin chose to prepare a second full version of the Cycle. It seems unlikely that R should be considered an acting-text. Perhaps he was commissioned by a Cheshire family to prepare R, and did so for a fee; the verse which follows XXIV. Finis may represent Bellin's prayer for his patron (see Textual Notes). It is clear, however, from correspondences not found in the other manuscripts that Bellin made considerable use of A in preparing R; but it is also clear—most notably in the final scene of XVIII—that he made important additional use for R of manuscripts other than A. A detailed account of these relationships will be presented in Volume II of this edition.

B: This manuscript is in the Bodleian Library, Oxford. According to the General Catalogue,[2] B was one of fifteen manuscripts given

---

[1] W. W. Greg, *Bibliographical and Textual Problems*, p. 35, and *Antichrist*, p. xvii.

[2] *Summary Catalogue of Western MSS. in the Bodleian Library*, v (Oxford, 1905), pp. 309–10.

to the Library in or shortly before August 1710, by Richard Middleton Massey of Brasenose College, Oxford, at one time Under-Keeper of the Ashmolean Museum, who died in 1743.[1]

The manuscript is bound in a vellum wrapper, much repaired, inside the front of which is an inscription, apparently in a late-seventeenth-century hand:

> Wm. Bedford's twenty-four pageantes or playes played by the twenty-four craftseller (?) of the City of Chester.

The binding measures approximately $7\frac{3}{5}$ by $11\frac{3}{5}$ inches. It has been strengthened by the addition of at least three sheets at the back and front, those at the front being cut away to reveal the inscription. These provide two additional blank leaves at the start and also at the end of the manuscript. The binding also contains 179 paper folios measuring approximately $7\frac{1}{2}$ by $11\frac{1}{2}$ inches. The tightness of the binding makes foliation difficult. The first and last gatherings are set somewhat deeper than the others and the stitching is obscured—it is possible that they have been resewn. Small sections of letters are occasionally lost at the edges, suggesting a later cropping, perhaps to fit the present binding.

Foliation seems to be 1^{13}, $2-4^{16}$, 5^{14}, $6-11^{16}$, 11^{8}. There is a watermark of a pot with one handle on 89 folios[2] which has no exact counterpart in Briquet or Heawood; the remaining folios have no watermark. The folios are numbered in pencil in the top right corner. Folios 1 (repaired) and 177–9 are numbered in a different hand from the others, and this hand has also numbered the first of the two final modern sheets 180 (*ult*). Additionally, some of the early pages are given a folio number in ink in the top right-hand corner, viz. folios 4 (*fol* only visible), 5 (*f* only visible), 7 (bottom of *f* only visible), 9 (*fol* only visible), 10 (*fol 1* with most of *o* visible), 11 (*fol* only visible), 13 (*fol: 1* with part of next figure visible), 14 (*fol. . 1* with part of next figure visible), 18, 19, 20, 21 (all visible), and 24 (*fol. 2* only visible).

The plays occupy 3^r–176^r and are preceded by a version of the

---

[1] *Massey* is the name of an important Cheshire family with several branches in the county.

[2] This occurs on folios 1, 2, 4, 7, 8, 10, 14, 15, 16, 17, 19, 20, 21, 25, 30, 31, 33, 35, 37, 39, 41, 43, 47, 49, 52, 53, 56, 57, 59, 60, 61, 62, 63, 64, 69, 70, 71, 72, 77, 78, 80, 81, 83, 85, 88, 89, 93, 95, 97, 98, 100, 103, 105, 107, 110, 112, 113, 115, 117, 120, 122, 123, 124, 126, 128, 129, 131, 133, 136, 138, 140, 141, 142, 147, 149, 150, 151, 152, 156, 157, 159, 161, 162, 163, 167, 169, 173, 175, and 176.

Banns beginning with the Drapers (perhaps the reference to the Tanners has been lost in the damage to the top of the page). 176^v–179^v are blank. The scribe seems to prefer to begin each play on a recto page and breaks this practice only three times: at Plays XXII–XXIII (155^v) he continues on the same page, for no apparent reason; at Play III (20^v) and Play XVIII (135^v) he seems to have changed his practice because he has broken off the previous play midway down the previous page and left the preceding recto page blank. In other cases, beginning a new play on the recto page has meant that a preceding verso may be blank, as at: 25^v, 33^v, 40^v, 50^v, 71^v, 88^v, 96^v, 103^v, 109^v, 116^v, 123^v, 143^v, 165^v. 14^r–16^v, continuing a gap beginning at 13^v, and 60^r are also blank and, since there is no break in the text itself, seem to reflect some scribal idiosyncrasy.

The manuscript is written in black ink in one hand, and the final inscription after XXIV. Finis indicates that it was written in 1604 by William Bedford, who after 1606 was clerk to the Brewers' Guild.[1] The first word of each verse of the Banns, *thee* at the start of the Guild-ascriptions to I and II, and the Finis-formula to XXIV are in heavy black capitals. Otherwise there are no notable decorations, no running titles, and apart from *the* at 1^v, no catchwords. The pages were apparently unruled and the handwriting is hasty, often with blots, cancellations, intersecting letters which make readings difficult, and scrawls which make many forms in final position—especially -*st* and -*e*—doubtful. The beginnings of stage directions are usually set 3–4 letter-spaces to the left of the text-margin. Speech-headings are centred. Quatrains are marked by a slightly wider gap than that between the lines fairly consistently to the end of IV, but the practice is less consistently observed after that (see 27^r, 41^r(Gabriel's speech), 41^v(Elizabeth's speech), 89^{r-v}(Jesus's speech), 139^v). The scribe occasionally changes to an almost non-cursive script for a short stage direction or Latin quotation in a margin or within a line.

B is in fair condition. The binding is battered. On 1^r the top two inches have been lost and the page skilfully repaired; the damage extends to a depth of five inches for a maximum width of $\frac{7}{10}$ inch at the top right of the page. There are two small holes that carry through to folio 2. The page is also stained along the right side, and over-all grimy. The staining continues, diminishing, to

[1] See F. M. Salter, *RES* xv (1939), 435–6.

10^r. On 1^v the loss is less extensive at the top, extending in rough diagonal from 1$\frac{2}{5}$ inches depth at the left midway across the page. There is further slight loss at the top of 2^r and 2^v. The right side of 82^r has an irregular strip torn off, of maximum width $\frac{1}{4}$ inch to a depth of 7$\frac{1}{2}$ inches. About 2 inches have been cut from the bottom of 176 and 2$\frac{3}{4}$ inches torn from the top of 177. The corners have worn. The coarse paper is beginning to yellow, especially at the edges, and the ink varies from black to brown. All pages show signs of three folds, at about two-inch intervals along the length of the manuscript, but the folds do not affect the readings. Whatever its purpose, the manuscript was not a presentation copy.

H: This manuscript is in the British Museum. It is part of the collection formerly belonging to Randle Holme, concerning which see the description of R above. It has regularly been designated H. A note on the recto of the back vellum cover reads: '2 die Junii, 1624: lent iis. upon this boke for a fortnight. Per me R. H.', which Greg implies may indicate how H came into the possession of the first Randle Holme. On 142^r, among other writing, is *Rich. Ledsham*, and on the verso of the front vellum cover, vertically from bottom to top, *Broome fam* (?) and *Williame Broome*; nothing is known of these men.

The manuscript is bound in the same manner as R, with, in gold letters on the spine: *Rundle Holmes Collection: Chester Plays: Brit. Mus. Harley 2124*; the cover is embossed with the arms of the Earl of Oxford. The binding, measuring 8$\frac{7}{10}$ inches by 12$\frac{1}{4}$ inches, contains modern leaves at the beginning and end. The manuscript, of 142 paper folios, is preceded and followed by two sheets of vellum, the front measuring 7$\frac{2}{5}$ inches by 11$\frac{1}{2}$ inches and the back 7$\frac{3}{5}$ inches by 11$\frac{3}{4}$ inches. The cover appears to be from a service book; the front sheet is much worn but preserves traces of blue and gold capitals, while the back is in better condition, with the colours of the illumination still fresh. The pages of the manuscript vary in length, but reach a maximum of approximately 7$\frac{1}{2}$ inches by 11$\frac{4}{5}$ inches, which suggests that if the vellum sheets are the original wrapper, they have been much trimmed.

The manuscript has been bound by separating the folios and attaching them to guards, thereby destroying the original gatherings. The folios are usually attached in pairs to each guard and there are throughout the volume groups of guards with no folios attached. The paper is thick and the watermark not always clearly distinguishable, but seventy folios bear the watermark of a pot with one handle, and of these some also bear letters and markings.[1] The marks have no exact counterpart in Briquet. The remaining 72 folios have no watermark. The Cycle occupies 1^r–141^r; 141^v–142^r contains a list of the plays and performing guilds with the page-number on which the play begins in the manuscript; the list is headed *A Table Wherby Any of the Pageants May Easely Be Found And In What Page* and appears to be in the hand of Scribe C. Another hand, which Greg identifies with that of antiquarian notes on the front cover, has added the play-titles, with occasional errors or omissions.[2]

Three scribes wrote the manuscript. Scribe A wrote 1^r–44^v complete. Scribe B, who writes a similar hand to A, wrote 45^r–56^v and 59^r–62^v excluding rubrics, for which he left spaces. Scribe C inserted rubrics in B's section and wrote 57^r–58^v and 63^r–142^r complete, in a hand distinctively different from that of A and B. The characteristics of these hands are described by Greg. Scribe A set out the page by ruling single-line margins to left and right and a further feint margin $\frac{1}{5}$ inch in from the left ruling; he also ruled lines for the text which are still visible. At I. 76 he begins his characteristic practice of starting each quatrain with one, or sometimes two, words in red ink. His initial capitals are set against the left margin-ruling and the text indented in line with the feint ruling. Scribe B uses the same general format but has a feint ruling $\frac{2}{5}$ inch in from the left of the page against which he aligns the speech-headings. Gaps were left for C's red-ink additions, which included the quatrain-rulings. Scribe B, perhaps because of C's activities, does not continue A's practice of beginning every quatrain with a word in red ink; only the first word of the first quatrain of each play is so treated. His ruled lines for the text are visible.

Scribe C does not have a ruled margin to the right of the page or a feint margin within the left ruling to inset the text, but he con-

---

[1] This pot occurs on folios 1, 4, 6, 8, 10, 11, 13, 16, 18, 19, 21, 24, 26, 27, 29, 31, 34, 35, 38, 40, 42, 45, 47, 49, 51, 54, 56, 58, 59, 62, 64, 65, 67, 70, 71, 74, 76, 77, 79, 82, 84, 86, 88, 89, 92, 93, 95, 97, 99, 102, 103, 106, 107, 110, 111, 113, 115, 118, 119, 122, 123, 126, 127, 129, 132, 134, 135, 138, 139, 142.

Of those bearing letters, the forms appear to be *WC* at 86, 102, 106, 118, 119, 122, 123, 127, 129; *NC* at 95, 97, 99, 107, 126, 132, 139, 142; *IC* at 88, 89, 92, 93, 103, 110, 111, 135, 138. It is, however, difficult to be certain of these last details.

[2] See description in W. W. Greg, *Antichrist*, pp. xviii–xx. These notes will be treated further in our Volume II.

tinues B's practice of having a ruling ⅔ inch in from the left side of the page, although his ruling is in red ink. No rulings for the text are visible in his section. Usually, although not invariably, he discontinues B's practice of writing the first word of each play in red ink, a notable exception being the start of XI on 58ᵛ, which is within B's section. Scribe C's section of the manuscript shows a number of other characteristics:

  (i) the use of a short diagonal stroke at the end of a complete segment—usually a line of verse, but sometimes a Latin text or a stage direction.

 (ii) a tendency to number stanzas in long speeches.

(iii) the use of brackets, usually in cases where there is some abnormality, as where two quatrains have been written in one quatrain-space or where the quatrains contain shorter lines than is usual. Sometimes, however, the brackets merely enclose extended stage directions or Latin texts.

(iv) the use of a stylized hand-symbol (also found, but less frequently, in A's section). This symbol serves a variety of functions. Often it is used apparently decoratively in rubrics to fill blank spaces to right and left, as in centred Guild-ascriptions or Finis-forms; there are two such indicators to the left of the Play-heading to XXIV. Sometimes, however, it is used to draw attention to some textual irregularity, such as a misplacement or insertion.

Of these characteristics, only (ii) is consistently noted in the Textual Notes.

Scribe C signs himself *James Miller* and, while nothing certain is known about him, Greg notes that 'Professor Salter would identify this scribe with the James Miller who was a minor canon of St. Werburgh's [Chester] from 1605 to 1618'. Miller gives a number of dates at the end of certain plays (see Textual Notes) which enable us to date the manuscript to 1607 and which indicate his manner of working. He completed XXIV on 4 August 1607, and then returned to B's section, since the Finis to X includes his signature and the date 6 August 1607. The work was therefore finally Miller's responsibility. Nothing is known of the identities of A and B.

Miller's work on 57ʳ–58ᵛ raises the question of the omission of XI. 40–211. Each page contains eleven quatrains, and the missing

171 lines thus correspond roughly to an omission of two folios. The folios in H bear two sets of numberings in the right-hand corner of the recto pages. The lower, modern numbering runs consecutively from 1 to 143, the latter being on the recto side of the back vellum sheet. The higher numbering, apparently scribal, is in red ink and takes the form *Fol. i, ii*, etc., although damage to the corners in the early and later plays has obscured parts of this numbering. At 43ʳ there is a change in the ink colour which corresponds to a slight change in format after *Fol* from full stop to colon. When Scribe C takes over, at 57ʳ, the *Fol* is omitted and the pages numbered *lvii* and *lviii*. The *Fol* form resumes at 59ʳ, but this folio is numbered *Fol: lxi* and henceforth the scribal numbering remains two more than the later numbering. At 63ʳ, when Miller resumes, the numbering takes the form *65, 66*, etc. and so continues to the end of the manuscript. The rubricated numerals thus indicate a period in the history of H when there were extra folios corresponding to the omission. Greg suggests that at 57–8 Miller 'was supplying a lacuna', but it is also possible that he was rewriting B's work, especially since he follows B's practice of beginning XI with a word in red ink and also uses Roman numerals for the folio-numbering. If so, it is unlikely that Miller copied only two of the missing folios, and the separation of the pages from their original gatherings suggests a point at which further loss may have occurred.

Apart from these scribal idiosyncrasies, the manuscript has a uniform format throughout. The speech-headings are in the left margin. Quatrains and speeches are marked by red-ink rulings. Each play begins on a fresh page, with the exception of XIII, which follows directly after XII. There are no notable decorations and no catchwords or running titles. All Play-headings, Guild-ascriptions, stage directions, Latin texts, and speech-headings are in red ink and, in addition, red ink is used in the text to mark the names of characters, the animals entering the ark, the shepherd's list of remedies and any other information apparently felt to be significant. The practice is so frequent that such instances are not recorded in the Textual Notes. Stage directions are written without indentation, in specially ruled sections; on occasion they are written to the right of the text, as are the occasional biblical texts, peculiar to H and apparently cited in support of the narrative. The manuscript is otherwise written in black ink.

The manuscript is in generally good condition, although there is some staining, particularly at the edges. The right edge of 1ʳ has been repaired and the repair affects a small part of the left margin of 1ᵛ. Folio 1 is grimy and folio 23 particularly shows marked signs of creasing and dirt. The final pages are also somewhat grimy. The writing of Scribes A and B is usually clear; that of C is thicker, which occasionally makes the distinction of *e* and *o* difficult to discern, but otherwise it is easily legible. C's sections, however, contain more blots and stains. The manuscript was evidently prepared with some care, since the pages seem to have been pre-ruled on occasion, with a clear understanding of the position of stage directions and, for B, of places in the text at which C would insert red-ink words. The addition of supporting biblical texts suggests a certain scholarly interest. The manuscript seems to have been a presentation copy for someone of antiquarian taste.

II. SELECTION OF THE TEXT

Two earlier editions of the Cycle have appeared: Wright (1843 and 1847) and Deimling–Matthews (1893–1916). Wright printed A, with some corrections from R and a few readings from H; he did not consider a full collation of the five cyclic manuscripts worth the effort. Deimling–Matthews used H as base text, and provided variant readings from the other manuscripts. Their effort was towards a critical text, with readings from the other four cyclic manuscripts at times substituted for H's readings, and with not infrequent unattested emendations. Such factors as the late dates of the manuscripts and the evidence for changes in the text over the 200 years of staging lead us to doubt that a solid base can be provided for establishing the text—line by line—as it was originally written and subsequently changed.[1] Also—unlike Wright—we could see no justification for selecting a base text without comparing all the manuscripts.

The problem of which manuscript to use as base text was difficult: no one of the five cyclic manuscripts closely approaches presentation of all the lines available from a conflation of all five manuscripts. Deimling demonstrated that H differs markedly from A, R, and B.[2] Later scholars have shown that Hm (D) is close to

[1] These matters will be discussed in more detail in Volume II.
[2] See his Introduction to the EETS edition.

A, R, B and distant from H;[1] Hm, A, R, B are consequently called 'the Group', as opposed to H. Obviously, the first question before us was whether to use H or one of the Group-manuscripts as base text.

By listing every variation between H and Hm (D)—the latter as representative of the Group—we found that, amid a host of minor variants, H has eight major differences:

1. Presence of the Raven-and-Dove scene in III (see Appendix IA), a scene seemingly essential to the play but absent from the Group-manuscripts.

2. Large differences in V (see Appendix IB) which make that play in H an Advent play closely linked to the following Nativity play, rather than the final Old Testament play, as it is in the Group-manuscripts.

3. Lack in H of VII. 597–640, the Shepherds' Boys' Gifts.

4. Lack in H of XI. 41–210 because the original H folios 59 and 60 are lost.

5. Presentation of XVI as a single play in H rather than as the two plays in the Group-manuscripts, and lack—in this segment of H—of Peter's denial of Christ, a necessary foreshadowing of Peter's remorse in XVIII.

6. A different version in H of the ending of XVI (see Appendix Ic), lacking references—present in the Group-manuscripts—to XVIII.

7. Lack in H of the final sixty lines of XVII, the scene of the Ale-wife, arguably a thematic scene, present in the Group-manuscripts.

8. Presence in H of the final lines of XVIII (see Appendix ID); the play is unfinished in the Group-manuscripts, except for R.

The eight large differences which characterize H obviously affect the total structure and meaning of the Cycle. Yet they do not seem to form a pattern which can remove from the area of subjective judgement an opinion that H is a better 'text' than Hm and the other Group-manuscripts, or vice versa. One could say, of course, that the first and fourth differences are detrimental to H, and that the second and seventh differences are detrimental to Hm. But whether the effect of the differences in V, VII, XVI, and XVII makes H or Hm 'better' must remain a matter of personal

---

[1] See particularly entries under Greg and under Salter in the Bibliography.

Judgement. H has continuity at V–VI which Hm lacks; H has a kind of finality at XVI–XVII not present in Hm. The effect is two differing versions of the Cycle, neither demonstrably 'better' than the other.

It is similarly impossible to prove one version 'better' than the other in many of the minor variants. Several examples will perhaps suffice; numerous others can be observed in the Variant Readings. In XVI. 1–100, with Hm as base text, 88 variants occur in the verse-text in the four other cyclic manuscripts. Of these 88, H has 63; among these 63, 43 occur only in H and 13 additionally occur in H in a form different from their occurrence in A, R, or B. Here are two specific instances: for Hm's *that one man dye witterly* (18), H has *that one must dye witterlye*; for Hm's *herden* (36), H has *hard him*. In such instances a reader may say that he subjectively prefers one reading to the other; but he cannot prove that his preference is 'better' than the other.

In the absence of any firm foundation for deciding whether to use H or a Group-manuscript as base text, after consideration of both major and minor variants, and discounting as impractical, both because of space and also because of cost, a parallel-text edition presenting H and one of the Group-manuscripts in full, we decided to consider whether any of the manuscripts could be chosen as base because it would simplify problems of presentation and provide a more convenient edition for the reader to use.

Anyone using the Deimling–Matthews edition for detailed work will be greatly inconvenienced, particularly in V and XVI, where he is faced with the considerable problem of establishing the extensive differences of the Group from H which are presented in a mass of material printed in small type as variants at the bottom of the pages. This same difficulty exists in that edition when one deals with the numerous smaller differences from H in the four Group-manuscripts. We could see that much of this complexity might be avoided by using a Group-manuscript as base text and printing H's large variations as an Appendix. As a consequence, the reader would have both versions of the Cycle easily available in a readily usable form. Here, we decided, was good reason for using a Group-manuscript, rather than H, as base text.

As an approach for deciding which Group-manuscript to use as base text, we listed the lines missing from each of the four when compared to a conflation of all four Group-manuscripts. Here is the list, with play- and line-numbers referring to the Text and Variant Readings in this volume:[1]

Hm

I whole play
VI four lines after 364
IX one line after 124, four lines after 183
XI one line after 110
XIII one line after 50, four lines after 270
XVI four lines after 16+

Annas, four lines before 98, four lines before 102
XVII one line after 254
XVIII ninety-five lines (see Appendix ID)
XX two lines after 148
XXIII four lines after 636

A[2]

I one line after 17, 46–51, 78–81, 122–3, 258
II 40, 537–40
IV 333–6
VI 277–92
VII 37–40, 137–40, 189–90, 310, 570
VIII 345, 419
IX one line after 124
X 197–208, 217–24, 229–32, 313–20, 369–72
XIII one line after 50, 256, 258, four lines after 270

XIV 421–4
XV 95
XVI as in Hm
XVIA 142
XVII 42, 66–9, one line after 254
XVIII 77–80, and as in Hm
XX two lines after 148
XXI 149–52, 155–8, 215–18
XXII 90–3, 247, 288
XXIII 217–20, 225–36, 460, 679–90, 695–8
XXIV 585–8, 593–6, 613–708

R

I one line after 17
IV 333–6
VI 79–80, 91–2, 214–17, 233–6, 277–88, 293–6, 616–19

VII 37–40, 310, 570
VIII 345

IX one line after 124, 204–7

---

[1] Although the totals depend to some extent upon whether a divided line is counted as one line or two, the over-all picture is not significantly affected by this variation.

[2] A damaged line in plays I, II, and XXIV in this manuscript was considered missing if less than half of the line remains.

X 35–8, 197–208, 217–32,
    245–52, 309–20, 349–
    60, 369–76
XIII as in Hm
XIV 421–4
XVIA 142, 330–6
XVII 42, one line after 254

XVIII 152–3
  XX two lines after 148
XXII 90–3, 288
XXIII 45–56, 185–8, 209–12,
    217–36, 371–6, 419,
    679–98
XXIV 57–64, 69–72, 341–8

B

I 174–7
II 681–704
IV 442
VI 671–4
VII 521, 570
IX 172–5, four lines after 183
XIII 361–4
XIV 349–52

XV 253–6, 347–66
XVIA 181–212
XVII 3
XVIII 425–32, and as in Hm
    and A
XXI 158
XXII 276
XXIII 393, 398–401, 711
XXIV 29

The totals of lines missing for each play and each manuscript appear in the following table:

	Hm	A	R	B
I	301	14	1	4
II	0	5	0	24
III	0	0	0	0
IV	0	4	4	1
V	0	0	0	0
VI	4	16	32	4
VII	0	12	6	2
VIII	0	2	1	0
IX	5	1	5	8
X	0	36	72	0
XI	1	0	0	0
XII	0	0	0	0
XIII	5	7	5	4
XIV	0	4	4	4
XV	0	1	0	24
XVI	12	12	0	0

	Hm	*A*	*R*	*B*
XVIA	0	1	8	32
XVII	1	6	2	1
XVIII	95	99	2	103
XIX	0	0	0	0
XX	2	2	2	0
XXI	0	12	0	1
XXII	0	6	5	1
XXIII	4	33	67	6
XXIV	0	105	20	1
Total	430	377	236	220

In bulk B has fewest lines omitted. But analysis of the function of omitted lines proved unfavourable to B. Its omission in III of Cain's report to his parents and their laments (681–Finis), a scene announced in 677–81, is a serious defect. In XV its omission of 349–Finis results in the loss of a passage important for connection with XVI, and its omission of 253–7 results in the loss of Jesus' promise of joy. In XVIA its omission of 565–97 sharply reduces the effectiveness of the scene in which the four Jews nail Christ to the Cross. And in XVIII it omits more from the end of the play than either Hm or A.

A proved to be even less attractive than B: it lacks folios at the end and has damage to numerous lines near the beginning, as well as frequent other sizeable omissions. At first glance, R seemed the best choice because it alone among the four Group-manuscripts includes the final scene of XVIII, also present in H. But closer examination showed that R's omissions, particularly those in VI, X, and XXIII, are seriously damaging to the sense and effect of the Cycle.

For Hm, the listing above makes obvious that it presents the largest number of plays with no lines omitted—fifteen, as opposed to B's eight—and that, apart from its lack of I (301 lines), it has fewest lines omitted from the conflation (127). Also obvious from the listing is the fact that R presents the fullest version for I. That Play was supplied for Hm by Collier's copy from R (see Textual Notes).

From the considerations set forth above[1] we concluded that we could present the *whole* of the Cycle, as it has come down to us,

[1] See further, Bibliography, p. xliii, Lumiansky–Mills.

most conveniently for the reader by using Hm as base text with Play
I in full from R, and with H's large differences—as well as the
variants in the ending of XVIII in R—included as an Appendix.
In addition, the three non-cyclic manuscripts could be presented
in full in a second Appendix. Such a presentation, which we have
adopted, most successfully avoids the taxing complexity resulting
from lengthy important differences appearing in Variant Readings;
and it most fairly presents the two versions of the Cycle—that of
the Group, and that of H.

Although we began by considering the reader's convenience,
there are other arguments for using Hm as base text. It is the
earliest of the five cyclic manuscripts; and it has in the past been
least readily available to readers, since its variants from the conflation were not considered by Wright and were very awkwardly presented in Deimling–Matthews. Further, although we have not yet
fully examined the matter, our sampling suggests that Hm has fewest indisputable errors in meaning among the smaller variations in
the Cycle.[1] But our primary consideration has been to present the
text of the whole Cycle in the form which would distract the reader
least by the necessity for complicated cross-reference.

III. TREATMENT OF THE TEXT

We have attempted to present the Text of the Cycle as it appears in
the manuscripts, except for certain modernizations and regulariza-
tions in form. The principle behind these changes is the same as
that behind our selection of the Text: convenience for the reader,
and thus service to the Cycle. The changes are as follows:

1. The plays have been numbered I–XXIV above the Guild-
   ascription. 'The Trial and Flagellation' and 'The Passion' form
   a single play, XVI, in H, but appear as two separate plays in
   the Group. We have numbered 'The Trial and Flagellation'
   XVI and 'The Passion' XVIA.

2. In the few instances where the manuscript omits a speech-
   heading indisputably necessary to the meaning of the Text,
   that speech-heading is entered within the Text in square
   brackets. At the request of the EETS Council we have supplied
   readings in instances where the Hm reading seems palpably
   nonsensical: these readings are also entered within the Text in

[1] This matter will be discussed in more detail in Volume II.

square brackets. We have not emended the Text in any other way.

3. Line-numbering, stanza-numbering, and folio-numbering have been added.

4. Speech-headings are regularly centred, and stage directions and Latin texts placed within the body of the Text. Where this practice conflicts with that of a manuscript, we have noted the position in the manuscript in the Textual Notes.

5. Our modern method of stanza-division is not to be found in any of the manuscripts. The Cycle is written almost entirely in the eight-line 'Chester stanza', rhyming aaabcccb or aaabaaab. The manuscripts either do not indicate this stanza-division, or else they mark it in quatrains. Since the eight-line grouping has functional point within the structure and meaning of the Cycle, we decided to use it as the basis for our stanza division. We consider a *stanza* a verse-paragraph defined by a link of rhyme and/or sense. In some cases our decisions about stanza-division are debatable; these instances will be dicussed in Volume II.

6. Word-division and capitalization have been changed in many cases to conform with modern practice. We have not felt it necessary to indicate such changes.

7. Modern equivalents have been used for graphs in certain positions in words in the manuscripts; again we have not felt it necessary to indicate such changes in the Text—*ever* for *euer*, *us* for *vs*, *Jesus* for *Iesus*. Initial *ff* is usually transcribed as *F*. But we have not transformed the manuscripts' roman numerals into words: *iiii* is presented as *iiii*, not *four*.

8. Abbreviations and suspensions are expanded and raised letters placed within the line, again without indication in the Text, as in the following examples: wth to *with*, wch to *which*, m^r to *master*, you^r to *your*, a tilde over a letter to *m* or *n*, *Ihu* to *Jesus*. The frequently used symbol at the end of a word to indicate the plural or the genitive is regularly expanded as -*es*. We had originally supplied modern punctuation in the case of the genitive by adding an apostrophe. Subsequently, however, this apostrophe was omitted at the request of the Society.

9. Modern punctuation is used; the manuscripts include almost no punctuation. In many passages a different punctuation from that which we have adopted is possible and will change the meaning of the passages. These instances will be discussed in the Explanatory Notes in Volume II.

IV. SELECTION AND TREATMENT OF VARIANT READINGS

Like others facing this editorial problem, we have listed the 'significant variants'. We define 'significant variants' primarily as 'variants which affect the meaning of the text'. Meaning is affected in a number of ways—by the absence of material which is present in Hm and by the presence of material which is absent from Hm; by differences in the choice of word, or in its inflection; by differences in word-order or syntax. Since, however, the Cycle is written in stanzaic rhyming verse, we have assumed also that meaning is affected by differences in rhyme and, on occasion, in metre. We have not listed variants which do not seem to affect meaning, as here defined; such instances we regard as 'spelling-variants'.

In determining whether meaning is affected, we have considered not merely the form of the variant, but also the context in which it appears. We have not assumed that a given variation will be significant in all contexts. Thus in B, for example, *thie* is a variant of *thy* and of *thee*, but it is listed as a variant only in contexts in which it could have either meaning. We have also included formal variants which tend to obscure meaning, such as *worldly*] *wordly*— variants often indicative of scribal practice or even scribal error.

Having established our list of variants, we also included forms from the manuscripts other than those fulfilling the above criteria. We did so where such forms might be regarded as intermediate forms which could indicate how the variant might have arisen or what the meaning might be—for example, *the*] *thee, thie, thy*.

We have throughout assumed that ARBH have the same reading as Hm unless we are certain that this is not so. Where the exact reading is not clear—as, for example, in many endings in B—we have assumed that the reading is not a variant. Where we are in doubt about a reading, we have indicated our difficulty in the Textual Notes. We have also felt that, since our purpose in this edition is to present late-sixteenth- and early-seventeenth-century manuscript-readings without attempting to reconstruct earlier forms of the Cycle, so in the Variant Readings we should try to present the English of the late sixteenth and early seventeenth centuries without speculations on the spellings, forms, and pronunciation of earlier periods in which we know the Cycle to have been performed.

Variations in pronunciation could have a significant effect upon the verse of the Cycle and hence upon the meaning as defined above. We have attempted, within the limits of available space, to present the reader with the forms in the manuscripts and thus allow him to decide. We have, therefore, noted a number of variants in rhyme-position which we do not note in medial position—for example, *anoye*] *anye* In doing so, we do not intend to suggest that these variants necessarily represent different pronunciations; we merely draw the reader's attention to the different forms. We recognize that the presence or absence of an unstressed vowel in an inflectional ending may also be 'meaningful', because it affects the number of syllables in a line and hence the metre. However, the variations in the representation of such endings are so frequent that we have felt compelled by considerations of space to make certain assumptions:

(a) final *e* was not pronounced at the time at which our manuscripts were written.

(b) unstressed *e* was not pronounced in final syllables before *s* unless preceded by *s*, *z*, *sh*, *ch*, or *dg*.

(c) in all other circumstances, unstressed *e* was pronounced in final syllables.

Thus, verbal inflections—*e*, *es*, *s*, *est*, *st*—are not noted as variants; the context makes the 'person' of the subject clear, and the assumptions above mean that these different forms of ending do not necessarily indicate variation in the number of syllables in the line. Where such forms are included in the Variant Readings, it is because they may represent a variation between indicative and subjunctive moods. An exception is the variation *lett*] *lettes* which is often noted because the latter may mean 'let us'. When, however, a variation exists between any of these endings and a third-person singular ending in *eth*, this is usually noted because it may indicate a variation in the number of syllables; hence *likes*] *liketh* would be listed. Where the verb-stem ends in a semi-vowel (*y*, *w*), this variation is not noted since the verb-stem is an open syllable; thus *say*] *saith*, *sayeth* would not be listed.

In presenting the Variant Readings we have listed the manuscripts in the chronological order ARBH and given the variant in the form in which it appears in the manuscript immediately following the form. The order HmARBH is, of course, adopted for the occasional references to a variant in Hm.

Spelling in the Variant Readings has been modernized in the same fashion as in the Text, and names, including *God*, are regularly capitalized. Word-division follows modern practice unless a different meaning is otherwise possible. Only extensive additions to or replacements of segments of the Text are punctuated in Variant Readings. Just as we assume that all manuscripts have the Hm form unless a variant reading is clear, so we also assume that no manuscript has a unique variant form unless that is clear. Where one manuscript has *have* and another *haue* or *hane*, for example, we list both as *have*.

The following terms and signs, regularly used in the Variant Readings, need to be explained:

(*a*) *Guild-ascription*: occurs at the start of the variants for each play; indicates the section of the heading which gives the name of the performing guild or guilds.

(*b*) *Play-heading*: comes after the Guild-ascription; indicates all other material preceding the first speech-heading for the play.

(*c*) *SD*: indicates all instructions to actors in the Text, unless a SD is attached to a speech-heading.

(*d*) *Latin*: indicates Latin texts which are neither lines nor SD's.

(*e*) *SH*: indicates a speech-heading; in the Variant Readings, as in the Text, speech-headings appear in capital letters.

(*f*)]: divides the entry from Hm from the entry or entries from other manuscripts. When it follows a number, or any of the items listed above —(*a*)–(*e*)—the following entry refers to the whole line or the item in Hm.

(*g*) To identify a SD or Latin text accurately, the form 125+SD is used where the position of the SD or SH reference in the list of variants could be ambiguous.

When the position of SD's or SH's is different from that in the Hm Text, we usually note the fact in the Textual Notes, but when the position is so far removed from that in Hm as to suggest that the action occurs at a different point, the position is indicated in the Variant Readings. The exact position of SD's or SH's not in Hm is regularly noted in the Variant Readings. When a word for which there are variants occurs twice or more often in a line, the specific variation is indicated by (1) or (2) or (3) after the variant: for example, *he*(2)] *his* B. Occasionally, when a particular variation occurs often—for example, omission of a word in a SH throughout a play—we have entered a general statement at the first occurrence and have not made further entry of the same variant. On a few occasions, we have listed a lengthy omission by entering only the first and last words of the passage.

Since not infrequently we found the distinction between entry in Variant Readings and entry in Textual Notes difficult to make, the reader is urged regularly to consult both for a complete picture of differences. In general we have included in Variant Readings material corresponding to material in Hm, and material applicable to the production of the plays. But we have not included such material as the Latin texts cited in H to substantiate the play-texts; such material is to be found in Textual Notes. For A, we have included in Variant Readings what is visible in the damaged portions: if such facts were placed in Textual Notes, the reader might assume from Variant Readings that A agreed at these points with the readings in Hm.

We have tried to assess each aspect of variation individually, and to present the 'significant variants'—as we define them—in the simplest and clearest possible way in order to make the reader aware of the possible readings in the manuscripts.

V. SELECTION AND TREATMENT OF TEXTUAL NOTES

The 1728 manuscript pages upon which this edition is based contain a great many peculiarities in addition to those which are included in our descriptions of the manuscripts. Within the Textual Notes, the peculiarities which we wish to include are presented in one of two ways:

(*a*) In a series of generalized accounts which describe the feature as it occurs throughout the whole of each manuscript. This method of presentation is used for material in the five cyclic manuscripts but not for material in the three shorter ones. The sections appear at the start of the Textual Notes for each manuscript. They include, in order of presentation:

  (i) Folio-numbering (AR)

  (ii) Position of Guild-ascriptions and Play-headings (ARBH)

  (iii) Content of pages (ARBH)

  (iv) Form of play-endings (HmARBH)

  (v) Marginalia (A)

(b) Play by play, and line by line within each play, throughout each manuscript in turn. This method of presentation is used for all eight manuscripts and includes the following information:

  (i) Items in the manuscript which have no counterpart in the Hm text (except the A-Marginalia above).

  (ii) Irregularities within the written text of the manuscript. These include erasures, cancellations, alterations, insertions, unusual or difficult abbreviations, unusual letter-forms and doubtful readings, re-inkings and possible changes of hand (other than those noted in manuscript-descriptions).

  (iii) Variations in format in each manuscript from the scribe's usual practice. These include changes in the line-division presented in Hm, stage directions which are set in a slightly different position on the page from the position in Hm (but not where the position is so markedly different as to suggest that the action takes place at a different point in the text), changes in spacing, ruling, and indentation, and changes in the usual line-grouping.

  (iv) Manuscript-damage, such as faded ink, wear, staining, holes, damage to letters from binding or trimming.

The list indicates the main kinds of information given, but we have also noted anything which seems significantly unusual in each manuscript. The information may tell the reader something of the scribe's exemplar, his understanding, his manner of working; or about the kind of reader for whom the manuscript was intended; or about the meaning of the Text and the way in which variants may have arisen.

Throughout the Textual Notes, roman numerals refer to plays and Arabic numerals refer to lines within the plays, as given in the text of Hm. In using the sections headed *Content of Pages*, the reader should check the pertinent *Variant Readings* for the possibility of omitted or added lines, and the pertinent *Textual Notes* to individual plays for the possibility of doubled or divided lines. When a single line in Hm is divided in another manuscript, the Textual Notes will indicate the division in the following manner: 'I. 69 two lines, *begyninge/*.' We hope that all other entries in the Textual Notes will be immediately understandable.

BIBLIOGRAPHY

THE listing below is limited to editions and discussions of the texts of the Cycle. A listing of items concerning other aspects of the Cycle will be included in Volume II of this edition. For the listing below, we have consulted Carl J. Stratman, *Bibliography of Medieval Drama* (second ed., revised and enlarged, New York, 1972), and the annual bibliographies in *PMLA*.

A. Editions of the Full Cycle

Wright, Thomas, *The Chester Plays*, Shakespeare Society Publications, 1843 and 1847, reprinted 1853.

Deimling, Hermann, and Dr. Matthews, *The Chester Plays*, EETS, E.S. 62 (1892) and E.S. 115 (1916); 62 reprinted 1926, 1959; 115 reprinted 1935, 1959.[1]

B. Some Editions of Parts of the Cycle

Markland, J. H., *Chester Mysteries: De Deluvio Noe. De Occisione Innocentium* (Roxburghe Club, 1818) (see Textual Notes for manuscript B).

Collier, J. P., *Five Miracle Plays or Scriptural Dramas* (London, 1836). Includes the Chester 'Antichrist'.

Collier, J. P., *The Advent of Antichrist. A Miracle Play. Now First Printed from the Duke of Devonshire's Manuscript* (London, F. Shoberl, 1836).

Marriott, W., *A Collection of English Miracle-Plays or Mysteries* (Basel, 1838). Includes the Chester 'Deluge' and 'Antichrist'.

Pollard, A. W., *English Miracle Plays, Moralities and Interludes* (Oxford, 1890, revised 1927). Includes the Chester 'Abraham and Isaac' and 'Noah'.

Manly, J. M., *Specimens of the Pre-Shaksperean Drama* (Boston and New York, 1903–4), volume I. Includes the Chester 'Balaam and Balaak' and 'Antichrist'.

Barne, H. H., *The Shepherds' Offering. One of the Chester Miracle Plays* (London, 1906).

Bridge, J. C., *Three Chester Whitsun Plays* (Chester, 1906). Includes the 'Salutation and Nativity', the 'Shepherds', and the 'Adoration of the Magi'.

Hemingway, S. B., *English Nativity Plays* (New York, 1909). Includes the Chester Nativity plays.

[1] See note below, at end of Bibliography.

Conroy, F. M., and Mitchell, R., *The Nativity and Adoration Cycle of the Chester Mysteries* (New York, 1917).

Isaacs, J., *The Chester Play of the Deluge* (Waltham St. Lawrence, Berkshire, 1928).

Adams, J. Q., *Chief Pre-Shakespearean Dramas* (Boston, 1924). Includes the Chester 'Deluge', 'Balaam and Balak', 'Christ's Ministry', and 'Harrowing of Hell'. The volume is now being extensively revised by Professor David Bevington of the University of Chicago.

Greg, W. W., *The Play of Antichrist from the Chester Cycle* (Oxford, 1935).

Salter, F. M., '*The Trial and Flagellation:* a new manuscript', *Chester Play Studies* (The Malone Society, 1935), pp. 1–73.

Greg, W. W., 'The Manchester Fragment of the *Resurrection*', *Chester Play Studies* (The Malone Society, 1935), pp. 85–100.

Cawley, A. C., *Everyman and Medieval Miracle Plays* (London and New York, 1956). Includes the Chester 'Flood' and 'Harrowing of Hell'.

Thomas, R. G., *Ten Miracle Plays* (London, 1966). Includes the Chester 'Balaam and Balak' and 'Christ's Passion'.

Rourke, J. F., 'An Edition of Play V, "Balaam and Balack", in the Chester Cycle of Mystery Plays' (unpublished dissertation submitted for the degree of M.A. in the University of Liverpool, 1967).

Clopper, L. M., Jr., *The Structure of the Chester Cycle: Text, Theme, and Theatre* (Ann Arbor: University Microfilms, 1969). Includes an edition from Hm of 'Balaam and Balack'.

c. Discussions of the Texts

A number of the editions listed above include discussion of the texts.

Deimling, H., *Text-Gestalt und Text-Kritik der Chester Plays* (Berlin, 1890). Inaug. diss. Berlin.

Greg., W. W., *Bibliographical and Textual Problems of the English Miracle Cycles* (London, 1914). Also published in *The Library*, v (1914), 1–30, 168–205, 280–319, 365–99. Four lectures; the second particularly concerns the Chester texts.

Frank, G., 'Revisions in the English Mystery Plays', *MP*, xv (1917–18), 565–72.

Dustoor, P. E., 'Textual Notes on the Chester Old Testament Plays', *Anglia*, lii (1928), 26–36, 97–112.

Salter, F. M., review of Greg's edition of 'Antichrist', *RES*, xiii (1937), 341–52.

Greg, W. W., reply to Salter's review, *RES*, xiii (1937), 353–4, and xiv (1938), 79–80.

Craig, H., review of Greg's edition of 'Antichrist', *JEGP*, xxxvii (1938), 97–9.

Salter, F. M., 'The Banns of the Chester Plays', *RES*, xv (1939), 432–57, and xvi (1940), 1–17, 137–47.

Coffee, B. F., *The Chester Plays: Interrelation of Manuscripts* (Ann Arbor: University Microfilms, 1956).

Lumiansky, R. M., and Mills, David, 'The Manuscripts of the Chester Cycle: A Statistical Survey', *LSE* (forthcoming). Presents detailed statistics of B's unique readings and R's reliance on A.

D. Facsimile

The Chester Mystery Cycle: A Facsimile of MS. Bodley 175, Leeds Texts and Monographs, Drama Facsimiles I (Leeds, 1973). Introduction by R. M. Lumiansky and David Mills.

Note to Bibliography

The EETS volumes indicate that Hermann Deimling edited the first of the two volumes, and Dr. Matthews the second. Hermann Wilhelm Deimling was born in Carlsruhe on 29 September 1867. He defended his dissertation (see Bibliography) at the Friedrich Wilhelms University in Berlin on 8 March 1890. His early death is noted by Furnivall in Volume I (p. vii) of the first EETS edition of the Chester Cycle.

We have not been able to identify Dr. Matthews. Professor Norman Davis kindly informed us that he also has been unable to make the identification, but that he is certain that neither J. Brander Matthews nor Godfrey W. Mathews, to the latter of whom E. K. Chambers attributes the second volume in *English Literature at the Close of the Middle Ages* (p. 213), was our editor. Professor Davis has also generously provided the following information: The earliest reference to Volume II, after the publication of Volume I in 1892, seems to be that in the advertisements bound with o.s. 100 and 103 of 1894. 'The Texts for the Extra Series in 1895 and 1896 will be chosen from . . . Part II of *The Chester Plays*, re-edited from the MSS., with a full collation of the formerly missing Devonshire MS., by Mr. G. England (at press).' The same statement appears in 104 (1895) and 106 (1896), but the projected dates are altered to 1896 and 1897. The same appears in 108 (1897) with projected dates as 1898 and 1899. The same again appears in 113 (1899), with projected dates as 1901 and 1902. Here 'and Dr. Matthews' is added after 'G. England'; also '(at press)' is deleted in the advertisement but retained on the wrapper, where 're-edited by Dr. Matthews'—without 'Mr. G. England'—is the description. That circumstance is repeated in 124 (1904), with projected dates as 1906 and 1907. In 141 (1911) projected dates are dropped, and the same statement is preceded by 'Later Texts . . .'.

No initial for Matthews is ever given; perhaps Furnivall did not know him. It is not now known what happened to the EETS records when Furnivall died in 1910 and Israel Gollancz became Director. In 1914 Gollancz sent a note, now in the possession of R. M. Lumiansky, to W. W. Greg stating that Dr. Matthews 'cannot be found, tho' he must have done a good deal of the work (still in type) of Part II'. David Mills's search in English university lists around

1890 has not produced an English graduate named Matthews. We have not searched for an appropriate Ph.D. recipient from a German university around 1890. 'Dr. Matthews' remains a mystery.

It should be added that Gollancz, in the note mentioned above, asked Greg 'to take in hand the edition of the Chester Plays Part II, concluding the text with collations, for the E.E.T.S.'. Professor Davis states that James Maxwell, who examined Greg's papers, informed him that there is no trace of any work by Greg in collating the Chester manuscripts. It would seem—from Gollancz's 'still in type' in his note to Greg (1914), and from his 'long been printed off' in his Prefatory Note to Volume II (1916)—that the collations in the footnotes to Volume II had been made and printed off at the same time as the Text. Just what part England and Matthews may have taken in that work forms an additional aspect of the puzzle.

4ʳ

THE TANNERS PLAYE

Pagina Prima: De Celi, Angelorom, et Infirne Speciun
Creacion Pagina

DEUS

1 Ego sum alpha et oo,
primus et novissimus.
It is my will it shoulde be soe;
hit is, yt was, it shalbe thus.

2 I ame greate God gracious,   5
which never had begyninge.
The wholl foode of parente is sett
in my essention.
I ame the tryall of the Trenitye
which never shalbe twyninge,   10
pearles patron ymperiall,
and Patris sapiencia.
My beames be all beawtitude;
all blisse is in my buyldinge.
All meirth lyeth in mansuetude,   15
cum Dei potentia,
bouth viscible and inviscible.

[The manuscript references are given in the sequence ARBH. The Variant
Reading is given in the form in which it appears in the manuscript listed immediately after it.]

Guild-ascription] The Tan . . . beinge the A, The Tanners playe being the
ff. . . . of the wholle booke B   playe] *om* H   *Play-heading*] *om* A, The
First Pageant of the Fal of Lucifer H   angelorom] angelorum B   infirne]
inferni B   speciun] specium B   creacion pagina] creatione B   DEUS]
GOD A, *om* B, DEUS PATER H   1 oo] o A, ø B, ω H   2 novissimus] *om* A
3 shoulde be] shalbe B   4 hit is yt was] yt was it is H   5 greate God
gracious] God greate and glorious H   6 which never had] without H
7 wholl] holy H   parente] parentes BH   8 essention] assention B,
licentia H   10 which] that BH   twyninge] turninge B   13 beaw-
titude] bewtitude A, beatitude BH   14 blisse is] this B   15 lyeth]
is H   in] in my BH   17 and] and eck BH   *After* 17] all lyes in my
weldinge BH (lyes] is H)

C 9206   B

As God greatest and glorious,
all is in mea licencill.

3 For all the meirth of the majestye   20
  is magnifyed in me.
  Prince principall, proved
  in my perpetuall provydence,
  I was never but one
  and ever one in three,   25
  set in substanciall southnes
  within selestiall sapience.
  The three tryalls in a throne
  and true Trenitie
  be grounded in my godhead,   30
  exalted by my exelencie.
  The might of my makeinge
  is marked in mee,
  dissolved under a deadem
  by my devyne experience.   35

4 Nowe sithe I am soe soeleme
4v and set in my solatacion,
  a biglie blesse here will I builde,
  a heaven without endinge,
  and caste a comely compasse   40
  by comely creation.
  Nyne orders of angells,
  be ever at onste defendinge;
  doe your indevoure and doubte you not
  under my dominacion   45
  to sytt in celestiall saftye.
  All solace to your sendinge!
  For all the likeinge in this lordshipp

18 greatest] so greate H   19 is] lyeth H   mea] my H   licencill]
licentia B, *om* H   20 meirth] mighte AH   23 provydence] prudence
BH   26 in] in my A   28 the] these BH   29 true] *om* H
31 exelencie] excellence BH   32 of] of all H   33 in mee] all in one H
34 dissolved] dissovlinus A   36 soe] thus H   37 in] *om* H   solata-
cion] solation BH   38 biglie] lightlie B   41 by] by my BH   42 nyne]
ten H   43 at] to H   onste] one BH   defendinge] de A, attendinge H
44 indevoure] devour B   and doubte you not] *om* A   45 under] nder A
dominacion] domy A   46] *om* A   47] *om* A   48] dshippe A

be laude to my laudacion.
Through might of my most majestie   50
your meirth shall ever be mendinge.

LUCIFFER

5 Lorde, through thy mighte thou hast us wrought,
nine orders here that we maye see:
Cherubyn and Seraphin through thy thought;
Thrones and Dominationes in blisse to bee;   55

6 with Principates, that order brighte,
and Potestates in blisfull lighte;
also Vertutes, through thy greate mighte,
Angell and also Arkeangelle.

7 Nine orders here bene witterlye,   60
that thou hast made here full right.
In thy blisse full brighte the bee,
and I the principall, lorde, here in thy sighte.

DEUS

8 Here have I you wrought with heavenly mighte,
of angells nine orders of greate beautye,   65
iech one with others, as it is righte,
to walke aboute the Trenitie.

9 Nowe, Luciffer and Lightborne, loke lowely you bee.
The blessinge of my begyninge I geve to my first
operacion.

49] dacion A   be laude] by lawe B, be love H   50] my moste magistie A
through] throught B, through the H   51] ever be mendinge A
52 lorde] om A   mighte] grace and mighte H   us] s me H   53 nine]
om A, x H   here] of angelles here H   that we] as you H   54 Cherubyn]
erubyn A   thy] your H   thought] grace A   55 Thrones] hones A
and] om H   to] for to H   56 Principates] Principatus H   57 Potes-
tates] Potestantes B   blisfull] blisse full BH   lighte] heighte H   58 thy]
your H   59 Angell] Angeli BH   and] om ABH   Arkeangelle] Arcangeli
BH   60 here] nowe heare A   bene] be full H   61 thou hast] you have
H   right] brighte H   62 thy] your H   brighte the bee] righte youe bye
H   63 principall lorde] x^{th} H   thy] your H   DEUS] GOD A   64 you]
om H   65 nine] x H   beautye] beinge B   66 others] other AH
67 aboute] above with B, about with H   68 Lightborne] Lighborne B
lowely] lovelic H   bee] be atending BH   69 begyninge] benignitie H
first] om A

For crafte nor for cuninge, cast never comprehension; 70
exsalte you not to exelente into high exaltation.
Loke that you tende righte wisely, for hence I wilbe
    wendinge.
The worlde that is bouth voyde and vayne, I forme in
    the formacion,
with a dongion of darkenes which never shall have endinge.
This worke is nowe well wrought by my devyne formacion. 75

5ʳ 10 This worke is well donne, that is soe cleane and cleare.
As I you made of naughte, my blessinge I geve you here.

ANGELIE

11 Wee thanke thee, lorde, full soveraignely,
that us hath formed soe cleane and cleare,
ever in this blesse to byde thee bye.   80
Graunte us thy grace ever to byde here.

ARCKEANGELIS

12 Here for to byde God grante us grace
to please this prince withouten peare;
him for to thanke with some solace,
a songe now let us singe here.   85

'Dignus Dei'

DEUS

13 Nowe seeinge I have formed you soe fayer
and exalted you so exelente—
and here I set you nexte my cheare,

70 cast] te A, craft B   comprehension] comprehending BH   71 exsalte]
alte A   exelente] exellency H   into] o A, in no BH   72] om H   loke]
ke A   that] om B   for] or A   73 vayne] vayle H   I] om A   the]
this BH   74 which] ch A, that H   75 this] om A, these H   worke is]
workes H   wrought] iwrought B, be done H   by my] om A   76 this
worke] orcke A, these workes H   is well donne] well I wrought H   that is
soe] om A, that are H   soe] thus H   77 as I you] om A   my blessinge]
om A   ANGELIE] om A, ANGELI H   78] soveraignlye A   thee] yow B
soveraignely] soverayntlie H   79] cleane and cleare A   80] ee by A
ever] even B, and H   byde] abyde H   81] to byde heare A   ever] aye
BH   byde] abide BH   ARCKEANGELIS] ARCKEANGELL A, ARCHANGELY BH
82 byde] abyde H   us grace] om A   83 to] and H   peare] om A
84 some] somp H   85 here] in feare ABH   SD] A songe: dignus es
Dei A, Then a songe: dignus es domine B, Tunc cantabunt H   DEUS]
GOD A   86 seeinge] sithens that B, sithe H

my love to you is soe fervente—
loke you fall not in noe dispaier.   90
Touche not my throne by non assente.
All your beautie I shall appaier,
and pride fall oughte in your intente.

LUCIFFER

14 Ney, lorde, that will we not in deed,
for nothinge tresspasse unto thee.   95
Thy greate godhead we ever dreade,
and never exsaulte ourselves soe hie.
Thou hast us marked with greate might and mayne,
in thy blesse evermore to byde and bee,
in lastinge life our life to leade.   100
And bearer of lighte thou hast made me.

LIGHTEBORNE

15 And I ame marked of that same moulde.
Loveinge be to our creator
that us hase made gayer then goulde,
under his dieadem ever to indure.   105

DEUS

I have forbyd that ye nearc shoulde;
but keepe you well in that stature.
The same covenante I charge you houlde,
in paine of heaven your forfeyture.

16 For I will wende and take my trace   110
and see this blesse in every tower.
Iche one of you kepe well his place;
and, Lucifer, I make thee govcrnour.
Nowe I charge the grounde of grace
that yt be set with my order.   115

93 and] yf B   94 we not] not wee H   96 we ever] we will ever A,
we will aye B, ay will we H   97 ourselves] ourselfe H   98 us marked]
marked us BH   might] myrth H   99 byde] abyde H   101 bearer]
bord B   102 that] the H   105 ever] aye H   DEUS] GOD A
106 neare] ney B, ne H   107 that] this H   109 your] ever H
113 thee] thie B   114 the] here the H   115 yt] they H   with] in H

Behoulde the beames of my brighte face,
which ever was and shall indewer.
This is your health in every case:
to behoulde your creator.
Was never none so like me, soe full of grace,   120
nor never shall as my fygure.
Here will I bide nowe in this place
to be angells comforture.
To be revisible in shorte space,
it is my will in this same houre.   125

LUCIFFER

17 Aha, that I ame wounderous brighte,
amongest you all shininge full cleare!
Of all heaven I beare the lighte
though God hymselfe and he were here.
All in this throne yf that I were,   130
then shoulde I be as wise as hee.
What saye ye, angells all that bene here?
Some comforte soone now let me see.

VERTUTES

18 Wee will not assente unto your pride
nor in our hartes take such a thoughte;   135
but that our lorde shalbe our guyde,
and keepe that he to us hath wroughte.

CHERUBYN

19 Our lorde comaunded all that bene here
to keepe there seates, bouth more and lesse.
Therfore I warne the, Luciffer,   140
this pride will torne to greate distresse.

116 face] *om* A   119 to] for to H   creator] creature A   120 so]
om BH   soe full of grace] under lace H   121 shall] shalbe H   fygure]
fyg A   122] in this place A   bide] abyde H   123] comforture A
to] for to H   124 to be] *om* A   125 it is] *om* A   *After* 125] Tunc
cantant et recedet Deus H   126 Aha] Ah Ah H   127 full] so H
133 soone] send B   134 assente] sent H   137 that he to us] to us that
he BH   139 there seates] his hestes H   141 this] thie B

LUCIFFER

Destresse? I commaunde you for to cease
and see the beautie that I beare.
All heaven shines through my brightnes
for God himselfe shines not so cleare.   145

DOMINACIONES

20 Of all angells yee beare the price
and most beautie is you befall.
My counsell is that you be wise,
that you bringe not yourselves in thrall.

PRINCIPATES

Yf that ye in thrall you bringe,   150
then shall you have a wicked fall;
and alsoe your ofspringe,
away with you they shall all.

CHERUBYN

21 Our brethers counsell is good to here,
to you I saye, Lucifer and Lightborne.   155
Wherfore beware you of this cheere,
least that you have a fowle spurne.

LIGHTEBORNE

22 In fayth, brother, yet you shall
sitt in this throne—arte cleane and cleare—
that yee maye be as wise withall   160
as God himselfe, yf he were heare.
Therfore you shalbe set here,
that all heaven maye ye behoulde.
The brightnes of your bodie cleare
is brighter then God a thousandfoulde.   165

142 for] all H   DOMINACIONES] DOMINATIONS H   149 yourselves] your-
self BH   PRINCIPATES] PRINCIPATUS H   150 yf] and yf BH   151 then]
om A   152 and] om A   your] all your BH   153 away] ye A
CHERUBYN] CHERAPHIN A, CERAPHINE B, CHERUB: H   154 brethers] breth-
rens ABH   good to here] go A   155 Lightborne] Lightbo A, Lighthurne
BH   156 this cheere] this chayer B, that chayre H   158 yet] but yet H
159 arte] that is A, both BH   160 maye] mighte A   162] om H

THRONES

23 Alas, that beautie will you spill
    yf you keepe it all in your thought;
    then will pride have all his will
    and bringe your brightnes all to naughte.
    Let yt passe out of your thought,   170
    and caste awaye all wicked pride;
    and keepe your brightnes to you is wrought,
    and let our lorde be all our guyde.

6ᵛ   POTESTATES

24 Alas that pride is the wall of beautye
    that tornes your thought to greate offence.   175
    The brightnes of your fayer bodyes
    will make yee to goe hense.

LUCIFFER

25 Goe hense? Behoulde, sennyors one every syde,
    and unto me you caste your eyen.
    I charge you angells in this tyde   180
    behoulde and see now what I meane.
    Above greate God I will me guyde
    and set myselfe here; as I wene,
    I ame pearlesse and prince of pride,
    for God hymselfe shines not so sheene.   185

26 Here will I sitt nowe in his steade,
    to exsaulte myselfe in this same see.
    Behoulde my bodye, handes and head—
    the mighte of God is marked in mee.
    All angells, torne to me I read,   190
    and to your soveraigne kneele one your knee.

THRONES] ANGELI H   166 spill] spoyll B   170 thought] thoughtes B
172 to] that to H   173 our(2)] your H   POTESTATES] om BH   174–7]
om B   174 beautye] lewtye H   176 the] the great H   fayer] om H
bodyes] bodye AH   177 to] sone for to H   LUCIFFER] POTESTATES B
178 goe hense] om H   179 you] om H   eyen] dene(?) B   181 now]
om H   I] I doe H   183 wene] wine B   185 sheene] shine B
186 his steade] this stide B, this stid H   187 see] om A   188 handes]
both hand H   head] h A   189 in mee] om A   191 kneele one your
knee] kn A

I ame your comforte, bouth lorde and head,
the meirth and might of the majestye.

LIGHTEBORNE

27 And I ame nexte of the same degree,
repleth by all experience.   195
Methinkes yf I mighte sit him bye
all heaven shoulde doe us reverence.
All orders maye assente to thee and me;
thou hast them torned by eloquence.
And here were nowe the Trenitie,   200
we shoulde him passe by our fullgens.

DOMINACIONES

28 Alas, why make yee this greate offence?
Bouth Luciffer and Lightborne, to you I saye,
our soveraigne lorde will have you hense
and he fynde you in this araye.   205
Goe too your seates and wynde you hense.
You have begone a parlous playe.
Ye shall well witt the subsequcnce—
this daunce will torne to teene and traye.

7ʳ   LUCIFER

29 I redd you all doe me reverence,   210
that ame repleth with heavenly grace.
Though God come, I will not hense,
but sitt righte here before his face.

'Gloria tibi Trinitas'

DEUS

30 Saye, what araye doe ye make here?
Who is your prince and principall?   215

192 I ame your com] *om* A   193 the meirth] *om* A   and] *om* A, and the H
the] your B   195 by all] all by H   196 mighte] should B   sit]
sett B   him bye] by thie BH   197 us] me H   198 all] our H
maye] arc H   199 them] us H   by] by thy H   DOMINACIONES] DOMINA-
TIONS H   206 wynde] wende AH, weende B   you] *om* H   208 witt]
weete B   209 will] shall A   to] yow to H   210 redd] rade B
212 come] come here H   *To right of* 212] Et sedet H   *SD*] oria
Trenits A, *om* H   DEUS] GOD A   215 who] where H   *To right of*
215] Tunc quatiunt et tremescunt H

I made thee angell and Lucifer,
and here thou woulde be lorde over all.
Therfore I charge this order cleare,
faste from this place looke that yee fall.
Full soone I shall chaunge your cheare—   220
for your fowle pride to hell you shall.

31 Lucifer, who set thee here when I was goe?
What have I offended unto thee?
I made thee my frende; thou arte my foe.
Why haste thou tresspassed thus to me?   225
Above all angells there were no moe
that sitt so nighe my majestye.
I charge you to fall till I byd 'Whoo,'
into the deepe pitt of hell ever to bee.

Nowe Lucifer and Lightborne fall.

PRIMUS DEMON

32 Alas that ever we were wroughte,   230
that we shoulde come into this place!
Wee were in joye; nowe we be naughte.
Alas, we have forfayted our grace!

SECUNDUS DEMON

And even heither thou hast us broughte
into dungeon to take our trace.   235
All this sorrowe thou hast us soughte—
the devill maye speede thy stinckinge face.

7ᵛ   PRIMUS DEMON

33 My face, false feature, for thy fare!
Thou hast us broughte to teene and treay.

216 angell and] an angell H   220 shall] shall doe H   223] why hast
thou trespast unto mee H   224 I made] ade A   225] what have I
trespased unto thee H   why] *om* A   thus] this A   226 above] *om* A
were] was H   227 that] *om* A   sitt] *om* A, sett B, sate H   my] the H
228 I charge you] u A   to] all A, *om* H   whoo] hoe H   *To right of* 228]
Tunc cadent Lucif. et Light H   229 into the deepe] epe A, to the H   pitt]
om B   ever] for ever B, evermore H   *SD*] Nowe Lucifer and Light A,
om H   232 we be] be we B   235 into] into the A, into a BH
236 us] yt H

I cumber, I congere, I kindle in care.   240
I sincke in sorrowe; what shall I saye?

SECUNDUS DEMON

34 Thou haste us broughte this wicked waye
    through thy mighte and thy pryde,
    out of the blesse that lasteth aye
    in sorowe evermore to abyde.   245

PRIMUS DEMON

35 Thy witt yt was as well as myne,
    of that pryde that we did shewe;
    and nowe bene here in hell fier
    till the day of dome that [beames] shall bloo.

SECUNDUS DEMON

36 Then shall we never care for woo,   250
    but lye here like two feeyndes blacke.
    Alas, that ever we did forgett soe
    that lordes love to lose that did us make.

PRIMUS DEMON

37 And therfore I shall for his sake
    shewe mankynde greate envye.   255
    As soone as ever he can hym make,
    I shall sende, hym to destroye,

38 one—of myne order shall he bee—
    to make mankinde to doe amisse.
    Ruffyn, my frende fayer and free,   260
    loke that thou keepe mankinde from blesse

240 congere] canker H   DEMON] om H   243 and] all and H   244 the
blesse] joy H   aye] ever A   245 to] for to ABH   DEMON] om H
248 bene] lyve B, lyethe H   fier] pine BH   249 that] tell A   beames]
beanes R   shall] om A   SECUNDUS DEMON] om H   250 care] wante A
252 ever] om H   forgett] forfayt H   253] the lordes love that did us
forsake H   lose] loose B   PRIMUS DEMON] om H   256 make] ma A
257 to] for to H   258] er shall he be A   one] some H   259 to make]
om A   260 Ruffyn] yne A, ruffian H   fayer] feare B   261 loke] e A
blesse] blisse BH

39 that I and my fellowes fell downe for aye.
    He will ordeyne mankinde againe
    in blesse to be in greate araye,
    and wee evermore in hell paine.   265

8r   SECUNDUS DEMON

40 Out, harrowe! Where is our mighte
    that we were wonte to shewe,
    and in heaven bare soe greate lighte,
    and nowe we be in hell full lowe?

                      PRIMUS DEMON

41 Out, alas! For woo and wickednesse   270
    I ame so fast bounde in this cheare
    and never awaye hense shall passe,
    but lye in hell allwaye heare.

                          DEUS

42 A, wicked pryde! A, woo worth thee, woo!
    My meirth thou hast made amisse.   275
    I maye well suffer: my will is not soe
    that they shoulde parte this from my blesse.
    A, pryde! Why mighte thou not braste in two?
    Why did the that? Why did they thus?
    Behoulde, my angells, pride is your foe.   280
    All sorrowe shall shewe wheresoever yt is.

43 And though they have broken my comaundement,
    me ruse yt sore full sufferently.
    Neverthelesse, I will have myne intente—
    that I first thought, yet soe will I.   285

263 ordeyne] ordeyne ordeyne B mankinde] manking B   264 in(2)] with
BH   SECUNDUS DEMON] om H   267 we] om H   to] for to H   269 we
be] lye H   PRIMUS DEMON] om H   271 I] that I A, that B   273 all-
waye] alwaye still B, all still H   DEUS] GOD A   274 a woo] aye woe B,
aye H   275 thou hast] hast thou H   277 this] thus BH   blesse]
blisse BH   278 why] when H   mighte] hast B   not] om H   279 that]
so H   thus] this H   281 wheresoever] wherever H   282 comaunde-
ment] comaundementes B   283 sufferently] soveraignlye AH   285 that]
what H

I and two persons be at one assente
a sollempne matter for to trye.
A full fayer image we have imente,
that the same stydd shall multiplye.

44 In my blessinge here I begyne   290
   the first that shalbe to my paye.
   Lightenes and darkenes, I byde you twene:
   the darke to the nighte, the lighte to the day.
   Keepe your course for more or myne
   and suffer not, to you I saye;   295
   but save yourselfe, bouth out and in.
   That is my will, and will allwaye.

8ᵛ   45 As I have made you all of noughte
   at myne owne wisheinge,
   my first day heare have I wroughte.   300
   I geve yt here my blessinge.

Finis

PLAY II

6ʳ   THE DRAPERS PLAYE

Incipit Pagina Secunda qualiter Deus docuit mundum.

DEUS

Ego sum alpha et omega, 1, primus et novissimus.

1 I, God, moste of majestye,
  in whom begininge none may bee;

286 be at one] are at H   288 we have imente] now have I ment H
289 the] this H   stydd] seede A   291 first] first thing H   292 and]
om H   twene] twinne BH   294 keepe] om A   your] yow this H   or]
a H   295 and] om A   296 but save] om A   297 that is my] om A
298 you all] all thinges H   noughte] no A   299] after my will and my
wisshing H   300 heare] now H   wroughte] om A   301 here] fullie H

   Guild-ascription] Drapers H   Play-heading] Pagina Secunda de Creatione
Mundi et Adam et Eva, be eorumque Tentatione H   docuit] docuett A,
creavit B   mundum] mundom dicat Jesus A   DEUS] GOD A, after Latin
and also before first line R   To left of DEUS] Minstrels play B   Latin]
om H   omega] o AR   1] om ARB   1 of] in ARBH

enlesse alsoe, moste of postee,
I am and have binne ever.
Now heaven and earth is made through mee. 5
The earth is voyd ondly I see;
therfore light for more lee
through my might I will liever.

2 At my byddynge made be light.
Light is good, I see in sight. 10
Twynned shalbe through my might
the light from thestearnes.
Light 'day' I wilbe called aye,
and thestearnes 'night', as I saye.
This morne and evene, the first day, 15
is made full and expresse.

3 Now will I make the firmament
in myddeste the water to bee lent,
for to bee a divident
to twynne the waters aye; 20
above the welkyn, beneath alsoe,
and 'heaven' hit shalbe called thoo.
This commen is morne and even also
of the seoconde daye.

4 Now will I waters everychone 25
that under heaven bine great one,
that the gather into one,
and drynesse sone them shewe.
That dryenesse 'yearth' men shall call.
The gatheringe of the waters all, 30
'seeyes' to [name] have the shall;
therby men shall them knowe.

5 I will one yearth yerbes springe,
ichon in kinde seede-gevinge;

3 enlesse] endles ARBH   alsoe] as H   6 ondly] onlye ARBH   8 might]
crafte H   liever] liver AR, be ever B, kever H   9 made] now made H
12 thestearnes] the steres B   14 thestearnes] the stares B   15 this
morne] thus morrow H   18 water] watters ARBH   22 thoo] oo H
23 this] thus AH   morne and even] even and morrow H   25 everychone]
everye ichone AB   26 one] won H   27 gather] together H   28 them]
him H   29 that] the A   31 name] man HmAR, men B   have] shewe R
32 them] om H   33 yearth] earth that ARBH   34 seede] seedes B

trees diverse fruite forth bringe   35
after ther kynde eachone;
the seede of which aye shalbe
within the fruite of each tree.
This morne and even of dayes three
is both commen and gonne.   40

6ᵛ   6 Now will I make through my might
             lightninges in the welkyn bright,
             to twyne the daye from the night
             and lighten the earth with lee.
             Great lightes I will too—   45
             the sonne and eke the moone also—
             the sonne for day to serve for oo,
             the moone for night to bee.

             7 Stares also through myne entente
             I will make one the firmamente,   50
             the yearth to lighten there the be lent;
             and knowne may be therby
             courses of planets, nothinge amisse.
             Now see I this worke good iwisse.
             This morninge and evon both made is,   55
             the fourthe day fullye.

             8 Now will I in waters fishe forth bringe,
             fowles in the firmament flyinge,
             great whalles in the sea swiminge;
             all make I with a thoughte—   60
             beastes, fowles, fruit, stone, and tree.
             These workes are good, well I see.
             Therfore to blesse all well liketh me,
             this worke that I have wrought.

35 fruite] frutes ARBH   36 after] fter A   37 the] om A   aye] for
aye H   38 within] thin A   39 this] om A, thus H   mornc] morrow H
40] men and gone A   41 might] om A   42 lightninges] lightninge
ARBH   45 I] also I H   will] will make H   too] towe A, two RBH
47 oo] aye R   49 and 50] reversed H   51 lent] sent H   55 this]
thus BH   morninge] morrow H   evon] eveninge R   57 waters] watter A
59 sea] seas R   61 fruit] om H   62 these] the H   63 well liketh]
lykes H   64 this worke] thees work B, these workes H .

9 All beastes, I byd you multyplye   65
   in yearth and water by and by,
   and fowles in the ayre to flye,
   the yearth to fulfill.
   This morne and evon through my might
   of the fiveth day and the night   70
   is made and ended well aright,
   all at my owne will.

10 Now will I one earth bringe forth anon
    all helpely beastes, everychone
    that crepon, flyen, or gone,   75
    eachon in his kynde.
    Now is this donne at my byddinge:
    beastes goinge, flyinge, and crepinge;
    and all my worke at my likinge
    fully now I fynde.   80

Then goinge from the place where he was, commeth to the place
where he createth Adam.

7ʳ   11 Now heaven and earth is made expresse,
                make wee man to our likenesse.
                Fishe, fowle, beast—more and lesse—
                to mayster he shall have might.
                To our shape now make I thee;   85
                man and woman I will there bee.
                Growe and multyplye shall yee,
                and fulfill the earth on hight.

12 To helpe thee thou shalt have here
    herbes, trees, fruit, seede in fere.   90
    All shalbe put in thy power,
    and beastes eke alsoe;

66 and] in ARBH   67 the] *om* H   to] for to H   69 this] thus AH
morne] morrow H   70 fiveth] fifte ARBH   the(2)] *om* H   71 aright]
and righte A   73 bringe forth] forth bringe H   anon] a man B
74 helpely] kindes of H   everychone] everye ichone AR   75 or] and B,
or els H   77 is this] this is A, is H   at] all H   79 worke] workes H
SD] **Tunc** recedet de illo loco ad locum ubi creavit Adamum et faciet signum
quasi faceret ipsum H   then] then God ARB   createth] created R
Adam] Adam sayinge R, man B   *After SD*] GOD A   81 expresse] exp A
83 fishe] she A   beast] *om* A, beastes B, both H   84 to] *om* A   88 the]
om H   on] with A, in RBH   90 fruit seede] sede fruite H   91 put] *om* H

all that in yearth bine livinge,
fowles in the ayre flyinge,
and all that gost hath and likinge, 95
to sustayne you from woe.

13 Now this is donne, I see aright,
and all thinge made through my might.
The sixt day heare in my sight
ys made all of the best. 100
Heaven and earth ys wrought all within
and all that needes to be therin.
Tomorrowe, the seaventh day, I will blinne
and of workes take my rest.

14 But this man that I have made, 105
with goste of lief I will him gladde.

Adam rysinge.

DEUS

Rise up, Adam, rise up, ryse,
a man full of sowle and liefe,
and come with mee to paradice,
a place of deyntee and delite. 110
But it is good that thou be wise;
bringe not thyselfe in striefe.

Then the creatour bringeth Adam into paradice, before the tree
of knowledge, and saith (minstrelles playe):

DEUS

15 Here, Adam, I give thee this place,
thee to comforte and solace,

93 livinge] sterring H   94 ayre] height H   95 and(1)] om H   97 this
is] is this R   aright] right B   98 thinge] thinges ARBH   100 all]
all here R   101 all] om H   within] with wyne ARB   103 blinne]
solempe A, sollempne R   104 workes] worcke ARBH   105 but] but
now H   SD] Heare Adam rissinge, and God saith A, om H   DEUS]
GOD A, om H   107 rise up ryse] up rayde B, rise up rade H   108 a]
om H   110 delite] delice BH   SD] Tunc creator adducet eum in
paradisum ante lignum II   saith] saith as followeth R   minstrelles playe]
ynstrilles ayinge A, mynstrills playinge R, om H   DEUS] GOD A, om H

7ᵛ

to keepe it well while thou hit hasse,   115
and donne as I thee bydd.
Of all trees that bine herein
thou shalt eate and nothinge sinne;
but of this tree, for weale nor wynne,
thou eate by noe way.   120

16 What tyme thou eates of this tree,
death thee behoves, leave thow mee.
Therfore this fruit I will thee flee,
and be thou not too bould.
Beastes and fowles that thou may see   125
to thee obedyent shall they bee.
What name they bee given by thee,
that name they shall hould.

Then God taketh Adam by the hande and causeth him to lye
downe, and taketh a ribbe out of his syde and saith:

DEUS

17 Hit is not good man only to bee;
helpe to him now make wee.   130
But excice sleepe behoves mee
anon in this man heare.
One sleepe thou arte, well I see.
Heare a bone I take of thee,
and fleshe alsoe with harte free   135
to make thee a feere.

Then God doth make the woman of the ribbe of Adam, wakinge
and sayth to God:

115 to] *om* ABH   it well] to yt H   hasse] haste AR   116 and] *om* A,
then H   donne] doe BH   bydd] saye ARBH   117 all] all the H   herein]
heare AR, therein B   119 weale] wayle ARH   nor] or RH   120 by]
of by R, not by H   122 thee] *om* H   leave] beleeve AR   123 thee]
thou ARB, not H   flee] fley A, flye R   124 thou not] not thou B   too]
so H   125 thou] yow H   126 shall they] aye shall H   *SD*] Tunc
creator capiens manum Adami et faciet ipsum jacere et capiet costam H
DEUS] GOD A, *om* RH   130 helpe] a helpe R   *To right of* 130] Dormit H
131 excice] excesse AR, excite BH   behoves] behoveth H   mee] thee H
132 anon in] to make one AR   133 well] nowe well ARBH   134 heare]
therfore H   of] from R   136 feere] make R   *SD*] *om* H   wakinge
and] then Adam wakinge AR   sayth to God] speaketh unto God as followeth
R, saith B

ADAM

18 A, lorde, where have I longe bine?
For sythence I slepte much have I seene—
wonder that withouten weene
hereafter shalbe wiste.   140

DEUS

Ryse, Adam, and awake.
Heare have I formed the a make;
hir to thee thou shalt take,
and name hir as thee liste.

Adam, rysinge up, saith:

ADAM

8ʳ   19 I see well, lord, through thy grace   145
bonne of my bones thou hir mase;
and fleshe of my fleshe shee hase,
and my shape through thy sawe.
Therfore shee shalbe called, iwisse,
'viragoo', nothinge amisse;   150
for out of man taken shee is,
and to man shee shall drawe.

20 Of earth thou madest first mee,
both bone and fleshe; now I see
thou haot her given through thy postee   155
of that I in me had.
Therfore man kyndely shall forsake
father and mother, and to wife take;
too in one fleshe, as thou can make,
eyther other for to glad.   160

137 A] O ARB   lorde] *om* H   138 sythence] seithen AB, since R, sithe H
139 wonder] wonders H   DEUS] GOD A   141 ryse] rise up ARBH
143 hir] here H   144 thee] thy AR, thie B, thou H   SD] Adam
surgit H   Adam] heare Adam A   146 bones] bone H   149 therfore]
wherfore R   shee shalbe] shall she be H   152 shee shall] shall she H
153 thou madest first] first thou madest H   154 now] as now H
155 thy] her A   156 that] that life R   157 therfore] thearfhe H
158 take] betake R

Then Adam and Eve shall stand naked and shall not bee ashamed.
Then the serpente shall come up out of a hole, and the dyvell
walkinge shall say:

DEMON

21 Owt, owt, what sorrowe is this,
   that I have loste soe much blysse?
   For onste I thought to doe amysse,
   out of heaven I fell.
   The bryghtest angell I was or this,   165
   that ever was or yet is;
   but pryde cast me downe, iwisse,
   from heaven right into hell.

22 Gostlye paradice I was in,
   but thence I fell through sinne.   170
   Of yeartly paradice now, as I weene,
   a man is given masterye.
   By Belsabubb, I will never blynne
   till I may make him by some gynne
   from that place for to twyne   175
   and trespasse as did I.

23 Should such a caytiffe made of claye
   have such blisse? Nay, by my laye!
   For I shall teach his wiffe a playe
   and I may have a whyle.   180
   For her to disceave I hoppe I may,
   and through her brynge them both awaye;
   for shee will doe as I her saye,
   hir hoppe I will begylle.

8ᵛ   24 That woman is forbydden to doe   185
   for anythinge the will therto.

SD] Tunc Adam et Eva stabunt nudi et non verecundubunt; et veniet serpens
ad paradisum positum in specie demonis et ambulando dicat H   162 blysse]
blesse AR   163 onste] ones A, once RBH   to doe] I did R   168 into]
downe to AR, to H   169 gostlye] tlye A   170 but thence] nse A
sinne] my sinne BH   171 yeartly] earthly ARBH   weene] wen A, wyne R,
mynne BH   173 I will] shall I H   174 gynne] sinne BH   175 twyne]
twayne A   180 whyle] wyle A   181 to] om H   184 will] to BH
185 forbydden] forbyd H   186 the will therto] therto will shooe H

Therfore that tree shee shall come to
and assaye which it is.
Dight me I will anone tyte
and profer her of that ylke fruite;   190
soe shall they both for her delyte
bee banyshed from that blysse.

25 A maner of an edder is in this place
that wynges like a bryde shee hase—
feete as an edder, a maydens face—   195
hir kynde I will take.
And of the tree of paradice
shee shall eate through my contyse;
for wemen they be full licourouse,
that will shee not forsake.   200

26 And eate shee of hyt, full witterlye
they shall fare both as dyd I:
be banyshed both of that valley
and hir osprynge for aye.
Therfore, as brooke I my panne,   205
the edders coate I will take one;
and into paradice I will gonne
as faste as ever I maye.

Supremus volucris, penna serpens, pede forma, forma puella.

SERPENS

27 Woman, why was God soe nyce
to byd you leave for your delice   210

187] that tree she shall therfore come to B   shee shall] shall shee AH
189 dight] disguise H   anone] as H   190 ylke] same AR   191 her]
there RH   192 from that blysse] of that valleye A, from the blisse H
194 like] as H   bryde] birde ARBH   hase] hath B   195 feete] foote H
196 kynde] kindenes H   197 the] that H   198 contyse] curteise B
199 they be] are H   licourouse] liccoris AR   200 will shee] she will H
201 full] as H   203 be] and be R   both] out H   valley]
baylie H   204 hir] their H   osprynge] ofspringe ARBH   aye] ever
R   205 brooke] brocke H   panne] penne H   206 the] my H
take] putte ARH   207 I will] will I H   SD supremus] superius AR,
spinx H   pede forma] pede fronte H   forma puella] torma puella AR,
puella H   To left of SD] Versus H   210 for] so H   delice]
delite AR

and of each tree in paradice
to forsake the meate?

EVA

Nay, of the fruite of yche tree
for to eate good leave have wee,
save the fruite of one wee muste flee;   215
of hyt wee may not eate.

28 This tree heare that in the middest is,
eate wee of hit wee doe amysse.
God sayde we should dye iwys
and if we touch that tree.   220

SERPENS

Woman, I saye leave not this;
for hyt shall yee not loose the blysse
nor noe joy that is his,
but be as wyse as hee.

29 God is subtyle and wisse of witte   225
and wotteth well when ye eate it
that your eyne shalbe unknyt.
Like godes yee shalbe
and knowe both good and evill alsoe.
Therfore hee warned you therfroe.   230
Yee may well wotte hee was your foe;
therfore doe after mee.

30 Take of this fruite and assaye;
yt is good meate, I dare laye.
And but thou finde yt to thy paye,   235
say that I am false.

211 in] of H   214 good] god B, *om* H   215 the] *om* H   flee] fleye A,
fley R, fly B   216 wee may] maye we ABH   eate] eaten B   217 heare
that] that heare ARBH   the] *om* H   218 hit] that B   220 if] *om* H
touch] touched H   222 shall yee] ye shall R, shall H   loose the] lose
yow H   blysse] blesse AR   225 subtyle] subtilte AR, coynt H
226 wotteth] wotte you AR, wottes H   227 that] then ARB   228 like]
and like R   230 warned] counselled H   231 wotte] wytte ARH

And yee shall knowe bothe welle and woe
and bee like godes both too,
thou and thy husband alsoe.
Take thou one apple and noe moo.   240

EVA

31 A, lord, this tree is fayre and bryght,
greene and seemely to my sight,
the fruite sweete and much of myght,
that godes it may us make.
One apple of yt I will eate   245
to assaye which is the meate;
and my husbande I will gett
one morsell for to take.

Then Eve shall take of the fruite of the serpente, and shall eate
therof and say to Adam:

EVA

32 Adam, husbande liffe and deare,
eate some of this apple here.   250
Yt is fayre, my leeffe feare;
hit may thou not forsake.

9ᵛ   ADAM

That is soothe, Eve, withouten were;
the fruit is sweete and passinge feare.
Therfore I will doe thy prayer—   255
one morsell I will take.

Then Adam shall take the fruite and eate therof, and in weepinge
manner shall saye:

240] *before* 237 H   237 welle] weale ARB, wayle H   238 bee like]
lyke to H   both] *om* A   240 take] eate ARBH   apple] morsell R   moo]
more R   242 to] in H   243 much] full AR   245 one] an H
248 take] eate H   *SD*] *om* H   serpente] tree of the serpent R   say] shall
saye R   Adam] Adam followinge R   EVA] *om* H   251 leeffe] lyffes B
After 252] Tunc Adam comedit, et statim nudi sunt, et lamentando di H
253 Eve] Eva AR   withouten] without H   254 sweete] fayer A   passinge
feare] sweete in fere A, fayer in fere RBH   *SD*] *om* H   saye] saye followinge A

ADAM

33　Out, alas, what ayleth mee?
　　I am naked, well I see.
　　Woman, cursed mote thou bee,
　　for wee bothe nowe shente.　　　　　　260
　　I wotte not for shame whyther to flee,
　　for this fruite was forbydden mee.
　　Now have I brooken, through reade of thee,
　　my lordes commandemente.

EVA

34　Alas, this edder hathe done mee nye!　　265
　　Alas, hir reade why did I?
　　Naked wee bine bothe forthy,
　　and of our shappe ashamed.

ADAM

　　Yea, sooth sayde I in prophecye
　　when thou was taken of my bodye—　　270
　　mans woe thou would bee witterlye;
　　therfore thou was soe named.

EVA

35　Adam, husbande, I reade we take
　　this figge-leaves for shames sake,
　　and to our members an hillinge make　　275
　　of them for thee and mee.

ADAM

　　And therwith my members I will hide,
　　and under this tree I will abyde;
　　for surely come God us besyde,
　　owt of this place shall wee.　　　　　　280

ADAM] *om* ARBH　　　257 ayleth] eales H　　　259 mote] moth AR, maye B,
must H　　　260 wee bothe nowe] we be bouth nowe AR, bothe now we be
H　　　261 wotte] can H　　whyther] wheither A, whether RBH　　flee] fley
AR, flye B　　265 nye] n A　　270 when] whe H　　271 witterlye] witlie H
272 therfore] wherfore R　　274 this] thes AH, these RB　　shames]
shame H　　275 an] *om* H　　hillinge] hillinges RH　　277 and] *om* H
279 surely] sickerlie H

Then Adam and Eve shall cover ther members with leaves,
hydinge themselves under the trees. Then God shall speake
(minstrelles playe).

10ʳ   DEUS

36 Adam, Adam, where arte thou?

[ADAM]

A, lorde, I harde thy voyce nowe.
For I naked am, I make avowe,
therfore now I hyd mee.

DEUS

Whoe tould thee, Adam, thou naked was   285
save only thy trespasse,
that of the tree thou eaten hasse
that I forbydd thee?

ADAM

37 Lord, this woman that is here—
that thou gave to my feare—   290
gave mee parte at hir prayer,
and of hyt I did eate.

DEUS

Woman, why hast thou donne soo?

EVA

This edder, lorde, shee was my foe
and sothly mee disceaved alsoe,   295
and made mee to eate that meate.

SD] om H   speake] speake and A, speake to Adam sayinge R   playe] playinge
AR   DEUS] GOD A   After 281] Tunc Adam et Eva cooperiant genitalia
sua cum foliis et stabunt sub arbore, et venit Deus clamans cum alta voce H
ADAM] om Hm   282 nowe] right now H   283 for] om H   naked am]
am nacked ARBH   284 now] om H   hyd] hyde ARBH   DEUS] GOD A
285 whoe] om A   286 save only] e A   thy] thyn owne ARBH   287 that
of the] om A   288] bade thee A   forbydd] forbade RBH   ADAM] om A
289 lord this] om A   290 that thou] om A   gave] gave me ARBH
291 gave mee] om A   at] I did H   292 and of hyt] tt A, of it H
DEUS] GOD A   293 woman] oman A   294 this] the H   shee] om H
295 mee disceaved alsoe] deceved me thoo AH, deceived thoe RB

DEUS

38 Edder, for that thou haste donne this anye,
    amongste all beasts on earth thee by
    cursed thou shalt bee forthy,
    for this womans sake.   300
    Upon thy brest thou shalt goo,
    and eate the yearth to and froo;
    and emnytie betweene you too
    I insure thee I shall make.

39 Betweene thy seede and hirs alsoe   305
    I shall excyte thy sorrowe and woe;
    to breake thy head and be thy foe,
    shee shall have masterye aye.
    Noe beast one earth, I thee behett,
    that man soe little shall of seett;   310
    and troden bee full under foote
    for thy mysdeede todaye.

10ᵛ   DEUS (ad Evam)

40 And, woman, I warne thee witterlye,
    thy much payne I shall multyplye—
    with paynes, sorrowe, and great anye   315
    thy children thou shall beare.
    And for that thou haste done soe todaye,
    man shall master thee alwaye;
    and under his power thou shalte bee aye,
    thee for to dryve and deare.   320

DEUS (ad Adam)

41 And, man, alsoe I saye to thee—
    for thou haste not donne after mee,

DEUS] GOD A   297 anye] anoye A, noye H   299 thou shalt] shalt thou H
303 betweene] betwixt BH   too] towe A, two RBH   304] henceforth I
will make H   305 betweene] betwixt H   306 thy] om H   307 to]
and R   308 shee] yt ARB   *To right of* 309] Tunc recedet serpens, vocem
serpentinam faciens H   309 behett] behite B   310 seett] lette ARBH
311 bee] om B   full] fowle H   foote] his feete ARB, feete H   312 mys-
deede] misdeedes B   DEUS ad Evam] DEUS et Eva B, om H   314 much
payne] payne A, mischeife H   shall] shall moch AR   315 paynes] pennance H   anye] anoye ARH   316 thou shall] shalt thou H   317 that]
om H   318 man] the man H   320 dryve] derne H   DEUS ad Adam] om H

thy wyves counsell for to flee,
but donne soe hir byddinge
to eate the fruite of thys tree, 325
in thy worke warryed the earthe shalbe;
and with greate travell behoves [thee]
one earth to gett thy livinge.

42 When thou one earth traveled hasse,
fruite shall not growe in that place; 330
but thornes, brears for thy trespasse
to thee one earth shall springe.
Herbes, rootes thou shalte eate
and for thy sustenance sore sweate
with great mischeyfe to wynne thy meate, 335
nothinge to thy likinge.

43 Thus shall thou live, soothe to sayen,
for thou haste byne to mee unbayen,
ever tyll the tyme thou turne agayne
to yearth there thou came from. 340
For earth thou arte, as well is seene;
and after this worke, woe and teene,
to earth there thou shalt, withouten weene,
and all thy kynde alsoe.

Adam shall speake mourninglyc.

ADAM

44 Alas, now in longer I am ilente! 345
Alas, nowe shamely am I shente!
For I was unobedyente,
of weale now am I wayved.

323 flee] fley AR, flye B   324 soe] to AR   326 warryed] wearied B
327 with] in H   behoves thee] behoves Hm, behoveth the H   329 thou one
earth traveled] on the earthe traveyled thou H   hasse] haste AR   330 in] on
H   that] eich R   331 brears] and bryers H   332 shall] the shall AR
333 rootes] and rootes ARBH   334 sweate] swe A   335 thy] thee B
339 the] om H   340 to] to the A   there] wher A   from] froe ARII
342 this worke] thes worckes AR, this world H   343 there] om AH   SD]
om H   Adam] heare Adam A   shall speake] speakeinge R   mourninglye]
mournglye A, mournefullie B   345 now in longer] in languor now H
I am ilente] am I lente ARB, I am lent H   346 shamely] shamfullie H
am I] I am H   347 unobedyente] inobedyente H   348 wayved] weined
ARB

Nowe all my kynde by mee ys kente
to flee womens intycemente.   350
Whoe trusteth them in any intente,
truely hee is disceaved.

45 My licourouse wyfe hath bynne my foe;
the devylls envye shente mee alsoe.
These too together well may goe,   355
the suster and the brother.
His wrathe hathe donne me muche woe;
hir glotonye greved mee alsoe.
God lett never man trust you too,
the one more then the other.   360

DEUS

46 Nowe wee shall parte from this lee.
Hilled behoveth you to to bee.
Dead beaste skynes, as thinketh mee,
ys best you one you beare.
For deadly nowe both bine yee   365
and death noe way may you flee.
Such clothes are best for your degree
and such shall yee weare.

Then God, puttynge garmentes of skynnes upon them:

DEUS

47 Adam, nowe hast thou thy wyllynge,
for thou desyred above all thinge   370
of good and evell to have knowinge;
nowe wrought is all thy will.

350 flee] fleye A, fleey R, flye B   womens] wemens A, womans BH
351 whoe] that H   trusteth] trustes H   in any] ought in his H   353 licou-
rouse] liccorise A, lyckorous R   354 shente] hath shente A   355 these
too] they twayne H   358 greved] hath greved AR   359 you] them H
DEUS] GOD A   361 wee shall] you shall AR, shall ye B, shall they H
from] _om_ H   362 hilled] hilled it AR   behoveth you] behoves you A, yow
behoves H   to to] to ARBH   363 beaste] beastes ABH   364 you
one you] for you to R   365 nowe both] bothe now H   366 and] for R
noe way may you] maye you noe waye A, no waye ye may B   368 shall
yee] now ye shall H   _SD_] Tunc Deus induet Adam et Eva tunicis pelliciis H
upon them] one Adam and Eve saith A, one them saith R   DEUS] GOD A
369 Adam] am A   hast thou] thou haste A   370 for thou] hou A
desyred] desiereste AR, dcsiredest H   above] over ARBH

Thou wouldeste knowe both weelle and woe;
nowe is it fallen to thee soe.
Therfore hence thou muste goo,   375
and thy desyre fullfilled.

48 Now lest thou [covett]este more
and doe as thou haste donne before—
eate of this fruite—to live evermore
heare may thou not bee.   380
To yearth thyder thou muste gonne;
with travell leade thy liefe therone.
For syccere there is noe other wonne.
Goe forthe; take Eve with thee.

Then God shall dryve Adam and Eve out of paradice, and sayth
to the Angell
11ᵛ (minstrelles playe):

DEUS

49 Nowe will I that there lenge within   385
the angelles order Cherubynn,
to keepe this place of weale and wynne
that Adam lost thus hathe,
with sharpe swordes one everye syde
and flame of fyer here to abyde,   390
that never a yearthly man in glyde;
forgiven the bynne that grace.

PRIMUS ANGELUS

50 Lorde, that order that is righte
is readye seett heare in thy syghte,
with flame of fyer readye to fyghte   395
agaynst mankynde, thy foe,

374 is it] yt is H   375 thou muste] now must thou B   376 fullfilled]
fulfill H   377 covetteste] cannot este HmAR, covett BH more] anie more
B, elswheare H   379 live] lief H   381 thyder thou] thou gather H
383 noe] non H   wonne] one H   SD] Tunc Deus emittet eos de para-
diso H   sayth] saye AR   Angell] angelles AR   minstrelles] and mynstrilles
A, minstres B   playe] shall playe A, playinge R   DEUS] GOD A, om H
385 lenge within] linge AR   387 and] or A   388 lost] lorne H   hathe]
hase H   389 swordes] sworde ARBH   391 a] om H   392 forgiven]
forgright H   393 that] as H

to whom noe grace is claymed by righte.
Shall none of them byde in thy sighte
tyll Wysdome, Right, Mercye, and Mighte
shall buy them and other moe.   400

SECUNDUS ANGELUS

51 I, Cherubyn, muste here bee chyce
to keepe this place of great pryce.
Sythenn man was soe unwyse,
this wyninge I muste weare—
that hee by crafte or countyce   405
shall not come in that was hise,
but deprived bee of paradyce,
noe more for to come there.

TERCIUS ANGELUS

52 And in this herytage I wilbe,
still for to ever see   410
that noe man come in this cyttye
as God hath me beheight.
Swordes of fyer have all wee
to make mann from this place to flee,
from this dwellinge of greate dayntee   415
that to him first was dighte.

QUARTUS ANGELUS

53 And of this order I am made one,
from mankynde to weare this wone
that through his gilte hath forgone
this wonninge full of grace.   420

397] to whom grace cleane is gright H   by righte] arighte AR, of right B
398] is readye sette heare in thy sighte AR   byde] lenge H   thy] my H
400 shall] om H   401 I] a R   muste] most H   here] ther AR   bee]
by H   chyce] coyse A, choyce RH, chyffe B   403 sythenn] seinge A, sith
that H   404 wyninge] woninge ARB, woming H   I muste weare] for to
lose A   405 hee] om R   or] nor ARB, ne no H   countyce] covetice B
407 deprived] pryved H   of] from H   409 in] om H   410 still] freely
B, sleelie H   to ever see] ever to see AR, to oversee H   411 in] into A
412 me] now H   413 swordes] sword H   all] shall H   415 this]
his H   417 and] om H   419 hath] he hath H, hath so B   forgone]
gone AR   420] for gright they bene that grace H

12ʳ   Therfore departe the must eycheone.
Our swordes of fyer shall bee there bonne
and myselfe there verye fonne,
to flame them in the face.

Minstrelles playe.

ADAM

54 Hight God and highest kynge,   425
that of nought made all thinge—
beast, fowle, and grasse growinge—
and me of yearth made,
thou gave me grace to doe thy wyllinge.
For after great sorrowe and sikinge   430
thou hast mee lent greate likinge,
too sonnes my hearte to glade:

55 Cayne and Abell, my childrenn deare,
whome I gate within xxx yeare
after the tyme wee depryved weare   435
of paradyce for our pryde.
Therfore nowe them will I lere,
to make them knowe in good manere
what I sawe when Eve, my feere,
was taken of my syde.   440

56 Whyle that I slepte in that place
my gost to heaven banished was;
for to see I ther had grace
thinges that shall befall.
To make you ware of comberouse case   445
and lett your doinge from trespasse,
sonne, I will tell before your face—
but I will not tell all.

421 departe] eschue H   422 our] and R, or H   swordes of fyer] els
sword H   423 there verye] also there H   SD] om H   minstrelles]
nstrilles A, minstres B   playe] ayinge A, playinge R   425 hight] highe
ARBH   429 gave] geve H   433 childrenn] childer H   435 depryved]
waved H   436 for] om B   437 them will I] I will them AH, them I
will R   439 sawe] see H   441 whyle] whyles H   442 banished]
ravished H   443 I ther had] ther I hade ARB, there had I H   444 thinges]
inges A   445 to make] ake A   446 your] you ARBH   doinge from]
for to doe H   447 sonne] some BH

57 I wott by things that I there see
    that God will come from heaven on hie,   450
    to overcome the devill soe slee
    and light into my kynde;
    and my blood that hee will wyne
    that I soe lost for my synne;
    a new lawe ther shall begine   455
    and soe men shall them sure.

58 Water or fyer also witterlye
    all this world shall distroye,
    for men shall synne soe horryblye
    and doe full much amysse.   460
    Therfore that yee may escape that nye,
    doe well and be ware me bye.
    I tell you heare in prophecye
    that this will fall ywisse.

59 Alsoe I see, as I shall saye,   465
    that God will come the laste daye
    to deeme mankynde in fleshe verey,
    and flame of fyer burninge,
    the good to heaven, the evell to hell.
    Your childrenn this tale yee may tell.   470
    This sight saw I in paradyce or I fell,
    as laye there sleepinge.

60 Nowe will I tell howe yee shall doe
    Godes love to underfoo.
    Cayne, husbandes crafte thou must goe to;   475
    and Abell, a shepharde bee.
    Therfore of cornes fayre and cleane
    that growes one ridges out of reane,
    Cayne, thou shalt offer, as I meane,
    to God in majestee.   480

12ᵛ — margin note next to line 461 area

449 I there] ther I AR   450 on] *om* ARH   451 soe slee] so slye AH,
to fley B   455 ther] then H   456 them sure] yt finde H   457 also]
as H   459 horryblye] horrlebly H   460 full] so H   461 yee] they H
nye] noy H   462 me bye] by me B   463 in] by H   464 that this will
fall] this will befall H   466 the] in the B   467 deeme] judge R
470 childrenn] childer H   471 sight] *om* H   472 as] as I ARBH
474 love] lawe AR   476 and] *om* H   bee] shalbe H   478 growes]
groweth H   of] of the ARH

61 And Abell, while thy lief shall laste
   thou shalt offer—and doe my heste—
   to God the first-borne beaste;
   therto thou make thee bowne.
   Thus shall yee please God almight   485
   if yee doe this well and righte,
   with good harte in his sight
   and full devotyon.

62 Nowe for to gett you sustenance
   I will you teach withou distance.   490
   For sythen I feele that myschaunce
   of that fruite for to eate,
   my leefe children fayre and free,
   with this spade that yee may see
   I have dolven. Learne yee this at mee,   495
   howe yee shall wynne your meate.

EVA

63 My sweete children, darlinges deare,
   yee shall see how I live heare
   because enbuxone so wee weare
   and did as God would not wee shoulde.   500
13ʳ   This payne, theras had bine no neede,
   I suffer on yearth for my misdeede;
   and of this wooll I will spyn threede by threede,
   to hill mee from the could.

64 Another sorrowe I suffer alsoe: 505
   my childrenn must I beare with woo,
   as I have donne both you too;
   and soe shall wemen all.

481 while thy] thou while H   shall] maye ARBH   482 heste] best H
485 thus] this AR   486 righte] aright B   488 full] good AR   489 you]
your H   490 withou] without ARBH   491 sythen] sithence B, sith H
feele] feelde AR, fell H   that] that fowle H   493 leefe] leiffe AR, lief B,
life H   494 that] s as H   495 yee] *om* H   *After* 496] Tunc Adam
fodiet terram et docebit filios, et Eva colum habebat H   499] bycause that
we unbuxom weare H   enbuxone] unobedient R   500 would not wee
shoulde] nowld H   501 theras] heare as A, ther is H   503 I] *om* H
will] *om* RH   504 hill] hyde R   mee] *om* H   506 must I] I muste
ARBH

This was the divell, our bytter foe,
that made us out of joy to goe.   510
To please, therfore, sonnes bee throwe,
in sinne that yee ne fall.

CAYNE

65   Mother, for sooth I tell yt thee,
a tyllman I am and soe wilbe.
As my father hath taught yt me,   515
I will fulfill his lore.

Hear he bringe in the plough.

CAYNE

Of corne I have great plentee;
sacrifice to God sonne shall yee see.
I will make too looke if hee
will sende mee any more.   520

ABELL

66   And I will with devotyon
to my sacrafice make mee bowne.
The comelyest beaste, by my crowne,
to the lorde I will choyse
and offer yt before thee here,   525
meeklye in good manere.
Noe beast to thee may bee deare
that may I not leese.

Heare Adam and Eve goe out tyll Cayne have slayne Abell.

509 this] thus R   was] *om* A   511 therfore sonnes] God sonnes therfore ARBH   512 in] from AR   ne] maye AR, not H   514 wilbe] will I be ARH   515 father] daddye A   yt] *om* H   *SD*] *om* H   he] Cayme A bringe] bringes ARB   plough] plough and saith AR   cayne] *om* RH 517 corne] cornes H   518 sonne] sone A, soone RB, as H   shall yee] yow shall H   519 will] *om* B   521 with] *om* B   523 comelyest] cleanest H 524 to] *om* A   the] my B, thee my H   choyse] chouse AR, chose H   526 in] and in H   527 deare] to deare H   528 that may I] for that I may H leese] lese A, lose R, loose H   *SD*] *om* H   heare] then R   have] hath AR   Abell] Abell and Cayme saith A

CAYNE

67 I am the elder of us too;
therfore firste I will goe.   530
Such as the fruite is fallen froo
is good inough for him.
This corne standinge, as mote I thee,
was eaten with beastes, men may see.
God, thou gettest noe other of mee,   535
be thou never soe gryme.

13ᵛ 68 Hit weare pittye, by my panne,
those fayre eares for to brenne.
Therefore the devill honge mee then
and thou of hit gett ought.   540
This earles corne grewe nexte the waye;
of these offer I will todaye.
For cleane corne, by my faye,
of mee gettest thou nought.

69 Loe, lord, here may thou see   545
such corne as grew to mee.
Parte of hit I bringe to thee,
anone withouten lett.
I hope thou wilte white mee this
and sende mee more of worldly blisse;   550
ells forsooth thou doest amisse
and thou bee in my debt.

ABELL

70 Now my brother, as I see,
hathe done sacrafice to thee.
Offer I will, as falleth for mee,   555
suche as thou haste mee sente.

534 men] as men H   535 noe] non H   other] better AR   537–40] *om* A
537 panne] penne H   538 those] these R, thes B, this H   fayre eares] eared
corne H brenne] brunc B   539 then] than H   540 thou] he H   hit] this
RBH   541 this] thes AR   corne] cornes AR   nexte] nye H   542 these]
this H   544 thou] he H   545 lord] God ARBH   549 white] quite H
550 worldly] wordlie B   blisse] blesse AR   551 ells] or elles AR
552 bee] long H   *After* 552] Tunc Abell mactabit animalia H   553 as]
hath H   554 hathe done] offred H   to] nowe to ARBH   555 falleth]
falles H

The beste beaste, as mote I thee,
of all my flocke with harte free
to thee offered it shalbe.
Receave, lorde, my presente.   560

Then a flame of fyer shall descende upon thee sacrafice of Abell.

ABELL

71   Ah, high God and kinge of blisse,
nowe sothly knowe I well by this
my sacrafice accepted is
before the lorde todaye.
A flame of fyer thou sende hase   565
from heaven one high into this place.
I thanke thee, lorde, of thy grace
and soe I shall doe aye.

CAYNE

72   Owt, owt! How have I spend my good?
To see this sight I am neare wood.   570
A flame of fyer from heaven stood
one my brothers offeringe.

14ʳ   His sacrafice I see God takes,
and my refuses and forsakes.
My semblant for shame shakes   575
for envy of this thinge.

DEUS (ad Cayne)

73   Cayne, why arte thou wroth? Why?
Thy semblant changes wonderously.
If thou doe well and truely,
thou may have meede of mee.   580

---

558 all] *om* AR   559 it shalbe] shall yt be AR   *SD*] Tunc flamma ignea veniet super sacrificium Abell H thee] the ARB   ABELL] *om* H   561 blisse] blesse AR   562 by this] iwis H   565 thou sende] thou sent B, send thou H hase] haste AR   566 high] it H   into] unto R   567 thee] the B   thy] his B   568 I shall] shall I H   aye] ever A   570 am] waxe ARBH 574 my] myne ARBH   ad Cayne] *om* H   577 why(2)] now why H 578 wonderously] wonderlie H   580 meede] need RH

Wottys thou not well that for thy deede
yf thou doe well thou may have meede;
if thou doe fowle, fowle for to speede
and syccere therafter to bee?

74 But, Cayne, thou shalt have all thy will,   585
thy talent yf thou wilt fulfill.
Synne of hit will thee spill
and make thee evell to speede.
Thy brother buxone aye shalbe
and fully under thy postee;   590
the luste therof pertaynes to thee.
Advyse thee of thy deede.

CAYNE

75 A, well, well, ys yt soe?
Come forth with mee. Thow must goe
into the fyeld a little froo;   595
I have and errande to saye.

ABELL

Brother, to the I am ready
to goe with thee full meekly.
For thou arte elder then am I,
thy will I will doe aye.   600

CAYNE

76 Say, thou caytiffe, thou congeon,
weneste thou to passe mee of renowne?
Thou shalt fayle, by my crowne,
of masterye yf I may.
God hath challenged mee nowe heare   605
for thee, and that in fowle manere;
and that shalt thou abye full deare
or that thou wende away.

581 thy] this B   582 have] *om* AR   583 for] *om* ARB   584 syccere]
sicurre B   therafter] therof ARBH   586 thy] the H   590 fully] fulfill H
under thy] after this B   591] frewill graunted is to thee H   592 thee]
thie B   thy] thee B   593 ys yt] then is it B, then it is H   594 come]
me A   forth] forth brother H   thow must] to H   595 into] *om* A   the]
om B   froo] here froe H   596 I have] *om* A   and] an ARBH   598 full]
moste A   600 aye] ever A   601 thou congeon] tho conjoyne H
605 challenged] challensed R   607 abye] abyde AR   608 that] *om* H

77 Thy offeringe God accept hase,
　　I see by fyer that one yt was.　　　　　610
　　Shalt thou never efte have such grace,
　　for dye thou shalt this night.

14ᵛ　　Though God stoode in this place
　　for to helpe thee in this case,
　　thou should dye before his face.　　　615
　　Have this, and gett thee right!

Then Cayne kylleth his brother Abell, and God comminge sayth
(minstrelles playe):

DEUS

78 Cayne, where is thy brother Abell?

CAYNE

I wote nere; I cannot tell
of my brother. Wottys thou not well
that I of him had noe keepinge?　　　620

DEUS

What hast thou done, thou wicked man?
Thy brothers blood askes thee upon
vengeance as fast as it can,
from yearth to me cryinge.

79 Cayne, cursed one earth thou shalt bee aye.　　625
　　For thy deede thou haste donne todaye,
　　yearth warryed shalbe in thy worke aye
　　that wickedly haste wrought.
　　And for that thow haste donne this mischeyfe,
　　to all men thou shalt bye unleeffe,　　　630
　　idell and wandringe as an theyfe
　　and overall sett at nought.

609 accept] accepted ARBH　　hase] hath B　　611 shalt thou] thou shalt H
efte have] have efte A, more have R, have H　　grace] a grase A　　After 612]
Tunc Cayne fratrem Abell occidet H　　613 in] heare in ARBH　　614 this]
om H　　616 thee] thie B, the H　　SD] om H　　God] om B　　sayth] to them
sayth ARB　　minstrelles playe] om AR　　DEUS] GOD A　　DEUS] GOD A　　621 man]
m A　　622 askes] asketh B　　626 thy] the AR, this H　　627 shalbe in thy
worke] shalbe in the work B, in thy work shall be H　　629 that] om BH
630 shalt bye] shalbe ARBH　　631 wandringe as] waved like H

Cayne speaketh mornefullye.

CAYNE

80 Out, alas! Where may I bee?
    Sorrowe one eache syde I see.
    For yf I out of the lande flee   635
    from mens companye,
    beastes I wott will werrye mee.
    And yf I lenge, by my lewtye,
    I muste bee bonde and nothinge free—
    and all for my follye.   640

81 For my sinne soe horryble is
    and I have donne soe muche amysse,
    that unworthy I am iwysse
    forgevenes to attayne.
    Well I wott where-ever I goe   645
    whoesoe meetes me will mee slowe,
    and yche man wilbe my foe.
    Noe gracc to mee may gayne.

15ʳ   DEUS

82 Naye, Cayne, thou shalte not dye soone,
    horrybly if thou have aye donne.   650
    That is not thy brothers boone,
    thy blood for to sheede.
    But, forsoth, whosoever slayeth thee
    sevenfolde punished hee shalbee.
    And great payne maye thou not flee   655
    for thy wicked deede.

83 But for thou to thys deede was bowne,
    thou and thy children trust mon—

SD] om H   Cayne] then Cayne R   mornefullye] mourningly RB   CAYNE]
om A   634 I] nowe I R   635 the] om ARBH   636 mens] enimyes
AR, mans H   637 beastes] beast B   werrye] worrye AR   638 by]
for AR   639 bonde] bounde ARBH   646 meetes] metteth A, meeteth R
648 may] is H   DEUS] GOD A   649 soone] sone A   650 aye] om AH, ye R
651 that] it H   652 to] to be H   653 whosoever] who so H   654 hee
shalbee] shall he be ARBH   655 payne maye thou] pennance thou may H
flee] fleye AR, flye B   657 but for] because R   658 children] childer H

into the seaventh generation—
punishment for the whole.   660
For thou todaye hase donne soe,
thy seede for thee shall suffer woe;
and whyle thou one yearth may goe,
of vengeance have the dole.

CAYNE

84 Owt, owt, alas, alas!   665
I am dampned without grace.
Therfore I will from place to place
and looke where is the best.
Well I wott and witterly,
into what place that come I,   670
iche man will loath my companye;
soe shall I never have rest.

85 Fowle hape is mee befall:
whether I bee in house or hall,
'cursed Cayne' menn will me call.   675
Of sorrowes may non nowe cease.
But yett will I, or I goe,
speake with my dam and syre alsoe.
And there maleson both too
I wott well I must have.   680

86 Dam and syre, rest you well,
for one fowle tale I can you tell.
I have slayne my brother Abell
as we fell in a stryffe.

ADAM

Alas, alas, is Abell deade?   685
Alas, rufull is my reade!

659 into] unto ABH   660] great pennance for to thole H   punishment]
unished A, be punished R   663 yearth] the eairth ARH   may] *om* R
goe] groo A   664 the] thie BH   dole] deale AR   CAYNE] CAYNE
lamentat H   673 mee] my B   674] where ever I stand in street or stall H
676] from sorrow may non me save H   677 will I] I will H   678 dam
and syre] dadde and mam A, sire and dame RBH   679 maleson] walson AR
680 well] that B   681–*Finis*] *om* B   681 dam and syre] mame and
dadd A, father and mother H   682] but one tydinges I shall you tell H

Noe more joye to me is leade,
save only Eve my wyfe.

15ᵛ   EVA

87 Alas, nowe is my sonne slayne!
Alas, marred is all my mayne!   690
Alas, muste I never be fayne,
but in woe and morninge?
Well I wott and knowe iwysse
that verye vengeance it is.
For I to God soe did amysse,   695
mone I never have lykinge.

CAYNE

88 Yea, dam and syre, farewell yee;
for owt of land I will flee.
A losell aye I muste bee,
for scapit I am of thryfte.   700
For soe God hath toulde mee,
that I shall never thryve nee [thee].
And now I flee, all yee may see.
I grant you all the same gifte.

Finis

687 to me is] is to me H   EVA] *om* H   690 alas] alas now H
691 muste I] I can H   694 that verye vengeance] verey vengeance that H
695 I to God soe did] I to God did so moche AR, to God did I so H
696] that I shall never have gladinge H   mone] must R   697 yea] then
A, nowe H   698 land] lande to lande AR, the land H   699 losell aye]
losscell ever A, lurrell alway H   700 scapit I am of] I am escaped H
701 mee] yt me H   702 shall] shold H   thee] three HmARB
703] now I goe to all that I see H   all yee] you all AR   704 you all]
om H

PLAY III

16ʳ   THE WATERLEADERS AND DRAWERS
OF DEE

The Thirde Pageante of Noyes Fludd

And firste in some high place—or in the clowdes, if it may bee—
God speaketh unto Noe standinge without the arke with all his
familye.

GOD

1   I, God, that all this world hath wrought,
     heaven and yearth, and all of nought,
     I see my people in deede and thought
     are sett fowle in sinne.
     My goost shall not lenge in mone   5
     that through fleshe-likinge is my fone
     but tyll six score yeares be commen and gone
     to looke if the will blynne.

2   Man that I made will I distroye,
     beast, worme, and fowle to flye;   10
     for on yearth the doe mee noye,
     the folke that are theron.
     Hit harmes mee so hurtefullye,
     the mallice that doth now multiplye,
     that sore it greeves mee inwardlye   15
     that ever I made mon.

3   Therfore Noe, my servante free,
     that righteous man arte as I see,
     a shippe sonne thou shalt make thee
     of trees drye and light.   20

Guild-ascription and] and the AR   of] in BH   Dee] Dee playe AR
After Guild-ascription] 3 pagena B   *Play-heading*] *om* AR, Pagina Tertia
de Deluvio Noe H   *SD*] *om* AR, Et primo in aliquo supremo loco—sive
in nubibus, si fieri poterat—loquatur Deus ad Noe extra archam existentem cum
tota familia sua H   GOD] DEUS BH   1 this] the H   4 sett fowle]
fowle sotted H   5 mone] man RBH   6 fleshe] fleshlie H   7 commen
and] come and B, *om* H   9 will I] I will ARBH   11 noye] nye ARH
12 are] is H   13 so] sore AR   hurtefullye] hartfullie H   14 that
doth now] now that can H   15 it greeves mee] it greveth me B, me greves H
inwardlye] hartelye AR   16 mon] man ARBH   19 sonne] sone AH,
soone R   thou] that thou B

Little chambers therin thou make
and bindinge sliche alsoe thou take;
within and without thou ne slake
to annoynte yt through all thy might.

4 Three hundreth cubitts yt shalbee longe   25
and fiftye broade to make yt stronge;
of height sixtye. The meete thou fonge;
thus measure thou hit aboute.
One window worke through thy witt;
a cubytt of length and breade make hit.   30
Upon the syde a doore shall shutte,
for to com in and owt.

5 Eatinge-places thou make alsoe
three, [rowfed] chambers one or too,
for with water I thinke to flowe   35
mone that I can make.
16ᵛ   Destroyed all they worlde shalbe—
save thou, thy wife, thy sonnes three,
and there wyves alsoe with thee—
shall fall before thy face.   40

NOE

6 A, lorde, I thanke thee lowde and still
that to mee arte in such will
and spares mee and my houshould to spill,
as I nowe soothly fynde.
Thy byddinge, lorde, I shall fulfill   45
nor never more thee greeve ne gryll,
that such grace hath sente mee tyll
amonges all mankynde.

23 without] out H   thou ne] neye thou AR   26 broade] of breade B, of
breadeth H   27 sixtye] fiftie A, 50 H   meete] nexte AR, melt H
28 thus] om R   thou] om H   hit] this AR   29 witt] will B, might H
30 a] one H   breade] breadeth RBH   31 shutte] sutte A, shoote B, sit H
34 three] om A   rowfed] ronett HmAB, rounde R   or too] a roe R
35 flowe] slowe H   36 mone] man AR   37 they] the ARBH
38 thy sonnes] and children AR   39 and] and all H   40] shall saved
he for thy sake H   41 A] O AR   43 houshould] house H   44 I nowe]
now I H   45 shall] will R   46 nor] and ARBH   48 mankynde] other
men R

7 Have donne, you men and weomen all.
  Hye you, leste this water fall,   50
  to worche this shippe, chamber and hall,
  as God hath bydden us doe.

SEM

Father, I am allreadye bowne:
an axe I have, by my crowne,
as sharpe as any in all thys towne   55
for to goe therto.

CAM

8 I have an hatchett wonder keene
  to bytte well, as may bee seene;
  a better grownde, as I weene,
  is not in all this towne.   60

JAFETT

And I can well make a pynne
and with this hammer knocke yt in.
Goe wee worch bowte more dynne,
and I am ready bowne.

NOES WIFE

9 And wee shall bringe tymber to,   65
  for wee mon nothinge ells doe—
  women bynne weake to underfoe
  any great travell.

SEMES WYFE

Here is a good hackestocke;
one this you may hewe and knocke.   70
Shall none be idle in this flocke,
ne nowe may noe man fable.

50] helpe for ought that may befall H   51 hall] all B   55 thys] the B
CAM] HAM H   58 as] it B   59 grownde] gronde one AR, grownden H
61 well make] make well AR   63 wee] and H   bowte] without H
more] *om* AR   NOES WIFE] UXOR NOE H   65 to] too AR   66 wee
mon] women H   SEMES WYFE] UXOR SEM H   69 hackestocke]
hacckinge stoccke AR   70 you] we B   may] must H   71 this] the B
72 fable] fayle ARBH

CAMES WIFE

10 And I will goe gather slytche,
    the shippe for to clam and pitche.
    Annoynte yt muste bee with stitche—   75
    borde, tree, and pynne.

JAFETES WIFE

And I will gather chippes here
to make a fyer for you in feare,
and for to dighte your dinnere
agayne you come in.   80

Then Noe beginneth to buyld the arke.

NOE

11 Nowe in the name of God I beginne
    to make the shippe that wee shall in,
    that wee may be ready for to swyme
    at the comminge of the fludd.
    These bordes I pynne here together   85
    to beare us safe from the weather,
    that wee may rowe both hither and thither
    and safe be from this fludd.

12 Of this tree will I make a maste
    tyed with gables that will laste,   90
    with a seale-yard for cych baste,
    and yche thinge in there kynde.

CAMES WIFE] CAIMES WIFE B, UXOR HAM H   73 goe] goe to H   slytche]
slyche ABH, flyche R   74 clam] caulke AR, cleane H   75 annoynte]
amounte A, amounted R, anoynted H   with] bout R, every H   stitche] slich B
76 borde] brod B   JAFETES WIFE] UXOR JAPHET H   80 agayne] againste
ARBH   you come] your cominge A   SD] Tunc faciunt signa quasi
laborarent cum diversis instrumentis H   arke] arcke and speaketh Noye A,
arke and then speaketh R, arke and then speaketh Noy B   81 I] I will H
83 may] om H   84 fludd] froude R   85 I pynne here] heare I pynne
A, I joyne here B, I joyne H   86 beare] kepe H   87 both] om AR
thither] thether B, thider H   88 this] the AR   89 make] have H   a] the
ARBH   90 gables] cabbelles A   91 baste] blaste ARBH   92 there]
the H

With topcastle and bowespreete,
bothe cordes and roopes I have all meete
to sayle forthe at the nexte weete—   95
this shippe is at an ende.

13 Wife, in this vessell wee shalbe kepte;
my children and thou, I would in yee lepte.

NOES WIFE

In fayth, Noe, I had as leeve thou slepte.
For all thy Frenyshe fare,   100
I will not doe after thy reade.

NOE

Good wiffe, do nowe as I thee bydd.

NOES WIFFE

By Christe, not or I see more neede,
though thou stand all daye and stare.

17ᵛ   NOE

14 Lord, that weomen bine crabbed aye,   105
and non are meeke, I dare well saye.
That is well seene by mee todaye
in witnesse of you eychone.
Good wiffe, lett be all this beare
that thou makest in this place here,   110
for all the weene that thou arte mastere—
and soe thou arte, by sayncte John.

94 bothe] with RH   have] hold H   meete] mette A   *After* 96] Tunc Noe
iterum cum tota familia faciunt signa laborandi cum diversis instrumentis H
At 97] NOE H   97 in this vessell wee shalbe] we shall in this vessell be AR,
in this shipe wee shalbe B, in this castle we shall be H   kepte] kepit B, keped H
98 children] childer H   in yee] ye in A, in we B, in H   lepte] lepitt B,
leaped H   NOES WIFE] UXOR NOE H   99 Noe] Noye A, no B   slepte]
sleppit B, had slepped H   100 Frenyshe] frynishe A, frunishe R, frankish H
101 I] for I H   thy] the B   102 nowe] *om* H   NOES WIFFE] UXOR
NOE H   104 all] all the H   106 non] never H   I dare well] that
dare I BH   107 that] this H   109 beare] lere B   110 makest] maiste
AB   111 that] *om* RH

Then Noe with all his familye shall make a signe as though the
wrought upon the shippe with divers instrucments. And after that
God shall speake to Noe as followeth:

DEUS

15 Noe, take thou thy meanye
and in the shippe hye that yee bee;
for non soe righteouse man to mee   115
ys nowe one yearth livinge.
Of cleane beastes with thee thoe take
vii and vii or then thou slake;
hee and shee, make to make,
bylyve in that thou bringe;   120

16 of beastes uncleane ii and ii,
male and female, bowt moo;
of cleane fowles seaven alsoe,
the hee and shee together;
of fowles uncleane twayne and noe more,   125
as I of beastes sayde before.
That man be saved through my lore,
agaynst I sende this wedder,

17 of meates that mon be eaten,
into the shippe loke the be getten,   130
for that maye bee noe waye forgotten.
And doe this all bydeene
to sustayne man and beastes therin
aye tyll the water cease and blynne.
This worlde is filled full of sinne,   135
and that is nowe well seene.

SD] *om* H   as followeth] sayinge A, *om* R   DEUS] GOD A   115 righteouse man] righte nor non AR   117 thoe] to AR, thou BH   118 then]
om H   120 bylyve] be leeve B   122 bowt] but B, without H   124 hee]
liie AR   125 twayne] two H   more] moe AR   126 as I of beastes]
of beastes as I H   127 man be] non be B, shalbe H   128 this] the H
wedder] weither AR, wether B   129 of] of all ARBH   mon] must RH
130 loke] see R, look that B   the] *om* A, there H   131 maye bee noe
waye] no way may be H   forgotten] forgetten B, foryeten H   132 this
all] all this ARH   133 beastes] beaste ARB   134 aye] *om* A, ye B
135 is] ye AR

18 Seaven dayes bynne yett cominge;
   you shall have space them in to bringe.
   After that, it is my likinge
   mankynde for to anoye.   140
   Fortye dayes and fortye nightes
   rayne shall fall for there unrightes.
   And that I have made through myghtes
   nowe thinke I to distroye.

18ʳ   NOE

19 Lord, at your byddinge I am bayne.   145
   Sythen noe other grace will gayne,
   hyt will I fulfill fayne,
   for gracyouse I thee fynde.
   An hundreth winters and twentye
   this shippe-makinge tarryed have I,   150
   if throughe amendemente thy mercye
   would fall to mankynde.

20 Have donne, yee men and weomen all;
   hye you lest this water fall,
   that eyche beaste were in stall   155
   and into the shippe broughte.
   Of cleane beastes seaven shalbe,
   of uncleane two; thus God bade mee.
   The flood is nigh, you may well see;
   therfore tarrye you nought.   160

Then Noe shall goe into the arke with all his familye, his wyffe
excepte, and the arke muste bee borded rownde aboute. And one
the bordes all the beastes and fowles hereafter reahersed muste
bee paynted, that ther wordes may agree with the pictures.

139 it] *om* H   140 anoye] nye H   143 myghtes] my mightes AR, my
mighte H   145 at your] to thy AR   146 sythen] seinge AR, sith H
noe] non H   149 winters] wyntter AB   150 this] of this B
151 amendemente] a memdant B   thy] any H   152 to] unto H
155 in] in his H   156 the] *om* H   158 two] *om* A   thus] this ARH
159 the] this H   you may well] well may we H   *SD*] Tunc Noe introibit
archam, et familia sua dabit et recitabit nomina animalium depicta in cartis et,
postquam unusquisque suam locutus est partem, ibit in archam, uxore Noe
excepta, et animalia depicta cum verbis concordare debent, et sic incipiet primus
filius H   and(1)] *om* R   one] upon R   beastes] beast A   hereafter
reahersed] *om* A, herafter receaved B   muste bee paynted that ther wordes
may agree with the pictures] painted A

SEM

21 Syr, here are lions, leopardes in;
horses, mares, oxen, and swynne,
geates, calves, sheepe, and kyne
here sytten thou may see.

CAM

Camelles, asses, man may fynde,   165
bucke and doe, harte and hynde.
All beastes of all manere of kynde
here bynne, as thinketh mee.

JAFETT

22 Take here cattes, dogges too,
otters and foxes, fullimartes alsoe;   170
hares hoppinge gayle can goe
here have colle for to eate.

NOES WIFE

And here are beares, wolves sett,
apes, owles, maremussett,
wesills, squerrells, and fyrrett;   175
here the eaten there meate.

18ᵛ   SEMES WIFFE

23 Heare are beastes in this howse;
here cattes maken yt crowse;
here a rotten, here a mowse
that standen nere together.   180

161 lions] lyons and B   163 geates calves] goote and cavlfe A, goate and calve
R, goat and calvern B   CAM] HAM H   165 man] men H   166 bucke] buckes R
and (1)] *om* H   167 all(1)] and ARBH   of(2)] *om* ARBH   168 thinketh]
thinke R, thinckes H   169 cattes] cattes and H   170 otters and foxes]
atter and foxe AR, otter and fox B, otter fox H   fullimartes] fillie mare AR,
fulmerd B, fulmart H   171 gayle] gile A, goale R, gaye B, gaylie H
172 here have colle] heare have coule A, here have coale R, here have call B,
have cowle here H   NOES WIFE] UXOR NOE H   173 beares] beares and B
174 owles] owles and B   175 squerrells] squirrles H   SEMES WIFE]
UXOR SEM H   177 heare are beastes] yet more beastes are H   178 yt]
it full B, in full H   179 a(1)] is a R   a(2)] is a R   180 that] they H
standen] stand H   nere] nighe ARBH

C 9206   E

CAMS WYFFE

And here are fowles lesse and more—
hernes, cranes, and byttoer,
swanes, peacockes—and them before
meate for this wedder.

JAFETTES WYFFE

24 Here are cockes, kytes, crowes,   185
    rookes, ravens, many rowes,
    duckes, curlewes, whoever knowes,
    eychone in his kynde.
    And here are doves, digges, drakes,
    redshankes ronninge through lakes;   190
    and eyche fowle that leadenn makes
    in this shippe man may fynde.

NOE

25 Wyffe, come in. Why standes thou there?
    Thou arte ever frowarde; that dare I sweare.
    Come, in Godes name; halfe tyme yt weare,   195
    for feare lest that wee drowne.

NOES WYFFE

Yea, syr, sett up your seale
and rowe forthe with evell hayle;
for withowten any fayle
I will not owt of this towne.   200

26 But I have my gossips everyechone,
    one foote further I will not gone.
    They shall not drowne, by sayncte John,
    and I may save there life.

CAMS WYFFE] UXOR HAM H   183 and] have H   184 wedder] weither AR, wether B   JAFETTES WYFFE] UXOR JAPHET H   185 cockes] coke AR kytes] kitte A, kytes and B   186 rookes] rockes R   many] and many B 187 duckes] cuckoes H   whoever] whoso H   188 his] theire R   189 and] om A   drakes] and drakes B   190 redshankes] edshonckes A   through] over R, through the H   192 man] nowe AR, men H   194 that dare I] I dare well AR   195 in] in one ARB, on H   name] om BH   196 wee] thou R   NOES WYFFE] UXOR NOE H   197 seale] saile ARBH   198 hayle] heale H   199 withowten] without H   any] om AR   fayle] faile I will not out R   200 I will not] om R   204 life] lyves B

The loved me full well, by Christe.   205
But thou wilte lett them into thy chiste,
elles rowe forthe, Noe, when thy liste
and gett thee a newe wyfe.

NOE

27 Sem, sonne, loe thy mother is wraowe;
by God, such another I doe not knowe.   210

SEM

Father, I shall fetch her in, I trowe,
withowten any fayle.
Mother, my father after thee sende
and byddes thee into yonder wende.
Looke up and see the wynde,   215
for wee benne readye to sayle.

19r   NOES WYFFE

28 Sonne, goe agayne to him and saye
I will not come therin todaye.

NOE

Come in, wiffe, in twentye devylles waye,
or ells stand there withowte.   220

CAM

Shall we all fetch hir in?

NOE

Yea, sonne, in Chrystes blessinge and myne,
I would yee hyed you betyme
for of this fludd I stande in doubte.

205 loved] loven A   206 wilte] om A   into] in H   thy] that R   chiste]
cheiste A, chest B   207 forthe Noe] nowe A   when] wher AR, whether H
thy] thou RBH   liste] listes B   209 wraowe] wrawe AH, ny R   210 by
God] forsooth H   knowe] see R   211 shall] will R   212 withowten]
without H   214 byddes] prayes R   yonder] yeinder shippe ARBH   NOES
WYFFE] UXOR NOE H   217 sonne] Seme AR   and] I AR   219 devylles]
devill B   220 there] om H   withowte] all daye AR   CAM] HAM H
222 sonne] sonnes ARBH   Chrystes] Christe A   223 you] yea B
224 stande] am ARH

THE GOOD GOSSIPS

29　The fludd comes fleetinge in full faste,　　225
　　one everye syde that spredeth full farre.
　　For fere of drowninge I am agaste;
　　good gossippe, lett us drawe nere.

30　And lett us drinke or wee departe,
　　for oftetymes wee have done soe.　　230
　　For at one draught thou drinke a quarte,
　　and soe will I doe or I goe.

31　Here is a pottell full of malnesaye good and stronge;
　　yt will rejoyse both harte and tonge.
　　Though Noe thinke us never soe longe,　　235
　　yett wee wyll drinke atyte.

JAPHETT

32　Mother, wee praye you all together—
　　for we are here, your owne childer—
　　come into the shippe for feare of the wedder,
　　for his love that [you] bought.　　240

NOES WYFFE

That will I not for all your call
but I have my gosseppes all.

SEM

In fayth, mother, yett thow shall,
whether thou will or nought.

225–32] *after* 242 H　　　THE GOOD GOSSIPS] THE GOOD GOSSIPPES SONGE A,
GOSSIP H　　　225 fleetinge in full faste] flittinge in full faste AR, fleeting in
apace B, in full fleetinge fast H　　　226 that] it BH　　spredeth full farre]
breadeth in hast H　　　228 gossippe] gossippes AR　　us drawe nere] me
come in H　　　229 and] or H　　　230 ofte] often H　　　231 one] a ARBH
draught] tyme H　　drinke] drinkes ARBH　　　232 doe or] or that H
233–6] *om* H　　　233 malnesaye] malmsme A, malmesey R, malmesy B
234 rejoyse] rejoye B　　　235 Noe] Noy B　　　236 yett] heare A　　atyte]
alike AR　　　238 owne] *om* H　　childer] children AR　　　239 wedder]
weither AR　　　240 you] *om* Hm　　NOES WYFFE] UXOR NOE H　　　242 but]
but if H　　　243 thow] you ABH　　　244 thou] yow BH　　nought] note A,
not RH　　　*To right of* 244] Tunc ibit H

NOE

33 Welcome, wyffe, into this boote.   245

NOES WYFFE

Have thou that for thy note!

NOE

Aha, marye, this ys hotte;
yt is good for to be still.
19ᵛ   Ah, chyldren, meethinke my boote remeeves.
Our tarryinge here mee highly greeves.   250
Over the lande the water spreades;
God doe hee as hee will.

Then the singe, and Noe shall speake agayne.

NOE

34 Ah, greate God that arte soe good,
that worchis not thy will is wood.
Now all this world is one a flood,   255
as I see well in sight.
This windowe I will shutt anon,
and into my chamber I will gonne
tyll thys water, soe greate one,
bee slaked through thy mighte.   260

Then shall Noe shutt the windowe of the arke, and for a little space
within the bordes hee shalbe scylent; and afterwarde openinge the
windowe and lookinge rownde about sayinge:

245 boote] boate B   NOES WYFFE] UXOR NOE H   246 have] and have H
note] mote H   To right of 246] Et dat alapam vita H   247 Aha] Ha ha
AR   248 yt] t A   for] om AII   249 chyldren] childer H   my] this H
remeeves] remewes A, renewes R   250 mee highly] highlye me ARB,
hugelie me H   252 hee(1)] om ARBH   SD] om H   and Noe shall
speake agayne] om A   NOE] om ABH   253 that] thou H   254] om H
is] as AR   255 this] the B   257 I will shutt] will I steake H
258 I will] will I H   259 one] wone ARB   SD] Tunc Noe claudet
fenestram archae et per modicum spatium infra tectum cantent psalmum "Save
mee, O God" et aperiens fenestram et respiciens H   shall Noe] Noye shall B
within] om A   the bordes] om A, borde RB   hee] om A, they R   shalbe] be
A   openinge the windowe] om A   and] om A, Noe R   rownde about] about
hym R   sayinge] shall saye A   After SD] forty-seven lines in H (see
Appendix IA)   After SD] NOYE AB

35 Lord God in majestye
　　that such grace hast granted mee
　　wher all was borne, salfe to bee!
　　Therfore nowe I am boune—
　　my wyffe, my children, and my menye—　　　265
　　with sacryfice to honour thee
　　of beastes, fowles, as thou mayest see,
　　and full devotyon.

GOD

36 Noe, to me thou arte full able
　　and thy sacrafice acceptable;　　　　　270
　　for I have founde thee treeue and stable,
　　one thee nowe muste I myne.
　　Warrye yearth I will noe more
　　for mans sinnes that greeves mee sore;
　　for of youth man full yore　　　　　275
　　hasse bynne enclyned to sinne.

37 Yee shall nowe growe and multiplye,
　　and yearth agayne to edifye.
　　Eache beast and fowle that may flye
　　shalbe feared of you.　　　　　　280
　　And fishe in saye, all that may fleete,
　　shall sustayne you, I thee behett;
　　to eate of them yee ne lett
　　that cleane bynne you mon knowe.

20ʳ　　38 Thereas yee have eaten before　　　285
　　trees and rootes since yee weare bore,
　　of cleane beastes nowe, lesse and more,
　　I give you leave to eate—

262 mee] *om* B　　　　263 wher] when H　　　salfe] false AB, saffe RH
265 children] childer H　　and] *om* H　　menye] meyne B　　267 of] with H
268] I offer here right sone H　　　GOD] DEUS RBH　　270 thy] to my A
272 myne] mynde R　　　273 I will] will I H　　　274 for] that H　　mans]
mens B　　sinnes] synne H　　mee] *om* H　　276 hasse] halfe AR　　to]
unto B　　278 and] on AR　　agayne to] you H　　279 flye] fley R,
flee B　　280 feared of] afrayd for H　　281 and] all B　　all] *om* ARH, ye B
fleete] flitte ARH　　　282 thee] that B, yow H　　behett] behitte A, beheit B,
behite H　　284 mon] may H　　knowe] knowne B　　286 trees] grasse H
287 nowe] *om* H

save blood and fleshe bothe in feare
of wrauge dead carryen that is here.   290
Eate yee not of that in noe manere,
for that aye yee shall leave.

39 Manslaughter also aye yee shall flee,
for that is not playsante unto mee.
They that sheden blood, hee or shee,   295
ought-where amongste mankynde,
that blood fowle shedd shalbe
and vengeance have, men shall see.
Therfore beware all yee,
you fall not into that synne.   300

40 And forwarde, Noe, with thee I make
and all thy seede for thy sake,
of suche vengeance for to slake,
for nowe I have my will.
Here I behette thee an heeste   305
that man, woman, fowle, ne beaste
with water whille this worlde shall laste
I will noe more spill.

41 My bowe betwene you and mee
in the fyrmamente shalbe,   310
by verey tokeninge that you may see
that such vengeance shall cease.
The man ne woman shall never more
be wasted by water as hath before;
but for synne that greveth me sore,   315
therfore this vengeance was.

---

289 fleshe] fishe H   290 wrauge] ronge A, wronge RH, wrang B
carryen] carrine A, carryn R, carren H   291 yee] *om* H   292 aye] *om*
AR   leave] let H   293 also aye] *om* A, ever R, also H   294 is] *om* A
unto] to BH   295 they] *om* BH   sheden] shedes H   297] that
sheedes blood his blood shed shall be H   298 men] that men H   299 all]
now all H   300 into] to B, in H   301 and] a AR   Noe] now H
thee] yow H   303 of] *om* A   to slake] thie sake B   307 this] the H
308 spill] destroye R   311 by] and R   verey] every AR   tokeninge]
tocken ARB, tokens H   may] shall A   313 the] *om* A, that BH   ne] *om*
A, the R   woman] *om* A   314 by] with AR   hath] he hath bene A,
they were R, is H   315 greveth] greeves R   me] *om* H   316 vengeance]
vengeane H

42 Where clowdes in the welkyn bynne,
that ylke bowe shalbe seene,
in tokeninge that my wrath and teene
shall never thus wroken bee.   320
The stringe is torned towardes you
and towardes me is bente the bowe,
that such wedder shall never showe;
and this behett I thee.

20ᵛ   43 My blessinge nowe I give thee here,   325
to thee, Noe, my servante deare,
for vengeance shall noe more appeare.
And now farewell, my darlinge dere.

Finis

PLAY IV

21ʳ   THE BARBERS PLAYE

Incipit Quarta Pagina qualiter reversus est a cede quatuor regum.
Occurrit rex Salim etc. equitando et Lothe; et dicat Abraham.

Preco dicat:

1 All peace, lordinges that bine presente,
and herken mee with good intente,
howe Noe awaye from us hee went
and all his companye;

318 ylke] same A, same rainebow R   319 tokeninge] tocken ARB   and]
I B   320 shall] shold H   thus] this AH, more this R   322 is bente]
bend is H   323 such] never such B   324 and] *om* AR   behett]
behighte A, beheigh R   325 nowe] Noye A   328 darlinge] lordinges B
    Guild-ascription] The Barbers and the Waxechaundlers Playe AR (the(2)]
om R), *om* B   playe] *om* H   *Play-heading*] Pagina Quarta de Abrahamo
et Melchisedech et Loth, qualiter Abraham reversus est de caede 4 regum; et
occurret ei Melchisadech equitando, et erit Loth cum Abrahamo; et dicat
Preco H   quarta pagina] pagina quarta A   qualiter] qualiter Abraham
B   occurrit] occurette A   Salim] Salem R   etc] *om* R   equitando]
equitand A   dicat] dicit B   Preco] NUNTIUS H   dicat] dicit B, *om* H
To left of Preco dicat] Here beginneth the Preface B   1 peace] *om* AR
presente] heare presente AR   2 and] now R   herken] listen B   mee]
now H   3 Noe] Noy B   hee] is H

and Abraham through Godes grace, 5
hc is commen into this place,
and yee will geeve us rowme and space
to tell you thys storye.

2 This playe, forsothe, begynne shall hee
in worshippe of the Trynitie 10
that yee may all here and see
that shalbe donne todaye.
My name is Goobett-on-the-Greene.
With you I may no longer beene.
Farewell, my lordinges, all bydene 15
for lettynge of [your] playe.

Abraham, having restored his brother Loth into his owne place,
doth firste of all begine the play and sayth:

ABRAHAM

3 Ah, thou high God, graunter of grace,
that endinge ne begininge hase,
I thanke thee, lorde, that thou hase
todaye give mee the victorye. 20
Lothe, my brother, that taken was,
I have restored him in this case
and brought him home in this place
through thy might and masteryc.

4 To worshippe thee I will not worne, 25
that iiii kynges of uncouth landes
todaye hath sent into my hand,
and ryches with greate araye.

6 commen] come B   7 us] him H   8] om H   thys] of AR, of the B
9 forsothe begynne] beginne forsouth B   10 in] in the H   11 yee] we H
here and] withe eye H   14 I may no longer] no longer I may H   15 my]
om H   lordinges] lordes A   all] om AR   16 your] you Hm   SD] Et
exit H   Abraham] heare Abraham AR   into] unto B   of all] om R   and
sayth] sayinge R   17 Ah] om H   graunter] and graunt H   18 ne]
no B   hase] hath AB   19 thou] to me H   hase] hath A, hast RB
20 give] geven ARBH   mee the] this AR, om H   22 him] om H   23 in]
to B, into H   this] his B   24 and] and thy H   25 I will] will I B
not worne] nowe wonne AR, not woone B, not wond H   26 uncouth]
unquoth R   landes] lande ARH   28 ryches with] of riches H

Therfore of all that I have wone
to give the teath I will begynne,   30
the cyttee sonne when I come in,
and parte with thee my praye.

5 Melchysedech, that here kinge is
and Goddes preyste allsoe iwisse,
the teathe I will give him of this,   35
as skyll is that I doe.
Godd that hase sende mee the vyctorye
of iiii kynges gracyously,
with him I praye parte will I,
the cyttie when I come to.   40

21ᵛ Here Lothe, torninge him to his brother Abraham, doth saye:

LOTH

6 Abraham, brother, I thanke thee
that this daye haste delyvered mee
of enimyes handes and ther postee,
and saved mee from woo.
Therfore I will give teathinge   45
of my good whille I am livinge;
and nowe alsoe of his sendinge
the teath I will give alsoe.

Tunc venit Armiger Melchysedech ad ipsum et gratulando dicit
Armiger (Here the Messenger doth come to Melchysedech, kinge
of Salem, and rejoysinge greatly doth saye):

7 My lorde the kinge, tydinges on right
your hart to glade and to light—   50
Abraham hath slayne in fight
iiii kinges since hee went.

29 have wone] can wyn H   30 the] thee AH, thie B   teath] teith B, tyth H
31 sonne] soone BH   32 and] to H   35 teathe] tenth B, tyth H
37 the] om H   39 I(1)] a AR, my BH   parte] departe H   SD] om H
doth saye] sayth R   LOTH] LOTH FRATER ABRAHAMI B   41 thee] it thee BH
43 of] from R   46 good] goodes B   livinge] levinge AB   48 the]
om H   alsoe] here R   SD Latin] om R   Armiger] Armiger ad H   ad ipsum]
ipsom A, om H   et gratulando dicit Armiger] et gratulando dicat Armiger A,
om H   SD English] om H   Melchysedech] the B   rejoysinge] rejoyced A
saye] saye as followeth R   After SD] MESSINGER A, MESSINGER dicat R,
ARMIGER H   49 on right] arighte H   50 hart] hard B, harte for H
to(2)] om H   52 hee] I H

Here hee will bee this ylke night,
and ryches enough with him dight.
I harde him thanke God almight   55
of grace hee had him sente.

Here Melchysedech, lookinge up to heaven, doth thanke God for
Abrahams victorye, and doth prepare himselfe to goe present
Abraham.

MELCHYSEDECH, REX SALEM

8 Ah, blessed bee God that is but one.
Agaynste Abraham will I gonne
worshipfullye and that anonne,
myne office to fulfill,   60
and presente him with bread and wyne,
for grace of God is him within.
Spede for love myne,
for this is Godes will.

ARMIGER (cum pocula)

Here the Messenger, offeringe to Melchysedeck a standinge-cuppe
and bread alsoe, dothe saye:

9 Sir, here is wyne, withowten were,   65
and therto bred white and cleare
to present him with good chere,
that soe us holpenn hasse.

Here Melchysedeck answeringe sayth:

To God I wott hee is full deare,
for of all thinges in his prayer   70
hee hath withowten dangere,
and speciallye his grace.

53 ylke] same AR   54 enough with him] with hym enough H
56 hee] God H   SD] Melchis extendens manus ad coelum H   goe] goe
and A   Abraham] Abraham et dicat R   REX SALEM] om H   58 will I]
now will I R, I will H   60 to] for to AR   61 and (1)] a B   62 for]
for the H   To right of 62] Armiger cum cuppa H   63 for] fast for BH
ARMIGER cum pocula] om R, ARMIGER H   SD] om H   here] om B
offeringe] doth offer A   Melchysedeck] meete Melchesedech with B   alsoe]
om ARB   65 withowten] without H   66 therto] hereto AR, tharf H
white] both white BH   67 with] in H   chere] manere ARBH   68 soe
us] God so H   hasse] hath ARB   SD] om RH   answeringe] answereth
and B   After SD] MELCHESADECKE ARBH   70 of] om AR   in] om H
prayer] power R   71 withowten] without H   72 his] great H

Melchysedeck, comminge unto Abraham, doth offer to him a cuppe full of wynne and bred, and sayth unto him:

22^r 10 Abraham, welcome moste thou bee—
Godes grace is fullye in thee.
Blessed ever muste thou bee   75
that enimyes soe can meeke.
Here is bred and wyne for thy degree;
I have brought as thou maye see.
Receyve this present nowe at mee,
and that I thee beeseche.   80

Here Abraham, receyvinge the offeringe of Melchysedeck, dothe saye:

11 Syr kynge, welcome in good faye;
thy presente is welcome to my paye.
God that hath holpen mee todaye,
unworthye though I were,
ye shall have parte of my praye   85
that I wan sinse I wente awaye.
Therfore to thee that take it maye,
the teathe I offer here.

Here Abraham offereth to Melchysedeck an horse that is laden. Melchysedeck, receivinge the horse of Abraham verey gladly, doth saye:

SD] Tunc Melchisedech equitabit versus Abraham et offerrit calecem cum vino et pane super patenam, et dicit Milchisedech BH (et offerrit] offerens H pane] panem H   et dicit Milchisedech] *om* H)   Melchysedeck] here Melchesadecke A   unto] to B   to] unto ARB   and sayth unto him] and saithe AB, a sayth as followeth R   *After SD*] MELCHESADECKE R   73 moste] muste AH, mayst R   75 muste] moste A, mayst R, more H   thou bee] be he H   77 *and* 78] *reversed* H   77 here is] *om* H   78 thou] you ARBH   79 at] of A, here of R   80 and] one AR   beeseche] beseeke A   SD] *om* H   doth offer Melchesadecke a horse that is loden A, and then doth offer unto him a horse that is loden and saith as followeth R   *After SD*] ABRAHAM ARH, Abraham taketh the cup B   81 faye] fayne B   83 that] *om* AR   85 ye] he H   86 sinse] sith H   87 that] thou RH   88 teathe] tenth H   *After* 88] Tunc tradit equum oneratum sibi dicens B, *to right of* 86–7 H (dicens] *om* H)   SD] *om* H   here Abraham offereth to Melchysedeck an horse] *om* AR   that is] *om* ARB   laden] *om* AR   Melchysedeck] here Melchesadecke R   verey] *om* R   doth saye] doe saie A, sayth as followeth R   *After SD*] MELCHESADECKE ABH

12 And your present, syr, take I
    and honoure hit devoutlye,   90
    for much good it may signifye
    in tyme that is commynge.
    Therfore horse, harnesse, and petrye,
    as falles for your dignitye,
    the teathe of hit takes of mee   95
    and receyve here my offeringe.

Here Loth doeth offer to Melchysedeck a goodly cuppe, and
sayth:

LOTH

13 And I will offer with good intente
    of such goodes as God hath mee lente
    to Melchysedeck here presente,
    as Gods will is to bee.   100
    Abraham, my brother, offered hasse,
    and soe will I through Godes grace.
    This royall cuppe before your face
    receyve yt nowe at mee.

Here Melchysedeck receaveth the cuppe of Loth.

MELCHYSEDECK

14 Syr, your offeringe welcome ys;   105
    and well I wott, forsoth iwys,
    that fullye Godes will yt is
    that is nowe doone today.
    Goe wee together to my cyttie;
    and God nowe hartely thanke wee   110

90 honoure] honours R   92 commynge] to come B   *At* 93] ABRAHAM H
93 petrye] perye H   94 your] my R   95 teathe] teith B, tythe H
takes of mee] taketh of me A, I take of thee R, takes at me H   96 here]
om ARBH   my] thy R   SD] Tunc Abraham recipiet panem et vinum,
et Melchis equum oneratum nomine decimae H   doeth offer to] offeringe unto
R, offereth to B   and sayth] sayth as followeth R   98 goodes as] good
as A, good H   lente] sent H   100 Gods] Christ H   is to] so yt H
101 offered] offereth R   hasse] hath B   102 through] by B   103 your]
my A   104 nowe] *om* H   at] of A   SD] Tunc Loth offeret cuppam
cum vino et pane, et recipiet Melchisadech H   here] *om* AB   receaveth]
receivinge AR   of] at B   Loth] Loth saith A, Lot saith as followeth R
108 nowe] *om* H   109 my] the B   110 God nowe] God B, now God H

that helps us aye through his postee,
for soe wee full well maye.

Here they doe goe together, and Abraham dothe take the bred and
wyne, and Melc. the laden horse.

22ᵛ   EXPOSITOR (equitando)

15 Lordinges, what may this signifye
I will expound yt appertly—
the unlearned standinge herebye   115
maye knowe what this may bee.
This present, I saye veramente,
signifieth the newe testamente
that nowe is used with good intente
throughout all Christianitye.   120

16 In the owld lawe, without leasinge,
when these too good men were livinge,
of beastes were there offeringe
and eke there sacramente.
But synce Christe dyed one roode-tree,   125
in bred and wyne his death remenber wee;
and at his laste supper our mandee
was his commandemente.

17 But for this thinge used should bee
afterwardes, as nowe done wee,   130
in signification—as leeve you mee—
Melchysedeck did soe.
And teathinges-makinge, as you seene here,
of Abraham begonnen were.
Therfore to God hee was full deare,   135
and soe were both too.

111 that helps] to helpe H   us] *om* B   aye] ever A, *om* R   112 wee full
well] full well we AR   *SD*] *om* ARH   doe] *om* B   the laden horse] *om* B
equitando] equitandon A, equitandum R, *om* H   113 lordinges] lordes H
may this] this may H   114 yt] *om* H   115 the] that the ARB, that H
unlearned] lewed H   117 present] offring H   122 too] *om* B
123 were] was all H   124 eke] *om* H   125 synce] sith H   one] on
the H   126 in] with H   his death] *om* B, him H   remenber] remember
ARB, worship H   127] and on Sherthursday in his maundye H   our]
one our AR   129 this thinge] that after thinges B   130 nowe] *om* B
131 as] *om* H   133 teathinges] teaching B, tythes H   seene] see BH
135 to God hee was] he was to God H   136 were] wee B, were they H

18 By Abraham understand I maye
   the Father of heaven, in good faye;
   Melchysedecke, a pryest to his paye
   to minister that sacramente   140
   that Christe ordayned the foresayde daye
   in bred and wyne to honour him aye.
   This signifyeth, the sooth to saye,
   Melchysedeck his presente.

Here God appeareth to Abraham and saythe:

DEUS

19 Abraham, my servante, I saye to thee   145
   thy helpe and thy succour will I bee.
   For thy good deede myche pleaseth mee,
   I tell thee witterly.

Here Abraham, torninge to God, saythe:

ABRAHAM

   Lord, on thinge that wouldest see,
   that I praye after with harte full free: 150
   grante mee, lorde, through thy postee
   some fruite of my bodye.

20 I have noe chylde, fowle ne fayre,
   save my nurrye, to bee my hayre;
   that makes mee greatly to appeare.   155
   One mee, lord, have mercye.

23ʳ   DEUS

   Naye Abraham, frend, leeve thou mee—
   thy nurrye thine hayre hee shall not bee;
   but one sonne I shall send thee,
   begotten of thy bodye.   160

137 understand I] I understand B   141 the foresayde daye] that said
daye B, on Sherethursday H   143] *om* H   144 Melchysedeck his]
Melchesadeckes AH, Melchesadecke here R   *SD*] *om* H   to] unto AR
DEUS] GOD AR   146 thy(2)] *om* BH   will I] I will H   147 deede] deedes B
pleaseth] pleased A   *SD*] *om* H   149 on] in one H   that] thou A,
that thou RBH   wouldest] wilt H   150 full] *om* AH   154 save]
but B   155 appeare] appayre BH   DEUS] GOD A   157 naye Abraham
frend] my frend Abraham H   158 hee] *om* BH   160 begotten] gotten H

21 Abraham, doe as I thee saye—
    looke and tell, yf thou maye,
    stares standinge one the straye;
    that unpossible were.
    Noe more shalt thou, for noe neede,   165
    number of thy bodye the seede
    that thou shalt have withowten dreede;
    thou arte to mee soe dere.

22 Therfore Abraham, servante free,
    looke that thou bee trewe to mee;   170
    and here a forwarde I make with thee
    thy seede to multiplye.
    Soe myche folke forther shalt thou bee,
    kinges of this seede men shall see;
    and one chylde of greate degree   175
    all mankynde shall forbye.

23 I will hethen-forward alwaye
    eyche man-chylde one the eyght daye
    bee circumsysed, as I thee saye,
    and thou thyselfe full soone.   180
    Whoesoe cyrcumsysed not ys
    forsaken shalbe with mee iwys,
    for unobedyent that man ys.
    Looke that this bee done.

ABRAHAM

24 Lord, all readye in good faye.   185
    Blessed bee thou ever and aye,

162 and] up and H   yf] and yf AR, me if H   163 straye] shaye H
165 noe neede] thy meede H   166 of] *om* AR   bodye the] bodelye AR
167 withowten] for thy good H   dreede] deed BH   169 therfore] wherfore H   171 here a forwarde] forward here H   with] to AR   173–4] *om* H
173 folke] more A, *om* B   forther] *om* R   shalt thou] thou shalte R
174 this] thy ARB   175 of greate] great of H   177 hethen forward]
hense fourth forwarde A, hence forewarde R, hether forward B, that from
henceforth H   alwaye] awaye B   178 man] man a B, knaves H   one]
om H   179 as I thee saye] on the eighte daie AR, as I saye B, as you say H
181 whoesoe] who s B, and who H   not] ne H   182 shalbe with] with
shalbe H   mee] *om* BH   183 unobedyent that] disobedient B, inobedyent
that H   184 looke] therfore looke H   186 ever] now B

for therby knowe thou maye
thy folke from other men.
Cyrcumsysed they shalbe all
anon for ought that maye befall. 190
I thanke thee, lorde, thyne one thrall,
kneelinge one my kneene.

25 Lordinges all, takys intent
what betokens this commandement:
this was sometyme an sacrament 195
in the ould lawe truely tane.
As followeth nowe verament,
soe was this in the owld testamente.
But when Christe dyed away hit went,
and then beganne baptysme. 200

26 Alsoe God a promise behett us here
to Abraham, his servant dere:
soe mych seede that in noe manere
nombred yt may bee,
and one seede mankinde for to bye. 205
That was Christe Jesus wytterlye,
for of his kynde was our ladye,
and soe alsoe was hee.

23ᵛ

DEUS

27 Abraham, my servante Abraham!

ABRAHAM

Loe, lord, alreadye here I am. 210

187 therby knowe thou] that we knowe A, that everye one knowe R, that verely
know I B, that men verey knowe H   190 anon] mon AR   191 thanke
thee] thrall thou H   one] owne ARBH   192 kneene] knye A, kneey R,
knee B   EXPOSITOR] EPOSITOR H   193 takys] take this ARB, takes
good H   195 sometyme] sometymes R   196 the ould] thould H
197 nowe] is now H   198 the] om B   199 when] om B   hit] he B
200 then beganne baptysme] baptisme then began H   201 alsoe] and also R
God a] God AH, Godes RB   promise] promysed A, om H   behett us] behitte
us B, behetes H   203 mych seede] Melchesedeh B   204 nombred]
mombered R, numbrer B   yt] om ABH   may] mighte ARBH   bee] not
be II   205 one] om H   for to bye] oughte to be AR, for to be B, to
forby H   206 Christe Jesus] Jhesus Christ H   207 his] this AR
kynde] om B   our] one R   DEUS] GOD A   210 lord] here H

DEUS

Take Isaack, thy sonne by name
that thou lovest the best of all,
and in sacryfyce offer him to mee
upon that hyll there besydes thee.
Abraham, I will that yt soe bee 215
for ought that maye befall.

ABRAHAM

28 My lord, to thee is myne intent
ever to bee obedyent.
That sonne that thou to mee haste sent
offer I will to thee, 220
and fulfill thy commandement
with hartye will, as I am kent.
High God, lorde omnipotent,
thy biddinge, lorde, done shalbee.

29 My meanye and my chyldren eycheone 225
lenges at home, both all and one,
save Isaack, my sonne, with mee shall gonne
to an hyll here besyde.

Here Abraham, torninge him to his sonne Isaack, sayth:

Make thee readye, my dere darlinge,
for we must doe a little thinge. 230
This wood doe thou on thy backe bringe;
wee may noe lenger byde.

30 A sworde and fyer that I will take,
for sacrifyce mee behoves to make.

DEUS] GOD A 211 name] nam R 212 the best] best B, most H
213 offer] *om* A 214 there] *om* H 215 that] *om* H soe bee] be
soe AR *To left of* 217–19] Here Abraham answereth very meekly to God
and saith B 219 that thou to mee] to me that thou B, that to me thou H
223 God lorde] lorde God AR 224 lorde done] *om* A, lorde R, done lord
God B, done H 225 chyldren] childer H 226 lenges] henges B
227 my sonne with mee shall] shall with me H 228 besyde] besydes R
SD] *om* H him] *om* RB 229 dere] *om* H 231 doe thou on thy
backe] doe one thy backe it AR, upon thy back thou H 232 may noe
lenger] must not long H byde] abyde ARBH 233 that] *om* H
234 mee behoves to] me behoves me to R, me hoves to B, I must H

Godes biddinge will I not forsake,   235
but ever obedyent bee.

Abraham taketh a sworde and fyer.
Here Isaack speakes to his father, taketh the bundell of stickes, and
beareth after his father.

ISAACK

Father, I all readye
to doe your byddinge moste meekely,
and to beare this wood full beane am I,
as ye commande mee.   240

ABRAHAM

31 O Isaack, my darlinge deare,
my blessinge nowe I give thee here.
Take up this fagott with good chere,
and on thy backe yt bringe.
And fyer with us I will take.   245

24ʳ   ISAACK

Your bydding I wyll not forsake;
father, I will never slake
to fullfill your byddinge.

ABRAHAM

32 Nowe Isaack, sonne, goe wee our waye
to yonder monte, yf that wee maye.   250

Here they goe both to the place to doe sacralice.

235 Godes] his H   not] never R   236 ever] aye H   SD(1)] *To left of*
233–5 A, *to right of* 233–4 R, *to left of* 233–4 B, *om* H   Abraham] heare
Abraham AR   a sworde and fyer] up a sworde R   SD(2)] Here Isaack,
taking the bundell of stickes, speaketh to his father *to left of* 237–40 B, *om* H
speakes] speaketh AR   taketh the] and taketh a AR   bundell] burne A,
faggot R   father] father and saieth A, father sayinge R   237 I] I am
ARBH   238 moste] *om* H   239 and] *om* H   full beane] bowne H
240 commande] commaunded AR   241 Isaack] Isack Isack BH
242 nowe] *om* H   here] in feare B   245 with us] *om* B, with me H
After 248] Tunc Isaak accipiet lignum super tergum, et ad montem pariter
ibunt H   250 monte] mowntayne H   *SD*] . . . are the goe . . . to they . . .
to doe . . . .ice A, *after* 248 R, *om* H   here] *om* B   both] both together B

ISAACK

My dere father, I will assaye
to follow you full fayne.

Abraham, beinge minded to slea his sonne, lifte us his handes to
heaven and sayth:

ABRAHAM

O my harte will breake in three!
To here thy wordes I have pittye.
As thou wilte, lorde, soe muste yt bee;   255
to thee I will bee beane.

33 Laye downe thy fagott, my owne sonne.

ISAACK

All readye, father; loe yt here.
But why make yee soe heavye chere?
Are ye any thinge adread?   260
Father, yf yt bee your will,
where is the beaste that wee shall kyll?

ABRAHAM

Therof, sonne, is none upon the hill
that I see here upon this stedde.

Isaack, fearinge leste his father will slea him, sayth:

ISAACK

34 Father, I am full sore afrayde   265
to see you beare that drawen sworde.
I hope for all myddylarde
you will not slaye your chylde.

SD] *om* H   minded] myded A   sonne] sonne Isaake A   lifte us] leiftes up
A, lifteth up R, list up B   handes] hand B   to heaven] *om* A   sayth] saith
fowlowinge A   257 owne] *om* H   sonne] sonne deare ARBH   *To left
of 257–9]* Isack layeth downe the wood and goeth to his father and saith B
258 yt] yt is H   259 but] and H   soe] sucke A, such R   262 wee]
ye B   263 therof sonne is none] ther is non sonne B   the] this ARBH
264 upon] in ARBH   this] *om* AR   SD] *om* H   will] woulde ARB
slea] kill B   ISAACK] ISAACKE dicat R   266 that] this RH   267 myd-
dylarde] myddellyarde AR, middell land B, middleyorde H   268 you]
wee B   slaye] slow B

Abraham, comfortinge his sonne, sayth:

ABRAHAM

Dreade thee not, my chylde. I reade
our lorde will sende of his goodheade   270
some manner of beast into this fyelde,
eyther tame or wylde.

ISAACK

35 Father, tell mee or I goe
whether I shall harme or noe.

ABRAHAM

Ah, deare God, that mee ys woe!   275
Thou breakeste my harte in sunder.

ISAAC

Father, tell mee of this case:
why you your sworde drawen hase,
and beares yt naked in this place.
Therof I have great wonder.   280

24ᵛ   ### ABRAHAM

36 Isaack, sonne, peace, I praye thee.
Thou breakest my harte anon in three.

ISAACK

I praye you, father, leane nothinge from mee;
but tell mee what you thinke.

ABRAHAM

Ah, Isaack, Isaack, I muste thee kyll.   285

SD] *om* H   Abraham] here Abraham R   comfortinge] comfortes AR
sayth] and saicth A, sayinge R, *om* B   ABRAHAM] *om* R   269 thee not]
not thou H   270 goodheade] godheade ARBH   271 of] *om* BH   fyelde]
stydd H   274 harme] bc harmcde AR, have harme H   276 breakeste]
burstes H   281 praye thee] thee praie A   282 anon in three] in sunder
A, even in three BH   285 Ah] O H

ISAACK

Alas, father, ys that your wyll,
your owne chylde for to spyll
upon thys hilles bryncke?

37 If I have trespassed in any degree,
with a yarde you may beate mee.   290
Put up your sworde yf your wyll bee,
for I am but a chylde.

ABRAHAM

O my deare sonne, I am sorye
to doe to thee this great anoye.
Godes commandement doe must I;   295
his workes are aye full mylde.

ISAACK

38 Would God my mother were here with mee!
Shee would kneele downe upon her knee,
prayeinge you, father, if yt might bee,
for to save my liefe.   300

ABRAHAM

39 O comely creature, but I thee kyll
I greeve my God, and that full yll.
I may not worke agaynste his wyll
but ever obedyent bee.
O Isaack, sonne, to thee I saye   305
God hase commanded mee todaye
sacryfyce—this is noe naye—
to make of thy bodye.

· ISAACK

40 Is yt Godes will I shalbe slayne?

287 for] here for RB   288 hilles] hill H   290 may] might H
293 deare] *om* H   294 to thee] *om* H   anoye] anye H   296 aye] ever A
298 downe] *om* H   299 might] maye A   301 creature] creator A
306 todaye] this daye BH   308 of] yt of ARH   bodye] bloode H
309 shalbe] shold be H

ABRAHAM

Yea, sonne, yt is not for to leane;   310
to his byddinge I will bee beane,
ever to him pleasinge.
But that I doe this deolfull deede,
my lorde will not quite mee my meede.

ISAACK

Marye, father, God forbydde   315
but you doe your offeringe.

41 Father, at home your sonnes you shall fynde
that you muste love by course of kynde.
Be I once out of your mynde,
your sorrowe may sonne cease.   320
But yet you must doe Godes byddinge.
Father, tell my mother for nothinge.

25ʳ Here Abraham, wringinge his handes, sayth:

ABRAHAM

For sorrowe I maye my handes wringe;
thy mother I cannot please.

42 O Isaak, Isaack, blessed most thow bee!   325
Almoste my wytt I loose for thee.
The blood of thy body soe free
I am full loth to sheede.

ISAACK

Father, synce you muste needes doe soe,
lett yt passe lightly and over goe.   330
Kneelinge upon my knees too,
your blessinge one mee spreade.

310 for] *om* H   312 ever] and ever ARB   him] his H   313 that] *om* H
314 my meede] in my nede AR   315 marye] nay B   318 muste]
moste A   319 once out] out once H   321 yet] *om* H   *SD*] *om* H
wringinge] wrynges AR, wringeth B   sayth] and saith A, sayinge R, *om* B
325 O] *om* B   Isaack(2)] sonne R   most] muste AB, moth R, mot H
326 loose] lose ARH   327 soe] *om* H   328 I am] methink H
After 328] Here Isaake askinge his father blessinge one his knyes, and saith AR
(one] kneelinge one R   and saith] *om* R), Here Isack kneleth on his knees and
asketh his father blessing *to left of* 329–32 B   329 synce] seinge AR, sith H
331 upon] on ABH

ABRAHAM

43 My blessinge, deare sonne, give I thee,
    and thy mothers with harte soe free.
    The blessinge of the Trinitye,   335
    my deare sonne, one thee light.

ISAACK

Father, I praye you hyde my eyne
that I see not the sworde soe keene.
Your strooke, father, would I not seene
leste I agaynst yt gryll.   340

ABRAHAM

44 My deare sonne Isaack, speake noe moare;
    thy wordes make my harte full sore.

ISAACK

O deare father, wherfore, wherfore?
Sythenn I muste needes bee dead,
of one thinge I would you praye.   345
Sythen I must dye the death todaye,
as fewe strokes as yee well maye
when yee smyte of my head.

ABRAHAM

45 Thy meekenes, chylde, makes mee affraye.
    My songe maye bee 'Wele-Awaye'.   350

ISAACK

O deare father, doe away, doe away
your makinge of myche mone.

ABRAHAM] *om* AR   333–6] *om* AR   334 soe] *om* H   ISAACK] *om* AR
337 father] also father R   338 the] your RH   339 your] you A
father] *om* H   seene] see AR   340 agaynst yt gryll] agaist did sliere B
344 sythenn] seinge AR, sithens B, syth H   345 would] will A   346] *om* H
sythen] since B   todaye] this day RB   347 as(2)] *om* A   yee well] well
yee B, you H   349 affraye] afraid B   350 wele] wayle AR, well BH
352 of myche] so moche ARB, so mickle H

Now truely, father, this talkinge
doth but make longe taryinge.
I praye you come of and make endinge,   355
and lett mee hence bee gone.

ABRAHAM

46 Come hyther, my chylde; thow art soe sweete.
Thow must be bounden hand and feete.

Here Isaack ryseth and cometh to his father, and hee taketh him
and byndeth him and layeth him one the alter for to sacrifyce him.

25ᵛ   ISAACK

Father, we muste noe more meete
by ought that I cane see.   360
But doe with mee then as thou will;
I muste obey, and that is skyll,
Godes commandement to fulfill,
for needes soe must it bee.

47 Upon the purpose that you have sett you,   365
forsooth, father, I wyll not lett you;
but evermore to doe your vowe
while that ever yee maye.
Father, greete well my brethen yonge,
and praye my mother of hir blessinge;   370
I come no more under her winge.
Farewell, for ever and aye.

48 But, father, I crye you mercye
for all that ever I have trespased to thee;
forgiven, father, that hit may bee   375
untill domesdaye.

355 of] *om* AR   356 bee] *om* H   357 thow] that BH   358 bounden]
bounde both A   feete] foote A   SD] *om* B, Tunc colliget eum et ligavit H
byndeth him] byndeth A   one] upon A   for] *om* AR   him] hym and saith A
359 father] A father H   360 by] be A   cane] maie AR   361 then]
right H   thou] you ARB   364] and let me hence gone H   365 you(2)]
om B   366 you] *om* B   367 to] unto H   doe your vowe] you bowe
ARBH   368 ever] *om* H   yee] I ARBH   369 brethen] brethren
ARBH   371 I] since B   under] I shall under B   374 for all that]
om H   ever] *om* B, of that H   375 father] *om* H   376 untill] unto H

ABRAHAM

49 My deare sonne, lett bee thy mones;
my chylde, thow greeves mee every ones.
Blessed bee thow, body and bones,
and I forgive thee here.　　　　　　　　　　380
Nowe, my deare sonne, here shall thow lye.
Unto my worke nowe must I hye.
I had as leeve myselfe to dye
as thow, my darlinge deare.

ISAACK

50 Father, if yee bee to mee kynde,　　　　　385
about my head a carchaffe bynde
and lett mee lightly out of your mynde,
and soone that I were speede.

ABRAHAM

Farewell, my sweete sonne of grace.

Here kisse him and binde the carchaffe about his head, and lett
him kneele downe and speake.

ISAACK

I praye you, father, turne downe my face　　　390
a little while, while you have space,
for I am full sore adreade.

ABRAHAM

51 To doe this deede I am sorye.

ISAACK

Yea, lorde, to thee I call and crye!
Of my soule thow have mercye,　　　　　　395
hartely I thee praye.

378 greeves] greaved H　　　every] ever AR, but H　　　381 nowe] loe H
384 darlinge deare] deare darlinge AR　　　　　　388 speede] spedd H
SD] Here Abraham doth kisse his sonne Isaake and byndes a charschaffe aboute
his heade; here let Isaake kneele downe and speake A, *om* H　　here] here
Abraham B　　kisse] kisseth B　　binde] bindeth B　　the] a B　　downe] *om* B
speake] speaketh B, speake as followeth R　　391 while while] while A, tyme
while R　　395 of] one RBH

ABRAHAM

Lord, I would fayne worke thy will.
This yonge innocent that lieth soe still,
full loth were mee him to kyll
by any manner of waye. 400

26^r   ISAACK

52 My deare father, I thee praye,
let mee take my clothes awaye,
for sheeding blood on them todaye
at my laste endinge.

ABRAHAM

53 Harte, yf thow would breake in three, 405
thou shall never mayster mee.
I will noe longer lett for thee;
my God I may not greeve.

ISAACK

A, mercye, father, why tarrye yee soe?
Smite of my head and lett mee goe. 410
I praye you rydd mee of my woo,
for nowe I take my leave.

ABRAHAM

54 My sonne, my harte will breake in three
to here thee speake such wordes to mee.
Jesu, one mee thow have pyttye, 415
that I have moste of mynde.

ISAACK

Nowe, father, I see that I shall dye.
Almighty God in majestie,
my soule I offer unto thee.
Lorde, to yt bee kynde. 420

399 were mee] me weare H   400 of] a A   401 thee] you RH
405 breake] borste A   411 you] God H   rydd] ryde AB   413 my]
Ah ARBH   416 of] in ARBH

Here lett Abraham take and bynde his sonne Isaack upon the
aulter, and leett him make a signe as though hee would cutt of
his head with the sword. Then lett the Angell come and take the
sworde by the end and staye yt, sayinge:

ANGELUS

55 Abraham, my servante deare!

ABRAHAM

Loe, lord, I am all readye here.

ANGELUS

Laye not thy sworde in noe manere
one Isaack, thy deare darlinge;
and doe to him none anoye.   425
For thou dreades God, well wott I,
that of thy sonne hasse noe mercye
to fulfill his byddinge.

ANGELUS SECUNDUS

56 And for his byddinge thow doest aye,
and sparest neyther for feare nor faye   430
to doe thy sonne to death todaye,
Isaack to thee full deare,
therfore God hath sent by mee in faye
a lambe that is both good and gaye.
Loe, have him right here.   435

SD] Tunc accipiet gladium, faciens occidendi signum, et Angelus veniens capiet
punctum gladii illius, ac postea dicat Angelus H   lett] *om* B   take and bynde]
om R, takes and bindes B   his sonne Isaack] *om* R, his sonne B   upon the
aulter] *om* R   and leett] let A, *om* R, and B   him] *om* RB   make] makes B
cutt] slaye and cutt R   the sword] his sorde AR   then lett] then B   come]
comes B   take] takes B   staye] stayeth B   *After* 422 ANGELUS] ANGELUS
2 H   425 and] naie H   doe] doe thou BH   to] *om* H   none] no ABH
426 for] *om* B   wott] se H   ANGELUS SECUNDUS] SECUNDUS ANGELLUS AR,
ANGELUS 2 H   429 aye] this daye B   430 and] not B   sparest]
spare B   faye] fraye ARH   431 todaye] this daye B   433 by mee]
to thee R   *After* 434] into this place as thou se maye H   435 have
him] it is H

57 Ah, lorde of heaven and kinge of blysse,
thy byddinge shall be donne iwys.
Sacrifyce here mee sent ys,
and all, lorde, through thy grace.
An horned wether here I see;   440
amonge these bryers tyed is hee.
To thee offered now shall hee bee,
anonright in this place.

Then lett Abraham take the lambe and kyll him, and lett God saye:

DEUS

58 Abraham, by my selfe I sweare:
for thou hast bine obedient ayere,   445
and spared not thy sonne to teare
to fulfill my byddinge,
thou shall bee blessed that pleased mee.
Thy seede shall I soe multiplye
as starres and sande, soe many highe I   450
of thy bodye comminge.

59 Of enimyes thou shalte have power,
and thy blood alsoe in feare.
Thow haste beene meeke and bonere
to doe [as] I thee bade.   455
And of all natyons, leeve thow mee,
blessed evermore shalbee
through fruyte that shall come of thee,
and saved through thy seede.

---

436 blysse] blesse AR   437 shall be donne] I shall doe H   438 here
mee sent] sente me here AR, here sent B, here to me send H   439 through]
of B   *At* 440] BRAHAM H   441 these] the ARBH   tyed is hee] died
to be B   442] *om* B   now] *om* AH   shall hee] it shall H   *SD*] Tunc
Abraham mactabit arietem H   and lett God saye] then God speaketh R
DEUS] GOD A   445 ayere] ever ARH   446 spared] sparest B   to teare]
so deare H   448 that pleased mee] that pleaseth me B, thou art worthy H
449 shall I] I shall ARBH   soe] *om* BH   450 as] as the B   sande]
sandes R   many] *om* B   highe] het H   453 and] and of AR   454 thow]
because thou B, for thou H   haste beene] art B   455 to] and A   as]
a Hm   456 of] *om* H   leeve] lyve B   457 shalbee] shall thou be AR
458 through] the H   shall] shalbe B   459 saved] saved be A, be saved R

Here the Docter saythe:

EXPOSITOR

60   Lordinges, this significatyon   460
     of this deede of devotyon—
     and yee will, yee wytt mon—
     may torne you to myche good.
     This deede yee seene done here in this place,
     in example of Jesus done yt was,   465
     that for to wynne mankinde grace
     was sacrifyced one the roode.

61   By Abraham I may understand
     the Father of heaven that cann fonde
     with his Sonnes blood to breake that bonde   470
     that the dyvell had brought us to.
     By Isaack understande I maye
     Jesus that was obedyent aye,
     his Fathers will to worke alwaye
     and death for to confounde.   475

Here lett the Docter kneele downe and saye:

62   Such obedyence grante us, O lord,
     ever to thy moste holye word;
     that in the same wee may accorde
     as this Abraham was beyne.
     And then altogether shall wee   480
     that worthye kinge in heaven see,
     and dwell with him in great glorye
     for ever and ever. Amen.

SD] *om* ARH   Docter] Expositor B   462 wytt] witten A   mon] mone
AR, more B   463 you to] to you B   464 yee] that B, that yee H
seene] see ARH, *om* B   here] is B, *om* H   465 in] an AR   466 to]
om B   mankinde] mankindes AR   467 roode] tree H   469 of] in B
fonde] fand H   470 Sonnes] *om* H   bonde] bande AH   471 that]
om H   had] *om* B   472 understande I maye] I maie understande A
475 and] his H   for] *om* BH   confounde] underfonge H   *SD-Finis*] *om* H
SD lett] *om* R   kneele] kneeleth R   downe] *om* B   saye] sayeth R
480 and] *om* A   then] *om* B   481 that] the B

Here the Messenger maketh an ende:

27ʳ   63 Make rowme, lordings, and give us waye,
           and lett Balack come in and playe,   485
           and Balaham that well can saye,
           to tell you of prophecye.
           That lord that dyed one Good Frydaye,
           the same you all, both night and daye.
           Farewell, my lordings, I goe my waye;   490
           I may noe lenger abyde.

Finis

PLAY V

27ᵛ   THE CAPPERS PLAYE

Incipit Pagina Quinta de Moyses et de lege sibi data.

DEUS (ad Moysen)

    1 Moyses, my servant leeffe and dere,
       and all my people that bine here,
       yee wotten in Egipte when yee weare
       out of thraldome I you brought.
       I will you have noe God but mee;   5
       no false godes none make yee.
       My name in vayne name not yee
       for that liketh mee nought.

    2 I wyll you hould your holy daye
       and worshippe yt eke alwaye,   10
       father and mother all that yee maye,
       and slea noe man noewhere.

SD maketh an ende] endeth the playe R   *After SD*] MESSINGER R
489 the same] he save ARB   you] us B   491 farewell my] fare you well B
    Play V: for H, see Appendix IB   *Guild-ascription* Cappers] Cappers and
Lynnan Drapers AR   *Play-heading*] *om* B   quinta] quint A, quinto R
data] data et dicat R   3 wotten] wotte B   weare] were ther B   5 noe]
no other B   6 no] nor B   7 name(2)] nam A

Fornication yee shall flee.
Noe meanes goodes steale yee,
nor in noe place lenge ne bee   15
false wytnes for to beare.

3 Your neighbours wyefe desyre you nought,
   servante nee goodes that hee hath bought,
   oxe nor asse, in deede nor thought,
   nor nothinge that is his,   20
   nor wrongefullye to have his thinge
   agaynst his love and his likinge.
   In all these keepe my byddinge,
   that yee doe not amysse.

MOYSES

4 Good lorde that art ever soe good,   25
   I will fulfill with mylde moode
   thy commandementes, for I stood
   to here thee nowe full styll.
   Fortye dayes now fasted have I,
   that I might bee the more worthye   30
   to lerne this tokenn trulye.
   Nowe wyll I worke thy will.

Tunc Moyses in monte dicat populo:

5 Good folke, dread yee nought.
   To prove you with God hath this wrought.
   Take theese wordes in your thought;   35
   nowe knowne yee what ys sinne.
   By this sight nowe yee may see
   that hee is pearles of postee.
   Therfore this token looke doe yee,
   therof that yee ne blynne.   40

---

13 flee] fleye AR, fly B   14 meanes] mens A, mans R, manner B   15 lenge
ne] leinge nor A, lying not B   17 nought] not A   18 goodes] good ARB
19 nor(2)] or B   22 and] or AR   23 keepe] doe A   25 art ever
soe] ever was B   27 commandementes] commaundment AR   28 thee]
them B   33 good] Godes AR   34 you with] that A, to you R, you B
this] us A   35 take] thinke A, thinkes R   36 knowne] knowe AR
sinne] sieene B   39 this] his B   yee] you R

DOCTOR

6 Lordings, this commandement
  was the firste lawe that ever God sent;
  x poynctes there bine—takes intent—
  that moste effecte ys in.
28ʳ   But all that storye for to fonge   45
  to playe this moneth yt were to longe.
  Therfore moste fruitefull ever amonge
  shortly wee shall myn.

7 After, wee reden of this storye
  that in this monte of Synaye   50
  God gave the lawe witterlye
  wrytten with his hand
  in stonye tables, as reede I;
  before, men honored mawmentrye.
  Moyses brake them hastelye,   55
  for that hee would not wond.

8 But after, played as yee shall see,
  other tables owt carved hee
  which God bade wrytten should bee,
  the wordes hee sayde before.   60
  The which tables [shryned] were
  after, as God can Moyses leare;
  and that [shryne] to him was deare
  therafter evermore.

Here God appereth agayne to Moyses.

DEUS

9 Moyses, my servant, goe anon   65
  and kerve owt of the rocke of stone
  tables to wryte my byddinge upon,
  such as thou had before.

43 takes] that takes AR, that taken B   48 wee] you R   myn] menne AR
49 of] on ARB   52 his] his owne R   53 I] we A   56 wond]
wonne A   61 shryned] shryved Hm   63 shryne] shryve Hm
SD] Iterum apparet Deus ad Moysen B   here] then AR   appereth] appeared
AR   Moyses] Moses sayinge R   DEUS] om B   67 byddinge] biddinges B   upon] one ARB   68 had] hadest B

And in the morninge looke thou hye
into the monte of Synaye.   70
Lett noe man wott but thow onlye,
of companye noe more.

MOYSES

10   Lord, thy byddinge shalbe donne
and tables kerved owt full soonne.
But tell mee—I praye thee this boone—   75
what wordes I shall wryte.

DEUS

Thou shalt wryte the same lore
that in the tables was before.
Hyt shalbe kepte for evermore,
for that is my delyte.   80

Tunc Moyses faciet signum quasi effoderet tabulas de monte et,
super ipsas scribens, dicat populo.

MOYSES

11   Godes folke of Israell,
herkens you all to my spell.
God bade ye should keepe well
this that I shall saye.
Syxe dayes bodely worke all;   85
the seaventh sabboath ye shall call.
That daye for ought that maye befall
hallowed shalbe aye.

12   Whoe doth not this, dye shall hee.
In howses forever shall noe man see   90
firste fruyctes—to God offer yee,
for soe himselfe beode;
purpur and [byse] both too
to him that shall save you from woo
and helpe you in your neede.   95

70 into] unto AR   75 this boone] *om* A, what bene R   78 was] were B
SD effoderet] effanderet A   de] et B   populo] populo et dicat A   81 folke]
people A   82 you all to] all unto AB, ye all unto R   88 aye] forever A,
for aye R   90 forever] farr B   92 soe] *om* AR   beode] byde A,
bydd R, bade B   93 purpur] purple AR   byse] kyse HmA, gkyse R

28ᵛ Tunc descendet de monte, et veniet rex Balaack equitando
juxta montem et dicat.

BALAACK

13 I Balaack, kinge of Moab land,
    all Israell and I had in hand,
    I am soe wrath I would not wond
    to slea them everye wight.
    For there God helpes them so stowtly   100
    of other landes to have mastery
    that yt is boteles wytterly
    agaynst them for to fight.

14 What natyon doth them anoy,
    Moyses prayeth anon in hye;   105
    then have the ever the victorye
    and there enemyes the worse.
    Therfore, how I will wroken bee
    I am bethought, as mote I thee:
    Balaham shall come to mee,   110
    that people for to curse.

Florish.

15 Noe knife nor sworde maye not avayle
    that ylke people to assayle.
    That foundes to fight, hee shall fayle,
    for sycker yt is noe boote.   115

Caste up.

    All natyons they doe anoye,
    and my folke commen for to distroye,
    and oxe that graweth buselye
    the grasse right to the roote.

SD montem] monten R, mont B   dicat] dicat Balacke rex A   BALAACK]
BALACKE REX ARB   96 Moab] Mobe AR   97 and] land B   had] hande
ARB   98 wond] wonne A   107 worse] worste A   108 how] *om* A
bee] me AR   112 knife nor sworde] sworde nor knife ARB   113 ylke]
same AR   to] for to A   114 that] he that AR   hee] *om* AR   115 boote]
boonte B   116 doe] do me B   117 commen] comon B   for to] to
AR, doe B   118 and] as AB, as the R   graweth] draweth AR   buselye]
bestely B

16 Whosoever Balaham blesseth, iwys,   120
    blessed that man sothlye is;
    whosoever he cursys fareth amyse,
    such name over all hath hee.

17 But yett I truste venged to bee
    with dynte of sword or pollicye   125
    on these false losells, leaves mee.
    Leeve this withowten dowbte,
    for to bee wroken is my desyre;
    my heart brennys as whott as fyre
    for vervent anger and for ire,   130
    till this bee brought abowte.

'Surgite dei patriae et opitulamini nobis et in necessitate nos
defendite.'

18 Therfore, my god and godes all,
    O mightye Mars, one thee I call!
    With all the powers infernall
    ryse now and helpe at neede.   135
    I am enformed by trewe reporte
    how the mediators doeth resorte
    to wynne my land to there comforte,
    desended of Jacobs seede.

19 Now shewe your power, you godes mighty,   140
    soe that these caytiffes I may destroye,
    havinge of them full victorye,
    and them brought to mischance.

Sworde.

    Beate them downe in playne battell,
    those false losells soe cruell,   145

---

121 that man sothlye] that man surely R, southly that man B   122 whoso-
ever] whoso B   cursys] cursed R   amyse] amesse A   125 dynte] dente
AR   126 on] of B   mee] ye ARB   131 till] that B   *Latin* surgite]
surget A, surgete R   patriae] patri A, patrie RB   opitulamini] opitulamine B
necessitate] sessetatem A, nesessetatem R   nos] mos R   defendite] defindite R
134 the] thie B   powers] power B   136 enformed] reformed A
137 mediators] meditators A   138 wynne] wyne A   land] love AR
140 power] powers A   you godes] *om* R   mighty] almightie AR   141 these]
the AR   145 those] these B   losells] loses R   cruell] fell R

that all the world may here tell
wee take on vengeance.

29^r　　20 Owt of Egipte fled the bee
and passed through the Red Sea.
The Egiptians that them pursued trewlye　　150
were drowned in that same fludd.
The have on God mickell of might
which them doeth ayde in wronge and right.
Whosoever with them foundeth to fight,
hee wynneth little good.　　155

21 They have slayne—this wott I well—
through helpe of God of Israell
both Seon and Ogge, kinges so fell,
and playnly them distroye.
Thearefore ryse up, ye goodes eiche one!　　160
Ye be a hundrethe godes for one.
I would be wroken them upon,
for all there pompe and pryde.

22 Therefore goe fetche hym, batchelere,
that he may curse these people heare.　　165
For sycker on them in no manere
may we not wroken be.

Miles rex Balack loquitur:

23 Syr, on your errannde will I goon,
that yt shalbe donne anone.
And he shall wreake you on your fanne,　　170
the peopell of Isarell.

REX BALACK

Yea, looke thou hett him gould great one
and landes for to live upon

147 on] one them ARB　　150 them pursued] pursued them B　　151 that]
the R　　same] om B　　To left of 151] Sword B　　153 and] or AR
154 with them foundeth] foundeth with them A　　155 little] but litill R
158 so] om R　　159 distroye] destroyed ARB　　160 goodes] godes ARB
164 goe] to B　　hym] in AR　　165 these] this AR　　166 sycker] suerlye A
167 we not] not we R　　SD loquitur] om ARB　　169 that] and R
170 fanne] fonne ARB

to destroye them as hee cann,
these freekes that bine soe fell.   175

Tunc Miles regis Balack ibit ad Balaham et dicat:

24   Balaham, my lorde greetes well thee
      and prayeth thee soone at him to bee,
      to curse the people of Judee
      that done him great anoye.

BALAHAM

Abyde a whyle there, batchelere,   180
for I may have noe power
but yf that Godes will were;
and that shall I wete in hye.

Tunc ibit Balaham ad consulendum dominum in oratione. Sedens
dicat Deus:

25   Balaham, I commande thee
      kinge Balackes byddinge for to flee.   185
      That people that blessed is of mee
      curse thou by noe waye.

BALAHAM

Lorde, I must doe thy byddinge
though yt to mee be unlikynge,
for therby mych wynninge   190
I might have had todaye.

29ᵛ   DEUS

26   Yett though Balack bee my foe
      thou shalt have leave thyther to goe.
      But look that thou doe right soe
      as I have thee taught.   195

SD regis] reges AR, rex B   *After SD*] MILES A, MILES REX BALACK B
177 thee soone at him] at hym sone A   182 that] *om* A   183 wete]
wytte AR   *SD* dominum] domine A   sedens dicat] sedences dicat A, *om* R,
et scedens dicat B   Deus] Deum B   *After SD*] Balaaham praieth to God on his
kneeyes AR, *to left of SD* B (Balaaham] here Balaham R)   *Before* 184] DEUS RB
186 of] for B   187 by] not by ARB   189 to mee be] be to me A
unlikynge] unwilling B   190 wynninge] woninge A   191 have] a AR
192 though] *om* B   193 thyther] theided A   194 that] *om* A

BALAHAM

Lorde, yt shall be donne in hight.
This asse shall beare me aright.
Goe we together anon, syr knight,
for leave nowe have I caught.

Tunc Balaham et Miles equitabunt simul, et dicat

BALAHAM

27 Knight, by my lawe that I live one,   200
nowe have I leave for to gonne,
cursed they shalbe everyeychone
and I ought wynne maye.
Hould the kinge that hee beheight,
Godes hoste I sett at light.   205
Warryed the shalbe this night,
or that I wynd awaye.

MILES

28 Balaham, doe my lordes will
and of gould thou shalt have thy fill!
Spare thou nought that folke to spill,   210
and spurne ther Godes speach.

BALAHAM

Frend, I have godes wonder fell;
both Ruffyn and Reynell
will worke right as I them tell.
Ther ys noe wyle to seeke.   215

Tunc Balaham ascendit super asinam et cum Milite equitabit; et
in obviam venit Angelus domini cum gladio extricto; et asina
videt ipsum et non Balaham, ad [terram] prostrata jacebit; et dicat

197 aright] righte AR   *SD* simul] fumel A   BALAHAM] *om* R   200 live]
leve AR   201 have I] I have ARB   205 hoste] hest B   I] I will AR
206 warryed] cursed R, worryed B   207 wynd] wende AB, wonde R
210 nought] not AR   212 frend] *om* B   godes] goodes A   fell] sett B
213 Reynell] Ranell R, Ragnell B   215 wyle] will RB   *SD* ascendit]
ascendet A   venit] venet A   domini] Deum A   extricto] extracto ARB
videt] vidit ARB   terram] terra Hm   jacebit] jacebet A

BALAHAM

29 Gooe forth, Burnell; goe forth, goe!
    What the divell? My asse will not goe.
    Served shee mee never soe,
    what sarrowe soever yt is.
    What the divell? Now shee is fallen downe.   220
    But thou ryse and make thee bowne
    and beare mee soone owt of this towne,
    thow shalt abye iwys.

Tunc percutiet Balaham asinam suam. Et hic oportet aliquis trans-
formiari in speciem asinae; et quando Balaham percutit, dicat
asina:

30 Mayster, thow doest ill secerly,
    soe good an asse as mee to nye.   225
    Now hast thow beaten mee here thrye,
    that bare the thus abowte.

BALAHAM

Burnell, whye begylest thow mee
when I have most neede to thee?

30ʳ   ASINA

    That sight that before mee I see   230
    maketh mee downe to lowte.

31 Am not I, mayster, thy owne asse
    to beare thee whyther thow will passe,
    and many winter readye was?
    To smyte me hyt ys shame.   235
    Thow wottest well, mayster, perdee,
    that thow haddest never non like to mee,
    ne never yett soe served I thee.
    Now am I not to blame.

218 shee mee] me she B   219 is] bee R   220 shee is] is shee AR
221 thou] nowe AR   thee] thie B   223 abye] abide B   *SD* percutiet]
percuciet B   et] et novum quod ARB   transformiari] transfornam AR, trans-
formari B   asinae] asine AB   asina] asinam B   *After SD*] The asse
peaketh ARB (peaketh] speaketh RB)   *Before* 224] ASSINA R   224 ill]
evill ARB   229 to] of AR   234 winter] wynters AR   235 hyt] this B
237 that] *om* ARB   never non] non never A, non ever B   238 never] ever B

Tunc videns Balaham Angelum evaginatum gladium habentem [adorans] ipsum dicat Balaham (Balaham on his knees shall fall sodenly downe and speaketh to the Angell).

BALAHAM

32 A, lorde, to thee I make avowe   240
    I had noe sight of thee or nowe.
    Little wyste I that yt was thowe
    that feared my asse soe.

ANGELUS

Why hast thow beaten thy asse, why?
Nowe am I commen thee to nye,   245
that changed thy purpose soe falsly
and nowe wouldest be my foe.

33 If this asse had not downe gonne,
    I would have slayne thee here anon.

BALAHAM

Lord, have pittye mee upon,   250
for synned I have sore.
Lorde, ys yt thy will that I forth gonne?

ANGELUS

Yea, but looke thow doe that folke no woe
otherwaye then God bade thee doe
and sayde to thee before.   255

Tunc Balaham et Miles equitabunt simul et in obviam veniet rex Balaack, et dicat rex

BALACK

34 Ah, wellcome, Balaham my frende,
    for all my anger thow shalt ende
    if that thy will bee to wende
    and wreake mee one my foe.

SD *Latin* evaginatum] evaquatum AR   habentem] *om* B   adorans] adoramus Hm, a adoriens A   *SD English* Balaham] here Balaham R   on his knees] *om* ARB   shall fall] falleth B   downe] *om* A, falle one his knees R   speaketh] speake AR   Angell] Angell saying R   240 A] O B   254 otherwaye] otherwayes AR   *SD* rex(2)] rex Balacke R   BALACK] BALACKE REX AB, REXE BALACKE R   258 wende] weend B   259 one] of AR

BALAHAM

Nought may I speake, as I have wyn,　　　　260
but as God putteth mee within
to forbye all the ende of my kyn.
Therfore, syr, me ys woe.

BALACK

35　Come forth, Balaham; come with mee.
For one this hill, soe mott I thee,　　　　265
the folke of Israell shall thou see
and curse them, I thee praye.
Gould and silver and eke pearle
thou shalt have, great plentee,
to curse them that yt sonne may bee,　　　　270
all that thou sayst todaye.

30ᵛ　Tunc Balaack descendit de equo et Balaham de asina et
ascendent in montem, et dicat Balaack rex.

BALAACK

36　Lo, Balaham, now thow seest here
Godes people all in feare.
Cittye, castle, and ryvere—
looke now. How lykes thee?　　　　275
Curse them now at my prayer
as thow wilt bee to mee full deare
and in my realme moste of powere
and greatest under mee.

Tunc Balaham versus austrem dicat.

BALAHAM

37　How may I curse here in this place　　　　280
that people that God blessed hasse?
In them is both might and grace,
and that is ever well seene.

260 wyn] wyne AR, wine B　　　262 forbye] forbidd B　　my] any B
263 syr] sure B　　　BALACK] BALACKE REX AR　　　266 Israell] Jacobe R
268 pearle] perre B　　　271 sayst] saide A, sayth R, seest B　　　SD asina]
asine AR　　ascendent] assendit A　　montem] monten R　　dicat] dicit B
BALAACK] BALACKE REX AR　　　272 now] om AR　　　274 ryvere] reiver A,
river B　　　275 lykes] likeste A, lyketh R　　　278 of] in R　　　SD austrem]
austrom A, austrum RB

Wytnes may I none beare
agaynst God that them can were, 285
his people that noe man may dare
ne trowble with noe teene.

38 I saye this folke shall have there will,
that noe natyon shall them gryll;
the goodnes that they shall fulfyll 290
nombred may not bee.
Theire God shall them keepe and save
and other reproffe shall they none wave;
but such death as they shall have
I pray God send to mee. 295

BALAACK

39 What the dyvell ayles thee, thow populart?
Thy speach is not worth a farte!
Doted I hope that thow arte,
for madly thou hast wrought.
I bade thee curse them everycheone 300
and thow blessest them blood and bone.
To this north syde thow shall gone,
for here thy deede is nought.

Tunc Balaack rex adducet Balaham ad borialem partem montis,
et dicat alta voce

BALAHAM

40 A, lord, that here is fayre wonninge:
halles, chambers great likinge, 305
valles, woodes, grasse growinge,
fayre yordes, and eke ryvere.

284 none] nowe A   285 were] leare R   286 may] can B   dare]
deare AR   288 this] thes A, these R   293 reproffe] hurte R   wave]
have AR   294 have] wave R   BALAACK] BALACKE REX A, REX BALACKE R
296 the] a A, om R   ayles] ayleth B   populart] popularde ARB   300 every-
cheone] everye ichone ARB   301 blessest] blessed R, blessesth B
302 thow shall] shalt thou B   SD Balaack] alaback B   adducet] addu-
cete A   304 A] O AR   306 valles] valleyes A, walles B   307 yordes]
yarde A, yardes RB   ryvere] reiver A, rivers R

I wott well that God made all this,
his folke to lyve in joye and blys.
That cursys them, cursed hee is;   310
whoe blesseth them to God is deare.

BALAACK

41 Thow preachest, populard, as a pye;
the dyvell of hell thee destroye!
I bade thee curse my enimye;
therfore thow come mee to.   315
Now hast thow blessed them here thrye,
for the meanes mee to anoye.

31ʳ   BALAHAM

Syr kinge, I told thee ere soe thrye
I might none other doe.

Tunc Balaham vertit se ad orientalem in plagam montis, et
respiciens coelum spiritu prophetico dicit: 'Orietur stella ex Jacobb
et exurget homo de Israell et consurget omnes duces alienigenarum,
et erit omnis terra possessio eius.'

BALAHAM

42 Now on thinge I will tell you all,   320
hereafter what shall befall:
a sterre of Jacobb springe shall,
a man of Israell,
that shall overcome and have in bond
all kinges and dukes of strange land;   325
and all this world have in his hand
as lord to dight and deale.

BALAACK

43 Goe wee hence; yt is noe boote
longer with this man to moote.

309 blys] blesse AR   310 that] he that R   BALAACK] BALACKE REX AR
312 preachest] preaches as AR   315 come] came A   mee to] to me AR
317 the] they R, thou B   to] here to R   318 ere] ever B   319 none]
no A   SD] om AR   prophetico] prophetica B   dicit] dicat B
BALAHAM] om AR   324 bond] bande AR   325 strange] strang B
BALAACK] om AR   328 yt] om A, for it R   329 this man] these men R

For God is both crop and roote, 330
and lorde of heaven and hell.
Now see I well noe man one lyve
agaynst him is able to stryve.
Therfore here, as mote I thrive,
I will noe longer dwell. 335

Here Balaham speaketh to Balaack: 'Abyde a while.'

BALAHAM

44 O, Balaack kinge, abyde a whyle.
I have imagined a mervelouse wyle
thy enimyes how thow shalt begyle,
my counsell yf thow take.

45 Ther maye no pestylence them dismaye, 340
neyther battell them affraye.
Plenteefull they shalbee aye
of gould, cattell, and corne.
There God of them takes the cure
from passions that hee makes them sure, 345
them to preserve in greate pleasure
as hee before hath sworne.

46 Yee shall not them distroye for aye,
but for a tyme vexe them yee maye.
Marke well now what I shall saye 350
and worke after my loore.
Send forth woomen of thy contrye
namely, those that bewtyfull bee—
and to thy enimyes lett them drawe nye,
as stales to stand them before. 355

47 When the yonge men that lustye bee
have percayved there great bewtye,
they shall desyre there companye,
love shall them soe inflame.

330 God] his God B   crop] crape A, crapp R   331 hell] eairth AR
333 is able to] no man is able to A, no man can R   334 as mote I thrive]
is a mote thrie A, is a mote thrive R   *SD* abyde a while] rex AR   336 a]
om R   337 wyle] wille B   340 them] then A   344 takes] taketh AR
345 passions] passion A, passiom R   that] *om* R   makes] maketh AR
347 hath] hade A   350 now] *om* AR   354 and to] unto AR   drawe]
stande A   355 them] *om* A   356 men] *om* AR

Then when they see the have them sure   360
in there love withowten cure,
the shall denye them theyre pleasure,
except the grante this same—

48 to love theyre great solempnitye
and worshipp the godes of thy contrye,   365
and all things commenlye
with other people to use.
Soe shall the theyre God displease
and torne themselves to great disease.
Then may thow have thy hartes ease,   370
there law when they refuse.

BALAAK

49 Balaham, thy counsell I will fulfill.
Hit shalbe done right as thow wyll.
Come nere, my knight that well can skyll
my message to performe.   375
Goe thou forth, thow valyant knight;
looke thow ne stopp daye nay night.
Bringe those women to [my] sight
that shall my enimyes destroye.

50 Spare thou neyther ryche ne poore,   380
wyddowe, mayde, ne ylke whoore;
yf shee bee fresh of coloure,
bringe her with thee, I saye.

MILES

My lord, I shall hye faste
to doe your wyll in goodlye haste.   385
Truste yee well, at the laste
your enimyes yee shall dismaye.

363 this] the A   365 the] their AR   thy contrye] trenetie AR
366 all] other A, *om* R   367 with] which RB   to] doe R, *om* B
369 disease] distres B   BALAAK] REX BALACKE R   372 will] shall ARB
375 performe] fulfill A   377 looke] take B   ne] no B   378 those]
these B   my] may Hm   379 enimyes] foes B   381 ylke] yet A, eke R
384 hye] hie me B   385 goodlye] good R   387 enimyes] foes B

The Doctor speaketh:

> 51 Lordes and ladyes that here bine lente,
> this messenger that forth was sente
> as yee have hard—to that intente, 390
> these women for to bringe—
> soe craftelye hee hath wrought,
> the fearest women hee hath owt sought;
> and to Godes people hee hath them brought—
> God knoweth, a perlouse thinge. 395

> 52 For when they had of them a sight,
> manye of them agaynste right
> gave themselfe with all theyre might
> those women for to please.
> And then soone to them they went; 400
> to have theyre [love] was there intent,
> desyringe those women of theyr consent
> and soe to live in pease.

> 53 But those women them denyed
> there love; the sayd yt should be tryed, 405
> which they might not elles abyde
> for fere of great disceyte.
> Those blynde people sware many an othe
> that neyther for leefe nor for lothe
> at any tyme they would have them wrothe, 410
> nor never agaynst them pleade.

> 54 Soe by these women full of illusion
> Godes people were brought to great confusion
> and his displeasure; in conclusion,
> his law they sett at naught. 415

the] *om* R   388 here bine lente] bene presente A, bene here lente R
390 to] of AR   that] what B   394 to] *om* AR   them] *om* R
395 God] godes R   knoweth] knowes AR   398 themselfe] themselves
ARB   with all] againste A   399 those] these A   401 love] lave Hm
402 those] these B   404 those] these B   405 love] lawe AR   406 which]
with A   they] their A   408 those] thes A, these R   409 neyther]
nother B   410 have them wrothe] have the wrath A, be wrath R, them
wroth B   412 full] so full A   413 brought] put A   great] *om* A
confusion] effuscion AR   415 sett] sete A

32^r

32^r   God to Moyses—leeve yee now—
bade him sett up a gallowes tree,
the princes of the tribes there hanged to bee
for sinnes that they had wrought.

55 With that Moyses was sore greved,   420
and generally hee them repryved.
Therfore the would him have mischived,
but God did him defend.
For the good people that tendered the lawe,
when they that greate mischyefe sawe,   425
wholye together the can them drawe
upon those wretches to make [an] ende.

56 Anon Phinees, a yonge man devowte,
captayne hee was of that whole rowte,
and of these wretches, withowt dowbt,   430
xxiiii thowsand the slewe.
And then God was well content
with Phinees for his good intent,
as the prophett wryteth verament,
and here wee shall yt shewe: 435

'Stetit Phinees, et placavit, et cessavit quassatio, et reputatum est
ei ad justitiam in generatione sua' etc.

57 Soone after, by Godes commandement,
to the Madianytes the went,
and ther they slewe verament
Balaham with fyve gyants moe.

416 to] spake to B   now] me ARB   417 bade him] byde hym A, *om* B
sett] sett thou B   gallowes] gallowe B   418 the(1)] they R   tribes]
tribe A   there] thereone R   419 sinnes] syn AR   420 was] *om* A
421 generally] generall B   repryved] reproved AR, repreved B   422 him
have] have hym ARB   427 an] and Hm   428 anon] and one ARB
Phinees] Phenes A, Phines R   429 whole] same A   430 these] those R
dowbt] all dowte A   431 xxiiii] twentye and fouer R   the] he AR
433 Phinees] Phenes A, Phines R   435 wee] I R   *Latin* stetit] stettet
AR   Phinees] Phenies A, Phines R, Phinies B   quassatio] quassaio A
reputatum] reputandum A   est] este R   ei] et A, *om* R   436 commande-
ment] verament B   437 the(2)] againe the AR, againe he B   439 moe]
more R

Lordings, mych more mattere 440
is in this storye then yee have hard here.
But the substans, withowten were,
was played you beforen.

58 And by this prophecye, leeve yee mee,
three kinges, as yee shall played see, 445
honored at his nativitye
Christe when hee was borne.
Now, worthye syrs both great and smale,
here have wee shewed this storye before;
and yf hit bee pleasinge to you all, 450
tomorrowe nexte yee shall have more.

59 Prayenge you all, both east and west
where that yee goe, to speake the best.
The byrth of Christe, feare and honest,
here shall yee see; and fare yee well. 455

Finis

PLAY VI

33ʳ THE WRIGHTES PLAYE

Pagina Sexta: De Salutatione et Nativitate Salvatoris
Jesu Christi

GABRIELL

1 Hayle be thow, Marye, mother free,
full of grace. God is with thee.
Amongst all women blessed thow bee,
and the fruite of thy bodye.

441 is] then AR   then] *om* AR   here] freey A, free R   443 was] is ARB
beforen] before AR   445 as yee shall played] played as yee shall B
449 here] you R, whom B   have wee] wee have B   this] you this A
453 that] as AR   best] lest B
 Guild-ascription Wrightes] Wrightes and Sklaters AB   playe] *om* BH
Play-heading Christi] Christie A   1 mother] maiden H   3 thow] shalt
thou B

PLAY VI

MARIA

Ah, lord that syttes high in see,   5
that wondrouslye now mervayles mee—
a simple mayden of my degree
bee greete this gratiously.

GABRIELL

2 Marye, ne dread thee nought this case.
With greate God found thow hase   10
amongst all other specyall grace.
Therfore, Marye, thow mone
conceyve and beare—I tell thee—
a childe. Jesus his name shalbe—
soe greate shall never non be as hee—   15
and called Godes Sonne.

3 And owr lord God, leeve thow mee,
shall give him Davyd his fathers see;
in Jacobs howse rayninge shall hee
with full might evermore.   20
And hee that shalbe borne of thee,
endlesse liffe in him shalbe,
that such renowne and ryaltye
had never non before.

MARIA

4 How may this bee, thow beast so bright?   25
In synne knowe I noe worldly wight.

GABRYELL

The Holye Ghoste shall in thee light
from God in majestee,
and shadowe thee seemely in sight.

MARIA] MARIE B   6 wondrouslye] wonderly H   8 this] thus RB
9 ne dread thee] thie dread B   10 and 11] reversed H   10 hase] haste
AR   11 other] wemen A   specyall] especiall AR   14 Jesus his name]
his name Jesus ARBH   15 shall never non be] shalbe never non AR, shall
never be none H   16 and] and be R   19 rayninge] raigne ARBH
21 hee] om R   MARIA] MARYE B   25 beast so] arte so AR, angell B
26 knowe] knewe AH   worldly] wordly B

Therefore that holye one, as I have height 30
that thow shalt beare through Godes might,
hee Sonne shall called bee.

5 Elizabeth that barren was
as thow maye see conceyved has
in age a sonne through Godes grace, 35
the [bedill] shalbe of blysse.
The sixte moneth is gone now agayne
seeth men called her barren;
but nothinge to Godes might and mayne
impossible is. 40

33ᵛ   MARIA

6 Now syth that God will yt soe bee,
and such grace hath sent to mee,
blessed evermore bee hee;
to please him I am payde.
Loe, Godes chosen meekelye here— 45
and lorde God, prince of powere,
leeve that yt fall in suche manere
this word that thow hast sayde.

Tunc Angelus ibit, et Maria salutabit Elizabeth:

7 Elizabeth, nece, God thee see.

ELIZABETH

Marye, blessed mote thow bee, 50
and the fruites that commes of thee,
amonge weomen all.
Wonderlye now mervayles mee
that Marye, Godes mother free,
greetes mee thus of simple degree. 55
Lord, how may this befall?

30 one] om ARBH   height] teighte A   32 hee Sonne] his Sonne ARH,
Jesus B   36 bedill] kedyll HmAR   blysse] blesse R   37 agayne]
gaine H   38 seeth] since B   40 impossible] unpossible R   41 syth]
seeinge R   that] om B   soe bee] be so AR   42 such] suche a AR
sent] send H   45 chosen] cossen A, cozin R   SD Angelus ibit] ibit
Angellus ARBH   Maria] om H   Elizabeth] Elizabeth et dicat R   At 49]
MARIA H   50 mote] moste A, mayst R, might B   51 fruites] frute
ARBH   55 thus] this A   degree] gree H   56 this] that A, thus B

8 When thow mee greetest, sweete Marye,
  the childe stirred in my bodye
  for great joye of thy companye
  and the fruite that is in thee.   60
  Blessed bee thow ever forthy,
  that lived soe well and stedfastly;
  for that was sayde to thee, ladye,
  fulfilled and done shalbee.

Maria gaudiens incipiet canticum 'Magnificat' etc.

MARIA

9 Elizabeth, therefore will I   65
  thanke the lord, kinge of mercye,
  with joyfull myrth and melody
  and laud to his likinge.
  'Magnificat,' while I have toome,
  'anima mea dominum'   70
  to Christe that in my kind is come,
  devoutly I will singe.

'Et exultavit spiritus meus in Deo' etc.

10 And for my ghost joyed hase
  in God, my heale and all my grace—
  for meekenes hee see in mee was,   75
  his feare of meane degree—
  therfore blesse mee well maye
  all generacons for aye.

11 Mych has that lord done for mee,
  that moste is in his majestye.   80
  All princes hee passis of postee,
  as sheweth well by this.

57 mee greetest] greetest me H   59 thy] thee B   61 ever] forever B
62 lived] leived ARH   *SD* gaudiens] gaudens B, gaudentes H   incipiet]
incipite AR, incipit B   magnificat] magnificate A, magnifacite R   etc] et
dicat Maria A, *om* R, anima etc H   MARIA] MARIE B   69 magnificat]
magnificate AR   toome] to me ARB, tome H   70 mea] mei R   71 is]
now H   *Latin* exultavit] exaltavit B   Deo etc] Deo AR, Deo salutari
meo etc H   73 joyed] it joyed B   hase] haste AR, also B   74 heale]
health B   76 of meane] in manye AR   79–80] *om* R   81 of] in AR

34ʳ Therefore with full hart and free
his name allway hallowed be;
and honored evermore be hee 85
one height in heaven blysse.

12 Mych hase God done for me today;
his name eye hollowed be,
as he is bound to doe mercy
from progenye to progenye. 90
And all that dredene him veryly,
his talent to fullfill,
hee through his myght gave maystery.
Disparcles proud dispytuusly
with myght of his harte hastely 95
at his owne will.

13 Deposethe myghty oute of place,
and mylde allso he hansed hasse;
hongry, nydy, wanting grace
with god hee hath fullfellede. 100
That rych power he hath forsakene;
To Iseraell, his Sonne he hath betakene.
Wayle to man throughe him his wakinge,
and myrcy hasse of his guylte—

14 as he spake to our fathers before, 105
Abrahame and his syde full yore.
Joy to the Father evermore,
the Sone, and the Holy Ghoste,
as was from the begininge
and never shall have endinge, 110
from world to world aye wendinge.
Amen, God of might most.

85 evermore] allwaie evermore A   86 one] and AR   height] highe ARB
heaven] heavens B   blysse] bleess R   88 eye] om R   hollowed] hallowed
ABH, blessed R   be] be aye AR   91–2] om R   93 gave] gave them H
maystery] majestie B   94 disparcles] dispersces AR, dispercing B, dis-
percles H   proud] pride B   dispytuusly] did pitiouslye A   97 deposethe]
disposeith AR   98 mylde] meeke ARBH   100 god] good ARH
103 his wakinge] is wacken ARBH   104 of] in R, for B   his] om R
guylte] owine A, store R   106 syde] seede ARBH   full] for AR
111 wendinge] weildinge A, weldinge R   112 might] mightes RBH

ELIZABETH

15　Marye, now redd I that wee gone
　　to Joseph thy husband anon,
　　lesse hee to misse thee make mone;　　　　　115
　　for now that is moste neede.

34ᵛ

MARIA

　　Elizabeth, nece, to doe so good is,
　　leste hee suppose one mea amysse;
　　but good lord that hath ordayned this
　　wyll witnes of my deede.　　　　　　　　120

ELIZABETH

16　Joseph, God thee save and see!
　　Thy wife here I brought to thee.

JOSEPH

　　Alas, alas, and woe is mee!
　　Whoe hasse made her with chyld?
　　Well I wist an ould man and a maye　　　　125
　　might not accord by noe waye.
　　For many yeares might I not playe
　　ne worke noe workes wild.

17　Three monethes shee hath bine from mee.
　　Now hasse shee gotten her, as I see,　　　　130
　　a great bellye like to thee
　　syth shee went away.
　　And myne yt is not, bee thow bould,
　　for I am both ould and could;
　　these xxxᵗⁱᵉ winters, though I would,　　　135
　　I might not playe noe playe.

---

113 now redd I] I rede nowe A, I red R　　115 lesse] lest BH　make] make
great B, makes H　　　MARIA] MARIE B　　　*To right of* 117] Tunc ibunt ad
Joseph H　　118 mea] me ARBH　　119 but] but the A　　122 here I]
I have AR, here I have BH　　123 woe is] woes AR　　125 an] and B
maye] maide R　　126 accord] agree R　　127 for] nor AR　yeares]
wynters A　　129 monethes] moneth B　　130 her] here A　　132 syth]
since A　　135 these] this BH　winters] wynter H　　136 playe]
plea A　noe] that H　playe] leaie A

18 Alas, where might I lenge or lende?
    For loth is mee my wife to shende,
    therfore from her will I wende
    into some other place.   140
    For to dyscreeve will I nought,
    feeblye though shee have wrought.
    To leave her privelye is my thought,
    that noe man knowe this case.

19 God, lett never [an] ould man   145
    take to wife a yonge woman
    ney seet his harte her upon,
    lest hee beguyled bee.
    For accorde ther maye be none,
    ney the may never bee at one;   150
    and that is seene in manye one
    as well as one mee.

20 Therfore have I slept a while,
    my wife that mee can thus beguyle,
    for I will gone from her; yt to fyle   155
    mee ys loth, in good faye.
    This case makes mee so heavye
    that needes sleepe nowe muste I.
    Lord, one hir thow have mercye
    for her misdeede todaye.   160

35ʳ   ANGELUS
21 Joseph, lett bee thy feeble thought.
    Take Marye thy wife and dread thee nought,
    for wickedly shee hath not wrought;
    but this is Godes will.
    The child that shee shall beare, iwys   ·   165
    of the Holy Ghost begotten yt is
    to save mankynd that did amisse,
    and prophecye to fulfill.

141 will] her will ARBH   142 feeblye] fowlye AR   have] hath B
144 this] the B   145 an] and Hm   146 to wife] hym ARBH
147 seet] sette AR   149 for] om B   151 one] a one AR   152 one]
in B   153 have I] when I have AR   154 mee can thus] can me thus
AR, thus can me BH   155 for] om BH   gone] goe ARBH   yt] for her
AB, for it RH   158 sleepe nowe] now sleepe H   To right of 159] Tunc
dormit H   166 begotten] gotten BH   yt] om AR

JOSEPH

22 A, nowe I wott, lord, yt is soe,
    I will noe man bee her foe;   170
    but while I may one yearth goe,
    with her I will bee.
    Nowe Christe is in our kynde light,
    as the prophetes before hight.
    Lord God, most of might,   175
    with weale I worshipp thee.

NUNTIUS

23 Make rowme, lordinges, and give us waye
    and lett Octavian come and playe,
    and Sybell the sage, that well fayre maye,
    to tell you of prophecye.   180
    That lord that dyed on Good Frydaye,
    hee have you all both night and daye.
    Farewell, lordinges. I goe my waye;
    I may noe lenger abyde.

OCTAVIANUS

24 I, preeved prince most of powere,   185
    under heaven highest am I here;
    fayrest foode to fight in fere,
    noe freake my face may flee.
    All this world, withowten were—
    kinge, prynce, baron, batchlere—   190
    I may destroy in great dangere
    through vertue of my degree.

25 My name Octavian called is—
    all me about full in my blys,
    for wholey all this world, iwys,   195
    is readye at my owne will.

170 man] more H   174 prophetes] prophescye AR   before hight] yore
beheight H   NUNTIUS] MESSINGER R   179 that] tha A   fayre] fraye A
182 have] save AB   183 goe] mus B   184 abyde] bide B   OCTAVIANUS]
OCTAVYAN AH   185 preeved] proveid AR, prived B   powere] postie A
186 here] om A   187 fayrest] the fayrest B   to fight in] faightest A, to
fraught with B   194 all me about] at my above H   blys] blesse R
196 owne] om B

Noe man one mould darre doe amisse
agaynst mee—I tell you this—
nay no man saye that ought is his
but my leave be thertyll. 200

26 For I halfe multiplyed more
the cittye of Rome sythe I was bore
then ever did any before,
syth I had this kingdome.
For what with strenght and strokes sore, 205
leadinge lordshipp, lovely lore,
all this world has bine yore
tributarye unto Rome.

35ᵛ 27 Segneurs, tous si assembles a mes probes
estates!
Jeo posse fayre lerment et leez, et mette in
languoure! 210
Vous tous si prest ne sortes
de fayre intentes ma volentes,
car je su soveroyne ben sages et de mande
emperoure.

28 Jeo si persone, nulle si able; jeo sa tent fayre
et leable.
En treasoroce ne treasagyle, mes de toyle
plerunt. 215
Destret et sage sua en counsell—ami, ou dame,
et ou pusele.
De clare et sanke mater frayle, un teell n'est
paas viva.

197 mould] live A   199 nay] maye AR   201 halfe] hals B   203 any]
anye me ARBH   204 syth] since R   205 strenght and strokes] strockes
and strenghte A   206 leadinge] lending B   lordshipp] lordshippes ARB
207 has] nowe hase   ARH (see TN for R 209-12)   209 si assembles] se
asmeles A   probes] proles BH   210 jeo] jey H   mette] metten H
211 vous] om A, vas R   tous] toutes H   si] se A   ne] me AR   sortes] fortes AR
212 mavolentes] movelentes A, movalentes R, movolentes BH   213 je su] Jhesu H
214–17] om R   214 jeo] jay H   nulle] mile ABH   si able] seable A, si alle B
jeo sa] jeo su A, jeo sic B, jey su H   tent] tous B   fayre] farre H   leable]
beable H   215 treasoroce] trausorce A, tresarois H   ne treasagyle] me
creaca A   mes] meas A   toyle] tole A   216 sua] sa A, sont B, su H
counsell] comecch A   ou dame] ou dem A   217 clare] claan A   et sanke]
sanke et AB, sake et H   viva] vum A, vivant B, vumame H

29 Kinge, coysell, clarke, or knight,
    saudens, senatoures in sight,
    princes, pryest here nowe dight   220
    and present in this place,
    peace! Or here my truthe I plight—
    I am the manfulst man of might—
    takes mynde on my manece.

30 All leedes in land bee at my likinge: 225
    castle, conquerour, and kinge
    bayne be to doe my byddinge;
    yt will non other bee.
    Right as I thinke, soe must all bee;
    for all the world dose my willinge   230
    and bayne bine when I bydd bringe
    homage and feoaltye.

31 Sythen I was lord, withowten lesse
    with my witt I can more increase
    the empire here then ever yt was,   235
    as all this world yt wiste.
    Syth I was soverayne, warre cleare can cease,
    and through this world now is peace,
    for soe dreade a duke sate never on dayes
    in Rome—that you may trust.   240

32 Therfore as lorde nowe likes mee
    to preeve my might and my postee,
    for I will send about and see
    how many heades I have.
    All the world shall written bee,   245
    great and smale in eych degree

218 kinge] kinges B   coysell] carsell H   or] and H   knight] kinge A
219 saudens] soundens A, saundence R   senatoures] solitaryes A
220 pryest] prese A, preistes RBH   222 truthe] wordes B   223 man-
fulst] manlieste AR   224 on] of AR   manece] mase AR, manace BH
225 leedes] lordes AR   227 doe] *om* AR   229 as] *om* AR   must all
bee] moste it be A, must it be R, is all thing BH   231 bayne bine] bayne
A, bene bayne R   bydd] byde AB, did H   232 feoaltye] feoalitie A
233–6] *om* R   233 sythen] since B, sithe H   234 witt] will B
236 yt] is H   237 syth] since AR   cleare] cleane AH, *om* RB   239 dayes]
dese AR, deys BH   241 nowe] *om* B   242 preeve] prove ARH, prive B
243 send] send and B   246 eych] his B

that dwell in shire or in cittye—
king, clarke, knight, and knave.

33　Eych man one penye shall paye.
　　Therfore, my bedell, doe as I saye.　　　　250
　　In middest the world by anye waye
　　this gammon shall begine.
　　The folke of Jewes, in good faye,
　　in myddest bine; that is noe naye.
　　Therefore thyder, daye by daye,　　　　255
　　and travayle or thow bline.

36ʳ　　34　Warne him that there ys president
　　that this is fully myne intent:
　　that eych man appere present,
　　his penye for to paye.　　　　260
　　And by that penye as well appent
　　knowledge to bee obedyente
　　to Rome, by gifte of such a rent,
　　from that tyme after aye.

35　When thus is done thus in Judye,　　　　265
　　that in the middest of the world shalbe,
　　to eych land, shire, and cyttye
　　to Rome make them soe thrall.
　　Warne them, boye—I commande thee—
　　they doe the same, saye thus from mee;　　　　270
　　soe all this world shall witt that wee
　　bine soveraygne of them all.

36　Have donne, boye! Art thow not bowne?

PRECO

All readye, my lorde, by Mahounde.
Noe tayles tupp in all this towne　　　　275
shall goe further withowten fayle.

248 and] or R　　256 or] all B　　257 warne] ware R　　there ys] is
there R　　264 aye] ever A　　265 thus(1)] this ARBH　　thus(2)] this A
266 of] *om* R, in B　　268 them] *om* B　　269 thee] *om* B　　270 thus]
this ARH　　271 this] the B　　witt] weet B　　273 bowne] bounde R,
bow H　　275 tayles tupp] tuppe tayles B, talls tup H　　all] *om* B
276 withowten] without ARBH

OCTAVIANUS

Boye, therfore by my crowne
thow muste have thy warrysoun!
The highest horse besydes Boughton
take thow for thy travell. 280

PRECO

37 Grauntemercye, lord, perdye;
this hackney will well serve mee,
for a great lord of your degree
should ryde in such araye.
The bine hye in dignitye, 285
and alsoe high and swifte is hee.
Therefore that reverans takes yee,
my deare lord, I you praye.

38 But your arrand shalbe donne anone.
First into Judye I will gonne 290
and sommon the people everychone,
both shire and eke cyttye.

OCTAVIANUS

Boye, there bine ladyes manye one;
amonge them all chose thee onne.
Take the fayrest or els none, 295
and freely I give her thee.

PRIMUS SENATOUR

39 My lord Octavyan, wee be sent
from all Rome with good entent.
Thy men there have eychone iment
as God to honour thee. 300
36ᵛ And to that poynct we be assent,
poore and ryche in parleament.
For soe loved a lord, veramente,
was never in this cyttye.

OCTAVIANUS] *om* AR   277–88] *om* AR   278 thy] thee B   279 highest] heigh BH
280 travell] travayle H   285 bine] lyve B   287 reverans] remanes B
289–92] *om* A   289 but] *om* R   290 will] wilbe B   291 everychone]
every eichone RB   292 both] both in H   eke] *om* H   OCTAVIANUS]
OCTAVIAN AH, *om* R   293–6] *om* R   293 one] a one A   297 my] from
my AR   298 good] full H   301 assent] sente AR   303 lord] lord in B

SECUNDUS SENATOR

40 Yea sicker, syr, ther will is this: 305
    to honour thee as God with blys,
    for thow did never to them amysse
    in worde, thought, ne deede.
    Peace hath bine longe and yett is.
    Noe man in thy tyme lost ought of his.   310
    Therfore there wyll is soe, iwys,
    to quite you this your meede.

OCTAVIANUS

41 Welcome, my frendes, in god faye,
    for you bee baynable to my paye.
    I thank you, all that ever I maye,   315
    the homage yee doe to mee.
    But follye yt were by manye a waye
    such soveraygntye for to assaye,
    syth I must dye I wotte not what day,
    to desyre such dignitye.   320

42 For of all flesh, blood, and bonne
    made I am, borne of a womane;
    and sycker other matter nonne
    sheweth not right in mee.
    Neyther of iron, tree, no stonne   325
    am I not wrought, you wott eychone.
    And of my life moste parte is gone,
    age shewes him soe in mee.

43 And godhead askes in all thinge
    tyme that hath noe begininge   330
    ne never shall have endinge;
    and none of this have I.

305 sicker syr] seckerly B   306 blys] blesse AR   310 ought] nought H
311 soe] now BH   312 quite] quitte A   this] in H   meede] neede H
OCTAVIANUS] OCTAVIAN A, OCTAVION R   313 god] good ARBH   314 bayn-
able] welckome AR, penyble H   319 syth] seinge AR   I(2)] and R
321 of] om AR   all] all the AR, om BH   322 made] man AR   326 am
I] I ame B   you wott] wott ye R   328 shewes] sheweth ARB   in mee]
I see ARBH   329 thinge] thinges RB   331 never] neyther R
332 this] thes A, these RH

Wherfore by verey proofe shewinge,
though I bee highest worldly kinge,
of godhead have I noe knowinge.   335
Hit were unkynde.

44 But yett enquyre of this will wee
of hir that hase grace to see
thinges that afterward shalbe
by ghoost of prophecye.   340
And after hir lore, by my lewtye,
discussinge this difficultye
worke; and take noe more one mee
then I am well worthye.

45 Sybbell the sage, tell mee this thinge,   345
for thow wytt hase as noe man livinge:
shall ever be any earthlye kinge
to passe mee of degree?

37ʳ   SYBBELL

Yea, syr, I tell you withowt leasinge
a bab borne shalbe, blys to bringe,   350
the which that never hase begininge
ne never shall ended bee.

OCTAVYANUS

46 Sybbyll, I praye thee speciallye
by signe thow would me certyfye
what tyme that lord soe royallye   355
to raigne hee shal beginne.

Sybyll speaketh:

Syr, I shall tell you witterlye
his signes when I see verelye;

333 proofe] proose B   334 bee] *om* H   worldly] wordlie B   336 un-
kynde] unkindly BH   337 of] if A   will wee] wilbe A   338 of] at
ARBH   to] for to ARBH   341 lore] lawe AR   lewtye] bewtie ARB
342 difficultye] difficallitie AR   343 one] of R   347 ever] there ever
RB   350 bab] barne ARBH   borne shalbe] shalbe borne A, shall borne
be RH   351 hase] hade A   352 ended] endinge AR   bee] have A
OCTAVYANUS] OCTAVIAN AR   353 speciallye] especiallye AR   Sybyll
speaketh] SYBBELL ARBH   357 syr] yea AR   358 verelye] very R

for when hee comes, through his mercye
one mankynde hee will mynne.   360

47 Well I wott, forsooth iwys,
    that God will bringe mankinde to blys,
    and send from heaven—leeves well this—
    his Sonne, our savyour.

48 But what tyme, syr, in good faye   365
    that hee will come can I non saye.
    Therfore in this place I will praye
    to greatest God of might.
    And yf I see ought to your paye
    ghoostlye by anye waye,   370
    warne you I shall anon this daye,
    and shew yt in your sight.

Tunc orat Sibilla, et dicat Preco alta voce.

PRECO

49 Peace I byd, kinge and knight,
    men and weomen and eych wight;
    tyll I have tould that I have tight,   375
    stonde styll, both stronge and stoute.
    My lord Octavyan, myche of might,
    commandes you should be readye dight:
    trybute hee wyll have in height
    of all this world about.   380

50 Hee wyll have written eych countree,
    castle, shyre, and eke cyttye—
    men and weomen, leeve you mee—
    and all that bee therin.

359 when] then B   360 mynne] wynne B   361 forsooth] and south AR
362 blys] blesse AR   *After* 364] *in* ARBH:
            Jesu Christe, nothinge ameisse,
            called he shalbe and ys:
            to overcome the devill and his countise,
            and be our conquerower.
                    (3 to] and R, *om* BH)   4
366 non] not ARBH   367 I will] will I AR   369 to] in AR   371 I
shall anon] I shall AR, anone I shall B   373 byd] byde A   376 stonde]
stall B   styll] stiffe A   stronge] still A, stiffe RBH   stoute] stronge AR
378 should be] shalbe R   382 eke] each H

A penye of eych man have will hee—   385
the valewe of ten pences hit shalbee—
to knowledge that hee hase soverayntee
fullye of all mankynd.

JOSEPHE

51 A, lord, what doth this man nowe here?
   Poore mens weale ys ever in were.   390
   I wott by this bosters beere
   that trybute I muste paye.

37ᵛ   And for greate age and noe powere,
      I wan noe good this seaven yere.
      Nowe comes the kinges messinger   395
      to gett all that hee maye.

52 With this axe that I beare,
   this perces and this naugere
   and hammer, all in fere,
   I have wonnen my meate.   400
   Castle, towre, ney riche manere
   had I never in my power;
   but as a symple carpenter
   with those what I might gett.

53 If I have store, anye thinge,   405
   that must I paye unto the kinge.
   But yett I have a likinge,
   the angell to mee towlde:
   hee that should man owt of bale bringe
   my wife had in her keapinge.   410
   That seemes all good to my likinge,
   and makes mee more bowld.

54 A, leeffe syr, tell mee I thee praye:
   shall poore as well as rych paye?

385 have] *om* H   386 pences] pence ARBH   389 A] O B
391 bosters] boisters A, bostes H   393 age] ayde R   398 perces]
perscer ARBH   naugere] nagere AR, maugere B   399 and] a A, and a R,
axe BH   400 wonnen] wonnan AR, woman B, wonne H   401 riche]
om AR   404 those] thes A, these RH, this B   what] that H   405 store]
store nowe ABH, store of R   409 should] *om* AR

My faye, syr, I hoope naye;   415
that were a wonders wronge.

PRECO

Good man, I warne thee in good faye
to Bethlem to take the waye,
leste thow in danger falle todaye
if that thow bee to longe.   420

JOSEPHE

55 Nowe syth yt may non other bee,
Marye, sister, now hye wee.
An oxe I will take with mee
that there shalbe soulde.
The silver of him, soe mote I thee,   425
shall fynde us in that cyttye,
and paye tribute for thee and mee;
for therto wee bine howlde.

MARIA

56 A, lord, what may this signifye?
Some men I see glad and merye   430
and some syghinge and sorye.
Wherfore soever yt bee?
Syth Godes Sonne came man to forbye—
is commen through his great mercye—
methinke that man should kindlye   435
be glad that sight to see.

ANGELUS

57 Marye, Godes mother dere,
the tokeninge I shall thee lere.
The commen people, as thow seest here,
are glad—as they well maye—   440

415 my] by my AR   416 wonders] woundrous ARB   420 that] *om* A
421 non] no AB   *To right of* 425-8] Tunc Joseph ligabit bovem et
canctam(?) asinae, et colliget Mariam super asinam; et cum ad stabulum pervenerit,
dicat Mar: H   426 that] this H   428 bine howlde] be houlde AR
429 A] O B   431 syghinge] all sickinge A   433 forbye] buy B   434 is
commen] comon is B, is come H   435 methinke] methinketh R   kindlye]
kindlie be B   436] that sight full gladlie for to see B   439 as] that H

that they shall see of Abrahams seede
Christe come to helpe them in there neede.
Therfore the joyen withowten dreede
for to abyde this daye.

58　The morneinge men—take this in mynde—　　445
are Jewes that shalbe put behinde,
for they passed owt of kinde
through Christe at his comminge.
For they shall have noe grace to knowe
that God for man shall light soe lowe;　　450
for shame on them that soone shall showe.
Therfore they bine mourninge.

JOSEPH

59　Marye, suster, sooth to saye
harbour, I hope, gett wee ne maye;
for great lordes of stowte araye　　455
occupye this cyttye.
Therfore wee muste in good faye
lye in this stable tyll yt bee daye.
To make men meeke, leeve I maye,
shew him here will hee.　　460

MARIA

60　Helpe me downe, my leeffe fere,
for I hope my tyme bee neere.
Christe in this stable that ys here,
I hope borne wilbee.

Tunc Joseph accipiet Mariam in brachia sua.

441 seede] blood seede H　　443 therfore] wherfore A　the] they RBH
joyen] joye ARH　withowten] without H　　446 shalbe] should be B
447 they passed] the passeth AR, they have passed B, it passes H　of] of their H
450 shall] should B, will H　　454 gett] non gett R　wee ne] we non A,
we R, yf wee B, we nay H　456 occupye] do occupye AR　cyttye] plase A
457 therfore] wherfore AR　460 hee] I B　461 my] then my BH
leeffe] lief B, life H　fere] dere B, in fere H　462 bee] is RH　SD] Tunc
in sua brachia Mariam accipiet after 468 H　accipiet] accepiet A

JOSEPH

Come to me, my sweete dere,   465
the treasure of heaven withowten were.
Welcome in full meeke manere.
Him hope I for to see.

Tunc statuet Mariam inter bovem et asinam.

61 Marye, sister, I will assaye
to gett too middwives yf I maye;   470
for though in thee bee God verey—
and commen agaynst kynde—
for usage here of this cittye
and manners sake, as thinkes mee,
too I will fetch anon to thee   475
yf I may any fynde.

38ᵛ   JOSEPH (ad obstetrices)

62 Weomen, God you save and see!
Is yt your will to goe with mee?
My wife ys commen into this cyttye
with child, and tyme is nere.   480
Helpes her nowe for charytee,
and bee with her tyll day bee;
and your travayle, soe mote I thee,
I shall paye you right here.

TEBELL

63 All readye, good man, in good faye.   485
Wee will doe all that ever wee maye.
For too such middwives, I dare well saye,
are not in this cyttye.

SALOME

Come, good man, leade us awaye.
By Godes helpe or hit bee daye   490

466 withowten] without ARBH   472 and commen] a comen A   474 and]
as A, of R   thinkes] thinketh B   JOSEPH] om H   ad obstetrices] abste-
trices AR, om H   479 commen] come RH   into] to H   480 nere] nye A
483 mote] mothe B   484 shall paye you] paye you shall B   TEBELL]
TEBELL a midwief B   487 well] om A   SALOME] SALOME the other
midwyffe B   489 awaye] the waie ARBH   490 by] with ARBH

that we can good thy wife shall saye;
and that thow shalt well see.

JOSEPH

64 Loe, Marye, harte, brought I have here
too middwives for the mannere,
to bee with thee, my darlinge deare,   495
tyll that hit bee daye.

MARIA

Syr, the be welcome withowt were.
But God will worke of his power
full sonne for mee, my lefe fere,
as best is nowe and aye.   500

Tunc paululum acquiescunt.

65 A, Joseph, tydinges aright!
I have a sonne, a sweete wight.
Lord, thanked bee thow, full of might,
for preeved is thy postee.
Payne felte I non this night.   505
But right soe as hee in mee light,
commen hee is here in this sight—
Godes Sonne, as thow maye see.

Tunc stella apparebit.

JOSEPH

66 Lord, welcome, sweete Jesu!
Thy name thow haddest or I thee knewe.   510
Nowe leeve I the angells worde is trewe,
that thow arte a cleane maye.

493 harte] sweete harte A, *om* R   brought I have] I have brought H
497 withowt] withouten AR   499 lefe] lyffes B, life H   500 aye]
ever A   *SD* acquiescunt] acquiescant H   503 full] moche ARBH
504 preeved] proved AR   505 payne] penance H   felte I non] non I felte
ARBH   506 light] heighte R   507 hee is] is he H   this] my ARBH
508 thow] you H   *SD* apparebit] apparebet AR   509 Jesu] Jesus A
511 worde is] wordes ARBH

For thow arte commen mans blys to brewe
to all that thy lawe will shewe.
Nowe mans joy beginns to newe   515
and noye to passe awaye.

MARIA

67 Lord, blessed most thow bee
    that [symple] borne art, as I see;
    to preeve the divell of his postee,
    commen thow arte todaye.   520
    Diversorye is non for thee.
    Therfore thy sweete bodye free
    in this cratch shall lye with lee,
    and lapped abowt with haye.

                TEBELL

68 A, dere lord, heaven kinge,   525
    that this is a marvelous thinge!
    Withowten teene or travaylinge,
    a fayre sonne shee hasse onc.
    I dare well saye, forsooth iwys,
    that cleane mayden this woman ys,   530
    for shee hath borne a chyld with blys;
    soc wiste I never none.

                SALOME

69 Be styll, Tebell, I thee praye,
    for that is false, in good faye.
    Was never woman cleane maye   535
    and chyld withowt man.
    But never the latter, I will assaye
    whether shee bee cleane maye,
    and knowe yt if I cann.

513 commen] come H   514 lawe] saw H   515 beginns] begineth AR
516 noye] joye AR   517 most] muste A, mayst RB   518 symple]
smple Hm   art] is B   519 preeve] prive A, prove R, reave B   520 thow
arte] art thou B   521 diversorye] fyne clothes A, fyne lynnen R, diverse
sorye B   522 thy] thee B   523 shall] *om* B   524 and] and be AR,
all B   TEBELL] TEBELLA H   525 heaven] heavens B   527 travay-
linge] brawlinge B   531 blys] blesse AR   536 and] and had BH
withowt] withoutten H   537 latter] later R   538 bee] be a BH

Tunc Salome tentabit tangere Mariam in sexu secreto, et statim
arentur manus eius, et clamando dicit:

70 Alas, alas, alas, alas,   540
 mee ys betyde an evyll case!
 My handes bee dryed up in this place,
 that feelinge none have I.
 Vengeance on mee ys nowe light,
 for I would tempte Goddes might.   545
 Alas, that I came here tonight
 to suffer such anoye.

Tunc apparet stella et veniet Angelus, [dicens] ut sequitur.

[ANGELUS]

71 Womann, beseech this childe of grace
 that hee forgive thee thy trespasse;
 and ere thow goe owt of this place   550
 holpen thou maye bee.
 This miracle that now thow seest here
 is of Godes owne powere,
 to bringe mankinde owt of dangere
 and mende them, leeve thow mee.   555

SALOME

72 Ah, sweete child, I aske mercye
 for thy mothers love, Marye.
 Though I have wrought wretchedlye,
 sweete childe, forgive yt mee.
 Ah, blessed bee God! All whole am I!   560
 Nowe leeve I well and sickerlye
 that God is commen, man to forbye.
 And thou, lord, thou art hee.

SD Salome] Salom B in] *om* AR sexu] sepu AR secreto] secrecto A
arentur] arement ARB, arenent H manus] manibus R dicit] dicat ARH
541 an evyll] a sorye ARBH 544 ys nowe] nowe is ARB, is H
545 tempte] tempe A 546 tonight] this nighte R *SD* apparet]
aparit R dicens] *om* Hm ANGELUS] TEBELL Hm, *om* B
548 womann] wemen AB 550 ere] ever A 551 maye bee] shalbe A
552 that now thow] nowe that thou A, that thou now RB 555 them] them
here H leeve] liere B 557 thy] thee B 558 wretchedlye] wickedly R
561 well] will B sickerlye] seckeretlye A 562 commen] com BH
563 thou(1)] *om* A, now B

73 Loe, lordings all, of this miracle here
    freere Bartholemewe in good mannere   565
    beareth wytnes, withowten were,
    as played is you beforne.
    And other myracles, yf I maye,
    I shall rehearse or I goe awaye,
    that befell that ilke daye   570
    that Jesus Christ was borne.

74 Wee reade in cronicles expresse:
    somtyme in Rome a temple was
    made of soe greate ryches
    that wonder was witterlye.   575
    For all thinges in hit, leeve you mee,
    was silver, gould, and rych perlye;
    thryd parte the worlde, as read wee,
    that temple was worthye.

75 Of eych province, that booke mynde mase,   580
    ther goddes image sett there was;
    and eych on abowt his necke has
    a silver bell hanginge,
    and on his brest written also
    the landes name and godes too.   585
    And sett was alsoe in middest of tho
    god of Rome, right as a kinge.

76 Abowt the house alsoe mevinge there
    a man on horse—stoode men to steare—
    and in his hand hee bare a spere,   590
    all pure dispituouslye.
    That horse and man was made of brasse;
    torninge abowt that image was.

564 all] *om* BH   565 freere] free AR   566 withowten] without H
567 beforne] before RB   568 and] an ARB   myracles] mirackle ARB
570 ilke] same AR   574 soe] suche AR   577 perlye] pearle A, araye
R, perrye BH   578 thryd] the thirde A   580 province] provinges AR
581 sett there] their sette ARB, set H   582 on] *om* B   584 written]
was wrytten H   585 name] names A   godes] goodes AR   too] bouth
too ARBH   586 was] *om* AR, wa B   alsoe] als BH   of tho] altho H
587 Rome right] renowne H   588 alsoe] als B, was H   589 steare]
feare B   591 all] a R   pure] pewer AR   592 of] on H

Save certayne preystes ther might non passe
for devylls phantasie.   595

77 But when that any lande with battell
    was readye Rome for to assayle,
    the godes [image] withowten fayle
    of that land range his bell
    and torned his face dispituouslye   600
    to god of Rome, as reade I,
    in tokeninge that there were readye
    to feyghtinge freshe and fell.

78 The image alsoe above standinge,
    when the bell beneath begane to ringe,   605
    torned him all sharpely, shewinge
    towarde that lande his spere.
    And when they see this tokeninge,
    Rome ordayned withowt tareinge
    an oste to keepe there comminge,   610
    longe or they came there.

79 And on this manere sothlye,
    by arte of neagromancye,
    all the world witterlye
    to Rome were made to lowt.   615
40ʳ   And in that temple there dowbtles
    was called therfore the Temple of Peace,
    that through his sleyt battell can cease
    throughowt the world, the worlde abowte.

80 But hee to coyntly this worke caste   620
    asked the devyll or hee paste
    howe longe that temple hit should laste
    that hee there can buylde.

596 that] *om* RH   598 image] I may Hm, I meane AR   withowten]
without H   602 tokeninge] token B   there] they BH   were] wente A
604 above] about H   606 torned] torninge A   him] himself B
608 see] saw H   610 comminge] torninge AR   611 there] thether B
612 on] in ARBH   615 to] *om* AR   616–19] *om* R   616 in] *om* H
618 that] *om* A   his] this BH   619 the world the worlde] the worlde
ABH   620 to] that H   coyntly] cuninglye AR   622 longe] *om* A
hit] there R   623 that] tha A

The devill answered suttillye,
and sayd yt should last sickerlye   625
untyll a mayden wemmostlye
had conceyved a chylde.

81 They hard, and beleeved therfore
yt should endure for evermore.
But that tyme that Christ was bore,   630
hit fell downe soone in hye.
Of which howse is seene this daye
somewhat standinge, in good faye.
But noe man dare well goe that waye
for feendes phantasye.   635

82 That daye was seene verament
three sonnes in the firmament,
and wonderslye together went
and torned into one.
The oxe, the asse, ther they were lent,   640
honored Christe in theyr intent;
and moe miracles, as wee have ment
to playe right here anon.

Tunc ostendet stellam, et veniet Sibilla ad imperatorem.

SIBILLA

83 Syr emperour, God thee save and see.
I tell you sicker that borne ys hee   645
that passeth thee of postee.
Looke up on height after mee.
That baron thow seest that great shalbee—
to passe all kinges, and eke thee,
that borne are or ever were.   650

626 wemmostlye] womanlye AR, woman slye B, wemmouslie H   634 well
goe] goe AR, goe well H   638 wonderslye] wonderlye ARH   640 were]
be A   642 wee] I R   SD ostendet] ostendent ARB, ostendant H
Sibilla] Sybbill H   imperatorem] imprecatorem A   645 sicker] trulye AR
646 postee] power H   647 on height] on highe ARB, an height H   648 that
great] greate AR, so great H   To right of 648] as none lyke him in any degree H
650 borne are] is borne A, borne was R   were] shalbe A

OCTAVYAN

84 A, Sibbell, this is a wondrouse sight,
for yonder I see a mayden bright,
a yonge chylde in her armes clight,
a bright crosse in his head.
Honour I wyll that sweete wight   655
with incense throughowt all my might,
for that reverence is most right,
if that yt bee thy reade.

85 Incense bringe, I command, in hye
to honour this child, kinge of mercye.   660
Should I bee God? Naye, naye, witterlye!
Great wronge iwys yt were.

40ᵛ   For this childe is more worthye
then such a thowsande as am I.
Therfore to God moste mightye   665
incense I offer here.

Tunc Angelus cantabit 'Haec est ara Dei caeli'; fiat notam secundum arbitrium agentis, etc.

86 A, Sybbell, heres not thow this songe?
My members all yt goeth amonge.
Joy and blys makes my harte stronge
to heare this melody.   670
Sycker yt may non other bee
but this childe is prince of postye
and I his subject, as I see.
Hee is moste worthye.

SYBBELL

87 Yea, syr, thow shalt leeve well this: 675
somewhere one yearth borne he is;
and that hee comes for mans blys,
his tokeninge this can shewe.

651 A] O AR   654 a] and a B   656 throughowt all] with all AR, through all B, through H   662 iwys] I wiste A   SD haec] hic A, hec RBH est] este A   caeli] cela AR   fiat] fiant R   arbitrium] arbitrum R   agentis] agentes A   667 not thow] thou not BH   669 makes] maketh AR   stronge] full strong H   671–4] om B   671 sycker] trulye A, surely R   SYBBELL] SIBBELLA R, SIBILLA H   675 thow] you H   leeve] lyve B   676 one] in ARBH   677 comes] cometh AR   blys] bless R   678 tokeninge] tocken AR

Reverence him, I read iwys,
for other God there none ys;   680
that hopes otherwise, doth amys,
but him for Christe to knowe.

OCTAVYAN

88 Syr senators, goes home anone
and warne my men everychone
that such worshipp I must forgonne   685
as they would doe to mee.
But this child worshipp eych maye
with full harte all that you [can],
for hee is worthye to leeve upon;
and that nowe I wyll see.   690

[PRIMUS SENATOR]

89 A, lord, whatever this may bee,
this is a wondrous sight to see;
for in the stare, as thinkes mee,
I see a full fayre maye.
Syr, shall this child passe yee   695
of worthines and dignitee?
Such a lord, by my lewtye,
I wend never had binne.

EXPOSITOR

90 Lordings, that this is verey
by verey sygne knowe yee maye;   700
for in Rome in good faye,
thereas this thinge was seene,

681 that] he that AR   hopes] hopeth AR   otherwise] otherwise he B, otherwayes he H   OCTAVYAN] OCTAVYON R   683 syr] sires ARB   684 every-
chone] everye iche one ARB, every one H   687 maye] man ABH, mone R
688 can] *om* Hm   689 leeve] lyve B   690 nowe I wyll] I nowe well A,
now I well R, I now will B   PRIMUS SENATOR] *om* HmARB, SENATOR H
691 A] and AR   692 this] it B   wondrous] wounderous ARB, wonders H
693 thinkes] thinketh ARB   *After* 694] PRIMUS SENATOR A   695] this
childe shall passe all wee R   696 of] in R   697 lewtye] bewtie A
698 never had] had never B   binne] bene non ABH, bene borne R
700 verey sygne] signes true B   702 this thinge] thes thinges AR

was buyld a church in noble araye—
in worshipp of Marye, that sweete maye—
that yett lastes untyll this daye,   705
as men knowe that there have binne.

41ʳ   91 And for to have full memorye
of the angells melodye
and of this sight sickerlye
the emperoure ther knewe,   710
the church is called St. Marye.
The surname is Ara Caeli,
that men knowe nowe well therby
that this was fullye trewe.

92 Another miracle I fynd also,   715
at Christes byrth that fell thoo:
when Salome attempted to knowe
whether shee was a maye,
hyr hand roted, as you have seene.
Wherby you may take good teene   720
that unbeleeffe is a fowle sinne,
as you have seene within this playe.

Finis

703 buyld] builded B   705 lastes] lasteth AR   untyll] unto ARH
706 binne] bene AR   712 is Ara Caeli] in a racali A, in racali R, in
aracali B   713 nowe] *om* AR   714 that] tha A   716 at] a A
that] *om* AR   thoo] right tho H   718 maye] mayde R   722 within]
in AB   playe] place AR

PLAY VII

41ᵛ   THE PAYNTERS PLAYE

Incipit Pagina Septima de Pastoribus.

PRIMUS PASTOR

1 On wouldes have I walked wylde
under buskes my bowre to bylde,
from styffe stormes my sheepe to shilde,
my seemely wedders to save.
From comlye Conwaye unto Clyde   5
under tyldes them to hyde,
a better shepperd on no syde
noe yearthlye man maye have.

2 For with walkynge werye I have mee rought;
besydes the suche my sheepe I sought.   10
My taytfull tuppes are in my thought,
them to save and heale
from the shrewde scabbe yt sought,
or the rotte, yf yt were wrought.
If the cough had them caught   15
of hyt I could them heale.

3 Loe, here bee my herbes saffe and sownde,
wysely wrought for everye wounde—
the woulde a whole man bringe to grownde
within a little whyle—   20
of henbane and horehounde,
tybbe, radishe, and egermonde,
which hee my herbes save and sounde,
medled on a rowe.

Guild-ascription] The Paynters and the Glasiors Playe A, The Paynters and
Glasiers H   *Play-heading*] Pagina Septima de Pastoribus Greges Pascenti-
bus H   pagina septima] septima pagina B   PRIMUS PASTOR] *om* B
1 wouldes] worldes B   have I] I have ARB   wylde] full wylde ARBH
2 to] for to H   3 sheepe] ship B   5 Clyde] glide H   6 under]
on the H   tyldes] hilles B   hyde] hid B   9 rought] thoughte ARB
10 thc] thee AR, all B   suche] sluch H   sheepe] shee AB   11 taytfull]
talefull AR, toylefull B, tytefull H   12 save] have B   13 shrewde]
shewde R   22 tybbc] bybbey A, bybbe R, tibbie B, ribbie H   radishe]
ridshe R   egermonde] egremounde ARBH   *After* 24] fynter fanter and
fetterfoe R

4 Here be more herbes, I tell yt you;   25
   I shall recken them on a rowe:
   fynter, fanter, and fetterfowe,
   and alsoe penyewrytte.
   This is all that I knowe.
   For be yt wether or be yt yowe,   30
   I shall heale then on a rowe
   cleane from theyre hurte.

5 Here is tarre in a pott
   to heale them from the rott;
   well I can and well I wott   35
   the talgh from them take.
   And yf sworne yt had the thursse,
   yett shall the talgh be in my purse,
   and the sheepe never the worse
   to renne on the rake.   40

42ʳ   6 But noe fellowshippe here have I
   save myselfe alone, in good faye;
   therfore after one faste wyll I crye.
   But first will I drinke, if I maye.

Hic potat Primus Pastor.

7 Howe, Harvye, howe!   45
   Drive thy sheepe to the lowe.
   Thow maye not here excepte I blowe,
   as ever have I heale.

Hic flabit Primus Pastor.

26 recken them] them reckone B   rowe] rooe A   27 and] *om* H   30 yt(2)]
om B   31 heale then] them heale A, heale them RBH   rowe] rooe A,
thraw H   32 from] of BH   theyre] the B   34 to] for to H   heale]
helle B   from] of H   36 talgh] caughe A, taylinge B, talch H   take]
to take H   37–40] *om* AR   37 yt] *om* B   38 yett shall the] *om* B
talgh] talch H   *To right of* 39] Tunc ad sedem H   44 will I] I will R
SD] Tunc potat *to right of* 42 H   potat] potet A   45 Harvye]
Harrye B   howe(2)] how how H   46 thy] the H   47 excepte] but if H
48 have I] I have B   heale] feale H   SD] Tunc flat cum cornu et reddit
'Aho! Io! O!' Tunc venit Secundus Pastor gerens plumam cornicis cum vestis
parte veteris H   Primus] Prius A

SECUNDUS PASTOR

Yt is no shame for mee to shewe
how I was set for to sowe   50
with the fether of a crowe
a clowte upon my heele.

Sitt downe.

8 Fellowe, nowe be we well mett.
   And though methinke us needes,
   had wee Tudd heere by us sett,   55
   thenn might wee sitte and feede us.

PRIMUS PASTOR

9 Yea, to feede us frendly in faye,
   how might wee have our service?
   Crye thow must lowd, by this daye;
   Tudd is deafe and may not well here us.   60

Secundus Pastor vocat submissa voce:

10 How, Tudd; come, for thy fathers kyn.

PRIMUS PASTOR

Naye, faye; thy voyce is wonders dym.
Why, knowys thow not him?
Fye, man, for shame!
Call him Tudd, Tybbys sonne,   65
and then wyll the shrewe come;
for in good fayth yt is his wonne
to love well his damys name.

49 no] not H   mee] *om* A   50 set] taught R   for] *om* A   sowe] sowe
with the Hm   *SD*] *om* H   sitt] he sittes R   53 be we] we be ARB
mett] mete A   54 and though] one thing H   us] *om* AR   needes]
neede is B   PASTOR *here and in all SHs*] *om* H   58 how] now H
service] service aye AR   60 may] *om* A   *SD* Secundus Pastor] tunc H
submissa voce] submisse vece A, humili voce how Tud Tud H   *At*
61] SECUNDUS H   61 fathers] father ARBH   62 naye] may B   faye]
fye H   wonders] wounderous AR, wondrous BH   63 knowys] knoweth B
To right of 65–6] Tunc vocat voce canora, ut antea H   65 Tybbys] Tybbes
ARH, Tibbies B

SECUNDUS PASTOR

11 How, Tudd, Tybbys sonne!

TERTIUS PASTOR

Syr, in fayth nowe I come,   70
for yett have I not all donne
that I have to done:
to seeth salve for our sheepe
and—lest my wiffe should yt weete—
with great gravell and greete   75
I scowre [an] ould panne.

12 Hemlocke and hayriffe—take keepe—
with tarreboyste must bene all tamed,
penyegrasse and butter for fatt sheepe;
for thys salve am I not ashamed.   80

42ᵛ   13 Ashamed am I not to shewe
no poynt that longeth to my crafte;
noe better—that I well knowe—
in land is nowhere lafte.

14 For, good men, this is not unknowen   85
to husbandes that benne here abowt:
that eych man muste bowe to his wife,
and commonly for feare of a clowte.

15 Thus for clowtes now care I;
all ys for feare of our dame-keynn.   90
Now wyll caste my ware hereby,
and hye faste that I were at Hankeynn.

16 Hankeyn, hold up thy hand and have mee,
that I were on height there by thee.

69 Tybbys] Tybbes AR, Tibbs H   71 all] half H   72 to] for to BH
done] doe ARBH   73 our] my R   75 and] or R   76 an] and Hm
77 hemlocke] hemlockes H   hayriffe] hereife A, heriff RH, horyffe B
78 must] most B, *om* H   bene all tamed] be tamde A, bene to me all good H
79 penyegrasse] penyegresse AR   80 for] of H   am] an A   81 am I]
I am H   82 that] to B   longeth] longes ARH, longis B   83 well]
will H   84 lafte] lefte AR   85 for] for to A   86 abowt] aboutes AR
87 bowe to his wife] to his wife bowne ARBH (to) unto R)   89 thus] this
AR   90 our] *om* H   dame] dames B   keynn] kenye A, kenny R, kynne
B, kin H   91 wyll] will I ARBH   94 on] on a H

PRIMUS PASTOR

Gladly, syr, and thow would bee by me,   95
for loth me is to denye thee.

SECUNDUS PASTOR

17 Nowe sythen God hath gathered us together,
with good harte I thanke him of his grace.
Welcome be thow, well fayre wedder.
Tudd, will we shape us to some solace?   100

TERTIUS PASTOR

18 Solace would best be seene
that we shape us to our supper;
for meate and drinke, well I deeme,
to eych deede is most dere.

PRIMUS PASTOR

19 Laye forth, eych man ilych,   105
what hee hath lafte of his liverye.
And I wyll put forth my pyche
with my parte firste of us all three.

SECUNDUS PASTOR

20 And such store as my wife had
in your sight soone shall you see,   110
at our begininge us to glade;
for in good meate ther is mych glee.

21 Here is bredd this daye was bacon,
onyons, garlycke, and leekes,
butter that bought was in Blacon,   115
and greene cheese that will greese well your cheekes.

TERTIUS PASTOR

22 And here ale of Halton I have,
 and whot meate I had to my hyer;
 a puddinge may noe man deprave,
 and a jannock of Lancastershyre.   120

23 Loe, here a sheepes head sowsed in ale,
 and a grayne to laye on the greene,
 and sowre milke. My wyffe had ordayned
 a noble supper, as well is seene.

43ʳ   ### PRIMUS PASTOR

24 Nowe will I caste of my cloacke   125
 and put ont parte of my liverye,
 put owt that I have in my poacke,
 and a pigges foote from puddinges purye.

TERTIUS PASTOR

25 Abyde, fellowes, and yee shall see here
 this hott meate—wee serven yt here— 130
 gambonns and other good meate in fere,
 a puddinge with a pricke in the ende.

PRIMUS PASTOR

26 My sotchell to shake out
 to sheppardes am I not ashamed.

117 ale] is ale R, alle B   118 whot] hot RB, what H I had] *om* R
119 a] and a H   120 Lancastershyre] Lankeshier RH   121 here]
heares A sowsed] sawsed AR ale] alle B   122 grayne] groyne BH
123 had] hath R ordayned] on sale H   *After* 124] *in* H:

> And as it is well sene, ye shall see
> and that somewhat I have in my sacke:
> a piggs foote I have here, pardye,
> and a panch-cloute in my packe.
> A womb-clout, fellowes, now have I, 5
> a lyveras as it is no lack;
> a chitterling boyled shall be;
> this burden I beare on my backe.

PRIMUS PASTOR] SECUNDUS PASTOR B, SECUNDUS H   126 put] pull BH ont]
outt B   127 put] and put A, pull BH poacke] pocke A, poke RBH
128 pigges] gygges AR puddinges] puddinge AH   130] that what meate
be served here R wee serven yt here] serveid here A, we shall it hend H
131 gambonns] gammons AR meate] *om* H   132 the ende] thend B
133 my] and that is in my H

And this tonge pared rownd aboute 135
with my teeth yt shalbe atamed.

Tunc commedent, et dicat Primus Pastor:

27 Byd me doe gladly, and I thee,
for by God here is good growsinge;
come eate with us, God of heavon hye,
but take noe heede though here be noe howsinge. 140

SECUNDUS PASTOR

28 Howsinge ennough have wee here
while that wee have heavon over our heddes.
Now to weete our mouthes tyme were;
this flackett will I tame, if thow reade us.

TERTIUS PASTOR

29 And of this bottell nowe will I bibbe, 145
for here is bowles of the best.
Such lickour makes men to live;
this game may noewhere be leste.

PRIMUS PASTOR

30 Fellowes, nowe our bellyes be full,
thinke wee on him that keepes our flockes. 150
Blowe thy horne and call after Trowle,
and bydd him, sonne, of our bytlockes.

SECUNDUS PASTOR

31 Well sayd, Hankyn, by my soothe,
for that shrewe I suppose us seekes.

135 and] *om* H   this] this oxe H   rownd] *om* H   136 with my] for
your H   teeth] tonge A, tooth H   atamed] tamed RB   *SD*] Tunc comedent H   Primus Pastor] *om* R, *as SH* B   137–40] *om* A   137] sit
downe by me R   138 by God] surclic H   139 of] on H   hye] hie
thee RB   140 but] and H   SECUNDUS PASTOR] *om* A   142 that] *om* H
143 were] it were H   144 flackett] flagette AR, flaggen H   thow] you B
145 and] nowe H   nowe] *om* H   bibbe] bibble B, fele H   146 bowles]
but ARBH   147 men] me A   148 noewhere] no way BH   leste]
lost BH   149 bellyes] bellye A   150 flockes] sheepe H   151 call]
blowe A   152 sonne] some ARBH   154 shrewe] shew B   us seekes]
seekes us AR, seke us BH

My horne to lille I wyll not lesse 155
tyll that lad have some of our leekes.

TERTIUS PASTOR

32 Leekes to his liverye is likinge;
such a lad nowhere in land is.
Blowe a note for that meetinge
whyle that horne nowe in thy hand ys. 160

43ᵛ   PRIMUS PASTOR

33 With this horne I shall make a 'Hooe'
that hee and all heaven shall here.
Yonder lad that sittes on a lowe
the lowd of this horne shall here.

Tunc cantabit, et dicat Garcius:

34 Good lord, looke on mee 165
and my flocke here as the fed have.
On this wold walke wee;
are no men here, that noe waye.

35 All is playne, perdee;
therefore, sheepe, we mon goe. 170
Noe better may bee
of beast that blood and bonne have.

36 Wotte I not, day or night,
necessaryes that to mee beelongen.

155 lille] blowe A, bill R, tilt H   lesse] lette A, leese BH   156 some]
bine B   leekes] leckes A   157 is] is to your H   158 nowhere in land]
in land nowhere H   159 note] mote ARBH   meetinge] mittinge A,
mytinge RB, mytting H   160 nowe] *om* H   161 hooe] howe ARH,
howte B   163 sittes] still is B   164 lowd] lowt BH   shall] he shall BH
SD cantabit] cantant H   dicat] venit H   Garcius] Trowle AR, *om* B
After SD] ɢᴀʀᴛɪᴜs BH   165 on] *om* B   166 here] *om* H   the] they
RBH   fed] feed A, fede B, foode H   167 walke] walkinge R   wee] we
woe A   168 men] man A   noe waye] maye A, me wold have H
169 playne] plaine plaine H   170 we mon goe] mon we good have H
171 may bee] maye be of beastes A, then these be H   172 of beast] *om* A,
of beastes RBH   173 or] nor ARH   174 beelongen] nedone AR,
nedon B, needen H

Tarboyste and tarboll   175
yee shall here;

37   nettle, hemlock, and butter abydinge,
     and my good dogge Dottynolle
     that is nothinge cheeffe of his chydinge.
     Yf any man come mee bye   180

38   and would wytt which waye beste were,
     my legge I lifte up wheras I lye
     and wishe him the waye easte and west where.
     And I rose where I laye,

39   me would thinke that travell lost.   185
     For kinge ne duke, by this daye,
     ryse I will not—but take my rest here.
     Nowe wyll I sitt here adowne

40   and pippe at this pott like a pope.
     Would God that I were downe   190
     harmeles, as I hastelye hope.
     Noe man drinke here shall

41   save myselfe, the devyll of the sope.
     All this lottes I seet at little;
     nay, yee lades, sett I not by yee.   195
     For you have I manye a fowle fitt.
     Thow fowle filth, though thow flytt, I defye thee.

175] *om* H   tarboyste] tarbox B   tarboll] tarreboyle AR   176] you shall
here sone see in sight H   here] see heare AR   *After* 176] *in* H

          of small hannes that to me needen;
          tarboist, tarboyle, and nettle,

177] hemlockes and butter abyding H   179 cheeffe] choyse ARH, chysse B
181 beste were] were beste AR   182 wheras] as ARB, where H
183 easte] by east H   and] or AR   where] *om* A   184 where] when ARB
185 me] I A   travell] travill A, labour R, traveyle H   lost] best were H
186 ne] or H   187 ryse] nay H   here] *om* A   188] nowe here sitte
downe I will A, nowe here adowne sitt I will R   sitt here adowne] set me
downe H   189–90] *om* A   191] *before* 189 R   *After* 191] *in* H

          At me all men learne mon
          this Golgatha grimly to grope.

192 drinke here shall] heare shall drinke AB, here drinke R, here drink mon H
193 of the] a B   194 this lottes] this bottill AR, thie lottes B, thy lathes H
I] Ile A   at] at a H   195 sett] kepe ARB   not] nett B   by] to lye
ARB   yee] thee ARBH   196 I] *om* AR   197 flytt] flye B, flite H

PRIMUS PASTOR

42 Trowle, take tent to my talkinge.
    For thy tooth here is good tugginge.
    While thy wedders benne walkinge,   200
    on this loyne thow may have good lugginge.

GARCIUS

43 Fye on your loynes and your liverye,
    your liverastes, livers, and longes,
    your sose, your sowse, your saverraye,
    your sittinge withowt any songes!   205

44 One this hill I hold mee here.
    Noe hape to your hot meate have I.
    But flyte with my fellowes in feare,
    and your sheepe full sycerly save I.

44^r   SECUNDUS PASTOR

45 For thow saves our sheepe,   210
    good knave, take keepe.
    Sythen thow may not sleepe,
    come eate of this sowse.

GARCIUS

    Nay, the dyrte is soe deepe,
    stopped therin for to steepe;   215
    and the grubbes theron do creepe
    at whom at thy howse.

46 Therfore meate, if I maye,
    of your dightinge todaye
    will I nought by noe waye   220
    tyll I have my wages.

198 tent] teene AR   199 tooth] teeith AH   201 on] and on A
GARCIUS *here and throughout the play*] TROWLE AR   202 and] and on A
203 liverastes] lyvarstes R, lyveras H   204 your(1)] you A   sose] sause
ARH, sowse B   sowse] sausces AR, sawse B, jawce and H   205 sittinge]
sittinges R   207 your hot] you what H   208 flyte] sitte A, flett R
feare] freye A   209 sycerly] securlye A, securely RB   save] keep R
210 for] for that H   211 take] take and H   212 sythen] seith AH
213 sowse] sauce AR   214 is] therin is H   soe] to B   215 stopped]
stomped A, stamped H   steepe] sleepe H   216 do] *om* H   220 nought]
not H   noe] the B   221 wages] wage H

I wend to have binne gaye
but, see, soe ragged is myne araye;
aye pinches is your paye
to any poore page.   225

TERTIUS PASTOR

47 Trowle, boy, for Godes tree,
come eate a morsell with me;
and then wrastle will wee
here on this wold.

GARCIUS

That shall I never flee!   230
Though yt bee with all three
to laye my liverye,
that will I hold.

Tunc ibit ad magistros suos, et dicat

GARCIUS

48 Nowe comes Trowle the Trewe;
a torne to take have I tight   235
with my masters. Or I rewe
put him forth that moste is of might.

PRIMUS PASTOR

Trowle, better thow never knewe.
Eate of this, meate for a knight.

GARCIUS

Naye, spare! Though I spewe,   240
all upon your heades shall yt light.

222 wend] mente R, went B   to] or this to H   223 but] *om* ARBH
224 pinches] pynckes AR, pinchinge B, pinkes pinkes H   225 any] everye
ARBH   226 tree] fee AR, three B, pitty H   228 then] *om* H   229 on]
in B   wold] greene AR   GARCIUS] TROWLE B, *om* H   230 shall] will H
flee] fleye AR   231 bee with] were with you H   233 that] that wages
ARB, that wager H   *SD* ibit] ibunt A   magistros] magistratos A, maiis-
tros B   suos] *om* BH   et dicat] et dicat Trowle A, *om* H   GARCIUS] *om*
ARH, GRATIUS B   235 tight] tithe B   237 moste is] is most H
238 thow never] never thou ARH   knewe] kever H   240 naye] non R
spare] spare I will ARBH   241 your] thy ARB   heades] heade ARB   shall
yt] shall ARB, it shall H

SECUNDUS PASTOR

49　Howe should wee suffer this shame,
　　of a shrewe thus to be shente?

TERTIUS PASTOR

This ladd lusts to be lame
and lose a lymme or hee went.　　　　　　245

GARCIUS

Have donne! Beginne wee this game.
But warre lest your golyons glent.
That were little dole to our dame,
though in the myddest of the daye yee were drent.

44ᵛ　　　　　### PRIMUS PASTOR

50　False lad, fye on thy face!　　　　　　250
　　One this grownd thow shall have a fall.
　　Hent one, and hould that thow hasse.
　　Yf thow happe have, all goe to all.

GARCIUS

And this, syrs, here to solace.
Hankyn, sheoparde, shame thee I shall.　　255
Wroth thow art, worse then thow was.
Warre lest thow walter here by the wall.

Tunc projiciat Primum Pastorem, et dicat Secundus Pastor.

SECUNDUS PASTOR

51　Boye, lest I breake thy bones,
　　kneele downe and axe me a boone.
　　Lest I destroy thee here on these stones,　　260
　　sease, lest I shend thee to soone.

242 this] all this AR　　　243 thus] this A　　　244 lusts] luste AR, list H
lame] lamde A　　　GARCIUS] GERTIUS B　　　247 glent] glette AR, gleett B
248 our] your H　　　249 the(1)] *om* AR　of the] *om* AR, of BH　　daye]
dde A, Dee RBH　　yee] the A, they RB　　252 hasse] haste AR　　253 happe]
have all H　　254 this] these AR, thes B, here H　　here to] to doe you H
256 wroth] worth AR　　257 walter] walte ARBH　　*SD*] Tunc Primus
prejicitur *to right of* 255 H　　projiciat] proistiat AR　　Primum Pastorem]
Primam Pastorem AR, Primus Pastor B　　SECUNDUS PASTOR] *om* AB
258 thy] there thy H　　261 shend] shame AR

GARCIUS

Gole thee to groyns and grownes!
Good were thee thy ould ragges to save soone.
Little dowbt of such drownes,
lyther tyke, for thy deedes donne.   265

TERTIUS PASTOR

52 Owt, alas, hee lyes on his loynes!
But lett mee goe now to that lad.
Sheppardes he shames and shendes,
for last now am I owt shad.

GARCIUS

Both your backes here to mee bendes;   270
for all your boastes I hould you to bad.
Hould your arses and your hinder loynes;
then hope I to have as I have hadd.

53 The better in the bore,
as I had before   275
of this bovearte,
yea, hope I more.
Keepe well thy scorc
for feare of a farte.

Tunc projiciat Tertium Pastorem, et dicat Garcius:

54 Lye ther, lither, in the lake.   280
My liverye nowe will I lach:
this curye, this clowt, and this cake.
For yee be cast, now will I catch.

262 gole] gloe AR   thee to] that so H   groyns] greynes A, greoynes R,
greonis B, grennes H   grownes] groundes A   263 ragges] ruggcs B   soone]
sounde AR, sonne B, sone H   *To right of* 263] Tunc 2us projicitur H
264 drownes] drones H   265 tyke] tycke AR, like H   donne] are done
ARBH   267 goe now] now goe H   268 shendes] shyndes A, sheindes
R, shenes B   269 now am I] ame I now B   shad] shade AR, shutt B
270 here] *om* H   bendes] bend B, byndes H   271 boastes] boste ARBH
to] full ARB, but H   273 I(1)] *om* H   have(2)] tofore A, now B, ere H
274 in] and H   276 bovearte] bosiart H   278 score] store ARB   *SD*]
Tunc 3us projicitur *to right of* 278 H   Tertium Pastorem] Tercius Pastor B
Garcius] Gertius B   280 lake] lacke A   281 will I] will AB, I will H
282 curye] cup H

To the devyll I you all betake,
as traytors attaynt of your tache!   285
On this would with this will I walke;
all the world wonder on the wache.

Et sic recedat Garcius, et dicat Primus Pastor:

55 Fellowes, this a fowle case ys,
    that wee bine thus cast of a knave.
    All agaynst our willes hee hase his;   290
    but I must needes hould the harmes that I have.

45^r   SECUNDUS PASTOR

56 That I have needes must I hold;
    of these unhappie harmes ofte here I.
    Therfore will I wayte on this would
    upon the wedder, for I am werye.   295

TERTIUS PASTOR

57 Though wee bine werye noe wonder,
    what betweene wrastlinge and wakinge.
    Ofte wee may bee in thought wee be now under.
    God amend hit with his makinge.

Tunc sedebunt, et stella apparebit, et dicat Primus Pastor:

58 What is all this light here   300
    that blasses soe bright here
    on my black beard?
    For to see this light here
    a man may bee afright here,
    for I am afeard.   305

284 you all] all you ARBH   285 as] and ARBH   attaynt] taynt H
286 with] on A, *om* H   walke] wake H   *SD*] *om* H   289 thus] this AR
of] out of AR   290 willes] will H   his] this B   291 harmes] harme
ARH, horne B   that] *om* R   293 these] this B   I] *om* H   294 wayte]
weete H   this] the B   295 the wedder] the weather R, this would H
297 wakinge] walkinge ARB   298 wee may] may we H   in thought]
over though H   now under] no wonder H   *SD*] Tunc sedebunt aut
ambulabunt et apparebit stella H   stella] stellum A   *At* 300] PRIMUS H
301 blasses] blackes A, blakes R, blak is B, shynes H   303 light] sight H
305 afeard] freayde AR, afrad B

SECUNDUS PASTOR

59 Feard for a fraye nowe
   may wee bee all nowe;
   and yett it is night,
   yett seemes yt day nowe.
   Never, soothly to saye nowe,   310
   see I such a sight.

TERTIUS PASTOR

60 Such a sight seeminge
   and a light leeminge
   lettes mee to looke.
   All to my deeminge,   315
   from a starre streaminge
   yt to mee stroacke.

GARCIUS

61 That starre if it stand
   to seek will I fond,
   though my sight fayle mee.   320
   While I may live in lond
   why should I not fond,
   yf it will avayle mee?

Tunc respiciens firmamentum dicat Garcius:

62 A, Godes mightis!
   In yonder starre light is;   325
   of the sonne this sight is,
   as yt nowe seemes.

306 feard] freayde AR, aferd H   a] I B   307 all] able B   308 and]
a AB, ah R   309 nowe] light R   310] om AR   313 leeminge]
gleming H   314 to] for to H   315 my] me B   317 stroacke]
strocke A, stroke RBH   318 stand] stonde RH   319 seek] see ARBH
320 my sight] mighte lighte AR   mee] om ARBH   321 lond] land BH
322 not] om ARBH   fond] stand H   323 mee] om ARBH   SD firma-
mentum] firmantum H   dicat] et dicat AR   324 Godes] God ARB
mightis] mighte is ARBH   326 the] this H   sight] light R   327 seemes]
sheines A

PRIMUS PASTOR

63 Hit seemes, as I nowe see,
a bright stare to bee,
there to abyde.   330
From yt wee may not flee
but aye gloe on the glee,
tyll yt downe glyde.

45ᵛ   PRIMUS PASTOR

64 Fellowes, will wee
kneele downe on our knee   335
after comford
to the trewe Trinitee,
for to lead us for to see
our elders lord?

TERCIUS PASTOR

65 Our lord will us lere   340
in our prayer
wherto yt will apent;
and why on high here
the eare is soe cleare,
nowe shall wee be kent.   345

GARCIUS

66 Lord, of this light
send us some sight
why that it is sent.
Before this night
was I never soe afright   350
of the firmament.

PRIMUS PASTOR

67 Ne, fye! By my faye,
nowe is it nigh daye;
so was it never.

329 to] for to H   330] *om* H   332 gloe] glye A, gleoy R, gloo B
PRIMUS] SECUNDUS ARBH   336 comford] comfortes AR, comfort H
338 for(2)] *om* ARBH   341 in] in this H   342 will] well H   343 high]
highte ABH   344 eare] eayre A, ayer RBH   347 send] guyde ARB
348 that] *om* H   sent] fayre H   352 ne fye] wyste I AR, wies I B,
nor I H   353 is it] it is H

Therfore I praye   355
the sooth us to saye,
or that we desever.

Tunc cantet Angelus: 'Gloria in excelsis Deo et in terra pax
hominibus bonae voluntatis.'

68 Fellowes in feare,
may yee not here
this mutinge on highe?   360

SECUNDUS PASTOR

In 'glore' and in 'glere'?
Yett noe man was nere
within our sight.

TERTIUS PASTOR

69 Naye, yt was a 'glorye.'
Nowe am I sorye   365
bowt more songe.

GARCIUS

Of this strange storye
such mirth is merye;
I would have amonge.

PRIMUS PASTOR

70 As I then deemed,   370
'selsis' it seemed
that hee songe soe.

46ʳ   SECUNDUS PASTOR

Whyle the light leemed,
a wreakinge mee weened;
I wyst never whoo.   375

357 that we] that R, we H   SD cantet] cantat B, cantabit H   excelsis]
excellis R   bonae] bone AR, bona B   After SD] PRIMUS PASTOR ARB,
PRIMUS H   360 on] of B   highe] heighte ARBH   SECUNDUS PASTOR]
om H   361 in] a AR, one BH   glore] glorie B   in] one BH
365 am I] I ame BH   sorye] sorye but A   366 bowt] om A, but R,
without H   368 is merye] more I ARBH   369 I] om A   370 then]
them AR   371 selsis] scellsis AR, caelcis H   372 songe soe] sange A
374 mee] we H   weened] deemed R   375 whoo] woo AR

TERTIUS PASTOR

71 What songe was this, saye yee,
    that he sange to us all three?
    Expounded shall yt bee
    erre wee hethen passe;
    for I am eldest of degree   380
    and alsoe best, as seemes mee,
    hit was 'grorus glorus' with a 'glee.'
    Hit was neyther more nor lasse.

GARCIUS

72 Nay, yt was 'glorus glarus glorius';
    methinke that note went over the howse.   385
    A seemely man hee was, and curiouse;
    but soone awaye hee was.

PRIMUS PASTOR

    Nay, yt was 'glorus glarus' with a 'glo,'
    and mych of 'celsis' was therto.
    As ever have I rest or woo,   390
    much hee spake of 'glas.'

SECUNDUS PASTOR

73 Naye, yt was neyther 'glas' nor 'glye.'
    Therfore, fellowe, nowe stand bye.

TERTIUS PASTOR

    By my fayth, hee was some spye,
    our sheepe for to steale.   395
    Or elles hee was a man of our crafte,
    for seemely hee was and [wounder] defte.

377 he] the A, was R   sange] songe R   379 hethen] hense ARB
382 grorus glorus] glore glare A, glorie glare R, glor glor B, glorum glarum H
383 lasse] lesse ARBH   GARCIUS] om H   384–7] om H   384 glorus
glarus] glori glory A, glorie glora R, glor glor B   385 methinke]
methoughte ARB   went] ronne AR   PRIMUS PASTOR] GARTIUS H   388 glorus
glarus] glory glory A, glory glore R, glor glar B, glorum glarum H   389 mych]
mirth B   390 woo] roo ARBH   392 glye] glee H   393 nowe stand]
stande thou R   394 hee] it BH   some] a B   397 wounder] worders
Hm, wondrous H   defte] dafte AR

GARCIUS

Nay, hee came by night—all thinges lefte—
our tuppes with tarre to teale.

PRIMUS PASTOR

74 Naye, on a 'glor' and on 'glay' and a 'gly'   400
gurd Gabryell when hee so gloryd.
When hee sange I might not be sorye;
through my brest-bonne bletinge hee bored.

SECUNDUS PASTOR

75 Nay, by God, yt was a 'gloria,'
sayde Gabryell when hee sayde soe.   405
He had a mych better voyce then I have,
as in heaven all other have soe.

TERTIUS PASTOR

76 Wyll hee here howe hee sange 'celsis'?
For on that sadly hee sett him;
nayther singes 'sar' nor soe well 'cis,'   410
ney 'pax merye Mawd when shee had mett him.'

46ᵛ   ### GARCIUS

77 On tyme hee touched on 'tarre,'
and therto I tooke good intent;
all heaven might not have gonne harre,
that note on high when hee up hent.   415

PRIMUS PASTOR

78 And after a 'pax' or of 'peace,'
up as a pye hee pyped;

398 came] come BH   all] and all H   thinges] thinge A   lefte] loste B,
lafte H   399 teale] tell ARB, tayle H   400 and on] on a AR, and a H
glay] glory AR, glare H   and a] on a A, and B   401 gurd] good BH
gloryd] glorcd H   403 through] for through H   bletinge] bloting H
bored] borned ARB   404 by] be AB   God] my faith H   405 sayde]
beganne ARB, sang H   406 I have] had I H   408 hee(1)] ye AB, you RH
410 singes] sing B, sang H   sar] sir AR   411 ney] ner H   had] so A
GARCIUS] GRATIUS B   412 on tarre] on terre AR, upon tar H   413 and
therto] on ther H   414 have] a ARB   415 note on] not one B   high]
heighte ABH   up hent] had howted H   416 a] of ARB, on H   417 a]
om AR

such a loden—this is noe lesse—
never in my life me so lyked.

SECUNDUS PASTOR

79 Upon 'hominibus' hee muted;   420
that much mervayle to mee was.
And aye I quoked when hee so whewted;
I durst not hede wher that yt was.

TERTIUS PASTOR

80 Yett, yett, hee sange more then all this,
for some word is worthye a forder.   425
For hee sange 'bonae voluntatis';
that is a cropp that passeth all other.

GARCIUS

81 Yett and yett he sange more to;
from my mynde yt shall not starte.
Hee sange alsoe of a 'Deo';   430
me thought that heled my harte.

82 And that word 'terra' hee tamed—
therto I toke good intent.
And 'pax' alsoe may not be blamed;
for that to this songe I assent.   435

PRIMUS PASTOR

83 Nowe pray wee to him with good intent,
and singe I wyll and me [unbrace]:
that hee will lett us to bee kent,
and to send us of his grace.

418 loden] ludden B, ledden H   this] that AB   lesse] las H   420 homini-
bus] onnibus A, omnibus RB   422 aye] ever AR   quoked] quocke ARBH
when] while H   whewted] shouted AR   423 not] not not A   hede]
here H   yt] I BH   424 yett yett] yet A   425] froo my mynde it shall
not starte A   word] wordes RB   worthye] worth RBH   forder] foder RB,
founder H   426 bonae] bene A, bone RBH   427 cropp] crape A,
crapp R   passeth] past H   428 and] om A   429 mynde] harte A
shall] may H   starte] astart H   431 that] om AR   432 terra] terre AR
435 to this songe] song to this H   437 unbrace] umbrace Hm, imbrace A,
ymbrace R

SECUNDUS PASTOR

84 Nowe syth I have all my will, 440
never in this world soe well I was.
Singe wee nowe, I rede us, shryll
a mery songe us to solace.

GARCIUS

85 Singe we nowe; lett see,
some songe will I assaye. 445
All men nowe singes after mee,
for musicke of mee learne yee maye.

Tunc cantabunt et postea dicat Tertius Pastor (Here singe 'troly,
loly, loly, loo.'):

86 Nowe wend we forth to Bethlem,
that is best our songe to bee,
for to see the starre-gleme, 450
the fruyt alsoe of that mayden free.

47ʳ   PRIMUS PASTOR

87 Nowe followe we the starre that shines,
tyll we come to that holy stable.
To Bethlem boyne the lymes;
followe we yt withowt any fable. 455

SECUNDUS PASTOR

88 Followe we hit and hyes full fast;
such a frende loth us were to fayle.

441 never] for never ARBH   I was] hase ARB   444 singe we nowe]
singe one now R, nowe sing on H   lett] lettes ARB, let us H   445 will I]
I will H   446 nowe] *om* H   singes] singe AB   447 of mee learne]
learne of me B   *SD*] Tunc omnes pastores cum aliis adiuvantibus cantabunt hilare carmen H   cantabunt] cantabit B   here] *om* ARB   troly loly
loly loo] troly loly troly loe A, troly loly lo R, troly holy holy loo B   *At*
448] TERTIUS H   448 Bethlem] Bethelem RB   450 for] *om* AR   gleme]
cleane maye A, gleene in R   451 the] and the R   alsoe] *om* AR   free]
freye A   452 nowe] and nowe H   shines] shyneth AR   454 Bethlem]
Bethelem ARB   boyne the] boune the A, boyne thy R, bend we our H
lymes] lym is B, lynes H   455 withowt] withowten B   456 and hyes
full] that hyeth so H   457 loth us were] loth us AR, us loth were B, loth
were us H

Launche on! I will not be the last
upon Marye for to mervayle.

Hic vadunt versus Bethlem.

TERTIUS PASTOR

89 Stynt nowe; goe no moe steppes,   460
for now the starre beginneth to stand.
Harvye, that good bene our happes
we seene—by our Savyour fonde.

Hic apparet Angelus et dicat:

90 Sheppardes, of this sight
be ye not afright,   465
for this is Godes might;
takes this in mynde.
To Bethlem nowe right;
there yee shall see in sight
that Christ is borne tonight   470
to cover all mankynde.

GARCIUS

91 To Bethlem take wee the waye,
for with you I thinke to wend,
that prince of peace for to praye
heaven to have at our ende.   475

92 And singe we all, I read,
some myrth to his majestee,
for certayne now see wee it indeede:
the kinge Sone of heavon is hee.

459 mervayle] marvell B   SD hic] tunc H   vadunt] vadint AR   Bethlem]
Bethelem RB   460 nowe] om H   goe] and goe R, goe we H   461 begin-
neth] begins BH   stand] stonde A   462 Harvye] hereby B, here we H
good bene our] bene our good AR, god bene our B   463 seene] see H
our] this our H   fonde] founde ARB, is found H   SD] Et apparebit
Angelus to right of 460 H   hic] hoc B   apparet] aparit AR, appariet B
Angelus et dicat] et dicat Angellus AR   After SD] ANGELUS RH
468 Bethlem] Bethelem ARB   nowe] wende R, goe now H   469 yee shall]
shall you H   471 cover] ken RB, kever AH   472 Bethlem] Bethelem
RB   473 wend] wynde H   474 that] the H   478 see wee] sheewe
AR, we see B   it] om H   479 kinge] kinges ARBH   is] it is B

PRIMUS PASTOR

93 Sym, sym, securlye 480
here I see Marye,
and Jesus Christ fast bye
lapped in haye.

SECUNDUS PASTOR

Kneele we downe in hye
and praye wee him of mercye, 485
and welcome him worthelye
that woe does awaye.

TERTIUS PASTOR

94 Awaye all our woe ys
and many mans moe ys.
Christ, lord, lett us kys 490
the cratch or the clothes.

47ᵛ   GARCIUS

Solace nowe to see this
byldes in my brest blys:
never after to do amys,
thinge that him loth ys. 495

PRIMUS PASTOR

95 Whatever this ould man that here ys?
Take heede how his head ys whore.
His beard is like a buske of bryers
with a pound of heare about his mouth and more.

SECUNDUS PASTOR

96 More ys this marveyle to mee nowe, 500
for to nappe greatly him needes.
Hartles is hee nowe
for aye to his heeles hee heedes.

480 securlye] sickerlye AR, soundlie H   489 mans] menes R   491 the(1)]
thy H   493 blys] blesse AR   495 thinge] thinges AR   498 is] om H
bryers] breeres H   501 greatly him] him greatlie B, greatlie he H
502 is hee] he is R   503 hee heedes] he hidis B, his head is H

TERTIUS PASTOR

97 Why, with his berde though hit be rough,
    right well to her hee hydes.   505
    Worthye wight, witt would wee nowe;
    wyll ye worne us, worthye in weedes?

MARIA

98 Sheppardes, sothlye I see
    that my sonne you hyther sent,
    through Godes might in majestye   510
    that in mee light and here is lent.
    This man maryed was to mee
    for noe sinne in such assent;
    but to keepe my virginitee,
    and truly in non other intent.   515

JOSEPH

99 Good men, Moyses take in mynde:
    as he was made through God allmight,
    ordayned lawes us to bynde
    which that wee should keepe of right;
    man and woman for to bynde   520
    lawefully them both to light;
    to fructifye, as men may fynde,
    that tyme was wedded every wight.

100 Therfore wedded to her I was
    as lawe would: her for to lere   525
    for noyse nor slander nor trespasse,
    and through that deede the devill to dere,
    as tould mee Gabriell, full of grace.
    When I had trussed all my gere
    to have fled and to have never seene her face,   530
    by him was I arested there.

504 be rough] hydes ARB   505 well] *om* H   hydes] heedes AR, heedis H
506 wee nowe] *om* ARB   507 ye] we AR, ne B   worthye] worthely B
in weedes] *om* ARB   511 in mee] me in H   lent] tent H   513 in]
ner A, ney RB, ne H   assent] intent B   515 in non] for no A, in no B
517 through] throug H   519 of right] arighte R   521] *om* B   526 nor
slander] slaunder R, and slaunder B, or sclaunder H   527 dere] dare A
530 to have never seene] never to have seene ARB, never to see H

101 For hee sayde to mee sleepinge
that shee lackles was of sinne.
And when I hard that tokeninge,
from her durst I noe waye twynne.   535
Therfore goes forth and preach this thinge,
all together and not in twynne:
that you have seene your heavenly kinge
common all mankynde to mynne.

48ʳ   PRIMUS PASTOR

102 Great God, syttynge in thy troone,   540
that made all thinge of nought,
nowe wee may thanke thee eychone:
this is hee that wee have sought.

SECUNDUS PASTOR

Goe wee neere anone
with such as we have brought.   545
Ringe, brooche, or pretiouse stone—
lett see whether we have ought to proffer.

TERTIUS PASTOR

103 Lett us doe him homage.

PRIMUS PASTOR

Whoe shall goe first? The page?

SECUNDUS PASTOR

Naye, yee be father in age.   550
Therfore ye must first offer.

535 noe waye] not AR   twynnc] twcyne AR   536 forth and preach] fourth
preach A, preache forth RBH   537 twynne] twene AR   539 all] and
all A, an all R, one all B   mynne] myne AR, mynd B   540 in] one R
541 thinge] thinges ARB   542 nowe] om H   eych] elke B   543 this]
for R, here H   is hee that] thou arte hee which R   545 with] which B
546 or] ner A   547 lett] lett us AR, lets H   whether] yf AR   549 goe
first] first goe H   page] pager B   550 father] fathers H   in] of ARBH
551 ye must] must you H   first] om A

PRIMUS PASTOR

104 Hayle, kinge of heavon soe hye,
    borne in a crybbe;
    mankynd unto thee
    thow hast made full sybbe.   555

105 Hayle, kynge, borne in a maydens bowre.
    Profettes did tell thow should be our succour;
    this clarkes do saye.
    Loe, I bringe thee a bell;
    I praye thee save me from hell,   560
    soe that I maye with thee dwell
    and serve thee for aye.

SECUNDUS PASTOR

106 Hayle, the emperour of hell
    and of heaven alsoe;
    the feynd shalt thow fell,   565
    that ever hath binne fals.

107 Hayle, the maker of the stare
    that stoode us beforne;
    hayle, the blessedesfull baronne
    that ever was borne.   570
    Loe, sonne, I bringe thee a flackett.
    Therby hanges a spoone
    for to eat thy pottage with at noone,
    as I myselfe full oftetymes have donne.
    With hart I praye thee to take yt.   575

TERTIUS PASTOR

108 Hayle, prince withowten any pere,
    that mankynde shall releeve.

553 crybbe] crebe AR   554 unto] to H   thee] thie B   555 full sybbe]
fullye AR, all sibbe H   558 this] thus ARB   do] doth AR, om H
560] om H   562 serve thee] farewell H   aye] ever A   563 the] thie B
564 alsoe] als H   565 feynd] finde B   shalt thow] shall thee AR, thou
shalt H   fell] fall H   569 blessedesfull] blessedfull ARB, blessedfullst H
baronne] barne ARBH   570] om ARB   was] yet was H   571 loe
sonne] om H   flackett] flaggette AR, flasket H   572 therby hanges] and
thereat H   573 for] om ARH   pottage] porage R, podage B   with]
withall AH   574 full] om B   oftetymes] ofte H   575 to take yt] to take
A, take it RH, for to take it B   576 withowten] without AR   any] om H

Hayle, the fooe unto Lucyfere,
the which beguyled Eve.

109 Hayle, the graunter of hope,   580
for one yearth now thow dwelles.
Loe, sonne, I bringe thee a cappe,
for I have nothinge elles.

110 This gifte, sonne, that I give thee ys but smalle;
and though I come the hyndmost of all,   585
when thow shalt men to thy blys call,
good lord, yett thinke one mee.

48ᵛ   GARCIUS

111 My deare, with dryrie unto thee I mee dresse,
my state on felloweshippe that I doe not lose;
and for to save mee from all yll sicknesse,   590
I offer unto thee a payre of my wyves ould hose.

112 For other jewells, my sonne,
have I none thee for to give
that is worthe anythinge at all,
but my good harte whyle I lyve   595
and my prayers tyll death doth mee call.

THE FIRST BOYE

113 Nowe to you, my fellowes, this doe I saye,
for in this place, or that I wynde awaye:
unto yonder chyld lett us goe praye,
as our masters have donne us beforne.   600

578 the] thee AR, *om* H   fooe] froo AR   580 the] *om* H   hope] happe
AR, happes H   581 for one] for in ARB, in H   thow] tho B   dwelles]
dwelleste AR   582 sonne] *om* H   cappe] cape A   584] to offer unto
thee this gifte sonne forsoth it is but small H   sonne] *om* R   that I give]
I bringe A, I give RB   thee ys] this R   585 and] *om* H   come the]
came H   hyndmost] last R, hyndermost H   586 men] them A   587 yett]
then H   588 dryrie] dutye A   589 state on] state and AR, flote on H
not lose] no lesse H   590 and] *om* A   for] *om* H   all] all that B
591 unto] to H   592 jewells] dremes A, jewell H   my] *om* H   593 have
I] I have H   thee] *om* ARH   give] geve ABH   596 doth] doe ARBH
mee] my B   THE FIRST BOYE] PRIMUS PUER R, *om* H   597–640] *om* H
597 you] *om* AR   doe] will AR   598 or that] or R, before B   599 goe]
goe and AR   600 beforne] before RB

THE SECOND BOYE

And of such goodes as wee have here,
lett us offer to this prince so dere,
and to his mother, that mayden clere,
that of her body hasse [him] borne.

THE FIRST BOY

114 Abyde, syrres, I will goe firste to yonder kinge.   605

THE SECOND BOYE

And I will goe nexte to that lordinge.

THE THYRD BOYE

Then will I be last of this offeringe;
this can I saye, noe more.

THE FIRST BOYE

Nowe, lord, for to give thee have I nothinge,
neyther gold, silver, brooch, ne ringe,   610
nor noe rich robes meete for a kinge
that I have here in store.

115 But thoe hit lacke a stopple,
take thee here my well fayre bottle,
for yt will hold a good pottle;   615
in fayth, I can give thee noe more.

THE SECOND BOYE

116 Lord, I know that thow art of this virgine borne,
in full poore araye sittinge one her arme.
For to offer to thee have I noe skorne,
althoo thou be but a child.   620

THE *here and in all succeeding English SHs in the play*] *om* R   604 hasse
him] hasse her Hm, hade bene A, hath him R   THE FIRST] THIRDE R
605 abyde] a toy B   I] and I R   607 I be] be I the A, I be the RB
of] at R   608 this] thus R   BOYE] PLAIE A   613 thoe] that AR
lacke] lackes AR   614 fayre] *om* A   617 I know that] *om* AR   this]
the R   618 one] in B   619 have I] I have ARB

For jewell have I none to give thee
to mayntayne thy royall dignitye;
but my hood, take yt thee,
as thow art God and man.

THE THYRD BOYE

117 O noble chyld of thy Father on hye,   625
    alas, what have I for to give thee?
    Save only my pype that soundeth so royallye,
    elles truely have I nothinge at all.
    Were I in the rocke or in the valey alowe,
    I could make this pipe sound, I trowe,   630
    that all the world should ringe
    and quaver as yt would fall.

49r   ### THE IIIIth BOYE

118 Nowe, chyld, although thou be commen from God
    and bee thyselfe God in thy manhoode,
    yet I knowe that in thy chyldhood   635
    thow will for sweetemeat looke.
    To pull downe apples, payres, and ploomes,
    ould Joseph shall not neede to hurte his handes;
    because thow haste not plentye of cromes,
    I give thee here my nuthooke.   640

PRIMUS PASTOR

119 Nowe farewell, mother and maye,
    for of synne nought thow wottest.
    Thow hast brought forth this daye
    Godes Sonne of mightis most.

621 jewell] jewells B   622 to] for to AR   623 take] that take A, then
take R, thou take B   625 thy Father on hye] thee AR, the B   626 for
to give thee] for thee A, *om* R, for B   627 that soundeth so royallyc] *om*
ARB   628 have I] *om* ARB   at all] *om* ARB   629 rocke] rockes ARB
the valey alowe] *om* ARB   630 sound I trowe] *om* ARB   631 the world]
this woode A, the wood RB   ringe] *om* B   632 quaver] quiver ARB
would fall] were ARB   634 thyselfe God] God thyselfe ARB   636 sweete-
meat] sweete meale A   637 apples payres] peares appells B   638 handes]
thombes AR, hondes B   639 not] no R   640 nuthooke] nutthocke A,
millhook B   644 of] which of H   mightis] mighteste ARB, might is H

120 Wherfore men shall saye: 645
     'Blessed in every coast and place
     be hee, memoriall for us all.'
     And that wee may from synne fall
     and stand ever in his grace,
     our lord God bee with thee.   650

                    SECUNDUS PASTOR

121 Brethren, lett us all three
     singinge walke homwardlye.
     Unkynd will I never in noe case bee,
     but preach all that I can and knowe,
     as Gabryell taught by his grace mee.   655
     Singinge awaye hethen will I.

                    TERTIUS PASTOR

122 Over the sea, and I may have grace,
     I will gange and goe abowt nowe
     to preach this thinge in every place;
     and sheepe will I keepe no more nowe.   660

                    GARCIUS

123 I read wee us agree
     for our mysdeedes amendes to make,
     for soe nowe will I;
     and to the chyld I wholey mee betake
     for aye securlye.   665
     Sheppardes craft I forsake;
     and to an anker herby
     I will in my prayers wach and wake.

647 hee] thou ARBH   for] for me and for ARBH   648 and] so H
649 his] thy ARBH   652 homwardlye] whomwardes ARBH   653 never]
om ARB   654 all] ever ARBH   knowe] crye ARBH   656 awaye]
alway H   hethen] hense AR   658 gange] henge AR   goe abowt] aboute
goe ARBH   659 thinge] om ARBH   660 no more] non ARB
661 agree] gree H   662 for] of B   mysdeedes] misd H   663 will I]
I will A   664 and] om H   the] that ARB   I wholey] whollye AR, hollie
will I BH   665 aye securlye] ever sickerlie ARH, ever securely B
666 I] heare I ARH, I here B   668 in] to H   wach] to watch BH

PRIMUS PASTOR

124 And I an hermitte
     to prayse God, to praye,   670
     to walke by stye and by streytt,
     in wildernes to walke for aye.
     And I shall noe man meete
     but for my livinge I shall him praye,
     barefoote one my feete.   675
     And thus will I live ever and aye.

49ᵛ   125 For aye, ever, and alwayse,
            this world I fully refuse,
            my mysse to amend with monys.
            Turne to thy fellowes and kys.   680

       126 I yelde, for in youth
            we have bine fellowes, iwys.
            Therfore lend me your mouth,
            and frendly let us kysse.

SECUNDUS PASTOR

From London to Lowth   685
such another shepperd I wott not where is.
Both frend and cowth,
God grant you all his blys.

TERTIUS PASTOR

127 To that blys bringe you
     great God, if that thy will bee.   690

---

669 an hermitte] am heare meke A, ame here mytte R   670 to praye] to
paie AH, and praye R   671 walke] wake H   stye] style AR   by] *om* A
streytt] streete ARBH   672 for aye] ever A, aye R   673 shall] will A
674 shall] will H   him] them AR   675 barefoote] barefoted H
676 thus] this AR   live] leeve R   677 and alwayse] ones AR, and onys
B, and honestie H   678 fully] will H   679 to] for to RH   monys]
mones ARH   680] *om* H   681 yelde] eylde A   for in] fore in R, and
in my H   683 me] us ARB   mouth] mouthes H   685 Lowth] Louth
such H   686 such] *om* H   wott not where is] not were A, ney were R,
not where B   687 frend] framed AR, tremed B, fremd H   cowth] cought H
688 grant] geve H   all his blys] amen ARB   689 you] us great God H
690 great God] God graunt B, *om* H   that] *om* A, it H

Amen, all singe you;
good men, farewell yee.

GARCIUS

128 Well for to fare, eych frend,
God of his might graunt you;
for here now we make an ende.   695
Farewell, for wee from you goe nowe.

Finis

PLAY VIII

50ʳ

THE VINTNERS PLAYE

Incipit Pagina Octava Trium Regum Orientalium.

PRIMUS REX

1 Mightye God in majestye,
that rules the people of Judee,
when thow one man wilt have pittye,
and his sinnes forbye,
send some tokeninge, lord, to mee,   5
that ylke starre that I may see
that Balaham sayd should ryse and bee
in his prophecye.

2 For well I wotte, forsooth iwys,
that his prophecye sooth is.   10
A starre should ryse tokninge of blys
when Godes Sonne is borne.

691] amend all thinges that be amisse H   you] wee R   692 men] men
now H   farewell yee] fares well AR, fare you well B, fares well yee H
693 fare] fayer B   695 for] and B   696 from you goe] goe from you A

   Guild-ascription playe] *om* H   *Play-heading*] Pagina Octava de Tribus
Regibus Orientalibus H   trium] trin A   regum] regnum AR   orientalium]
orientoalum et dicat Primus Rex A   2 rules] ruleth AR, ruled H
3 pittye] mercy H   5 lord] *om* B   6 ylke] same A   I] we H
10 sooth] truth R   11 tokninge] betockeninge ARH   of] *om* H   blys]
blesse AR

Therfore these lordes and I in fere
in this mounte make our prayer
devoutlye once in the yeare,   15
for therto we binne sworne.

SECUNDUS REX

3   Yea, we that binne of Balahams bloode,
    that prophecyed of that sweete foode—
    when Balaack, that kinge soe woode,
    to curse would hee have made   20
    Godes people of Israell.
    But power fayled everye deale;
    to prophecye mankyndes heale
    that tyme happe hee hadd—

4   therfore wee kinges of his kynde,   25
    I read wee take his wordes in mynde,
    grace in him if wee maye fynde
    that Godes Sonne shalbe.
    And goe wee praye, both one and all,
    into the Mounte Victoryall.   30
    Paraventure such grace may fall
    that starre that wee maye see.

TERTIUS REX

5   Syr, securlye I read on right;
    unto that hill I will me dight
    and there beseech God almight   35
    one us for to have mynde,
    and of that starre to have a sight.
    Worshippe wee all that sweete wight
    that Balaham to us beheight,
    that shall forbye mankynde.   40

6   Saye, fellowe, take this coursere
    and abyde mee right here.

13 in] *om* A   15 once] onste A   17 Balahams] Bethlems A, Bethelems
R, Balaam B   18 prophecyed] prophescieth AR   foode] flood B   22 but]
that H   fayled] fayled hym ARBH   25 therfore] wherfore A   27 in]
to H   33 securlye] sickerlye ARH   I] ye ARBH   36 have] *om* AR
37 and] out A   a] some ARBH   40 forbye] forlitte B   41 fellowe]
fellowes H   coursere] censore B

Goe wee, syres, to our prayer,
I read now in good faye.
I have donne this manye a yere,   45
and my auncetours that before mee were.
Highe God, prince of power,
thou comforte us todaye.

50^v   Hic descendunt de equis et ibunt in montem.

PRIMUS REX

7 Lord, what tyme ys yt thy will
Balahams prophecye to fullfill,   50
thou give us grace, both lowd and styll,
and by some signe us shewe.

SECUNDUS REX

Yea, lord, though wee bee unworthye,
one thy men thou have mercye;
and of thy birthe thou certefye   55
her to thy knightes three.

TERTIUS REX

8 Lord God, leader of Israell,
that dye would for mankyndes heale,
thow come to us and not conceale,
but bee our counselour.   60

PRIMUS REX

Of all this world thou art the well
that shalbe called Emanuell.
Deeme the, lord, with us to dwell,
and graunte us our prayer.

Tunc apparebit stella.

43 prayer] praiers AR   44 now] we now R   good] *om* R   *At* 45] PRIMUS
REX H   45 a] *om* R   46 auncetours] ansecestores A   47 highe]
hight B   *SD*] Descendunt et ibunt ad montem H   descendunt] decendet
A, decendit R   montem] monten et dicat A   PRIMUS REX] *om* H   49 ys
yt] it is AR, is H   51 thou give] geve thou H   56 knightes] kinges
ARH   TERTIUS REX] *om* H   58 dye would for] dyed for AR, die would B
mankyndes] mankind to B   59 conceale] counsaile H   61 well] weale
AH   62 that shalbe] thou shalt be H   63 the] thee ARH   dwell]
deale ARBH   *SD*] Tunc stella apparet H   stella] stalla A

PRIMUS REX

9 A, syr roy, si vous ploitt,   65
gardes sus sur vostre teste.

SECUNDUS REX

Une esteile issi est
que syr vous reploiste.

TERTIUS REX

10 Aloies, soit luy une semblant
de une virgin portant,   70
come le semble, de une enfant
em brace apportement.

[PRIMUS REX]

11 A, lord, blessed most thou bee,
that one thy people hase pittye.
Witterly now witten wee   75
that wrought is our askinge.

SECUNDUS REX

That our prayer hard hasse hee
I leve full well, well by my lewtee;
for in the starre a chyld I see
and verye tokeninge.   80

TERTIUS REX

12 Lordes, I read wee hethen hye,
for I dare saye, and nothinge lye,
fullfilled is Balahams prophecye;
by this wee maye well knowe.

51ʳ Tunc reges iterum genua flectent, et Angelus portans stellam.

PRIMUS REX] *om* H   65 A] O B   roy] rex AR   vous] veus AR   ploitt]
plaist H   66 gardes] gardez BH   sur] sir H   vostre] voutre H   teste]
lest AR   67 issi] essi H   68 syr] sur RBH   TERTIUS REX] *om* H
69 une] *om* H   70 une] vin A   virgin] firgin B   71 le] de B   72 em]
en AR   PRIMUS REX] *om* HmA   73 most] muste AB, mayst R
77 prayer] prayers ARB   hee] *om* AR   78 leve] lyve B   well well] well
ARBH   *To right of* 81] Et surgit H   81 hethen] hense A, hether B,
hithen II   SD] *after* 88 H   genua] genu ARB   flectent] flectente A,
flectunt H   portans stellam] portans stellam et dicat AR, stellam portans
dicat H

PRIMUS REX

Yea, lest this bee some fantasye   85
yett praye we all speciallye;
for if hee bee borne verelye
more sygnes he will us shewe.

ANGELUS

13 Ryse up, yee kinges three,
    and commys anone after mee   90
    into the land of Judee
    as fast as yee may hye.
    The chyld yee seeke there shall yee see,
    borne all of a mayden free,
    that kinge of heaven and yearth shalbee   95
    and all mankynde forbye.

Here the kinges ryse up.

PRIMUS REX

14 Lordes, hye wee heathen anone.
    Nowe wee binne bydden theder gonne,
    I will never byde—by my bonne—
    tyll I at him bee.   100

SECUNDUS REX

Yea, syrs, I read us everyechone
dromodaryes to ryde upon,
for swyfter beasts be there none.
One I have, ye shall see.

TERTIUS REX

15 A dromodarye, in good faye,   105
    will goe lightly on his waye
    an hundreth myles upon a daye;
    such beasts nowe take wee.

PRIMUS REX] *om* R   86 speciallye] especiallye ARH, perpetuallie B
89 ryse] arise H   92 may] can AR   94 free] freye A   *SD] om* H
up] upp et dicat A   *To right of* 97] Et surgit H   97 heathen] theider A,
theyther R   98 nowe] for AR   99 byde] abyde H   100 I] that I H
101 us] you H   everyechone] everye ichone AR, every one H   106 on]
in R   108 beasts] corsers H

PRIMUS REX

Lordes, and I leeve well maye
that child would shorten well our waye   110
that bringinge presentes to his paye,
and most is of degree.

Then goe downe to the beastes and ryde abowt.

PRIMUS REX

16 Alas, where is this starre iwent?
Our light from us awaye is glent.
Nowe wott I not where we bene lent,   115
nor whitherward lyes our waye.

SECUNDUS REX

Praye we to God with good intent,
to whome we bringe our present.
Hee will never suffer us to be shent;
that dare I bouldly saye.   120

51ᵛ   TERTIUS REX

17 It is good that we enquire
if any the waye can us lere.
Saye, [belamye] that rydes there,
tell us some tydinge.

THE MESSINGER

Syr, tell me what your will were.   125

PRIMUS REX

Can thou ought saye what place or where
a child is borne that crowne shall beare
and of the Jewes bee kynge?

109 and] *om* H   leeve well] well leve A   111 bringinge] bringen H
112 and] that B   *SD*] Descendunt et circumamblant bis et tunc ad eques H
then] then the kinges A   PRIMUS REX] *om* RBII   113 this] the A
114 from us awaye] awaie from us ARB   115 we bene lent] be we lente A,
we bene kente R   123 belamye] bellanye Hm, ballamy R   rydes] rideth B
there] heere H   124 tydinge] tydinges ABH   THE MESSINGER]
MESSINGER R, EXPLORATOR H   125 were] is A   126 ought saye] say
ought H   127 beare] weare H   128 the] *om* ARBH   bee] be the H

C 9206   M

SECUNDUS REX

18 We see the starre shine verey
    in the east in noble araye.   130
    Therfore wee come nowe this waye
    to worshippe him with wynne.

MESSINGER

Hould your peace, syrs, I you praye!
For if kinge Herode here you soe saye,
he would goe wood, by my faye,   135
and flye out of his skynne.

TERTIUS REX

19 And sythe a kinge is soe nere,
    goe wee to him in all manere.

MESSINGER

Yee may well see hee wonnys here,
a pallace in to dwell.   140
But maye hee wott withowten were
that anye is borne of more powere,
you bringe yourselves in greate dangere
such tidinges for to tell.

Here the Messinger must goe to the kinge. Minstrells here must
playe.

20 O noble kinge and worthye conqueroure,   145
    crowned in gould, sittinge on hye,
    Mahound thee save longe in honoure!
    License I require to speake to thee.
    Tidings now, my lord, I shall you tell
    that these three kinge doe shewe unto mee.   150
    From whense the binne I knowe not well;
    yonder the stond, as yee may see.

129 see] sawe ARBH   the] his H   verey] verelye AR   131 come]
comen H   MESSINGER] THE MESSENGER B, EXPLORATOR H   133 you]
can B   134 here] hard H   135 by] be A   137 sythe] seeinge R
MESSINGER] EXPLORATOR H   141 wott] witte AR   144 tidinges] tyding B,
thinges H   SD] Nuntius ibit ad Herodem H   must goe] goeth ARB
minstrells here] and the mynstrilles AR   must] om R   After SD]
MESSINGER R   145–52] om H   148 speake to] come A, come to RB
149 tidings now] now tydinges B   150 kinge] kinges ARB   shewe unto]
telle unto AR, show to B   151 knowe] woot B

PRIMUS REX

21 Syr roy, ryall and reverent,
    Deu vous gard, omnipotent.

52^r   SECUNDUS REX

    Nos summes veneus comoplent,   155
    novelis de enquire.

Staffe.

HERODES

    Bien soies venues, royes gent.
    Me detes tout vetere entent.

TERTIUS REX

    Infant querenues de grand parent,
    et roy de celi et terre.   160

HERODES

22 Syrs, avise you what you sayne!
    Such tydinges makes my harte unfayne.
    I read you take those wordes agayne
    for feare of velanye.
    There is none soe great that me dare gayne,   165
    to take my realme and to attayne
    my power, but hee shall have payne
    and punished appertlye.

23 I kinge of kinges, non soe keene;
    I soveraigne ayre, as well is seene;   170
    I tyrant that maye both take and teene
    castell, towre, and towne!

153 ryall] royall A   and] et H   154 vous] vos B   gard] gardes A,
gurdes R   155 summes] sums A, sumus H   vencus] venues H   como-
plent] complent A, coinopent H   156] noveles et enquerere A   novelis]
noviles B, novelles H   enquire] enquere R   SD] om BH   158 detes]
detez H   tout] tot BH   vetere] vesture H   159 querenues] queruns A,
querens R, queremus B, queramus H   parent] om A, paret H   160 et]
parente e A   celi] caelli H   terre] terra H   HERODES] HERODE H
161 sayne] say B   162 such] your H   163 those] thes AR   To left
of 163] Sword B   168 and] and be AR   170 well] non B

I weld this world withouten weene;
I beate all those unbuxone binne;
I drive the devills all bydeene   175
deepe in hell adowne.

24 For I am kinge of all mankynde;
    I byd, I beate, I loose, I bynde;
    I maister the moone. Take this in mynd—
    that I am most of might.   180

25 I am the greatest above degree
    that is, or was, or ever shalbe;
    the sonne yt dare not shine on me
    and I byd him goe downe.
    Noe raigne to fall, shall non be free;   185
    nor noe lord have that libertie
    that dare abyde and I byd flee,
    but I shall cracke his crowne.

26 Non farre nor neare that doth me nye—
    whoe wrathes me I shall him nye;   190
    for everye freake I dare defye
    that nyll me paye ne plaese.
    But ye be beane, I shall you beate;
    there is noe man for you shall treate.
    All for wrothe, see how I sweate!   195
    My hart is not at ease.

52ᵛ Staffe.

27 For all men may wott and see—
    both hee and you all three—
    that I am kinge of Gallilee,
    whatsoever he sayes or does.   200

Sword.

173 weld] weale H   174 those] them A   178 byd] byde A   loose]
lose AR, losse B   182 or(1)] that AR   or(2)] that A   184 and] if H
185 raigne] raine ARBH   non] nowe AR   free] freye A   189 non]
ner A, nor RBH   that doth] thad doe A   nye] noye H   190 him nye]
them nye A, hym wrye R, destroy H   192 nyll] will not RH   ne] and
R, me B   *SD*] Baculum H   197 wott and] witte and AR, wett and B,
well H   199 Gallilee] Galley R   *SD*] Staffe B, Gladius H

What the devell should this bee?
A boye, a growme of lowe degree,
should raygne above my ryalltee
and make me but a goose,

Cast up.

28 that ringes and raignes so riallye?   205
All grace and goodnes I have to give.
There is noe prince but hee shall plye
to doe my hartes ease.
But now you may both here and see
that I reconed up my rialtye.   210
I red you all be ruled by mee
and found mee for to please.

PRIMUS REX

'Vidimus stellam eius in oriente et venimus cum muneribus
adorare eum.'

29 Syr, wee see the starre appeare
in the east withouten were
in a merveilouse manere,   215
together as we cann praye.

SECUNDUS REX

Wee see never non soe cleare;
by it the waye we could lere.
But when we came to your land here
then vanished it awaye.   220

TERTIUS REX

30 By prophecye well wotten wee
that a child born should bee
to rule the people of Judee,
as was sayd many a yeare.

203 above] againste AR   *SD*] Jacc gladium H   205 riallye] royaltie H
206 give] geve ARBH   207 plye] please AR   208 my] me H
To left of 209–11] Staffe and another gowne ARB   *To right of* 209] Baculum
et toga alia H   210 I reconed] I receyved B, reconed I have H   my] *om* A
Latin] *om* A   vidimus] videmus B   stellam eius in oriente] stella in eius
moriente R, stellam eius in orient B   adorare] adoratum H   218 could]
can A   219 your] this AR   221 prophecye] prophesies H   223 to]
and H

HERODES

That is false, by my lewtee,   225
for in mauger of you all three
this realme moves all of mee;
other kinges non shall be here.

31 But sythen you speake of prophecye,
I will witt anon in hie   230
whether yee saye sooth or lye—
my clarke soone shall see.
Syr Doctor, that cheife art of clergie,
looke up thy bookes of prophecye
of Daniell, David, and Isaye,   235
and what thou seest say thou mee.

53ʳ   32 These kinges be come a farre way
to seeke a child, I hard saye,
that should be borne in this cuntraye
my kingdome to destroye.   240
Seeke eych leafe, I thee praye,
and what thou findes in good faye
tell now here, for I dare laye
that all these lordes lye.

DOCTOR

33 Nay, my lord, bee ye bould;   245
I trowe noe prophetes before would
write anythinge your hart to could
or your right to denye.
But syth your grace at this tyme would
that I the prophets declare should,   250
of Christes comminge as they have tould,
the trueth to certyfie,

HERODES] HERODE H   225 that] this A   lewtee] lewt B   226 mauger]
maungere A   227 of] on AR   228 kinges] kinge RB   non shall]
shall non ARBH   229 sythen] seinge AR, sithence B, sith H   231 saye]
speake AR   233 cheife art] arte cheifeste AR, art cheife H   234 thy]
the B   235] of . . . and H (see TNs)   236 seest say] seeiste tell A,
fyndest tell R   thou] to R, thou to B   237 come] comen H   238 hard]
harde them ARBH   242 what] that H   245 my] me B   bee ye
bould] by the bold B   246 prophetes] prophesye AR, prophett BH
247 anythinge] nothing H   249 syth] seeinge R

34 I beseech your ryall majestee
with patience of your benignitie
the trueth to here, and pardone mee   255
there sayenges to declare.

HERODES

Nay, my true clarke, that will not I
debate with thee; therfore in hye
looke well on everye prophecye.
For nothing that thou spare,   260

35 but search the trueth of Esaye,
Ezechiell, Nauum, and Jheremye,
Micheas, Abdias, and Zacharye,
of Christ what they doe saye.
Looke alsoe upon Malachye,   265
Aggeus, Oseas, and Sophonye,
Joell, Amos, and Abacuck in hye;
looke non be left awaye.

[DOCTOR]

'Non auferetur sceptrum de Juda et dux de foemore eius, donec
veniet qui mittendus est et erit ipse expectatio gentium.' Genesis,
quadragessimo nono.

36 The Holy Scripture maketh declaration
by patryarckes and prophettes of Christes nativitie,   270
when Jacob prophecied by playne demonstration,
sayde the realme of Juda and eke the regaltye
from that generation never taken should bee

254 your] *om* B   255 the trueth to here] to heare the truth H   256 sayen-
ges] sayinge RB   HERODES] HERODE H   261 Esaye] Esau A
262 Nauum] Maun A, Malichi R, Abdias Naum H   263 Micheas] Michea-
deas and A, Micheas and RH   Abdias] Abdies A, allso H   and] *om* H
Zacharye] Zachrye A, Zackeny B   265 upon] on H   266 Sophonye]
Sopheni A   267 Abacuck] Balahams A, Balackes R   DOCTOR] *om* Hm,
after Latin ARH   *Latin* Genesis quadragessimo nono] *before quotation* R
auferetur] auferitor A, auferitur R   sceptrum] secptrum A, septrum R   Juda]
Judi A   dux] dixe A, dex R   de foemore] more R   mittendus] mittendio A
gentium] gentum AR   nono] nonae et dicat Doctor A   269 Scripture]
scriptures AR   maketh] makes AB, make R   270 patryarckes] patrickes AR
Christes] Christ B   271 prophecied] prophesies H   272 Juda] Judy R
eke] *om* R   regaltye] ragalitie ARH   273 never taken should] shold never
taken H

untill hee were come that most mightye is,
sent from the Father, kinge of heavenly blys.   275

37 And now fulfilled is Jacobs prophecye;
53ᵛ   for kinge Herode that is nowe rayninge
is noe Jewe borne nor of that progenye,
but a stranger by the Romans made there kinge;
and the Jewes knowe non of ther blood descendinge   280
by succession to claime the scepter and regaltye;
wherfore Christe is nowe borne our kinge and messye.

HERODES

A bill.

38 That is false, by Mahound full of might!
That ould villard Jacob, doted for age,
shall withold by no prophecye the tytle and right   285
of Romans hye conquest which to mee in heritage
is fallen for ever, as prince of hye parentage.
If anye other kinge or messye intend it to wynne,
his head from his bodye with this sword shall I twynne.

Et dicat, 'Read one.'

DOCTOR

'Cum venerit sancta sanctorum cessabit unctio vestra.'

39 Daniell, fulfilled with heavenly grace,   290
prophecied alsoe by divine inspiration
that when he was come that of all holye was
most holiest in yearth, to take his habitation
in the wombe of a virgin, and by his blessed incarnation

274 untill] til H   hee] the AR   come] comen H   that] which BH
275 heavenly] heaven H   blys] blesse AR   279 the] *om* H   280 de-
scendinge] sendinge AR   281 regaltye] regallitie A, regally H   282 is
nowe] now is H   and] or A, and our RB   HERODES] HERODE H   SD]
om H   283 full] *om* B   284 doted] all doted H   285 by] with AR
and right] *om* A   286 hye] his H   heritage] herit A   287 fallen]
fallne to me ARB   as] as a ARBH   parentage] parage ARBH   *To left
of* 288] Sword B   288 to] for to H   289 this] this sharpe RBH   shall
I twynne] I shall twayne A, I shall twyne RH   SD] *om* AH   DOCTOR]
after Latin A   *Latin* cum] tunc A   unctio] uncio AR   vestra] vestra et
dicat A, vestra Danielis 9 H   291 alsoe] before H   292 come] comen H
that of] that A, which of H   293 most] the most H

out of Sathans band to deliver mankynd   295
whom synne originall most pitiously did bynd—

40 then both unctions, sacrifices, and rittes ceremonyall
of the ould testament with legall observation
shall utterly cease and take there end fynall
through Christes commynge, which for mans salvation 300
a newe testament should ordayne by devine operation,
offeringe himselfe in sacrafice for mankyndes offence,
which from heaven was exiled through his greate
    negligence.

HERODES

41 Fye on that dreame-reader! Such dotardes never shall,
ney noe sleepie sluggard, make my right title cease.   305
But I shall knightlye keepe yt, whatsoever shall befall,
agaynst that yonge godlinge. And if hee ones doe presse
this kingdome to clayme, or put mee to distresse,
his head of shall I hewe. Yett looke yf thou finde there
wher this boye is borne for whom these kinges
    enquire.   310

[DOCTOR]

'Et tu Bethlem quidem terra Juda nequaquam minima es in
principibus Judae. Ex te enim exiet dux qui reget populum meum
Israell.' Michei quinto et Mathei secundo.

42 Micheas, inflamed with ghostly inspiration,
prophecied that Bethlem should a child forth bringe.
Ruler of Godes people and of the Jewes nation
should hee be borne, of Israell to be kinge.

295 band to] bandes to B, band H   mankynd] all mankind H   296 origi-
nall] originallye A   most] *om* H   bynd] blynde H   299 there] the H
fynall] fyniall AR   301 should] shall H   302 offence] offences B
HERODES] HERODE H   *To left of* 304] Cast downe the sword B   304 dotar-
des] doctors B   305 sleepie] sleeping H   sluggard] sloparde R
306 whatsoever] whatever R   shall] *om* ARBH   307 godlinge] gedling H
ones] onste A   presse] prease H   310 kinges] knightes H   DOCTOR]
om Hm, *after Latin* R   *Latin*] *om* A   tu] in R   Bethlem] Bethelem R,
Bethleem H   quidem terra Juda] Juda quidem terra H   Judae] Juda RH,
Juda quia B   enim exiet] enim exie R, exiet enim B   reget] *om* R
311 inflamed] inspired A   312 prophecied] prophescieth AR   Bethlem]
Bethelem R, Beathlem B   should a child forth] a childe fourth AR, a child
forth should B, shold a prince furth H

Alsoe Esaye and Jheremye, full vertuous of beinge,   315
with divers others mo fulfilled with grace,
of Christes comminge prophecied while they were livinge.

54ʳ   DOCTOR

'Ambulabunt gentes in lumine tuo et reges in splendore ortus tui.'
Esaui sexagessimo.

43 Esawe, to whom the spirit of prophecye
    was singulerly given through the Holy Ghost,
    in his tyme prophicied that kinges witterlye   320
    and folkes of strange natyons and from sundrye coasts—
    that princes death to magnifie, which of might is
        moste—
    should walke in great light; and brightnes should apere,
    as did unto these kinges in a bright starre shininge clere.

HERODES

'Effundam super parvulum istum furorem meum et super con-
silium juvenum, disperdam parvulos de fores, et juvenes in plateis
morientur gladio meo.'

44 Alas, what presumption should move that pevish page 325
    or any elvish godlinge to take from me my crowne?

Cast downe the sword.

But, by Mahound, that boye for all his greate outrage
shall die under my hand, that elfe and vile [congion].

315 beinge] lyving BH   316 with] and B   divers] many H   others]
other ABH   317 Christes comminge] Christ B   while] when A   they]
the AR, ther BH   were livinge] livinge was ARBH   DOCTOR] om ARB
Latin Esaui] Esau A, Essays R, Esaias B   318 Esawe] Esay BH   to] unto
ARBH   320 his] this AR   that kinges] this kinge AR   321 folkes]
folcke AR   strange] strang B   natyons] nacion AB   and] om H   from]
om A   sundrye coasts] sundrye coste A, sundrye coast R, many a sondry coast H
322 death] birth ARBH   323 should(2)] om A   324 as] s A   unto]
to A   bright] om A   HERODES] after Latin A, HERODE cum gladio H
Latin] om R   parvulum] parmulum A   istum] om H   furorem] fuorem A
disperdam] et disperdam B   fores] fortes A, foris H   juvenes] javenes A
plateis] platies A   326 godlinge] gedling H   from me] awaye R
SD] to left of HERODES AR, to left of 325–6 B, om H   327 greate] om A
328 congion] coninge Hm, connyon R, conge B

And all his pertakers I shall slea and beate downe,
and both of him and his finall distruction make.   330
Such vengeance and eke crueltye on them all will I take

45 that non such a slaughter was seene or hard before,
syth Athalia here raigned, that fell and furiouse queene,
that made slea all men children that of kinges blood
   were
when her soone was dead. So for to wreake my teene   335
I shall hewe that harlott with my bright brond so keene
into peeces smale. Yett looke and search agayne
if these kinges shall him finde and his presence attayne.

DOCTOR

'Reges Tharsis et Insule munera offerent; reges Arabum et Saba
dona adducent.' [Psalmo] septuagesimo primo.

46 David, of all prophettes called most prepotent,
   prophecied that kinges of Tharsis and Arabye   340
   with misticall giftes shall come and presente
   that lord and prince, that kinge and hye messye,
   of Abrahams seede descendinge lineallye—
   which kinges with great treasure here in presence,
   to seeke him as soverraigne and lawde his
      magnificence.   345

47 My lord, by prophecie is proved you beforne
   that in Bethlem should bee borne
   a child to save that was forlorne
   and rule all Israell.

330 of] *om* A   finall] *om* A, fyniall R, a finall H   distruction] distructions R
331 eke] *om* A, ilke H   all] *om* B   will I] I will A   332 before] beforne H
333 syth] since B   Athalia] Athalye A   334 that(1)] which ARBH   were]
were borne H   335 soone] sonne AR   for] *om* H   336 that] that
yong BH   brond so keene] sorde A, sworde soe keene R   337 yett] yea A
Latin Tharsis] Thrasis AR   Insule] Iasule A, Insula BH   munera] mnera H
offerent] offerunt B   Arabum] Arabi H   psalmo] phalmo Hm   septuagesimo primo] sextuagessimo primo R, 70 B   339 prepotent] propotent A
340 of] from H   Tharsis] Thrasis A   Arabye] Arabia AR, Aralia B
341 shall] shoulde ARB   342 and prince] *om* AH, that prince RB
343 descendinge] descendid AH   344 treasure] treasure both H
presence] presentes R   345] *om* AR   as] as a H   346 my] *om* H
beforne] before A   347 Bethlem] Bethelem R, Beathlem B   should]
shall H   348 child] clylde H

HERODES

Breake a sword.

> By cockes sowle, thou art forsworne!   350
> Have donne! Those bookes were rent and torne.
> For hee shalbe noe kinge in crowne,
> but I fullye in my weale.

54ᵛ 48 And maugard David, that sheppard with his slinge,
    Esaye, Jheremye, with all there osspringe,   355
    here gett noe other messye or kynge
    from my right title to expell.

Cast up.

    49 What a devill is this to saye:
      that I should be disproved and put awaye—
      syth my right is soe verey—   360
      for a boyes boast?
      This realme is myne and shalbe aye,
      manfullye maynteane yt while I may,
      though hee bringe with him todaye
      the devill and all his hoaste.   365

Cast up.

    50 But goes you forth, you kinges three,
      and enquire if it soe bee.
      But algates come agayne by mee,
      for you I thinke to feede.
      And if hee bee of such degree,   370
      him will I honour as donne yee,
      as falles for his dignitie
      in word, thought, and deede.

PRIMUS REX

    51 By your leave, syr, and have good daye,
      tyll we come agayne this waye.   375

HERODES] HERODE H   SD] *om* H   351 those] these ARH   rent and torne] all totorne H   353 weale] wele A   354 maugard] maugere AH, maungere R   355 with] and R   osspringe] ofspringe AR, offpring H   356 noe] non RH   or] nor ARBH   357 to] me to R   expell] exspresse R   *SD*] *om* H   358 this] that R   360 syth] seinge AR   363 maynteane yt] manteyne R, to mainteyne it BH   I] that I H   *SD*] Staffe and another gowne B, Jacct gladium H   366 goes you] goe A   368 but] and B   by] to AR   371 donne] doe ARB   374 your] *om* ARBH   daye] aye B

SECUNDUS REX

Syr, as sonne as ever wee maye;
and as we seene, soe shall wee saye.

TERTIUS REX

And of his riches and his araye
from you wee shall not layne.

HERODES

Farewell, lordes, in good faye;   380
but hye you fast agayne.

The boye and pigge when they kinges are gonne.

52 Owt, alas, what the divell is this?
    For shame almost I fare amysse
    for was I never soe woe, iwisse;
    for wrath I am nere wood.   385
    For everye man may well say thus—
    that I maynteane my realme amysse,
    to lett a boye inherite my blys
    that never was of my blood.

Staffe.

53 But yett the lasse it greivouse mee   390
    that I lett goe those kinges three;
    for I shall knowe nowe which is hee
    when the commen agayne.
    Then will they tell mee in what contrey
    that this boye then borne is hee;   395
    then shalbe taken both they and hee,
    and that will make mee fayne.

55ʳ Sword.

377 as] *om* R   378 and(2)] and of AR   379 layne] leane AR   HERODES]
HERODE H   381 but] and H   *SD*] *om* B, Puer et nefrens cum reges
discescerunt H   they] the AR   385 for] of R   386 well say] say
well H   thus] this ARH   388 blys] blesse AR   *SD*] *om* B, Baculum H
390 greivouse] greves ARH, greveth B   391 those] these ARH
393 commen] come H   394 mee] *om* H   395 then] *om* ARBH
396 taken] tacke A   both] *om* R   they and hee] he and they H   *SD*] *to left
of* 401 AR, *om* H

54 By cockes sowle, come they agayne
all three traytors shall bee slayne,
and that ylke swedlinge swayne—   400
I shall choppe of his head.
Godes grace shall them not gayne,
nor noe prophecye save them from payne.
That rocked rybauld, and I may rayne,
rufully shalbe his reade.   405

55 By Mahound full of mightes,
tomorrowe I will send after my knightes
to rule my realme and my rightes
agaynst this boyes boaste,
and rayse the contrye one everye syde,   410
all that ever may goe or ryde.
Soe shall this boye loose his pryde,
for all his greatest hoste.

56 This boye doth mee soe greatly anoye
that I wax dull and pure drye.   415
Have done and fill the wyne in hye;
I dye but I have drinke!
Fill fast and lett the cuppes flye,
and goe wee heathen hastelye;
for I must ordeyne curiouslye   420
agaynst these kynges comminge.

Finis

400 ylke] same A   swedlinge] swelling B   401 choppe] swap H
402 them] the AR   not] never H   403 nor] no R   save them from
payne] make them feyne R   404 rybauld] reball A, ryball R   405 shalbe
his] shall he R   406 mightes] might AR   407 I will] will I H
knightes] knighte R   408 rightes] right R   409 this] ny B   boaste]
bostes B   411 all] and all R   412 loose] lose AR, losse B   413 greatest
hoste] greateste boste AR, great host BH   *To left of* 414] Caste up ARB
414 boye] boste ARBH   greatly] greate ARBH   anoye] nye R   415 dull]
cleane dulle A   pure] cleane AR   418 cuppes] cup H   419] *om* A
heathen] hense R   420 curiouslye] quintely H

PLAY IX

THE MERRCERS PLAYE

Pagina Nona: De Oblatione Trium Regum

PRIMUS REX

1 Myghtie God and moste of mayne,
  to honour thee wee may bee fayne:
  the starre I see yt common agayne
  that was owt of our sight.

SECUNDUS REX

  Thy lordshippe to us thou ney layne,   5
  that for mankynde would suffer payne.
  Thou send us grace, if thou be gayne,
  to come to thee tonight.

TERTIUS REX

2 A, lord, honored be thou aye,
  for nowe we shall knowe well the waye.   10
  I will followe yt in good faye,
  my forward to fullfill.

[PRIMUS REX]

  I hope withowt dreade todaye
  to see that childe and his araye.
  But methinkes, lordes, by my fayc,   15
  the starre yt standeth still.

SECUNDUS REX

3 That is a signe wee be neare,
  but high hall see I non here.
  To a child of such powere
  this howsinge standeth lowe.   20

Guild-ascription playe] *om* BH   *Play-heading* de] de presentacione sive
ARB   trium] tercium AR   regum] regum Primus Rex A, regnum et dicat R
1 and] *om* AR   3 yt] is BH   common] come AR   5 layne] leane R
7 thou(1)] now R   10 well] *om* R   PRIMUS REX] *om* Hm   14 and]
in A   15 my] me B

TERTIUS REX

Nowe wott I well, withouten were,
without prydc hee will apere
to make men meeke, in such manere
an example us to shewe.

PRIMUS REX

4 The starre yonder over the stable is.   25
I wotte wee be not gonne amys,
for yt hath sterred ever or this
and nowe there yt is glent.

SECUNDUS REX

I wotte hee wonnes here, iwysse,
and this simple house is his.   30
Ordeyne we nowe that kinge of blys
appertly our present.

56ʳ   ### TERTIUS REX

5 What present best will for him fall
cast we here amongest us all;
for though hee lye in an oxe stall,   35
his might is never the lesse.

PRIMUS REX

'Kinge of Jewes' wee shall him call;
therfore of mee have hee shall—
that am his subjecte and his thrall—
gould, or I passe.   40

6 For in our land is the manere
to approache noe kinge neare
but dayntye giftes rich and deare
after his dignitie.
And for a kinge gould cleane and cleare   45
is moste commendable. Therfore nowe here
hee shall have that of mee.

21 wott I well] well I wotte ARBH   PRIMUS] om A   27 sterred] storred A,
sturreth R   31 blys] blesse AR   34 we] us H   amongest] betwixt H
35 an] one R   45 cleane] fayer AR   After 46] to releeve him in this
manere H

7 Alsoe yt seemes by this place
  that little treasure his mother hasse.
  Therfore to helpe hir in this case   50
  gould shall be my present.

SECUNDUS REX

And I will offer through Godes grace
incense that noble savoure hasse.
Stynke of the stable yt shall wast,
theras they be lent.   55

TERTIUS REX

8 And myrre is best my offeringe to bee:
  to anoynte him, as thinkes mee,
  the childes members—head and knee,
  and other lymmes all.
  Thus shall we honour him all three   60
  with thinges that falles to his degree,
  towchinge manhoode and deitie.
  These giftes will well befall.

PRIMUS REX

9 You saye well, lordes, witterlye.
  As towchinge gould, prove maye I,   65
  yt should be given him dewlye
  because of temporalitye.
  Syth hee shall be kinge most mightye,
  trybute hee must have trulye;
  and gould therfore witterlye   70
  is beste, as thinkes me.

56ᵛ   ### SECUNDUS REX

10 And syth hee hath in him godhead,
  methinkes best—as eate I bread—
  incense to give him through my reade
  in name of sacrifice,   75

48 this] his B   50 to] *om* AR   53 noble] a noble R   hasse] mase
ARBH   54 stynke] stinch B, stench H   57 thinkes] thinketh B
61 falles] falle A   to] for ABH   62 and] and his AR   deitie] dieatie A,
dietie R   65 prove] see AR   66 dewlye] trulie B   67 temporalitye]
pacialitie A, parcialitie R, temporaltye H   68 syth] seinge AR
71 thinkes] thinketh B   73 best] *om* AR

for that may noe waye be lead.
Syth hee of Holy Church is head,
more dewe giftes, yf I should be dead,
I cannot devise.

TERTIUS REX

11 You saye full well, syrs, both two.   80
And myrre is good, methinkes alsoe.
Syth hee for man will suffer woo
and dye on roode—tree,
myrre—that puttes sinne him fro
and saves man from rowtinge woo;   85
for yt is best to balme him thoo,
that shall hee have of mee.

PRIMUS REX

12 By these giftes three of good araye
three thinges understand I maye:
a kinges powere, sooth to saye,   90
by gould here in my hand;
and for his godhead lastlye aye
incense wee must give him todaye;
and bodely death alsoe in good faye
by myrre I understande.   95

SECUNDUS REX

13 Gould love alsoe may signifye,
for yt men given not commonlye
but these they loven hartfullye—
this chyld as wee donne all;
and incense tokeneth, leeve I,   100
orysons and prayers done devoutlye;
myrre death that man hath bodelye.
And all these him shall fall.

---

76 may] waye B   77 syth] seinge AR   80 syrs both] bouth sires ARB
you sirrs H   84 sinne him] hym synne AR   85 rowtinge] rottinge
ARH   86 him] his A   92 lastlye] lasteth ARBH   93 him] om H
98 these] thoes AR, ther BH   hartfullye] hartelye AR   100 and] an A
101 done] om AR   103 him] thinges A

TERTIUS REX

14 By gould that wee to bringe are bowne,
that rychest mettall of renowne, 105
skyllfullye understand wee mon
most pretiouse godhead;
and incense may well be sayd
a roote of great devotyon;
by myrre, that waves corruptyon, 110
cleane flesh both quicke and dead.

57ʳ 15 And sycerlye this knowen wee:
hee wantes non of these three;
for full godhead in him hasse hee,
as gould maye signifie. 115
And sowle devout in him must bee
to come owt of the Trynitie;
and cleane flesh we hopen to see
in him full hastelye.

PRIMUS REX

16 Nowc we have proved yt here 120
these giftes to him bee most deare,
goe wee forth in good manere
and make we our present.

SECUNDUS REX

The starre yt shines fayre and cleare
over this stable aye entyre. 125
Here is his wonninge withowten were,
and herein is hee lent.

TERTIUS REX

17 A fayre mayden yonder I see,
an ould man sittinge at hir knee,
a child alsoe; as thinkes mee, 130
three persons therin are.

104 bowne] bounde ARB   105 that] the AB   106 mon] monc AR
116 devout in him] in him devoute R   118 hopen] happen AR   121 to
him bee] be to hym AR   124 yt] that B   shines] shineth B   fayre] both
fayre B   127 is hee] he is H   *After* 127] foure maidens sirres yonder I
see B   128 fayre] *om* B   yonder] sirs yender R, sirres yonger B, sirres
yonder H   130 thinkes] thinketh B   131 are] arne H

PRIMUS REX

I saye in certayne this is hee
that we have sought in farre countree.
Therfore now with all honestye
honour I will that baron.   135

Tunc appariet sciatuum cum auro.

PRIMUS REX

18 Hayle be thou, lord, Christe and messie,
    that from God art common kindly,
    mankynd of bale for to forbye
    and into blys bringe.
    We knowe well by prophecye—   140
    of Moyses, Davyd, and Esaye,
    and Balaam of our auncetrye—
    of Jewes thou shalt bee kinge.

19 Therfore, as falleth for thy crowne,
    gould I have here readye bowne   145
    to honour thee with greate renowne
    after thy royaltye.
    Take here, lord, my intentyon
    that I doe with devotyon,
    and give mee here thy benesoun   150
    ere that I goe from thee.

57ᵛ   SECUNDUS REX

20 Hayle be Christe Emanuell!
    Thou common art for mans heale
    and for to wynne agayne that wayle
    that Adam put awaye.   155
    Prophets of thee every one saye,
    both Esaye and Ezechiell;
    and Abraham might not conceale
    the sooth of thee to saye.

132 saye] saide A   this] that this AR   133 in farre] from AR, from our
BH   135 honour] to honour A   I will] will I H   baron] barne H
SD appariet] aperiet H   sciatuum] sciathum H   auro] auro et dicat R
PRIMUS REX] om B   136 lord] om A   137 common] come H   kindly]
kinely B   138 forbye] buy H   148 here lord] lord here H   152 be]
be thou RH   154 wayle] weale R   156 saye] said B, fayle H
157 Esaye] Esau A   159 sooth] truth A

21 Bushoppe I wotte thou must bee;   160
   therfore now, as thinkes mee,
   incense will fall best for thee;
   and that nowe here I bringe
   in tokninge of thy dignitie
   and that office of spiritualtye.   165
   Receave here, lord, at mee
   devoutly my offeringe.

TERTIUS REX

22 Hayle, conquerour of all mankynd!
   To doe mercye thou hasse mynde,
   the devills band to unbynd   170
   and releive all thyne.
   A full fayre waye thou can fynd
   to haunce us and put him behind,
   though thy Passyon to unbynd
   thy people that be in pyne;   175

23 for thou shalt mend us throgh thy might,
   dye and ryse the thyrd night,
   to recover agayne our right
   and breake the devills bande.
   Myrre to thee here have I dight   180
   to balme thy bodye fayre and bright.
   Receive my present, sweete wight,
   and blesse mee with thy hand.

MARIA

24 You royall kinges in rych araye,
   the high Father of heavon I praye   185

161 thinkes] thinketh B   165 spiritualtye] spirialitie AR   166 here
lord] lorde heare ARBH   at] of AR   172–5] om B   174 though]
through ARH   unbynd] unbyde R   175 pyne] payne A   180 have]
om H   After 183] in AR

GOD

You be welckome, kinges three,
unto my mother and to me,
and into the land of Judye.
And heare I geve you my blessinge. 4

(GOD) DEUS R   3 and] om R   4 blessinge] beneson R)

to yeeld you your good deede todaye,
for his micle might;
and give you will now and alwaye
to yerne the liefe that lasteth aye,
and never to fall out of the faye   190
that in your hartes is pight.

58ʳ   25 And leeves, lordes, withouten were,
that to my sonne you shall be deare,
that him todaye hath honored here
and me alsoe for his sake.   195
When tyme is come entyre
to prove his strenght and his powere,
to him you shall bee leeffe and deare—
that darre I undertake.

JOSEPHE

26 You kynges all comely of kynd,   200
full faythfully you shall yt fynd—
this menskie that God will have in mynd
and quyte you well your meede.
And leeves well: of noe mans strynde
ys hee, not gotten by leefe of kynde;   205
that soe beleevon are full blynde,
for I knowe yt in deede.

27 This mayden was betaken mee
when I had lost my jollitie,
and fayled might and postie   210
sinne for to assaye.
But for God would in chastitie
that we should together bee,
keeper of her virginitie
I have binne manye a daye.   215

186 yeeld] eylde A   187 his] this B   190 fall] faylle B   192 leeves]
leve AR   lordes] lorde A   withouten] with our A, withowt BH
196 when] when the H   197 his(2)] *om* A   201 full faythfully] faith-
full A, ful faythfull R   202 this menskie] these guyftes R, this goodnes B,
this menske H   that] *om* B   204–7] *om* R   204 strynde] strynte A
205 kynde] lynde H   206 beleevon] beleeveth B   208 mayden]
mayde RH

28 Therfore I wott, forsooth iwys,
   cleane mayden that shee ys
   and with man did never amysse;
   and therof be you bould.
   But of the Holye Ghost this ys   220
   for to bringe mankynde to blys.
   And this child is verey his;
   soe Gabriell me tould.

ANGELUS

29 I warne you comely kynges three,
   my lord would you not spilled bee.   225
   Therfore hee sendes you word by mee
   to torne another waye.
   Herodes felowshippe you shall flee;
   for you, harme ordayne hasse hee.
   Therfore goes not through his countree,   230
   ne the gate you come todaye.

58ᵛ   PRIMUS REX

30 A, high lord that wee honour here,
   that warnes us in thys manere—
   elles had we wend without were
   to him that would us spill.   235

SECUNDUS REX

Yea, lord, as thou can us lere,
we will doe to our powere.

TERTIUS REX

Goe we hethen all in fere,
and his byddinge fullfill.

220 ys] this A   221 blys] blesse AR   224 kynges] knightes B
225 you not] not B, not you H   226 sendes] sende ARH, sent B
228 Herodes] lordes B   229 you] your ARB   ordayne] ordaynde ARBH
231 come] came ARB   234 without] withouten AR   236 lere] loare H
238 hethen] hense A, hense then R

PRIMUS REX

31 Farewell, syr Jasper, brother, to you,   240
    kinge of Tharsis most worthye.
    Farewell, syr Balthasar; to you I bowe.
    I thanke you of your companye.
    Hee that made us to meete on playne
    and offered to Marye in her jesayne,   245
    send us saffe and sound agayne
    to the land we came froo.

SECUNDUS REX

32 You kinges, I saye you verament:
    syth God of his grace you hyther sent,
    wee will doe his commandement   250
    whatsoever may befall.
    Therfore stand we not in doubt
    for to walke our land about,
    and of his byrth that wee maye moote
    both to great and smale.   255

TERTIUS REX

33 Farewell, syr kynges, both in fere;
    I thanke you both of your good chere.
    But yett my witt in a were
    lest Herode make us some trayne.
    Hee that shoope both sea and sand,   260
    send us saffe into our land.
    Kynges to, give me your hand;
    farewell and have good daye!

Finis

To left of SH] Melchior nomine B   241 Tharsis] Thrasis A   worthye]
worthyly R   242 Balthasar] Balcsare A, bachelere R   244 to] *om* H
245 offered] offer H   247 we] that we ARBH   248 you] *om* AR
249 syth] seinge A   you] us ARBH   251 may] *om* ARBH   253 land]
landes BH   254 moote] talke AR   258 in] is in ARBH   259 trayne]
trame B   260 shoope both] shaped A, made bouth R   262 to] two
ARBH

PLAY X

THE GOULDSMYTHES PLAYE

Pagina Decima: De Occisione Innocensium ex Heredis
Tirannica Persuasione

HERODES

1 Princes, prelates of price,
    barronnes in blamner and byse,
    beware of mee, all that binne wise,
    that weldes all at my will.
    Saye noe man anythinge is his   5
    but onlye at my devyce;
    for all this world lyes
    to spare and eke to spill.

2 My subjectes all that here bine sett—
    barrones, burges, and barronett—   10
    bees bayne to mee, or you is lett,
    and at my biddinge bee.
    For leeves all this withouten lett,
    that I will doe as I have hett,
    marye that mysbegotten maremasett   15
    that thinkes to marre mee.

3 And those false traytours that mee beheight
    to have commen agayne this same nighte,
    by another way have taken ther flight;
    this waye darst the not take.   20
    Therfore that boye, by God almight,
    shall be slayne soone in your sight,
    and—though it be agaynst the right—
    a thousand for his sake.

Guild-ascription playe] and Massons plaie A, *om* BH   *Play-heading* ex]
et A   Heredis] Herodies A, Herodes R   tirannica] tioanica A   persuasionc]
perswacione et diat A   HERODES] HEROD B, HERODE H   1 prelates]
plelates A   2 blamner] balmer A, baunner B   3 mee] one R   5 man]
man that R   7 lyes] under me lies BH   11 is lett] I beate A, Ile
beate R   13 withouten] without RBH   15 marye] mare B, mar H
mysbegotten] begotten B   maremasett] marsmosette A, marmosett RBH
17 those] these AR   18 commen] come H   this] the AR   20 darst]
durste ARBH   22 your sight] height R   23 agaynst] againe BH

4 Alas, what purpose had that page   25
    that is soe yonge and tender of age,
    that would bereave my heritage,
    that am so micle of might?
    Forsooth that shrewe was wondrouse sage
    agaynst me anye warre to wage!   30
    That recked rybauld for all his rage
    shall not reve mee my right.

5 But syth it may noe other bee
    but these kinges are gone from me,
    and that shrewe would have my soveraintye,   35
    I thinke to put him agayne:
    all the knave-children in this contree
    shall by his guile, soe mote I thee.
    Because I knowe not which is hee,
    all for his sake shalbe slayne.   40

59ᵛ   6 How, prettye Pratte, my messingere,
    come hither to me withouten weare!
    For thou must goe with hastye bere
    into Judee this daye
    after my doughtie and comely knightes,   45
    and bydd them hye with all there myghtes
    and that the lett for noe feightes.
    Bringe them withouten delaye.

PRECO

7 Yes, my lord of great renowne,
    to doe your hest I am bowne,   50
    lightly to leape over dale and downe
    and speede if I were there.
    Farewell, my lord in majestee,
    for on my jorney I will hye me.

26 soe] *om* R   28 micle] mylde AR, much B   30 agaynst] againe H
31 recked] ricked A, rocked BH   rybauld] reballe A   33 noe] non ARH
34 but] that BH   35–8] *om* R   36 agayne] downe A   37 knave]
knaves ABH   38 guile] guilt BH   mote] mate A   40 all] and B
41 prettye] petty H   42 withouten] without RB   43 bere] leere B
47 that] *om* A   feightes] freight B   48 them] them all AR   withouten]
without ARBH   PRECO] DOCTOR H   49 great] hie AR   50 hest]
heistes ARBH   51 and] or H   52 if] and B   54] and ever to dwell
in feare R   I will] will I B

HERODE

Now mightie Mahound be with thee,   55
and ever to dwell in feare.

PRECO

8 How, awake out of your sleepe,
syr Grymball and syr Lancherdeepe!
And to me you take good keepe,
for hether I am send;   60
my lord, kinge Herode, begines to sowne
for a shrewe would have his crowne
and thus bereave him of his renowne,
and soone would have him shend.

PRIMUS MILES

9 Welcome, messenger, that art soe gent.   65
This tydinges which my lord hath sent
they be welcome veryment.
With thee nowe will I wend.

SECUNDUS MILES

Messinger, I will in good faye
wend with you this ylke waye   70
to here what my lord will saye,
of this matter to make an end.

PRECO

10 Hayle, comly kynge sittinge on hye!
Here bynne thy knightes common to thee
that be men of greate degree   75
to here of your talent.

HERODE] HERODES R   56] and well that thou maye speede R   dwell] be A
58 Grymball] Grymbalde ARH   Lancherdeepe] Lanclerdepe A, Launclet-
deepe R   60 send] sente ARB   61 sowne] swaine AR, stonne B,
swone H   63 thus] this A   renowne] crowne R   64 shend] shente
RB   66 this] thes A, these RBH   70 ylke] same AR   waye] daie
ARBH   73 on hye] in see ARBH   74 thy] these AR

HEROD

Messingere, for thy good deede
right well shall I quite thy meede:
have here of mee to doe thee speede
right a gaye garmente.   80

PRECO

11 Grantmercye, lord regent;
well am I pleased to myne intent.
Mightye Mahound that I have ment
keepe you in this steede!

PRIMUS MILES

12 Sir Lancherdeepe, what saye ye?   85
This is the fayrest king that ever I see.

SECUNDUS MILES

This daye under the sunne shininge
is there non soe seemely a kinge.

PRIMUS MILES

13 Hayle, comely kinge crowned in gould!
Eche kinge and [kesar] kennes not your bett.   90
If anye weare that with your grace feight would,
such strokes for your sake sore should be sett.

SECUNDUS MILES

14 Yf him wee may take or gett,
the devill ought him debt;
and soe hee shalbe quitt   95
such maystryes for to make.

HEROD] HERODES AR   79 thee] thie B   81 grant] graund H   82 to]
and B   84 this] his B   steede] steade A, stidd B, tyde H   PRIMUS
MILES] HERODE B   85 Lancherdeepe] Lansclerdepe A, Launclerdeepe R
90 eche] eck B   kesar] keason HmR, keison A, keson B   kennes] bendes A
not] at AR   bett] becke AR, lett B   91] if any with your worship
were which fight wold H   grace] worship B   92 sore] full sore RBH
should be] shalbe AH, shall I R   93 him wee] we hym H   95 quitt]
quite B

HERODE

15 Welcome, our knightes that be so gent.
   Nowe will we tell you our intent,
   what is the cause we for you sent
   soe soone and hastelye.   100
   Yesterdaye to this cittie
   when wee weare in our royaltye,
   there came to us kinges three
   and tould us there intent

16 to seeke a child that borne should bee,   105
   that was sayd by prophecye
   that should be kinge of Judee
   and manye another land.
   We gave them leave to search and see
   and come agayne to this cittie;   110
   and if hee weare of such degree,
   we would not him withstand.

17 But and they had commen agayne,
   all three traytours should have binne slayne,
   and alsoe that lyther swayne—   115
   and all for his sake.

60ᵛ   Out, alas, what may this bee?
   For I knowe not which is hee,
   therfore all knave-children in this contree,
   on them shall fall the wreake.   120

18 For wee knowe not that child well,
   though wee therfore should goe to hell,
   all the children of Israell
   wee deeme them to be slayne.
   Counselour, what is thy reade?   125

DOCTOR

   Deeme them, lord, for to be dead;
   for that is best, as eate I bread,
   to catch that lyther swayne.

HERODE] HERODES AR   97 knightes] knight B   gent] good B   98 nowe]
no B   103 kinges] knightes B   107 that] om B   108 and] and of A
114 have] a R   119 knave] knaves ARBH   children] childer H
contree] cittie AB   120 wreake] wracke A, wreck B   123 children]
childer H   124 wee] I R   128 catch] chatch B   lyther] litter A

19 Command your knightes anon to hye,
  to goe to the land of Gallile 130
  and into the land of Judye,
  to slaye all that they may fynd.

HERODE

That was well sayd, my counselour.
But yett I burne as doth the fire—
what for wroth, what for yre— 135
tyll this be brought to end.

20 Therfore, my knightes good and keene,
  have done belyve; goe wreake my teene.
  Goe slaye that shrewe; lett yt be seene
  and you be men of mayne. 140
  Preeves manfully what they binne,
  that non awaye from you fleene.
  Dryve downe the dyrtie-arses all bydeene,
  and soone that there were slayne!

21 So shall I keepe that vyle [congeon] 145
  that this would reave mee of my crowne.
  Therfore, my batchleres, make you bowne
  and found to save my righte.
  You must hye you out of this towne
  to Bethlem as fast as you mon. 150
  All knave-children, by my crowne,
  you must sley this nighte.

PRIMUS MILES

22 Alas, lord and kinge of blys,
  send you after us for this?
  A villanye yt weare, iwys, 155
  for my fellowe and mee

129 your] you B to] in ARBH 131 Judye] Judei B HERODE]
HERODES AR 133 was] is A 135 yre] fier B 138 have] hase BH
done] downe B 140 and] yf B men] mene B mayne] mighte A
141 binne] bene AR 142 non] nowe AR fleene] have fleeyen R
143 the] ther AR all] *om* AR 144 there] the A, they RBH
145 congeon] commen Hm, connion A, conine B, conioyne H 146 this]
thus ARBH 150 Bethlem] Bethelem R mon] mone A, cane R
151 knave] knaves ARBH 152 nighte] mighte A 153 blys] blesse AR
154 send] sent R

to sley a shitten-arsed shrowe;
a ladd his head [mightc] of hewe.
For rybbottes are not in this rowe,
but knightes of great degree.   160

SECUNDUS MILES

23 My leeffe lord of greate renowne,
we shall wreake you yf wee mon.
Whether hee be knight or champion
stiffer than ever Sampson was,
sickerly I shall dryve them downe.   165
But for to kyll such a conjoyne
mee shames sore, by saynct Mahound,
to goe in any place.

HERODE

24 Nay, nay, it is neyther on nor two
that you shall sley, as mott I goo,   170
but a thousand and yett moo;
takes this in your mynd.
Because I knowe not which this shrewe ys,
therfore, lest you of him mys,
you must slaye, forsooth iwys,   175
all that you may fynd.

25 You shall walke farre and neere
into Bcthlem. Spare for no beere
all knave-children within two yeere
and on daye ould.   180
Slea them downe both on and all.
Soe shall you meete with that stall
that would my kingdome clayme and call,
and my welth alsoe welde.

158 ladd] luddie B   his head mighte] his head migh Hm, head might B, might
his head H   of hewe] ihewe AR   159 rybbottes] riballes A, rybbattes R
160 knightes] kinges A   grcat] good H   162 wreake] wreckon B   you] us
AR   yf] as A   mon] mone ARB   163 knight] kinge AR   164 stiffer]
tiffer B   167 shames sore] seemes more B   saynct] om AR   Mahound]
Mahone B, Mahowne H   168 in] into H   HERODE] HERODES R
169 nay(2)] ne A   nor] or H   173 which] with H   this shrewe] that
shrewe ABH, he R   178 Bethlem] Bethelem R   179 knave] knaves
ARBH   yeere] years H   180 daye] daies AR   181 both] om A

PRIMUS MILES

26 Hit shalbe donne, lord, in hye;   185
shall non be lefte witterlye.
We shall goe search by and by
in Bethlem all about,
and wreake your teene full tenderly,
leave non unslayne syckerly.   190
Soe shall we soone that shrewe distroye,
and keepe him in the rowte.

Tunc ibunt milites simul.

27 But lookes you rich you to aray;
to Bethlem, that borrowe, I am bowne.
With this speare I thinke to assaye   195
to kyll manye a smale congeon.
If anye blacke-lypped boyes be in my waye,
they shall rewe yt, by Mahound,
though all they world would saye nay,
I myselfe shall dinge them all downe.   200

61ᵛ   28 If you will wytt what I height,
my name is syr Waradrake the knight.
Agaynst me dare no man fight,
my dintes they so dreade.

29 But fayne would I feight my fill,   205
as fayne as facoune would flye,
my lord to wreake at his will
and make those dogges to dye.
These congeons in there clowtes I will kill
and stowtly with strokes them destroye.   210
Shall never on skape by my will;
all babbes for that boye, full sore shall they bye.

186 lefte] lest B   188 Bethlem] Bethelem R, Beathlem B   190 non]
not B   192 keepe] kill A   the] that A   193 but lookes you] knowes
AR, buskes ye B, rewkes H   to] be A   aray] raye AR   194 Bethlem]
Bethelem RB   borrowe] barro A, borough H   195 speare] spart H
197–208] om AR   197 blacke] blab BH   198 yt] that B   by] by
mightie BH   Mahound] Mahowne H   199 they] the H   200 I] om B
all] om B   201 wytt] wight B, wot H   204 dintes] dentes H   208 to]
for to H   209 there] the A   212 babbes] babes ARBH   they bye]
bye A, rew R, die B

30 Shall never non overpasse
   of two yeres age and lesse;
   and this boy that kinge crowned was—   215
   shall non skape bout [scathe].

SECUNDUS MILES

31 And I alsoe, without boaste—
   though the kinge of Scottes and all his hoste
   were here—I sett by there boaste,
   to dryve them downe bydeene.   220
   I slewe ten thousand upon a daye
   of kempes in there best araye;
   there was not on escaped awaye,
   my sword yt was so keene.

32 Therfore to me you take good keepe;   225
   my name is syr Grymbald Lancherdeepe.
   They that mee teene I laye to sleepe
   on evirych a syde.
   I slewe of kempes, I understand,
   more then an hundreth thousand.   230
   Both on water and on land
   no man dare mee abyde.

33 Through Bethlem I will springe,
   for I must nowe at your byddinge;
   right all downe shall I dinge   235
   these laddes everychone.
   And then that false geldinge
   that borne was soe yonge,
   hee shall for nothinge
   away from us gonne.   240

213 non] one R   214 age] old B   216 non] not ARBH   bout] without ARH, withouten B   scathe] scatche Hm, searche AR   217–24] om AR
219 by] not by BH   boaste] best H   225–8] om R   225 you] om A
226 Grymbald] om A, Grimbold B, Grymball H   Lancherdeepe] Lanchler-
depe A   227 teene] tynne B, teenen H   228 evirych] everye iche AB
a] om B   229–32] om AR   233 Bethlem] Bethelem RB, Bedleem H
will] must H   234 byddinge] bydinge AR   236 everychone] every eche
one B   237 geldinge] gedlinge H   239 for] not for AR

PRIMUS MILES

34 Farewell, my lord, and have good-daye.
  For hardly thus dare I saye—
  not for noe boast; in good faye,
  yt is not my manere—
  I would I might fynd in my waye   245
  Sampsoun in his best araye,
  to looke whether I durst affraye
  to fight with him right here.

62ʳ

HERODE

35 Nay, nay, I knowe well or thou sweare
  that thou arte a doughtye man of warre;   250
  and though Sampsoun were here,
  soone hee should be slayne.
  But yett, yett my witt is in a were
  whether you shall fynd that losingere.
  But speedes you fast for my prayer,   255
  and hye you fast agayne.

Tunc ibunt milites et veniet Angelus.

ANGELUS

36 Josephe, aryse and that anon;
  into Egipte thou must gonne—
  and Marye alsoe—from your fonne.
  This is my lordes will.   260
  There staye, lest this child be slayne,
  tyll I warne thee to come agayne.
  False Herode would have you fayne,
  Jesus for to spill.

242 thus dare I] I dare this AR, this darre I BH   243–4] in R
             that he shall not escape, by my faye,
             and I can fynde him out.
243 not] that B   244 manere] minde B   245–52] om R   246 best]
bost B   248 with] om B   HERODE] HERODES R   249 nay(2)] ne A
250 warre] ware A   252 soone] right sone H   should] shal BH   253 yett
yett] yet H   witt] minde B   254 losingere] solingere AR, lossayne H
SD Angelus] om R   ANGELUS] om A   259 from your fonne] with your
sonne B   262 thee] om H   263 have you] om AR   After 264] Tunc
ibunt, Angelus cantabit: 'Ecce Deus ascendet super nubem levem, et ingradientur
Egiptum' R

JOSEPHE

37 A, lord, blessed most thou bee.   265
   Thyder anon we will flye.
   Have we companye of thee,
   we will hye one our waye.

ANGELUS

Yea, companye we shall you beare
tyll that you be commen there.   270
Herode buskes him you to deare
as fast as ever hee maye.

JOSEPHE

38 Marye, suster, now we must flytt;
   upon my asse shall thou sytt,
   into Egipte that wee hitt.   275
   The angell will us leade.

MARIA

Syr, evermore lowd and still
your talent I shall fulfill.
I wott yt is my lordes will;
I doe as you me read.   280

⁶²v   ANGELUS

39 Come nowe forth in Godes name.
   I shall you sheild from all shame;
   and you shall see, my leeffe dame,
   a thinge to your likinge.
   For mahometes both on and all,   285
   that men of Egipt godes can call,
   at your comminge downe shall fall
   when I beginne to synge.

265 most] muste ABH, maist R   266 flye] fleye AR, flee H   269 we] I B
271 buskes] lokes AR   deare] feare AR   274 shall thou] nowe shalte
thou A, now shall you R, shall thou now BH   275 that] tell AR, till BH
MARIA] MARY B   277 and] and and A   279 is] was R   280 I] Ile R
285 mahometes] mahomett B   286 of] on A

Tunc ibunt et Angelus cantabit, 'Ecce dominus ascendet super nubem levem, et ingrediatur Egiptum, et movebuntur simulachra Egipti a facie domini exercituum'; et si fueri poterit, [cadet] aliqua statua sive imago.

PRIMUS MILES

40 Have donne, fellowes, [hie] fast,
    that these queanes weare downe cast,   290
    and the children in thrust;
    and kyll them all to clowetes!

SECUNDUS MILES

Yea, syr, we dwell to longe;
therfore goe we them amonge.
They hopen to have some wronge   295
that gonne soe fast about us.

PRIMUS MULIER

41 Whom callest thou 'queane,' scabde dogge?
    Thy dame, thy daystard, was never syche.
    Shee burned a kylne, eych stike;
    yet did I never non.   300

SECUNDUS MULIER

Bee thou soe hardye, I thee behett,
to handle my sonne that is so sweete,
this distaffe and thy head shall meete
or wee heathen gonne.

SD] om AR   ascendet] ascendit B   ingrediatur] ingredetur B, ingredietur H Egipti] Egipt B   fueri] fieri BH   cadet] caldet Hm, cadat B   289 have donne] haste downe ARB, hase done H   fellowes] fellowe A   hie] hyses HmH, hastes downe A, hast downe hast downe R   291 the] their ARBH in thrust] in haste AR, all to thrast H   293 syr] sires A   to] all to ARBH 296 about us] awaie AR   PRIMUS MULIER] PRIMUS MILES B, PRIMA MULIER H 297 scabde] scabbe B   dogge] biche ARBH   298 daystard] daster AR, deighter B, drister H   syche] suche ARBH   299 kylne] knave AR   eych] ciche A   stike] stiche ARBH   SECUNDUS MULIER] SECUNDUS MILES B, SECUNDA MULIER H   301 behett] beheight B   302 that] it B 304 heathen] hense ARB

PRIMUS MILES

42 Dame, abyde, and lett mee see   305
    a knave-child if that yt bee.
    The kinge hase commanded me
    all such for to areste.

PRIMA MULIER

    Arest? Ribott, for-thee
    thou lyes, by my lewtye.   310
    Therfore I read fast that thou flee
    and lett mee have my peace.

63ʳ   SECUNDUS MULIER

43 Saye, rotten hunter with thy gode,
    stytton stallon, styck-tode.
    I reade that thou no wronge us bode   315
    lest thou beaton bee.
    Wherto should we longer fode?
    Laye we on them large lode.
    There bassnetts be bygge and broade;
    beates on now, letts see.   320

SECUNDUS MILES

44 Dame, thy sonne, in good faye,
    hee must of me learne a playe:
    hee must hopp, or I goe awaye,
    upon my speare ende.

PRIMA MULIER

    Owt, owt, and weale-awaye,   325
    that ever I abyd this daye!
    One stroke yett I will assaye
    to give or that I wend.

306 knave] knaves ARBH   PRIMA MULIER] PRIMUS MULIER A, *om* R
309-12] *om* R   309 ribott] riball A   310 lewtye] bewtie B   311 fast
that] that faste AB   flee] fleye A, flie B   SECUNDUS MULIER] *om* AR,
SECUNDA MULER B, SECUNDA MULIER H   313-20] *om* AR   313 gode] god B,
goade H   314 stytton] stibbon H   styck] stickt H   319 bassnetts]
basenetes H   SECUNDUS] SECUNDA H   PRIMA] PRIMUS AR   325 owt
owt] out and out AR   weale] wayle AR, well BH   326 abyd] abide A,
did abyd R, abode BH   327 yett] *om* A   328 or that] that ere B

SECUNDA MULIER

45 Owt, owt on thee, theife!
My love, my lord, my life, my leife, 330
did never man or woman greiffe
to suffer such torment!
But yet wroken I will bee.
Have here on, two, or three.
Beare the kinge this from me; 335
and that I yt him sennd.

PRIMUS MILES

46 Come hither to me, dame Parnell,
and shewe me here thy sonne snell.
For the kynge hase byd mee quell
all that we fynd mon. 340

PRIMA MULIER

My sonne? Nay, stronge theiffe.
For as I have good preeffe,
do thou my child any greiffe,
I shall cracke thy crowne.

Tunc Miles trasfodiet primum puerum et super lancea accipiet.

47 Owt, owt, and woe is me! 345
Theeffe, thou shall hanged be.
My chyld is dead; now I see
my sorrowe may not cease.

63ᵛ   Thow shall be hanged on a tree
and all thy fellowes with thee. 350
All the men in this contree
shall not make thy peace.

SECUNDA] SECUNDUS AR   MULIER] MULER A   329 on] out R   thee] this AR   theife] teiffe A   330 my life] *om* R, my lief BH   leife] leffe A 331 or] nor ARBH   greiffe] greffe A   334 or] and H   336 that I yt] saye it I B   sennd] sente RB   339 byd] beden A, byden R   quell] quaile AR   340 mon] mone RH, man B   PRIMA] PRIMUS AR   MULIER] MULER RB   342 preeffe] proffe A, preff R   343 do thou] thou do A greiffe] greffe AR   344 I] and I RB   *SD*] *om* A   trasfodiet] transfodiet RBH   primum] primus B   super] *om* H   *After SD*] PRIMA MULIER H   345 woe is] woes AR   346 hanged be] be hanged hie AR 349–60] *om* R   352 thy] thee A, the B

48 Have thou this, thou fowle harlott
    and thou knight, to make a knott!
    And on buffett with this bote   355
    thou shalt have to boote.
    And thow this, and thou this,
    though thou both shyte and pisse!
    And if thou thinke we doe amysse,
    goe buskes you to moote.   360

SECUNDUS MILES

49 Dame, shewe thou me thy child there;
    hee must hopp uppon my speare.
    And hit any pintell beare,
    I must teach him a playe.

SECUNDA MULIER

    Naye, freake, thou shalt fayle;   365
    my child shall thou not assayle.
    Hit hath two hooles under the tayle;
    kysse and thou may assaye.

50 Be thou soe hardy, styck-toode,
    to byde any wronge or boade!   370
    For all thy speach and thy goade,
    I read yee do but good.
    For and thou do me any harme
    or my child upon my arme,
    I shall found to keepe thee warme,   375
    bee thou never so wood.

Tunc Secundus Miles transfodiet secundum puerum.

51 Owt, owt, owt, owt!
    You shalbe hanged, the rowte.
    Theves, be you never so stout,
    full fowle you have donne.   380

356 boote] bowte A   358 thou] you ABH   pisse] pesse A   359 thou]
you ABH   360 goe] to A   361 thou] om ARBH   there] here AH
362 uppon] pon H   363 hit] if it H   SECUNDA] SECUNDUS AR   366 shall
thou] thou shalt H   367 hit] he ARBH   the] his AR   369–72] om AR
369 styck] stuckt H   370 byde] bid BH   or] om H   371 speach]
spear H   and] or H   372 good] goad H   373–6] om R   SD tunc]
om R   secundum] secundus AR   transfodiet] tranfodiet H   378 the]
all the BH   379 theves] theffe AB   you] thou B

This child was taken to me
to looke to. Theves, who binne yee?
Hee was not myne, as you shall see;
hee was the kinges sonne.

52 I shall tell while I may drey: 385
his child was slayne before my eye.
Theeves, ye shall be hanged hye,
may I come to his hall.

64ʳ   But or I goe, have thou one,
and thou another, syr John!   390
For to the kinge I will anon
to playne upon you all.

Tunc ibit ad Herodem.

53 Loe, lord, looke and see
the child that thou tooke mee.
Men of thy owne contrey   395
have slayne yt—here the bine.

HERODES (iratus)

Fye, hoore, fye! God give the pyne!
Why didest thou not say that child was myne?
But yt is vengeance, as drinke I wyne,
and that is now well seene.   400

SECUNDA MULIER

54 Yes, lord, they see well right
thy sonne was like to be a knight.
For in gould harnesse hee was dight,
paynted wonders gaye.
Yett was I never so sore afright,   405
when the theire speares through him thright;
lord, so little was my might
when they beganne to fraye.

381 to me] me to kepe B   382 who] wo H   383 shall] maie A
385 drey] drye ARH, dree B   392 playne] plainte AR   SD] om H
ad] et R   393] lord lord see see H   394 mee] to me ABH
395 contrey] meanye ARBH   396 bine] bene ARB, be H   HERODES]
HERODIAS R   iratus] irates A   398 not] om AR   was] was not A
SECUNDA] SECUNDUS AR   401 yes] yeas B   see] saw B   right] arighte
ARBH   402 be] have bene ARBH   404 wonders] wounderous ARBH
406 theire] om A   him] his B

HERODES

55 Hee was right sycker in silke araye,
    in gould and pyrrie that was so gaye.   410
    They might well knowe by this daye
    he was a kinges sonne.
    What the divell is this to saye?
    Whye weare thy wyttes soe farre awaye?
    Could thow not speake? Could thou not praye 415
    and say yt was my sonne?

56 Alas, what the divell is this to meane?
    Alas, my dayes binne now donne!
    I wott I must dye soone.
    Booteles is me to make mone,   420
    for dampned I must bee.
    My legges roten and my armes;
    that nowe I see of feindes swarmes—
    I have donne so many harmes—
    from hell comminge after mee.   425

57 I have donne so much woo
    and never good syth I might goo;
    therfore I se nowe comminge my foe
    to fetch me to hell.
    I bequeath here in this place   430
    my soule to be with Sathanas.
    I dye now; alas, alas!
    I may no longer dwell.

64ᵛ Tunc faciet signum quasi morietur et veniet Demon.

DEMON

58 Warre, warre, for now unwarely wakes your woo!
    For I am swifter then is the rowe.   435

HERODES] IIERODE BH   410 pyrrie] pearle AR   411 by] be B   this
daye] his araye ARBH   414 farre] om ARBH   417 meane] mone A
419 I wott] for well I wotte B   420] om H   mone] anie mone B
423 and 424] reversed H   425 after] for H   428 nowe] om AR   com-
minge] comes B   432 now] I dye H   SD] om R, Tunc moritur H
faciet] facient A   morietur] morientur A   434 unwarely] unwakely B
wakes] walkes AR   your] you ARH   435 is] was ARB   rowe] doe H

I am commen to fetch this lord you froe,
in woe ever to dwell.
And with this crocked crambocke your backes
    shall I clowe;
and all false beleevers I burne and lowe,
that from the crowne of the head to the right tooe   440
I leave noe right whole fell.

59 From Lucifer, that lord, I am sent
to fetch this kinges sowle here present
into hell, there to bringe him, there to be lent,
ever to live in woe;   445
ther fyre burnes bloe and brent.
Hee shall there be, this lord, verament.
His place evermore therein is hent,
his bodye never to goe froe.

60 No more shall you trespas. By my lewtye,   450
that filles there measures falselye
shall beare this lord companye;
the gett none other grave.
I will you bringe thus to woe,
and come agayne and fetch moe   455
as fast as I maye goe.
Farewell, and have good-daye.

Exit Demon.

ANGELUS

61 Joseph, aryse, and that in hye,
for dead is now your enimye.
Take Jhesu, the child, and eke Marye   460
and wend into Judye.

437 ever] evermore A   438 crambocke] camrocke AR, cambroke BH   shall I clowe] I shall cloe A, will I clo R, shall I clowte B   439 false] farse A and] in a H   lowe] bloe AR   440 right] om AR   441 right] om H whole] wholye B   442 I am] heither I am AH, hether ame I R, heigher I ame B   444 into] and to H   there to(i)] to ARB, om H   445 ever] and ever R   live] abide B   446 ther] teire A   447 hee shall there be] in their shalbe A, there shall B, he shall be ther H   lord] lord be B 448 is] his R   450 you] you that R, thou B   trespas] tapstars BH   lewtye] bewtie B, lowtye H   451 there] your A   453 none] no A   grave] grace ARBH   454 you] om H   thus] this ARH   to] into ARH, unto B 456 I] ever I BH   457 and have good] tell onother R   460 Jhesu] om B   461 wend] goe A

Herode, that would have had you slayne,
hee is marred, both might and mayne.
Therfore hyes you whome agayne;
in peace now you shall be.   465

JOSEPHE

62 A, lord that madest all of nought,
yt is skyll thy will be wrought.
Now is hee dead that us hase sought;
we shall never cease
tyll that we a whome bee   470
agayne in our countree.
Now hope we well to live in lee
and in full great peace.

63 Marye, sister, we must goe
to our land that we came froe.   475
The angell hase bydden us soe,
my owne deare sweete.
On my asse thou shalt bee
and my mantell under thee,
full easylie, sister, leeve thou mee   480
and that I thee behett.

MARIA

64 I thanke you, syr, as I can.
Helpe me that I weare upon.
Hee that is both God and man
keepe us in this tyde.   485

JOSEPHE

Come hither, deare hart-roote;
I shall soone be thy boote.
Thou shalt soonne ryde eych foote,
and I will goe by thy syde.

65ʳ

463 both] *om* R   464 whome] whon H   465 you shall] shall you B
469 cease] dasse B   470 a whome bee] be againe AR, againe be BH
471 agayne] at whom ARBH   473 great] good H   478 bee] sitt and
be R   481 behett] beheete H   485 keepe] helpe R   486 deare]
deert H   hart] *om* H   488 soonne] *om* ABH

ANGELUS

65 Nowe you be readye for to goe—   490
Josephe and Marye alsoe—
forsooth I will not departe you froe
but helpe you from your foe.
And I will make a melodie,
and singe here in your companye   495
a worde was sayd in prophecye
a thousands yeares agoe:

'Ex Egipto vocavi Filium meum, ut salvum faciet populum meum.'

Finis

PLAY XI

65ᵛ   THE BLACKSMYTHES PLAYE

Pagina Undecima: De Purificatione Beatae Virginis

SYMEON

1 Mightie God, have mynd on me,
that most art in majestee.
For many a winter have I bee
preist in Jerusalem.
Mych teene and incommoditie   5
followeth age, full well I see;
and nowe that fytt may I not flee,
thinke me never so swem.

2 When I am dead and layd in claye,
wend I mote the same waye   10
that Abraham went, the sooth to saye,
and in his bosome be.

ANGELUS] *at* 494 H   492 departe] parte R   493 but] to H   foe] fone H
497 thousands] thousande ARB, hundreth H   yeares] yeare H   *Latin* ex]
et A   vocavi] vocami A   faciet] facitt A, faciat B   populum] policulum A
meum] *om* R

Guild-ascription playe] pagent B, *om* H   *Play-heading* undecima] *om* R
de] et A   beatae] beate AB, beati R   virginis] virginis et dicat Semeon A
1 on] of AR   3 a] *om* AR   winter] winters R   7 fytt] flitt H
not] now R   8 swem] swene A, sweyne R   10 mote] muste AR

But heaven-blysse after my daye—
tyll Godes Sonne come, the sooth to say,
to ransome his folke, in better araye   15
to blysse come never wee.

3 That Christe shall come well I wott,
   but daye nor tyme may noe man wott.
   Therfore my booke looke I mott,
   my hart to glad and light.   20
   When Esaye sayth I will see,
   for well I wott how yt shalbe;
   or I deed, well were me
   of him to have a syght.

Tunc respitiens librum legat prophetiam: 'Ecce virgo concipiet et
pariet filium' etc.

4 A, lord, mich is thy power;   25
   a wonder I fynd written here.
   It sayth a mayden clean and cleare
   shall conceive and beare
   a sonne called Emanuell.
   But of this leeve I never a deale;   30
   it is wronge written, as have I heale,
   or elles wonder yt were.

5 He that wrote this was a fonne
   to writte 'a virgin' hereupon
   that should conceive without helpe of man;   35
   this writinge mervayles me.
   I will scrape this awaye anon;
   thereas 'a virgin' is written on
   I will write 'a good woman'—
   for so yt should be.   40

13 heaven] hevens B   14 the] om H   17 well] that well B   wott]
note B   18 may] om H   19 booke] bokes ARBH   21 when] what
ARBH   Esaye] Esau A   will] well B   23 or] and AR   deed] were
deade AR, dead were B, dyed H   SD respitiens librum] librum respiciens H
ecce virgo] after filium AR   pariet] parie A, parictes H   filium] om H
etc] om ARB   25 A] O B   26 I fynd] fynde I A   27 clean] faier AR
32 yt] om ARBH   35 should] shall H   man] mon B

66ʳ   Tunc fabricabit librum quasi deleret hoc verbum (virgo); et
post ponit librum super altare. Et veniet Angelus et accipiet librum,
faciens signum quasi scriberet; et claudet librum et vuanesset; et
dicat Anna Vidua.

ANNA VIDUA

6   Simeon, father, sooth I see
    that Christe shall come, our boote to be,
    from the Father in majestie
    on mankynd for to myne.
    And when he comes, leeves you mee,   45
    hee will have mercye and pittie
    on his folke, to make them free
    and salve them of there synne.

SIMEON

7   The tyme of his comynge knowe I nought;
    yett manye bookes have I sought.   50
    But wonderlye hee that this writinge wrought,
    and marvell thinkes mee.
    My booke to looke yf I fynde ought
    what maner mankynde shalbe bought
    and what tyme yt shalbe.   55

Tunc accipiet librum et admirando dicat:

8   A, lord, how may this be? Todaye
    that I wrote last I fynd awaye
    and of red letters in stowte araye
    'a virgin' written therin.
    Nay, faye, after I will assaye   60
    whether this miracle be verey,
    and scrape this word written so gaye
    and write 'a good woman.'

Tunc iterum fabricat ut antea.

SD] *om* AR   fabricabit librum] fabicabit librum B, librum fricabit H   *paren-*
theses] *om* H   ponit] ponet H   altare] altera B   accipiet librum] libro
accepto H   faciens] faciet H   quasi scriberet] scribendi H   claudet librum
et vuanesset] libro clauso recedet H   ANNA VIDUA] *om* H   41–210] *om* H
45 comes] cometh AR   you] thou ARB   48 salve] save AR   of] from R
49–52] *after* 53–5 B   51 wonderlye] wonderousle B   that] *om* B
52 and] which B   thinkes] thinketh ARB   55 yt] he B   SD admirando]
admirand B   56 A] O ARB   59 therin] theron ARB   60 nay faye]
nay here A, maye R, may fay B   SD iterum] eterum R   antea] antea et
dicat A, ante R

9 Dame Anne, thou may se well here
this is amended in good manere;   65
for a wonder thinge yt weare
to fall by any waye.
Therfore, as yt was amisse,
I have written that soother ys:
that 'a good woman' shall iwys   70
conceive, and not a maye.

Tunc ponit librum super altare, et faciet Angelus ut antea.

ANNA

10 Syr, marvayle yoe nothinge thereon;
forsooth God will take kynd in man.
Through his godhead ordayne hee can
a mayd a child to beare.   75
For to that high comly kinge
impossible is nothinge.
Therfore I leeve yt no leasinge,
but sooth all that is here.

66ᵛ   SIMEON

11 My faye, yet eft will I see   80
whether my letters changed be.

Accipiet librum.

A, hye God in Trinitee,
honored be thou aye.
For goulden letters, by my lewtye,
are written through Godes postie   85
syth I layd my booke from mee
and my writinge awaye,

12 thereas 'a good woman' written was
right nowe here before my face;
yet stirred I not owt of this place,   90
and my letter changed is.

71 maye] mayd RB   *SD* faciet] facit B   antea] antea dicat A   72 yoe]
you ARB   73 forsooth] for AR   in] of B   77 is] ther is B   SIMEON]
SEMION accepe librum AR   80 my] by my AR   faye] fayretest B
eft] *om* ARB   *SD*] *om* AR, *below and to left of* 82 B   83 aye] ever AR
84 lewtye] bewtie B   86 syth] since AR   89 nowe here] here nowe A
90 I not] not I B   91 letter] letters AR

This must be needes by Godes grace,
for an angell this written hase.
Nowe leeve I a mayd in this case
shall beare a barron of blysse.   95

13 Now, lord, syth that yt so is—
that thou wilt be borne with blisse
of a mayd that never did amysse—
on mee, lord, thou have mynd.
Lett me never death tast, lord full of grace,   100
tyll I have seene thy childes face
that prophecied is here in this place
to kever all mankinde.

ANGELUS

14 Simeon, I tell thee sickerly
that Godes owne ghost am I,   105
common to warne thee witterly:
death shall thou never see
tyll thou have seene Christe verey
that borne is of meaden Marye
and common mankynd for to forbye.   110

SIMEON

15 A, lord, I thanke thee of thy grace
that thy goste sent to mee hase.
Nowe hope I syckerlye in this place
thy Sonne for to see,
that of a virgin must be borne   115
to save mankynd that was forlorne,
as Esaues bookes tould me beforne.
Lord, blessed must thou bee.

Tunc Simeon sedebit expectans consolationem; de alio loco
[procull] a templo

92 be needes] nedes be A   94 mayd] mayden AR   95 blysse] blesse R
96 lord syth] seith lorde AR   so is] is so B   97 that] om A   blisse]
bless R   98 mayd] mayden AR   99 thou have] have thou B   101 thy]
that A, the B   103 kever] ever A, eyver R   105 am] an A   108 have]
hast B   110 for] om AB   After 110] from God in magistie ARB
111 A] O RB   112 hase] haste A   115 must be] shalbe B   117 Esaues]
Esayes RB   bookes] boke AR   SD] om A, after 110 R   de] et B
procull] plocul Hm   templo] templo dicat Maria B

MARIA

16 Joseph, my owne trewe fere,
   now redde I—if your will weare— 120
   syth fortye dayes are gonne entere,
   the temple that wee goe to
   and, Moyses lawe for to fulfill,
   my sonne to offer Simeon tyll.
   I wott well that yt is Godes will 125
   that we nowe soe doe.

JOSEPHE

17 Yea, Marye, though yt be no neede—
   syth thou art cleane in thought and deede—
   yett yt is good to do as God bade
   and worke after his sawe, 130
   and to the temple that we goe
   and take with us dove-byrdes two
   or a turtle to offer too,
   and soe fulfill Goddes lawe.

MARIA

18 Ryghtwise Simeon, God thee see! 135
   Here am I common here to thee
   purified for to be
   with myld harte and meeke.
   Receave my sonne nowe at mee
   and to my offringe bryddes three, 140
   as falles, syr, for your degree
   and for your office eke.

JOSEPHE

19 A signe I offer here alsoe
   of virgin waxe, as other moo,
   in tokeninge shee hase lived oo 145
   in full devotion.

119 owne trewe] trewe owine ARB   126 nowe] mone A   129 yt is]
is it A   130 sawe] lawe AR   131 goe] gone AR   132 take] take
we A   133 turtle] turckell A   too] also AR   136 here(2)] nowe ARB
141 your] our B   143 signe] singe B   144 virgin] virgins B   145 oo]
thoe AR

And, syr Simeon, leeve well this:
as cleane as this waxe nowe is,
as cleane is my wife, iwys,
of all corruption.   150

Tunc Simeon accipiet puerum in ulnas.

SIMEON

20   Welcome, Christ my saviour!
Welcome, mankyndes conqueroure!
Welcome, of all fruites the flowre,
welcome with all my harte!
To thee worshippe, joye, and honour!   155
For nowe I see my saviour
is commen to leech my langour
and bringe me unto blys.

21   Though I bere thee nowe, sweete wight,
thou rulest mee as yt is right;   160
for through thee I have mayne and myght
more then through waye of kynde.
67ᵛ   Therfore a songe, as I have tyght,
and laudes to thee with hart right
I will shewe here in thy sight;   165
of mee, lord, thou have mynde.

Tunc cantabit 'Nunc dimittis servum tuum, domine' etc.

22   Nowe, lord, lett thy servant bee
after thy word in peace and lee,
for with my eyes nowe I see
thou art mankyndes heale.   170
And thou hast ordayned there thy postie
to people which thou hast pittie.
Lightninge is commen nowe through thee
and joye to Israell.

149 as] soe R   150 of] as of AB, from R   *SD*] *om* AR   accipiet]
accipett B   151 Christ] my Christe ARB   153 fruites] frute ARB
157 commen] come B   leech] see A, heale R   158 unto] into A   blys]
blesse AR   164 hart] handes B   166 of] on A   *SD* cantabit]
cancabit B   dimittis] denittes B   servum] servam AR   domine] deu A
etc] in pace B   167 nowe lord] nowe A, no lord B   171 and] for AR
there] through B   173 lightninge] light B

23 And Marye, mother, to thee I saye: 175
 thy sonne that I have seene todaye
 is commen—I tell thee in good faye—
 for fallinge of many fonne;
 and to releeve in good araye
 manye a man, as hee well maye,   180
 in Israell or hee wend awaye
 that shall leeve him upon.

24 Manye signes hee shall shewe
 in which untrewe shall non trowe.
 And suffer thou shalt many a throwe,   185
 for sword of sorrowe it shall goe
 through thy hart, that men shall knowe
 thoughtes in harte—on a rowe—
 of men that shall contrarye you
 and found to worke thee woe.   190

ANNA VIDUA

25 And I acknowledge to thee, lord, here:
 to leeve on thee through thy power,
 that fore score and fore yeares
 hase send me might and grace
 to live in pennance and prayer.   195
 Nowe wott I well withowten were
 that thou art Christ in godhead cleare,
 in thee wholey thou hast.

26 And openly here sooth I saye
 to all thy people that I see maye—   200
 the which have wayted many a daye
 after thee, saviour—
 that thou art commen, Christ verey;
 this wott I well by many a way.
 Therfore I honour thee now and aye,   205
 my Christ, my creatour.

178 many] manye a A 182 leeve] lerne B 184 untrewe] untruth R
non] not ARB 185 throwe] harde thrawe A 186 sword] soe A
187 thy] my A that] then A 190 thee] thie B 192 thy] my ARB
193 yeares] yeaire AR 195 live] leve AR 198 thou] thow it B
200 thy] the B 201 wayted] wayled AR 202 thee] the B saviour]
our savyoure AR 203 that] and that B 205 now and] for AR

27 Josephe, husband leeffe and deare,
    our child is gonne upon his waye.
    My harte were light and hee weare here;
    lett us goe seech him, I thee praye.   210
    For sodenlye hee went his waye
    and left us both in Jerusalem—
    greatly in likinge manye a day—
    that wilbe lord over all the realme.

                    [JOSEPH]

28 Marye, of myrthes we may us meane,   215
    and truely tell betwixt us two
    of fearly sightes that wee have seene
    syth wee came the cittye froe.

                    [MARYE]

29 Deare Josephe, you will not weene
    syth our child hath binne us with—   220
    homward I read, I read we hye—
    hee kept us both from growne and gryth.
    In all the might that ever we maye—
    for dread of wicked companye,
    lest any us meete upon the waye—   225
    homwarde therfore I read wee hye.

                PRIMUS DOCTOR

30 Here our reason right on a rowe,
    you clarkes that be of great cunninge:
    methinkes this child will learne our lawe;
    hee taketh great tent to our talkinge.   230

208 his] this R   209 here] *om* A   210 I] we A   211 his waye]
awaie ARBH   212 left] lest B   JOSEPH] *om* HmAR   215 myrthes]
mirth BH   meane] mone R   216 betwixt] betwene ARBH   217 fearly]
fearefull B   MARYE] *om* HmARH   219 you will not] will
you A   weene] wende AR   221 *and* 222] *reversed* H   221 I read I
read] I rede ARBH   we] us B   222 kept] kepe AR   gryth] greiffe A,
greff R   223 that] *om* BH   we] I A   225 any] aye H   227 a]
om H   228 that] *om* B   229 methinkes] me H   will] woulde A
230 tent] heede AR

DEUS

31 You clearkes that be of great degree,
unto my talkinge you take good heede.
My Father that sitteth in majestie,
hee knowes your workes in thought and deede.
My Father and I together bee   235
in on godhead withouten dread.
We be both on in certayntie,
all these workes to rule and reade.

PRIMUS DOCTOR

32 Hearkes this child in his bourdinge!
Hee weenes hee kennes more then hee knowes. 240
Certes, sonne, thou art over-yonge
by cleargie cleane to knowe our lawes.
Therefore, if thou wouldest never so fayne,
further in age tyll thou have drawe—
yett art thou neither of might nor mayne   245
to knowe yt as a clarke might knowe.

SECUNDUS DOCTOR

33 And thou wilt speake of Moyses lawe,
take good heede and thou may see,
in case be that thou can knowe,
herc in this booke that written bee.   250

68ᵛ   DEUS

34 The kingdome of heaven is in me light
and hath me annoynted as a leach,
and given me playne power and might
the kingdome of heaven to tell and teach.

SECUNDUS DOCTOR

35 Behould how hee hase learned our lawes,   255
and he learned never on booke to reade.

231 degree] cuninge AR   232 talkinge] talke H   234 workes in thought]
thoughtes in worde A   237 certayntie] Trynitie B   239 hearkes] hearc
AR   244 tyll] then A   245 neither] never AH   246 yt] *om* A
might] shoulde A, may H   249 can] maye A   250 that] they BH
252 annoynted] noynted H   as] like A   253 given] geve B   254 tell]
till R   255 learned] lead H   256 never on booke] never one booke R,
one booke never B

Methinkes hee sayes suttle [sawes]
and very trueth, if you take heede.

TERTIUS DOCTOR   .

Lett him wend forth on his wayes;
for and he dwell, withouten dread,   260
the people full sonne will him prayse
well more then wee, for all our deede.

PRIMUS DOCTOR

36   This is nothinge to my entent;
     such speach to spend I read we spare.
     And wyde in world as I have went,   265
     yett found I never so farrely fare.

SECUNDUS DOCTOR

By matters that this child hath ment
to knowe our lawes, both lesse and more,
owt of heaven I hope him sent
into the earth to salve our sore.   270

DEUS

37   You that be maisters of Moyses lawe
     and worthye doctours of great degree,
     one commandment you to me shewe
     that God on earth bade kept should be.

PRIMUS DOCTOR

38   I read this is the first biddinge,   275
     and is the most in Moyses lawe:
     to love our God above all thinge
     with all our might and all our lawe.

257 sawes] suwes Hm   259 wend] weend on B   260 withouten]
without H   261 full sonne will] will sone AR, will full sone H   262 well]
will A   wee] he AR   deede] deedes A   264 spend] speake B
265 and] as H   wyde] welde AR   went] mente AR   266 farrely] vereye
AR   fare] a fare ARBH   267 matters] matter B   268 both] om A
273 you to me] to me you ARBH   PRIMUS DOCTOR] om H   277 thinge]
thinges H   278 lawe] sawe H

DEUS

39 That for to do, looke yee be bayne
with all your harte with good intent. 280
Take you not his name in vayne;
this is my Fathers commandment.

40 Alsoe you honour your holye daye;
no workes save almes-deedes you doe.
These three, the certayne for to saye, 285
the first table belongen to.
69ʳ   Alsoe father and mother worshippe aye.
Take no mans goodes without the right.
All false witnesse you put awaye,
and slea no man by day nor night. 290

41 Envy do by no woman,
to do her shame by night or daye.
Other mens wives desyre you not;
all such desyres you put awaye.
Looke ye ne steale by night nor daye, 295
whatsoever that you be lent.
These wordes understand you maye;
they are my Fathers commandment.

TERTIUS DOCTOR

42 Syr, this child of mycle pryce
which is yonge and tender of age, 300
I hould him sent from the high justice
to wynne agayne our heritage.

MARIA

43 Nowe blessed be hee us hither brought;
in land lyves non so bright.

DEUS] *om* H   280 harte] hartes B   with(2)] in H   285 the] be B
for] sooth H   286 belongen] belonge A   to] unto A, one
to R   287 alsoe] and B   288 goodes] good H   without] againste A
289 all] also all AR   291 envy] evill B   by] to B   292 do her
shame] shame her ether B   or] nor AR   293 not] note A   294 you
put] put you B   295 ne] doe not AR   by] *om* AR   296 whatsoever]
whersoever H   that] to A, that to R   298 they] for they B   299 syr]
sires AR   this] this a B   301 sent] *om* AR   303 us] that us AR
304 land] land there H   bright] lighte ARBH

See where hee sittes thatt wee have sought   305
amonge yonder maisters micle of might.
Wend forth, Josephe, upon your waye
and fetch our sonne—and lett us fare—
that sytteth with yonder doctours gaye;
for we have had of him great care.   310

JOSEPHE

44 Marye, wife, thou wottes right well
that I must all my traveyle teene;
with men of might I cannot mell,
that syttes soe gaye in furres fine.

MARIA

45 My deareworthy sonne, to mee so deare,   315
wee have you sought full wonder wyde.
I am right glad that you be here,
that we found you in this tyde.

DEUS

46 Mother, full ofte I tould you tyll:
my Fathers workes, for wayle or woe,   320
hither was I sent for to fulfill;
that must I needes doe or I goe.

69ᵛ   MARIA

47 They sawes, sonne, as have I heale,
[I] can nothinge understand.
I shall thinke on them full well   325
and fownd to doe that the command.

305 sittes] sitteth H   thatt] which AB, *om* H   306 maisters] master B
307 wend] goe AR   upon] on AB   314 syttes] sitteth AR   in] with B
MARIA] MARYE B   315 deareworthy] worthy ARB   316 you] thee AR
full] *om* A   317 you be] thou arte AR   318 we] we have ARBH   you]
thee AR   320 wayle] weale B   321 was] was was A   322 that
must I] which I must B   needes] neede H   doe or] before B   323 they]
thy ARBH   sawes] sayinge A, sayinges R   heale] seale H   324 I can]
can HmR, cane I BH   326 the] you A, thee R, they BH

ANGELUS

48 Now have you hard, all in this place,
that Christ is commen through his grace—
as holye Esau prophecied hase—
and Symeon hase him seene.   330
Leeve you well this, lordes of might,
and keepe you all his lawes of right,
that you may in his blisse so bright
evermore with him to leene.

Finis

PLAY XII

70r   ## THE BOWCHERS PLAYE

Incipit Pagina Duodecima qualiter Jhesus ductus est in desertum
a Spiritu. Incipiat Diabolus.

DIABOLUS

1 Nowe by my soverayntie I sweare
and principallitye that I beare
in hell-pine, when I am theare,
a gamon I will assaye.
There is a doseberd I would deare   5
that walkes abroad wydewhere.
Who is his father I wott neare,
the sooth if I should saye.

2 What maister mon ever be this
that nowe in world commen is?   10
His mother I wott did never amisse,
and that now mervayles mee.

329 Esau] Esay RBH   hase] hath B   330 Symeon] Symond R   seene]
sende A   331 this] you B   lordes] lord H   332 all] well H   of right]
arighte AR   334 to leene] live AR, to lyve B, to beene H

Guild-ascription playe] om H   _Play-heading_] Pagina Duodecima de
Tentatione Salvatoris H   desertum] deseitor A   Diabolus] om B   DIABOLUS]
SATHANAS H   1 my] om A   soverayntie] soverante A, soveraint R,
soveraigne B   6 abroad] about H   wyde] wilde A, whelke B   where]
were AR   9 mon] man R   10 nowe] om H   in] into the AR, to B,
in the H   commen] thus comen H

His [father] cannot I find iwys,
for all my crafte and my couintise.
Hit seemes that heaven all should be his,   15
so stowte a syre is hee.

3 He is man from foote to crowne,
and gotten without corruption;
so cleane of conversation
knewe I non before.   20
All men of him mervayle mone,
for as man hee goeth up and downe;
but as God with devotion
[he has bene honoured yore].

4 Sythen the world first begane   25
knewe I never such a man
borne of a deadlych woman,
and hee yet wembles.
Amonge sinfull synne dose hee none,
and cleaner then ever was anyone;   30
blotles eke of blood and bonne,
and wiser then ever man was.

5 Avarice nor any envye
in him could I never espie.
He hase no gould in tresorye,   35
ne tempted ys by no syght.
Pryde hasse he none, ne gluttonye,
ne no likinge of lecherye.
His mouth hard I never lye
neather by day nor night.   40

13 his] this R   father] *om* HmARB   cannot I] can I not H   14 and] ne H
couintise] countise A, covetise B, quayntyce H   15] it seemes he thought
heaven were his H   all should be] shoulde albe A, shalbe R   17 is] is a H
18 corruption] corrptcion A   20 I] I never ARBH   before] *om* R
24] his hasse him honoure youre Hm AR (his] this R), him honor now doe you B
25 sythen] since AR, sithens B, sith H   26 man] mon B   28 hee yet
wembles] howe it wembles A, how it wymbles R, how yet wemles B, yet she is
wemlesse H   29 sinfull] the sinfull H   30 ever was] was ever B
31 blotles] he semes to be H   eke] *om* ARH   and] or R   33 any] no H
34 espie] spie B   36 ys] *om* B, is he H   syght] waye R   38 no] nor
no AR   40 neather by] nother H

6 My heighnes he puttes aye behynd,
  for in him faulte non can I fynd.
  If hee be God in mans kinde,
  my crafte then fully fayles.

70ᵛ   And more then man I wott hee is,   45
  elles somethinge he did amys;
  save only [hongarye he is], iwis,
  elles wott I not what him ayles.

7 And this thinge dare I soothly saye:
  if that hee be God verey   50
  honger should greeve him by no waye;
  that weare agaynst reasoun.
  Therfore nowe I would assaye
  with speach of bread him to betraye,
  for he hasse fast nowe manye a daye;   55
  therfore bread were in seasoun.

Diabolus dicit:

8 Thou, man, abyde and speake with mee.
  Goddes Sonne yf that thou be,
  make of these stones—nowe lett see—
  bread through thy blessinge.   60

DEUS

Sathan, I tell thee sycerly
bread man lives not only bye,
but through Goddes word verelye
of his mouth [cominge].

41 my] by H   he puttes aye] he puttes ever A, he putteth aye R, he puttes
allwayes B, aye he putes H   42 non can I fynd] cane I non fynde ARH,
cane I finde none B   44 crafte] craftes B   fayles] fayleth AR   45 and]
a B, for H   46 somethinge] some thinges B, somewhat H   47 only]
he is H   hongarye] honge Hm   he is] he hasse HmB, om H   48 wott I]
I wot H   him] he H   50 be] were H   51 should] shall AR
53 would] will RH   55 fast] fasted ARH   nowe] om H   56 therfore
bread] now meat H   SD] om RBH   58 yf that] and yf A   59 nowe
lett] nowe lettes AR, that thou may H   DEUS] JHESUS H   61 sycerly]
securely B   62] mans lyves not by bread onely H   lives] liveth AR
64 cominge] commimge Hm

9   Therfore thou pynes thee, Sathanas,   65
     to suplant mee of my place
     by meate, as sometyme Adam was,
     of blys when hee was brought.
     Disceaved hee was that tyme through thee,
     but nowe must fayle thy postee;   70
     therfore to meeve that thinge to mee
     yt shall serve thee of nought.

10   Sathan, through thine inticement
     honger shall nought torne myne intent,
     for Goddes will omnypotent   75
     is my meat withouten fayle,
     and his word perfect sustenance
     to mee always without distance;
     for thou shalt finde no varyance
     in mee that shall thee avayle.   80

DIABOLUS

11   Owt, alas! What is this?
     This matter fares all amysse;
     hongree I see well hee is,
     as man should kindlye.
     But through no craft ne no coyntyse   85
     I cannot torne his will, iwys;
     that neede of any bodely blys
     in him nothinge hasse hee.

12   For hee may suffer all maner of noye
     as man should, well and stifflye;   90
     but aye hee winneth the victorye
     as godhead in him weare.
71ʳ   Some other sleight I mott espye
     this disobedient for to destroye;

65 Sathanas] Sathan AR   67 sometyme Adam] sometymes Adas B, Adam sometyme H   74 nought] not H   76 withouten] boute ARB, without H   77 his] this BH   78 to] and to A   alwayes] also A   80 thee] om H DIABOLUS] SATHANAS H   82 fares] falles out B   83 hongree] hongarye AR, for hongry H   well] that H   84 kindlye] kindlye be ARBH 86 can] may H   not] om R   87] no neede of meate ne worldly blisse H blys] blesse AR   88 hee] om R   89 of] om ARH   noye] anoye ARB, nye H 90 stifflye] steadfastlye AR   91 aye] ever ARH   winneth] wynnes H 93 mott] muste ARH   94 disobedient] doscibeirde AR, dosaberd H

for of mee hee hasse the maistrie   95
unhappingely nowe here.

13 Adam, that God himselfe wrought,
through my discent in bale I brought;
but this syre that I have sought,
borne of on woman,   100
for no neede that himselfe hasse,
with no counsell in this case
to greeve him I may have no grace,
for no craft that I can.

14 Yett will I seeke some sutteltie.   105
Come forth, thou Jhesu, come with me
to this holy cittie;
I have an errande to saye.
Verey God if that thou bee
nowe I shall full well see,   110
for I shall shape honour for thee
or that thou wend awaye.

Tunc statuat Jesus super pinnaculum templi, et dicat Diabolus:

15 Say thou nowe that syttes so high:
if thou be Goddes Sonne, by sleight
come downe, and I will saye in sight   115
thou diddest a fayre maistrye.
Thine owne angells mon keepe to thee
that thou hurt no foote ne knee.
Shewe thy power; now lett see
that thou may have maistrye therbye.   120

Jesus dicit ad Diabolum.

96 unhappingely] unhappelye ARBH   98 discent] deceate ARBH
102 with] ne H   105 yett will I] but I will H   107 to this] unto the H
109 if that] and if A   110 well] sone ARBH   111 shall] om B   shape]
ordayne H   SD statuat] statuit B, statuet H   et dicat Diabolus] et
Diabolus B, om H   113 nowe that syttes] that siteth nowe AR, that sittes
now B, that sittes there H .   114 by sleight] by sleigh R, the sleigh B, be
slye H   115 saye] see AR   in sight] I see H   116 thou diddest]
that thou dideste A, thee doe H   117 angells] angell H   to] om BH
118 no] nether H   119 lett] lettes AR   120 that] om H   maistrye]
honour H   SD] om H   Diabolum] Diabolus ARB

JESUS

16 Sathan, securlye I thee saye
hit is written that thou ne maye
tempt God, thy lord, by no waye,
what matter soever be ment.

Discendens de pinnaculo dicat Diabolus:

Alas, that me is woe todaye!   125
This have I fayled of my praye.
Was I never rent in such araye
ne halfe so foule reprived.

Tunc Sathan adducet Jhesum super montem, et dicat Diabolus:

71ᵛ   17 Yett, fellowe, if it be thy will,
goe we playe us to a hill;   130
another poynte I must fulfill
for ought that may befall.
Looke abowte thee nowe and see
of all this realme the royaltie;
for to kneele downe and honour me   135
thou shall be lord of all.

JESUS

18 Goe forth, Sathanas, goe forth, goe!
It is written and shalbe soe:
'Thy lord God thou shalt honoure oo
and serve him though thee nye.'   140

JESUS] om ARB   121 securlye] sickerlye ARH   124 ment] mooved H
SD discendens] descedens B, descendet H   pinnaculo] pinoglo A, pinaclo R,
pinacula B   dicat Diabolus] om H   After SD] DIABOLUS B, SATHANAS H
125 that me is woe] woe is me H   126 this] thus B, twise H   127 rent]
tormented B, rowted H   128 halfe] om H   reprived] deprived AR,
reproved H   SD] om H   adducet] addcet B   Jhesum] Jesus R   dicat]
dicit B   129 yett] but yet H   fellowe] om H   130 to a] upon this H
131 I] thou H   134 this realme] these realmes H   135 honour] worshipe
AR   JESUS] DEUS AR   137 Sathanas] Satan H   138 is] was A
and] it AR   139 thy lord God] God thy lord H   oo] om AR
140 serve him] him serve B   though] through AR, thought it B, though it H
thee nye] thyn eye AR, thie nye B, thee noye H

DIABOLUS

Owt, alas! That me is woe
for found I never so great a foe.
Though I to threepe be never soe throe,
I am overcommen thrye.

19 Alas, my slight nowe am I qwyt.   145
   Adam I founded with a fytt,
   and him in comberans soonne I knyt
   through contyse of my crafte.
   Nowe soone of sorrowe he mone be shitt
   and I punished in hell-pitt.   150
   Knewe I never man of such wytt
   as him that I have [lafte].

20 Alas, for shame I am shent.
   With hell-houndes when I am hent
   I must be ragged and all torent   155
   and dryven to the fyre.
   In sorrowe and woe nowe am I brought,
   and all my cunninge is sett at nought;
   endles payne must I have unsought
   to my reward and hyre.   160

21 But I am nowe of good intent
   to hould a court ful diligent,
   and call my servants verament
   shortly for to appeare;

DIABOLUS] SATHANAS H   141 that] now H   142 great] mickle H
143 threepe] the people AR   be] were AR   144 overcommen] overcome
ARBH   thrye] thrise AR   147 comberans] cumberances A, combers B
148 contyse] covetise B   149 of] out of H   he] the R   mone] must BH
shitt] sutte A, shutt RH   150 punished] pyned H   151 knewe] know B
man] non ARH   wytt] a witt H   152 him] he AR   lafte] laste HmAR
153 I am] now ame I R   155 ragged] rugged B   156 to the fyre] all
to dyrt H   After 156] in H

                    Therfore is nowe myne intent
                    or I goe to make my testament:
                    to all that in this place be lent
                    I bequeath the shitte. Exit   4
157–68] om H   157 in] and in AR, into B   158 cunninge] coming B

then to reward with dignitie   165
that all their life have served mee.
In burninge blys there shall they bee
and sytt with Luciferre.

DOCTOUR

22 Loe, lordinges, Godes righteousnes,
    as Gregorye makes mynd expresse: 170
    syns our forfather overcommen was
    by three thinges to doe evill—
    gluttonye, vaynglorye, there bine too,
    covetous of highnes alsoe—
    by these three poyntes, bowt moe,   175
    Christ hasse overcommen the devill.

23 That Adam was tempted in gluttonye
    I may well prove appertly,
    when of that fruite falsly
    the devyll made him to eate.   180
    And tempted hee was in vayneglorye
    when hee height him great maistrie,
    and have godhead unworthelye
    through eatinge of that meat.

24 Alsoe hee was tempted in avarice   185
    when he height him to be wise,
    knowe good and evill at his devise
    more then he was worthye.
    For covetousnes, Gregorye sayth expresse,
    sinnes nought greatly in riches   190
    but in willinge of highnes
    and state unskylfullye.

---

165 then] them ARB   168 with] with me B   DOCTOUR] EXPOSITOR H
170 as] as St. H   makes] maketh A   mynd] paine B   173 too] towe
AR, twoo BH   174 covetous] coveteousnes BH   175 poyntes bowt]
thinges without H   176 overcommen] overcome RH   177 gluttonye]
glorye AR   178 prove] prove it B   appertly] apartelie B   179 that]
the H   181 vaynglorye] vainegolie B   182 maistrie] magistie ARB
183 and] to BH   187 knowe] to know B   189 covetousnes] *om* R,
covetous H   sayth] doth B   expresse] exspesse A   190 nought] not BH
greatly] onlye ARBH

25 Alsoe Christe in these sinnes three
    was tempted, as yee might well see;
    for in gluttonye—leeve yee mee—   195
    hee moved him sleightely here
    when he entysed him through his read
    to torne the stones into bread,
    and soe to move his godhead
    which hee was in a weare.   200

26 In vayneglorye he tempted him alsoe,
    when hee bade him down to goe
    the pinnacle of the temple froe
    an unskilfull gate.
    And in covetousnes he tempted was   205
    when hee shewed him such ryches
    and height him londes more and lesse,
    and that through great estate.

27 This overcome thrise in this case
    the devill, as playd was in this place,   210
    of the three sinnes that Adam was
    of wayle into woe weaved.
72ᵛ But Adam fell through his trespas,
    and Jhesu withstoode him through his grace;
    for of his godhead soothnes   215
    that tyme was cleane disceived.

Tunc venient duo Pharasei adducentes mulierem in adulterio
deprehensam. Dicat

PRIMUS PHARASEUS

28 Maister, I read by God almight
    that we lead this wretched wight,

193 sinnes] signes A   194 as] *om* H   might] maie AR   195 leeve]
lyve B   196 sleightely] yea sleilye A, as yee did B, you saw H   198 the]
om H   199 move] prove H   200 a] *om* H   201 him] *om* H
202 bade] excited H   205 covetousnes] covetous H   207 more] both
more H   208 that] there H   209 this] thus BH   thrise] Christe H
210 as playd was] was as is was played B   211 of the] with those H
212 of] from B   wayle] weale B   weaved] wayved ARB, waved H   215 for]
and B   soothnes] Sathanas H   *SD* venient] veniet AR, venint H
Pharasei] Pharasie A, Judeorum H   adducentes mulierem] cum muliere H
in adulterio deprehensam] deprehensam adulterio H   dicat] ut Jesum tentarent
quorum dicit primus H   PHARASEUS] JUDEUS H   217 maister] maysters A
by] us by H

that was taken thus tonight
in fowle advowtrye,   220
before Jhesu in his sight;
for so to tempt him I have tyght
to wyt whether hee will deeme the right
or elles unlawfullye.

SECUNDUS PHARASEUS

29 That is good read, fellowe, by my faye.   225
Soe mone we catch him by some waye;
for if hee doe hir grace todaye,
he dose agaynst the lawe.
And if hee byd punish her sore,
hee dose agaynst his owne lore   230
that hee hasse preached here before:
to mercye mon should drawe.

Tunc adducent mulierem inter se coram Jesu, et dicat

PRIMUS PHARASEUS

30 Mayster, this woman that is here
was wedded lawfully to yeare;
but with another then her feare   235
we found her doe amisse.
And Moyses lawe byddes us stone
all such as binne uncleane.
Therfore to thee we can us meane
to give a dome of this.   240

Jesus scribens in terra dicat:

31 Nowe which of you everychon
is bowt synne, buske him anon

220 advowtrye] advoultrye AB, addulterye RH   222 so] to A, *om* H
have] ame B   223 wyt] se A   PHARASEUS] JUDEUS H   225 that] hit H
good] well A   fellowe] *om* H   226 mone we] maye we A, we may H
232 to]no R   should] shall H   *SD*] Tunc venient ad Jesum H   adducent]
adducente A, addcent B   et] ad R   PRIMUS PHARASEUS] *om* H   234] is
a wedditt wyfe without weer H   to] this other A, the other R   235 another]
one other R, another man H   236 we] was H   her] here H   238 such]
such women H   *SD*] Tunc Jesus scribit super terram *to right of* 244 H
scribens] scribenes A   dicat] dicat Jesus A   *After SD*] JESUS R   *At* 241]
JESUS H   241 everychon] everye ichone ARB   242 bowt] without H

and cast at her the first stonne
belyve or that ye blynne.

PRIMUS PHARASEUS

Speake on, maister, and somewhat saye: 245
shall shee be stoned or elles naye;
or do her mercye as thou maye,
to forgive her this synne?

73ʳ   SECUNDUS PHARISEUS

32 Mayster, why art thou so styll?
    What writest thou, if it be thy will?   250
    Whether shall we spare or spill
    this woman found in blame?
    What writest thou, maister? Now lett me see.
    Owt, alas that woe is mee!
    For no longer dare I here bee,   255
    for dread of worldly shame.

Et fugiet, et postea dicat Primus Pharaseus:

33 Why fleest thou, fellowe, be thy faye?
    I will see soone and assaye.
    Alas, that I weare awaye
    farre beyonde France!   260
    Stond you, Sybble, him besyde.
    No longer here dare I abyde
    agayst thee for to chyde,
    as have I good chance.

PHARASEUS] JEW H   245 and somewhat] somewhat to H   247 as thou
maye] here today H   PHARISEUS] JEW H   250 thou] thou master H
251 spare] save H   To right of 252] Tunc inspiciunt scripsionem H
253 lett me] lettes AR, lett H   At 254] PRIMUS JEW H   254 woe is]
woes AR   255] here no longer dare I be H   dare I here] here dare I B
After 255] I see my synnes so clearly H   256 worldly] wordlie B, worlds H
SD] om H   fugiet] fugett AB   postea dicat] dicat et postea AR   257 fleest]
fleddest B   thy] my H   To right of 258] Tunc inspicit secundus H
259 awaye] not away H   260 beyonde] behynde ARH   261 you]
thou H   him] here B   262 dare I] I darr H   263 agayst] againste
ARBH   for] now for H   264 have I] I have H

Et fugiet, et dicat Jesus ad mulierem:

34 Woman, where binne these men eychon   265
   that putten this gilt thee upon?
   To dampne thee nowe there is none
   of tho that were before.

MULIER ADULTERIA

Lord, to dampne mee there is non,
for all they binne awaye gonne.   270

JESUS

Nowe I dampne thee not, woman.
Goe forth and synne noe more.

MULIER

35 A, lord, blessed most thou be,
   that of mischeiffe hasse holpen mee.
   Hethenforth filth I will flee   275
   and serve thee in good faye.
   For godhead full in thee I see
   that knowes worke that doe wee.
   I honour thee, kneelinge one my knee,
   and so will I doe aye.   280

DOCTOR

36 Nowe, lordes, I pray you marke here
   the great goodnes of Godes deede.
   I will declare, as hit is neede,
   these thinges that playd were,

SD] om H   fugiet] fugett ARB   After SD] jesus RH   265 these]
those H   266 putten] putt H   267 dampne] condempne B   nowe
there is] is ther H   268 tho] thoes ARBH   ADULTERIA] ADULTRIAM A,
ADULTERIAM R, om H   269 dampne] condempne B   271] neyther
condempne I the woman B, neither do I damne thee thow woman H
273 most] muste ARBH   275 hethen] hense AB, from hence H   filth]
nowe A, om R, synne H   277 full] fully H   278 knowes] knoweth H
worke] worckes ARB, all workes H   doe] done ARH   wee] be H   279 thee]
thee lord H   one] upon R   280 will I] I will H   aye] ever AR
DOCTOR] EXPOSITER H   281 lordes] lordings H   marke here] take hede H
282 the] of the H   deede] deere AR   284 these thinges] this thing H
were] was ARBH

73ᵛ   as Augustine speaketh expressely   285
         of hit in his homely
         upon St. Johns Evangelye;
         this hee sayes in that case:

37 two wayes the casten him to anoye
    syns he had preached mych of mercye,   290
    and the lawe commandeth expressely
    sych women for to stone
    that trespassen in advowtrye.
    Therfore they hoped witterlye
    varyans in him to espye—   295
    or blenquyshe the lawe cleane.

38 That wyst Jesu full well their thought,
    and all theire wyttes hee sett at nought—
    but bade which synne had not wrought
    cast first at her a stonne;   300
    and wrote in claye—leeve yee mee—
    their owne synnes that they might see,
    that ichone fayne was to flee,
    and they lefte hir alonne.

39 For eychon of them had grace   305
    to see theire sinnes in that place;
    yett non of them wiser was,
    but his synnes cych man knewe.
    And fayne the were to take the waye
    lest they had dampned binne that daye.   310
    Thus helpe that woman in good faye,
    our sweete lord Jesu.

Finis

285 Augustine] Austyne AR   speaketh] sayeth H   287 Johns] John ARH
288 that] this H   289 anoye] anie B   290 syns] sith H   mych] mirth B
291 commandeth] comaunded ARBH   293 trespassen] tresspasseth R,
trespassed H   advowtrye] advoultrye AB, addultery RH   294 hoped]
hopen AR   296 blenquyshe] blemyshe ARH   297 that] thcn H   full]
om AH   298 hee] om H   299 bade] bad he B   synne had not] no
synne hadd H   301–4] after 305–8 H   302 synnes] sunnes H   might]
maie AR   303 that] the B   304] omd ther lafte never one H   they]
so B   305 eychon] eche one B   307 them] other H   308 his]
ther B   synnes] owne H   man] one B   309 the(1)] om H   the(2)]
their H   310 had dampned] dampned had B   311 thus] this AR
helpe] helped ARB, holpe H   that] the H

PLAY XIII

74r

THE GLOVERS PLAYE

Pagina Decima Tertia: De Chelidonio et de Resurrectione Lazari

JESU

'Ego sum lux mundi. Qui sequitur me non ambulat in tenebris sed habebit lumen vitae.'

1 Brethren, I am Filius Dei, the light of this world.
Hee that followeth me walketh not in dearknes
but hath the light of life; the scriptures so recorde;
as patriarches and prophets of me bearen wytnes,
both Abraham, Isaack, and Jacob in there sundrye
   testimonies,   5
unto whom I was promised before the world beganne
to paye there ransome and to become man.

2 Ego et Pater unum sumus: my Father and I are all on,
which hath me sent from the throne sempiternall
to preach and declare his will unto man   10
because hee loveth him above his creatures all
as his treasure and dearlinge most principall—
man, I say agayne, which is his owne elect,
above all creatures peculiarlye select.

3 Wherfore, deare brethren, yt is my mynd and will   15
to goe to Bethenye that standeth herebye,
my Fathers hestes and commandmentes to fulfill.
For I am the good sheppard that putteth his life in
   jeoperdye
to save his flocke, which I love so tenderlye;

Guild-ascription playe] *om* H   *Play-heading* decima tertia] decimo tercio B   Chelidonio] Chelidonis A, Chelidanis R, Cheledonio B, Chelidonio ceco H   Lazari] Lazarrus A, Lazarre et dicat Jesu R   JESU] *om* R *Latin* non] not B   sequitur] sequitor A   ambulat] ambulabat A   vitae] vite ARB   *After Latin*] JESUS AR   4 patriarches] patrickes A   bearen] beare AB, beareth RH   5 and Jacob] *om* B   8 all] *om* R   9 the] his ARBH   11 loveth] loved R   12 as] and R   14 peculiarlye] seculierlye A   17 Fathers] Father B   19 so] *om* A

as yt is written of mee—the scripture beareth
    wytnes—   20
'bonus pastor ponit animam suam pro [ovibus] suis.'

4 Goe we therfore, brethren, while the day is light,
    to do my Fathers workes, as I am fully mynded;
    to heale the sicke and restore the blynd to sight,
    that the prophecye of mee may be fulfilled.   25
    For other sheepe I have which are to me commytted.
    They be not of this flocke, yet will I them regard,
    that there may be one flocke and one sheppard.

5 But or we goe hence, printe these sayinges in your
    mynd and harte;
    recorde them and keepe them in memorye.   30
    Contynue in my worde; from yt doe not departe.
    Therby shall all men knowe most perfectlye
    that you are my disciples and of my familie.
    Goe not before me, but let my word be your guide;
    then in your doinges you shall alwayse well speede.   35

'Si vos manseritis in sermone meo, veri discipuli mei eritis, et
cognoscetis veritatem, et veritas liberabit vos.'

74ᵛ   [PUER] (ducens Caecum)

6 If pittie may move your jentyll harte,
    remember, good people, the poore and the blynd,
    with your charitable almes this poore man to comforte.
    Yt is your owne neighbour and of your owne kynd.

CAECUS

7 Your almes, good people, for charitie,   40
    to me that am blynd and never did see,

20 scripture] scriptures ARH   21 ponit] penit AR   suam] suom AR
ovibus] omnibus HmAR   24 restore] to restore B   25 may] mighte AR
27 I] I not R   29 printe] wryte AR   these] this B   mynd and] *om* A
harte] har B   30 them] them ofte AR   and] *om* A, and ofte BH
35 alwayse] ever R   *Latin* eritis] erite AR   cognoscetis] cognoserittis A
veritas liberabit] veretatus liberavit A, veritatibus liberavit R   PUER]
PUCER Hm   Caecum] Celoum A, Celcon R, Coelum B   36 harte] hartes AR
38 this] the AR   39 yt] he AR   CAECUS *here and in SHs throughout*
the play] CACUS AR, CHELODONIUS H

your neighbour borne in this cittie;
helpe or I goe hence.

PETRUS

Maister, instruct us in this case
why this man borne blynd was.   45
Is it for his owne trespas
or elles for his parentes?

JOHN

8 Was synne the cause oryginall,
   wherin we be conceived all,
   that this blynd man was brought in thrall?   50

JESUS

9 Hit was neither for his offence,
   neither the synne of his parentes,
   or other fault or negligence
   that hee was blynd borne;
   but for this cause spetiallye: 55
   to sett forth Goddes great glorye,
   his power to shewe manifestlye,
   this mans sight to reforme.

10 While the daye is fayre and bright,
    my Fathers workes I must worke right   60
    untyll the comminge [of] the night
    that light be gonne awaye.
    In this world when I am heare,
    I am the light that shyneth cleare.
    My light to them shall well appeare   65
    which cleeve to mee alwaye.

Tunc Jesus super terram spuit et lutum faciat, et oculos Caeci
manibus fricabit; postea dicat.

43 helpe] helpe me ARBH   45 borne blynd] blynd borne H   49 con-
ceived] decived A   *After* 50] or his forefathers offence BH   52 synne]
sinnes H   53 or(1)] nor BH   negligence] negigence H   55 spetiallye]
especially R   58 reforme] restore R   61 comminge] comnge H   of]
of of Hm   63 in] for R   64 shyneth] shines R   *SD* Jesus super
terram] super Jesus tarram A   faciat] faciet AH   Caeci] Cci A   postea]
et postea A   dicat] dicat Jhesu H

JESUS

11 Doe, man, as I say to thee.
Goe to the water of Siloe,
there washe thy eyes, and thou shalt see;
and give to God the prayse.   70

75ʳ Tunc Caecus quaerit aquam et abiit Jesus.

CAECUS

Leade me, good child, right hastely
unto the water of Siloe.

Tunc lavat, et postea dicat:

Praysed be God omipotent
which nowe to me my sight hath sent.
I see all thinges nowe here present.   75
Blessed be God alwaye.

12 When I had donne as God me badde,
myc perfect sight forthwith I haddc;
wherfore my hart is now full gladde
that I doubt where I am.   80

PRIMUS VICINUS

Neighbour, if I the trueth should saye,
this is the blynd man which ycsterdayc
asked our almes as we came this waye.
Yt is the verey same.

SECUNDUS VICINUS

13 No, no, neighbour, yt is not hee,   85
but yt is the likest to him that ever I see.
One man to another like may bee,
and so is hee to him.

JESUS] om H   69 there] and H   73 omipotent] omnipotente ARBH
75 all] all all A   76 alwaye] alwayes H   77 God] he R, Christ BH
79 my hart is now full] my harte is wounder A, now my harte is R   VICINUS]
PHARASEUS A, PROXIMUS H   81 neighbour] neightboures AR   SECUNDUS
VICINUS] SECUNDUS PHARASEUS A, om B   85 neighbour] neightboures AR
86 yt] om H   see] did see R

CAECUS

Good men, truely I am hee
that was blynd, and nowe I see. 90
I am no other verelye;
enquire of all my kynne.

PRIMUS VICINUS

14 Then tell the trueth, we thee praye,
how this his happened to us saye—
thou that even yesterdaye 95
couldest see no yearthly thinge,
and nowe seest so perfectly.
No want of sight in thee we see.
Declare therfore to us truelye
withowt more reasoninge. 100

CAECUS

15 The man which we call Jesus,
that worketh miracles daylye with us
and whom we finde so gratiouse,
anoynted my eyes with claye.
And to the water of Siloe 105
he bade me goe immediatelye
and wash my eyes, and I should see;
and thyder I tooke my waye.

16 When the water on my eyes light,
immediately I had my sight. 110
Was there never yearthly wight
so joyfull in his thought.

SECUNDUS VICINUS

Where is hee nowe, we thee praye?

CAECUS

I knowe not where he is, by this daye.

75ᵛ

---

91 no] not B   VICINUS] PHARASEUS A   94 how] and how B   his] is
ARBH   happened] happened here H   99 therfore to us] to us therefore
BH   105 Siloe] Siloei H   108 my] the BH   112 in his thought]
as was I R

SECUNDUS VICINUS

Thou shalt with us come on this waye   115
and to the Pharasyes these wordes saye.
But yf thou would these thinges denye,
yt shall helpe thee right nought.

17 Looke up, lordinges and judges of right!
We have brought you a man that had no sight   120
and one the sabaoth day through on mans might
was healed and restored forsooth.

PRIMUS VICINUS

Declare to them, thou wicked wight,
who did restore thee to thy sight,
that we may knowe anonright   125
of this matter the trueth.

CAECUS

18 Jesus annoynted my eyes with claye
and bade mee washe in Siloe,
and before I come awaye
my perfect sight I hadd.   130

PRIMUS PHARASEUS

This man, the trueth if I should saye,
is not of God—my head I laye—
which doth violate the saboath daye.
I judge him to be madd.

SECUNDUS PHARASEUS

19 I cannot enter into my thought   135
that hee which hath thys marveyle wrought
should be a synner—I leeve yt nought;
hit is not in my creede.
Saye what is hee that did thee heale.

115 this] thy H   116 Pharasyes] Pharasittes A   these wordes] *om* B
117 but] that B   thinges] wordes AR   119 of right] arighte AR
124 thee to] to thee AR   128 bade] byde A   Siloe] Silo B   129 come]
came ARBH   135 I] it ARBH   136 which] that RB   137 nought]
not H   139 is hee] he is B

CAECUS

A prophet hee ys, withowt fayle.   140

PRIMUS PHARASEUS

Surely thou arte a knave of kynde
that faynest thyselfe for to be blynde;
wherfore nowe this is my mynde,
the trueth to trye indeede.

20 His father and mother, both in feere,   145
shall come declare the matter heere,
and then the trueth shall soone appeare
and we put out of doubt.
Goe forth, messinger, anon in hye,
and fetch his parentes by and by.   150
This knave can nought but prate and lye;
I would his eyes were out.

NUNTIUS

21 Your byddinge, maister, I shall fulfill
and doe my dutye as is good skill,
for this daye hither I knowe the will,   155
and I shall spie them out.

Tunc circumspectat, et adloquitur eos:

Syr and dame, both in feare,
you must afore the Pharasies appeare.
What there will is, there shall you heare.
Have donne and come your waye.   160

MATER

22 Alas, man, what doe we heere?
Must we afore the Pharasyes appeare?
A vengeance on them farre and neare;
they never did poore men good!

141 of] by AR   142 that] and ARBH   143 is] *om* H   NUNTIUS]
MESSINGER AR   153 byddinge] bydinge R, biddinges B   maister] maysters
ARBH   *SD*] *after* 152 R   circumspectat] circumspetat AR   adloquitur
eos] loquitur ad eos B, loquitur H   158 afore] before AR   Pharasies]
Pharasites AR   162 afore] before AR   Pharasyes] Pharasittes A
164 men] man RH

PATER

Dame, here is no other waye   165
but there commandment wee must obeye,
or elles they would without delaye
course us and take our good.

NUNCIUS

23 Here I have brought as you bade me
these two persons that aged bee.   170
They be the parentes of him truely
which sayd that he was blynde.

PRIMUS PHARASEUS

Come neare to us both too,
and tell us truely or ere wee goe
whether this be your sonne or noe—   175
looke noe descent we fynde.

76ᵛ   PATER

24 Maysters, we knowe certaynlye
our sonne hee is we cannot denye—
and blynd was borne, undoubtedly,
and that we will depose.   180

25 But whoe restored him to his sight
we be uncertayne, by God almight.
Wherfore of him, as is right,
the trueth you must enquyre.

MATER

For he hath age his tale to tell,   185
and his mother-tonge to utter hit well;
although hee could never bye nor sell,
lett him speake, we desyre.

165 here] their ARBH   no] non R   168 course] curse ARBH   NUNCIUS]
MESSINGER AR   174 ere wee] you A, ever you R, that you BH
176 descent] deceate ARBH   183 of] at H   as] as it ARBH   184 must]
maye R   186 hit] om R   187 never] nether R

PRIMUS PHARASEUS

26 Give prayse to God, thou craftie knave,
   and looke hereafter thou do not rave   190
   nor saye that Jesus did thee save
   and restored thee to thy sight.

SECUNDUS PHARASEUS

Hee is a sinner and that wee knowe,
disceavinge the people to and froe.
This is most true that wee thee showe.   195
Beleeve us as is right.

CAECUS

27 If he bee sinfull I doe not knowe,
   but this is trueth that I doe showe.
   When I was blynd and in great woe,
   hee cured me, as yee see.   200

PRIMUS PHARASEUS

28 What did hee, thou lither swayne?

CECUS

I tould you once; will you here hit agayne?
Or his disciples will [you] become,
of all your sinnes to have remission?

SECUNDUS PHARASEUS

29 O cursed caytyffe, yll moote thow thee!   205
   Would thou have us his disciples to bee?
   No, no! Moyses disciples binne wee,
   for God with him did speake.

30 But whence this is, I never knewe.

191 nor] andr H   192 thee to thy] to thee thy A, thie to thie to thie B
198 is] *om* H   CECUS] *om* H   202 once] onste AR   will] would B
203 you] hee Hm, yea B   PHARASEUS] PARASEUS A   207 no no] no R   wee]
all we ARBH   209 whence] when B   this] he A   I] we ARBH

CECUS

I marvayle of that, as I am trewe—   210
that you knowe not from whence hee should bee
that me cured that never did see—
knowinge this most certaynlye:
God wyll not sinners here.
77ʳ   But hee that honoreth God truely,   215
him will hee here by and by
and grant his askinge gratiously,
for that man is to him deare.

31   And to this I dare be bould,
there is noe man that ever could   220
restore a creature to his sight
that was blynd borne and never sawe light.
If he of God were not, iwis,
hee could never worke such thinges as this.

PRIMUS PHARASEUS

32   What, sinfull knave! Wilt thou teach us   225
which all the scriptures can discusse,
and of our livinge be so vertuous?
We curse thee owt of this place.

JESUS

Beleeves thou in God Sonne trulye?

CAECUS

Yea, gratious lord. Whoe is hee?   230

JESUS

Thou hast him seene with thy eyee.
Hee is the same that talketh with thee.

211 from] of B   212 me] hath me BH   215 honoreth]
honoured AR   218 is to him] to hym is RH   219 to this] that R
221 to] unto ARBH   224 thinges] thinge R   226 discusse] excusse R
229 God] Godes ARBH   trulye] truly restored B   231 eyee] eyne AR,
eye BH   232 talketh] calketh B

CAECUS

Then I here, I honour him with hart free,
and ever shall serve him untill I dye.

PRIMUS JUDEUS

33 Saye, man that makest such maistrye,   235
    or thow our sowles doe anoye,
    tell us here appertly
    Christ yf that thou be.

JESUS

That I spake to you openlye
and workes that I doe verelye   240
in my Fathers name almightie
beareth wytnes of mee.

34 But you beleeve not as you seene,
    for of my sheepe yee ne beene;
    but my flocke, withowten weene,   245
    here my voyce alwaye.
    And I knowe them well eychon,
    for with me alwaye the gonne;
    and for them I ordayned in my owne
    everlastinge life for aye.   250

35 No man shall reave my sheepe from me,
    for my Father in majestie
    ys greater then binne all yee,
    or any that ever was.

SECUNDUS JUDEUS

Thou shalt abye, by my bone,   255
or thou heathen passe.

---

233 I(1)] *om* ARBH   234 shall] will AR   untill] till R   235 makest]
maketh AB   236 thow] thou tow B   anoye] anie any BH   239 spake]
speake ARH   to] unto H   240 doe] did B   242 beareth] beare A
249 ordayned] ordayne AR   owne] name AR   250 for aye] *om* R
JUDEUS *here and in all following SHs in the play*] JEW H   255 abye] by R
by my bone] or thou passe A   256] *om* A   heathen] hense R

36 Helpe, fellowe, and gather stones
and beate him well, for cockes bones.
He scornes us quiantlye for the nones
and doth us great anoye.   260

Tunc lapides colligunt.

Yea, stones nowe here I have
for this rybauld that thus can rave.
One stroke, as God me save,
he shall have soone in hye.

JESUS

37 Wretches, manye a good deede   265
I have donne, yea in great neede;
nowe quite you fowle my meede
to stone me on this manere.

PRIMUS JUDEUS

38 For thy good deede that thou hast wrought
at this tyme stone we thee nought.   270
Both in word and thought
there thou lyes falselye.

JESUS

39 But I doe well and truely
my Fathers biddinge by and by,
elles may you hope well I lye   275
and then leeves you me nought.

258] *om* A   well for] welby R   260 anoye] anye H   261 nowe here]
here nowe ARB, anow here H   262 rybauld] riball AR   264 in] one B
266 yea] you ARBH   in] on H   great] your AR   neede] meed R
269 thy] the AR   deede] deedes ARB   270 we thee] thie wee B
After 270] *in* BH:
                but for thie leasinge falsely wrought
                thou shewest apartelie here;
                thou, that art man as well as I,
                makes thieself God here openly.   4
                (1 leasinge] leasongs H)
271 *and* 272] *reversed* ARBH   272 there] here B   falselye] fowle and falslye
ARBH   275 may you] you may H
C 9206   R

40 But sythen you will not leeve me,
nor my deedes that you may see,
to them beleevinge takes yee,
for nothinge may be soother.   280
Soe may you knowe well and verey
in my Father that I ame aye,
and hee in mee, sooth to saye,
and eyther of us in other.

Tunc colligunt lapides et statim evanescit Jesus.

SECUNDUS JUDEUS

41 Owt, owt, alas where is our fonne?   285
Quyntly that hee is heathen gonne.
I would have taken him, and that anone,
and fowle him all to-frapped.
Yea, make we never so much mone,
nowe there is noe other wonne,   290
for hee and his men everychone
are from us clearly scaped.

78ʳ   PRIMUS JUDEUS

42 Nowe by the death I shall one dye,
may I see him with my eye,
to syr Cayphas I shall him wrye   295
and tell that shall him deare.
See I never none, by my faye,
when I had stones, soe soone awaye.
But yet no force! Another daye
his tabret we shall feare.   300

---

277 sythen] seinge AR   278 that you may] which you now H   281 may
you] you may H   verey] wreye B   *SD* colligunt] colligent ARBH   statim]
statine AR   evanescit] evanescet H   286 quyntly] quicklye AR, quaintely B
heathen] hense ARB   287 have] a AR   288 fowle] woulde AR
all to-frapped] all to-clapped AR, to have wrapped B   290 there] here AR
291 everychone] everye iche one ARB   292 scaped] escaped R   PRIMUS
JUDEUS] *om* H   293 nowe] o now B   one] on AH   295 I shall]
I shall I B   296 deare] dare AR, dere BH   299 another] one other R
300 tabret] taberte AR

MARIA

43 A, lord Jesu, that me is woo
    to wytt my brother syckly soo!
    In feeble tyme Christ yoode me froo.
    Well were we and hee were here.

MARTHA

    Yea, sister, abowt I will goe   305
    and seeke Jesu too and froo.
    To helpe him hee would be throo
    and hee wyst how hit were.

Tunc venit Jesus.

44 A, my lord, sweete Jesus, mercye!
    Lazar, that thou loved tenderlye,   310
    lyeth sicke a little herebye
    and suffereth mych teene.

JESUS

    Yea, woman, I tell thee wytterlye,
    that sickenes is not deadly
    but Godes Sonne to glorifie.   315
    Loe, I am him, as may be seene.

Tunc ibit Martha ad Mariam.

MARIA

45 A, Martha, sister, alas, alas!
    My brother ys dead syth thou heere was.
    Had Jesus my lord binne in this,
    this case had not befalne.   320

MARTHA

    Yea, sister, neare is Godes grace.
    Manye a man hee holpen hasse.
    Yett may hee doe for us in this case
    and him to life call.

301 A] O B   303 tyme] teene B   304 we] me AR   305 I] we AR
307 would be] wilbe A   309 A] O AR   310 loved] loved soe R,
lovest BH   316 loe I am] by ARBH   SD] om H   318 syth] since ARH
319 this] this plase ARBH   320 befalne] bene fallne AR

MARIA

46 Here will I sitt and mourninge make   325
tyll that Jesu my sorrowe slake.
My teene to harte, lord, thou take,
and leeche mee of my woe.

MARTHA

In sorrowe and woe here wyll I wake,
and lament for Lazar my brothers sake.   330
Though I for coulde and pennance quake,
heathen will I not goe.

Tunc pariter juxta sepulchrum sedebunt plorantes, et Jesus procul
sit.

JESUS

47 Brethren, goe we to Judye.

PETRUS

Maister, right nowe thou well might see
the Jewes would have stoned thee,   335
and yett thou wilt agayne?

JESUS

Wott you not well this is vereye,
that xii houres are in the daye
and whoeso walketh that tyme a waye
trespasseth not, the sooth to saye?   340

48 Hee offendeth not that goeth in light;
but whosoever walketh abowte in night,
hee tresspasseth all agaynst the right,
and light in him is non.

326 Jesu] my Jesu H   sorrowe] soveraigne B   328 leeche] ease
AR   331 coulde and pennance] payne and coulde A, colde and paine R
332 heathen] hense ARB   *SD* pariter] pariet A   juxta] jusu B   sepul-
chrum] sepulcroum R, sepulcrum Lazari H   Jesus procul ait] Jesus AR, ait
Jesus H   334 nowe thou well might] well thou maye A, well thou
might R, now thou might well H   335 have] a R   339 a] his ARBH
341 goeth] geeth H   342 whosoever] whoso H   abowte] *om* A
343 tresspasseth] trespassed A

Whye I saye this, as I have tight,   345
I shall tell you soone in height.
Have mynd on hit through your might
and thinkes well thereupon.

49 To the daye myselfe may likened be,
and to the xii houres all yee   350
that lightened be through followinge mee
that am most likinge light.
For worldes light I am verey,
and whoesoe followeth me, sooth to saye,
hee may goe no Chester waye,   355
for light in him is dight.

'Oportet me operari opera eius qui misit me donec dies est; venit
nox quando nemo potest operari. Quamdiu sum in mundo, lux
sum mundi.'

50 Brethren, I tell you tidinges:
Lazar my freinde is sleepinge.
Thether wee must be goinge,
upon him for to call.   360

JOHN

Lord, if hee sleepe, saffe hee may bee,
for in his sleepe no perrill is hee.
Therfore yt is not good for thee
goe thider for soe smale.

79r   JESUS

51 I tell you, brethren, certenlye;   365
Lazar is deade, and thyder will I.
Fayne I am, I wott, that I
was not there, as you may see.
We goe thider anon in hye.

345 as] that AR   tight] toulde AR   347 on] of AR   348 well] om AR
349 the] om B   may likened] lickned maie AR   350 and] om AR
355 Chester] thester H   Latin donec] donet R   sum] sunt B
sum mundi] som R, fiunt mundi B   After Latin] JESUS A
357 tidinges] tydinge H   358 Lazar] Lather B   359 wee must] must
we H   JOHN] JOHANNES EVANGELISTA H   361–4] om B   364 goe]
to goe ARH   JESUS] om B   367 I(2)] you ARBH   that] not A, not
that R   369 we goe] goe wee BH

THOMAS

Followe him, brethren, to his anoye,   370
and dye with him devoutly,
for other hit will not bee.

Tunc versus locum ibit Jesus ubi Maria et Martha sedent, et
Martha fuit obviam.

MARTHA

52 A, lord Jesu, haddest thou binne here leade,
Lazar my brother had not binne deade;
but well I wott thou wilt us reade,   375
nowe thou arte with us here.
And this I leeve and hope aright:
what thinge thou askest of God almight,
hee will grant yt thee in height
and grant thee thy prayer.   380

JESUS

53 Thy brother, Martha, shall ryse, I saye.

MARTHA

That leeve I, lord, in good faye,
that hee shall ryse the last daye;
then hope I him to see.

JESUS

Martha, I tell thee withowt naye,   385
I am risynge and life verey;
which liffe shall last for aye
and never shall ended be.

54 Whosoever leeveth steedfastlye
in mee—I tell thee trulye—   390
though he dead bee and downe lye,
shall live and fare well.
Leeves thou, woman, that this maye?

370 anoye] any H   371 dye] I AR   372 other] non other A, no other R
SD locum] locom R   Jesus] om B   et Martha fuit obviam] et Martha fuet
obviam AR, fit obviam B, om H   373 leade] layd H   377 this] thus B
378 askest] asketh AB   380 thee] to thie B   381 thy brother Martha]
Martha thy brother H   387 liffe] lyfe I say H   393 maye] may be ARBH

MARTHA

55 Lord, I leeve and leeve mon
that thou arte Christ, Godes Sonne,   395
is commen into this worlde to wonne,
mans boote for to bee.
This have I leeved steedfastlye;
therfore on mee thou have mercye,
and on my sister eke Marye.   400
I will fetch her to thee.

Tunc Martha ibit et vocabit Mariam, dicens

79ᵛ   MARTHA

56 A, Marye, sister leeffe and deare,
hye thee quickly and come neare.
My sweete lord Jesu hee is here,
calleth thee him to.   405

MARIA

A, well were we and hit so were!
But had my lovely lord of leere
seene my brother lye one beare,
some boote might have binne donne.

57 But nowe he stinketh, sooth to saye,   410
for nowe this is the fourth daye
syth hee was buryed in the claye,
that was to mee so leeffe.
But yet my lord I will assaye,
and with all my hart him I praye   415
to comforte us, and that hee may
and mend all our mischeiffe.

396 is] and H   into] unto R   this] the B   398 this] thus H   SD ibit
et vocabit] vocat H   MARTHA] om H   402 Marye sister leeffe and]
leffe Marye sister A   404 is] was R   405 calleth] and calleth ARBH
MARIA] MARYE B   406 we] me RB   and] yf R   so were] were so AR
408 seene] since B   lye] lyne AR   one] in B   409 boote] helpe AR
have] a AR   412 syth] since ARH   413 leeffe] leffe A, deere R
415 I] will I BH   416 and] yf BH

Tunc Maria videns Jesum prosternat se ad pedes, dicens:

58   A, lord Jesu, haddest thou binne here,
     Lazarre my brother, thy owne deare,
     had not binne dead in this manere.   420
     Mych sorrowe is me upon.

JESUS

Where have yee donne him? Telles mee.

MARYE

Lord, come hither and thou may see,
for buryed in this place is hee
fore dayes nowe agonne.   425

Tunc venient Judei, quorum dicat Primus.

PRIMUS JUDEUS

59   See, fellowe, for cockes soule,
     this freake beginneth to reeme and yowle
     and make great dowle for gowle
     that hee loved well before.

SECUNDUS JUDEUS

Hee hadd cunninge, meethinke hee might   430
from death have saved Lazarre by right,
as well as send that man his sight,
that which so blynd was borne.

JESUS

60   Have donne, and put away the stone.

MARTHA

A, lord, foure dayes be agone   435
syth hee was buried, bloodd and bonne.
He stynkes, lord, in good faye.

SD Jesum] Jesus R   prosternat se] se prosternit H   422 donne] layd H
mee] to me AR, it me B   MARYE] MARIA ARH   424 is] was R
SD venient] veniet A, veniunt H   Primus] Primus Judeus AR   PRIMUS
JUDEUS] *om* AR   427 freake] fellow B   beginneth] begines A   reeme]
weepe R   428 and make] that makes A   gowle] a gowle BH
430 hee] yf he ARBH   hadd] have R   431 have] a R   435 be
agone] bene gone AR, be gone B, be now gone H   436 syth] since AR
bloodd] both blood B

JESUS

Martha, sayd I not to thee
if that thou fullye leeved in mee
Godes grace soone shalt thou see?   440
Therfore doe as I thee saye.

Tunc deponent lapidem de sepulchro, et Jesus tergum vertens,
manibus elevatis, dicit.

JESUS

61   Father of heaven, I thanke yt thee
that so soone hasse hard mee.
Well I wist and soothly see
thou hearest myne intent.   445
But for this people that stande hereby
speake I the more openlye,
that they may leeve steedfastly
from thee that I was sent.

JESUS

62   Lazarre, come forth, I bydd thee!   450

LAZARUS

A, lord, blessed most thou be
which from death to life hast raysed mee
through thy micle might.
Lord, when I hard the voyce of thee,
all hell fayled of there postie,   455
so fast from them my soule can flee;
all divells were afrayd.

JESUS

63   Loose him nowe and lett him goe.

439 fullye leeved] leeved fullye AR, fullie beleeved B   440 grace] graces H
shalt thou] that thou shalt B, shouldst thou H   SD deponent lapidem]
lapidem deponunt H   sepulchro] sepultro AR   elevatis dicit] elivat et dicat
Jesus AR, levatis H   JESUS] om AH   442 yt] om AR   446 stande
hereby] standeth by A, standeth hereby R   448 leeve] beleeve AR   JESUS]
om ARBH   450 bydd] byde A   451 A] O B   most thou] must
thou R, thou must B   452 which] om ARH, that B   453 micle] much
B, great and mikle H   455 postie] poste A   456 can] could H   flee]
fleye A, fley R, flie B   458 loose] losse A, lose R

MARTHA

A, lord, honored be thou oo
that us hast saved from mych woe   460
as thou hast oft beforne.
For well I wist hit should be soo,
when ye were full farre froo.
The, lord, I honour, and no moo,
kneelinge upon my kneene.   465

MARIA

64 A, lord Jesu, mych is thy might,
for nowe my harte is glad and light
to see my brother ryse in my sight
here before all these men.
Well I hoped that soone in height   470
when thou came yt should fare aright.
The, lord, I honour with all my might,
kneelinge upon my knees.

80ᵛ 65 A, lord Jesu, I thanke thee,
that one my brother hase pittie.   475
By verey signe nowe men maye see
that thou arte Godes Sonne.
With thee ever, lord, will I bee
and serve thee with harte free
that this daye hase gladdedd mee,   480
and alwaye with thee wonne.

[JESUS]

66 Have good-day, my doughter deare.
Whereever you goe, farre or neare,
my blessinge I give you here.
To Jerusalem I take the waye.   485

Finis

459 A] O ARB   460 saved] waved H   461 beforne] before A   463 froo]
us froo B, me froe H   464 the] thee AR, thie B   465 kneene] knye A, knee
RBH   MARIA] MARIE BH   466 A] O AR   468 to] I B   my(2)] om B
469 these men] thes meny H   471 yt] I A   fare] fall B   aright] right B
472 the] thee ARH, thie B   473 knees] knye A, kneey R, knee BH   At 474]
MARTHA H   474 A] O AR   476 signe] signes ARBH   477 that] om R
478 thee] thie B   ever lord] lorde ever RB, ever H   JESUS] om Hm
482 doughter] daughters AR, deghter H   483 goe] om H   or] and H

PLAY XIV

81ʳ   THE CORVISORS PLAYE

Pagina Decima Quarta: De Jesu Intrante Domum Simonis
Leprosi et de Aliis Rebus

JESUS

1 Brethren, goe we to Bethenye
   to Lazarre, Martha, and Marye;
   for I love mych that companye,
   thidder now will I wend.
   Symon the lepper hath prayed me   5
   in his house to take charitie.
   With them nowe yt liketh mee
   a while for to lend.

PETRUS

2 Lord, all readye shall we be
   in life and death to goe with thee.   10
   Great joye they may have to see
   thy comminge into there place.

PHILIPPUS

   Lazarre thou raysed through thy pittye,
   and Simon also—mesell was hee—
   thou clensed, lord, that wotten we,   15
   and holpe them through thy grace.

Tunc ibunt versus domum Simonis leprosi.

SIMON

3 Welcome, Jesu, full of grace,
   that mee that fowle and mesell was
   all whole, lord, thou healed hase,
   over all for to showe.   20

Guild-ascription Corvisors] Corvsars H   playe] pagent B, *om* H   *Play-
heading* pagina decima] paginae decimae R   3 that] their AR   4 wend]
weend B   7 liketh] lykes H   10 in] I B   PHILIPPUS] PHILIPPE AB,
PHILLIPPI R   13 through] throught H   pittye] posty H   14 Simon]
Symonde A   *SD*] *om* H   leprosi] leposi B   18 mee] I AR   was]
face B   20 over all] overll all lorde A

Well is me that I may see thy face
here in my house, this poore place.
Thou comfortes me in manye a case
and that I full well knowe.

LAZARUS

4 Welcome, lord, sweete Jesu.   25
Blessed be the tyme that I thee knewe.
From death to life through thy vertue
thou raysed me not yore.
Fowre dayes in yearth when I had layne
thou grantest me life, lord, agayne.   30
Thee I honour with all my mayne
nowe and evermore.

81ᵛ   ### MARTHA

5 Welcome, my lovely lord and leere;
welcome, my deareworth darlinge dearc.
Fayne may thy freindes be in feere   35
to se thy freelye face.
Syttes downe, if your will weare,
and I shall helpe to serve you here
as I was wonte in good manere
before in other place.   40

Tunc Jesus sedebat, et omnes cum eo, et veniet Maria Magdalena
cum alablastro unguenti, et lamentando dicat.

MARIA MAGDALENA

6 Welcome, my lovely lord of leale;
welcome, my harte; welcome, my heale;
welcome, all my worldes weale,
my boote and all my blys.

23 case] place A   25 Jesu] Jesus B   29 had layne] lyne A, had lyne R
30 life lord] life A, helpe lord B, lord lyfe H   33 and] of H
34 deareworth darlinge] deere darlinges A, deare darlinge R   36 freelye]
sweetlye AR   39 in good manere] to serve you heare A   SD sedebat]
sedabat R, sedebit BH   eo] ipso H   veniet] venit et A   cum] at cum A,
ac cum R   alablastro] albastro A, alabastro BH   dicat] cica Maria Magdelena
A, dicat Maria Magdalena R   42 my(2)] in A   43 weale] heale A
44 blys] blesse AR

From thee, lord, may I not conceale   45
my fylth and my faultes fayle.
Forgive mee that my flesh so frayle
to thee hath donne amysse.

7 Oyntment I have here readye
to anoynte thy sweete bodye.   50
Though I be wretched and unworthye,
wayve me not from thy wonne.
Full of synne and sorrowe am I,
but therfore, lord, I am sorye.
Amend me through thy mercye,   55
that makes to thee my monne.

Tunc aperiet pixidem, et faciet signum unctionis, et rigabit pedes
Jesu lachrymis et tergebit capillis suis.

SIMON

8 A, Judas, why doth Jesus soe?
Methinke that hee should lett her goe,
this woman full of synne and woe,
for feare of worldes shame.   60
And if hee verey prophet were,
hee should knowe hir life here
and suffer her not to come him nere,
for payringe of his fame.

JUDAS ISCARIOTH

9 Naye, Simon, brother, sooth to saye,   65
hit is nothinge to my paye;
this oyntment goeth to fast awaye
that is so mych of pryce.
82ʳ   This ylke boyst might have binne sould
for three hundreth penyes tould   70

45 thee] the ARH   46 fylth] fayth H   fayle] feale H   49 oyntment]
oyntementes B   I have here] heare I have ARBH   52 thy] the B
55 mercye] great mercy H   *SD* aperiet pixidem] apariet pixidem AB,
pixidem aperiet H   unctionis] viccionis AR   et rigabit pedes Jesu] *om* H
lachrymis] lacrinis AR, *om* H   et tergebit capillis suis] et capillis rigabit H
SIMON] SIMEON B   59 *and* 60] *reversed* A   61 were] be A   ISCARIOTH]
ISCARIOTTE A, ISCARIOTA H   65 Simon] Symonde A   67 to] so ARBH
69 ylke boyst] oyle boxe AR

and dealt to poore men, whosoever would,
and whosoever had binne wise.

JESUS

10 Simon, take good heed to mee.
I have an errand to saye to thee.

SIMON

Maister, what you will maye bee,   75
saye on, I you beseech.

JESUS

By an example I shall thee showe
and to this companye on a rowe,
whereby I say thou may knowe
to answere to my speache.   80

11 Two detters somtyme there were
oughten money to a userer.
The on was in his dangere
five hundreth penyes tould;
they other fiftie, as I saye here.   85
For they were poore, at there prayer
he forgave them both in feare,
and nought take of them he would.

12 Whether of these two, read if thou can,
was more behoulden to that man?   90

SIMON

Lord, as much as I can thereon
I shall saye or I passe.
Five hundreth is more then fiftie;
therfore methinke skylfullye
that hee that hee forgave more partie,   95
more houlden to him he was.

71 whosoever] whoever A, whosoere B, whosere H   72 and] om B
whosoever] whosoere B, whosere H   75 you] your ARBH   76 beseech]
beseeke AR   JESUS] om H   77–80] om H   81 somtyme there were] ther
were sometyme B   82 oughten] ought B   a] one R, an BH   84 penyes]
poundes AR   85 they] the ARBH   87 them] om H   88 take] toke B
of] at H   91 as(2)] as as H   93 hundreth] hundrye B   then] om B
94 methinke] methinketh H   95 that hee that hee] that he that ARH,
that he B   more] the more B

JESUS

13 Simon, thou deemes soothlie, iwysse.
   Sees thou this woman that here is?
   Sycker shee hath not donne amysse
   to worke on this manere.   100
   Into thy house here thou me geete;
   no water thou gave mee to my feete.
   Shee washed them with her teares weete
   and wyped them with her heare.

82ᵛ   14 Kisse syth I came thou gave non,   105
   but syth shee came into this wonne
   shee hath kyssed my feete eychon;
   of weepinge shee never ceased.
   With oyle thou hast not me anoynt,
   but shee hat donne both foot and joynt.   110
   Therfore I tell thee on poynt,
   mych synne is her released.

Ad Judam Iscarioth:

15 And Judas, also to thee I saye:
   wherto wouldest thee mispaye
   with this woman by any waye   115
   that eased me this hasse?
   A good deede shee hath donne todaye,
   for poore men you have with you aye,
   and me yee may not have, in faye,
   but a little space.   120

16 Therfore, woman, witterlye,
   for thou hast loved so tenderly,
   all thy synnes nowe forgive I;
   beleeffe hath saved thee.

100 on] in ARBH   101 geete] gate B   102 mee] *om* BH   103 teares]
tear H   105 kisse] kisses B   syth] since ARBH   gave] gave me BH
106 syth] since H   wonne] woone B   108 weepinge] wyping H
109 anoynt] anoynted AR   110 hat] hath ARBH   112 her] here H
SD] *om* ARB   113 also to thee] to thie also B   114 wherto] where-
fore R   wouldest] wouldest thou BH   116 this] thus BH   hasse] hath B
119 me] wee R   faye] good faye A   *To right of* 120] Ad Mariam Magda H
To left of 121] Ad Mariam B

And all that preach the evangelye   125
through the world by and by
of thy deed shall make memorye
that thou hasse donne to mee.

MARIA MAGDALENA

17 My Christ, my comfort and my kinge,
I worshippe thee in all thinge,   130
for nowe my hart is in likinge,
and I at myne above.
Seaven devills nowe, as I well see,
thou hast dryven nowe owt of mee,
and from fowle life unto great lee   135
releeved me, lord, for love.

Tunc surget Jesus, et stando dicat ut sequitur:

JESUS

18 Peter and Phillipe, my brethren free,
before you a castle you may see.
Goe you thider and fetch anon to mee
an asse and a foale alsoe.   140
Loose them, bringe them hither anone.
Yf any man grytch you as yee gonne,
and you say that I will ryde thereon,
soone will they let them goe.

83r   PETRUS

19 Maister, we shall doe your byddinge   145
and bringe them soone for anythinge.
Phillippe, brother, be we goinge
and fetch these beastes too.

---

127 of] and of A   128 to mee] todaye R   MAGDALENA] MAGDELEN B
133 as] *om* R   134 thou hast] hast thou B   dryven] removed H   nowe]
om B   owt of] from H   136 me] my B   *SD* surget] fraget A
stando] stand B   dicat] dicat discipulis suis H   139 anon to] it B
140 a] her ARBH   142 you] ther H   143 say] will saye R   148 too]
towe A, two RBH

PHILLIPPUS

Brother, I am readye bowne.
Hye that we were at the towne.   150
Great joye in hart have we mone
on this arrand for to goe.

Tunc ibunt in civitatem, et dicat Petrus Janitro:

20 How, how! I must have this asse.

JANITOR

Here thou gettest neither more then lesse
but thou tell me or thou passe   155
whither they shall goe.

PHILLIPPUS

My maister Jesu, leeve thou mee,
thinkes to come to this cittie
and bade both brought to him should bee,
himselfe to ryde upon.   160

JANITOR

21 All readye, good men, in good faye!
And syth hee will come todaye,
all this cittie I will saye
and warne of his comynge.
Take asse and foale and goe your waye,   165
for eyche man of him marvayle maye.
Lazarre, that fowre daye dead laye,
hee raysed at his callinge.

Tunc ibit Janitor ad cives.

22 Tydinges, good men evrye one!
The prophet Jesus comes anone.   170
Of his disciples, yonder gonne
twayne that were nowe here.

PHILLIPPUS] PHILLIPE ARB   *SD*] *om* R   Petrus] primus A   Janitro]
Janitor A, Janitori BH   *After SD*] PETRUS ARBH   154 thou gettest]
getts thou H   then] nor ARB, or H   155 tell] shalte tell A, shall tell R
thou] the B   156 whither] wheither A, whether RBH   PHILLIPPUS]
PHILLIPE ARB   159 brought to him] to him brought B   163 saye]
assaie AR   164 comynge] conninge H   167 Lazarre] Lazarrous R
daye] dayes ARBH

For his marvayles leeve aye upon
that hee is verey Goddes Sonne
although hee in this wonne—   175
for elles wonder were.

PRIMUS CIVIS

23 A, lord, blessed most thou bee!
Him will I goe nowe and see;
and so I read that all wee
thidderward take the waye.   180

83ᵛ   SECUNDUS CIVIS

Fellowes, I leeve that Christ is hee,
commen from God in majestie;
elles such marveyles, as thinkes mee,
hee ney did daye for daye.

TERTIUS CIVIS

24 Lazarre he raysed, as God me save,   185
that foure dayes hath binne in grave.
Therfore devotion nowe I have
to welcome him to this towne.

QUARTUS CIVIS

Branches of the palme tree
eycheon in hand take wee,   190
and welcome him to this cittie
with fayre processionn.

QUINTUS CIVIS

25 With all the worshippe that I maye
I welcome him will todaye,
and spread my clothes in the waye   195
as soone as I him see.

173 leeve aye] aye leev H   174 verey] veryly H   175 this] this worlde ARB
176 for] or ARB   wonder] it wonder B, it great wonder H   177 most]
mayst R, must BH   178 and] to H   179 that] *om* H   180 the] our R
CIVIS *here and in following SHs in the play*] CIVES ARBH   185 raysed]
saved A   as] so AR   186 hath] had RB   192 processionn] proffession
AR   194 him will] will him H   195 the] his R

SEXTUS CIVIS

These miracles preeven appertlye
that from the Father almightie
hee is commen, mankynd to bye;
yt may not other bee. 200

PRIMUS PUER

26 Fellowes, I hard my father saye
Jesu the prophet will come todaye.
Thidder I read we take the waye
with branches in our hand.

SECUNDUS PUER

Make wee myrth all that we maye 205
pleasant to that lordes paye.
'Hosanna!' I read, by my faye,
to synge that we founde.

Tunc ibunt pueri versus Jerusalem cantantes 'Hosanna!' cum
ramis palmarum in manibus. Et cives prosternent vestimenta sua
in via: 'Hosanna, filio David! Benedictus qui venit in nomine
domini! Hosanna in excelsis!'

Tunc Jesus sedens super asellam, videns civitatem, flebit et dicat.

JESUS

27 A, Jerusalem, holye cittie!
Unknowne todaye yt is to thee 210
that peace thou hast—thou canst not see—
but bale thou shalt abyde.
84¹   Mych must thou dreigh yet some daye
when woe shall fall on everye waye,
and thou begyled, sooth to saye, 215
with sorrowe one all syde;

197 these] his B   preeven] approven AR, appreven BH   199 commen]
come B   200 not] no AB, non RH   202 Jesu] that Jesu AR
204 hand] handes AR   205 make] maye B   208 founde] fonde H
SD pueri] purie A   cantantes hosanna] om H   ramis] rames R   palmarum]
palmar A, palmas R   vestimenta] vestemente A   via] via et cantabunt H
domini] domine ARB   Jesus sedens] sedens Jesus A   flebit] flebet AR,
flebat B   et dicat] et dicat Jesus AR, et dicet B, om H   211 thou canst]
canste thou ARBH   see] fley R   212 shalt] muste A   213 dreigh]
drighte ARH, drye B   214 waye] om A, syde way H   215 sooth] the
south AR

28 destroyed, dilfullye dryven downe.
   Noe stone with other in all this towne
   shall stand, for that they be unlevon
   to keepe Christes commen   220
   and Goddes owne visitation,
   donne for mankyndes salvation;
   for the have no devotyon,
   ne dreiden not his dome.

Tunc Jesus equitabit versus civitatem, et omnes cives pannos suos
in via prosternent. Et cum venerit ad templum, descendens de
asina dicat vendentibus, cum flagello:

29 Doe awaye, and use not this thinge,   225
   for hit is not my likinge.
   You make my Fathers wonnynge
   a place of marchandize.

PRIMUS MERCATOR

What freake is this that makes this fare
and casteth downe all our warre?   230
Come no man hither full yare
that did us such anoye.

SECUNDUS MERCATOR

30 Owt, owt, woe is mee!
   My table with my money
   is spread abroade, well I see,   235
   and nought dare I saye.
   Nowe yt seemes well that hee
   would attayne royaltee;
   elles this bould durst hee not bee
   to make such araye.   240

217 dryven] beaten AR   218 this] the B   220 Christes] Christe B
commen] commaundmente A, commaundementes R, coming B, come H
222 donne] downe B   SD civitatem] Jeru H   pannos] pamos R   in]
in in R   prosternent] posternent AR   descendens de asina] descendes de
asina R, de asina descendens H   vendentibus] videntibus R   flagello]
flagello et dicat Jesus R   After SD] JESUS R   227 wonnynge] dwellinge AR   229 this(2)] om AR   230 warre] ware ARBH   231 come]
came BH   232 anoye] anye H   MERCATOR] MECATOR H   233 woe is]
woes AR   238 attayne] attayne to H   239 this] thus BH

PRIMUS MERCATOR

31 Hit seemes well hee would be kinge
    that casteth downe thus our thinges
    and sayes his Fathers wonninge
    in this temple is.
    Saye, Jesus, with thy janglinge,   245
    what evidence or tokeninge
    shewest thow of thy rayninge,
    that thou darest doe this?

84ᵛ   SECUNDUS MERCATOR

32 What signes nowe shewest thou here
    that preeves such power   250
    to shend our ware in such manere,
    maisterlye through thy mayne?

JESUS

This temple here I maye destroye,
and through my might and my maistrye
in dayes three hit edifie   255
and buyld yt up agayne.

PRIMUS MERCATOR

33 Aha, Jesu, wilt thou soe?
    Thys worde, as ever mote I goe,
    shalbe rehearsed before moe.
    Cayphas I shall tell.   260

Tunc Jesus ejiciet cum flagello ementes et vendentes.

JESUS

Hye you fast this temple froe,
for marchandize shall be here noe more.

242 thus our] every B   thinges] thinge ARBH   245 janglinge] javeling B
247 shewest] showewest B   248 thou darest] thou nowe dareste AR, thow
darest now B   249 signes] signe AR   nowe shewest thou] sheweth thou
now B, shewest thou H   250 preeves] thou preeves of B, thou preves H
251 such] this H   255 edifie] reedify H   257 Aha] Ah R   258 thys
worde] these wordes B   260 Cayphas] and Cayphas ARBH   SD ejiciet]
ejecit B   cum] fcum A   vendentes] videntes R, vendentes inquiens H
JESUS] om H   262 marchandize] marchandes R   more] moe ARBH

In this place, be you never soe throe,
shall you no lenger dwell.

JUDAS ISCARIOTH

34 By deare God in majestie,   265
    I am as wroth as I may be,
    and some waye I will wreake mee
    as soone as ever I maye.
    My maister Jesu, as men might see,
    was rubbed head, foote, and knee   270
    with oyntment of more dayntee
    then I see many a daye.

35 To that I have great envye,
    that hee suffered to destroye
    more then all his good thrye,   275
    and his dammes too.
    Had I of yt had maistrye,
    I would have sould yt soone in hie
    and put hit up in treasurye
    as I was wont to doe.   280

36 Whatsoever was given to Jesu
    I have kept syns I him knewe;
    for hee hopes I be trewe,
    his pursse I alwaye beare.
    Him had binne better, in good faye,   285
    had spared oyntment that daye,
    for wroken I wilbe some waye
    of waste that was donne there.

85ʳ   37 Three hundeth penyes-worth yt was
    that hee lett spill in that place.   290
    Therfore God give me hard grace
    but himselfe shalbe sould

276 as(1)] so AR   267 wreake] wrecken AR   269 might] maye AR
260 knee] knye A   271 oyntment] oyntmentes B   276 too] towe A,
twoo B   281 whatsoever] whatseer H   283 hopes] hope R   be]
wilbe AR   284 I alwaye] allwaie I ARBH   285 had binne better]
better had bene B   286 had] to have B   288 of] for B   that] that
that H   289 hundeth] hundreth ARBH   penyes-worth] penny-worthes
AR, peniworth B

to the Jewes, or that I sytt,
for the tenth pcnye of hit;
and thus my maister shalbe quytte   295
my greeffe an hundrethfould.

38 Syr Cayphas and his companye
conspyrne Jesus to anoye.
There speech anon I will espye,
with falsshood for to fowle him.   300
And if the gladlye will do whye,
I shall teach them to him in hye,
for of his counsell well knowe I.
I may best beguyle him.

Tunc Judas pro tempore abiit, et Cayphas dicit.

CAYPHAS

39 Lordinges, lookers of the lawe,   305
herkyns hether to my sawe.
To Jesu all men can drawe
and likinge in him hase.
If we letten him longe gonne,
all men will leeve him upon;   310
so shall the Romanes come anon
and pryve us of our placc.

40 Therfore yt is fullye my readd
we cast howe hee best were dead;
for yf hee longe on life be leade   315
our lawe goeth all to nought.
Therfore saye cychon his counsell,
what manere of waye will best avayle
this ylke shrewe for to assayle—
some sleyght there must be sought.   320

295 thus] this AR   quytte] quite ARB   298 conspyrne] conspier B
299 espye] spie AR   300 falsshood] falesed H   him] his A   *SD* abiit]
discedet H   dicit] dicat R, loquitur H   305 lookers of] lokes on A, looke
one R   307 can] maye AR   308 likinge in him hase] lyken him in haste B
309 letten] let A   314 howe hee best] best how he R, how he H   were]
may be H   317 saye eychon] saye one ech B   318 of] a AR, *om* BH
319 ylke] same A

PLAY XIV

ANNAS

41 Syr, you saye right skylfullye;
    but needesly men must espie
    by him we catch noe vilanye,
    to fownd and fowle to fayle.
    For you knowe as well as I,   325
    oft we have fownded to do him anoye;
    but ever he hath the victorye—
    that noe waye maye avayle.

85ᵛ

PRIMUS PHARASEUS

42 Yea, syr, in temple hee hath binne
    and troubled us with mych teene,   330
    that when we wended and did weene
    of him to have had all our will,
    or ever we wist, he was awaye.
    This maketh the people, in good faye,
    to leeve that hee is Christ vereye,   335
    and our lawe for to spill.

SECUNDUS PHARASEUS

43 Yea, lordes, one poynt may doe gayne.
    That lourden, Lazarre, should be slayne,
    for he raysed him up agayne
    that foure dayes had binne dead.   340
    For that miracle mych of mayne,
    to honour him eychon is fayne;
    and Lazarre, that dead was, will not layne,
    and hee one life be leade.

CAYPHAS

44 Noe more, forsooth, will many moe   345
    that hee hase made to speake and goe;
    and blynd that have theire sight alsoe
    loven him steadfastlye

---

322 needesly] nedelye ARBH   326 oft] *om* B   anoye] nye ARH, noye B
328 noe] we noe AR   329 binne] bene AR   331 wended] winded B
332 all] *om* B   337 yea] yee B   gayne] againe AR   338 lourden]
lorden RH, lurden B   342 eychon] eich man R   343 Lazarre] Lazarus R

and followen him both farre and neare,
preachinge to the people his powere.   350
Therfore my witt is in a weare
to ordayne remedye.

ANNAS

45 And remedye must ordayned be
    before this great solempnitie,
    or elles may other as well as we   355
    trusse and take our waye.
    For when hee comes to this cittie,
    all the world, as you might see,
    honored him upon there knee
    as God had comon that daye.   360

PRIMUS PHARASEUS

46 Alsoe, lordinges, you sawe there
    how that he fared with chaffere—
    cast hit downe, God give him care,
    that was so great of price!
    And alsoe lowdlye hee can lyc—   365
    called the temple apertlye
    his Fathers house full falslye,
    right as yt had binne his!

86ʳ   SECUNDUS PHARASEUS

47 Lordinges, there is noe more to saye—
    but loost is owr lawe, I dare laye,   370
    and hee come one our saboath daye
    that nowe aprocheth nye.
    Heale he any, lesse or more,
    all men will leeve on his lore.
    Therfore yt is good to slea him before,   375
    yf that wee will be slye.

349–52] *om* B   349 both] *om* A   350 to] *om* H   356 waye] naye B
357 comes] come A, came RBH   358 might] maie ARH   359 knee]
knye A   360 comon] come ARB   362 that] *om* H   fared] fareth A
chaffere] our chaffer H   369 to] t B   374 leeve] beleve H

CAYPHAS

48 Amonge our wittes lett us see
to take him with some subteltye.
Hee shall have sylver, gould, and fee,
this thinge that would fulfill.   380

JUDAS

Lordes, what will you give mee
and I shall soone helpe that hee
sleelye betrayed bee,
right at your owne will?

CAYPHAS

49 Welcome, fellowe, as have I roo.   385
That bargayne fayne would I goe too.

JUDAS

Lett me see what ye will doe,
and laye downe sylver here.
For the devill swappe of my swyre
and I doe yt without hyre,   390
other for soveraigne or syre—
yt is not my manere.

CAYPHAS

50 Saye on what we shall give thee
to helpe that he taken bee;
and here is readye thy moneye   395
to paye thee or thou passe.

JUDAS

As ever mote I thrive or thee,
and I shewe my subtilltye,
thirtie penyes yee shall give mee
and not a farthinge lasse.   400

JUDAS] JUDAS ISCARIOTH R   381 lordes] lord H   383 sleelye] slielye that
he B   386 fayne would I goe too] woulde I fayne knowe A   389 swappe]
swope A, swopp R   390 and] if H   without] withoutten B   391 sove-
raigne] swaine B   397 ever] evill H   thee] three R   398 *and*
399] *reversed* H   400 a] one R   lasse] lesse ARB

PRIMUS PHARISEUS

51 Yea, but thy trueth thou must plight
for to serve us aright
to betraye thy maister through thy might,
and have here thy money.

86ᵛ   JUDAS

Have here my trueth, as I have tight,   405
or Fridaye that hit be night
I shall bringe you to his sight
and tell which is hee.

PRIMUS PHARISEUS

52 Yee binne brethren on a rowe.
Which is he I cannot knowe.   410

JUDAS

Noe. A verey signe I shall you showe.
Aspies whom I kysse,
and that is hee, sooth to saye.
Takes him manlye, as you maye,
and lead him sleelye awaye   415
whither your likinge ys.

CAYPHAS

53 Nowe looke thou serve us truely,
thy maysters comminge to espie.

JUDAS

Trust well therto and sickerlye
that he shall not eschewe.   420

401 yea] nay B   thy] the B   trueth] troth ARBH   plight] pighte A
405 here] he B   trueth] troth BH   tight] pighte A   406 or] on A
that] or AR, that ere B   407 you to his] him to your H   411 noe] nowe
AR, *om* H   412 aspies] espices A, aspyes ye H   414 manlye] man-
fullye A   416 whither] whether as R   418 maysters] maiste is A,
master is RB   comminge] coning BH   to] us to AR   420 eschewe]
eskape A

And would God almightie
the kinge of France might so afye
in this realme and baronye
that they were all so treu!

54 On Fridaye in the morninge   425
espies all on my comminge,
for where that he is walkinge
I will goe and espie.
With him I thinke to eate and drinke
and after, tydinges to you to bringe   430
where he shapes his dwellinge,
and come and tell you in hye.

Finis

PLAY XV

87ʳ   THE BAKERS PLAYE

Pagina Decima Quinta: De Caena Domini et de eius Proditione

JESUS

1 Brethren all, to me right deare,
come hither to me and ye shall here.
The feaste of Easter you knowe draweth neare
and nowe yt is at hand.
That feaste needes keepe must we   5
with verye great solempnitie.
The pascall lambe eaten must bee
as the lawe doth commande.

421–4] om AR   421 almightie] almightie the B   422 the] om B
might] may H   423 this] his H   and] or H   426 all] om AR   my]
his R   comminge] conning BH   427 that] as R   428 espie] spye R
430 to(2)] om ARH   431 dwellinge] dwellinges R   432 in] one B

    Guild-ascription playe] om H   Play-heading caena] coona AR
de(2)] om R   proditione] proditione et dicat Jesus R   4 nowe] how B
5 needes keepe] keepe needes B   6 solempnitie] solempeintie A   7 eaten
must bee] eate muste we A   8 doth] do A

2 Therfore, Peter, looke that thou goe,
and John with thee shalbe alsoe. 10
Prepare all thinges that longeth therto
acordinge to the lawe.

PETRUS

Lord, thy biddinges doe will we.
But tell us first where yt shalbe
and we shall doe yt speedelye, 15
and thidder will we drawe.

JESUS

3 Goe into the cittie which yee doe see,
and there a man meete shall yee
with a water pott that beareth hee,
for so you may him knowe. 20
Into what house that hee shall goe,
into the same [howse] enter ye alsoe
and saye the maister send you too
his message for to shewe.

4 Saye 'The maister to thee us sent 25
to have a place convenient
the pascall lambe to eate.' There is my entent,
with my disciples all.
A fayre parlour hee will you shewe.
There prepare all thinge dewe 30
where I with my retynewe
fulfill the lawe we shall.

PETRUS

5 All readye, lorde. Even thy will
shortlye we two shall fulfill,

---

10 shalbe] shall B   11 longeth] belonges AR, longes B, belongeth H
PETRUS] PETER R   13 biddinges] byddinge ARBH   22 howse] house
house Hm   enter] goe B   23 the] your B   too] two RH   25 the]
thie B   27 to eate there] their to eate AR, to eate B   my] his B   28 my]
his B   29 you shewe] shew you H   30 thinge] thinges ARBH
PETRUS] JOHN A, PETER R

and the fayre cittie we shall goe tyll   35
as fast as we maye.

87ᵛ Tunc Petrus et Johannis ibunt ac hominem vas aquae
testaceum portantem alloquerentur.

PETRUS

All hayle, good fellowe, hartelye.
To thy maisters house I praye thee hye;
and wee must keepe thee companye
our message for to saye.   40

SERVUS

6 Come on your waye and followe mee;
my maisters house soone shall you see.
Loe, here yt is, verelye.
Saye nowe what yee will.

Tunc domum intrant.

PETRUS

Syr, the maister saluteth thee   45
and as messingers send we bee.
Therfore we praye thee hartelye
take heede us untill.

7 The maister hath sent us to thee.
A place preparde for him must bee;   50
the pascall lambe there eate will hee
with his disciples all.

PATER FAMILIUS

Loe, here a parloure all readye dight
with paved flores and windowes bright.
Make all thinges readye as you thinke right,   55
and this have you shall.

SD Johannis] Johannes ARBH   ac] et H   hominem] horinem AR   testa-
ceum] testacem AR   portantem] protamtem A, protantem R   alloquerentur]
alloquerentibus A, alloquerentum R, alloquerentur et annuntiabit eis domum
heri sui H   PETRUS] PETER R   38 I] we RBH   39 must] will H
SERVUS] SERVANUS AR   45 the] thie B   50 preparde] prepare ARBH
bee] we ARBH   FAMILIUS] FAMILIAS H   54 flores] flowers AR

JOHANNIS

8 Nowe, brother Peter, lett us hye
the pascall lambe to make readye;
and to our maister then will you and I
as fast as we maye. 60

Tunc adornent mensam et revertunt.

PETRUS

Thy commandment, lord, donne have wee.
The pascall lambe is made readye.
Therfore come on and you shall see,
and we shall lead the waye.

JESUS

9 Nowe, brethren, goe to your seate; 65
this pascall lambe nowe lett us eate,
and then we shall of other thinges entreate
that be of greater effecte.
For knowe you nowe, the tyme is come
that sygnes and shadowes be all donne. 70
Therfore, make haste, that we maye soone
all figures cleane rejecte.

88ʳ 10 For nowe a newe lawe I will beginne
to helpe mankynd owt of his sinne
soe that hee may heaven wynne, 75
the which for synne hee loste.
And here, in presence of you all,
another sacrifice beginne I shall,
to bringe mankynd out of his thrall,
for helpe him neade I muste. 80

Tunc accumbet Jesus ac Johannis in gremio dormit.

JOHANNIS] JOHANNES ARBH   59 and to our maister then] then to our master
ARH   you and I] wee B   SD] Tunc mensa preparata revertentur H
adornent] adornant ARB   revertunt] revertime A, revertuns R   PETRUS]
PETER R   To right of 64] Tunc eviunt H   67 and then we shall] then
shall we H   68 greater] greate ARB   70 sygnes] figures H   74 his]
om R   78 another] one other B   79 his] om R, this B   SD accumbet]
occumbit A, accumbit RH, accumberit B   ac] et B   Johannis] Johannes ARBH
gremio] suo gremio H   dormit] dormiet H   After SD] JESUS RBH

11 Brethren, I tell you bye and bye,
with greate desyre desyred have I
this Passeover to eate with you trulye
before my Passion.
For I saye to you syckerlye,   85
my Fathers will allmightye
I must fullfill meekelye,
and ever to be bowne.

Tunc Jesus accipiet panem, frangit, et discipulis suis dat, dicens:

12 This bread I give here my blessinge.
Takes, eate, brethren, at my byddinge,   90
for, leeve you well, withowt leasinge,
this is my bodye
that shall dye for all mankynde
in remission of there synne.
This give I you on me to mynd   95
aye after evermore.

Tunc accipit calicem in manibus, oculis elevatis, dicens:

13 Father of heaven, I thanke thee
for all that ever thou doest to mee.
Brethren, takes this with hart free;
that is my blood   100
that shalbe shedd on the tree.
For more together drinke not wee
in heaven-blys tyll that we bee
to tast that ghostly foode.

Tunc edit et bibit cum discipulis, et Judas Iscarioth habebit manum in patina.

85 saye] said B   88 to be] to it be AR   bowne] bounde B   *SD* accipiet
panem] accipite panem AR, accipit panem B, panem accipit H   frangit]
franget A   discipulis suis] discipulis suat AR, suis discipulis H   dicens]
dicens Jesus A   *After SD*] JESUS R   90 eate] eates you H   91 for
leeve] beleeve AR   95] *om* A   96 aye] here A   *SD* accipit calicem]
accipetet calicem A, accipet calicem R, calicem accipiet H   oculis elevatis]
occulus lavates A, occuliis levatis RB, levatis oculis H   dicens] dicens Jesus R,
dicit B   100 that] for this A, for yt R   103 bee] see R   *SD*] Tunc
omnes simul edent et Judas Isca manum in patina habebit H   et(2)] ad R
manum] manibus R   in patina] in patina et dicat Jesus A

14 Brethren, forsooth I you saye, 105
one of you shall me betraye
that eatethe here with me todaye
in this companye.

88ᵛ

PETRUS

Alas, alas and weale-awaye!
Whoe that may be, knowe I nay maye— 110
for I yt is not, in good faye,
that shall doe such anoye.

ANDREAS

15 Hard yt is for us all
to whom this case shall befall.
We be but twelve within this hall— 115
lord, tell yf yt be I.

JACOBUS

Sorrowfull for these wordes be wee.
Who ys yt? I cannot see.
If this case shall fall to mee,
lord, tell mee hastelye. 120

Tunc Judas intingit in patinam.

JESUS

16 Through his deceipte I am but dead
that in my cuppe weetes his bread.
Mych woe for his wicked read
that wretch must thole iwys.
Well were him had hee binne unborne, 125
for bodye and soule hee is forlorne
that falselye soe hath donne beforne
and yett in will hee ys.

PETRUS] PETER R 109 weale] wayle AR, well B 112 anoye] anye H
ANDREAS] ANDREWAS AR 115 within] in A 118 ys yt] it is ARBH
SD intingit] intinget ARH patinam] patinam Jesus dicens A 122 cuppe]
dishe R 124 thole] hold B 126 hee] *om* ABH forlorne] bouth
forlorne AH 128 will] witt B hee ys] is he AR

C 9206 T

JUDAS

17 Leeffe maister, ys yt not I
that shall doe thee this villanye? 130

JESUS

Thou hast read, Judas, redealye,
for sycker thou arte hee.
That thou shalt doe, doe hastelye.

JUDAS

Farewell, all this companye,
for on an errand I must hye; 135
undonne hit may not bee.

JESUS

18 Brethren, take up this meate anon;
to another worke we must gonne.
Your feete shall washen be eychone
to shewe all charitie. 140
And first myselfe I wyll begynne
and washe you all that be herein,
one thys deede that you may mynne
and meeker for to bee.

89ʳ Tunc Jesus precinget corpus lintheolo.

PETRUS

19 A, lord, shalt thou washe my feete? 145

JESUS

That doe I, Peeter, I thee beheight.
The while more thou shalt not wytt,
but thou shalt afterwarde.

130 thee] *om* H   132 sycker] suerlye A   133 doe(2)] it B   139 shall
washen be] washen shalbe B   141 myselfe] my feete AR   142 you
all] all ye B   143 mynne] mynde A   *SD* precinget] precinge AR,
precingit B   lintheolo] lintheolo et dicit Petrus A   146 doe I] I do H
beheight] beheat B   147 wytt] weete B

PETRUS

Naye, lord, forsooth in no manere
my feete shalt thou not washe here!   150

JESUS

But I washe thee, withowten were
of joye gettes thou noe parte.

PETRUS

20 Naye, lord, my feete may well be layde;
but wash my handes and my head.

JESUS

All ys cleane. Therfore doe I read   155
thy feete shall washen bee
and you cleane—but not all.

PETRUS

Lord, of wayle thou arte the wall,
and, though yt not well befall,
have here my feete to thee.   160

Tunc lavabit pedes omnium singulatim et abstergit lintheo.

JESUS

21 My deare brethren, well wytt yee
that lord and maister you call mee;
and well you saye as should bee—
I am, and have binne yore.
Syth I have washen your feete here—   165
lord and maister, in meeke manere—
doe eychon to other in fere
as I have done before.

Tunc invicem omnes aliorum pedes lavant.

149 naye] no B   150 shalt thou not] thou ney A   152 joye] joyes B
153 layde] leade AR   155 doe I] I doe AR, doe my H   157 cleane] are
clean H   159 not] do not H   SD omnium] omnes R   abstergit]
abstreget A, abstregit R, obstringit B, absterget H   lintheo] lintheolo H
162 call] will calle AR   163 as] as I B, as it H   164 have] om B
166 lord] your lorde AR   167 to] so to ARBH   SD] Tunc alius alios
pedes lavabunt H   After SD] JESUS AR

22 My litle children and my brethren free,
  little while maye I with you bee,   170
  but thidder shall you not goe with mee
  as I am nowe in waye.
  But this soothly my biddinge:
  you love together in all thinge
  as I before, withowt fletchinge,   175
  have loved you trulye aye.

89ᵛ   23 Soe all men may knowe and see
  my disciples that you bee,
  falshood if you alwayes flee
  and loven well in feere.   180

PETRUS

Lord, whither arte thou in waye?

JESUS

Peter, thidder as I goe todaye
come syckerlye thou ney maye
this tyme in noe manere;

24 but thou shalt thidder goe.   185

PETRUS

Whye shall yt not, lord, be soe?
My lyffe I will put in woe
and for thy sake be slayne.

JESUS

Peter, I saye thee syckerlye,
or the cocke have crowen thrye   190
thou shalt forsake my companye
and take thy word agayne.

169 litle] *om* BH   children] brethren B   170 little] a littill AR   maye I]
I maye ARBH   173 soothly] southlye is AH   biddinge] bydinge R
175 I] I have H   fletchinge] flytinge R   176 aye] ever AR   177 all
men may] may all men B   179 alwayes] ever R   JESUS] JE A
183 come] come ney ARB, come nye H   184 manere] manner a waye
AR, manner way B   PETRUS] PE A, PETER H   186 yt not] not it A
lord] *om* AR, lord now BH   JESUS] JE A   190 have] hath H

25 Brethren, lett not your hartes be sore,
but leeve in God evermore
and in mee as you have before,   195
and care not for this case.
For in my Father house there is
manye wonnynges of great blys,
and thidder I will goe now, iwys,
to purvaye you a place.   200

26 And though I goe from you awaye
to purvaye a place to your paye,
I come agayne another daye
and take you all with mee.

THOMAS

Lord, we wotte not, in good faye,   205
what manere of gate thou wilt assaye.
Tell us, that we knowe maye
that gate and goe with thee.

JESUS

27 Thomas, I tell thee withowt stryfe,
in me is waye, soothnes, and life,   210
and to my Father no man ney wife
may come withowt mee.
And yf you knowe me verelye,
my Father you might knowe in hye.
From henceforth, I say you syckerlye,   215
knowe him all shall yee.

90ʳ   PHILLIPP

28 Lord, lett us see thy Father anon
and yt sufficeth us everychone.

193 hartes] hardes B   197 Father] Fathers ARBH   house] *om* H
198 blys] blesse AR   202 to(2)] for AR   206 manere of] a AR, maner a H
210 waye] very H   212 mee] *om* A   213 you knowe] thou knew H
214 might] maye R   215 you] *om* AR   PHILLIPP] PHILIPPUS H
218 everychone] everye iche one ARB

JESUS

A longe tyme you have with me gonne,
Phillipp; why sayest thou soe?　　　　　　　　220
Sickerlye, whoe seeth mee
seeth my Father, I tell yt thee.
Whye willest thou my Father to see
while I with you goe?

29　Phillipp, leeves thou not this:　　　　　　225
that my Father in mee ys,
and I in him alsoe, iwys,
and both we be one?
The workes that I doe are his;
for his helpe maye I not mys.　　　　　　230
Therfore, to wynne you heaven-blys,
my deedes you leeve upon!

30　Whatsoever ye aske my Father deare
in my name in good mancre,
to fulfill yt I have power.　　　　　　235
All that ys to my paye,
that my Father in majestie
by mee glorified may bee;
and eyther, as I saye to thee,
for one have binne aye.　　　　　　240

31　Yf that you love mee hartfullye,
keepe my biddinge truelye,
and to my Father praye will I
to send you the Holye Ghoste
to abyde with you evermore—　　　　　　245
for the world knoweth not his lore,
but you, that have knowen mee yore,
in you he shall be most.

32　Though I goe now to distresse,
I will not leave you comfortles;　　　　　　250

---

221 sickerlye] suerlye A　　　　223 willest] willeth A　　　229 that] *om* AR
231 therfore] wherfore A　　heaven] hevens B　　blys] blesse AR　　　235 I
have] in full AR　　　236 my] his H　　　240 aye] ever A　　　241 hartfullye]
hartely RH　　　242 biddinge] bydinge R, biddinges B

but leeves this well and expresse,
efte I will come agayne;
and then your hartes on a rowe
shall gladlye be, my blys to knowe,
with joye noe man shall take you froo,   255
would he never so fayne.

90ᵛ   33 Ryse up and goe heathen anon.
To my prayer I must gone,
but syt you styll everychwonne,
my Father while I call.   260
Wakes and have my benisonn
for fallinge into temptation.
The sprite aye to bale is bowne
and the flesh readye to fall.

Tunc it Jesus oratum, et discipuli pre dolore dormiunt.

34 Father of heaven in majestie,   265
glorifie, yf thy will bee,
thy Sonne, that hee may glorifie thec,
nowe or I heathen wend.
In yearth thou hast given me postie,
and I have donne with harte free   270
the worke that thou charged mee
and brought yt to an ende.

35 Thy name have I made men to knowe
and spared not thy will to showe
to my disciples one a rowe   275
that thou hast given mee.
And nowe they knowe verelye
that from the Father sent am I.
Therfore, I pray thee especiallye,
save them through thy mercye.   280

253–6] *om* B   254 shall gladlye be] shalbe glade AR   255 with] which
ARH   noe man shall] shall no man H   257 and goe heathen] and goe
wheathen AR, goe we hencc B, and goe we heathen H   259 everychwonne]
everye eiche one A, every eichone R, everyechone BH   263 sprite] speritte
ARBH   264 and] but B   readye] ever readye A, aye ready RBH
SD it Jesus oratum] et Jesus oratum AR, iit Jesus oratum B, Jesus oratum ibit H
discipuli] discipule A   pre] prae H   dormiunt] dormient H   *After SD*]
Jнᴇsᴜs H   268 heathen] hense ARB   269 postie] poste A   277 nowe]
that H

Tunc venit ad discipulos et invenit eos dormientes, et dicit:

36 What! Sleepe you, brethren all, here?
Ryse up and make your prayer
lest temptation have power
to make you for to fall.
The flesh is, as I sayd before,   285
inclininge aye to synne sore,
and ghooste occupyed evermore;
therfore nowe wakes all!

Tunc iterum ad orationem, et alta voce loquitur:

37 My hart is in great mislikinge
for death that is to me commynge.   290
Father, if I dare aske this thinge,
put this awaye froe mee.
Eych thinge to thee possible is;
neverthelesse, nowe in this
at your will I am, iwys.   295
As thou wilt, lett yt bee.

91ʳ Tunc redit ad discipulos iterum.

38 You sleepen, brethren, yett, I see.
Sleepes one nowe all yee.
My tyme ys common taken to bee.
From you I must awaye.   300
He that hath betrayed mee,
this night from him will I not flee.
In sorye tyme borne was hee
and soe he may well saye.

Tunc Judas cum militum cohorte, laternis facibus et armis, venit illuc.

SD] Tunc ad discipulos redit, eos dormientes inveniens H   discipulos] discipulis A, discipulus R   eos] om AR   dicit] dicat R, ait B   286 inclininge]
enclyned B   aye] om AR   287 ghooste] so is B   288 wakes] wake you B
SD orationem] orandum H   loquitur] loquitor dicit A   292 this] it BH
293 eych] all ARBH   thinge] thinges RB   294 nowe] yet A   295 your]
thy R   SD redit] rediet B   iterum] om H   297 sleepen] slepe B
298 all yee] lettes see R   299 common] come H   301 hath betrayed]
betraeth B   SD laternis] laterrens A   armis] armes AR   venit]
veniet H   illuc] illuc et dicat AR, om H

JESUS

39 You men I aske, whom seeke yee?   305

MALCHUS

Jesus of Nasareth, him seeke we.

JESUS

Here, all readye—I am hee.
What have you for to saye?

JUDAS

A, sweete maister, kysse thou mee,
for yt is longe syth I thee see,   310
and togeather we will flee
and steale from them awaye.

JESUS

40 What seeke you men with such a breath?

PRIMUS JUDEUS

Wee seeke Jesus of Nazareth.

JESUS

I saye yore, and yet I saye,   315
I am hee, in good faye.
Suffer these men to goe there waye
and I am at your will.

MALCHUS

41 False theefe, thou shalt gone
to bysshopp Cayphas, and that anon;   320
or I shall breake thy bodye and bonne
and thou be to late.

JESUS] *om* R   *After* 306 JESUS] *om* H   JUDAS] JUDAS ISCA H   309 thou]
om H   310 for] *om* H   syth] synce A   313 breath] breach B
JUDEUS] JEW H   315 saye(1)] said B   321 and] or R

PETRUS

Theefe, and thou be so bould
my maister soe for to hould,
thou shalt be quytte an hundrethfould,   325
and onward take thou that!

91ᵛ   42 Be thou so bould, as thrive I,
to hould my maister here in hye,
full deare thou shalt hit abye
but thou thee heathen dight.   330
Thy eare shall of, by Goddes grace,
or thou passe from this place.

Tunc extrahet gladium et abscindet auriculam Malchi.

Goe playnt nowe to Cayphas
and bydd him do the right.

MALCHUS

43 Owt! Alas, alas, alas!   335
By cockes bones, my eare hee hase!
Mee is betyde a hard case
that ever I come here.

JESUS

Peeter, put up thy sword in hye.
Whosoever with the sword smiteth gladlye   340
with sword shall perish hastelye,
I tell thee withowten were.

Tunc Jesus tetigerit auriculam et sanabit.

---

243 soe] *om* R   326 thou that] thou this A, thee this R   329 thou shalt]
shalt thou H   abye] bye AR   330 heathen] hense RB   *SD* extrahet
gladium] extrahit gladium B, gladium extrahet H   abscindet auriculam
Malchi] abscidit auriculum Malche A, abscidit auriculum Malchi R, abscidit
auriculam Malchi B, Malchi auriculam abscidet H   333 playnt] *om* A
334 bydd] byde A   the] thee AR, thie B   336 cockes] cocke H   hase]
hath B   337 mee] my B   338 come] came RBH   340 whosoever
with the sword smiteth] whosoe smyteth with sorde R, whosoever with sword
smiteth BH   *SD* tetigerit] tetigent B, tangit H   auriculam] auriculum
AR   sanabit] sanat eam H

MALCHUS

44 A, well is mee, well is mee!
My eare is healed nowe, I see.
So mercifull a man as ys hee   345
knewe I never none.

PRIMUS JUDEUS

Yea, though hee have healed thee,
shutt from us shall hee not bee,
but to syr Cayphas, as mott I thee,
with us shall hee goe.   350

JESUS

45 As to a theeffe you came here
with sword and staves and armerye
to take me in fowle manere
and end your wicked will.
In temple with you when I was aye,   355
noe hand on mee would you laye,
but nowe is common tyme and daye
your talent to fulfill.

PRIMUS JUDEUS

46 Come, caytiffe, to Cayphas
or thou shalt have a hard grace.   360
Trott upon a prowder pase,
thou vilde popelard.

92ʳ   Though Belzebubb and Sathanas
come to helpe thee in this case,
both thy hand that thou hase   365
shalbe bounden hard.

Finis

MALCHUS] *om* B   334 nowc] well AR   345 as] *om* AR, as now B
PRIMUS JUDEUS] *om* B, PRIMUS JEW H   347–*Finis*] *om* B   347 have] has H
350 goe] gone AR   351 came] come ARH   352 sword] swordes RH
armerye] armerer A, armere R, armyre H   355 with you when I was]
when I was with you AR, whyl I was with you H   361 pase] space AR
362 vilde] vile ARH   popelard] popilerde A, poplard H   365 hand]
handes ARH   366 bounden] bounde AR

PLAY XVI

92ᵛ THE FLETCHERS, BOWIERS, COWPERS,
AND STRINGERS PLAYE

Incipit Pagina Decima Sexta de Passione Christi.

Et primo venient Judei adducentes Jesum ad Annam et Caypham;
et primo incipiet

PRIMUS JUDEUS

1 Syr byshopps, here we have brought
a wretch that mych woe hase wrought
and would bringe our lawe to naught—
right soe hath hit spurned.

SECUNDUS JUDEUS

Yea, wydewhere we have him sought,   5
and deare alsoe we have him bought,
for here manye mens thought
to him he hase turned.

ANNAS

2 A, janglinge Jesus, art thou nowe here?
Nowe thou may prove thy postie powere,   10
whether thy cause be cleane and cleare;
thy Christhood we must knowe.

CAYPHAS

Meethinke a maistrye that yt were
other for pennye or prayere
to shutt him of his dangere   15
and such sleight to shewe.

Guild-ascription] The Boyers, Fletchers, and Iremengers H   and Stringers]
Stringers and Iremongers B   playe] pagina XVI B   *Play-heading*] Pagina
Decima Sexta de Passione Jesu Christi H   sexta] sexta et A   adducentes]
addulcentes A   Annam] Amani A, Annes R   incipiet] incipit AR   JUDEUS
here and in SHs throughout the play] JEW H   2 wretch] wreth B   4] for
it he hath spurned H   hath hit] at it hath he ARB   5 we have] have
wee B   7 mens] mans H   9 janglinge] javeling B   thou nowe] then H
10 thou may] may thou H   postie] *om* H   12 must] shall H
13 maistrye that yt] maister if he H   15 shutt] shunt H   his] this BH
16 sleight] *om* A, sleightes B, a sleight H

ANNAS

3 Syr, yt is needfull—this saye I—
that one man dye witterlye
all the people to forbye
so that the perish nought.   20

TERTIUS JUDEUS

4 Syr Cayphas, herken nowe to mee!
This babelavaunt would our kinge bee,
whatsoever hee sayes nowe befor thee.
I hard him saye full yore
that prince hee was of such postee,   25
destroye the temple well might hee
and buyld yt up in dayes three
right as yt was before.

93ʳ   QUARTUS JUDEUS

5 Yea, sycker, that I hard him saye,
he maye not denye by no waye;   30
and also, that he was God vereye,
Emanuell and messye.
He maye not nycke this ne say neye,
for more then fortye, in good faye,
that in the temple were that daye   35
harden as well as I.

CAYPHAS

6 Saye, Jesu, to this what sayne yee?
Thow wottest nowe what is put on thee.

After ANNAS] *in* RBH

Sir Cayphas, I saye seckerly
we that bene in companye
must needes this dosebeirde destroye
that wickedly hase wroughte.   4
CAYPHAS
(3 dosebeirde] disabeard H)

17 syr] *om* H   18] that one must dye verely H   19 all] then all B
20 so] and H   nought] not H   21 nowe to] unto R   22] this babliant
that king would be H   would our kinge] or kinge woulde ARB   23 what-
soever] whatsere H   nowe] *om* B   25 such] *om* H   29 that] *om* H
30 not denye] demy it H   33 nycke] nye A, denye R   34 fortye]
twenty H   36 harden] hard him H

Put forth, prince, thy postie
and perceive what the preven.   40
What devill! One worde speakes not hee!
Yett, Jesu, here I conjure thee;
if thou be Goddes Sonne, before mee
answere to that the meven.

JESUS

7 As thou sayes, right soe saye I.   45
I am Goddes Sonne almightye,
and here I tell thee truelye
that me yet shall thou see
sytt on Goddes right hand him bye,
mankynd in clowdes to justefye.   50

CAYPHAS

'Justifie!' Marye, fye, fye on thee, fye!
Wytnes of all this compenye
that falsely lyes hee!

8 Ye hearen all what he sayes here.
Of wytnes nowe what neede were,   55
for before all these folke in feere
lowdlye thou lyes?
What saye you men that nowe binne here?

PRIMUS JUDEUS

Buffetes him that makes this bere,
for to God may he not bee dere   60
that owr lawe so destroyes.

39 forth] force B   40 preven] proven A, sayne H   41 devill] devell
of hell A, the devill H   one worde speakes not] not on worde speakes A, not
one worde speaketh R   43 before] here before A   44 meven] moven AR
45 right soe] soe righte R, so H   49 right] *om* H   50 clowdes] clowd H
CAYPHAS] OMNES SIMULL H   51] *om* H   justifie marye] marye justiffye A,
marye justiffye marye R   fye fye] fye ARB   52 of] *om* H   *At* 54]
CAYPHAS H   54 hearen] herken H   55 nowe] *om* H   56 these] thes A,
this H   58 nowe] *om* H   60] a new law we shall him leer H   may
he] he maye A   61 lawe] lawes B

CAYPHAS

9 Distroye shall hee not hit.
Yee wretches, ye wanton wytt!
Found that freake a fitt
and gurd him in the face.   65

93ᵛ   ANNAS

Despice him, spurne and spyt.
Let see, or you sytt,
whoe hase happe to hitt
that thus us harmed hase.

Tunc Judei statuent Jesum in cathedram, et dicat torquendo

PRIMUS JUDEUS

10 For his harminge here   70
[nighe] will I nere
this fameland freare
that makes our lawe falsc.

SECUNDUS JUDEUS

Hee ys, withowt were,
to the devyll full deare.   75
Spytt we in fere
and buffett him alls.

TERTIUS JUDEUS (exputans)

11 Yee herden him in this place nowe
howe he lyed hase nowe;
in mydest his face nowe   80
fowle will I fyle him.

63 ye wanton] you wante R, without H   64 that] this H   65 in] on AR
66 spyt] spite B   67 let] letes B   69 thus us harmed] us this harmed
AR, us thus harmed H   hase] hath B   SD cathedram] catheram B,
cathedra H   et dicat torquendo] dicentes ut sequitur H   70 harminge]
harmes H   71 nighe] nygnahe Hm   will I nere] well I were B
72 fameland] same lewd H   freare] fere ARH   74 withowt] but a H
75 full] om H   76 spytt] spite B   77 alls] elles AR, all B   exputans]
om H   78 yee herden] yea harcken AR, you hard H   him] om ARBH
80 mydest] midds of H   81 fowle] fully H   fyle] fowle AH, fielle B

QUARTUS JUDEUS (exputans)

Passe he shall a pase nowe.
For God he him makes nowe,
gettes he no grace nowe
when I may beguyle him.   85

PRIMUS JUDEUS (dans alapam)

12 Fye upon the, freyke!
Stowpe nowe, nowe, and creake.
Thy breanes to breake
am I reddye bowne.

Tunc Secundus Judeus dans alapam velando faciem Jesu.

SECUNDUS JUDEUS

His face will I steake   90
with a cloth, ere he creake,
and us all wreake
for my warrysonn.

TERTIUS JUDEUS

13 And thou be messye
and loth for to lye,   95
whoe smote thee crye,
yf that thou be Christ.

94r   QUARTUS JUDEUS (percutiens)

14 Though he sore stryke
a buffett shall byte;

exputans] *om* H   85 may] *om* H   dans alapam] *om* H   86 upon] on H
the] this AR, thie B, thee H   87 stowpe] stope R, carpe H   nowe nowe]
nowe ARBH   88 to] will I H   89 am] as B   *SD*] *to right of*
JUDEUS B, *om* H   tunc Secundus Judeus] *om* B   faciem] facien R   Jesu]
Jesu et dicat A   90 steake] stecke A, seeke B, streake H   91 a] *om* H
92 all] all to H   97 that] *om* H   percutiens] peroutrens A, *om* RH
Before 98] *in* RBH

For all his prophesye
yet he fayles thrye;
though my fiste flye,
gettes he a feiste.   4

PRIMUS JUDEUS

(4 gettes he] gave I not H   feiste] feast B, fist H   JUDEUS] JUDEUS percutiens B)
98 sore stryke] sore skricke ARB, him beshitt H   99 byte] bytt H

may no man myne white,   100
though I do him woo.

SECUNDUS JUDEUS (percutiens)

15 And moe yett I maye.
I shall soone assaye
and shewe large paye,
thou prince, on thy pate.   105

QUARTUS JUDEUS

Yf he saye naye,
I shall, in faye,
laye on. I dare laye
yt is not to late.

Tunc cessabunt ab alapis, et dicit Cayphas.

CAYPHAS

16 Lordinges, what is your best read?   110
This man hase served to be dead,
and yf hee lightly thus be lead,
our lawe cleane will sleepe.

ANNAS

Syr, yt is fullye myne advise,
leade we him to the hye justice.   115
Syr Pilate is both warre and wise
and hase the lawe to keepe.

100 myne] me ARBH   white] witt H   percutiens] perutrens A, om RH
Before 102] in RBH

                        Hym fayles to flytt
                        or ought to despitte;
                        for he hase to lite,
                        now must he have moe.   4
                TERCIUS JUDEUS (percutum)
(1 hym] he H   to flytt] for to flyte H   2 despitte] despice B   4 have]
                hame H   percutum] percutiens B, om H)

102 yett] if H   104 and shewe] haste thou H   107 in] hym AR
108 on] one RB, om H   SD et dicit Cayphas] et dicat A, et dicat Cayphas
R, om H   110 lordinges] lordins B   114 fullye] full A   116 is both]
that is H

Tunc Cayphas et Annas et Judei adducunt Jesum ad Pilatum.
Dicat

CAYPHAS

17 Syr Pilate, here we bringe one
   that false is, and our elders fonne.
   Tribute may be given nonne   120
   to Caesar for him here.
   Whersoever he and his fellowe gonne,
   they turne the folke to them eychone.
   Nowe aske we donne here him upon
   of that he hasse power.   125

ANNAS

18 Sycker he is our elders foe.
   Whersoever he goeth, to or froo,
   that he is Christ, and kinge also,
   he preaches apertlye.
   Wist Caesar that, he would be woo,   130
   such a man and we let goo.
   Therfore to dampne him we binne throo,
   lest he us all destroye.

94ᵛ   PILATUS

19 Per vous, syr Cayphas; dye vos, syr Annas
   et sum desepte Judas; vel atres in fuit.   135
   Come up, lordinges, I you praye,
   and we shall here what he will saye
   amonge this fellowshippe here.

20 What sayst thou, man in miseraye?
   And thou be kinge of Jewes, saye!   140

SD adducunt] adducant ARB, adducent H   Jesum] eum H   dicat] dicitte
Cayphas A, dicat Caiphas B, om H   118 bringe] bringen H   122 fellowe]
felowes ARBH   123 folke] folkes AR   124 donne here him] dome
hym ARH, dome him here B   125] lest he us all destroy H   that he]
thee that ARB   126 he] hye B   foe] fone H   128 Christ and kinge]
kinge and Christ H   131 and] if AR   132 dampne] dome H
PILATUS] after 135 A   134–8] om H   134 vous] vos B   vos] vous AR
135 desepte] dispte A, despte R   139 miseraye] misserye A, mystarye R,
mis arraye BH   140 saye] then saye B

JESUS

So thou sayes; men heare maye
a kinge that thou me mase.

PILATUS

Noe cause fynd I, in good faye,
to doe this man to death todaye.

CAYPHAS

Syr, the people, us to mispaye,   145
converted to him all hee hase.

ANNAS

21 Yea, all the land of Gallilee
cleane turned to him hase hee.
Therfore [dome] nowe aske we,
this false man to do downe.   150

PILATUS

Syth he was borne ther as steyne yee,
to Herode send soone shall he be;
elles rafte I him his royaltie
and blcmished his renowne.

22 Goe, lcades him to Herode in hye,   155
and sayes I send him to justefie
this man of which he hath maistrye
at his owne likinge.

PRIMUS JUDEUS

Him shall he have full hastelye,
and lead him thidder anon will I.   160

141 men] as men H   143 cause] cuse A   145 us to mispaye] follow his
way H   146 converted to him] perverted them H   148 him] them H
149 dome nowe] downe nowe Hm, now doome of him B   150 do downe]
be done H   151 syth] wheras AR   as] om A   steyne] seene B, sayen R,
sayn H   152 send soone shall he] sone send he shall H   153 rafte]
rwast B, reft H   154 blemished] blemyshe RBH   155 in] one B
156 sayes] saithes B   him] om H   159 he] you AR   full] om H
160 and] for H   will I] in hye R

Come thou forth with thy rybaldrye
and speake with our kinge.

Tunc ibunt duo Judei adducentes Jesum ad Herodem; et dicat

PRIMUS JUDEUS

23 Syr kinge, here Pilate hath you sent
a shrewe that our lawe hasse shent,
for to have his judgment   165
or he hens awaye wend.

HERODES

A! Welcome, Jesu, verament!
And I thanke Pilate of his present,
for oftetymes I have binne in that intent
after thee to have sent.   170

95ʳ   24 Jesu, mych have I hard of thee.
Some vertue fayne nowe would I see.
If thou from God in majestie
be commen, tell us here.
I pray thee, say nowe to mee,   175
and prove some of thy postie,
and mych the gladder would I bee,
truly, all this yeare.

Jesus nihil respondebit; et dicat

HERODES

25 What! I weene that man is wood,
or elles dombe and can no good.   180

161 rybaldrye] sigaldry H   162 our] the H   *SD* adducentes Jesum]
cum Christo H   et dicat] et dicat Primus Judeus A, et dicunt B, *om* H
PRIMUS JUDEUS] *om* ARH   163 Pilate] sir Pilate A   165 his] hye H
166 hens awaye] heathen H   167 Jesu] Jesu a A   168 and] *om* H   of]
for H   his] this ARH   169 oftetymes] oftetyme H   I have] have I B   in that]
om H   170 to] for to B   have sent] have sende A, sende H   171 have
I] I have H   172 vertue fayne nowe] signe now fayne H   175 say nowe]
that thou say H   176 some] some now B, here some H   177 would I]
I must H   *SD*] Nihil resondet H   nihil] nichell A, nighell R, nill B
respondebit] respondet B   dicat] dicit Herodes A, Herodes dicat B   HERODES]
om ABH   179 that] this H   180 dombe] dompe A, dome B   can
no] cannot R

Such a scalward never before me stood,
so stowt and sterne is hee.
Speake on, Jesu, for cockes blood,
for Pilate shall not, by my hood,
do the non amys; but mend thy mood   185
and speake somwhat with mee.

26 Alas, I am nigh wood for woo.
    Methinkes this man is wonders throo,
    dombe and deafe as a doted doo,
    or frenticke, in good faye.   190
    Yett sythen that Pilate hasse donne soo,
    the wrath that was betweene us two
    I forgive—no more his foe
    to be after this daye.

27 Cloth him in white, for in this case   195
    to Pilate hit may be solace,
    for Jewes custome before was
    to cloth men that were wood
    or madd, as nowe hee him mase,
    as well seemes by his face;   200
    for him that hase lost his grace
    this garment is full good.

Tunc Judei induent eum veste alba et dicat

PRIMUS JUDEUS

28 Have this, Jesu, upon thee
    a worshipfull weede, as thinkes mee,
    of the kinges liverye   205
    that nowe is on thee light!

181 scalward] stalwarde RB, stanold H   never before me] before me AR,
before me never H   182 so] and H   185 non] om H   but] now H
186 and] then B   with] to BH   187 nigh] near H   188 wonders]
wounder ARB, wondrous H   throo] froe H   191 sythen] seinge A, sith B,
since H   that] om B   192 betweene] betwixt B   193 no more] no more
to be A, to be no more R, him no more H   195 in(2)] om H   198 to] so
to H   were] be H   wood] madd R   199 madd] wood R   as nowe hee him]
nowe as he hym A, as he hymselfe R, as he now him H   200 seemes]
seemed R   202 this] that H   SD] to right of 198 H   Judei] Juddi A,
om H   induent] indent AR, induunt H   veste] vestum B   et dicat] om H
204 thinkes mee] thinken we H   206] that on thee now is lifte H

SECUNDUS JUDEUS

Put thee forth. Thou may not flee.
Nowe thou art in thy royaltie!
Syr Herode, kinge, beleave on thee
and grantmercye this [guyfte].   210

95ᵛ Tunc exeunt duo Judei ad Pilatum adducentes Jesum in veste alba, et dicat

PRIMUS JUDEUS

29 Syr Pilate, here the kinge hath sent
Jesu agayne, and, syth we went,
he hasse forgiven his male intent
for thy deede todaye.

PILATUS

Yea, fault in him can I fynd none,   215
ne Herode, as seemes hereupon.
Therfore is best we lett him gonne
whither he will his waye.

SECUNDUS JUDEUS

30 Naye, all, all we cryen with on voyce,
nayle him, nayle him to the crosse.   220

PILATUS

Yee men, for shame! Lett bee your noyce!
My counsell will I saye.
Yee knowen eychonne the manere:
delivered must be a prisoner—
this feast that nowe approches neare—   225
for honour of the daye.

31 Will ye Jesu delyvered bee?

208 thou art] art thou H   209 Herode kinge] kinge Herode H   on thee]
of thee ARB, will ye H   210 this] *om* AR   guyfte] guyste Hm, guyse R
SD] Tunc redeunt ad Pilatum cum Christo H   veste] vest R   212 we]
he RH   213 forgiven] forgotten A   216 as seemes] has seene AR,
as seene is BH   217 is] it is AR   219] nayle him we cry with on
voyce H   all(1)] ney ARB   all we] we all A, we B   cryen] crynne B
220 nayle him nayle him] nayle hym A, nayle nayle him R   221 lett bee] be
still H   noyce] naye B

TERTIUS JUDEUS

Naye, suffer the death worthye is hee;
and thereupon all cryen wee,
and Barabas reserved.   230

PILATUS

What shall I doe with Jesu here
that Christ is called, and kinge in feere?

QUARTUS JUDEUS

Nayle him on the crosse in all manere,
for so he hath deserved.

PILATUS

32 Nowe sythen I see you so fervent   235
and shapen that he shalbe shent,
wash I will here in your present,
waxe ye never so woodd.
Yee shall all wytt verament
that I am cleane and innocent   240
and for to sheede in no intent
this rightwise mans bloodd.

Tunc Pilatus lavabit manus, et Cayphas et Annas recedent cum
Pilato; et dicat Pilatus.

96ʳ   PILATUS

33 Yee prelates here everychonne,
what will ye do? Lett him gonne?

CAYPHAS

Nayle, nayle him to the crosse anonne   245
and deeme him or thou leeve.

228 suffer the] to suffer H   229 all cryen] all crye AR, cry all H
230 Barabas] Barabam AR, Barraban B   233 the] *om* H   235 sythen]
seinge A, since H   237 I will] will I H   in your] you all H   240 cleane]
clear H   241 and] not H   242 rightwise] righteous B   *SD*] Tunc
Pilatus manus suas lavabit, et postea dicat H   manus] manibus AR
recedent] recedente A   cum] a B   et] *om* A   Pilatus] *om* AB
PILATUS] *om* H   243 everychonne] everye eichone ARB   245 nayle(1)]
nay BH   246 deeme] dome H

PILATUS

Takes ye him, that binne so gryme,
and after your lawe deeme ye him.

ANNAS

Nay, that is not lawfull, lyth ne lymme
for us no man to reeve.   250

PILATUS

34 What devill of hell ys this to saye?
Jesu, tell me, I thee praye,
arte thou kinge—saye yea or naye—
of Jewes by auncetrye?

JESUS

Whither hopes thou yt so be,   255
or other men tould hit the?

PILATUS

Naye, fay! Thyselfe may knowe and see
that no Jewe am I.

35 Men of thyne owne nation
shewen for thy dampnatyon   260
with many an accusatyon,
and all this day have.
Art thou kinge—say, for all ther crye?

JESUS

My realme in this world, as say I,
ys [not]—but were, witterlye,   265
with Jewes were I not tayne.

PILATUS] *om* H   247–8] *om* H   249 that] it H   lyth] lyfe H   250 reeve]
leve A   251 devill] the devill H   255 whither] wheither A, whether
RBH   256 hit the] thee of me H   257 naye] may B, ma H   thyselfe]
thieselvon B   261 an] *om* ARBH   262 have] soe have R, so han H
263 say] *om* B   264 as] *om* A   265 not] nowe Hm   were] were it
ARB, if it weer H

36 And if my realme in this world were,
stryve I would with you nowe here
and lead with me such powere
should pryve you of your praye. 270
But my might in this manere
will I not prove, ne nowe appere
as worldly kinge; my cause uncleare
were then, in good faye.

PILATUS

37 Ergo, a kinge thou art, or was. 275

96ᵛ JESUS

That thou sayes, yt is no lesse.
But nowe I tell thee here expresse
that kinge I am and be maye.
In world I came to beare wytnes
of soothnes, and therfore borne I was, 280
and all that leeven soothnes
take heede to that I saye.

PILATUS

38 What is soothnes, tell thou mee?

JESUS

Soothnes came from Goddes see.

PILATUS

In yearth then hath trueth no postie 285
by thyne opinion?

JESUS

Howe should on yearth bee
while so deemed in yearth is hee
of them that have non authoritie
in yearth, agaynst reason? 290

267 in] of B   268 I would with you] with you I would H   271 my]
om H   273 worldly] wordlie B   PILATUS] om H   275-82] om H
278 be maye] maye be A   280 and] om A   281 leeven] lyven B
284 came] comes H   285 hath trueth] truth hath H   286 by] in A
287 should] shoulde truth ARBH   on] in BH   288 is] his R
289 non] om H   290 agaynst] agayne H

PILATUS

39 Lordinges, I fynd no cause, iwys.
to dampne this man that here ys.

CAYPHAS

Pilate, he hath donne mych amysse.
Let him never passe.
By Moyses lawe liven wee   295
and after that lawe dead shall hee bee,
for apertly preached hase hee
Goddes Sonne that he was.

ANNAS

40 Yea, Pilate, he that makes him appere
other to kinge or kinges feere   300
withsayth Caesar of his power,
and so we have donne with him.
And whoso calles himselfe a kinge here
reves Caesar of his power.

PILATUS

Anone goe scourge this losingere   305
and beat him lymme and lythe.

PRIMUS JUDEUS

41 Come nowe with care,
freake, for thy fare.
On thy bodye bare
strockes shalt thou beare.   310

SECUNDUS JUDEUS

Cast of thy ware,
all thy clothes, yare.

291 lordinges] lordes H   fynd] fyne R   292 dampne] dome H   this]
thes H   that] that now B   295 lawe] lawes R   liven] leven ARBH
296 shall] should H   299 makes] maketh R   appere] peere H   301 with-
sayth] doth saith A, withsayth so R, wich saith B   302 we have donne]
he hath H   303 and] for H   calles] called A, calleth R   himselfe a]
him H   304 reves] depryves H   306 lymme and lythe] leith and lym A
PRIMUS] FIRST H   308 for] with H   SECUNDUS] SECOND H   311 thy]
this H   312 all] of all ARH

Start nowe and stare.
This stalward I would stere.

Tunc spoliabunt ipsum et ligabunt ad columnam; et dicat

TERTIUS JUDEUS

42 Nowe he is bounden.   315
    Be he never so wandon,
    soone he shalbe fownden
    with flappes in feere.

QUARTUS JUDEUS

In woo he ys wounden
and his grave is grounden.   320
No lade unto London
such lawe can him lere.

Tunc posteaquam flagellaverunt eum, postea induunt eum purpurea ponentes in cathedram, et dicat

PRIMUS JUDEUS

43 Nowe, syth hee kinge ys,
    whyte his clothinge ys.
    Beggere, I bringe thee this,   325
    thee for to wearc.

Tunc Secundus Judeus ponens coronam spineam super capite eius
et dicat

314 this stalward] thee stanold H   would] will AR, om H   SD spoliabunt]
poliabunt A   ipsum] eum H   ligabunt ad columnam] legabunt ad columnam R, ad columnam ligabunt H   et dicat] om H   TERTIUS] THIRD H
315 he is] is he H   316 wandon] wounden ARH, wendon B   317 he
shalbe] shall he be H   fownden] fonden R, fowden B   319 he ys] he was R,
shall he be H   320 grave is] grane is A, graynes H   SD] om AR
posteaquam] om H   flagellaverunt] flagellabunt H   postea] et postea H
induunt] induent H   eum] om B   purpurea] purpura H   ponentes]
potentes B, sedentem H   cathedram] cath H   et dicat] et dicat Primus
Judeus B, om H   PRIMUS] FIRST H   323 syth] since H   324 whyte]
whante R, whainte B, quoynt H   clothinge] clothis H   325 I bringe thee]
to thee I bringe H   326] for this thou shalt beare H   SD] om ARH
spineam] spinam B   capite] caput B

SECUNDUS JUDEUS

All in lythinge this ys
that of ould spronge ys;
of thornes this thinge ys,
thee for to were.   330

TERTIUS JUDEUS

44 Nowe thou hasse a weede,
have here a reede.
A scepter I thee bede,
a kinge for to bee.

QUARTUS JUDEUS

Hervye, take heede!   335
Thus must I neede
for my foule deede
kneele upon knee.

97ᵛ   ### PRIMUS JUDEUS

45 Hayle, kinge of Jewes!
That so many men shewes,   340
rybauld, nowe thee rewes,
with all thy reverence.

SECUNDUS JUDEUS

With yron on him hewes
and his hyde hewes.
An oyntment thee newes   345
for thyne offence.

SECUNDUS JUDEUS] *om* B, SECOND JEW H   327 in] ye A, of H   lythinge]
lething B, heathing H   328 that] and H   spronge] sprong B, spinge H   *To
right of* 328] Cum corona spinea H   329 this] thi H   TERTIUS] THIRD H
333 a] *om* H   bede] bide AR, beare B   *To right of* 333] Tradet sibi
arundinem H   QUARTUS] FOURTH H   335 Hervye] hevie B, harlott H
336 thus] this ARH   *To right of* 336] Tunc flectent genua H   337 my]
thy H   338 upon] upon my ARB, on my H   knee] knye A   PRIMUS]
FIRST H   340 men] *om* H   shewes] rewes A, shrews H   341 rybauld]
riball A   nowe] *om* AH   rewes] reaves B   342 with] *om* H   thy]
this H   SECUNDUS] SECOND H   343 yron] spould H   hewes] spues H
344 and] on A   345] annoynting thy brows H   an oyntment] anoyntmente ARB

TERTIUS JUDEUS

46 To wryte in his face—
thou that the kinge mase,
nowe my nose hase
good spice of the newe!   350

QUARTUS JUDEUS

With a hard grace
thou came to this place.
Passe thou this rase,
sore shalt thou rewe.

PILATUS

47 Lordinges, here you may se   355
your kinge all in his royaltie.

CAYPHAS

Nay, syr, forsooth, no kinge have wee
save the emperour of Rome pardee;
and but thou nayle him to the tree,
the emperour full wrath wilbee.   360

ANNAS

All we sayen right as sayes hee.
Deme him while thou hase tyme.

PILATUS

48 Whether of them will ye have,
Jesus Christ or Baraban?

TERTIUS] THIRD H   347 wryte] spitt H   his] thy H   348 thou] tho B,
om H   the] thee ARH   mase] was B   349 nowe] noe A   350] good
ostern new H   QUARTUS] QUARTU B, FOURTH H   353 thou] now H
this] the H   354 sore] so ever H   355 lordinges here] come hether
lordinges B   357 have wee] is he H   358 pardee] om H   359 and]
om BH   to] unto B   360 full] om A   362 tyme] tome H
363 will] would H   364 Jesus Christ] Christ Jesu H   Baraban] Barabam
ARB

CAYPHAS

Naye, Jesus this traytour that is tane 365
must nayld be to the tree,
and lett Baraban goe his waye.

PILATUS

Take him to you nowe as I saye,
for save him I ney maye,
undonne but I would bee. 370

98r ### PRIMUS JUDEUS

49 This [dome] is at an end.
Nowe read I that we wend
this shrewe for to shend
a little here besyde.

Secundus Judeus, ponens crucem super dorsum eius, dicat.

SECUNDUS JUDEUS

Here shalt thou not lend. 375
Come hither and behind
thy backe for to bende.
Here may thou not abyde.

THE DAMSELL (to Peter)

50 Was not thou with Jesus of Nazareth?

PETER

I knowe him not, nor what thou sayest. 380

365 this] that H   tane] here R   366 to] unto B, on H   367 Baraban]
Barrabam AR, Barabbas H   368 to you nowe] forth then H   I] ye R,
you H   369 him] him I see H   370 would] should H   *After*
370] Tunc Judei capiunt Jesum H   PRIMUS] FIRST H   371 dome]
donne Hm   372 read I that we] I redd us to H   *SD*] *om* AH, Pones
crucem super dorsum et dicat R   SECUNDUS JUDEUS] *om* B, SECOND JEW H
376 behind] be hynd A, be hende BH   378 here] hit A, he B   *To right of*
378] Tunc ibunt versus montem Calvariae H   THE DAMSELL to Peter] the
Damsell doth speake to Petter A, *om* H   379–*Finis*] *om* H   380 nor] or A
sayest] saies AR, saith B

THE DAMSELL

Syrs, syckerlye I tell you playne,
this man here is on of them
that was with him in the garden;
I knowe yt to be trewe.

PETER

51 Yt is not trewe, so mote I thee. 385
I knowe him not by any degree.

THE JEWE

One of [them] thou art assuredlye,
and thou art alsoe of Gallilee.
Thy speach clearly bewrayeth thee
in wytnes of us all. 390

PETER

52 In fayth and trueth, that ys no soe.
Shame have I, and myckell woo,
yf ever I did him before knowe
or keepe him companye.

Finis

PLAY XVIA

98ᵛ THE IRENMONGERS PLAYE

Incipit Pagina de Crucifixione Christi et de his qui fuerunt in
eundo versus locum Calvariae; et incipit Cayphas.

CAYPHAS

1 Nowe of this segger we binne seker.
Agaynst us boote he not to beker.

THE] *om* ARB 381 syckerlye] *om* AR THE] *om* R 387 them] then
HmB 391 trueth] troth A no] not ARB 394 keepe] kepte A

Guild-ascription] *om* H *Play-heading*] *om* H crucifixione] cruci-
fixionem R qui] que ARB fuerunt] fuerust A, fuerant B Calvariae]
Calvarre R, Calveri B Cayphas] *om* A 1 segger] sager H 2 agaynst]
all againste AR boote he] him boots H beker] leker B, bicker H

Though he flyre, flatter and flycker,
thys fiste shall he not flee.
Thou, Jesu, would be our kinge?   5
Goe forth! Evill joye thee wringe,
for wroken on thee at our likinge
full soone shall we bee.

2 Gurd on fast and make him goe,
this freake that ys our elders foe;   10
for all his wyles, from this woe
shall no man him warne.

ANNAS

Him seemes werye of his waye.
Some helpe to gett I wyll assaye,
for this crosse, in good faye,   15
soe farre he may not beare.

3 Come hither, Symon of Surrey,
and take this crosse anon in hye.
Unto the mount of Calverye,
helpe that yt were borne.   20

SYMON

The devill speede this companye!
For death hee is not worthye.
For his sake, syckerlye,
I hould you all forlorne.

4 To beare no crosse am I entent,   25
for yt was never myne assent
to procure thys profettes judgment,
full of the Holy Ghoost.

3 flyre] flyte H   and] or H   4 fiste] fytt H   5 would] wouldest RB,
would thou H   6 joye] John B   7 on] of R   9 on] him H
make] lett H   10 ys our elders] hath bene our H   11 his wyles]
this whyle H   from] form A   12 warne] weare H   13 of] on A
16 he may] may he H   17 of Surrey] Sirrye H   18 and] *om* H
19 unto] and to H   Calverye] Calvely B   SYMON] SIMON DE CIREN H
21 this] all this BH   25 am I] is my H

CAYPAS

Symon, but thou will be shent
and suffer payne and imprisonment,   30
this crosse upon thy backe thou hent
and lett be all thy bost.

SYMON

5 Alas, that ever I hither come!
Would God I had bynne in Rome
when I the waye hither come,   35
thus to be anoyed!

99ʳ But God I take to wytnes
that I do this by distresse.
All, iwys, through your falsnes
I hope will be destroyed.   40

ANNAS

6 Have donne! Bringe forth those theeves two!
On eyther halfe him they shall goe.
This freake shall be handled soe
with fellowshippe in fere.

PRIMUS JUDEUS

Take them here, bound fast,   45
while this whippecorde may last,
for the pryme of the daye is past.
How longe shall we be here?

PRIMA MARIA

7 Alas, alas, and woe is mee!
A doolfull sight this is to see.   50

CAYPAS] CAYPHAS ARBH   30 imprisonment] prisonment BH   SYMON]
SIMON DE SIREN H   33 come] came R   34 in] at A   35 come] nome H
36 thus] this A   37 God] lord H   38 and 39] reversed H   39 iwys
through your] Jewes for this H   To right of 40] Tunc crucem accipiet H
41 those] these AR   two] towe A, too B   42 on] om R   halfe] syde
A, syde of H   they shall] shall they H   43 freake] sir H   handled]
honored H   44 fere] feree B   PRIMUS JUDEUS] om H   45 them]
him H   bound] bounden H   46 this] a H   may] here will H   47 for
the] om H   48 shall we] will you H   After 48] Tunc Jesum et duos
latrones abducent, et venient mulieres, quarum dicat Prima H   MARIA]
MULIER H   49 woe is] woes AR   50 this is] is this AR, is it H

C 9206   X

So many sycke saved hath hee,
and nowe goeth this waye.

SECUNDA MARIA

Sorrowfull may his mother bee
to see thy flesh so fayre and free
nayled so fowle upon a tree,   55
as he mon be todaye.

JESUS

8 Yee weomen of Jerusalem,
weepe not for mee, ne make noe [swem];
but for your owne barme-[teame]
ye mon reame tenderlye.   60
For tyme shall come, withowten were,
ye shall blesse ballye that never child bere
and pappe that never milke came nere,
so nygh ys your anoye.

CAYPHAS

9 Have donne, you tormentours, tyte,   65
and spoyle him that hath donne us spyte.

PRIMUS JUDEUS

Yea, though hee both growne and stryke,
owt hee shalbe shaken.
Bee thou wroth or be thou fayne,
I will be thy chamberlayne.   70
This coate gettes thou never agayne
and I may be waken.

51 sycke] *om* H   52 this waye] this awaye AR, thus away B, his way H
SECUNDA MARIA] SECUNDUS MARIA AR, THE SECOND MARY B, SECUNDA MULIER H
54 see] witt H   thy] his R, thee B, the H   flesh] flecke A   55 so] *om* AR
56 mon] must H   58 swem] swene HmAR, mone B   59 barme] barne
ARBH   teame] teane HmR   60 mon] may H   reame] weepe RH, rue B
61 withowten] without H   62 ye] they H   ballye] ball A, bale R, balle B,
belye H   63 pappe] papps H   never milke] milke never AR   64 nygh]
niche A, much H   ys] as B   anoye] anye B   *To right of* 64] Tunc ibunt
super montem H   65 have] hase A, haste R   66 and] *om* H   spoyle]
spill AR   us] you B   spyte] spitte A   JUDEUS] JEW H   67 growne]
pisse H   stryke] skricke AR, skrike B, shyte H   69 or] *om* H   72 may]
om H

99ᵛ

10 This coate shalbe myne,
for yt is good and fyne
and seame is none therin   75
that I can see.

TERTIUS JUDEUS

Yea, God give me pyne
and that shalbe thine,
for thou art ever inclind
to drawe towardes thee.   80

QUARTUS JUDEUS

11 Naye, fellowes, by this daye,
at the dyce we will playe,
and there we shall assaye
thys weede for to wyn.

PRIMUS JUDEUS

A, fellowe, by this daye,   85
well can thou saye!
Laye forth those clothes; laye
on boord or we blyn!

SECUNDUS JUDEUS

12 Fellowes, nowe let see!
Here are dyce three.   90
Which of all wee
shall wynne this ware?

TERTIUS JUDEUS

Nay, parted they shalbe,
for that ys egallye.

SECUNDUS JUDEUS] SECUND H   75 is] is ther H   therin] within H
TERTIUS JUDEUS] THIRD H   79] aye thou art enclyne H   inclind] inclyne
ARB   QUARTUS JUDEUS] FOURTH H   81 fellowes] felowe ABH   this
daye] my fay H   PRIMUS JUDEUS] FIRST H   85 A] yea H   this daye]
my fay H   87 those] these BH   88 we] you A   After 88] Tunc
spoliabunt Jesum vestibis et stabit nudus quousque sortiati H   SECUNDUS
JUDEUS] SECOND H   89 fellowes] fellow H   let] lettes ABH, lett us R
92 ware] warre B   TERTIUS JUDEUS] THIRD H   93 parted they] departed
it H   94 egallye] equitye H

Therfore, as mote I thee,   95
or we hethen fare—

QUARTUS JUDEUS

13 This coate bowt seame,
to breake yt were shame,
for in all Jerusalem
ys non such a garment.   100

PRIMUS JUDEUS

His dame nowe may dreame
for her owne barme-teame;
for nother aunte nor eame
gettes this gaye garment.

SECUNDUS JUDEUS

14 His other clothes all   105
to us fowre can fall.
First parte them I shall,
and after playe for this.

100ʳ   This kyrtle myne I call.
Take thow this pawlle.   110
Iche man in this halle
wottes I doe not amysse.

Ad Tertium:

15 This kyrtle take to thee—

Ad Quartum:

and thou this to thy fee.
Iche man nowe maye see   115
that all wee be served.

95 therfore] in fowr parts H   96 hethen] hense ARB   QUARTUS JUDEUS]
FOURTH H   97 bowt] without H   98 shame] sweme H   99 all] *om* H
100 ys] ther is H   a garment] one other R, verament H   PRIMUS JUDEUS]
FIRST H   102 owne] *om* H   barme] barne ARBH   teame] teane AR
103 nother] mother B   eame] neeme B   104 gaye] *om* H   SECUNDUS
JUDEUS] SECOND H   106 can] mon H   107 parte] depart H   108 playe]
dice H   110 take] and take H   ad Tertium] ad Secundus A, *om* RBH
113 kyrtle] corsett H   ad Quartum] ad Tercium A, *om* RBH   115 nowe
maye] maye nowe AR, may H

TERTIUS JUDEUS

Yea, nowe I read that wee
sytt downe, as mote I thee,
and looke whose thys shalbe
that ys here reserved.   120

Tunc omnes sedent et dicat Primus Judeus jactans decios:

16 Nowe will I beginne
for to cast, or I blynne,
this coate for to wynne
that is both good and fyne.

SECUNDUS JUDEUS

By my fathers kynn,   125
noe parte hasse thou therin;
but, or I hethen wynne,
this coate shalbe myne.

17 Take! Here, I darre laye,
arc dubletts in good araye.   130

TERTIUS JUDEUS

Thou fayles, fellowe, by my faye,
to have this to thy fee,
for here is cator-traye.
Therfore goe thou thy waye,
and as well thou maye,   135
and leave this with mee.

QUARTUS JUDEUS

18 Fellowes, verament,
I read we be at on assent.

TERTIUS JUDEUS] THIRD H   117 nowc I read] I redd now H   118 as]
so H   119 looke] *om* H   *SD*] *om* A, Tunc sedebunt omnes H   et dicat
Primus Judeus] *om* R   decios] decias R, alias B   *After SD*] PRIMUS
JUDEUS AR, 1. FIRST H   122 for] *om* H   124 both] *om* H   *To right
of* 124] Jacet et perdit H   SECUNDUS JUDEUS] 2. SECOND H   125 fathers]
father ARBH   126 therin] in H   127 wynne] twynne H   130] a
rowndfull in good fay H   araye] faye AR   *To right of* 130] Jacet et
perdit H   TERTIUS JUDEUS] 3. THIRD H   131 fellowe] *om* H   133 here
is] it was H   traye] tree R   *To right of* 134] Jacet et perdit H   135 and]
for B   136 this] it H   QUARTUS JUDEUS] 4. FOURTH H   138 we be
at on] you all H

This gaye garment
that is bowt seame,   140
you give by judgment
to mee this vestement,
for synnce God hath me sent,
thinke you never so sweene.

100ᵛ   PRIMUS JUDEUS

19 As have I good grace,   145
well wonne yt thou hasse,
for synke ther was
that every man might see.

CAYPHAS

Men, for cockes face,
howe longe shall pewee-ars   150
stand naked in that place?
Goe nayle him on the tree!

SECUNDUS JUDEUS

20 Anon, mayster, anon.
A hommer have I wonne.
As farre as I have gonne   155
ys non such another.

TERTIUS JUDEUS

And here are, by my pon,
nayles good wonne
to nayle him upon
and he were my brother.   160

---

140 bowt] without B, withou H   141 you] nowe A   by] by my H
142] *om* AR   *To right of* 142] Jacet et vincit H   143 synnce] synnes
AR, syyes H   hath me] has H   144 so sweene] to wine B, so swem H
PRIMUS JUDEUS] FIRST H   146 well] *om* H   hasse] haste AR   147 synke]
synnes ARH, since B   148 that] *om* H   every] ever B, ech H   might]
maye AR   150 pewee-ars] pewdreas A, pewdras R, pewderas B, poydrace H
151 that] this H   152 on] to ARBH   SECUNDUS JUDEUS] SECOND H
154 wonne] one ARBH   156 ys non] ther is not H   another] one
other R   TERTIUS JUDEUS] THIRD H   157 pon] bones H   158 good
wonne] very good ones H   159 him upon] therupon H   160 and]
though H

QUARTUS JUDEUS

21 Goe we too as fast.
This caytyffe have I cast.
Hee shall be wronge wrast
or I wynd awaye.

PRIMUS JUDEUS

Here is a rope wyll last   165
for to drawe at the mast.
This poplard never past
so perrelous a playe.

SECUNDUS JUDEUS

22 Layes him therupon,
this ilke mased man,   170
and I shall dryve one
this nayle to the end.

TERTIUS JUDEUS

As broke I my ponn,
well cast him I con
and make him full wonne   175
or I from him wend.

QUARTUS JUDEUS

23 Fellowes, will yee see
howe sleight I shalbe
this fist, or I flee,
here to make fast?   180

101ʳ   ### PRIMUS JUDEUS

Yea, but, as mote I thee,
shorte-armed is hee.

QUARTUS JUDEUS] FOURTH H   161 too] to ARH   as] hit H   162 have I] I have
ARBH   163 hee] om H   PRIMUS JUDEUS] FIRST H   166 for] om A   drawe]
drawe hym AR   at the] a H   168 perrelous] parleues A   SECUNDUS
JUDEUS] SECOND H   170 ilke] madde A   171 shall] will AR   172 end]
head B   TERTIUS JUDEUS] THIRD H   174 con] can ARH   175] he
shall be well wonne H   wonne] wan B   After 176] Tunc ponent Jesum
super crucem H   QUARTUS JUDEUS] FOURTH H   178 shalbe] will be H
179 flee] fleye AR, flye H   PRIMUS JUDEUS] FIRST H   181–212] om B

To the booringe of this tree
hit will not well last.

SECUNDUS JUDEUS

24 A, therfore care thou nought.   185
A sleight I have sought.
Roopes must be bought
to strayne him with strenght.

TERTIUS JUDEUS

A rope, as I beheight,
yee shall have in brought.   190
Take yt here well wrought,
and drawe him a lenght.

QUARTUS JUDEUS

25 Drawes, for your fathers kynne,
while that I dryve yn
this ilke iron pynne   195
that I dare laye will last.

PRIMUS JUDEUS

As ever have I wynne,
his arme is but a fynne.
Nowe drive on bowten dynne
and we shall drawe fast.   200

SECUNDUS JUDEUS

26 Fellowe, be this light,
nowe were his feete dight,

183] to bringe to this tree H   booringe] boweringe A   184 hit] he AR
well] long H   SECUNDUS JUDEUS] SECOND H   185 A] and AR
187 bought] brought H   188 strayne] steyne A   with] *om* H   strenght]
strength RH   TERTIUS JUDEUS] THIRD H   189 I] *om* ARH   190 in
brought] unbought H   191 yt here] here one H   192 drawe him]
hym in AR   a lenght] a length R, on length H   *After* 192] Tunc ligabunt cordam ad sinistram manum quia dextra erat prius fixa H   QUARTUS
JUDEUS] FOURTH H   193 fathers] father ARH   195 ilke] same A
PRIMUS JUDEUS] FIRST H   199 on] in R   bowten] bout AR, but H
dynne] dimme H   *After* 200] Tunc tres trahent et quartus transfiget
clavem H   SECUNDUS JUDEUS] SECOND H   201 fellowe] fellowes ARH
be] by ARH   this] this daye A   202] now if his feet were pight H

this gamon went on right
and up hc should be raysed.

TERTIUS JUDEUS

That shall be donne in hight   205
anon in your sight,
for, by my trouth I plight,
I sarve to be praysed.

QUARTUS JUDEUS

. 27 Fellowes, will you see
howe I have stretched his knee?   210
Why prayse ye not mee .
that have so well donne?

PRIMUS JUDEUS

Yea, helpe nowe that hee
on height raysed bcc,
for, as mote I thee,   215
almost hit ys noone.

101ᵛ Tunc Pilatus, habens tabulam in manu, dicit.

PILATUS

28 Come hither thou, I command thee;
goe nayle thys table unto the tree.
Sythen he wyll kynge of Jewes bcc,
he must have a cognisens.   220
'Jesu of Nazareth,' mon may see;
'Kynge of Jewes'—howe lykys thee?—
is wrytten theron, for so sayd hee
withowten varyens.

203 on right] arighte RH   TERTIUS JUDEUS] THIRD H   205 hight] hye AR
207 by] *om* H   trouth] troth AR, trothe H   208 sarve] deserve H
To right of 208] Tunc pedes transfigent H   QUARTUS JUDEUS] FOURTH H
210 knee] knye A   PRIMUS JUDEUS] *om* B, FIRST H   214 height] highe
ARB   SD] Tunc Pilatus tabulam habens in manu tradet uni militum H
tabulam] tabulum AR   manu] manus A   dicit] dicat A, dicas Pilatus R
218 unto] upon AR, on H   219 sythen] seinge A, sithens B, sith H   wyll
kynge of Jewes] kinge of Jews will H   220 a] *om* H   221 mon] men
ARH   222 lykys] liketh AR   thee] ye H   223 is wrytten] I writt H
224 withowten] without H

SECUNDUS JUDEUS

29 Naye, syr Pilate, to us beede. 225
Kinge ys he non, so God me speede.
Therfore thou doest a sorye deede;
this writinge many a mon rewes.
Thou should wryte that men might reede
howe hee lyes to eych leede 230
and tould over all theras he yeede
that he was kynge of Jewes.

PILATE

30 That that ys wrytten I have wrytten.

TERTIUS JUDEUS

And in good fayth that ys fowle wrytten,
for everye mon may well wytten 235
that wronge thou hasse wrought.
What the devyll kynge ys he, mon?
But falslye thereas hee hath gone
hee hasse tould leasinges manye one,
that deere they should be bought. 240

Tunc venit Maria lachrimans.

MARYE

31 Alas, my love, my liffe, my leere!
Alas, nowe mourninge, woe ys mee!
Alas, sonne, my boote thou bee,
thy mother that thee bare.

SECUNDUS JUDEUS] SECOND JEW H   225 naye] now H   syr] yf AR   beede]
byde AR, thou bede B, take hede H   226 ys he non so] he is not as H
228 this] that H   a mon] one H   229 men] man AR, many H   might]
shoulde R   230 lyes] lyed H   231 over all] marvell B   theras] wher H
PILATE] PILATUS H   233 that that] that H   I have] that have I H
TERTIUS JUDEUS] THIRD H   234] yea would God thou were beshitten H
fayth] faye R   235 everye mon] all men H   may] shall H   236 wronge]
wrough A   237 ys he] he is B   mon] non ARBH   239 hee hasse]
om H   manye] to manye RBH   240 that] but R, that full H   they
should] they shalbe R, shall H   SD] Tunc omnes crucem exultabunt, et
veniet Maria H   lachrimans] licramans A, lachrinans R   MARYE] MARIA
AR, THE MOTHER OF JESUS to left of 241-2 B, MARIA MATER JESU CHRISTI H
241 liffe] leeffe R   leere] lee BH   242 nowe mourninge] mowrning now H
woe ys] woes AR, madds H   243 sonne] om H   thou] looke thou H
244 thy] the B

Thinke one, my fruyte, I fostred thee   245
and gave thee sucke upon my brest.
Upon my pyne thou have pittye;
thou feyles no power.

32 Alas, whye nyll my liefe forlorne
to fynd my sonne here me beforne,   250
tugget, lugget, and all totorne
with traytors nowe this tyde,
with nayles thrast and crowne of thorne?
Therfore I made, both evon and morne,
to see my byrth that I have borne   255
this bitter bale to byde.

102ʳ   33 Alas, my sorrowe when wyll thou slake
and to these traytors me betake
to suffer death, sonne, for thy sake
—and doe as I thee saye?   260
Alas, theeves, why doe ye soe?
Slayes ye mee and lett my sonne goe.
For him suffer I would this woe
and lett him wend awaye.

246 brest] knee H   247 thou have] have thou H   248 thou] thee H
feyles] feeleste AR   249 nyll] will A, ne were H   liefe] lyfe H   250 sonne]
foode H   here me] me here B, me H   251 and] om H   253 thrast]
throuste A, thrust RB, thast H   254 made] mone AR, madd H   both] om A
256 byde] abyde AR   After 256] in H

My sorrow, sweet sonne, thou cease,
or of my lyfe thou me releace.
How should I apayd be or in peace
to se thee in such penaunce?
Sith thou me to thy moder chose   5
and of my body borne thou was,
as I conceived thee wemlesse,
thou graunt me some legiaunce.

Alas, the sorrow of this sight
marrs my mynd, mayne and might, 10
but aye my hart methink is light
to looke on that I love.
And when I looke anonright
upon my child that thus is dight,
would death deliver me in height,   15
then were I all above.

257 when wyll thou] why wilt thou not H   262 ye] om AH   and] om AR
264 awaye] his way H

MARIA MAGDALENA

34 Alas, howe should my hart be light   265
     to see my seemely lord in sight
     deolfully drawne and so dight
     that did never man greivans?
     Marred I am mayne and might
     and for him fayles me to fight;   270
     but God, that rules aye the right,
     give you mickell mischance.

MARIA JACOBI

35 Alas, sorrowe syttys me sore!
     Myrth of thee I gett no more.
     Why wouldest thou dye, Jesu, wherfore,   275
     that to the dead gave liffe?
     Helpe me, Jesu, with some thinge
     and out of this bitter bale me bringe,
     or elles slaye me for anythinge
     and stynt me of this stryffe.   280

MARIA SALOMEE

36 Come downe, lord, and breake thy bandes.
     Lose and heale thy lovely handes.
     Or tell me, Jesu, for whom thou wondes,
     syth thou art God and man.
     Alas, that ever I borne was   285
     to see thy bodye in such a case.
     My sorrowe wyll never slake nor seace,
     such sorrowe is me upon.

ANNAS

37 Nowe this shrewe ye hoven on height
     I would see, for all his sleight,   290

MARIA] MARIE B   MAGDALENA] MAGDALEA A, MAGDALEN B   267 drawne]
torne AR   so] all to H   268 greivans] vreavance A   270 fayles me]
me fayles H   271 rules aye] rules ever AR, aye rules H   272 give]
he geve H   mickell] much H   273 syttys] settes H   274 I gett]
gett I H   275 wherfore] therfore AR   281 downe lord] lord downe H
282 thy] they B   283 me] om H   thou wondes] thou wonnes A, thou wones
R, thou woundes B, thy woundes H   284 syth] seinge A, since H   286 thy
body] my lord H   a case] unpeace H   287 slake] slacke A   289 ye
hoven] hoven AR, we haven B, is hoven H   on] an H   290 would] will AR

for his crowne howe he can feight
and ferre from us to flee.
He that hasse healed so manye one
nowe save himselfe give that he can,
and then all we shall leeve him upon   295
that hit soothly so ys.

JESUS

102^v 38 Father of heaven, yf thy will be,
forgive them this they donne to mee;
for they be blynd and may not see
howe fowle they donne amys.   300

CAYPHAS

If thou be of such postee,
and Godes Sonne in majestie,
come downe and we will leeve on thee
that yt soothly so ys.

PRIMUS LATRO (The First Theefe)

39 If thou be Christ verrey   305
and Godes Sonne, nowe as I saye
save us from this death todaye
and thyselfe also.

SECUNDUS LATRO (The Second Theefe)

A, man, be still, I thee praye!
Dreede God, I read thee aye,   310
for folylye thou speakest in faye.
Make not thy freind thy foe.

291 can] would H   292 ferre] fownd H   293 so] *om* A   one] a
one B   294 give] yf ARBH   295 then all] *om* H   shall] will A
him] thee R   296] that Gods Sonne is he H   hit] is B   *After*
296] Tunc Jesus in lignum pendens ait ut sequitur H   297 of heaven]
om H   298 donne] do ARB   299 for] *om* H   300 fowle] *om* B
donne] have done B, do H   304] that soothly so it is H   PRIMUS
LATRO] *om* R   The First Theefe] *before SH* A, *to left of SH* B, *om* H
306 as I saye] assay H   SECUNDUS LATRO] *om* R   The Second Theefe]
before SH A, *to left of SH* B, *om* H   310 I read] or I dreed H   311 folylye]
foulye ARB, folishly H

40 Mon, thou wottest well, iwys,
that rightwisely we suffer this,
for he hath not donne so mych amys   315
to suffer so great anoye.
But, lord, I beseech thee,
when thou art in thy majestie,
then that thou wilt thinke on mee
and on mee have mercye.   320

JESUS

41 Mon, I tell thee, in good faye,
for thy beleeffe is so verey,
in paradyce thou shalt be todaye
with me there in my blys.
And, woman, to thee also I saye   325
by the thy sonne there thou se maye
that cleane virgine hasse binne aye
right as thyselvon ys.

42 And, John, there thy mother thou may see.

JOHN

Yea, lord, her keper I shalbe.   330
Welcome, Marye, mother free;
together we must goe.

MARY THE FIRST

Alas, my hart will brast in three!
Alas, death, I conjure thee!
The liffe, sonne, thou take from mee   335
and twyn me from this woe.

313 wottest] knows H   314 rightwisely] righteouslie BH   315 for he]
but this man H   so mych] *om* H   316 so] suche AR   318 thy] *om* B
319 wilt] wouldest B   322 thy] this AR   323 in] and in AR
324 there] *om* H   blys] blesse A   325 woman to thee] to thee woman H
326 by the] by thy B, ther H   there] *om* H   328 right] lyke H   selvon]
selfe one AR, self H   329 there thy mother thou may] thy moder ther may
thou H   JOHN] JOHANNES EVANGELIS H   330–6] *om* R   330 shalbe]
will be H   331 Marye mother] mother Marye A   MARY THE FIRST]
MARIA H   333 brast] barste A, burst B, break H   335 the] my H
take] takest B

43 Comforte thee nowe, sweete Marye,
    for though we suffer this anoye,
    suster, I tell thee sekerlye,
    on lyve thou shalt him see   340
    and ryse with full victorye
    when he hasse fullfilled the prophecye.
    Thy sonne thou shalt se, sekerlye,
    within these dayes three.

JESUS

44 Eloye, Eloy! My God, I speake to thee!   345
    Eloy lamazabathany!
    Why hasse thou thys forsaken mee?

PRIMUS JUDEUS

A, herke, herke howe hee cryeth upon Elye
to delyver him of his anoye.

SECUNDUS JUDEUS

Abyde, and we shall see in hye   350
whether Elye dare come here or noe.

JESUS

45 My thyrst ys sore, my thyrst ys sore.

TERTIUS JUDEUS

Yea, thou shalt have drynke therfore
that thow shalt lyst to drynke no more
of all thys seaven yeare.   355

JOHN] *om* R, JOHANNES EVANG H   337 nowc] *om* H   338 for] *om* ARH
anoye] anye H   339] I tell thee suster sickerly H   340 lyve] lyfe H
341 ryse] ryse up H   343] thou shalt him se full sickerly H   thou shalt
se] shalt tho B   *After* 344] *in* H
                    Hely, Hely, Hely, Hely!
                    My God, my God, I speak to thee!

345] *om* H   346] hely lama sabacthany H   lamazabathany] lazama-
bathanye A   347 thys] thus B, *om* H   PRIMUS JUDEUS] FIRST JEW H
348 herke herke howe] harcke howe A, hark H   349 to] for to H   of his
anoye] from this anoye B, hastely H   SECUNDUS JUDEUS] SECOND H
350 we] well B   see] witt H   351 Elye] Eloye AR   here] heither A, I B
352] my thirst is sore H   TERTIUS JUDEUS] THIRD JEW H   353 drynke]
a drink H   354 to] *om* ARB

JESUS

46 Mightie God in majestie,
    to worke thy wyll I would never wend.
    My [spiritte] I betake to thee;
    receyve yt, lord, into thy handes.

'Consummatum est.'

CENTURIO

47 Lordinges, I say you sickerlye,   360
    this was Godes Sonne almightie.
    No other, forsooth, leeve will I,
    for needes so yt must be.
    I knowe by manner of his crye
    hee hasse fulfilled the prophecye   365
    and godhead shewed apertlye
    in him, all men may knowe.

CAYPHAS

48 Centurio, as God me speede,
    thou must be smutted; thou canst not read.
    But when thou seest his hart bleede,   370
    lettes se what thou can saye.
    Longys, take this speare in hand
    and put from thee—looke thou ne wond.

103ᵛ   LONGYUS

    A, lord, I see ne sea ne lond
    this seaven yeare, in good fay.   375

QUARTUS JUDEUS

49 Have this speare and take good heede.
    Tho must doe, as the bushoppe thee bade,
    a thinge that ys of full great neede.
    To warne I hould thee wood.

356 mightie] almighty H   in] of R   357 would] will RH   never] ever R
wend] wonde BH   358 spiritte] speete Hm   359 handes] hand H
Latin] *om* H   *For* 359+SH—*Finis in H, see Appendix* IC.   363 so
yt must] soe must it R, it so must B   368 as] so ARB   371 lettes]
lett us AR   372 Longys] Longes A, Longeus R   this] the AR   373 looke
thou ne wond] thou ney wonnde A, ney thou wonde R   374 A] O AR
ne(1)] no R   375 yeare] yeares R   377 tho] thou ARB   bade] bede A,
byde R   379 thee] you AR

LONGYUS

I will do as ye byd mee,   380
but on your perill hitt shalbe.
What I doe I may not see,
whether yt be evell or good.

Tunc Longyus lancia perforat latus Christi, dicens:

50 High kinge of heavon, I thee here.
    What I have donne well wott I neere,   385
    but on my hand and on my speare
    owt water runneth throwe;
    and on my eyes some can fall
    that I may see both one and all.
    A, lord, wherever be this wall   390
    that this water came froe.

51 Alas, alas, and wellawaye!
    What deede have I donne todaye?
    A mon I see, sooth to saye,
    I have slayne in this stead.   395
    But this I hope be Christ verey
    that sycke and blynd hasse healed aye.
    Of mercye, lord, I thee nowe praye,
    for I wyste not what I did.

52 Jesu, mych have I hard speake of thee,   400
    that sycke and blynd through thy pittie
    hasse healed before in this cittie
    as thou hasse me todaye.
    Thee will I serve and with thee bee,
    for well I leeve in dayes three   405
    thou will ryse full in postee
    from enemyes. Lord, I thee praye.

380 byd] byde ARB   *SD* Longyus] Lungius ARB   lancia perforat] laricia
perforat A, perferat cum lancia B   *After SD*] LONGEUS R   384 kinge]
God R   here] praye A   386 hand] handes ARB   390 A] O AR   this]
that R   wall] wale R   391 came] come A   392 well] wayle AR
394 see] see now B   395 this stead] the streete AR   396 be] by B
398 I thee nowe] I thee AR, now I thie B   400 speake] *om* ARB
406 full in] in thye A, in full B

  C 9206   Y

JOSEPHE

53 A, lord God, what hartes have yee
    to slea this mon that I here see
    dead, hanginge upon roode-tree,   410
    that never yett did amys?
    For, sekerly, Goddes Sonne ys hee.
    Therfore a tombe is made for mee
    therin his bodye buryed shalbe,
    for hee is kinge of blys.   415

104ʳ   NYCODEMUS

54 Syr Joseph, I saye sekerly,
    this ys Godes Sonne almightie.
    Goe aske at Pilate his bodye,
    and buryed shall hee bee.
    I shall helpe thee, witterlye,   420
    to take him downe devowtlye,
    though Cayphas goe horne-wood thereby
    and all his meanye.

Tunc veniet Joseph ab Aramathia ad Pilatum et dicat

JOSEPH

55 Syr Pilate, speciall I thee praye
    a boone thou grant me as thou maye.   425
    This prophett that ys dead todaye,
    thou grant me his bodye.

PILATUS

    Joseph, all ready, in good faye!
    If that Centurio he will saye
    that hee ys dead withowten naye,   430
    him will I not denye.

56 Centurio, is Jesus dead?

410 upon] one B   412 sekerly] suerlye A   415 blys] blesse AR
419 shall hee bee] he shalbe A   *SD* veniet] venit ARB   ab] ad AR
dicat] dicat Josephe AR, dicit B   424 speciall] speciallye ARB

CENTURIO

Yea, syr, as broke I my head,
in him ther is no liffe lead,
for I stood therby.   435

PILATUS

Joseph, take him then to thee
and burye him where thy will be.

JOSEPH

Grantmercy, syr, perdee.
I thanke you hartfullye.

Tunc ibit Joseph super montem, et dicat Joseph:

57 A, sweete Jesu, sweete Jesu,   440
    as thou art God, faythfull and true,
    in a tombe ys made full newe
    thy bodye shall in be layd.
    Shouldest thou never have such vertue
    as thou hast shewed synce I thee knewe   445
    but yf godhead thy deede should shewe
    as thou before hasse sayde.

58 Therewith, Jesu, come hyther to mee.
    Thy blessed bodye buryed shalbe
    with all worshipp and honestie   450
    and menske all that I may.
    Yett hope I within these dayes three
    in flesh and blood alyve to see
    thou that art nayled on a tree
    unworthely todaye.   455

104ᵛ   NICODEMUS

59 Joseph, brother, as I well see,
    this holy prophet is given to thee.

433 broke I my head] eate I bread A   JOSEPH] PILATUS R   439 hart-
fullye] hartelye AR   SD dicat] dicit B   After SD] JOSEPHE R
441 God] good AR   443 in] om B   444 have] have had B   446 yf]
that B   deede] deedes B   448 therewith] therefore B   449 buryed
shalbe] shall buryed be AR   451 menske] mirth AR   I] we R
453 alyve] on live ARB   454 thou] thee AR, thie B

Some worshipp hee shall have of mee
that ys of myghtiest most.
For as I leve by my lewtye,   460
verey Goddes Sonne ys hee,
for wonders sightes men might see
when that he yeeld the goost.

60 For the sonne lost all his light;
yearthquake made men afright;   465
the rocke that never before had clyft
clayve, that men might knowe;
graves opened in mens sight;
dead men did ryse. Therfore, by right
I may saye this was Goddes Sonne almight   470
that so great sygnes can shewe.

61 Therefore here brought have I
a hundreth poundes of spicerye.
Myr, alloes, and many more therbye
to honour him with I bringe,   475
for to balme his sweete bodye
in sepulcher for to lye,
that hee maye have on me mercye
in heaven where hee ys kinge.

Finis

459 myghtiest] mighte A, mightes R, mightest B   460 leve] love B
462 wonders] wounderous AR, worders B   sightes] sighte A   might] maie
AR   463 yeeld] eylde A   465 made] om B   466 rocke] rockes RB
had] om AR   clyft] clyst R   472 here] om A   473 poundes] pounde B
474 and] om ARB   therbye] ther be B   475 with] will AR, which B
478 on] of A

PLAY XVII

105ʳ **THE COOKES PLAYE**

Hic incipit Pagina Decima Septima de Decensu ad Inferna et de
his qui ibidem fiebant secundum Evangelium Nicodemi.

Et primo fiat lux in inferno materialis aliqua subtilitate machinata,
et postea dicat Adam.

ADAM

1 O lord and soveraigne saviour,
 our comfort and our counselour,
 of this light thou art author
 as I see well in sight.
 This ys a signe thou wilt succour   5
 thy folkes that lyven in great langour,
 and of the devill be conquerour,
 as thou hast yere beheight.

2 Mee thou madest, lord, of claye,
 and gave me paradyce in to playe;   10
 but through my synne, the soothe to saye,
 depryved I was therefroe,
 and from that weale put awaye,
 and here have longett sythen aye
 in thestearnesse both night and daye,   15
 and all my kynd also.

3 Nowe, by this light that I nowe see,
 joye ys come, lord, through thee,
 and one thy people hast pittye
 to put them out of payne.   20

Guild-ascription playe] and Inkepers H *Play-heading*] Pagina Decima
Septima de Descensu Christi ad Inferos H decima septima] *om* B de-
censu] dcensum A, desensum R qui] que B in] *om* R Adam]
Adamus B ADAM] *om* B, ADAMUS H 1 O] A H 3] *om* B
5 wilt] would H 6 folkes] folke H lyven] lyve A, lyen R, bene H
8 yere] eyer AR, earst B, yore H 11 through] after H the] *om* H
12 depryved] pryved H 14 longett] lenged H sythen aye] south to
saye A, sithens aye B 15 thestearnesse] this distres B 17 by] be B
18 joye ys] joyes are B come] comon ARH lord] now B 19 one]
of ABH hast] thou hase AR, thou have B, thou hast H 20 put] take B

Sycker, yt may non other bee
but nowe thow hast mercye on mee,
and my kynd through thy postye
thou wilt restorc agayne.

ESAYUS

4 Yea, secerlye, this ilke light   25
comys from Goddes Sonne almight,
for so I prophecyed aright
whyle that I was livinge.
Then I to all men beheight,
as I goostlye sawe in sight,   30
these wordes that I shall to myght
rehearse withowt tarienge:

'Populus qui ambulabat in tenebris vidit lucem magnam.'

5 The people, I sayd that tyme expresse,
that yeeden abowt in thesternesse
seene a full great lightnesse,   35
as we donne nowe ychone.
Nowe ys fullfilled my prophecye
that I, the prophet Esaye,
wrote in my booke that will not lye,
whoso will looke theron.   40

105ᵛ   SIMEON JUSTUS

6 And I, Symeon, sooth to saye,
will honour God all that I maye;
for when Cryst child was, in good faye,
in temple I him tooke

ESAYUS] ESAYAS R, ESAIAS B, ESAY H   25 secerlye] suerlye A, secker R,
securely B   ilke] same A   30 sawe] se H   31 these wordes] this
word H   shall] om H   to myght] to my mighte ARB, throrgh Gods might H
32 rehearse] shall rehearce H   *Latin* ambulabat] ambulabant B, ambulat H
vidit] videbant B   33 I sayd that tyme] that tyme I sayd H   34 yeeden]
eylden A, yelden R, went H   thesternesse] the esternes A   35 seene]
seithen AR, se H   36 we] you AR   donne] do ARB   37 fullfilled]
filled H   39 booke] books H   SIMEON] SIMON B   41 Symeon]
Simon B   42] om AR   43 child] a child H

and, as the Holye Gooste that daye 45
taught me or I went awaye,
these wordes I sayd to Godes paye
that men may fynd in booke:

'Nunc dimittis servum tuum, domine, secundum verbum tuum,
in pace.'

7 There I prayed, withowten les,
that God would lett me be in peace. 50
For he is Christ that commen was,
I had both feld and seene,
that he had ordeynt for mans heale,
joye to the people of Israell,
nowe ys yt wonne, that ylke weale, 55
to us, withowten weene.

JOHANNES BAPTISTA

8 Yea, lord, I am that prophett Johan
that baptysed thee in flood Jordan
and prophecyed to every natyon
to warne of thy commynge 60
to bringe the people to salvatyon
by merrytt of thy bitter Passyon,
through fayth and penance to have remyssion
and with thee to have wonnynge:

'Penitentiam agite! Appropinquat enim regnum caelorum.'

9 And with my finger I shewed expresse, 65
when I lyved in wildernesse,

48 that] as H   may] might B   *Latin* nunc] tunc B   dimittis] demittes Π
domine] domini A   secundum] secundus B   49 withowten] without H
50 would] will AR   be] dye H   51 he is] swet H   52 feld] felte B
53 heale] health B   54 the] *om* H   55] that he hath wonnen with ilk
weale H   yt] is B   ylke] eke A   weale] wayle AR   57 I] and I H
prophett] ilk H   Johan] John ARH   58 baptysed] followed H   59] and
that in world about can gone H   prophecyed] preached AR   every]
many a R   61–4] *om* H   62 merrytt] mirrette AR   *Latin*] *om* H
penitentiam] penitentia B   appropinquat] appromquat A, approquinquat R
caelorum] celorum et dicat A   65 and] all B   finger] fingers R   shewed]
shewe A   66–8] *om* A, *in* H

a meke lamb in thy lyknes,
in token that thou common was
mankynd of bale to bringe,

a lambe in tokeninge of thy lycknesse,
our ransome for to bee.
At thy commynge we had forgivenesse;
mercye concluded ryghtwisenesse.   70
Wherfore these wordes I doe rehearse
with honour unto thee:

'Ecce agnus Dei, ecce, qui tollit peccata mundi.'

SEETHE

10 And I, Seethe, Adams sonne, am here,
that livinge went, withowten were,
to aske at paradyce a prayer   75
at God, as I shall saye:
that he would grant an angell in hye
to give me oyle of his mercye
to anoynt my father in his anoye,
in sycknes when he laye.   80

106ʳ   11 Then to me appeard Mychaell
and bade me travell never a deale,
and sayde for remynge nyf prayers felle
that grant me not to seeke;
nyf of that might I have none,   85
made I never so mych mon,
tyll fyve thousand yeres were gonne
and fyve hundreth yeeke.

Omnibus flectibus dicat David:

12 A, high God and kinge of blys,
worshipped be thy name, ywys!   90
I hope that tyme nowe commen ys
delyvered to be of languor.

67 tokeninge] token B   69] *om* AH   70–2] *om* H   70 concluded]
concludeth B   ryghtwisenesse] righteousnes B   71 wherfore] therfore AR
Latin ecce(2)] *om* B   tollit] tollet AR   peccata] peccat B   mundi]
nundi B   74 withowten] without H   75 at] a A   76 at] of B
77 an] the H   78 me] to me AR, *om* BH   79 his anoye] nye H
82 travell] travayle AR   83 for remynge] wepinge H   nyf] nor ARH, nys B
84 that grant me not] avayled me nothing H   85 nyf] ner A, nor R,
nys B, nay H   that] that oyle ARBH   might] migh H   86 never]
neve H   87 tyll] untill H   *SD*] Omnes genu flectantes H   flectibus]
flectentibus B   *To left of SD*] DAVID H   *After SD*] DAVID R   89 blys]
blesse AR   91 commen] come H   92] to deliver us of danger H

Come, lord, come to hell anon,
and take owt thy folkes everychon,
for the yeares be all comen and gonne   95
sythen mankynd first came here.

Tunc Sathan sedens in cathedra dicat daemonibus:

13   Hell-houndes all that binne here,
     makes you boune with boste and beere,
     for to thys felowshippe in fere
     there hyes a feerly freake.   100
     A noble morsell ye have mone;
     Jesu that ys Godes Sonne
     comes hither with us to wonne.
     One him nowe ye you wreake.

14   A man hee ys fullye, in faye,   105
     for greatly death hee dread todaye,
     and these wordes I hard him saye:
     'My soule is threst to death.'
     Such as I made halt and blynd,
     he hasse them healed into theire kynd.   110
     Therfore this bolster looke ye bynd
     in bale of hell-brethe.

SECUNDUS DAEMON

15   Syr Sathanas, what man ys hee
     that should thee pryve of thy postie?
     Howe darre he doe agaynste thee   115
     and dread his death todaye?
     Grayter then thou he seemes to be,
     for degradit of thy degree
     thou must be soone, well I see,
     and pryved of thy praye.   120

94 folkes] folke ARBH   everychon] everye eichone AR, echone B   95 the]
those H   be all] al be ARB, are fully H   comen and] om H   96 sythen]
since A, sithens B, sith H   first came] came firste AR   SD dicat daemoni-
bus] dicens demones A   After SD] SATHAN H   103 hither] he heither A,
he there R   104 wreake] wrecke A   105] om H   108 is] om H
threst] thirste ARBH   to] unto H   After 108] Tristis est anima mea usque
ad mortem BH   110 them] om H   into] to AR   111 this bolster]
that boyster H   ye] that you ARBH   112 hell] hells B   116 his]
the H   117 he] hym AR

TERTIUS DEMON

16 Who ys he so styffe and stronge
that so maysterlyke comes us amonge,
our felowshippe as he would fonge?
But therof he shall fayle.
Weyt he us with any wronge,   125
he shall synge a sorye songe;
but on thee, Sathan, or yt be longe,
and his will ought avayle—

106ᵛ   SATHANAS

17 Agaynst thys shrewe that commys here
I tempted the folke in fowle manere.   130
Aysell and galle to his dinere
I made them for to dight,
and sythen to hange him on roode-tree.
Nowe ys he dead, right so through mee,
and to hell, as yee shall see,   135
hee comys anonne in hyght.

SECUNDUS DAEMON

18 Syr Sathanas, ys not this that syre
that raysed Lazour out of the fyre?

SATHANAS

Yea, this ys hee that would conspire
anonne to reave us all.   140

TERTIUS DAEMON

Owt, owt! Alas, alas!
Here I conjure thee, Sathanas,
thou suffer him not come in thys place
for ought that may befall.

121 he] this H   122 so] *om* H   maysterlyke] maisterly H   123 as]
that H   125 weyt] witte A, weete B   127 Sathan] Sathanas H   or yt
be] that it be ARB, it is H   SATHANAS] SATHAN H   129 commys]
sittes A   131 aysell] ascill A   133 sythen] since AR, sithens B, *om* H
to] *om* H   on] on a H   135 as] *om* H   136 hyght] heigh B   137 syr
Sathanas] Sathan H   138 Lazour] Lazarie A, Lazarrous R, Laser B   out]
one B   SATHANAS] SATHAN H   139 would] will H   140 reave]
rulle B   TERTIUS DAEMON] *om* H   141 alas(1)] out R   143 not come]
come not B, not to come H   in] to H

SECUNDUS DAEMON

19 Yca, sekerly, and he come here,   145
    passed ys cleane our power,
    for all this felowshippe in fere
    have home away he would;
    for at his commandement
    Lazour, that with us was lent,   150
    maugre our teythe awaye hee hent,
    and him might we not hould.

Tunc venit Jesus et fiat clamor, vel sonitus magnus materialis; et
dicat Jesus: 'Attollite portas, principes, vestras, et elevamini portas
aeternales, et introibit rex gloriae.'

JESUS

20 Open up hell-gates anonne,
    ye prynces of pyne everychon,
    that Godes Sonne may in gonne,   155
    and the kinge of blys.

SECUNDUS DAEMON

Go hense, poplard, owt of thys place
or thou shalt have a sorye grace.
For all thy boaste and thy manace
theise men thou shalt amys.   160

SATHANAS

21 Owt, alas, what ys thys?
    Seghe I never so mych blys
    towardes hell come, iwys,
    sythen I was warden here.

148] he may take away when he would H   home] whom A   149 at] all
be at H   150 Lazour] Lazarro A, Lazaour R, Laseour B   with us was]
was with us H   151 awaye] om AR   hent] wente AH   SD venit]
veniet H   fiat] fiet H   magnus materialis] materialis magnus H   et dicat
Jesus] Jhesus ait H   attollite] aholite A   portas(2)] porte ARB, portae H
introibit] introibis H   gloriae] glorie et dicat Jesus R, glorie B   JESUS]
om B   153 up] open B, om H   154 everychon] everye eichone ARB
156 blys] blesse AR   157 owt of] out from AR, from H   158 or] for H
160 amys] anyse AR, mis BH   SATHANAS] SATHAN H   162 seghe]
seinge AR, sith B, see H   blys] blesse A   164 sythen] sith H   warden]
prince H

107ʳ   My masterdome fares amys,   165
for yonder a stubberne fellowe ys,
right as wholye hell were his,
to reave me of my power.

TERTIUS DAEMON

22 Yea, Sathanas, thy soverayntie
fayles cleane. Therfore thou flee,   170
for no longer in this see
here shalt thou not sytt.
Goe forth! Feight for thy degree!
Or elles our prynce shall thou not bee;
for nowe passys thy postee   175
and hethen thou must flytt.

Tunc surgens Sathanas de sede dicat.

SATHANAS

23 Owt, alas, I am shent!
My might fayles, verament.
This prynce that ys nowe present
will pull from me my praye.   180
Adam by myne intycement,
and all his blood, through me were shent.
Nowe hethen they shall all be hent,
and I in hell for aye.

DAVID REX

24 I, kinge Davyd, nowe well may saye   185
my prophecye fulfilled is, in faye,
as nowe shewes in sight verey,
and soothly here ys seene.

165 fares] farre it B, now fares H   167 wholye] hollye AR   hell] all H
168 reave me of] pryve H   170 thou] *om* H   flee] fleye A, flye R
174 shall thou] thou shall A, thou shalte R, thalt thou B   176 hethen]
hense ARH, hethenc B   *SD*] Jaceant tunc Sathanam de sede sua H
surgens] surgit B   de sede] dece A   dicat] et dicat Sathanas A,
et dicat RB   SATHANAS] *om* AB, SATHAN H   179 ys nowe] now
is B   180 pull] powle A, poll R, spoyle H   182 me] hym R
shent] blent H   183 hethen] hense ARH, hethence B   184 aye] ever A
DAVID REX] REX DAVID R, *om* H   185–92] *om* H

I taught men thus here in my lyefe-daye
to worshippe God by all waye,   190
that hell-yates he should afraye
and wonn that his hath bynne.

'Confiteantur domino misericordiae eius et mirabilia eius, filius
hominis contrivit portas aereas et vectes ferreas confregit.'

Tunc item dicat Jesus.

JESUS

25 Open up hell-yates yett I saye,
ye prynces of pyne that be present,
and lett the kinge of blys this waye   195
that he may fulfill his intent.

SATHANAS

26 Staye! What, what ys hee, that kinge of blys?

DAVID REX

That lord the which almightie ys,
in warre no power like to his,
of all blys ys gretest kynge.   200
107ᵛ   And to him ys non like, iwys,
as ys soothly seene by thys,
for men that somtyme dyd amysse
to his blys he will them bringe.

Hic extrahuntur patriarchi. (Here must God take owt Adam.)

---

189 thus] this AR   here] *om* R   daye] dayes B   190 waye] wayes B
191 should] shall AR   192 wonn] wone A, wonne R, wine B   *Latin] om* H
misericordiae] misceriacordie A, misericordie R, misericordia B   aereas] preas
A, proreas R   vectes] victes A   confregit] confreget AR, confringitt B
SD] om BH   Jesus] *om* A   193 up hell] the H   194 pyne] peace H
SATHANAS] SATHAN H   197 staye] saye BH   what what] what ARH   hee]
om H   blys] blesse AR   DAVID REX] REX DAVID R, JHESUS H   199 in
warre] ther is H   200 blys ys gretest] joy he is H   203 men] man H
204 his] this R   them] us A, *om* H   *SD*] Tunc Jesus accipiet Adam per
manum H   extrahuntur] extravitur A, extrauntr R   patriarchi] patriarici A
here] and here B   must God take] God doth take A, God taketh R

JESUS

27 Peace to thee, Adam, my dearlynge,   205
and eke to all thy osspringe
that ryghtwise were in yearth livinge.
From mee yee shall not severe.
To blys nowe I wyll you bringe
there you shalbe withowt endinge.   210
Mychaell, lead these men singinge
to blys that lasteth ever.

MYCHAELL

28 Lord, your will donne shalbe.
Come forth, Adam, come with mee.
My lord upon the roode-tree   215
your synnes hath forbought.
Nowe shall ye have likinge and lee,
and be restored to your degree
that Sathan with hys subtyltye
from blys to bale had brought.   220

SATHANAS

29 Owt, alas! Nowe goes awaye
all my prysoners and my praye;
and I myselfe may not starte awaye,
I am so stretlye tyed.
Nowe comes Christe, sorrowe I maye   225
for me and my menye for aye.
Never sythen God made the first daye
were we so sore afrayd.

Here must Adam speake to Enocke and Helye.

jesus] *om* H   206 osspringe] ofspringe ARBH   207 ryghtwise]
rightious AH   yearth] ther H   208 yee shall] shall they H   209 you]
them H   210 there] where B   212 blys] joy H   lasteth] lastes B
213 your] thy R   220 had] hath B, you H   *After* 220] Tunc Michael
adducet Adam et sanctos ad paradisum et in obviam venient Henoc et Helias,
latro salvatus; et Sathan dicat H   SATHANAS] SATHAN H   221 alas]
out H   222 all] *om* H   my(2)] all my H   223 myselfe] *om* H   may]
might H   starte awaye] sture away B, stirr one stry H   224 tyed] dight H
226 for] to H   my] to my H   227 sythen] seith A, since R, sithens B,
sith H   made the] *om* H   228 sore afrayd] afraid B, fowle afright H
SD] Tunc Adam videns Enock et Heliam ait H   must Adam speake] Adam
speaketh R

ADAM

30 Syrs, what manner of men bene yee
that bodelye meete us, as I see, 230
that dead come not to hell as wee,
sythen all men dampned were?
When I trespassed, God height mee
that this place closed should bee
from yearthly men to have entree, 235
and yett I fynd you here.

ENOCKE

31 Syr, I am Enocke, the sooth to saye,
put in this place to Goddes paye;
and here have lyved ever synce aye
at likinge all my fill. 240
And my fellowe here, in good faye,
ys Helye the prophet, see yee maye,
that ravished was in this araye,
as hit was Godes will.

108ʳ HELIAS PROPHETA

32 Yea, bodely death, leeve thou mee, 245
yett never suffred wee,
but here ordaynt we are to bee
tyll Antechriste come with hise.
To fight agaynst us shall hee
and slea us in this holye cittye; 250
but sekerly, within dayes three
and a halfe, we shall ryse.

ADAM] ADAMUS H   229 syrs] say H   of] *om* H   230 meete] meten H
231 that] and H   come] came ARB   as] as well as AR   232 sythen]
seinge A, sithens B, since H   233 trespassed] treasspaseth AR   height]
hett H   234 closed] closed alway H   235 yearthly] earthy R
men] man H   236 I fynd] fynd I H   237 the] *om* H   238 in]
into H   to] for R   Goddes] goods A   239 lyved] livered B   aye] that
day H   240 at] at my R   242 see yee] as you se H   243 this] his B,
that H   HELIAS PROPHETA] HELY PROPHETTE A, HELIAS H   247 we] *om* H
248 with hise] *om* A, in hast R   249 to] *om* H   250 this] the H
251 sekerly] suerlye A   within] in A   252 a halfe] half one H

ADAM

33 And who ys this that comes here,
that lives with you in this manere?

LATRO

I am that theeffe, my father dere,   255
that honge on roode-tree.
For I beleeved withowten were
that Christ might save us both in feere,
to him I made my prayer,
the which was granted mee.   260

34 When I see synnys full verey
that hee was Goddes Sonne, sooth to saye,
to him devoutely did I praye,
in his regyon when he come
that he would thinke on me alwaye;   265
and hee answered and sayd: 'This daye
in paradice thou shalt with me playe.'
Hederward I nome.

35 Then he betaught me this tokeninge,
this crosse upon my backe hanginge,   270
to Michaell angell for to bringe,
that I might have entree.

ADAM

Nowe goe wee to blys, ould and yonge,
and worshippe God all willinglye;

ADAM] *om* H   253 this] that H   comes] cometh B   254] *om* H   in this
manere] *om* B   *After* 254] with crose on shoulder in this manner BH (this)
such H)   256 honge] hanged H   257 for] but for H   beleeved]
leeved H   withowten] without AH |258 save us both] us both
save B   261 synnys] signes ARH, sines B   full] *om* AH   263 did I]
I can H   264 regyon] realme H   he] I H   come] came ARB   265 that
he would] to H   alwaye] by all way H   266 this] to H   267] in
paradice with me thou shalt be aye H   268] heitherwarde anon A, therein
anon R, so hither the way I noome H   269 then] and H   betaught]
betooke H   270 this] a H   271 to Michaell angell] the angell Michael H
272 entree] enterye A, entrance R, entrye BH   ADAM] ADAMUS H
273 nowe] *om* H   ould] bouth oulde ARB, then owld H   274 all
willinglye] all willinge A, alway weldinge H

and thiderward I read we singe 275
with great solempnitie.

Tunc eant omnes, et incipiat Michaell 'Te Deum laudamus.'

MULIER

36 Woe be the tyme that I came here,
I saye to thee nowe, Lucifere,
with all thy felowshipp in fere
that present be in place. 280
Wofull am I with thee to dwell,
syr Sathanas, sargeant of hell.
Endles sorrowe and paynes cruell
I suffer in this case.

37 Sometyme I was a taverner, 285
a gentle gossippe and a tapster,
of wyne and ale a trustie bruer,
which woe hath me wrought.
Of kannes I kept no trewe measure.
My cuppes I sould at my pleasure, 290
deceavinge manye a creature,
thoe my ale were nought.

108ᵛ 38 And when I was a bruer longe,
with hoppes I made my alle stronge;
esshes and hearbes I blend amonge 295
and marred so good malt.
Therfore I may my handes wringe,
shake my cuppes and kannes ringe.
Sorrowfull maye I syke and singe
that ever I so dalt. 300

275 thiderward] afterward H   To right of 276] 'Te Deum laudamus, te
domine confitemur' H   SD] Et sic ibunt glorificantes Deum cantantes
'Te Deum' H   eant] eante A, eunt R, cantant B   incipiat] incipiant AR
laudamus] laudamus dicat A   MULIER] om H   277–Finis] om H
277 the] to the AR   281 am I] I ame B   283 sorrowe and paynes]
paines and sorowe A, paines and sorrowes R   284 case] place AR
289 kept] kepe R   294 hoppes] hoopes A   298 cuppes and kannes]
cannes and cuppes AR   299 sorrowfull] sorrowfully R   syke] sicke A,
sigh R   300 dalt] dealed A, dealte R, delt B

39 Tavernes, tapsters of this cittye
   shalbe promoted here with mee
   for breakinge statutes of this contrye,
   hurtinge the commonwealth,
   with all typpers-tappers that are cunninge,   305
   mispendinge much malt, bruynge so thinne,
   sellinge smale cuppes money to wynne,
   agaynst all trueth to deale.

40 Therfore this place nowe ordayned ys
   for such yll-doers so mych amysse.   310
   Here shall they have ther joye and blys,
   exalted by the necke,
   with my master, mightie Mahound,
   for castinge malt besydes the combes,
   myche water takinge for to compound,   315
   and little of the secke.

41 With all mashers, mengers of wyne, in the night
   bruynge so, blendinge agaynst daylight,
   sych newe-made claret ys cause full right
   of sycknes and disease.   320
   Thus I betake you, more and lesse,
   to my sweete mayster, syr Sathanas,
   to dwell with him in his place
   when hyt shall you please.

SATHANAS

42 Welcome, dere daughter, to us all three.   325
   Though Jesu be gonne with our meanye,
   yett shalt thou abyde here still with mee
   in payne withowt ende.

SECUNDUS DAEMON

43 Welcome, sweete ladye! I will thee wedd,
   for manye a heavye and dronken head   330

301 tavernes] taverners ARB   302 with] by AR   303 contrye] citie R
304 hurtinge] and hurtinge R   305 typpers-tappers] tiplinge tapsters A,
tipplers tapsters B   306 thinne] theyne A   309 nowe] om ARB
310 for] so B   311 blys] blesse A   314 combes] combe ARB
316 secke] sacke R   317 mengers] minglers AR   321 thus] this AR
323 his] this RB   325 daughter] darlinge AR   SECUNDUS] DECUNDUS B
329 sweete] dere A   will] shall A   wedd] weed R

cause of thy ale were brougt to bedd
farre worse then anye beaste.

TERTIUS DAEMON

Welcome, deare darlinge, to endles bale.
Usynge cardes, dyce, and cuppes smale,
with many false othes to sell thy ale— 335
nowe thou shall have a feaste!

Finis

PLAY XVIII

109ʳ

THE SKYNNERS PLAYE

Pagina Decima Octava: De Resurrectione Jesu Christi

PILATUS

1 Per vous, sir Cayphas,
  et vous e vous, syr Annas,
  et sum disciple Judas
  ou le treison fuite;
  et grande luces de lucite 5
  a moy perfoyte deliverie,
  nostre dame fuit judge,
  per loer roy estreite.

2 You lordes and ladyes so lovely and lere,
  you kemps, you knowne knightes of kynde, 10
  herkens all hitherward my hestes to here,
  for I am most fayrest and freshest to fynd,

---

331 brougt] broughte ARB   333 darlinge] daughter A

Guild-ascription playe] *om* H   2 e] a BH   3 disciple] discipule A
4 ou le] cu le AR, ubi B, gule H   5 luces] lices A   lucite] lucete R,
lucide B   6 perfoyte] perfoy A, perfeyt H   deliverie] et judge A,
deluverie R, delivere H   7 nostre] mostre A   judge] deliverie A
8 loer] locs A, loier B, loys H   estreite] escreite A, distreite R   9 lordes]
lordinges H   lovely] loving B   10 kemps] kennes A   knowne]
knowes AR   12 fynd] fyne H

and most highest I am of estate;
for I am prynce pereles, most royall man of ryches.
I may deale and I may dresse.   15
My name ys syr Pilate.

3   For Caesar, lord most of postie,
    honored my estate and my degree
    when that he sent Jesus to me
    to delyver him to the dead.   20
    The cryed on mee all with on voyce;
    the Jewes one me made great noyce.
    I gave them leave to hange him on crosse.
    This was through Jewes read.

4   I dread yett lest hee will us greeve,   25
    for that I sawe I may well beleeve.
    I sawe the stones begane to cleave
    and dead men up can ryse.
    In this cyttye all aboute
    was non so stearne ne so stowte   30
    that up durst looke, for great doubt;
    they could so soone agryse.

5   And therfore, syr Cayphas, yett I dread
    leste there were parrell in that deed.
    I sawe him hange on roode and bleed   35
    tyll all his blood was shedd.
    And when he should his death take,
    the wedders waxed wondrous blacke—
    layte, thonder—and earth beganne to quake.
    Therof I am adread.   40

109ᵛ   CAYPHAS

6   And this was yesterdaye, about noone?

                           PILATUS

    Yea, syr byshoppe, this ys one.
    To speake therfore we have to donne.

---

14 man] *om* B   17 lord] prince A   22 great] piteous BH   24 Jewes]
Jesus AR   25 lest] lesse B   31 up durst looke] up loked ARB, durst
look up H   32 could] were A   soone] sore A   agryse] agased A, agrie B
34 were] be A   38 wedders] weither ARBH

For I lett burye him full soone
in a tombe of stonne.   45
And therfore, syrs, amonge us three
lett us ordayne and oversee
yf there anye parrell be,
or we hence gonne.

CAYPHAS

7 Syr Pilate, all this was donne,   50
as we sawe after sone;
but betyme at afternoone
the wedder begane to cleare.
And, syr, yf yt be your will,
such wordes you lett be styll   55
and speake of another skyll,
least any man us heare.

ANNAS

8 Yea, syr Pilate, nought forthy!
I sawe him and his companye
rayse men with sorcerye   60
that longe before were dead.
For, and there be any more such lafte
which can of such wytchcrafte,
yf that bodye be from us rafte,
advyse you well, I redd.   65

CAYPHAS

9 Yea, syr Pilate, I tell you right.
Lett us ordayne manye a hard knight,
well armed, to stand and feight
with power and with force,
that noe shame to us befall.   70
Lett us ordayne here amonge us all,
and trewe men to us call
to keepe well the coarse.

44 full] *om* H   52 betyme] belyve H   55 be] to be B   62 lafte]
lefte AR   63 of] of any H   66 you] thee H   67 hard] hardie BH
73 coarse] corse ARB

PILATUS

10 Nowe by Jesu that dyed on roode,
   methinke your counsell wondrous good.   75
   The best men of kynne and blood
   anonne I wyll in.
   Syr Colphram and syr Jeragas
   Aroysiat and syr Jerophas,
   we praye you, syrs, here in thys case   80
   anonne looke you ne blynne.

110ʳ   11 A, my knightes styffe and stearne of hart,
   you be bould men and smart.
   I warne you nowe at wordes short,
   with you I have to donne.   85

PRIMUS MILES

Syr, we be here all and some
as bowld men, readye bowne
to dryve your enemyes all adowne
while that wee may stand.

12 We be your knights everychon.   90
   Fayntnes in us there shalbe nonne.
   We wilbe wroken upon thy fonne
   wherever he may be found—
   and for no dread that we wyll wend.

PILATUS

That I am well to understand.   95
You be men doughtie of hand;
I love you withowt lacke.

13 But that prophett that was donne and drawes
   throwe the recountinge of your lawes—

74 roode] roade R   75 wondrous] is wounderous AR   76 men] man A
77–80] om A   77 in] have in R, call in BH   78 Colphram] Colphran BH
Jeragas] Jerafas H   79 Aroysiat] Araysat H   syr] om H   Jerophas]
Gerophas R, Gerapas H   80 here] om H   81 ne] no A   82 A] and AR
85 with] for with AR   I] we R   86 all] both all B   87 readye] all
ready H   88 adowne] downe A   89 while] why A   90 everychon]
everye eichone ARB   94 wend] wonne AR, wounde B, wond H
98 drawes] draw H   99 your] our B   lawes] law H

but yett somethinge me standes in awes　　100
of wordes that he spake.
Forsooth, this I hard him saye:
that hee would ryse the thyrd daye.
Nowe surely and he so maye,
he hath a wonderous tatch.　　105

SECUNDUS MILES

14 Yea, lett him ryse yf that him dare;
for, and I of him be awarre,
hee bode never a worse charre
or that hee wend awaye.
I helped to slea him yerre while.　　110
Weenes he to doe us more guyle?
Ney, yt ys no parrayle,
my head heare dare I laye.

TERTIUS MILES

15 Yea, lett him quicken! Hardlye,
whiles my fellowes here and I　　115
may awake and stand him by,
he scapeth not uncaught.
For and he ones heave up his head,
but that he be soone dead,
shall I never eate more bread　　120
ne never more be saught.

110ᵛ　　### PRIMUS MILES

16 Have good-day, syr. Wee wyll be gonne.
Geeve us our charge everychon.

PILATUS

Nowe fares-well, the best of blood and bonne,
and takes good heede unto my sawe.　　125

---

100 me standes] we stand AR　　awes] awe H　　102 I hard] harde I A
104 and] if H　　106 him(2)] he BH　　107 for] om H　　I] yf I B, I may H
be] maye be ARB　　awarre] warr H　　110 yerre] ere ARH, her B
112 parrayle] perille ARB　　113 heare] their AR　　114 hardlye]
hardelie BH　　115 whiles] whyle ARBH　　117 scapeth] skaped A
118 ones] ofte A　　heave up] leave us B　　122 syr] sirs H　　be] om H
123 everychon] everye eichone AR, every one H　　*To left of* 125]
CAYPHAS H　　125 and] now H　　good] om H　　heede] head R

For as I am a trewe Jewe,
yf that you anye treasonn sue,
there ys none of you all shall yt eschewe
but he shall be to-drawe.

SECUNDUS MILES

17 Nowe, fellowes, we be charged hye.   130
Our prynce hath sworne that we shall dye
withowt anye prophecye
or anye other encharre
but yf we donne as the wyse.
I read us we right well advise.   135
Though he be bould, hee shall not ryse
but one of us be warre.

TERTIUS MILES

18 Syr, the most wytt lyeth in thee
to ordayne and to oversee.
You binne the eldeste of us three,   140
and man of most renowne.
The tombe ys here att our hand.
Sett us there as we shall stand.
Yf that he ryse, we shall found
to beate him adowne.   145

PRIMUS MILES

19 And I shall nowe sett us soe,
yf that he ryse and would goe,
one of us, or elles two,
shall see of his upryste.
Stand thou there, and thou here,   150
and I myselfe in myddle mere.
I trowe our hartes will not feare
but yt were stowtly wyste.

127 sue] shewe A   128 yt] *om* AR   eschewe] esue A, eshew R
133 encharre] in charge A, in chare R, encure B   134 we] the AR
135 us] *om* A   we] here R   139 to(2)] *om* H   141 and] a H
145 him] him all H   149 upryste] uprise AR   150 there] heare ARBH
here] there RBH   152–3] *om* R

Tunc cantabunt duo angeli: 'Christus resurgens a mortuis' etc.,
et Christus tunc resurget; ac postea, cantu finito, dicat ut sequitur.
Jesus resurgens et pede eos milites quatiat.

[JESUS]

20 Earthlye man that I have wrought,
 awake out of thy sleepe.   155
 Earthly man that I have bought,
 of me thou take noe keepe.

111ʳ   From heaven mans soule I sought
 into a dungeon deepe;
 my deare lemmon from thence I brought,   160
 for ruth of her I weepe.

21 I am verey prynce of peace
 and kinge of free mercye.
 Whoe wyll of synnes have release,
 one me the call and crye;   165
 and yf they will of synnes sease,
 I grant them peace trulye
 and therto a full rych messe
 in bread, my owne bodye.

22 I am verey bread of liffe.   170
 From heaven I light and am send.
 Whoe eateth that bread, man or wiffe,
 shall lyve with me withowt end.
 And that bread that I you give,
 your wicked life to amend,   175
 becomes my fleshe through your beleeffe
 and doth release your synfull band.

23 And whosoever eateth that bread
 in synne and wicked liffe,
 he receaveth his owne death—   180
 I warne both man and wiffe;

SD cantabunt] cantabit AR   mortuis] mortus A   resurget] resurgit B
postea] *om* H   *SD*(2)] *om* H   pede] pedes B   eos] omnes R   JESUS]
om HmB, JESUS resurgens H   155 thy] the B   156 earthly] earth B
that] whom H   157 take] have AR, takes B   161 of] or A   168 therto]
threto H   messe] messye AR   171 send] sent B   172 that] this H
175 to] for to AR   177 band] bond B   178 eateth] eathe H   179 and]
or ARBH

the which bread shalbe seene instead
the joye ys aye full ryffe.
When hee ys dead, through fooles read
then ys he brought to payne and stryffe.　　185

Tunc duo angeli, posteaquam Christus resurrexit, sedebunt in
sepulchro, quorum alter ad caput, alter ad pedes, sedeant.

PRIMUS MILES

24　Owt, alas! Where am I?
So bright abowt ys herebye
that my harte wholey
owt of slough ys shaken.
So fowle feared with fantasye　　　　　　190
was I never in non anoye,
for I wott not, witterlye,
whether I be on sleepe or waken.

Tunc socium surgere cogit.

111ᵛ　　　　　　SECUNDUS MILES

25　Where art thou, syr batchlere?
About me ys wonder cleare.　　　　　　195
Wytt me wantes withowten were,
for fearder I never was.
To remove farre or neare
mee fayles might and power.
My hart in my bodye here　　　　　　200
ys hoven owt of my brest.

Tunc tanget socium et de somno surgere coget.

PRIMUS MILES

26　Yea, we are shent, syckerlye,
for Jesu ys rysen, well wott I,
owt of the sepulchre mightelye,
and therof I have in mynd.　　　　　　205

182 instead] in steede B, stydd H　　　183 the] their ARBH　　ryffe] rafte A
184 fooles] om H　　　SD posteaquam] postquam ARBH　　resurrexit] resur-
rexint H　　quorum] quarum AR　　189 slough] my breste A　　192 wott]
witt H　　193 on] in R　　SD] om BH　　cogit] cogett AR　　195 wonder]
wondrous B　　196 withowten] without H　　197 fearder] freader R
199 mee] my B　　SD] om H　　tanget] tangit B　　et de somno] somno de
ARB　　cogett dicat A　　PRIMUS MILES and 202–9] after
217 H　　204 owt] and out H　　205 have] ame R

And, as dead here can I lye,
speake might I not, ney espye
which waye he tooke, truelye—
my eyes the were so blynde.

TERTIUS MILES

27 Alas, what ys thys great light 210
shyninge here in my sight?
Marred I am, both mayne and might;
to moove have I noe mayne.
These two beastes that are so bright—
power I ney have to ryse aright— 215
mee fayle with them for to fight,
would I never so fayne.

SECUNDUS MILES

28 Yea, I will creepe forth upon my knee
tyll I this parrell passed bee,
for my waye I may not see, 220
neyther yearth ney stonne.
Yea, in a wicked tyme we
nayled him on the roode-tree.
For us, he sayd, in dayes three
that he would ryse agayne. 225

TERTIUS MILES

29 Hye we fast we were awaye,
for this ys Goddes Sonne vercy.
Stryve with him wee ney maye
that mayster ys and more.

112ʳ   I will to Cayphas, by my faye, 230
the sooth openlye for to saye.
Farewell, syrs, and have good-daye,
for I will goe before.

207 not] *om* A, non R   espye] spie AR   MILES] *om* H   212 both]
om A   213 mayne] meane H   *To left of* 212–15] The 3 knights must
say thes ii staves and com in at the right hand B   215 I ney have] have
I non A, non I have R   218 upon] on ARH   knee] knye A, kneey R
222 a] *om* A   224 us] as ARBH   225] risen he is and gone H
230 my faye] and by A

PRIMUS MILES

30 We to lenge here ys no boote,
for needes to syr Pilate we moote   235
and tell him both croppe and roote
so soothly as wee wist.
For and they Jewes knewe as well as wee
that he were rysen through his postie,
then should the last errour bee   240
worse then was the firste.

Tunc adeunt Pilatum.

SECUNDUS MILES

31 Herkens, syr Pilate, the sooth to sayne,
Jesu that was on Frydaye slayne
through his might ys rysen agayne.
Thys ys the thyrd daye.   245
There came noe power him to fett,
but such a sleepe he on us sett
that none of us might him lett
to ryse and goe his waye.

PILATUS

32 Nowe by the othe that I have to syr Caesar
   sworne,   250
all you dogges sonnes
shall dye therfore
yf yt be on you longe.
If that you have privylie
sowld him to his companye,   255
then are you worthye for to dye
right in your owne wronge.

234 to] two H   ys] were A, it were R, it is BH   boote] boute A
235 needes] nede A   we] me H   moote] mote A   236 both] *om* A
croppe] crape A, crapp R   238 they] the ARBH   knewe] knowe R,
wist H   240 errour] errande A   241 was] *om* AR   *SD* tunc] *om* B
242 sayne] saye B   247 he on us] he on me A, on us he H   249 waye]
wayes AR   250 that] *om* AR   syr] *om* ARH   251-2] *in* H

    all you doggs sonnes beforn tomorne
    shall dye; therfore think no scorne

251 all] a A   253] are it be overlong B   be on you longe] one you
belonge R

TERTIUS MILES

33 Nowe by the order that I beare of knight,
he rose up in the morninge light
by vertue of his owne might.　　　　260
I knowe hit well afyne.
Hee rose up, as I saye nowe,
and lefte us lyenge, I wott nere howe,
all bemased and in a swoone
as we had binne stycked swyne.　　　　265

PILATUS

34 Fye, theeffe; fye, traytour;
fye on thee, thy truth ys full bare!
Fye, feynd; fye, feature;
hye hence. Fast I read that thou fare!

112ᵛ ### PRIMUS MILES

35 That tyme that hee his waye tooke　　　　270
durst I neyther speake nor looke,
but for feare I laye and quooke,
and laye in sownd dreame.
He sett his foote upon my backe
that everye lythe beganne to cracke.　　　　275
I would not abyde such another shacke
for all Jerusalem.

PILATUS

36 Fye, harlott; fye, hownde;
fye on thee, thou taynted taken dogge!
What! Laye thou styll in that stound　　　　280
and lett that losingere goe so on the rogge?

258 that] *om* AR　　　259 light] bright B　　　261 knowe] knew H　　well
afyne] vereye well A　　　264 bemased] me mased H　　and] *om* ARBH
swoone] soune A, sowne H　　　267 truth] truste ARB, thrift H　　　269 that]
om A　　　273 in] in a BH　　sownd] sowne B　　　275 lythe] joynt B
276 abyde] byde H　　such] *om* B　　shacke] shake ARB　　　279 taken]
om AH　　　280 what] why H　　stound] stonde B　　　281 goe] *om* H
so] *om* AR, so fie B　　the] thee H

37 Syr Cayphas and syr Annas,
    what saye you to thys trespas?
    I praye you, syrs, in this case
    advyse me of some reede.   285

CAYPHAS

38 Nowe, good syr, I you praye,
    herkens to mee what I you saye—
    for mych avayle us yt maye—
    and doe after my spell.
    Praye them nowe, syr, pardye,   290
    as the loven well thee,
    here as they standen all three,
    to keepe well our counsell.

ANNAS

39 Syr byshoppe, I saye to you verament,
    unto your counsell I fullye assent.   295
    This foolishe prophet that we all torent
    through his witchcrafte ys stollen awaye.
    Therfore lett us call our counsell together
    and lett us conclude to the whole matter,
    or elles our lawes are donne forever.   300

PILATUS

40 Nowe in good fayth, full woe ys mee,
    and so I trowe bynne all yee,
    that he ys rysen thus privelye
    and ys from us escaped.
    Nowe I praye you, syrs, as yee love mee,   305
    keepe this in close and privetye
    untyll our counsell and tyll wee
    have hard howe hee is scaped.

113ʳ Tunc tradet eis pecuniam, ac discedunt; et venient [mulieres]
plorantes ac Jesum querentes.

287 herkens] harke R   you] can B, *om* H   292 standen] stand AR
295 assent] me assent B   296 foolishe] foolihe H   300 forever] for
ever hereafter ARBH   301 woe ys] woes AR   303 thus] this A
308 hee] it H   scaped] shaped H   *SD* tradet] tradit B   ac discedunt]
addiscedunt A, ac discendunt R, et discedunt H   mulieres] muliere Hm
Jesum] Jesu R

MARIA MAGDALENA

41 Alas, nowe lorne ys my likinge.
For woe I wander and handes wringe. 310
My harte in sorrowe and sighinge
ys sadlye sett and sore.
That I most loved of all thinge,
alas, ys nowe full lowe lyenge.
Whye am I, lord, so longe livinge 315
to loose thy luxonne lore?

MARIA JACOBI

42 Alas, wayle awaye ys went.
My helpe, my heale from me ys hent.
My Christ, my comfort that me kent,
is clongen nowe in claye. 320
Mightie God omnipotent,
thou give them hard judgment
that my soveraygne hath so shent,
for so I maye well saye.

MARIA SALOME

43 Alas, nowe marred ys my might. 325
My lord through whom that I was light
shamefullye slayne here in my syght!
My sorrowe ys aye unsought.
Syth I maye have no other ryght
of these dyvelles that have my lord so dight, 330
to balme his bodye that ys so bryght
boyst here have I brought.

MARIA MAGDELENA

44 Suster, which of us everychon
shall remove this great stonne
that lyeth my sweet lord upon, 335
for moove yt I ne maye?

311 sighinge] in sickinge A, in sighinge R   319 comfort] counsell H
320 clongen] lodged B   325 ys] is all ARBH   326 that I] my hart H
329 maye] om A   333 everychon] everye one A, every eichone RB,
echone H

MARIA JACOBI

Suster, maystrye ys hit nonne.
Hit seemes to mee as he were gonne,
for on the sepulcher sytteth one,
and the stonne away.   340

MARIA SALOMEE

45 Two children I see ther syttinge—
all of whyte ys there clothinge—
and the stonne besydes lyeinge.
Goe we nere and see.

113ᵛ   Tunc ibunt, et aspiciunt in sepulchrum.

ANGELUS PRIMUS

46 What seeke ye women here   345
with weepinge and unlykinge chere?
Jesus, that to you was deare,
ys rysen, leeve you mee.

ANGELUS SECUNDUS

Be not afrayde of us in fere,
for he ys wente, withowten were,   350
as hee before can you leere,
forth into Gallylye.

ANGELUS PRIMUS

47 This ys the place, therfore be apayde,
that Jesu our lord was in layde;
but he ys rysen as he sayde,   355
and heathen went awaye.

337 ys hit] it is ARB   338 hit] he H   341 I see ther] here I see AR,
ther I see H   342 clothinge] clothnge H   SD] Tunc ibunt, et in
sepulcrum circumspicient H   aspiciunt] asspituit AR   ANGELUS PRIMUS]
PRIMUS ANGELLUS AR   345 women] women what seeke ye H   346 and]
and with RH   ANGELUS SECUNDUS] SECUNDUS ANGELLUS AR   349 afrayde
of us] of us afrayd H   fere] free R   350 wente] gone BH   withowten
were] as we did see R   ANGELUS PRIMUS] PRIMUS ANGELLUS AR
353 therfore be] be ye H   apayde] payde AR   356 heathen] hense A,
hethence B

ANGELUS SECUNDUS

Hye you, for ought that may befall,
and tell his disciples all;
and Peter allso saye you shall
there fynde him that you maye. 360

MARIA MAGDALENA

48 Ah, hye wee faste for anye thinge
and tell Peter this tydinge.
A blessedfull word we may him bringe,
sooth yf that hit were.

MARIA JACOBI

Yea, walke thou, suster, by on waye 365
and we another shall assaye
tyll we have mett with him todaye,
my dereworth lord so deare.

Tunc discedent, et palisper circumambulabunt; et tunc obvient
discipulis, Petro et Johanni.

MARIA MAGDALENA

49 A, Peter and John, alas, alas!
There ys befallne a wondrous case. 370
Some man my lord stollne hase
and put him I wott not where.

PETRUS

What? Ys he removed owt of the place
in the which he buryed was?

MARIA MAGDALENA

Yea, sickerlye, all my solace 375
ys gonne and ys not there.

ANGELUS SECUNDUS] SECUNDUS ANGELLUS ARB   359 saye] tell H   JACOBI]
JACOBE B   368 dereworth] worthy AR   SD discedent] discedunt BH
obvient] obvenient B   Petro] Petrus A   Johanni] Johanni et dicat Maria
Magdelena A   372 wott] om B   375 sickerlye] sicker A

C 9206   A a

50   Peter, goe we thither anon,
      runninge as faste as we maye gonne,
      to looke whoe hath removed the stonne
      and whether hee be awaye.   380

PETRUS

Abyde, brother, sweete John,
leste wee meete with anye fonne;
but nowe I see non other wonne,
to runne I will assaye.

Tunc ambo simul concurrunt, sed Johannes precurreret citius
Petro, et non intrat sepulchrum.

JOHANNES

51   A, Peter, brother, in good faye,   385
      my lord Jesu is awaye,
      but his sudarye, sooth to saye,
      lyenge here I fynd
      by hitselfe, as thou se maye;
      farre from all other clothes yt laye.   390
      Nowe Maryes wordes are sooth verey,
      as we may have in mynd.

PETRUS

52   Yea, but as God keepe me from woe
      into the sepulcher I wyll goe
      to looke whether yt be verey soe   395
      as Marye to us can saye.

Tunc introibit in sepulchrum.

PETRUS

A, lord, blessed be thou ever and oo,
for as thou towld me and other moo

EVANGELIST] EVANGELISTA B   378 maye gonne] can A   379 to] and H
383 non] no AR   *SD* ambo] *om* H   concurrunt] concurrent A,
concurrerint H   precurreret] procuret A, procucurrit B, precucurrent H
citius] *om* H   non intrat] non intrant A, not intrat B, prior veniet ad H
387 sudarye] shouldarye AR   395 whether] yf AB   PETRUS] *om* AH

I fynd thou hasse overcome our foo
and rysen art in good faye.   400

Tunc Petrus lamentando dicat.

PETRUS

53 A, lord, howe shall I doe for shame—
    that have deserved so mych blame
    to forsake thy sweete name—
    to meete with thee by any waye,
    I that in pennance and great anoye   405
    my sweete lord forsooke thrye?
    Save endlesse hope of his mercye,
    therto trust I maye.

54 For ne hit were his great grace
    and sorrowe in hart that in me was,   410
    worse I were then was Judas,
    my lord so to forsake.

114ᵛ   JOHANNES

    Peter, comforte thee in this case,
    for sycker my lord Jesu hase
    greate repentance for thy tresspasse;   415
    my lord in hart will take.

55 Goe we seeke Jesu anon in hye,
    one waye thow, another way I.

PETRUS

    Yea, well I hope through his might
    my pennance shall him please.   420

Tunc abeunt, hic per aliam viam ille per alteram. Mulieres venient.

---

399 overcome] overconon A, overcommen H   *SD* lamentando] et lamentando A   dicat] dicit B   PETRUS] *om* AR   401 lord] lore A
403 sweete] holye A   405 anoye] anye H   409 ne hit] it ne B
410 in] of A   that] as R   411 was Judas] Judas was A   JOHANNES]
JOHANNES EVANG H   413 this] thes H   414 sycker] suerlie AR   hase]
accepted hase ARBH   418 another] and another BH   way] *om* B
SD abeunt] abiunt B, vadunt H   mulieres venient] *om* H

MARIA MAGDALENA

56 Heathen will I never, syckerlye,
tyll I be comforted of myne anoye
and knowe where hee is readelye.
Here will I sitt and weepe.

ANGELUS PRIMUS

57 Woman, whye weepest thou so aye?   425

MARIA MAGDALENA

Sonne, for my lord ys taken awaye
and I wott nere, the sooth to saye,
whoe hath donne that thinge.
Alas, whye were I not dead todaye,
clought and clongen under claye   430
to see my lord that here laye
once at my likynge?

Finis

PLAY XIX

115ʳ   THE SADLERS PLAYE

Pagina Decima Nona: De Christo Duobus Discipulis ad Castellum
Emaus Euntibus Apparente et Aliis Discipulis

LUCAS

1 Alas, nowe wayle ys went awaye.
My owne, my mayster ever I maye
that is nowe clongen under claye,
that makes my hart in care.

---

421 heathen] hense ARBH   422 anoye] anye H   ANGELUS PRIMUS]
PRIMUS ANGELLUS AR, ANGELUS H   MARIA MAGDALENA] *om* B   425–*Finis*]
om B   427 nere] not where AR   428 that] this H   430 clought]
clough R   RH *continuation—see Appendix ID.*

    Guild-ascription] *om* H   *Play-heading* Christo] Christ B   castellum]
castellam RB   apparente] aparent A   et] et et A   discipulis] discipulis et
dicat Lucas A   3 clongen] logged B

Sorrowe and sighinge, the sooth to saye,   5
makes me both, that ys no naye.
When I thinke on him both night and daye
for deole I drowpe and dare.

CLEOPHAS

2 Yea, mych myrth was in mee
my sweete soveraygne when I might see,   10
and his likinge lore with lee,
and nowe so lowe ys layde.
Brother, nowe ys dayes three
syth hee was nayled on the tree.
[Lorde], whether he rysen bee   15
as hee before hath sayd?

LUCAS

3 Leyffe brother Cleophas,
to knowe that were a coynte case.
Syth he through hart wonded was,
howe should he lyve agayne?   20

CLEOPHAS

If that godhead in him hasse
and commen to bye mans tresspas,
he may ryse through his owne grace
and his death to us gayne.

LUCAS

4 A mystie thinge yt is to mee   25
to have beleyffe yt should so bee,
howe hee should ryse in dayes three—
such wonders never was wyst.

6 me both] mone AR, me half dead H   7 both] om ARBH   8 deole]
deale AB   drowpe] droppe A, drope R   CLEOPHAS] CLEAPAS H   10 when]
whyl H   might] did B   12 and] which H   13 ys] are H   14 on]
upon BH   the] om A   tree] roode tree AR   15 lorde] bord Hm
16 hath] hade AR   17 Cleophas] Clephas H   18 that] this A   a]
om H   coynte] cuninge AR, quainte B   CLEOPHAS] CLEOPAS H   21 that]
that he ARBH   22 commen] come B   mans] makynds H   24 to]
do H   gayne] againe B   25 to] om A   28 never was] was never B

CLEOPHAS

Sooth thou sayst, nowe well I see.
Leeve maye I not by any lewtye;   30
but God maye of his majestye
doe whatsoever him liste.

Tunc veniet Jesus in habitu peregrino et dicat eis.

115ᵛ   JESUS

5 Good men, yf your will weare,
   tell me in good manere
   of your talkinge. That in fere   35
   and of your woe wytt I would.

CLEOPHAS

A, syr, yt seemes to us here
a pylgryme thou art, as can appeare.
Tydinge and tales all inteere
thou may here what ys towld.   40

6 In Jerusalem that other daye
   thou, that walkest manye a waye,
   maye thou not here what men doe saye,
   abowt theras thou yeede?

JESUS

What are those? Tell me, I thee praye.   45

LUCAS

Of Jesus of Nazareth, in good faye,
a prophett to eych mans paye
and wyse in word and deede!

CLEOPHAS] CLEOPAS H   29 nowe] full AR   30 maye] om H   any]
my ARBH   lewtye] bewtie B   32 whatsoever] whatever B   him] he H
SD veniet] venit ARB   habitu] habet A, habit R   peregrino] periogrem A,
periogrine R, peregrine B, peregrinae H   dicat eis] dicat Jesu AR, ait H
35 talkinge] calling B   CLEOPHAS] CLEOPAS H   37 seemes] seeme H
38 can] doth AR   39 tydinge] tydinges ARH, good tytinges B   42 thou
that] that thou A   43 doe] om A   45] tell me what are those I thee
pray B   48 and(2)] in H

7 To God and man wyse was hee,
  but bushoppes—cursen motte the bee—   50
  dampned him and nayled him on a tree,
  that wronge never yett wrought.

CLEOPHAS

Witterlye, before wend wee
that Israell he should have made free,
and out of payne through his postye   55
the people he should have brought.

LUCAS

8 Yea, syr, nowe ys the thyrd daye
  sythe they made thys affraye,
  and some weomen there as hee laye
  weare yarlye in the morne   60
  and feared us fowle, in faye.
  The towld us hee was stollen awaye
  and angelles, as they can saye,
  the sepulchre syttinge beforne.

CLEOPHAS

9 Yea, syr, these weomen that hard I   65
  sayde hee was rysen redelye,
  and some men of our companye
  thyder anon can goe
  and found yt so, lesse and more.
  And yett our hartes are full sore   70
  lest yt be not so.

116ʳ   JESUS

10 Ah, fooles, and feeble in good faye;
  latt to beleeve unto Goddes lawe!
  The prophetes before can thus saye—
  leeve you on this soothlye—   75

50 cursen] cursed AR, cursten H   motte] mought B   52] that wroughte
yet never wronge AR   54 he] om AR   have] a R   57 ys] this is H
60 weare] were their A   yarlye] erlye ARB, yerly H   64 beforne] before A
CLEOPHAS] CLEOPAS H   65 these] ther B   69] and found it so as it towld
of yore H   After 69] and they sayd so neither lesse nor more H   74 thus
saye] this sawe AR

that yt needes be alwaye,
Christ to suffer death, the sooth to saye,
and to joye that lasteth aye
bringe man through his mercye.

11 And first at Moyses to beginne,   80
    what he sayth I shall you mynne:
    that God was a greave within
    that burned aye, as him thought.
    The greave payred nothinge therbye—
    what was that but mayd Marye   85
    that bare Jesu synleslye
    that man hath nowe forbought?

12 Also Esaye sayd this:
    'As a woman comfortes iwys
    her child that hath donne amys   90
    to amend, leeve ye mee
    so God would man reconcyled here
    through his mercye, in good manere,
    and in Jerusalem in better were
    forbought they should bee':   95

'Quemadmodum mater consolatur filios suos, ita et ego consolabor
vos; et in Jerusalem consolabimini.' Esaias, capitulo sexagesino
sexto.

CLEOPHAS

13 A, lord give thee good grace,
    for greatly comforted mee thou hasse.
    Goe with us to this place.
    A castell ys herebye.

JESUS

Nowe, good men, soothly to saye,   100
I have to goe a great waye.
Therfore at this tyme I ne maye,
but I thanke you hartelye.

82 a greave within] agreve with hym AR, a grave within B   83 that] and B
him] he H   86 synleslye] sincerlye AR   94 in(2)] if H   SD filios]
filies AR   consolabor] consolabom A   capitulo sexagesino sexto] capitula
sexage sexto et dicat A, om R, 66 B, capitulo sexagemio sexto H   CLEOPHAS]
CLEOPAS H   100 to] for to ARBH

LUCAS

14 Syr, you shall in all manere
dwell with us at our suppere,   105
for nowe night approcheth nere.
Tarrye here for anythinge!

CLEOPHAS

Nowe God forbyd that we weare
so uncurtysse to you here
for, saffe my lovely lord of lere,   110
thy lord ys most likinge.

116ᵛ   Tunc ibit Jesus cum illis ad castellum.

LUCAS

15 Sytt downe, syr, here I you praye
and take a morsell yf you maye,
for you have walked a great waye
syth todaye at noone.   115

JESUS

Grantmercye, good men, in good faye.
To blesse this bread, sooth to saye,
I will anon in good araye
rightly you beforne.

Tunc frangit panem et dicat:

16 Eates on, men, and do gladlye   120
in the name of God almightie,
for this bread blessed have I
that I give you todaye.

Tunc Jesus evanescit.

111 lord] lore BH   SD] Tunc omnies ad castellum evunt H   castellum]
castillum A, castellam RB   112 syr here] here sire ARB   113 yf] and A
114 great] longe A   115 noone] morne H   116 men] me A
119 rightly] righte by A   beforne] before R   SD frangit] franget A
dicat] ait H   After SD] JESUS A   SD evanescit] evaneset A,
evanescet H

LUCAS

Grantmercye, syr, syckerlye.
Nowe read I you be right merye.　　　　　125
What! Where ys hee that sate us bye?
Alas, he ys awaye.

CLEOPHAS

17　Alas, alas, alas, alas!
This was Jesus in this place.
By breakinge the bread I knewe his face　　　130
but nothinge there before.

LUCAS

A burninge hart in us hee made,
for while [he] with us here was
to knowe him we might have no grace
for all his luxon lore.　　　　　135

CLEOPHAS

18　Goe we, brother, and that anon,
and tell our brethren everychon
howe our mayster ys from us gonne;
yee, soothly wee may saye.

LUCAS

Yea, we maye make our monne　　　　　140
that sate with him in great wonne,
and we no knowledge had him upon
tyll he was passed awaye.

Tunc ibunt ad alios discipulos in alio loco congregatos.

---

124 syr] om AR　　　125 read I] I read H　　　CLEOPHAS] CLEOPAS H
130 the] om R, of BH　　　132 made] masse H　　　133 he] hee hee Hm,
he heare AR, that he H　　here] om AR　　was] stayde R　　134 might]
migh H　　135 luxon] luxom ARH, lixsom B　　CLEOPHAS] CLEOPAS H
137 everychon] everye eichone ARB　　140 we maye] well may we H
142 had him] hym hade A　　SD alios] cateros H　　congregatos] congregatos
dicat A

CLEOPHAS

19 A, reste well, brethren one and all.
 Wondrously ys us befall! 145
 Our lord and wee were in a hall
 and him yett knewe not wee.

117ʳ

ANDREAS

 Yea, leeve thou well this, Cleophas,
 that hee ys rysen that dead was
 and to Peter appeared hase 150
 this daye appertlye.

LUCAS

20 With us he was a longe fytt
 and undyd his holy wrytt;
 and yett our wyttes were so knytt
 that him we might not knowe. 155

CLEOPHAS

 Nowe sycker awaye was all my wytt
 tyll the bread was broken eych bytt;
 and anon when he brake hitt
 he vanished in a thrall.

PETRUS

21 Nowe we breathren all in feere, 160
 I reade we hyde us somewhere here
 that Jewes meete us not in no manere
 for malice, leeve you mee.

ANDREAS

 Lenge wee here in this place.
 Peradventure God wyll shewe us grace 165
 to se our lord in little space
 and comforted for to bee.

144 well] *om* B   145 befall] befalne B   146 lord] master R   a]
on AR   ANDREAS] ANDREWAS R   152 us] *om* H   153 undyd]
opened H   wrytt] write B   CLEOPHAS] *om* AR, CLEOPAS H   156 awaye]
awas A   159 thrall] thrawe AR   160 we] we be BH   all] *om* AR
ANDREAS] ANDREWAS AR   167 and comforted] our comfortes B

Tunc omnes eunt infra castrum, et veniet Jesus stans in medio
discipulorum; et postea dicat

JESUS

22 Peace amonge you, brethren fayre!
    Yea, dread you nought in no manere.
    I am Jesus, withowt were,   170
    that dyed on roode-tree.

PETER

A, what ys hee that comys here
to this fellowshippe all in fere
as hee to me nowe can appeare?
A ghooste methinke I see.   175

JESUS

23 Brethren, whye are ye so frayd for nought
    and noyed in harte for feeble thought?
    I am hee that hath you forbought
    and dyed for mans good.
    My feete, my handes you may see;   180
    and knowe the soothe also may yee,
    soothly that I am hee
    that dead was upon a tree.

117ᵛ   24 Handle me, both all and one,
           and leeve well this everychone: 185
           that ghooste hath neyther fleshe ne bonne
           as you see nowe on mee.

ANDREAS

A, lord, mych joye is us upon!
But what he ys, wott I ney can.

SD eunt] erunt H   castrum] castellum H   veniet] venient AR, venit B
medio] media B   et] ac H   dicat] dicat Jesus A   169 yea] ye B
nought] not H   PETER] PETRUS BH   174 nowe can] can now B,
he can H   176 so] *om* B   177 noyed] moved R   181 soothe]
truth AR   185 leeve] beleeve AR   well this] this R, this well H   every-
chone] everye eichone ARB   ANDREAS] ANDREWAS AR

JESUS

Nowe sythe you leeve I am no man,   190
more sygnes you shall se.

25 Have you any meate here?

PETRUS

Yea, my lord leeffe and dere,
rosted fyshe and honye in fere,
therof we have good wonne.   195

JESUS

Eate we then in good manere.
Thus nowe you knowe withowt were
that ghooste to eate hath no powere,
as you shall see anon.

Tunc commedit Jesus, et dabit discipulis suis.

JESUS

26 Brethren, I towld you before   200
when I was with you not gayne an howre,
that nedelye both lesse and more
must fulfilled bee.
In Moyses lawe as wrytten were,
all other prophettes as nowe weare,   205
ye fulfilled in good manere
of that was sayd of mee.

27 For thys was wrytten in prophecye:
that I must suffer death nedelye
and the thyrd day with victorye   210
ryse in good arraye
and preach remission of synnes
unto all men that his name doth mynne.
Therfore, all you that bee herein
thinke on what I saye.   215

191 sygnes] signe H   193 leeffe] life A   197 nowe you] you now H
SD commedit] comedent A, comedet H   discipulis] discipulus R   suis]
om H   JESUS] om H   201 an] one R   202 both] om A   204 lawe]
lawes B   205 prophettes] prophesyes H   nowe] then H   206 ys]
is now B   208 in] by AR   211 in] with AR   212 synnes] sinne H
213 men] om A   doth] doe A, om R   mynne] myne A, mynes R

Tunc evanescit Jesus, et ibunt discipuli Bethaniae; et obviantes
Thomas dicat Petrus.

PETRUS

28 A, Thomas! Tydinges good and neewe!
    We have seene the lord Jesu.

118ʳ   THOMAS

    Shall I never leeve that this ys trewe,
    by God omnypotent,
    but I see in his handes two   220
    holes the nayles can in goe
    and put my fynger eke alsoe
    thereas the nayles went.

ANDREAS

29 Thomas, goe we all in feere;
    for dread of enemyes better were   225
    then Jewes should have [us] in there dangeire
    and all our fraternitie.

THOMAS

    Wherever you goe, brethren deare,
    I will goe with you in good manere;
    but this talke you tell mee here   230
    I leeve not tell I see.

PETRUS

30 Nowe, Thomas, bee thou not awaye
    and in happe se him thou maye
    and feele him also, in good faye,
    as we have donne before.   235

SD tunc] iterum H   evanescit] evanescet H   ibunt discipuli Bethaniae]
ibunt discipuli Bethanie B, discipuli versus Bethaniam ibunt H   obviantes
Thomas] Thomas obviantes H   dicat Petrus] *om* A, dicat Peter B   218 that]
om R   220 his handes] hand H   221 the] that H   223 went]
were B   ANDREAS] ANDREWAS R   226 us] *om* Hm   there] *om* B
228 wherever] whether ever R   brethren deare] farre or nere A   233 happe]
hope A

THOMAS

Wherever you bee, I will be aye;
but make mee leeve this thinge verey—
you pyne you not! Therfore I you praye
to speake of that no more.

*Tunc ibunt omnes iterum ad mansionem et recumbent. Et
subito apparebit Jesus dicens.*

JESUS

31 Peace, my brethren, both on and all.   240
Come hither, Thomas; to thee I call.
Showe forth, for ought that maye befall,
thy hand and put in here;
and see my handes and my feete,
and put in thy hand; thou ne lett.   245
My woundes are yett freshe and wett
as the first were.

32 And be thou no more so dreadinge,
but ever trulye beleevinge.

Tunc emittet manum in latus et vulnera.

THOMAS

My God, my lord, my Christ, my kinge!   250
Nowe leeve I withowt weeninge.

118ᵛ   JESUS

Yea, Thomas, thou seest nowe in mee.
Thou leevest nowe that I am hee.
But blessed must they all bee
that leeve and never see   255

238 you] and B   pyne] payne H   you(3)] *om* H   *SD* iterum] *om* H
dicens] *om* A   240 both] *om* A   245 hand thou] handes and B   lett]
leet H   246 wett] weette ARBH   247 the] they BH   248 no more
so] so no more H   249 ever trulye] evermore true B   *SD*] Tunc
immittct in latus et vulnera manum H   emittet] emittit ARB   vulnera]
velnare A   252] yee now seeth you Thomas in me B, yea Thomas now
thou seest me H

33 that I am that same bodye
    that borne was of meeke Marye
    and on a crosse your sowles did bye
    upon Good Frydaye.
    Whoeso to this wyll consent,   260
    that I am God omnipotent,
    as well as they that be present
    my dearlynges shalbe aye.

34 Whoeso to this wyll not consent
    ever to the daye of judgment,   265
    in hell-fyer they shalbe brent
    and ever in sorrowe and teene.

35 Whosoever on my Father hath any mynd
    or of my mother in any kynd,
    in heaven blysse they shall yt fynd   270
    withowt any woe.
    Christe give you grace to take the waye
    unto that joye that lasteth aye,
    for there is noe night but ever daye,
    for all you thyder shall goe.   275

Finis

256 that] the B   261 omnipotent] onnipotent B   262 be] did B
263 aye] ever A   266 brent] brende B   268 on] of ARH   any] *om* A
mynd] mine B   270 heaven] heavens B   273 that] the AR   274 for]
om R   there is] thers H   275 goe] com B

PLAY XX

THE TAYLORS PLAYE

Incipit Pagina Vicesima de Assentione Domini. Et primo dicat
Jesus 'Pax vobis; ego sum; nolite timere.'

JESUS

1 My brethren that sytten in companye,
with peace I greate you hartfullye.
I am hee that standes you bye;
ne dread you nothinge.
Well I knowe and wytterlye 5
that yee be in greate extacye
whether I be rysen verelye—
that makes you sore in longinge.

2 [You] ys no neede to be anoyed soo
neyther through thought to be in woo. 10
Your handes puttes nowe you froo
and feele my woundes wyde.
And leeves this, both all and one,
that ghoost hath neyther fleshe ne bonne
as yee may feele mee upon 15
on handes and on feete.

'Spiritus quidem carnem et ossa non habet sic me videtis habere.'

PETRUS

3 A, what ys this that standeth us bye?
A ghoost meethinke he seemeth, wytterlye.
Meethinke lightned mych am I
this spryte for to see. 20

Guild-ascription playe] *om* H   *Play-heading*] Pagina Vicesima de Ascen-
tione Salvatoris Jesu Christi H   incipit] hic incipit B   domini] dominum
AR   ego sum] *om* B   timere] timere et dicat Jesus AR   JESUS] *om* B
To right of JESUS] 'Pax vobis; ego sum; nolite timere' H   1 sytten] sit H
2 hartfullye] hartelye AR   5 wytterlye] wittely H   6 greate] an H
9 you] your Hm, ther BH   ys] have R   10 through] for B   11 nowe
you] nowe AR, you now H   12 wyde] weet H   13 leeves]
beleeve AR   both] *om* A   16 and] or AR   *Latin* quidem] quidam
A, *om* H   non] not B   habet] habit R, habete B   sic] sicut H
videtis] videtes A   habere] habere dicat Petrus A, Luca 24 H   17 standeth]
standes BH   18 meethinke he] me hym ARBH   seemeth] seemes B
19 ame] ane A   20 spryte] spirritte ARBH

ANDREAS

Peeter, I tell thee prevelye
I dread me yett full greatlye
that Jesu should doe such maystrye,
and whether that this be hee.

JOHANNES

4 Brethren, good yt is to thinke evermore   25
what wordes he sayd the daye before
he dyed on roode—gonne ys not youre—
and bee we steadfast aye.

JACOBUS MAJOR

A, John, that makes us in weare
that alwaye when he will appere—   30
and when us lyst beste to have him here,
anonne hee ys awaye.

119ᵛ   ### JESUS

5 I see well, brethren, sooth to saye,
for any signe that I shewe maye
yee be not steadfast in the faye,   35
but flittinge I you fynd.
Moe signes therfore yee shall see.
Have you ought may eaten bee?

SIMON

Yea, lord, here—meate innough for thee,
and elles we were unkynd.   40

JESUS

6 Nowe eate we then for charitie,
my leeve brethren fayre and free,
for all thinges shall fullfilled bee
wrytten in Moyses lawe.

ANDREAS] ANDREWAS R, ANDREUS B   JOHANNES] JHON H   25 brethren]
brother H   yt is] is it H   thinke] thinke on H   28 bee we] we be H
steadfast] wisted faste AR   31 lyst beste] best list H   34 that] om H
36 flittinge] flechinge H   39 here] heare is AR, heres B, om H   meate]
om A   40 and] or ARBH

Prophetes in psalmes sayden of mee   45
that death I behoved on the roode-tree,
and ryse within dayes three
to joye mankind to drawe

7 and preach to folke this world within
   pennance, remyssion of there synne;   50
   in Jerusalem I should begynne,
   as I have donne for love.
   Therfore, beleeve steadfastlye
   and come ye with mee to Bethanye.
   In Jerusalem yee shall all lye   55
   to abyde the grace above.

Tunc commedet Jesus cum discipulis suis, et postea dicat

PHILIPPUS

8 Lord, from us thou nought conseyle!
   What tyme that thou art in thy weale,
   shalt thou restore Israell
   agayne her realme that daye?   60

JESUS

Brother, that ys not to thee
to knowe my Fathers privetie
that towcheth to his owne postie—
wytt that yee ne maye.

9 But take ye shall, through my beheste,   65
   vertue of they Holye Ghoste
   that send shalbe to helpe you moste
   in world where ye [shall] wend.
120r My wytnesse all yee shalbee
   in Jerusalem and Judee,   70
   Samarye also, and eych countree
   to the worldes end.

45 sayden] said ARBH   46 I behoved on] I behoveth on AR, behoved
me H   47 within] in A   49 this] the R   50 synne] sines B
53 beleeve] brethren beleevs H   54 come ye] comes H   55 all] om AR
SD commedet] comedit AB   et postea dicat] om H   57 thou nought]
do not H   58 what] that AR   that] om H   weale] wayle ARH
59 shalt] wilt B   63 to] om H   64 yee] thou H   66 they] the
ARBH   68 in] in the B   shall] wynne Hm, mooye A, maye R
71 Samarye] Samaria ARBH   72 to] unto H

10 Goe yee all the worlde, and through my grace
preach my word in eych place.
All that steadfast beleeffe hasse,   75
and fullye, save shall [be].
And whoeso beleeveth not in your lore,
the wordes ye preach them before,
dampned shalbe evermore;
that payne may them not flee.   80

11 By this thinge ye shall well knowe
whoso leeveth steadfastlye in you;
such signes, soothlye, the shall shewe
whersoever the tyde to goe.
In my name well shall they   85
devylles powers to putt awaye;
newe tonges yee shall have to preach the faye,
and edders to mayster also;

12 and though the poyson eate or drynke,
yt shall nye them nothinge;   90
sycke men with ther handlinge
shall healed redelye bee,
such grace shall be in there doinge.
Nowe to my Father I am goinge.
Yee shall have, brethren, my blessinge,   95
for to heaven I must stee.

Tunc adducet discipulos in Bethaniam; et cum pervenerit ad
locum, ascendens dicat Jesus, stans in loco ubi assendit. Dicat
Jesus, 'Data est mihi omnis potestas in caelo et in terra.'

73 yee] ye in R, in H   and] *om* BH   75 all] and B   76 save] saved
ABH   be] *om* Hm, yee R   77 whoeso] *om* B   beleeveth] leeves H
78 ye] that you H   them] then H   79 evermore] for evermore ARBH
80 may them not] shall not them A, shall they not R, they may not H
81 ye] they H   82 leeveth] liveth B, leves H   in] on H   83 soothlye]
apertly H   the] they RBH   86 powers] power B   to] *om* R   putt]
doe H   87] new tonges to preach have shall they B   yee] *om* ARH
88] and other misteries moe H   89 the] they B   91 handlinge]
helpinge H   93 in] *om* AR   95 brethren] here H   96 stee] hie B,
stye H   *SD* adducet] adducit A, abducet H   discipulos] discipulis R,
discipulos suos et B   ascendens] *om* H   dicat] *om* H   stans] stan B
assendit] assendus B, ascenderit H   Jesus] *om* H   omnis] omnes AR
caelo] cela A   terra] terra dicat A

JESUS

13 My sweete brethren leeffe and deare,
to mee ys granted full powere
in heaven and yearth, farre and neare,
for my godhead is moste. 100
To teach all men nowe goe yee
that in world will fullfilled bee
in the name of my Father and mee
and of the Holy Ghooste.

Tunc Jesus ascendet, et in ascendendo cantet (God singeth alonne).

120ᵛ JESUS

Ascendo ad Patrem meum et Patrem vestrum, Deum meum et Deum vestrum. Alleluya. [a]

Cum autem impleverit Jesus canticum, stet in medio quasi supra nubes, et dicat major angelus minori angelo. [b]

Primus Angelus cantat:

Quis est iste qui venit de Edom, tinctis vestibus de Bosra? [c]

Minor Angelus respondens cantat:

Iste formosus in stola sua, gradiens in multitudine fortitudinis suae? [d]

Jesus cantat solus:

Ego qui loquor justitiam et propinquator sum ad salvandum. [e]

Chorus cantat:

Et vestimenta tua sicut calcantium in torculari. [f]

102 world] word H   fullfilled] folowe A, followed RBH   bee] me A
SD ascendet] ascendit ARB   in] om H   ascendendo] ascendo AH   cantet]
cantat B, cantabit Jhesus ut sequitur H   God] om H   singeth] almighti AR,
om H   alonne] om H   Latin alleluya] alleguus R, alleluia
alleluya H   SD] om R, Et cantico finito stabit Jhesus in medio quasi supra
nubes H   nubes] nubens A   Primus Angelus] Angelus Primus H
cantat] cantet AR, om H   Minor Angelus] Angelus Secundus H   respon-
dens] respondentem AR, responden B, om H   cantat] cantet A, om H
Latin iste] ista B   suae] sua R, sue B   cantat solus] cantet solus R, om H
Latin propinquator] propungnavor AR, propugnabor B, propugnator H
chorus cantat] chorus cantet R, Anelus Tertius H   Latin calcantium]
calcantrum A   torculari] torquilarie A

Jesus cantat solus:

Torcular calcavi solus, et de gentibus non est vir mecum.   [g]

Primus Angelus dicat in materna lingua: [h]

14 Who ys this that cometh within   105
the blysse of heaven that never shall blynne,
bloodye, owt of the world of synne—
and harrowed hell hath hee?

SECUNDUS ANGELUS

Comely hee ys in his clothinge,
and with full power goinge,   110
a nomber of sayntes with him leadinge.
Hee seemeth great of postee.

Jesus autem pausans eodem loco dicat.

JESUS

15 I that spake rightwisenesse
and have brought man out of distres,
forbyer called I am and was   115
of all mankynd through grace.
My people, that were from me rafte
through synne and through the dyvelles crafte,
to heaven I bringe—good never one lafte—
all that in hell were.   120

TERTIUS ANGELUS

16 Whye ys thy cloathinge nowe so reedd,
thy bodye bloodye and also head,
thy clothes also, all that binne ledd,
like to pressars of wyne?

cantat solus] cantet solus R, *om* H   *Latin* torcular] torcalas A, torculor BH
Primus Angelus] Angelus Primus H   dicat in materna lingua] in lingua
materna dicat AR, in materna lingua dicat B, *om* H   107 bloodye]
bluddelye AR, bodie B   SECUNDUS ANGELUS] ANGELUS SECUNDUS H
111 a] and B, *om* H   112 seemeth] semes H   *SD* Jesus]
tunc Jesus H   autem pausans] autem pausas R, stans paulisper H   eodem
loco] in loco eodem H   dicat] dicat Jesus A   113 spake] speak BH
rightwisenesse] righteousnes H   114 brought] bought R   man] men B
115 called I am and] I ame and called R, I am called and H   119 good]
om ARB   never one] and never one AR, one never H   lafte] lefte ARBH
120 all] of all B   were] was H   TERTIUS ANGELUS] ANGELUS TERTIUS H
121 nowe] *om* AR   122 head] rede B   123 all] *om* ARB   ledd] leade ARH

121^r   JESUS

For the devill and his powere   125
that mankynd brought in great dangere.
Through death one crosse and blood so clere
I have made them all myne.

17 These bloodye droppes that yee nowe see
all the freshe shall reserved bee   130
tyll I come in my majestie
to deame the laste daye.
This blood I shedd, wytnes bere to mee,
and dyed for man on roode-tree,
and rose agayne within dayes three—   135
such love I loved thee aaye.

18 Theise droppes nowe with good intent
to my Father I will present
that good men that on yearth be lent
shall knowe appertlye   140
howe gratiouslye that I them bought;
and for good workes that I have wrought
everlastinge blysse that they sought,
to preeve the good worthye;

19 and that the wycked may eychone   145
knowe and see all one
howe worthelye they [forgone]
that blysse that lasteth aye.
For theise causes, leeve yee mee,
the droppes I shedd on roode-tree.   150
All fleshe shall reserved bee
ever, tyll the laste daye.

127 one] and H   clere] deere R   129 bloodye droppes] droppes so
bloodye AR   nowe] may H   130 the freshe] they H   132 deame]
dome H   133 I shedd] shall H   134 and] I H   on] on the H
roode] bloddie B   135 agayne] om H   136 thee] them H   141 that]
om AR   142 I have] they H   145 may] om B, men H   146 knowe]
maye know BH   one] and one H   147 forgone] forgive Hm   148 aye]
ever AR   After 148] 137–8 repeated B (nowe] om B)   151 fleshe]
freshe ARBH

Tunc ascendet, et in ascendendo cantent angeli canticum sub-
scriptum. Cantent 'Exaltaremus, domine, in virtute tua; cantabimus et psallemus virtutes tuas.'

Tunc descendent angeli, et cantent 'Viri Gallilei, quid aspicitis in
caelum?'

QUARTUS ANGELUS

20 Yee men that binne of Gallilee,
whereupon nowe wonder yee,
waytinge him that through postye   155
ys nowe gonne you froo?

PRIMUS ANGELUS

Jesu Christe, leeve yee mee,
that steede to heaven, as ye see,
right so come agayne shall hee
as yee seene him goo.   160

121ᵛ

PETRUS

21 Loo, brethren, what these angelles sayen,
that Jesu, that through his great mayne
to heaven ys gonne, will come agayne
right as he forth went.

ANDREAS

Manye sethen so height hee   165
to send his Ghooste, with hart free,
and in Jerusalem we shalbee
tyll yt were to us sent.

SD] *om* AR   ascendet] ascendit B   cantent] cantant H   subscriptum]
subsequentem H   cantent] *om* ARH   exaltaremus] exaltare BH
psallemus] psalmus B   virtutes] virtute B   tuas] tuas alleluya H
SD] *om* AR   cantent] cantabunt H   caelum] celum etc B   QUARTUS ANGELUS]
ANGELUS QUARTUS H   154 whereupon] therupon AR   wonder]
marvayll A   PRIMUS ANGELUS] ANGELUS PRIMUS H   158 steede]
went B, stayed H   see] might se H   160 seene] saw H   161 loo]
om B   162 that(2)] *om* B, which H   his] is B   ANDREAS] ANDREWAS R
165 sethen] days sith H   166 with] ech B   free] so free ARH, to free B
167 shalbee] should be H

SIMON

22 Brethren, I read us, in good faye,
    that we thether take the waye   170
    and with devotion night and daye
    lenge in our prayer.

PHILIPPUS

For knowe we mone by sygne vereye
that hee ys Godes Sonne, sooth to saye.
Therfore yt ys good we goe to praye   175
as he commanded here.

JOHANNES

23 Nowe mon we leeve yt no leasinge,
    for both by syght and handlinge,
    speakinge, eatinge and drinkinge
    hee prooves his deitee.   180

JACOBUS MAJOR

Yea, also by his uppsteyinge
hee seemes fully heaven-kinge.
Whoe hasse therin full leevinge,
saved liffe and soule ys hee.

PETRUS

24 Goe we, brethren, with one assent   185
    and fullfill his commandement;
    but looke that none through dread be blent,
    but leeves all steadfastlye.
    Praye we all with full intent
    that hee to us his Ghoost will sent.   190
    Jesu, that from us nowe ys went,
    save all this companye! Amen.

Finis

SIMON] SIMOND B   173 knowe we mone] now we know H   sygne] signes H
175 to] and H   177 nowe mon] for now must H   179 drinkinge]
handlinge A   180 prooves] proved H   deitee] dietie B   JACOBUS]
JACOBI B   182 heaven] heavenlye AR, heavens B   184 saved] soved A,
saved in H   soule] soules R   190 his] he R   sent] sende A   191 from
us nowe ys] nowe is from us ARB, from us is H   192 amen] om ARH

PLAY XXI

122ʳ   THE FISHEMONGERS PLAYE

Incipit Pagina Vicesima Prima de Electione Matthei et de Emissione
Spiritus Sancti qualiter apostoli fecerunt simbolum apostolicum—
viz. 'Credo in Deum Patrem' etc.

Et primo inter apostolos incipiat

PETRUS (ad condiscipulos)

1   My deare brethren everychone,
you knowe well, both all and one,
howe our lord ys from us gonne
to blysse that lasteth aye.
Comforte nowe maye wee have nonne   5
save his beheste to trust upon.
Therfore leeve we in this wonne
that never one wend awaye.

2   Lenge we styffe in our prayer,
for well I wott, withowt were,   10
he will send us a counselour,
his Ghoost, as hee beheight.
Therefore lenge we right here,
this faythfull fellowshippe in fere,
tyll our lord, as he can us lere,   15
send us of heaven light.

Tunc exurgens Petrus in medio fratrum et dicat:

3   My deare brethren fayer and free,
Holye Scripture, leeve yee mee,

Guild-ascription Fishemongers] Fishemonders B   playe] *om* H   *Play-
heading* incipit] *om* H   vicesima] vissicima A   Matthei] Mathia AR,
Mathie BH   sancti] sancti de symbolo apostolorum H   qualiter . . .
incipiat] *om* H   apostolicum] aplicamini A   credo] dredo R   incipiat]
icipiat Patrus ad condiscipulus A, incipiat Patrus ad condiciplus R, incipiet B
SH ad condiscipulos] *om* ARH, ad discipulos B   1 everychone] everye
eichone ARB, every one H   2 both] *om* A   one] wan A   4 aye]
ever A   5 maye wee] we maye R, we H   6 trust] leeve H   7 leeve]
lyve H   wonne] one B   9 lenge] lynge R, long B   10 wott] wotten B
withowt] withouten ARBH   13 we] we all H   *SD* exurgens Petrus]
Petrus exurgens H   fratrum] fratrum ibit H   dicat] dicat Petrus A

fullye must fullfilled bee
that Davyd sayd beforne.   20
All of the Holye Ghooste had hee.
Towchinge Judas [wytten] yee
that sould our mayster for money
and nowe ys cleane forlorne.

4 Amonge us nombred that wretch was,   25
the fayth to preach in eych place;
and nowe his hyre fullye hee hasse,
for hanged himselfe hasse hee.
His bodye bursten for his tresspasse,
soule dampned as a man withowt grace.   30
Therfore, as the psalter mynd mase,
fullfylled nowe must bee:

'Fiat habitatio eius deserta et non [sit] qui habitet in eo. Episcopatum eius accipiat alter.'

122ᵛ   5 Therefore, men that nowe binne here
and fellowes that aye with us were
with Jesus Christe, our mayster dere,   35
in yearth livinge was—
that yee that seene his powere,
his myracles manye in good manere,
dyinge, rysinge, both in fere,
maye best nowe beare witnesse.   40

6 Mattheus I read here be one,
and Josephe that aye with us hath gonne,
for whom we caste to lottes anonne
and buske us all to praye

20 beforne] before ARH   21 all] also AR   holye] hely H   22 wytten]
wrytten Hm, witt H   24 forlorne] forlore H   26 the fayth to preach]
to preach the fayth H   27 hasse] hathe B   28 himselfe] hisself B
hee] see B   29 bursten] borsen AR, hanged B   30 soule] his sowle H
as a man] om H   withowt] bout AR   Latin deserta] in deserto B   non sit]
non sic HmAR, not sit B   habitet] habite B   eo] ea ARBH   accipiat]
accipiet BH   alter] alter dicat Petro A   34 aye] ever A   35 with]
which B, while H   36 yearth] youth B   livinge] lyeinge R   37 seene]
see H   38 manye] om AR   good] om AR   39 dyinge] drying B,
dinnge H   41 Mattheus] Mathias ARBH   here] he B   42 that aye
with us] with us that ever A, with us that aye R

whether of them yt ys Godes will   45
this same office to fullfill.

Tunc respondent omnes (all speake together):

Wee assenten us theretyll,
for this ys the beste waye.

Tunc omnes apostoli genuflectent et dicat

PETRUS

7 Thow, lord, that knowest all thinge,
eych hart and will of man livinge,   50
shewe us here by some tokeninge
whom that we shall take,
and whether of theise ys thy likinge
in Judas steed that be standinge,
thy name to preach to olde and yonge,   55
and whither that thou wilt make.

Tunc Petrus mittet sortem et sors cadet super Mattheum; et dicat

PETRUS

8 This lott ys falne, brethren free,
one Matthewe—all men may see.
To us therfore I take thee
and apostle thee make.   60

MATTHEUS

Yea, honored be God in Trynitie,
though I unworthye therto bee
that to you have chosen mee;
dye wyll I for his sake.

46 this] the H   same] *om* A   *SD*] Tunc omnes una voce respondeant,
et sors cadet super Mathiam H   omnes] omnes apostoli una voce B   all
speake together] *om* RBH   *At* 47] OMNES H   47 assenten] assente
ARH   us] all AR, us all BH   tyll] tell R   48 this] that H   *SD*] Tunc
genua flectent H   apostoli] populi B   genuflectent] genuflecten R, flecten B
dicat] dicat Petrus AR   PETRUS] *om* A   49 thinge] thinges B
56 whither] wheither A, whether RBH   make] take A, choose R   *SD*]
Tunc colliget Petrus sortes et Deus inmittet sortem H   Mattheum] Mathiam
ARB   dicat] dicat Petrus RB   PETRUS] *om* RBH   58 Matthewe]
Mathi B, Mathias H   60 apostle] an apostle H   MATTHEUS] MATHIAS
ARBH   63 that] and H   you] you that H

ANDREAS

9 Nowe, Peeter, brother, goe we and praye, 65
for evermore I myne maye
my sovereygne howe I hard him saye
here in your companye—

JACOBUS MAJOR

hee would not leave us by noe waye
fatherles children, in good faye, 70
but ryche us sone in better araye
with his Ghooste gratiouslye.

JOHANNES EVANGELISTA

10 Yea, brethren, also verament
to us hee sayd in good intent
in yearth here while he was present 75
and with us could lend—

THOMAS

but yf so were that hee ne went,
his Ghooste to us should not be sent;
and yf hee yood, where wee were lent
hitt hee would us send. 80

JACOBUS MINOR

11 Yea, sweete and likinge was his lore,
and well yee wytten that there wore
but a little while before,
or hee to heaven steede—

PHILIPPUS

hee bade wee should not goe awaye 85
from Jerusalem to no countrey
but there abyde, soothe to saye,
his heste from an highe.

ANDREAS] ANDREWAS AR 65 nowe] no B 66 I] *om* AR myne]
mynde R 71 us] is H EVANGELISTA] EVANGELESTE A, EVANGELIST R
74 in] to AR 77 hee] *om* AR 79 wee were] he AR 80 hitt]
yet B 82 well yee] we B wytten] wotten R, wot H that] what B
there wore] they wore B, not yore H 84 steede] stead ARB, steight H
85 bade] bydde A, byde R wee] me I AR 87 abyde] to abide B
88 an] on RB highe] height H

BARTHOLOMEUS

12 Also hee sayd to us eychone
    that his forgoer, Saynt John,   90
    with water baptysed manye one
    while that hee was here.

MATHIAS

But we shall baptyse without boste
fullye with the Holye Ghooste
through helpe of him that ys moste,   95
sone after, without were.

'Tunc Johannes quidem baptizavit aqua; vos autem baptazimini
Spiritu Sancto non post multos hos dies.'

SIMON

13 Wee mynd theron, lasse and more.
    Yett some that standen him before
    asked whither hee should restore
    that tyme all Israell.   100

123ᵛ   THADDEUS

And he answered anonright:
'That tyme knowe yee ne might,
that in his Fathers will was pight'—
for that hee must conseyle.

'Non est vestrum nosse tempora vel momenta quae Pater posuit
in sua potestate.'

MATTHEUS

14 Yea, brethren, that tyme hee us behight   105
    the Holye Ghoost should in us light,
    that wee might tell to eych wight
    his deedes all bydeene

BARTHOLOMEUS] BARTHOLEMEWE A   MATHIAS] MATHEUS ARBH   96 with-
out] withoutten H   *Latin* tunc] quia B, *om* H   quidem baptizavit] quidem
baptazuit R, baptizavit quidem B   baptazimini] baptizbamini R, babtizabi-
mini B, baptizabimini H   Spiritu] supra AR   Sancto] scoko A, *om* R   hos]
hodies AR   SIMON] SYMION A, SIMEON R, SYMON ZELOTES H   99 asked]
asked him H   whither] wheither A, whether RBH   100 all] alsoe R
THADDEUS] JUDE A, THADDEUS JUDE R, JUDAS THADDEUS H   102 might] night H
Latin est] *om* B   tempora] pempora R   quae] qui AR, que B   sua] suae R
potestate] poteste A   MATTHEUS] MATHIAS ARBH   105 yea] ye B

in Jerusalem and Judee—
where in world soever walked wee—   110
and Samarye, that men should see,
as after maye be seene.

'Accipietis virtutem supervenientes Spiritus Sancti in vos, et eritis
mihi testes in Jerusalem et in Judea, Samaria et usque ad ultimum
terrae.'

PETRUS

15 Kneele we downe upon our knee
and to that lord nowe praye wee.
Sone I hope that hee will see   115
to his disciples all.

ANDREAS

Yea, in his liffe so taught hee:
aske and have with hart free;
rightwise boone shall granted bee
when men will on him call.   120

Tunc omnes apostoli genuflectentes cantent 'Veni, creator
Spiritus.' Postea dicat

JACOBUS MAJOR

16 Come, Holye Ghoost; come, creatour!
Visytt or thoughtes in this store—
thou art mans conquerour—
and grant us, lord, thy grace!

JOHANNES

Thou that art called 'conselor'   125
and send from heaven as savyour,

110 walked] walke AR, walken B   111 Samarye] Samaria ARBH
Latin accipietis] accipiet B   supervenientes] suprivementes A   Judea] omni
Judea H   terrae] terre dicat Petrus A, terre RB   ANDREAS] ANDREWAS R
119 rightwise] righteous H   boone] dome A   SD omnes apostoli]
apostoli omnes AR   genuflectentes] genibus flectentibus H   cantent] cantet
A, cantabunt H   postea dicat] poste A, postea R, et postea dicatt B, mentes
tuorum visita imple superna gratia que tu creasti pectora H   MAJOR] MAJOS A
122 or] our ARBH   thoughtes] hartes H   this] thie B   store] stowre
ARH, stoore B   123 art] *om* B   126 send] sente RB   savyour]
senyor B

well of liffe, lenght or langore
that prayen here in this place.

THOMAS

17 Hee that in seaven monethes would conseyle
grace of thy Ghooste about to deale,   130
as thou promised for mans heale,
appeare nowe synce I praye.

JACOBUS MINOR

Light our wyttes with thy weale;
put liffe in our thoughtes lele;
fulsome thy frendes that binne frayle   135
with vertues lastinge aye.

124^r   ### PHILIPPUS

18 Vanishe our enemyes farre awaye
and grant us peace, lord, to our paye,
for while thou art our leader aye
we may eschewe anoye.   140

BARTHOLOMEUS

Through thy might knowe wee maye
the Father of heaven, full in good faye;
and yee, his Sonne, all sooth to saye
thou art in companye.

MATHIAS

19 Worshipped be thou ever and oo,   145
the Father and the Sonne also.
Lett thy Ghooste nowe from thee goe
and faith that we may fynd.

127 lenght] lyght B, leach H   or] in B, of H   128 prayen] praye R
here] he B   129 hee] yea ARH, ye B   seaven monethes] seven moth B,
fyfty dayes H   133 light] lighten R   weale] wayle ARH   134 lele]
wholle B   135 fulsome] lixom A, luxsome R, full soone B   136 aye]
ever A   137-40] after 152 H   139 while] why H   140 anoye]
anye ARB   BARTHOLOMEUS] PHILIPPUS H   141 through] thow B
142 of] in BH   143 yee] thou H   all] in AR, om H   MATHIAS]
MATHIEUS AR, MATHEUS B, BARTOLOMEUS H   145 worshipped] worshipp H
ever and] and ever B   146 and] om H   147 thy] thee B

SIMONNDE

That we asken with hart throo—
to fulsome us agaynst our foe—   150
grant thy men here, both one and moe,
that have thee ever in mynd.

Christ must speake in heaven.

LYTTLE GOD

20 Gloryous Father fayre and free,
yee knowe well of your dutye
that I have donne your will.   155
They apostles that you have chosen to mee,
with grace, wisdome, and prosperitye
that you will them fullfill.

Tunc omnes apostoli contemplantes vel orantes quousque Spiritus
Sanctus missus fuit, Deus dicat:

21 My Sonne beloved, liffe and dere,
your healthfull askinge ever here   160
that you aske ys not to arere.
I knowe your cleane intent.
With will full lyberall and cleare
my Ghooste to them shall appere
to make them wyser then the were.   165
That ys my full assent.

22 My Ghoost to yearth shall goe downe
with seaven gyftes of renowne,
ther to have by devotyon.
Confyrme them to be sadd,   170

SIMONNDE] *om* A, SIMON RB, MATHEUS H   149–52] *om* A   149 asken]
aske H   150 fulsome] full soone B   151 thy] they B   both] *om* RBH
one and moe] and beloe B   152 that] to H   *SD*] *om* ARH, *to left of*
153 B   LYTTLE GOD] GOD THE SONNE A, DEUS R, JHESUS H   154 your]
om A   dutye] deitie H   155–7] *om* A   155 will] de(?) B
156 they] the RBH   157 prosperitye] prophesye R, posteritic B   158] *om* AB
SD contemplantes] contemplabunt H   orantes] orabunt H   Sanctus]
Sanctum R   missus] messus A   fuit] fuerit H   Deus dicat] *om* H   *At*
160] DEUS PATER H   160 healthfull] faythfull H   161 to] *om* H   arere]
deare AR   162 I] to AR   169 by] my A

that they may be ever readye bowne
in heaven-blysse to were the crowne,
ever to reigne in possession,
there to be merye and gladd.

124ᵛ   23 My patryarkes and propheetes here   175
that through your fayth to mee were deare,
angelles and archangelles cleare,
all in my blysse wonnynge,
yee wotten well withowten were
howe I have mended in good manere   180
man that was lorne through Lucifere
and through his owne lykinge.

24 My Sonne I send downe from my see
into a virgyn fayre and free
and manhood tooke, as lyked mee,   185
one man to have mercye,
that righteousnes might saved bee.
Synce man had loste his lybertye,
I made man in on degree;
his bale behovedd to bye.   190

25 Nowe man fullye have I bought
and out of bale to blysse brought.
His kynd also, as me good thought,
ys mixte within my godhead.
Thus man that [I] thus made of nought,   195
that Sathanas through synne hadd sought,
by this waye I have so wrought
non good in hell binne lead.

26 But while I was in that degree
in yearth wonynge, as man should bee,   200
chosen I have a good meanye
one which I must have mynd.

172 heaven] hevens B   175 patryarkes] patrickes A   176 your] ther
BH   to mee were] were to me B   179 wotten] wot H   183 send]
sente RB   185 manhood] mankynd H   187 righteousnes] rightious A,
rightwisenes R   188 synce] seimge H   190 behovedd] behoveth AR
to bye] to lye B, for to be H   193 thought] taughte A   194 mixte]
mighte AR   195 thus] this H   I] om Hm   thus] om AR, have H
196 hadd] om H   200 wonynge] abyding H

Nowe they have made there mone to mee
and prayed speciallye, as I see,
which I must suffice with hart free   205
or elles I were unkynd.

27 Throughout the world they shall gonne,
my deedes to preach manye one.
Yett steadfastnes in them ys nonne
to suffer for me anoye.   210
Fletchinge yett they binne ichone.
But when my Ghoost ys them upon,
then shall they after be styffe as stonne
my deedes to certyfie.

28 Dreade of death ne no distres   215
shall lett them of stydfastnes.
Such love in them, and such goodness,
my sprytte shall ever inspire
125ʳ   that to speake and expresse
all languages that ever yett was   220
they shall have cunnynge, more and lesse,
through force of heavenly fyre.

29 Alsoe they shall have full powere
to baptyze men in water clere
that beleeven, in good manere,   225
to have full mynd on mee.
And on all such, withowten were,
the Holye Ghooste at theire prayere
shall light on them, that they may lere
in fayth steadfast to bee.   230

30 Nowe will I send anon in hye
to my brethren in companye
my Ghooste, to gadd them gratiouslye—
for that ys there willinge—

204 speciallye] especially H   205 which] whom H   208 manye] to
manye a A, to manie BH   210 anoye] anye ARBH   211 fletchinge]
fleittinge A, flettinge R, flitting B   213 be] be as AR   215–18] om A
218 sprytte] spiritt RBH   224 water] watter watter A   229 may]
might R   233 gadd] glade ARBH

in lycknes of fyre freelye,   235
that they may styffned be therbye,
my workes to preach more steadfastlye,
and therby more connynge.

Tunc Deus emittet Spiritum Sanctum in spetie ignis, et in mit-
tendo cantent duo angeli antiphonam 'Accipite Spiritum Sanctum;
quorum remiseritis peccata, remittentur eis' etc. Et cantando
projecient ignem super apostolos. Finitoque Angelus in caelo
dicat.

ANGELUS

31 Rest well, all that binne here.
My lord you greetys, and his Ghooste dere.   240
Hee byddes you dread noe bost nor bere
of Jewes farre ne nere;
but looke yee goe anon in hye
into all the world by and by,
and also preach the fayth meekelye   245
and his workes so deare.

THE SECOND ANGELL

32 And through this Ghooste that I you bringe
yee shall have understandinge
of every lond speakinge,
whatsoever the saye;   250
and this world that ys flytchinge
yee shall despyce ever all thinge,
and heaven at your endinge
yee shall have to your paye.

236 styffned] strengthed H   238 therby] thereby be R, be therby B,
therby have H   connynge] coming B   SD] Heare the Holy Ghoste
descendes upon the xii appostles and then the angells speake followinge R
emittet] emittit A, immittet H   Sanctum] om A   cantent] cantat B
antiphonam] antiphonum A, om H   peccata . . . dicat] om H   remittentur]
remittantur AB   eis] eius A   cantando] cantendo A   finitoque] finitis A
dicat] dicit A   ANGELUS] PRIMUS ANGELLUS AR, ANGELUS PRIMUS H
240] into all the world by and by B   dere] heare AR   241 byddes]
bydes RB   242 ne] or B   nere] nye R   246 workes] word H
deare] dreade A   THE SECOND ANGELL] SECUNDUS ANGELLUS AR, ANGELUS
SECUNDUS H   247 this] his ARB   I] om A   249 lond] londes B,
leed H   251 flytchinge] flittinge ARB, flechinge H   252 ever] over
ARBH   254 to] at AR

PETRUS

33   A, mercye, lord, full of might!   255
     Both I feele and see in sight
     the Holye Ghoost ys on us light;
     [of] fyre this house full ys.

ANDREAS

Nowe have wee that was us beheight,
for full of love my hart ys pight   260
and wyser then ys any wight
meethinke I am, iwys.

JACOBUS MAJOR

34   Yea, lord, blessed moste thou bee,
     for both I feele and eke I see
     the Holye Ghoost ys light on mee.   265
     Thus quytte I am my meede.

JOHANNES

For such love, by my lewtee,
with this fyer in my hart can flee
that death to doe for my mayster free
I have no manner of dread.   270

THOMAS

35   And I thanke thee, both God and man,
     for synce this fyer light me upon
     of all languages well I can,
     and speake them at my will.

JACOBUS MINOR

I, before that was but a foone,   275
am waxen as wise as Salamon.
There ys no scyence but I can therone
and cunnynge to fullfill.

258 of] for Hm   full ys] is full A   ANDREAS] ANDREWAS AR   259 was
us] us was B   260 full] all H   pight] plighte A   263 moste] muste
ARBH   265 holye] holyest R   266 thus] this AR   JOHANNES]
JOHANNES EVANGE H   268] this fyre hath sett in my hart free H   in]
into B   flee] flie AR   269 doe] dye ARBH   free] truly H   270 of]
om ARB   275 before that] that before H   276 am] as B

PHILIPPUS

36 And I that never could speake thinge
     save Ebrewe as I learned yonge,   280
     nowe I can speake at my likinge
     all languages, both lowe and hye.

BARTHOLOMEUS

And soe styffe I am of beleevinge
that I doubt neyther prynce ne kynge
my maysters myracles for to mynge   285
and for his love to dye.

126^r

MATHIAS

37 A, blessed be my mayster deare!
     So lyttle while can us lere.
     All languages that ever were
     upon my tonge binne light.   290

SIMON

My beleeffe ys nowe so clere,
and love in harte so prynted lere,
to moove my mynd in no mannere
there ys no man hath might.

TADDEUS

38 Yea, sythen this fyre came from high   295
     I am waxen so wondrous sleigh
     that all languages farre and nigh
     my tonge will speake nowe aright.

---

280 as] that AH   282 both] *om* AR   BARTHOLOMEUS] BARTHOLOMES A,
BARTHOLOMEW R   284 neyther] no AR   MATHIAS] MATHIEUS AR,
MATHEUS BH   287 A] and R   288 so] that in so B, that so H   while]
a whille B   SIMON] SIMON ZE H   292 lere] here ARBH   TADDEUS]
JUDE AR   295 sythen] since A, sith BH   high] an highe AR, one high B,
an height H   296 wondrous] wounder A   sleigh] slighte A, sleighte RH
298 nowe] *om* B   aright] righte AH

MATTHEUS

Nowe sythen my lord to heaven steegh
and send his Ghooste as hee beheight,   300
to all distresses nowe am I drest
and dye for the love of God almight.

PETRUS

39 Nowe, brethren, I read us all in fere,
make wee the creede in good mannere
of my lordes deedes deare   305
that gladed us hath todaye;
and I will first beginne here,
synce Christ betooke me his power,
the lewd hereafter that we maye lere,
to further them yn the faye.   310

Tunc Petrus incipiat: 'Credo in Deum, Patrem omnipotentem,
creatorem caeli et terrae,'

40 I beleeve in God omnipotent
that made heaven and yearth and fyrmament
with steadfast hart and true intent,
and hee ys my comford.

ANDREAS

'et in Jesum Christum, Filium eius, unicum dominum nostrum,'

And I beleeve, where I be lent,   315
in Jesu, his Sonne, from heaven sent,
verey Cryste, that us hath kent
and ys our elders lord.

MATTHEUS] MATHIAS ARBH   299 sythen] sith BH   steegh] steight H
300 and send] and sente R, hath sent B   301 drest] dighte AR, dreight H
302 and] and will A, to RB   305 deare] here H   306 gladed] glad-
deth AR   us hath] hath us AB   308 synce] seinge H   309 the] om H
lewd] lawe A, truth R, lewte B   lere] leve A   310 to] and R   To right
of 310] Tunc venient duae alienigenae H   SD tunc Petrus] om H
incipiat] incipiet B, om H   in] om R   terrae] terre AR, terra B   To left
of SD] PETRUS H   After SD] PETRUS AR   311 omnipotent] onnipotent B   312 and(1)] om B   314 comford] comforte ARB   ANDREAS]
after Latin A, ANDREWAS R   Latin nostrum] nostrum et dicat A
315 where] more AR   be] am H   317 verey] verely H   318 lord]
lore A

PLAY XXI

JACOBUS MAJOR

'qui conceptus est de Spiritu Sancto, natus ex Maria virgine,'

41 I beleeve, without bost,
in Jesus Christe of mightes most,   320
conceyved through the Holy Ghooste
and borne was of Marye.

JOHANNES

'passus sub Pontio Pilato, crusifixus, mortuus et sepultus.'

And I beleeve, as I can see,
that under Pilate suffred hee,
scourged and nayled one roode-tree;   325
and buryed was his fayre bodye.

THOMAS

'Descendit ad inferna; tertia die resurrexit a mortuis,'

42 And I beleeve, and sooth can tell,
that hee ghoostly went to hell,
delyvered his that there did dwell,
and rose the third daye.   330

JACOBUS MINOR

'ascendit ad caelos, sedet ad dexteram Dei Patris omnipotentis,'

And I beleeve fully this,
that he stayed up to heaven-blysse
and on his Fathers right hand ys,
to raygne for ever and aye.

JACOBUS MAJOR] *after Latin* A   *Latin* Maria] Marie AR   virgine] virgine
dicit A, irgine B   319 I] and I ARH   without] with AR, withouten B
320 of] in AR   mightes] mightest A, might H   321 conceyved] con-
seveith A   JOHANNES] *after Latin* A   *Latin* Pilato] Pilatum A
sepultus] sepultus et dicat Johannes A   325 one] upon R   326 his]
he R   THOMAS] *after Latin* A   *Latin* ad] et A   mortuis] mortus dicit
Thomas A   JACOBUS MINOR] *after Latin* A   *Latin* ascendit] ascendiet R
caelos] celes AR   Dei] die A   omnipotentis] omnipotentes dixit A
332 stayed] sended B   heaven] hevens B   blysse] blesse AR

PHILIPPUS

'inde venturus est judicare vivos et mortuos.'

43 And I beleeve, with hart steadfast,   335
that hee will come at the laste
and deeme mankynd as he hath caste,
both the quycke and the dead.

BARTHOLOMEUS

'Credo in Spiritum Sanctum,'

And my beleeffe shall be moste
in vertue of the Holye Ghooste;   340
and through his helpe, without boste,
my lyffe I thinke to lead.

127ʳ   MATHIAS

'sanctam ecclesiam catholicam, sanctorum communionem,'

44 And I beleeve, through Godes grace,
such beleeffe as Holy Church hasse—
that Godes bodye granted us was   345
to use in forme of bread.

SIMON

'remissionem peccatorum,'

And I beleeve, with devotyon,
of synne to have remission
through Christes blood and Passion,
and heaven when I am dead.   350

PHILIPPUS] *after Latin* A   *Latin* inde] unde AR   venturus] ventrus AR
est] et A   judicare] judicas B   vivos] vivas AR   mortuos] mortuous dicat A
337 and deeme] to judge H   BARTHOLOMEUS] BARTHELEMEWE *after Latin* A
MATHIAS] MATHIEUS *after Latin* A, MATHEUS RBH   *Latin* ecclesiam] cctlam A
catholicam] cathelicam AR   communionem] communionem dicat A, com-
munione R   344 beleeffe] leefe H   345 Godes] God his H   SIMON]
after Latin A, SYMON ZELOT H   *Latin* peccatorum] peccatorem ARB
348 synne] sinnes H   349 Christes] Crist his H

TADDEUS

'carnis resurrectionem,'

45 And I beleeve, as all wee mon,
    in the generall resurrection
    of ych bodye, when Christe ys [bowne]
    to deeme both good and evell.

MATTHEUS

'et vitam aeternam.'

    And I beleve, as all wee maye,   355
    everlastinge liffe, after my daye,
    in heaven for to have ever and aye,
    and so overcome the devyll.

PETRUS

46 Nowe, brethren, I read all wee
    goe ychone to dyvers cuntree   360
    and preach to shire and to cyttee
    the fayth, as Christe us beede.

ANDREAS

    Yee, leeffe brother, kysse nowe wee
    yche one another before wee dye,
    for Godes will must fullfilled bee,   365
    and that ys nowe great neede.

Tunc venient duo alienigene, quorum dicat

PRIMUS ALIENIGENA

47 A, fellowe, fellowe, for Godes pittie,
    are not theise men of Gallilee?
    Our language the can as well as wee,
    as ever eate I bread!   370

TADDEUS] JUDE AR, *after Latin* A   *Latin* carnis] carnem R
351 all] well H   353] of Christes body eichone was borne R   bowne]
borne HmA, boone B   354 deeme] dome H   MATTHEUS] *after Latin* A,
MATHIAS RBH   *Latin* aeternam] eternum B, eternam amen H   355 all]
well H   357 for] *om* ARH   361 to(2)] *om* H   362 beede] bade
ABH, byd R   ANDREAS] ANDREWAS AR   363 yee] ye B   brother]
brethren AR, brether B   *SD*] *om* H   venient] venit B   dicat] dicat
Primus Alei A   ALIENIGENA] ALIENIGENE AR   367 fellowe(1)] leeffe R
Godes] cockes A   369 language] languages H

127ᵛ

SECUNDUS ALIENIGENA

Well I wotte, by my lewtee,
that within theise dayes three
one of them could not speake with mee
for to have binne dead.

PRIMUS ALIENIGENA

48 Of all languages that binne hereby   375
that come to Mesopotamye,
Capadocie and Jurye,
the jangle without weene—
of the Ile of Pontus, and Asye,
Fryzeland and Pamphilye,   380
Egipt, right into Lybie
that ys byesyde Syrene.

SECUNDUS ALIENIGENA

49 Yea, also men of Arabye
and of Greece that ys thereby
herden them prayse full tenderlye   385
God of his great grace;
and we herden them, witterlye,
prayse God faste, both thou and I.
Fellowe, goe we therfore and espye
howe goes this wondrous case.   390

Finis

ALIENIGENA] ALIENIGENE AR   371 well] yea well H   ALIENIGENA]
ALIENIGENE AR, om H   375 languages] languag B   376 come] came H
377 Capadocie] Capodorye A, Capedocia RBH   378 jangle] janglen H
without] withouten H   379 Pontus] Ponthus AR, Ponce H   Asye] Asia
RB   380 Pamphilye] Pamphami A   381 Egipt] of Egipt H   into]
in H   Lybie] Billi A   382 that] which H   ALIENIGENA] ALEINGENA A,
ALIENIGNE R   383 Arabye] Rabie A   385 herden] hard RBH   full]
om R   386 great] owine AR   387 herden] hard H   389 fellowe
goe we] folowe we AR, followe wee them BH   therfore and] and therefore B
espye] spye A

PLAY XXII

THE CLOTHEWORKERS PLAYE

'Facta est super me manus domini et eduxit me spiritus domini, et demisit me in medio campi qui erat plenus ossibus, et [circumduxit] me per ea in giro.' Hec in libro Ezechielis 37.

1 Herken, all that loven heale!
  I am the prophett Ezechiell.
  What I sawe I will not conceale
  but as mee thought I will tell.
  God his ghooste can with me deale   5
  that lead me longe with wordes leale
  into a feild where bones fell
  all bare without flesh.

2 Then spake that ghoost unto mee
  and sayd, 'Mans sonne, how likest thee?   10
  Thinkest thou not well that this may bee,
  these bones might turne and lyve?'
  Then bade hee mee tell and prophecye
  that hee would revyve them soone in hye
  with flesh and synewes and skynne therebye   15
  which soone hee can them give.

3 After that ghooste hee them geete,
  ryse of there graves hee them leete,
  and made them stande upon there feete,
  speake, goe, and see.   20

Guild-ascription] The Clothiars or Shermen H   *After Guild-ascription*]
Pagina Vicessima Secunda Ezechiell AR, Pagina Vicesima Secunda B, Pagina
Vicesima Secunda de Prophetis Prophetantibus; de Die Novissimo; de Antechristo; de Enock et Helia H   *Before Play-heading*] EZECHIELL B   *To left
of Latin*] EZECHIELL H   *Latin* facta] fatea AR   est] este A   manus]
manibus A   eduxit] aduxet A   demisit] dimisit H   circumduxit] circumdixit HmAR   hec] hic AR, haec H   libro] *om* B   Ezechielis] Ezechiell
RB   37] *om* R, capitulo tricesimo septimo H   *After Latin*] EZECHIELL AR
3 not] *om* AR   5 God his] Godes R   7 where] wherin BH   8 flesh]
fleshe or fell ARH, or shea B   9 unto] thus unto H   10 and] *om* ARH
likest] liketh ARB   11 that] *om* AR   may] mighte ARBH   14 in]
one B   15 synewes] senowe ARB, sinew H   16 can] came B   18 of]
out AR, out of H   leete] lette ARB

This sawe I right in my sight
to knowe that he was God almight
that heaven and yearth should deale and dight
and never shall ended bee.

EXPOSITOR

4 Nowe that you shall expresselye knowe   25
these prophettes wordes upon a rowe,
what the doe signifie I will shewe
that mych may doe you good.
By them understand may I
the daye of doome skyllfullye,   30
when men through Godes postee
shall ryse in flesh and blood.

5 Therefore this prophett sayd full yare
hee sawe a feild of bones bare,
and soone that ghoost with them can fare,   35
gave them fleshe and life.
128ᵛ   Beleeve this fullye withoutcn weene,
that all which dead and rotten beene
in fleshe shall ryse, as shalbe seene,
man, mayd, and wyfe.   40

6 They that shall be saved shall be as bright
as seaven tymes the sonne ys light;
the dampned thester shall be in sight,
theire doome to underfoe.
Both saved and dampned, after that daye   45
dye they may not by noe waye.
God give you grace to doe soe aye
that blisse you may come to.

'Levavi occulos meos et vidi; et ecce, quatuor quadrigc egredientes
de medio duorum montium.' Capitulo sexto.

35 with them can] can with them A, with him can H   36 gave] and gave B
38 which] wchch A   43 thester] sorte AR   44 theire] the B
underfoe] understande AR   48 come] goc A   *Latin* levavi] Zacharias
propheta levavi H   meos] meoes AR   ecce] dice AR   egredientes] agre-
dientes A   de] et B   duorum] quorum A, *om* R   montium] montim A
capitulo] capituo B, hac in libro Zachariae prophetae capitulo H   sexto]
sextu B

ZACHARIAS

7 I, Zacharye—men, leeves yee mee—
   lift up my eyes a sight to see,   50
   and as mee thought, by my lewtee,
   foure charettes came anon
   out of two hilles—leeve yee mee,
   sylver hilles they were, as wytten wee!
   Great wonder I had in my degree   55
   whither that they would gonne.

8 Redde horses in one were, reddelye;
   another blacke that went them bye;
   the third was white, I wott not whye;
   the forth of dyvers hewe.   60
   They were styffe, drawinge biglye.
   Then anone answered I
   to that angell in my bodye
   which tould me wordes true.

9 I asked him then what yt might bee   65
   and he answered anon unto mee.
   'These charettes,' he sayde, 'which thou doest see,
   foure wyndes the bee, iwys,
   which shall blowe and readye be
   before Christe, that prynce which ys of postye.   70
   There ys none soe fell there feete to flee
   nor wynne there wyll from this.'

EXPOSITOR

10 Nowe for to moralyze aright
    which this prophett sawe in sight,
    I shall found through my might   75
    to you in meeke mannere,

ZACHARIAS] *before Latin* ARB, *to left of Latin* H   51 mee] I B   by my
lewtee] verely H   54 as] at B   wee] me ARB   56 whither]
wheither A, whether RBH   60 hewe] hewes AR   61 biglye] lightlye AR
66 unto] to AH   67 charettes] charreth B   70 Christe that prynce]
that prince Christ H   which ys] high R   71 feete to] fitte may ARBH
75 found] shewe R

129ʳ and declare that soone in height
more playnlye, as I have teight.
Lystens nowe with hartes light
this lesson for to learne.   80

11 Fowre charettes this prophett see, howe they
out of two hilles tooke there waye—
the hilles of sylver, the soothe to saye,
the horses of dyvers hewe.
Which hilles signifie maye   85
Enock and Helye, in good faye,
that as good sylver shalbe aye
stydfast men and trewe.

12 Fowre charrettes hee sawe, as thinkes mee,
skylfullye may lickned bee   90
to sayntes of foure maners of degree
that then shall suffer anoye.
Fowre horses ys allso, certayntee,
of dyvers hewes that he coon see,
fowre manner of sayntes in dignitee— 95
licken them well maye I:

13 martyrs, confessours, there bee two;
men misbeleevinge converted also
that turned shalbe from synne and woe
through Enock and Helye;   100
virgens also, both on and moe.
Here be dyvers hewes too
that through Godes grace shall goe
for him to suffer anoye.

14 These redde horses call I maye   105
all maner of marters, in good faye,
for redd maye well betoken aye
mans blood sheedinge;

79 lystens] lightens A   81 see] saw se H   they] th A   84 hewe]
hewes AR   87 as] is B   89 charrettes] chareth B, charrtts H
90–3] om AR   91 maners] maner BH   92 anoye] anye H   93 ys allso]
also is H   certayntee] certanie B   94 coon] can ARBH   97 martyrs]
martrisse A   98 misbeleevinge] mislevinge H   101 both] loth H
104 anoye] anye H   106 marters] martrises A   108 sheedinge]
sheweeding R

they white hee sayth token there waye
above the yearth to goe astraye,   110
as such that neyther night nor daye
dreeden death nothinge;

15   the blacke horses which went them bye,
by them maye well signifie
preachers of Godes word, truely,   115
that confessors shalbe;

16   the skewed horses, by myne intent,
the which into the south forth went,
I maye well licken verament
to Jewes and paynims eke,   120
129ᵛ   yett through fayth with hart fervent
shall turne to good amendment
when Enock and Helye have them kent
salvatyon for to seeke.

DANYELL

'Ego, Daniell, videbam in visione mea nocte; et ecce, quatuor venti
pugnabant in magno mare, et quatuor bestiae gradentes ascende-
bant de mare.' Capitulo septimo.

17   I, Daniell, as I laye on a night,   125
methought I sawe a wondrous sight.
Fowre wyndes together the can fyght
above the sea upon hye.
Fowre beastes out of that sea the yeade.
To the fourth beast I tooke good heede;   130
for that to speake of nowe ys neede,
the other all I will leave.

109 they] the ARBH   token] betockeneth A, tokeneth R, toke B   there
waye] thereby R   111 as] are H   that] as ARBH   112 dreeden]
dread B   113 horses] horse B   which] om R   114 maye well] well
may H   117 horses] horse B   118 forth] parte AR   121 yett]
but AR   fayth] harte A   hart] faith A   122 turne] come H   good]
god AR   123 have] hath A, shall R   124 seeke] kepe A   DANYELL]
after Latin A   Latin nocte] nocke A, nock R   pugnabant] pugnabunt
AR   mare] mari H   bestiae] bestie ARB   gradentes] grandes ARBH
ascendebant] asendebunt AR   mare] mari H   capitulo septimo] capit
secptimo dicat A, haec in libro Danielis Cap. 7 H   128 upon] one B
129 sea] om H   the] om AR, ther B   130 fourth beast] foure bestes B
132 all] all nowe A, om B

18 That beaste was wondrous styffe and stronge,
of teeth and nayles sharpe and longe,
eatinge over all that hee could fonge. 135
The remnante he fortredde.
Unlike he was to anye of leede.
Ten hornes he had upon his head.
In the myddest on little horne can spread
above all other in hye. 140

19 That horne had mouthe to speake and eyes to see,
and spake great wordes, leeve you mee;
but of the ten, the first three
soone were consumed awaye.
That one horne had so great postee; 145
the remnant meeke to him to bee
that highest was in that degree,
and endured so, manye a daye.

20 Then was yt tould me right there
that ten hornes ten kinges were, 150
but all that on should feare
that sprange upward so fast,
and that hee should worke agaynst that kinge
that of nought made all thinge;
but lyttle while, without leasinge, 155
that kinge his might should last.

EXPOSITOR

21 By this beast understand I maye
the world to come nexte doomesdaye;
and by that horne, in good faye,
in myddest the ten can springe, 160
130ʳ Antechriste I maye understand,
that then great lord shalbe in land
and all the world have in hand
three yeares and halfe duringe.

---

136 fortredde] fortrade B 137 of] *om* AR 139 the] *om* BH 140 in]
on ARBH 141 eyes] hornes A 145 so] suche AR 151 but]
but them BH 161 Antechriste] Antichriste A 163 in] in his AR
164 halfe] a halfe ARB

'Tradentur in manu eius usque ad tempus et tempora et dimidium temporis, et usque ad annum duos annos et dimidium anni.' Danielis capitulo septimo.

22 Ten hornes ten kinges in land shalbe 165
of which Antechriste shall slea three.
The other seaven this case shall see
and put them to his grace.
This shal befall, witterlye,
by the understandinge that have I 170
of Danyelles prophecye
that here rehersed was.

JOHANNES EVANGELISTA

'Dabo duobus testibus meis et prophetabunt diebus mille, ducentis et sexaginta amicti saccis.' Apocalipsis capitulo undecimo.

23 I, John, Christes owne darlinge,
as I laye in greate longinge
upon my maisters brest sleepinge, 175
wonders sawe I manye one.
My ghoost was ravished, without leasinge,
to heaven before that highest kinge.
There sawe I manye a wondrous thinge.
One will I tell you anon. 180

24 There hard I God greatly commend
two wittnesses which he thought to send,
false faythes for to defende
that raysed were by his foe.
He sayde the should prophecye 185
a thousand dayes, witterlye;
two hundreth and sixtye
in sackes clad they should goe.

Latin] om R et] ad A tempora] tempore A dimidium] demidium B
et] om A annum] unum annum ABH duos] emos A annos] amos A
Danielis] haec in libro Danielis H 166 Antechriste] Antichriste A
167 this] that B 169 befall] be full R JOHANNES EVANGELISTA] JOHAN-
NES EVANGELISTE after Latin A, JOHANNES EVANGELESTI R Latin meis]
meius A, meus R amicti] amiciti A, om B saccis] om B, saccis haec in
libro H Apocalipsis] Apocalispis A, Apocalypsios H capitulo undecimo]
undcimo A 175 brest] barme H 176 wonders] wounders sightes R
180 you] om BH 181 commend] comaunde B 182 to] for to AR
188 sackes clad] sack cloth B

25 He called them chandelours of great light
   burninge before Godes sight.   190
   Fyre out of there mouthes the should feight,
   there enemyes for to destroye.
   Whosoever them harmed, as sayde hee,
   dead behooved him for to bee.
   To lett the raygne they had postee   195
   in tyme of there prophecye.

26 Hee sayde the should have power good
   to turne the water into blood,
   and overcome there enemyes that were wood,
   and maister them through [their might].   200
   And when they had donne there devoure,
   a beast should come, of great power,
   from beneath, withowten were;
   agaynst them he should feight.

27 And slea them also should hee   205
   in middest of the holye cyttye
   where Christ was nayled on a tree,
   forsooth as I you tell.
   But after three dayes and halfe one,
   they shall ryse, speake and gonne,   210
   and into heaven be taken anonne,
   in joye evermore to dwell.

EXPOSITOR

28 Nowe, lordinges, what these thinges may bee,
   I praye you herken all to mee.
   As expressely in certeyntye   215
   as I have might and grace,
   I shall expound this ylke thinge
   which saynt John sawe thus sleepinge
   through helpe of Jesu, heaven kinge,
   anonneright in this place.   220

130ᵛ (margin)

191 the] *om* R   feight] send B   192 for] *om* BH   193 sayde] saith AR
194 behooved him] behooveth them R   200 through their might] through
HmR, through their power A, throuly B   201 devoure] vower AR, devower B
206 of] *om* R   210 shall] shoulde R   215 as] and AR   217 I] and
I AR   ylke] same A   218 thus] this A   219 heaven] heavenlye AR

29 These two wyttnes, wytterlye,
    hee sayde the should come and prophecye,
    that one ys Enock, the other Helye—
    shall have great might and mayne
    that when Antechrist comes in hye   225
    Goddes people for to destroye,
    that he deceaveth falselye
    they shall convert agayne.

30 Manye signes they shall shewe
    which the people shall well knowe,   230
    and in theire token truely trowe
    and leeve yt steadfastlye.
    And all that turne, leeve you mee,
    Antechrist will slea through his postie;
    but verey martyrs they shalbee   235
    and come to heaven one hye.

31 They beast that John spake of here
    ys Antechrist, withowten were,
    which shall have the devilles power
    and with these good men meete;   240
    and at the last, witterlye,
    he shall slea Enock and Helye
    in Jerusalem, as read I,
    even in myddest of the streete.

131ʳ   32 Nowe, that you shall knowe and seene   245
           what men Enock and Helye beene,
           I will you tell, withouten wene,
           while that I have tyme.
           They are two good men, leeve yee mee;
           to paradyce through Goddes postee   250
           were ravished both, and there shalbee
           ever tyll the daye doe come.

221 wyttnes] wittnesses ARH   223 that] the ARBH   225 Antechrist]
Antichriste A   226 for] om B   227 deceaveth] deceaved AR   falselye]
full falslye AR   233 turne] tyme H   234 Antechrist] Antichriste A
235 martyrs] martrises A   237 they] the ARBH   of] one B   238 Ante-
christ] Antichriste A   withowten] without H   243 Jerusalem] Hieru-
salem H   245 and] om R   247] om A   252 doe] shall AR

33 They one was taken, for hee was good,
longe before Noe his flood,
and there he lyves in fleshe and blood,   255
as fullye leeven wee.
They other was taken, withouten were,
after that manye a hundreth yeare;
and there together they binne in fere
untyll that tyme shalbe.   260

Signa 15: Signa quindecim magna quae, secundum opiniones
doctorum, extremum precedunt judicium, ab antiquis Hebroeorum
codicibus selecta a doctore huius paginae reticenda.

34 Nowe xv signes, while I have space,
I shall declare by Goddes grace,
of which saynt Jerome mentyon mase
to fall before the daye of doome;
the which were wrytten on a rowe—   265
he found in booke of Hebrewe.
Nowe will I tell in wordes fewe,
a while yf you will dwell.

35 1 The first daye, as I wrytten fyand,
the sea shall ryse agaynst kinde,   270
and as a wall agaynst the wynd
above all hilles on hye
2 fortye cubytes, as read wee;
the seaconde daye so lowe shalbee
that scarslye a man the sea shall see,   275
stand he never so nye.

36 3 The third daye after, as read I,
great fishes above the sea shall lye,
yell and rore so hideouslye
that only God shall heare.   280

253 they] the ARBH   254 Noe his] Noyes AR   256 wee] yea A
257 they] the ARBH   258 manye] may H   signa 15] 15 signa *after
Latin* R, *om* B   *Latin* quae] que ARB   doctorum] dctroum R
precedunt] precedent H   judicium] judiciri A   ab] ab a A   codicibus]
codicilus A, cocdicibus R   paginae] pagina AB, pagine H   reticenda] reci-
tando A, recitanda RBH   264 fall] come B   265 on] upon H
266 booke] bookes BH   269–329] *sign numbers om* B   269 as] *om* A   fyand]
fynde ARBH   270 kinde] it kinde B   273 wee] I H   275 scarslye]
skarse R   a man the sea] the sea a man R   276] *om* B

4 The fourth daye next after then,
sea and water all shall burne
agaynst kinde, that men may kenne,
tynder as though yt were.

131^v   37   5 The fifte daye, as reade wee,   285
all manner of herbes and also tree
of blooddye dewe all full shalbee,
and manye a beaste all dased.
Fowles shall gather them, as I fynd,
to feildes; eicheon in there kynd   290
of meate and drinke shall have no mynd,
but stand all madd and mased.

38   6 The syxt daye in the world overall,
buylded thinges to ground shall fall—
church, cittie, house, and wall—   295
and men in graves dare.
Layte and fyre alsoe, verament,
from the sonne to the firmament
up and downe shall stryke and glent,
and all night so fowle fare.   300

39   7 The seaventh daye both rocke and stonne
shall breake asunder and fight as fonne.
The sound thereof shall here no man,
but onlye God almight.
8 The eight daye yearthquake shalbe,   305
that men and beast, leeve you mee,
to stand or goe shall fayle postee,
but fall to ground all right.

40   9 The nynthe day, as our bookes sayen,
hilles shall fall and waxe all playne,   310
stonne turne to sand through Goddes mayne,
so streat men shall be stadd.

---

282 burne] brene ARH   283 kenne] kene A   284 tynder] the ende
A, thende R   285 daye] day day H   286 of] om ARBH
288] om AR   manye a] main(?) and B, man and H   beaste] beastes B
291 of meate] to eate A   294 ground] earth B   296 graves] greeves H
297 layte] leate RH, late B   302 asunder] in sunder ARH   303 thereof]
whereof AR   304 almight] amight H   306 men] man R   beast]
beastes B   leeve] beleeve AR   311 stonne] stonnes B

10 The tenthe daye, men that hydd bee,
out of theire caves they shall flee—
to speake together have noe postee,   315
but goe as the were madd.

41 11 The elevon daye, from morrowe to even,
all buryalls in the world shall be open
that dead may ryse, withowten weene,
above the yearth standinge.   320
12 The twelffe daye starres shall fall in hye
and fyre shoote from them hideouslye.
All manner of beastes shall rore and crye
and neyther eate nor drynke.

42 13 The thirteene daye shall dye all men   325
and ryse anone agayne right then.
14 The foureteene daye, all shall brenne,
both yearth and eke heaven.
132ʳ   15 The fyfteene daye made shalbee
neewe yearth, neewe heaven, through Goddes
    postee;   330
which heaven God grant us in to bee,
for his names seaven.

43 Nowe have I tould you, in good faye,
the tokens to come before doomesdaye.
God give you grace to do so aye   335
that you them worthye bee
to come to the blysse that lasteth aye.
As mych as here wee and our playe,
of Antechristes signes you shall assaye.
Hee comes! Soone you shall see!   340

Finis

313 bee] have bene AB, hath bene RH   316 madd] made B
317 elevon] leventh A, xiᵗʰ R, eleventh BH   318 shall be open]
open shal bene ARBH   321 twelffe] twelffte AH, xiiᵗʰ RB
322 and] of AR   shoote] shotte AR, shote B   323 beastes] bastes H
rore] rere B   325 thirteene] xiiiᵗʰ ARB, thirdtenth H   326 anone
agayne] againe anon ARBH   327 foureteene] xiiiiᵗʰ AR, fourthenth B,
fourtenth H   329 fyfteene] xvᵗʰ AR, fiftenth BH   made] om B
332 seaven] sake RB   To left of 333] conclusio H   335 you] us B
336 you them] you maye B, then you H   338 here wee] we heare AR
339 Antechristes] Antichristes A, Antechriste B

PLAY XXIII

132ᵛ

THE DIARS PLAYE

Pagina Vicessima Tertia: De Adventu Antechristi

ANTECHRISTE

1 De celso throno poli, pollens clarior sole,
age vos monstrare [descendi], vos judicare.
Reges et principes sunt subditi sub me viventes.
Sitis sapientes vos, semper in me credentes
et faciam flentes gaudere atque dolentes.   5
Sic omnes gentes gaudebunt in me sperantes.
Descendi praesens rex pius et perlustrator,
princeps aeternus vocor, Christus, vester salvator.

2 All leedes in land nowe be light
that wilbe ruled throughout the right.   10
Your saviour nowe in your sight
here may you saffelye see.
Messias, Christ, and most of might,
that in the lawe was you beheight,
all mankind to joye to dight   15
ys commen, for I am hee.

3 Of me was spoken in prophecye
of Moyses, Davyd, and Esaye.
I am hee the call messye,
forbyar of Israell.   20
Those that leeven on me steadfastlye,
I shall them save from anoye,
and joye right as have I
with them I thinke to deale.

Guild-ascription] *om* B   playe] *om* H   *Play-heading* vicessima] vice-
simo B   tertia] tertio B   adventu] adventum AR   Antechristi]
Antechristi dicit A   ANTECHRISTE] ANTECHRISTIE A, ANTECHRISTI R,
ANTECHRISTUS H   2 vos] vobis H   monstrare] monstare A   descendi] descen
Hm   judicare] judicari A   3 sunt] scunc A, sunc R   viventes] vementes
AR   4 sitis] sites A   vos] vose A   5 atque] et que R   dolentes]
delentes BH   7 descendi] discindi R   8 princeps] principes AR
9 leedes] lordes R   15 to(1)] *om* H   16 commen] come B
21 those] thes H   leeven] leeve A   on] in H   22 them] then B
anoye] anye H   23 joye] such joy H   right] gright B   as have] have as B
24 them I] theth B

De me dicitur Ezechielis tricesimo sexto: 'Tollam vos de gentibus
et congregabo vos de universis terris, et reducam vos in terram
vestram.'

4 But one hath ligged him here in land,   25
  Jesu he height, I understand.
  To further falsehood he can found
  and fard with fantasye.
  His wickednes hee would not wond
  tyll he was taken and put in band   30
  and slayne through vertue of my sond.
  This ys sooth, sickerlye.

5 My people of Jewes he could twynne
  that there land came the never in.
  Then on them nowe must I mynne   35
  and restore them agayne.
133ʳ   To buyld this temple wyll I not blynne,
  as God honored be therein,
  and endelesse wayle I shall them wynne,
  all that to me benne bayne.   40

De me enim dicitur in psalmo: 'Adorabo ad templum sanctum
tuum in timore tuo.'

6 One thinge me glades, be you bould.
  As Danyell the prophett before me tould,
  all women in world me love should
  when I were come in land.
  This prophecye I shall well hould   45
  which ys most likinge to yonge and ould.
  I thinke to fast manye hould
  and theire fayrenes to found.

Latin] *om* R   de me dicitur] de me enim dicitur AB, dicitur enim de me H
Ezechielis] Ezechie B, Ezechiel cap H   vestram] vestrum et dicit A   25 hath]
had B   him] me AR, *om* B   27 found] fonde H   29 wond] wound B
31 sond] sound ARB, sand H   33 twynne] twayne AR   34 came]
come H   35 then on] on A, then of B   37 blynne] blene A   38 as]
so as B, and as H   *Latin*] *om* R   tuum] enim H   tuo] tuo et dicat A
42 before] afore H   44] and their fairenes to founde AR   45–56] *om* R
47 to fast manye] faste manye to A, to force many H   hould] fould H

7　Also he tould them, leeve you mee,
　　that I of gyftes should be free,　　　　　　50
　　which prophecye donne shalbe
　　when I my realme have wonnen;
　　and that I should grant men postee,
　　ryved ryches, land and fee—
　　hitt shalbe donne, that you shall see,　　　55
　　when I am hither commen.

'Dabit eis potestatem, et multis terram dividet gratuito.' Danielis
decimo tertio.

8　What saye you kinges that here be lent?
　　Are not my wordes at your assent?
　　That I am Christe omnipotent,
　　leeve you not this eychon?　　　　　　　　60

PRIMUS REX

Wee leeven, lord, withouten lett,
that Christ ys not common yett.
Yf thou be hee, thou shalbe sett
in temple as God alonne.

SECUNDUS REX

9　Yf thou bee Christe called messie　　　　　65
　　that from our bale shall us bye,
　　doe before us maistrye,
　　a signe that wee may see.

TERTIUS REX

Then will I leeve that yt ys soe.
Yf thou doe wonders or thou goe　　　　　　70
soe that thou save us of our woe,
then honored shalt thou bee.

---

49 them] then H　　　52 wonnen] wine B, nommon H　　　53 men postee]
mercye A　　　54 ryved] om B　　fee] great fee B　　　Latin eis] eius R
multis] multus AR　　　　dividet] dividitte A, dividit R　　　　gratuito]
gratimo A　　Danielis] Dameles A, Danielo B　　decimo tertio] dicimo tercia
et dicitt A, om R　　　61 withouten] without RBH　　　64 alonne] above A
68 may] om H　　　71 of our] from R　　woe] foe B

QUARTUS REX

10 Fowle have we leeved manye a yeare
and of our weeninge binne in were.
And thou be Christe commen here,   75
then may thou stynt all stryffe.

ANTECHRISTE

That I am Christ and Christ wilbe
by verey signe soone shall you see,
for dead men through my postee
shall ryse from death to liffe.   80

11 Nowe wyl I turne, all through my might,
trees downe, the rootes upright—
that ys marveyle to your sight—
and fruyt groinge upon.
So shall they growe and multiplye   85
through my might and my maisterye.
I put you owt of heresye
to leeve me upon.

12 And bodyes that binne dead and slayne,
yf I may rayse them up agayne,   90
then honoures mee with might and mayne.
Then shall no man you greeve.
Forsoothe, then after will I dye
and ryse agayne throwe my postee.
Yf I may doe this marveylouslye,   95
I read you on me leeve.

13 Men buryed in grave you may see.
What maistrye ys nowe, hope yee,
to rayse them up throwe my postye
and all through my owne accorde?   100

73 we] *om* H   74 binne in] manye a AR   75 commen] nowe
comon ARBH   ANTECHRISTE] ANTECHRISTIE A, ANTECHRISTI R, ANTE-
CHRISTUS H   78 signe] signes ARBH   soone] *om* AR   shall you] you
shall AR   81 might] thoughte A   84 and] with A, that R   86 might]
night H   maisterye] postee B   91 with] with with A   95 may]
om H   97 grave] graves AR, graves as B, grave as H   100 owne] *om* RH

Whether I in my godhead bee
by verey signe you shall see.
Ryse up, dead men, and honour me
and knowe me for your lord.

Tunc resurgent mortui de sepulchris.

PRIMUS MORTUUS

14 A, lord, to thee I aske mercye.   105
I was dead but nowe live I.
Nowe wotte I well and witterlye
that Christe ys hither commen.

SECUNDUS MORTUUS

Him honour wee and all men,
devoutlye kneelinge on our kneene.   110
Worshippe be thou there amen.
Crist, our [knave], ys commen.

134ʳ   ANTECHRISTE

15 That I shall fulfill Whollye Wrytte
you shall wotte and knowe well hitt,
for I am wall of wayle and wytt   115
and lord of everye land.
And as the prophett Sophonye
speakes of mee full wytterlye
I shall rehearse here readelye
that clarkes shall understand: 120

'Expecta me in die resurrectionis meae in futurum quia judicium
ut congregem gentes et colligam regna.' Sophoni 3.

102 signe] signes AR   104 lord] lord amen B   *SD* mortui] mortum
AR   de] *om* R   105 A] O AR   to] of B   108 commen] come AR
110 kneene] knye A, ken R, knee B   111 worshippe] worshipped ARB
112 Crist] Christ that BH   knave] naue Hm, name ARBH   commen]
named B, nummen H   ANTECHRISTE] ANTICHRISTIE A, ANTECHRISTI R,
ANTECHRIST B, ANTECHRISTUS H   113 whollye] and wholy B   wrytte]
wrytten AR, write B   115 of] *om* AR   118 speakes] speaketh R   full]
righte A   119 here] *om* AR   120 clarkes] clarke AR   *Latin* resur-
rectionis] resurpens A, resurrexones R   meae] me ARB   futurum] futrum R
judicium] judicia A   congregem] congregam A   regna] ragna A, ragula R
Sophoni] Sophin A, Sophonia B   3] *om* AR, 3 etc B

16 Nowe will I dye, that you shall see,
and ryse agayne through my postee.
I will in grave that you put mee
and worshippe me alonne.
For in this temple a tombe ys made,   125
therein my bodye shall be layde.
Then will I ryse as I have sayde—
take tent to me eycheone!

17 And after my resurrection
then will I sitt in greate renowne   130
and my ghooste send to you downe
in forme of fyre full soone.

18 I dye, I dye! Nowe am I dead!

PRIMUS REX

Nowe sythe this worthye lord ys deade
and his grace ys with us leade,   135
to take his bodye yt ys my reade
and burye yt in a grave.

SECUNDUS REX

Forsoothe, and so to us he sayde
in a tombe he would be leade.
Nowe goe we further, all in a brayde;   140
from disease hee may us save.

Tunc transeunt ad Antechristum.

TERTIUS REX

19 Take we the bodye of this sweete
and burye hit lowe under the greete.
Nowe, lord, comfort us, we thee beseech,
and send us of thy grace.   145

128 tent] teene AR   132] om H   135 grace] grave R   138 to us he]
he to us A   139 leade] layde ARBH   140 further] fourth ARBH
141 disease] destres A   SD transeunt] transunt AR, evunt H   143 burye]
laye BH   144 beseech] beseeke ARH

QUARTUS REX

And yf hee ryse soone through his might
from death to liffe, as hee beheight,
him will I honour both daye and night
as God in everye place.

Tunc recedent de tumulo usque ad terram.

PRIMUS REX

20 Nowe wotte I well that he ys dead,   150
for nowe in grave we have him lead.
Yf he ryse as hee hath sayde,
hee ys of full great might.

SECUNDUS REX

I cannot leeve him upon
but yf hee ryse himselfe alonne   155
as hee hath sayde to manye one,
and shewe him here in sight.

TERTIUS REX

21 Tyll that my savyoure bee rysen agayne,
in fayth my harte may not bee fayne
tyll I him see with eye.   160

QUARTUS REX

I must mourne with all my mayne
tyll Christ be rysen up agayne
and of that miracle make us fayne.
Ryse up, lord, that we maye see.

Tunc Antechristus levat corpus suum surgens a mortuis.

148 both] *om* ARBH   *SD* de] a H   tumulo] tunando A, tumulu B
151 lead] layde ARH   156 one] a one A   159 may] will B   *After*
159] my body eke will not be bayne H   160 I him] him I B   eye] joye R
162 be] were A   *SD* Antechristus] Extechristam A, Antechristum R
suum] sum A   a mortuis] mortus AR

ANTECHRISTUS

22 I rysc! Nowe reverence dose to mee, 165
God glorified created of degree.
If I be Christe, nowe leeve yee
and worche after my wise.

PRIMUS REX

A, lord, welcome most thou bee.
That thou arte Godd nowe leeve wee. 170
Therefore, goe sytt up in thy see
and keepe our sacrafice.

Tunc transeunt ad Antechristum cum sacrificio.

SECUNDUS REX

23 Forsoothe, in seate thou shalt be sett
and honored with lambe and geat
as Moyses lawe that lasteth yett, 175
as hee hath sayde before.

135ʳ   TERTIUS REX

O gratiouse lord, goe sytt downe then,
and wee shall kneelinge on our kneene
worshippe thee as thy owne men
and worke after thy lore. 180

Tunc anscendit Antechristus ad cathedram.

24 Hither wee be commen with good intent
to make our sacrifice, lord excellent,
with this lambe that I have here hent,
kneelinge thee before.

ANTECHRISTUS] ANTECHRISTIE A, ANTECHRISTI R   165 dose] nowe doe A
166 created] greatest H   167 yee] you me AR, ye me B   168 worche]
worch you H   my] the H   wise] will A   169 A] O AR   most] mayst
R, must BH   170 Godd] good R   SD] om A, Tunc sacrificant H
174 lambe and geat] lande greate AR, lambe goate B   176] hath ofte said
heretofore B   178 kneelinge] kneele ARB   on] upon ARB   kneene]
kene AR   179 worshippe] and worshipp R   180 lore] lorde R
SD anscendit] ascendit ARB, ascendet H   Antechristum] Antechristum B
ad] et ad A, at B   After SD] QUARTUS REX R, PRIMUS REX H   183 I have
here] here is B   184 thee] here H

Thou grant grace to doe and saye   185
that yt be pleasinge to thee aye,
to thy blysse that come wee maye
and never from yt be lore.

ANTECHRISTUS

25 I lord, I God, I high justice,
    I Christ that made the dead to ryse!   190
    Here I receave your sacrifice
    and blesse you fleshe and fell.

Tunc recedent Antechristo.

        I will nowe send my holye ghooste.
        You kinges, also to you I tell
        to knowe me lord of mightes moste   195
        of heaven, yearth, and hell.

Tunc emittet spiritum, dicens 'Dabo vobis cor novum et spiritum
novum in medio vestri.'

SEVERALIS REX

26 A, God! A, lord mycle of might!
    This holye ghoost is in me pight.
    Methinkes my harte ys verey light
    syth yt came into mee.   200

PRIMUS REX

        Lord, wee thee honour daye and night
        for thou shewest us in sight
        right as Moyses us beheight.
        Honored most thou be.

At 185] secundus rex H   185–8] *om* R   186 that] and yf A   188 lore]
borne A   antechristus] antichristi R, antechiristus H   189 I(1)] a A
SD] Tunc ab Antechristo reverterunt H   recedent] recedunt B   Ante-
christo] Antichristo A, Antichristi R   193 *and* 194] *reversed* H   194] you
kinges I tell withouten bost H   to] *om* AR   195 mightes] might H
196 and] and ecke of B   *SD*] Heare his ghoste decendes R   emittet]
emittit A   spiritum(1)] supram A   novum(2)] noum A   vestri] vestre B
severalis] quartus H   197 mycle] much B   198 me] us R, my B
201 daye] both daye B   204 most] muste ARB

ANTECHRISTUS

27 Yett worthye workes to your will   205
of prophecye I shall fulfill.
As Danyell prophecied you untyll
that landes I shall devise,
that prophecye yt shalbe donne
and yt you shall see right soone.   210
Worshipps me all that ye mon
and doe after the wise.

135ᵛ   28 You kinges, I shall advance you all,
and, because your regions be but smale,
citties, castells shall you befall,   215
with townes and towers gaye;
and make you lordes of lordshipp fayre,
as well yt fall for my power.
Yea, looke you doe as I you leere
and herkens what I saye.   220

29 I am vercy God of might.
All thinges I made through my might,
sonne and moone, daye and night.
To blysse I may you bringe.
Therefore, kinges noble and gaye,   225
token your people what I saye—
that I am Christ, God verey—
and tell them such tydinge.

30 My people of Jewes were put mee from.
Therefore great ruthe I have them one.   230
Whether the will leeve me upon
I will full soone assaye.
For all that will leeve me upon,
worldlye welth shall them fall one
and to my blysse the shall come   235
and dwell with mee for aye.

207 you] *om* AR   208 landes] baundes A   I] *om* R   shall] shoulde
ARBH   209–12] *om* R   210 yt] that ABH   217–20] *om* AR
217 lordshipp] lordshipes BH   218 fall] falles BH   221–4] *om* R
225–36] *om* AR   234 worldlye] wordly H   them fall] have full B

31 And the giftes that I beheight
　　you shall have, as ys good right.
　　Hence or I goe out of your sight
　　eichone shall knowe his dole.   240

32 To thee I give Lombardee;
　　and to thee Denmarke and Hungarye;
　　and take thou Pathmos and Italie;
　　and Roome yt shalbe thine.

SECUNDUS REX

Grantmercye, lord, your giftes todaye!   245
Honour we will thee alwaye,
for wee were never so rych, in good faye,
nor nonne of all our kynne.

ANTECHRISTUS

33 Therefore be true and stidfast aye,
　　and truely leeves on my lawe,   250
　　for I will herken on you todaye,
　　stydfast yf I you fynde.

Tunc resedet Antechristus et venient Enock et Helias.

136ʳ   ENOCK

34 Almightie God in majestie,
　　that made the heaven and yearth to bee,
　　fyre, water, stonne, and tree,   255
　　and man through thy might—
　　the poyntes of thy privitie
　　any yearthlye man to see
　　ys impossible, as thinkes mee,
　　for anye worldelye wight.   260

237 that I beheight] I shalbe height R   240 knowe] have H   243 Path-
mos] Ponthous AR   247 for wee were never so rych] never so rich were
we H   good] om RB   252 stydfast] sidfast H   I] om R   SD resedet]
recedet BH   Antechristus] Anechristus A   venient] venit R   256 thy]
his B   260 for] or R   worldelye] wordly BH

35 Gratiouse lord, that art so good,
   that who so longe in fleshe and blood
   hath granted lyffe and heavenlye foode,
   lett never our thoughtes be defyled;
   but give us, lord, might and mayne,   265
   or wee of this shrewe be slayne,
   to converte thy people agayne
   that hee hath thus beguiled.

36 Sythe the worldes begininge
   I have lyved in great likynge   270
   through helpe of high and heaven kinge
   in paradice withowt anoye,
   tyll we hard tokeninge
   of this theves comynge
   that nowe on yearth is rayninge   275
   and doth Goddes folkes destroye.

37 To paradice I was taken that tyde,
   this theeffe his comynge to abyde,
   and Helye my brother, here mee besyde,
   was after sent to mee.   280
   With this champion we must chide
   that nowe in worlde walketh wyde,
   to disproove his pompe and prydc
   and payre all his postee.

HELIAS

38 O lord, that madest all thinge   285
   and longe hath lent us livinge,
   lett never the devylls power springe
   this man hath him within.

264 thoughtes] though R   266 shrewe] shrewe we A, shewe B
268 beguiled] defiled R   269] synce first the worlde begane R   sythe]
synce A, sithens B   270 and 271] reversed R   271 through] throrgh H
and] om ARBH   heaven] heavenlye AR   274 comynge] commnge H
275 on] in A   276 folkes] folke H   277 I was taken] tacken I was
ARBH   278 theeffe his] thiffes ARH   comynge] commnge H
279 mee] om AR   HELIAS] HELYE A   285 thinge] thinges B
286 livinge] levinge A   288 this] that R

God gyve you grace, old and yonge,
to knowe disceate in his doinge,   290
that you maye come to that likinge
of blysse that never shall blynne.

39 I warne you, all men, wytterlye,
this ys Enock, I am Helye,
binne common his errours to destroye   295
that hee to you nowe shewes.
136ᵛ   Hee calles himselfe 'Christe' and 'Messye'.
Hee lyes, forsooth, apertlye.
Hee ys the devyll, you to anoye,
and for nonne other him knowes.   300

PRIMUS REX

40 A, men, what speake you of Helye
and Enocke? The binne both in companye.
Of our blood the binne, wytterlye,
and wee binne of there kynde.

QUARTUS REX

Wee readen in bookes of our lawe   305
that they to heaven were idrawe
and yett binne there—ys the common sawe
wrytten, as men may fynd.

ENOCK

41 Wee binne those men, forsooth iwysse,
common to tell you doe amysse,   310
and bringe your soules to heaven-blysse
yf yt were anye boote.

HELIAS

This devylls lymme that common ys,
that sayth heaven and yearth ys his,
nowe wee be readye—leeve you this—   315
agaynst him for to moote.

289 old] bouth ould ARBH   295 common] come B   296 to you nowe] nowe
to you A   297 calles] calleth B   himselfe] hym A   300 nonne] no B
knowes] knowe RB   PRIMUS] TERTIUS BH   304 kynde] kynne R, kine B
306 idrawe] drawe R   311 heaven] heavens B   blysse] blesse A
HELIAS] HELYE A   314 heaven] heave B   315 wee be] bene wee B, we H

PRIMUS REX

42 Yf that wee here wytt mon
by prooffes of disputacon
that you have skyll and reason,
with you wee wyll abyde.   320

SECUNDUS REX

And yf your skylles may doe him downe,
to dye with you we wilbe bowne
in hope of salvatyon,
whatever may betyde.

ENOCK

43 To doe him downe wee shall assaye   325
through might of Jesu, borne of a maye,
by right and reason, as you shall saye,
and that you shall well here.
And for that cause hither were we sent
by Jesu Christe omnypotent,   330
and that you shall not all be shent.
Hee bought you all full deare.

44 Be gladd, therefore, and make good cheare,
and I doe reede as I you leere,
for wee be commen in good maneere   335
to save you everychone.

137r And dreade you not for that false feynde,
for you shall see him cast behinde
or wee departe and from him wend,
and shame shall light him one.   340

Et sic transibunt Enock et Helias ad Antechristum.

317 mon] anon H   318 prooffes] proueffes B   321 and] *om* AR
324 whatever] whatsoever ARBH   may] *om* ARBH   328 you] *om* R
329 were we] we be AR, are we H   330 omnypotent] ommipotent B
334 I doe] doe I H   you] do AR   336 everychone] everye one ARBH
337 false] selfe A   339 and] or AR   wend] wynde R   340 shall]
shall shall R   light him] him light H   *SD* Antechristum] Antichristum
A, Antechristi R

ENOCK

45 Saye, thou verey devylles lymme
    that syttes so grysely and so gryme—
    from him thou camc and shalt to him,
    for manye a soule thou deceaves.
    Thou hast deceaved men manye a daye   345
    and made the people to thy paye,
    and bewitched them into a wronge waye
    wickedlye with thy wyles.

ANTECRISTUS

46 A, false faytures, from me yee flee!
    Am not I most in majestie?   350
    What men dare mayne them thus to mee
    or make such distance?

HELIAS

    Fye one thee, fayture, fye on thee,
    the devylls owne nurrye!
    Through him thou preachest and hast postee   355
    a while, through sufferance.

ANTECHRISTUS

47 O you ypocrytes that so cryne!
    Loselles, lardans! Lowdlye you lyne!
    To spill my lawe you aspine.
    That speeche ys good to spare.   360
    You that my true fayth defyne
    and needeles [my folke] devyne,
    from hence hastelye; but you hence hyne,
    to you comes sorrowe and care.

ENOCK] *om* AR   344 a soule] soules B   346 made] brought B
347 into] to B   348 wyles] willes AB   349 from me yee flee] you
from me fleyne A   351 mayne] name AR   HELIAS] HELYE A   354 owne]
one B   ANTECHRISTUS] ANTCHRISTUS A   358 lardans] lurdenes A,
lordens R, lurdans B, lordans H   lowdlye you] so loudlye AR   359 aspine]
spine AR   362 my folke] my folke my folke Hm   devyne] denyne H
363 but] *om* R   hence] *om* ARBH

ENOCK

48 Thy sorrowe and care come on thy head,   365
for falsely through thy wicked read
the people ys put to pyne.
I would thy bodye were from thy head,
twentye myle from yt layde,
tyll I hit brought agayne.   370

ANTECHRISTUS

49 Owt on the, roysard, with thy wyles,
for falselye my people thou begyles.
I shall thee hastely honge,
and that lurdayne that standes thee bye;
hee puttes my folke to great anoye   375
with his false flatteringe tonge.

137ᵛ   50 But I shall teach you curtesye,
your savyour to knowe anonne in hye,
false theeves with your heresye,
and yf you darre abyde.   380

HELIAS

51 Yes, forsoothe, for all thy pryde,
here we purpose for to abyde
through grace of God almight.
And all the world that ys so wyde
shall wonder on thee on everye syde   385
soone in all mens sight.

ANTECHRISTUS

52 Owt one you, theeves both too.
Eyche man may see you be so
all by your araye,
muffeled in mantelles. Non such I knowe.   390

---

365 come] comes B   367 put] put put R   369 myle] miles ARH,
milles B   layde] leade ARB   ANTECHRISTUS] ANTECHRISTE A, ANTECHRISTI R
371–6] *om* R   371 roysard] rasarde A, wiserde BH   374 thee] thie B,
thy H   375 to] in A   anoye] anye H   376 flatteringe] flattery B
HELIAS] HELYE A   382 *and* 383] *reversed* ARBH

I shall make you lowt full lowe
or I departe you all froo,
to knowe mee lord for aye.

ENOCK

53 Wee bee no theeves, wee thee tell,
thou false fyend common from hell.   395
With thee wee purpose for to mell,
my fellowe and I in feare,
to knowe thy power and thy might
as wee these kinges have behight,
and thereto wee be readye dight   400
that all men nowe maye heare.

ANTECHRISTUS

54 My might is most, I tell to thee.
I dyed, I rose through my postie.
That all these kinges sawe with theire eye,
and everye man and wyefe.   405
And myracles and marveyles I dyd also.
I counsell you, therefore, both too,
to worshippe me and noe moe,
and lett us nowe noe more stryve.

HELIAS

55 The were no myracles but mervelles thinges   410
that thou shewed unto these kinges
through the fyendes crafte.
And as the flower nowe springes,
falleth, fadeth, and hanges,
so thy joye; nowe yt raygnes   415
that shalbe from thee rafte.

392 all] *om* R   393] *om* B   398–401] *om* B   401 nowe maye] maye
nowe A   409 nowe] *om* BH   HELIAS] HELYE A   411 shewed]
shewest R   unto] to BH   *After* 411] into falsehood thou them bringes H
412 the] thy R   413 flower] flowrs H   414 falleth] fayleth R   fadeth]
faith AR   hanges] heinges R, henges BH   415 nowe] *om* AR   yt] *om* B
416 shalbe from thee] shall from thee be H

ANTECHRISTUS

56 Owt on thee, theeffe, that syttes so styll!
Whye wilt thou not one word speake them tyll
that commen me to reprove?

138ʳ   DOCTOR

O lord, maister, what shall I saye then?   420

ANTECHRISTUS

I beshrewe both thy knen.
Art thou nowe for to ken?
In fayth, I shall thee greeve.

57 Of my godhead I made thee wyse
and sett thee ever at micle pryse.   425
Nowe I would feele thy good advyse
and heare what thou would sayen.
These lowlers, the would fayne me greeve
and nothinge one me the will leeve,
but ever be readye me to repreeve   430
and all the people of my lawe.

DOCTOR

58 O lord, thou art so micle of might,
meethinke thou should not chyde ne fight;
but curse them, lord, through thy might.
Then shall they fare full yll.   435
For those whom thou blesses, they shall well
    speede,
and those whom thou cursest, they are but deade.
This ys my counsell and my reade,
yonder heretikes for to spill.

418 one word] *om* AR   *After* 418] but lett them speak all ther will H
419] *om* R   421 knen] kenne A, eyne R, kneene B   422 nowe] *om* H
423 in] I R   425 micle] mickles B   427 sayen] saye ARB
428 lowlers] lossilles AR, loullords H   fayne] *om* RH   429 will leeve]
wilbe leeve AR   430 be] are B   repreeve] reprove AR   433 not]
ne AR, *om* H   434 lord] all R   436 whom] *om* AR, whon B
437 whom] *om* RB   438 and] and and R   439 for] *om* H

ANTECHRISTUS

59 The same I purposed, leeve thou mee. 440
All thinges I knowe through my postee.
But yett thy wytt I thought to see,
what was thyne intent.
Hit shalbe donne full syckerlye;
the sentence given full openlye, 445
with my mouth, truelye,
upon them shalbe hent.

60 My cursse I gyve you, to amend your meeles,
from your head to your heeles.
Walke yee furth, in the xx devylles waye. 450

ENOCK

Yea, thou shalt never come in coelis,
for falselye with thy wyles
the people are put in pyne.

ANTECHRISTUS

61 Owt on you, theeves! Whye fare yee thus?
Whether had you leaver have, payne or blysse? 455
I maye you save from all amys.
I made the daye and eke the night
and all thinges that are on yearth growinge—
flowes fayre that freshe can springe;
also I made all other thinge— 460
the starres that be so bright.

441 thinges] thinge H   knowe] knew H   443 what] that A   thyne]
myne A   444 full] right R   syckerlye] witterlye AR   448 amend]
mende B   449 head to] heade unto ARH, heades unto B   450 the]
om AR   451 coelis] clisse AR   After 452] in H

all this people thou begyles
and puttes them all to pyne.

453] om H   are] is ARB   ANTECHRISTUS] ANTECHRIST H   454 thus]
this R   455 leaver] rather AR   blysse] blesse AR   456 you save] save
you H   457 the(2)] om H   458 thinges] om A, thinge H   that
are] that is ARH, om B   459 flowes fayre that freshe] flowers freshe that
faier ARBH   460] om A   thinge] thinges B   461 the] and
the A

138ᵛ

HELIAS

62 Thou lyest! Vengeance on thee beefall!
Owt on thee, wretche! Wroth thee I shall!
Thou callest thee 'kinge' and 'lord of all';
a fyend ys thee within.   465

ANTECHRISTUS

63 Thou lyest falselye, I thee tell.
Thou will be dampned into hell.
I made thee man of flesh and fell,
and all that ys lyvinge.
For other godes have yee nonne.   470
Therefore worshippe mee alonne,
the which hath made the water and stonne,
and all at my lykinge.

ENOCK

64 Forsoothe thou lyest falselye.
Thou art a fyende common to anoye   475
Goddes people that stande us bye.
In hell I would thou were.

HELIAS

Fye on thee, fellonne, fye on thee, fye!
For all thy wytchcrafte and sorcerye,
to mote with thee I am readye,   480
that all the people may heare.

ANTECHRISTUS

65 Owt on you, harlottes! Whence come yee?
Where have you anye other god but mee?

ENOCK

Yes, Christe, God in Trynitie,
thou false fayture attaynt,   485

HELIAS] HELYE A   462 beefall] fall R   467 will] shalt H   475 com-
mon] come BH   anoye] anye H   476 stande] standeth R   HELIAS]
HELYE A   481 the] thes A, this R   482 come] came H   483 god]
godes A

that sent his Sonne from heaven-see
that for mankynde dyed on roode-tree,
that shall full soone make thee to flee,
thou fayture false and faynt.

ANTECHRISTUS

66 Rybbauldes, ruled owt of raye!   490
    What ys the Trinitye for to saye?

HELIAS

Three persons, as thou leeve may,
in on godhead in feere—
Father and Sonne, that ys noe naye,
and the Holye Ghoost styrringe aye.   495
That ys one God verey;
binne all three named here.

139ʳ   ANTECHRISTUS

67 Owt on you, theeves! What sayen yee?
    Wyll you have on God and three?
    Howe darre you so saye?   500
    Madmen, madmen! Therfore leeve on mee
    that am on god—so ys not hee!
    Then may you lyve in joye and lee,
    all this land I darre laye.

ENOCK

68 Naye, tyrand! Understand thou this: 505
    withowt beginyge his godhead ys
    and also without endinge, iwys.
    Thus fullye leeven wee.
    And thou that ingendered was amys
    haste beginynge and nowe this blys,   510
    and end shall have—no dread there ys—
    full fowle, as men shall see.

486 sent his] Gods H   488 full soone make thee] make thee full sone A,
soone make thee RH   flee] fleye A, flie B   490 ruled] ruler B   HELIAS]
HELYE A   493 feere] free AR   500 so] so to B   501 madmen
madmen] madmen R   therfore] om A   506 beginyge] begininge ARBH
507 iwys] is AR   510 blys] blesse A   511 and] anAR   512 full]
fully A

ANTECHRISTUS

69 Wretches! Gulles! You be blent.
Goddes Sonne I am, from him sent.
Howe dare you maynteyne your intent,   515
syth hee and I bee one?
Have I not, syth I came him froo,
made the dead to speake and goe?
And to men I sent my ghoost alsoe
that leeved mee upon.   520

HELIAS

70 Fye on thee, fellonne, fye on thee, fye!
For through his might and his majestie,
by sufferance of God almightie,
the people are blent throwe thee.
Yff those men be raysed wytterlye   525
withowt the devylles fantasye,
here shalbe prooved apertlye
that all men shall see.

ANTECHRISTUS

71 Ah, fooles! I read you leeve mee upon
that myracles have shewed to manye on,   530
to the people everychone,
to put them owt of doubt.
Therefore I read you hastclye
convertes to me most mightie.
I shall you save from anoye,   535
and that I am abowt.

ENOCK

72 Nowe of thy miracles would I see.

---

513 gulles] glowes A, gowles R, goioles B, goles H   517 syth] synce R
518 speake] rise AR   519 sent] send H   520 leeved] leeve A
HELIAS] HELYE A   522 his(2)] *om* A   majestie] maisterye A, mastery R,
maistry H   524 are] is ARBH   527 apertlye] perfectlye AR
531 everychone] every eichone RB   534 mightie] mightelye ARB

HELIAS

Therefore common hither be wee.
Doe what ys thy great postee—
and some thereof to leere. 540

ANTECHRISTUS

Soone may you see, yf you wyll abyde,
for I wyll neyther fight nor chydc.
Of all the world that ys so wyde,
therein ys not my peare.

ENOCK

73 Bringe forth those men here in our sight 545
that thou hast reysed agaynst the right.
Yf thou bee so micle of might
to make them eate and drynke,
for verey God we will thee knowe
such a signe yf thou wylt shewe, 550
and doe thee reverence on a rowe
all at thy likynge.

ANTECHRISTUS

74 Wretches, dampned all bee yee,
but nought for that yt falleth mee,
as gratyouse god abydinge bee, 555
yf you wyll mend your liefe.
You dead men, ryse through my postye.
Come eate and drynke, that men may see,
and prove me worthye of deitee;
so shall we stynt all stryffe. 560

PRIMUS MORTUIS

75 Lord, thy biddinge I will doe aye
and for to eate I will assaye.

HELIAS] HELYE A 538 common] come A be wee] we be A 540 some]
soone R 542 for] and B 545 those] thes AR 548 them] *om* H
551 thee] thie B ANTECHRISTUS] ANTECHRIST B 556 your] you H
559 deitee] dyety B MORTUIS] MORTUUS ARBH

SECUNDUS MORTUUS

And I also, all that I maye,
wyll do thy byddinge here.

HELIAS

Have here breadd both too. 565
But I must blesse yt or yt goe,
that the fyend, mankyndes foe,
on hit have no power.

76 This bread I blesse with my hand
in Jesus name, I understand, 570
the which ys lord of sea and land
and kinge of heaven on hie.
In nomine Patris—that all hath wrought—
et Filii virginis—that deare us bought—
et Spiritus Sancti—ys all my thought— 575
on God and persons three.

PRIMUS MORTUUS

77 Alas, put that bread out of my sight!
To looke on hit I am not light.
That prynt that ys uppon hit pight,
hit puttes me to great feere. 580

140ʳ   SECUNDUS MORTUUS

To looke on hit I am not light.
That bread to me yt ys so bright
and ys my foe both daye and night,
and puttes me to great deare.

ENOCK

78 Nowe you men that have donne amys, 585
you see well what his power ys.
Convertes to him, I read iwys,
that you on roode hath bought.

563 also] will R   HELIAS] HELYE A   566 yt(2)] I AR   572 of]
in ARBH   on] so ARBH   576 on] one ARBH   MORTUUS] MORTUS R
580 hit] that R   MORTUUS] MORTUS R   583 both] om A   584 deare]
dreade AR   588 hath] om H

TERTIUS REX

A, nowe we knowe appertlye
wee have binne brought in heresye.　590
With you to death we will forthye,
and never efte torne our thought.

QUARTUS REX

79 Nowe, Enock and Helye, yt ys no naye.
You have taynted the tyrant this same daye.
Blessed be Jesu, borne of a maye!　595
On him I leeve upon.

PRIMUS REX

Thou fayture feard with fantasye,
with sorcerye, wytchcraft, and nygromancye,
thou hast us lead in heresye.
Fye on thy workes eychone!　600

SECUNDUS REX

80 Jesu, for thy mycle grace,
forgyve us all our trespasse
and bringe us to thy heavenlye place
as thou art God and man.
Nowe am I wyse made through thy might.　605
Blessed be thou, Jesu, daye and night!
This greesely groome greetes him to fight,
to flea us here anonne.

TERTIUS REX

81 Of our lyves lett us not wreache,
though we be slayne of such a wretche,　610
for Jesus sake, that maye us teache
our soules to bringe to blys.

589 A] and AR　592 efte] om A, more R　our thought] from thie B
594 taynted] taunted R　the] thy H　597 feard] fere AR　606 thou]
om A　607 this] the H　greetes] girts H　608 flea] slea ARBH
610 though] thorghe H　611 Jesus] Jesu his RB　teache] lech A, leech
RBH　612 blys] blesse A

QUARTUS REX

That was well sayd, and soe I assent.
To dye, forsooth, ys myne intent
for Christes love omnypotent,   615
in cause that ys rightwyse.

ANTECHRISTUS

82 A, false faytures, turne you nowe?
    You shall be slayne, I make avowe;
    and those traytors that so turned you,
    I shall make them unfayne,   620
140ᵛ   that all other by verey sight
    shall knowe that I am most of might,
    for with this sword nowe wyll I feight,
    for all you shall be slayne.

Tunc Antechristus occidet Enock et Heliam et omnes reges conversos cum gladio et redibit ad cathedram; cum dicat Michaell
cum gladio in dextera sua.

MICHAEL ARCHANGELUS

83 Antechriste, nowe ys common this daye.   625
    Reigne no lenger nowe thou maye.
    Hee that hath led thee alwaye,
    nowe him thou must goe to.
    No more men shall be slayne by thee.
    My lord will dead that thou bee.   630
    Hee that hath gyven thee this postee
    thy soule shall underfoe.

84 In synne ingendered first thou was.
    In synne ledd thy lyffe thou hasse.

615 love] sake R   ANTECHRISTUS] ANTECHRIST B   619 so] *om* H
623 nowe wyll I] I thinke to A   *SD*] Heare Antechristus kylles them R
occidet] occidit A   Enock] Enochum H   et omnes] omnesque H   con-
versos] conversus A, *om* H   et] posteavero H   cum dicat Micheall cum
gladio in dextera sua] et Michael cum gladio in dextra dicat H   ARCHANGELUS]
ARCKEANGELL A, *om* R, THARCHANGELL B   625 ys common] commen is H
this] thie BH   626 nowe thou] thou ne ARH   628] to him now must
thou goe H   631 this] his A   632 underfoe] underfree B   634 hasse]
haste AR

In synne an end nowe thow mase 635
that marred hasse manye one.
Nowe thou shalt knowe and wytt in hie
that more ys Goddes majestie
then eke the dyvell and thyne therebye,
for nowe thow shalt be deade. 640

85 Thou hase ever served Sathanas
and had his power in everye place.
Therefore thou gettes nowe no grace.
With him thou must gonne.

Tunc Michael occidet Antechristum et in occidendo clamat Antechristus 'Helpe, helpe, helpe, helpe!'

ANTECHRISTUS

86 Helpe, Sathanas and Lucyfere! 645
Belzebubb, bould batchellere!
Ragnell, Ragnell, thou art my deare!
Nowe fare I wonder evyll.
Alas, alas, where ys my power?
Alas, my wytt ys in a weare. 650
Nowe bodye and soule both in feare
and all goeth to the devyll.

Tunc morietur Antechristus et venient duo demones et dicunt ut
sequitur:

PRIMUS DEMON

87 Anonne, mayster, anonne, anone!
From hell-ground I hard thee grone.

635 an end nowe] now an ende RH   636 one] a one A   *After* 636] *in*
ARBH:
             Three yeairs and halfe on witterlye
             thou haste hade leave to destroye
             Godes people wickedlye
             through thy fowle reade.   4
             (yeairs] year H)
638 majestie] maistry H   639 dyvell] devilles ARBH   640 for] *om* A
643 thou gettes nowe] thou gettes AR, now getts thou H   no] no other AR
SD occidet] occidit AR   Antechristum] Antechristus ARB   clamat]
clamam A   Antechristus] *om* H   ANTECHRISTUS] *to left of SD* H
646 batchellere] balacher AR   648 wonder] wonderous B   650 wytt]
wittes R   *SD* morietur] morientur AR   dicunt] dicat Primus Demon H
PRIMUS DEMON] DEMON PRIMUS H   654 thee] thie B

I thought not to come myselfe alonne   655
for worshippe of thine estate.
With us to hell thou shalt gonne.
For this death wee make great mone.
To wynne more soules into our wonne—
but nowe yt ys to late!   660

SECUNDUS DEMON

88 With mee thou shalt. From mee thou come.
   Of mee shall come thy last doome,
   for thou hast well deserved.
   And through my might and my postee
   thou hast lyved in dignitie   665
   and many a soule deceyved.

                    PRIMUS DEMON

89 This bodye was gotten by myne assent
   in cleane whooredome, verament.
   Of mother wombe or that he went,
   I was him within   670
   and taught him aye with myne intent
   synne, by which hee shalbe shent.
   For hee dyd my commaundement,
   his soule shall never blynne.

                    SECUNDUS DEMON

90 Nowe, fellowe, in fayth great mone wee maye make   675
   for this lord of estate that standes in this steed.
   Manye a fatt morsell wee had for his sake
   of soules that should have bine saved—in hell be
      the hydd!

Tunc capient animam eius, et potius corpus.

657 thou] that thou B   658 this] thy R   659 wonne] pon AR
SECUNDUS DEMON] DEMON SECUNDUS H   661 come] came B   664 postee]
maisterye A   PRIMUS DEMON] DEMON PRIMUS H   671 aye with] eever A
SECUNDUS DEMON] DEMON SECUNDUS H   675 wee maye make] make wee B
676 standes] standeth AR   in this steed] us instead R, in this stidd BH
678 should] *om* R   have bine] bene A, be H   saved] hange A   be the
hydd] by the head AR, by thie B   *SD*] *om* A, Heare the devills carry
Antichristi away R, Tunc aufertur corpus Antechristi a demonibus H   capient]
capieint B

436 PLAY XXIII

PRIMUS DEMON

91 His soule with sorrowe in hand have I hent.
Yee, pennance and payne soone shall hee feele.   680
To Lucyfere, that lord, yt shalbe present
that burne shall as a brande; his sorrowe shall not
keele.

SECUNDUS DEMON

92 This proctor of prophecye hath procured manye one
one his lawes for to leeve, and lost for his sake
theire sowles be, in sorrowe, and his shalbe soone.   685
Such maistries through my might manye on I do make.

Posteaquam demones loqunti sunt, resurgens Enock et Helias ab
Antechristo [coesi] et auditoribus status suos commonstrabunt.

PRIMUS DEMON

93 With Lucyfere, that lord, longe shall he lenge;
in a seate aye with sorrowe with him shall he sytt.

SECUNDUS DEMON

Yea, by the heeles in hell shall hee henge
in a dungeon deepe, right in hell-pytt!   690

PRIMUS DEMON

94 To hell wyll I hye withowt anye fayle,
with this present of pryce thither to bringe.

SECUNDUS DEMON

Thou take him by the toppe and I by the tayle.
A sorrowfull songe, in fayth, shall hee singe.

PRIMUS DEMON] *om* AR, DEMON PRIMUS H   679–90] *om* AR   682 keele]
feele H   SECUNDUS DEMON] DEMON SECUNDUS H   684 one] in H
685 be] leve H   his] this B   686 maistries] maistres B   on] one
BH   I do] do I BH   *SD* posteaquam] postquam BH   loqunti]
loquti B, loqumti H   sunt] fuerint H   resurgens] resurgent BH   coesi]
coesti Hm   PRIMUS DEMON] DEMON PRIMUS H   SECUNDUS DEMON]
DEMON SECUNDUS H   689 henge] leng B   PRIMUS DEMON] *om* R, DEMON
PRIMUS H   691–4] *om* R   691 withowt anye] withouten B   fayle] faye A
SECUNDUS DEMON] DEMON SECUNDUS H   693 thou take] take thou H
and] *om* B   694 shall hee] he shall A

PRIMUS DEMON

95 A, fellowe, a dole lookc that thow deale   695
to all this fayre companye, hence or thou wend.

141ᵛ   SECUNDUS DEMON

Yea, sorrowe and care ever shall the feele.
In hell shall they dwell at theire last ende.

ENOCKE

96 A, lord, that all shall leade
and both deeme the quycke and deade!   700
That reverence thee, thou on them reade
and them through right releaved.
I was deade and right here slayne,
but through thy might, lord, and thy mayne
thou hast me reased up agayne.   705
Thee will I love and leeve.

HELIAS

97 Yea, lord, blessed must thou bcc.
My flesh glorifyed nowe I see.
Wytt ney sleight agaynst thee
conspired may be by noe waye.   710
All that leeven in thee stydfastlye
thou helpes, lord, from all anoye,
for dead I was and nowe lyve I.
Honored be thou aye!

MYCHAELL

98 Enock and Helyc, come you anon.   715
My lord wyll that you with mee gonne
to heaven-blysse, both blood and bone,
evermore there to bee.

PRIMUS DEMON] *om* AR, DEMON PRIMUS H   695–8] *om* AR   695 deale] delle
B, now deale H   SECUNDUS DEMON] DEMON SECUNDUS H   698] all sinnfull
shall dwell in hell at ther last ende H   699 all] all the world H   700 both
deeme] dome bothe H   703 I] and I H   704 lord] *om* A   706 thee]
thie B   HELIAS] HELYE A   707 yea] ye B   708 glorifyed nowe] now
glorified H   710 by] *om* BH   711] *om* B   leeven] leve AR
713 nowe] *om* B   714 honored] lord honored H   aye] ever A

You have binne longe, for you bynne wyse,
dwellinge in yearthly paradyce;   720
but to heaven, where himselfe ys,
nowe shall you goe with mee.

Tunc abducens eos ad coelos, cantabit Angelus 'Gaudete justi
in domino' etc.

Finis

PLAY XXIV

_{142^r} THE WEBSTARS PLAYE

Pagina Vicessima Quarta et Omnium Postrema: De Judicio
Extremo

DEUS

Ego sum alpha et omega, 1, primus et novissimus.

1 I God, greatest of degree,
in whom begyninge non may bee,
that I am pearles of postee,
nowe appertly that shalbe preeved.
In my godhead are persons three;   5
maye non in faye from other flee.
Yett soveraygne might that ys in mee
may justly be meeved.

2 It ys full youre syns I beheight
to make a reckoninge of the right.   10
Nowe to that doome I will mee dight
that dead shall dulye dread.

720 yearthly] earthie B   722 goe] *om* H   *SD*] Tunc Michael archangelus adducet Henochum et Heliam ad caelum, et cantabit 'Gaudete justi in
domino' etc H   ad] et A, ac R   coelos] celum ARB   cantabit] cantebit
AR   gaudete] gaudet B   justi] in justi A, just R   etc] *om* R

Guild-ascription] *om* B   playe] *om* H   *Play-heading* postrema] posterma
R   extremo] novissimo H   *Latin* 1] *om* ARBH   1 of] in AR
4 nowe] *om* H   that] *om* AH   preeved] proved ARH   6 faye] aye R
flee] fley AR, be H   7 might] lord B   8 justly] mystely H   meeved]
moved R   9 syns] sith H   11 doome] done B   mee] thie B   12 that]
that I A

Therefore, my angelles fayre and bright,
looke that you wake eych worldlye wight
that I maye see all in my sight   15
that I blood forth can bleede.

3 Shewe you my crosse appertlye here,
crowne of thorne, sponge and speare,
and nayles to them that wanted nere
to come to this anoye;   20
and what weede for them I weare,
upon my bodye nowe I beare.
The most stowtest this sight shall steare
that standeth by streete or stye.

ANGELUS PRIMUS

4 Lord that madest through thy might   25
heaven and yearth, daye and night,
withowt distance wee be dight
your byddinge for to donne.
And for to awake eyche worldlye wight
I shall bee readye, and that in height,   30
that they shall shewe them in thy sight.
Thou shalt see, lord, full soone.

SECUNDUS ANGELUS

5 Take wee our beames and fast blowe.
All mankynd shall them knowe.
Good accompt that nowe can shewe,   35
soone yt shalbe seene.
That have done well in there lyvinge,
they shall have joye withowt endinge.
That evell have done withowt mendinge
shall ever have sorrowe and teene.   40

142ᵛ

14 wake] awake A   worldlye] wordly H   15 my] *om* B   16 forth]
for ARBH   18 thorne] thornes H   sponge] songe H   19 nere] never
ARBH   20 anoye] anye H   24 standeth] standes A   ANGELUS
PRIMUS] PRIMUS ANGELLUS ARB   27 withowt] withou R   29] *om* B
worldlye] wordly H   32 thou] that RB   shalt see] shalbe R   SECUNDUS
ANGELUS] ANGELUS SECUNDUS H   33 beames] beanes ARB   34 mankynd]
manking B   35 accompt] accomptes H   nowe] non B   37 that] the
that R   well] evill A   lyvinge] levinge A   39 mendinge] amendinge H

Tunc angeli tubas accipient et flabunt, et omnes mortui de
sepulchris surgent, quorum dicat primus Papa Salvatus.

PAPA SALVATUS

6 A, lord, mercye nowe aske wee,
that dyed for us on the roode-tree.
Hit ys three hundreth yeares and three
synce I was put in grave.
Nowe through thy might and thy postye   45
thy beames blast hath raysed mee—
I, flesh and blood as I nowe see—
my judgment for to have.

7 While that I lyved in flesh and bloodd,
thy great godhead that ys so good   50
mee knewe I never, but ever was wood
worshipps for to wynne.
The wyttes, lord, thou sent to mee
I spend to come to great degree.
They highest office under thee   55
in yearth thou puttest me yn.

8 Thou grantest me, lord, through thy grace,
Peters power and his place.
Yett was I blent. Alas, alas,
I dyd not thyne assent.   60
But my fleshlye will that wicked was,
the which raysed nowe thou hasse,
I forthered, lord, before thy face
shall take his judgment.

9 When I in yearth was at my will,   65
this world mee blent, both lowde and styll;
but thy commandment to fulfill
I was full neglygent.

SD accipient] accipente A   sepulchris] sepulcor AR, secpulcris B, sepulchis H
surgent] surgente A, resurgent H   dicat primus Papa Salvatus] dicat primus
Papa Salvata A, dicat primus Papa R, dicat primus B, primus Papa Salvatus
dicat ut sequitur H   42 the] om A   46 beames] beanes ARB, bames H
47 I(1)] in ARBH   51 mee] ne ARBH   54 spend] spente AR
55 they] the ARBH   56 in] I B   57–64] om R   57 grantest]
grantedst H   62 hasse] haste A   66 mee] be H   both] om AR
68 was] way H   full] ever H

But purged yt ys with paynes yll
in purgatorye that sore can gryll.   70
Yett thy grace I hope to come tyll
after my great torment.

10 And yett, lord, I must dread thee
for my great synne when I thee see;
for thou art most in majestie,   75
of mercye nowe I call.
The paynes that I have longe in bee,
as hard as hell save hope of lee,
agayne to goe never suffer mee
for ought that may befall.   80

143ʳ   IMPERATOR SALVATUS

11 A, lord and soveraygne savyoure,
that lyvinge put mee to honour
and made me kinge and emperour,
highest of kythe and kynne—
my flesh, that fallen was as the flowre,   85
thou hasse restored in this stowre
and with paynes of great languowre
clensed mee of my synne.

12 In purgatorye my soule hath binne
a thousand yeares in woe and teene.   90
Nowe ys noe synne upon mee sccne,
for purged I am of pyne.
Though that I to synne were bayne and bowne
and coveted ryches and renowne,
yett at the last contrytion   95
hath made mee on of thyne.

13 As hard payne, I darre well saye,
in purgatorye are night and daye
as are in hell, save by on waye—
that one shall have an end.   100

69–72] *om* R   74 synne] synnes ARB, simnes H   thee see] see thie B
76 of] for AR   78 save] as AR   of] as AR   90 yeares] yearc H
91 synne] woe AR   93 that] *om* ARB   bowne] bounde R   97 payne]
paines ARBH   98 are] *om* A   100 one] onste A, once R

14 Worshipped bee thou, high justice,
that mee hasse made in flesh to ryse.
Nowe wott I well, those that have binne wyse
shall come unto thy welth.
Grant me, lord, amongest moe,   105
that purged am of synne and woe,
on thy right hand that I maye goe
to that everlastinge health.

REX SALVATUS

15 A, lord of lordes and kinge of kinges
and informer of all thinges,   110
thy power, lord, spreades and springes,
as soothly here ys seene.
After bale, boote thou bringes,
and after teene-tyde tydinges
to all that ever thy names mynes   115
and buxon to thee benne.

16 While I was lord of land and leede
in purple and in rych weede,
meethought to thee I had no neede,
so wronge the world me wyled.   120
Though thou for me thy blood can sheede,
yett in my hart more can I heede
my flesh to further and to feede,
but the soule was ever begyled.

143ᵛ   17 My fowle bodye through synne blent,   125
that rotten was and all torent,
through thy might, lord omnipotent,
raysed and whole yt ys.
My soule that ys in bales brent
to my bodye thou hast nowe sent   130
to take before the judgment
of that I have donne amys.

101 worshipped] worshipp H   high] righte AR   104 unto] into ARH
105 grant] and grante R   amongest] amonghte A, amogst H   108 health]
wealth R   109 lordes] lorde R   112 here] ther AR   113 after] and H
114 tyde] om B   115 that] om H   names] name ARBH   mynes] minges H
120 me] in A   121 sheede] bleed H   126 all torent] also rente A
129 in bales] in balleus AR, bale H   131 the] thee ARH   132 amys] mise B

18 But, lord, though I were synfull aye,
   contrytion yett at my last daye
   and almes-deedes that I dyd aye   135
   hath holpen me from hell.
   But well I wott that ylke waye
   that Abraham went wynde I maye,
   for I am purged to thy paye,
   with thee evermore to dwell.   140

REGINA SALVATA

19 Pearles prynce of most postye
   that after langwore lendeth lee,
   that nowe in bodye hasse raysed mee
   from fyre to rest and rowe—
   my flesh, that as flowre can flye   145
   and powder was, through thy pyttie
   together hasse brought, as I nowe see,
   the soule and bodye too.

20 While I in yearth rych can goe
   in softe sandalles and silke alsoe,   150
   velvet also that wrought me woe,
   and all such other weedes,
   neyther prayed I ney fastc.
   Saffe almes-deedes, yf any paste,
   and great repentance at the laste   155
   hath gotten me to thy grace,

21 that saved I hope fullye to bee,
   for purged synnes that were in mee.
   Thy laste doome may I not flcc,
   to come before thy face.   160
   All that might excyte lecherye—
   perrelles and precyouse perrye—

133 though] although A   135 I] om AR   140 with] to AR   evermore]
evermore more A   SALVATA] SALVATOR AR   141 of most] most of R
142 lendeth] sendeth H   145 flye] fley R, flee H   146 powder]
power AR   thy] om H   147 I nowe] nowe I AR   148 and] the ARBH
150 sandalles] sendal H   153–60] after 164 H   158 synnes] signes H
159 flee] fleye AR, flye H   162 perrelles] pearles ARH

agaynst thy byddinge used I,
and other wycked deedes.

22 After purgatorye-paynes 165
from me thy lordshippe thou ney laynes.
To warne thy doome mee ney gaynes,
though I were never so greate.

144ʳ   Sythe I have suffred woe and teene
in purgatorye longe too benne, 170
lett never my synne be on me seene
but, lord, thou hit forgett.

Tunc venient damnati.

PAPA DAMNATUS

23 Alas, alas, alas, alas!
Nowe am I worse then ever I was.
My bodye agayne the soule hasse 175
that longe hase benne in hell.
Together the bee—nowe ys noe grace—
fyled to bee before thy face,
and after my death here in this place
in payne ever to dwell. 180

24 Nowe bootelesse ys to aske mercye,
for, lyvinge, highest in yearth was I,
and cunynge closen in cleargye;
but covetousnes dyd me care.
Also sylver and symonye 185
made mee pope unworthye.
That burnes me nowe, full witterlye,
for of blys I am full bare.

25 Also, why spend I wronge my wytte
in covetousnes my hart to knytte? 190
Hard and hott nowe feele I hitt;
hell howldes me right here.

163 byddinge] biddinges B   165 purgatorye] purgation B   166 lord-
shippe] lordeshipes A   ney laynes] me lames B   167 warne] flee H
SD venient] venit R   damnati] damnata A, damnate R   174 am] as B
175 agayne the soule] the sowle againe ABH   178 fyled] defyled H   to]
they H   180 ever] evermore A   183 closen] chosen ARH   184 but]
and A   187 witterlye] worthelie B, bitterly H   189 also] alas BH
spend] spcnte R   192 howldes] howles R

My bodye burnes everye bytt.
Of sorrowe must I ncver be shutt.
Mee to save from hell-pytt   195
nowe helpeth noe prayer.

26 Of all the soules in Christianitie
that damned were while I had degree
nowe gyve accompt behoveth mee,
through my lawes forlorne.   200
Also damned nowe must I bee.
Accompt befalles, or elles to flee.
Make me deafe, I cojure thee,
as I had never binne borne.

IMPERATOR DAMNATUS

27 Alas, nowe sterred I am in this stowre.   205
Alas, nowe fallen ys my flowre.
Alas, for synne nowe cease succour.
No sylver maye mee save.
Alas, that I ever was emperoure.
Alas, that I ever had towne or towre.   210
Alas, hard bye I my honour;
hell-paynes for yt I have.

111ᵛ   28 Alas, in world whye was I ware?
Alas, that ever mother mee bare!
Alas, there ys noe yeane-chare!   215
Scape may I not this chance.
Alas, doe evell who ys that dare?
To threpe no more us ne dare,
for to payne we ordayned are,
ever withowt delyverance.   220

193 bytt] white B   196 helpeth] helpes AR   noe] to A   197 Christiani-
tie] Christiantie ARBH   200 lawes] laches H   201 nowe] om AR
203 cojure] counger A, conjure RBH   DAMNATUS] DAMPNATA A
205 sterred] storred A   207 cease] no H   209 I ever] ever I ARB
210 I ever] ever I ARBH   211 hard bye I] hardlye I bye AR, hard doe I
buy B, I buy hard now H   214 mother] my mother H   215 yeane]
joye A, eyme R, gayne H   chare] cheare AR   216 scape may I] scake I
may H   217 ys] om B   218 us ne dare] me ney dare R, now no
care H   219 we ordayned] ordeyned we R

29 Nowe ys manslaughter upon mee seene.
    Nowe covetousnes makes my care keene.
    Nowe wronge-workinge, withowten weene,
    that I in world have wrought,
    nowe traytorouse tornes do me teene,   225
    and false doomes all bydeene.
    In gluttonye I have in binne
    that shall nowe deare be bought.

30 Nowe knowe I what I dyd with wronge
    and eke my lyther lyvinge longe.   230
    Falsehoode to hell makes mee to fonge,
    in fyre ever fowle to fare.
    Misbegotten money ever I myxed amonge.
    Nowe ys me yeelded to hell yonge.
    Whye were I not dead as ys the donge?   235
    For deole I drowpe and dare!

REX DAMNATUS

31 Alas, unlykinge ys my lott.
    My weale ys gonne, of woe I wott.
    My synne ys seene I was in sett.
    Of sorrowe nowe may I synge.   240
    To hell-payne that ys so hott
    for my misdeedes wend I mot.
    Alas, that I hadd beene sheepe or goatte
    when I was crowned kinge.

32 When I was in my majestie,   245
    soveraigne of shyre and of cyttye,
    never did I good. In noe degree
    through me was any grace.

222 nowe] nowe towe AR   care] cares ARBH   225 traytorouse] traytores
AR   226 bydeene] by deme BH   227 in binne] bene in ARH
229 with] by H   233 misbegotten] my misbegotten AR, misgotten BH
ever] *om* H   I] *om* R   myxed] mixen A   234 me] in A   yeelded]
yelled A   yonge] thonge H   235 not] not as R   ys the] *om* R
236 deole] deale ARB, dole H   239 synne] sight B   in sett] a sott H
242 misdeedes] misdede H   wend] now wiend BH   243 alas] as las B
246 of(2)] *om* RH

Of poore had I never pittie.
Sore ne sycke would I never see. 250
Nowe have I languowre and they have lee.
Alas, alas, alas!

33 Wronge ever I wrought to eych wight.
For pennyes, poore in payne I pight.
Relygion I reaved agaynst the right. 255
That [keenlye] nowe I knowe.
Lecherye, I held hit light.
In covetousenes my hart was clight.
On good deede in God his sight
nowe have I not to shewe. 260

145ʳ REGINA DAMNATA

34 Alas, alas! Nowe am I lorne.
Alas! With teene nowe am I torne.
Alas, that I was of woman borne,
this bytter bale to byde.
I made my moane both even and [morne] 265
for feare to come Jesu beforne
that crowned for mee was with thorne
and thrust into the syde.

35 Alas, that I was woman wrought.
Alas, whye God made me of nought 270
and with his pretyouse blood me bought
to worke agaynst his wyll?
Of lecherye I never wrought,
but ever to that synne I sought,
that of that fylth in deede and thought 275
yett had I never that fyll.

36 Fye on pearles! Fye on prydee!
Fye on gowne! Fye on guyde!

253 ever I wrought] wrought I B, I ever wrought H   254 pennyes]
pynchinge A   256 keenlye] kneelye Hm, kinely B   257 hit] but H
259 God his] Godes ARH   DAMNATA] DAMNATUS R   262 nowe am I
torne] I am totorne H   263 I] ever I H   of] om ARH   264 byde]
abyde AR   265 both] om A   morne] norne Hm   267 for mee was]
was for me B   270 God made] made God H   272 agaynst] agayst H
275 that(1)] and H   fylth] synne A   276 that] my ARH, om B
277 prydee] pride ARBH

Fye on hewe! Fye on hyde!
These harrowe me to hell.   280
Agaynst this chance I may not chyde.
This bitter bale I must abyde.
Yea, woe and teene I suffer this tyde,
noe lyvinge tonge may tell.

37 I, that soe seemelye was in sight,   285
    where ys my blee that ys so bright?
    Where ys baron, where ys knight
    for mee to alledge the lawe?
    Where in world ys any wight
    that for my fayrenes nowe wyll fight,   290
    or from this death I am to dight
    that darre mee heathen drawe?

JUSTICIARIUS DAMNATUS

38 Alas! Of sorrowe nowe ys my sawe.
    Alas! For hell I am in awe.
    My fleshe as flowre that all to-flawe   295
    nowe tydes a fearely fytt.
    Alas, that ever I learned lawe,
    for suffer I must manye a hard thrawe;
    for the devyll will me drawe
    right even into his pytt.   300

39 Alas! While that I lyved in land,
    wrought] to worke I would not wond
    but falsely causes tooke in hand
    and mych woe dyd elles.
    When I sought sylver or rych sound   305
    of baron, burges, or of bound,
    his moote to further ever I would found,
    were yt never so false.

280 harrowe] arrow B   283 yea] with AR   284 may] can B   286 ys(2)]
was ABH   287 baron] the barron AR   knight] the knighte AR
288 alledge] leadge AR   291 I am] me R   292 mee] my B
heathen] hense AR   293 of] I B   294 am] stand A   295 flowre]
flowers AR   298 hard] om R   299 will] om A   300 into his] to his
AR, to hell H   302 wrought] wronge ARBH   303 falsely] false ARBH
tooke] to be hand B   304 elles] als H   305 rych sound] riches founde
A, riches sounde R   306 baron] barrons B   of(2)] a H   bound] bande
AR, bonde H   307 moote] matter AR   ever] om H   308 so] to B

145^v

40 Nowe ys the dyvell readye, I see,
his moote to further agaynst mee   310
for the judge of such postye
that mee wyll not avayle;
harte and thought both knoweth hee.
Though I would lye, noe boote wyll bee.
Alas, this hard fytt to flee   315
rufullye I must fayle.

41 All my lyeffe ever I was bowne
to trouble poore in towre an towne,
payre Holy Church possession
and sharpely them to shend.   320
To reave and robbe relygion,
that was all my devotyon.
Therefore mee tydes damnatyon
and payne withowten end.

MERCATOR DAMNATUS

42 Alas, alas, nowe woe ys mee!   325
My fowle bodye, that rotten hath be,
and soule together nowe I see.
All stynketh, full of synne.
Alas! Marchandize maketh mee,
and purchasinge of land and fee,   330
in hell-payne evermore to bee,
and bale that never shall blynne.

43 Alas! In world fervent was I
to purchase landes falselye.
Poore men I dyd such anoye,   335
made them theire landes to sell.
But when I dyed, wytterlye,
all that I had, my enemye

309 I] *om* H   310 moote] matter AR   311 for] before H   of] is of
AR   314 wyll] to AR   315 flee] fleye A, flie B   316 rufullye] ruthfullie B
317 ever I was] I was ever A, ever was I H   318 an] and ARBH
319 church] churches ARH   324 withowten] without A   325 woe ys]
woes AR   328 stynketh] stinckes A   329 maketh] make AR, marreth H
330 and] a A   of] after AR   335 poore] to pore B   such] much B
anoye] anye H   336 made] and made B   landes] land H   338 I] *om* H
my] was my B
C 9206   G g

both bodye and soule damned therebye
ever to the payne of hell.   340

44 Yett might not false purchase suffyce,
   but ofte I dealed with marchandyce;
   for there methought wyninge would ryse,
   I used yt manye a yeare.
   Ofte I sett upon false assyce,   345
   rayvinge poore with layinge myse.
   Falsely, by God and saynte Hyse
   a thousand tyme I sware.

45 Occurre I used wylfullye.
   Wanne I never so much therebye,   350
   to Holye Church never taythed I,
   for meethought that was lorne.

146ʳ   Why made thou me, lord, of nought? Whye?
        To worch in world so wickedlye
        and nowe burne in the dyvelles bellye?   355
        Alas, that ever I was borne!

Finitis lamentationibus mortuorum, [descendet] Jesus quasi in
nube, si fieri poterit, quia, secundum doctoris opiniones, in aere
prope terram judicabit Filius Dei. Stabunt angeli cum cruce,
corona spinea, lancea, et instrumentis aliis; ipsa demonstrant.

339 both] and H   341–8] *om* R   343 methought] ny thought B
345 sett] sitt B   346 rayvinge] ravening B   layinge] laynige A   347 and]
and by A   saynte] saintes BH   Hyse] his B   348 tyme] tymes A,
othes B, sythes H   sware] swore A   349–56] *in* R

        Why made thou me of naughte, lorde, why,
        to worke in worlde soe wickedly?
        To Holy Church never hyed I.
        Alas, that ever I was borne!
        Occoure I used willfully;   5
        wanne I never soe moch thereby—
        and now borne in the devills belly.
        Alas, alas, alas!

351 taythed] hyed A   353 lord of nought] of nought lord BH
354 wickedlye] wrechedlye A   355 burne] borne A   dyvelles] devill H
356 alas] alas alas A   *SD* mortuorum] mortuens R   descendet] descende
Hm, descendit AR   fieri] fiere A   poterit] potent R   quia] qua R
doctoris] doctori AR, doctorum BH   aere] quere AR, oerere B   spinea]
spina AR   et instrumentis aliis] et instrumentes aliis AR, aliisque instrumentis H   ipsa] ipse A, omnia H   demonstrant] demonstra dicat Jesus A,
demonstra R, demonstrantes BH

JESUS

46 You good and evell that here benne lent,
    here you come to your judgment,
    yf you wyst whereto hit would appent
    and in what manere.   360
    But all myne, as I have ment—
    prophettes, patriarches here present—
    must knowe my doome with good intent.
    Therefore I am nowe here.

47 But you shall heare and see expresse   365
    I doe to you all rightwysenes.
    Loovesome deedes more and lesse
    I wyll rehearse nowe here.
    Of yearth through mee made, man, thou was
    and putt in place of greate cleanes   370
    from which thou was, through wyckednes,
    away then wayved weare.

48 When thou had donne this trespasse,
    yett wayted I which way best was
    thee to recover in this case   375
    into my companye.
    Howe might I do thee more grace
    then that selfe kynd that thou hasse
    take—here nowe in this place
    appeareth appertlye—   380

49 after dyed on the roode-tree
    and my blood shedd, as thou may see,
    to pryve the devyll of his postie
    and wynne that was awaye;
    the which blood—behouldes yee—   385
    fleshe-houlden tell nowe I would should be

357 lent] blente AR   358 come] bene comen AR   your] *om* H
362 patriarches] patrickes A   363 with] in R   365 heare and see] see
and H   366 rightwysenes] rightiousnes ARBH   367 loovesome]
luxome AR   more] bouth more RB   371 from] rom A   was] hast H
372 away] aye A   then] they B, thou H   376 into] to AR   378 that]
om A   hasse] haste AR   379 nowe] nowe is A, now as BH   this] *om* H
380 appeareth] as appeareth A, as peareth R   383 pryve] depryve H
386 fleshe] freshe ARBH   tell] that AR, till BH   nowe I would should be]
I shall see AR

for certayne poyntes that lyked mee
of which I will nowe saye.

50 On cause was this, certeynlye,
that to my Father almightie   390
at my Assentyon offer might I
this blood, prayinge a boone:

146ᵛ   that hee of you should have mercye
and more gracyous be therebye
when you had synned horryblie,   395
not takinge vengeance to soone.

51 Also, I would, withowten were,
this bloodd should nowe be shewed here
that the Jewes dyd in this manere
might knowe appertlye   400
howe unkynd they them beare.
Behould on mee and you may lere
whether I be God in full powere
or elles man onlye.

52 Also, my blood nowe shewed ys   405
that good therebye maye have blys
that avoyded wyckednes, iwys,
and ever good workes wrought.
And evyll also, that dyd amysse,
must have greate sorrowe in sight of this   410
that lost that joye that was his
that him on roode-tree bought.

53 Yett, for all this greate torment
that suffered here while I was lent,
the more spared in your intent.   415
I am not as I feele.
For my bodye ys all torent
with othes false alwayes fervent;
noe lymme on mee but yt is lent
from head right to the heele.   420

387 lyked] liketh AR   389 this] this now B   391 I] *om* R   396 takinge]
taken B   397 withowten] without H   399 this] that A   401 unkynd]
unkindlye ARH   403 God] good B   406 blys] blesse A   407 avoyded]
awayved H   412 tree] *om* H   413 greate] *om* A   414 that] that I H
415 more] more I AR   419 on] of A   lent] rente AR, hent H

54 Nowe that you shall appertlye see
freshe blood bleede, man, for thee—
good to joye and full greate lee,
the evyll to damnatyon.
Behould nowe, all men! Looke on mee 425
and see my blood freshe owt flee
that I bleede on roode-tree
for your salvatyon.

Tunc emittet sanguinem de latere eius.

55 Howe durst you ever doe amys
when you unthought you of this, 430
that I bleede to bringe you to blys
and suffered such woo.
Me you must not white, iwysse,
though I doe nowe as right ys.
Therefore eych man reacon his, 435
for ryghtwysenes must goo.

147ʳ   PAPA SALVATUS

56 A, lord, though I lyved in synne,
in purgatorye I have [bene] in.
Suffer my bale for to blynne
and bringe mee to this blysse. 440

IMPERATOR SALVATUS

Yea, lord, and I have therein bee
more then three hundreth yeares and three.
Nowe I am cleane, forsake not mee,
although I dyd amysse.

422 man] om AR   424 the] om AR   425 looke] om ARBH   426 flee]
flye AR   427 bleede] blede AR, bled BH   SD emittet] emittitte A
sanguinem] sanguiene R   eius] eius et dicit A, eius et dicat R, suo H
430 unthought] unbethoughte AR, unthough H   431 bleede] blede AR,
bled BH   blys] blesse A   432 such] moche AR   435 man] one A
436 ryghtwysenes] rightiousnes ARBH   must] moste A   437 A]
O AR   438 bene] beeme Hm   440 this] thy H   blysse] blesse A
SALVATUS] SALVATOR A   441 I have therein] I theirin have AR, therin
have I H

REX SALVATUS

57 Lord, receyve me to thy grace 445
that payne hath suffered in this place.
Although I foule and wycked was,
washen yt ys awaye.

REGINA SALVATA

And I, lord, to thee crye and call,
thy owne christen and thy thrall, 450
that of my synnes am purged all,
of thy joye I thee praye.

JESUS

58 Come hither to mee, my dearlynges deare,
that blessed in world alwayse weare.
Take my realme, all in feare, 455
that for you ordayned ys.
For while I was on yearth here
you gave mee meate, in good manere;
therefore in heaven-blysse cleare
you shall ever lenge, iwysse. 460

59 In great thyrst you gave me drynke,
when I was naked also clothinge,
and when mee needed harboringe
you harbored me in cold.
And other deedes to my lykinge 465
you dyd on yearth there lyvinge.
Therefore you shall be quytte that thinge
in heaven an hundrethfold.

PAPA SALVATUS

60 Lord, on this can I not mynne:
earth when I was dwellinge in, 470
thee in myscheffe or any unwynne
to shewe such a will.

446 this] that AR   SALVATA] SALVATUS R   450 christen] thisten BH
451 am] are AR   452 of] f A   457 on] in AR   458 good] goad R
460 lenge] linge R, long B   461 great thyrst] Christ B   463 needed]
neadie B   467 that] this R   SALVATUS] SALVATA A   469 can I not]
cannot I R, I can not H   471 myscheffe] miserye R   472 shewe] shew
thie BH

IMPERATOR SALVATUS

Noe, syckerlye! I can have noe mynde
that ever to thee I was so kynd,
for there I might thee never fynd,   475
such kyndnes to fulfyll.

JESUS

61 Yes, forsoothe, my freindes deare,
    such as poore and naked weare,
    you cladd and fedd them both in feere
    and harbored them alsoe.   480
    Such as weare also in great dangere,
    in hard prysoun yn yearth here,
    you visited them in meeke mannere,
    all men in such woe.

62 Therefore, as I you ere tould,   485
    you shalbe quytt an hundrethfould.
    In my blysse, bee you bowld,
    evermore you shall bee.
    There neyther honger ys ney could
    but all thinges as yourselves would—   490
    everlastinge joye to yonge and old
    that in yearth pleased mee.

63 Therfore, my angelles, goe you anon
    and twyne my chosen everye one
    from them that have benne my foen   495
    and bringe them unto blysse.
    On my right hand they shall be sett,
    for soe full yore I them beheight
    when the dyd withowten lett
    my byddinge not amysse.   500

473 can] coulde A   474 kynd] unkinde B   475 I might thee never]
might I never thee H   479 fedd] feede A   482 yn] one A
483 meeke] like B   484 such] full B   485 you ere] ere yow B
489 ney] nye B   490 would] wou A   491 old] om A   493 you]
om A   494 everye one] everychon H   495 them] feble H   496 unto]
into ARBH   blysse] blesse A

PRIMUS ANGELUS

64 Lord, we shall never blynne
tyll we have brought them blys within,
those soules that benne withowten synne,
full soone, as you shall see.

SECUNDUS ANGELUS

And I knowe them well affyne   505
which bodyes, lord, that benne thyne.
The shall have joye withowten pyne
that never shall ended bee.

Tunc angeli ibunt ac cantabunt euntes ac venientes 'Letamini in
domino, salvator mundi, domine.' Ac omnes salvati eos sequentur;
postea veniunt demones, quorum dicat Primus.

DEMON PRIMUS

65 A, rightuouse judge, and most of might,
that there art sett to deeme the right,   510
mercye thou was, nowe ys gright,
to save these men from pyne.
148ʳ   Doe as thou hast yoare beheight.
Those that be synnfull in thy sight,
to reacon there deedes I am dight   515
to proove these men for myne.

66 Judge this pope myne in this place
that worthye ys for his trespace—
and ought to be thyne through grace—
through synne commynne myne.   520

PRIMUS ANGELUS] ANGELUS PRIMUS H   503 benne] are R   SECUNDUS
ANGELUS] ANGELUS SECUNDUS H   506 that] that have B   507 withowten]
without ARH   SD ibunt ac] om H   cantabunt] cantibunt AR   euntes]
emittes A, emittis R   domino] duo(?) A, domino vel H   domine] om AR
ac] tunc H   eos] omnes AB   sequentur] sequitur AR, sequntur B
veniunt] venient BH   dicat Primus] dicat Primus Demones A, dicat
Primus Demon R, Primus dicat H   DEMON PRIMUS] PRIMUS DEMON AR
510 deeme] judg B, dome H   514 those] thoes A, thes H   516 proove]
proves A   519 ought] made H   520 commynne myne] is commen
my hyne H

A christen man I wott hee was,
knewe good from evell in eych case,
but my commandment donne hee hase,
and ever forsaken thyne.

67 Through mercye hee should be thyne,   525
but myne through wyckednes and synne;
thyne through passion thou was in,
and myne through temptatyon.
To mee obedyent hee was aye,
and thy commandment put awaye.   530
Thou righteouse judge therefore I praye,
deeme him to my pryson.

68 This emperour also that standeth by,
I hould him myne full wytterlye,
that held him ever in heresye   535
and leeved not on thy lore.
Therefore I tell thee verament
myne hee ys withowt judgment.
Thou sayd, when thou on yearth went,
that leeved not, damned were.   540

'Qui non credit, jam judicatus est.'

69 This kinge and queene would never knowe
poore men, them almes to showe.
Therefore, put them all from you
that stand before thy face,
and I shall leade them tyll a lowe;   545
there fyre shall burne though no man blowe.
I have them tyed upon a rowe;
they shall never passe that place.

521 christen] christien ARB, chiristan H   I wott hee was] he was I
wotte A   522 knewe] newe A   523 but] t A   hase] hath B   524 and]
om A   525 through] h A   526 but myne] om A, but my B   wyckednes]
wretchednes H   527 thou] th A, that thou RBH   was in] om A, was is B
530 commandment] comaundmentes BH   536 leeved] lyved B   540 that]
all that H   leeved not] lyved B   Latin jam] om R   est] este A
545 a lowe] looe A   546 there] wher A   547 them tyed upon] tyed
them on H

SECUNDUS DEMON

70 Naye, I wyll spute with him this
that sytteth as high justice,   550
and yf I see he be righteous
soone I shall assaye.

148ᵛ   And other he shall, forsooth iwysse,
forsake that of him wrytten ys
or these men that have donne amysse,   555
deeme them us todaye.

71 These wordes, God, thou sayde expresse,
as Matthewe thereof bayreth wyttnes,
that right as mans deedes was
yeelden hee should bee.   560
And, lest thou forgett, good man,
I shall mynne thee upon,
for speake Latten well I can,
and that thou shall soone see.

'Filius hominis venturus est in gloria Patris, Patris sui cum angelis
suis, et tunc reddit unicuiquam secundum opus suum.'

72 Therefore, righteouse yf thou bee,   565
these men are myne, as mote I thee,
for on good deede here before thee
have they not to shewe.
Yf there bee anye, saye on! Lettes see!
Yf there be nonne, deeme them to mee;   570
or elles thou art as false as wee—
all men shall well knowe.

DEMON PRIMUS

73 Yea, this thou sayd, verament,
that when thou came to judgment

SECUNDUS DEMON] DEMON SECUNDUS H   549 spute] pute A, put R   this]
thus B   553 other] eyther H   554 that] om A   556 us] to us A, as B
557 thou] then R   558 bayreth] beare A   559 deedes] deed H
560 yeelden] helden AR   Latin hominis] omnes AR   venturus] ventrus
A, ventras R   gloria] om A   Patris Patris] Patris ARBH   angelis] angelus
AR   et tunc] om A   reddit] reddet H   unicuiquam] unicuique B   opus
suum] o A, opus R   566 I thee] om A   567 here] om B   before thee]
om A   569 yf] om A   lettes] lett BH   570 yf] om A   571 as(1)] om A
572 shall] it shall B   DEMON PRIMUS] PRIMUS DEMON AR   574 came] come R

thy angelles from thee should be sent 575
to put the evyll from the good
and put them into great torment,
there reemynge and grennynge verey fervent;
which wordes to clearkes here present
I wyll rehearse. 580

'Sic erit in consummatione seculi: exibunt angeli et [seperabunt]
malos de medio justorum, et mittent eos in caminum ignis, ubi
erit fletus et stridor dentium.'

74 Therefore delyver mee these men
and, as broke I my panne,
I shall make them to grynne
and rufullye to reeme.
And in as whott a chimneye 585
as ys ordayned for mee
bathed they all shalbee
in bitter bale and brenne.

149ʳ 75 This popelard pope here present
with covetousenes was aye fullye bent. 590
This emperour also, verament,
to all synne did enclyne.
This kinge also all righteouse men shent,
damned them through false judgment
and dyed so withowt amendment; 595
therefore I hould him myne.

76 This queene, while shee was lyvinge here,
spared never synne, in no mannere,
and all that myght, by Mahound so dere,
excyte her lecherye 600

575 angelles] angell R   thee] they B   576 put] part BH   from the]
for H   578 there] ther is Λ, wher H   reemynge] weeping B   and] om
ARBH   grennynge] greminge AR, grynnyng BH   verey fervent] veramente
AR, were fervent H   580 rehearse] rehearse nowe heare AR, reherse by
the rode BH   SD seculi] seculis A   seperabunt] sperabunt HmAR   malos]
males AR   justorum] justus A   eos] omnes A   erit] erat H   fletus]
flectus AR   dentium] dentum A   581 mee] om ARBH   these] thse H
men] men heine A, men home R, men hime B, men hence H   582 panne]
penne H   584 and] om A   reeme] crye AR   585-8] om A
587 bathed] baked B   they all shalbee] all they shalbe B, all shall they be H
588 and] to H   brenne] brune B   590 was aye] was ever A, aye was H
593-6] om A   593 all] om R

shee used, mans harte to styrre,
and thereto fullye ordayned her.
Therefore shee hath lost her lure,
heaven-blysse, right as dyd I.

JESUS

77 Loe, you men that wycked have benne,   605
   what Sathan sayth you heren and seene.
   Rightuouse doome may you not fleene,
   for grace ys put awaye.
   When tyme of grace was endurynge,
   to seeke yt you had no lykinge.   610
   Therefore must I, for anythinge,
   doe rightuousenes todaye.

78 And though my sweete mother deare
   and all the sayntes that ever were
   prayed for you right nowe here,   615
   all yt were to late.
   Noe grace may growe through theire prayere.
   Then rightuousenes had no powere.
   Therefore, goe to the fyre in feere.
   There gaynes noe other grace.   620

79 When I was hungrye and thyrstie both,
   and naked was, you would not mee clothe;
   also, sycke and in greate woe,
   you would not vysytt mee;
   nor yett in pryson to me come,   625
   nor of your meate to gyve me somee,
   nor mee to your harboure nome
   never yett in wyll were yee.

602 thereto fullye ordayned] fullie ordeyned therto B   603 her] a H
604 heaven] hevens B   605 loe] *om* A   606 what] *om* A   heren]
heare ARH   607 rightuouse] ous A   doome] deme B   fleene] flye H
608 for grace] ace A   609 when tyme] me A   endurynge] deweringe A
610 to seeke yt] *om* A   611 therefore] *om* A   I] *om* A   612 doe
rightuousenes] nesse to A   todaye] this daye B   613–*Finis*] *om* A
613 though] thou H   617 growe] goe RBH   620 noe] none H
623 in] *om* H   626 to] *om* H   somee] some RBH

PAPA DAMNATUS

80 When was thou naked or harborlesse,
    hongrye, thyrstie, or in sycknes;   630
    eyther in any prysoun was?
    Wee sawe thee never a-could.

IMPERATOR DAMNATUS

Hadd we thee hungrye or thyrstie seene,
naked, sycke, or in prysoun benne,
harborlesse or in anye teene,   635
have harbored thee we would.

JESUS

81 Naye! When you sawe the leaste of myne
    that on yearth suffered pyne,
    with your rychesse you would not ryne
    ney fulfill my desyre.   640
    And syth you would nothinge enclyne
    for to helpe my poore lyne,
    to mee your love yt was not fyne.
    Therefore, goe to the fyre!

PRIMUS DEMON

82 A, syr judge, this goeth aright.   645
    By Mahound mych of might,
    you bee myne, eych wyght,
    ever to lyve in woe.
    A dowlefull death to you ys dight,
    for such hyre I you beheight   650
    when you served me daye and night,
    to be rewarded soe.

83 Goe we forthe to hell in hye.
    Withowt end there shall you lye,
    for you have loste—right as did I—   655
    the blysse that lasteth ever.

---

632 sawe] see B   635 teene] other teene H   636 thee] they B
639 ryne] then relieve B, them ryne H   642 lyne] lyve B, hyne H
PRIMUS DEMON] DEMON PRIMUS BH   650 I] as I R   655 right as]
as righte R

Judged you be to my bellye
there endles sorrowe ys and noye.
One thinge I tell you truelye—
delyvered benne you never. 660

DEMON SECUNDUS

84 Naye, maister, forgett not these theves two,
for, by Mahound, the shall not goe!
Theire deedes, lord, amonge moe,
soone I can them spye.
This justice, lord, was ever thy foe, 665
but falsehood to further hee was ever throo.
Therefore deeme him to sorrowe and woe,
for hee ys full well worthye.

150ʳ 85 This marchant also that standeth here,
hee ys myne, withowten were. 670
As oftetymes hee him forswere
as seedes be in my secke.
And occurre also used hee
that my powche ys so heavye,
I sweare by Mahound so free, 675
hit well-nye breakes my necke.

Tunc demones exportabunt eos, et venient quatuor evangelistae.

MATTHEUS

86 I, Matthewe, of this beare wytnes,
for in my gospell I wrotte expresse
this that my lord of his goodnesse
hath rehearsed here. 680
And by mee all were warned before
to save theire soules evermore
that nowe through lykinge the benne lore
and damned to fyre in feare.

658 noye] nye R, anoy H   DEMON SECUNDUS] SECUNDUS DEMON R
661 two] to B   664 soone] some B   can] came B   666 but] *om* R
667 deeme] dome H   669 standeth] staneth H   here] by here R
671 tymes] tyme H   *SD* quatuor] *om* H   evangelistae] evangele R,
evangeliste B   MATTHEUS] MATHEAS R   682 evermore] for evermore
RBH   683 lykinge] lyvinge H

MARCUS

87 I, Marke, nowe appartlye saye   685
    that warned they were by manye a waye
    theire lyvinge how the should araye,
    heaven-blysse to recover;
    so that excuse them they ne maye
    that they benne worthye, in good faye,   690
    to suffer they doome given todaye
    and damned to be ever.

LUCAS

88 And I, Luke, on yearth lyvinge,
    my lordes workes in everyethinge
    I wrote and taught through my cunnynge   695
    that all men knowe might.
    And therefore I saye, forsooth iwys,
    excusation none there ys.
    Agaynst my talkinge they dyd amysse.
    This donne, yt goeth aright.   700

JOHANNES

89 And I, John the Evangeliste,
    beare wytnes of thinges that I wyste
    to which they might full well have truste
    and not have donne amysse.
    And all that ever my lord sayth here,   705
    I wrote yt in my mannere.
    Therfore, excuse you, withowten were,
    I may not well, iwysse.

Finis

MARCUS] MARKE R   685 nowe] *om* R   686 a] *om* R   689 they ne]
non R   691 they] the RBH   692 and] *om* R   ever] for ever RBH
LUCAS] LUKE R   694 workes] words H   698 none there] ther non B
699 agaynst] truste R   700 donne] dome RBH   aright] righte R
703 to] *om* R   705 sayth] sayde R   706 in] all in H

APPENDIX I A

The Raven-and-Dove Scene in Play III (Noah's Flood)

[After the Stage Direction following 260, H has forty-eight lines not present in the Group-manuscripts. Noah is speaking.]

1   Now 40 dayes are fullie gone.
    Send a raven I will anone,
    if ought-where earth, tree, or stone
    be drye in any place.
    And if this foule come not againe,   5
    it is a signe, soth to sayne,
    that drye it is on hill or playne,
    and God hath done some grace.

Tunc dimittet corvum, et capiens columbam in manibus, dicat:

2   Ah, lord, wherever this raven be,
    somewhere is drye, well I see;   10
    but yet a dove, by my lewtye,
    after I will sende.
    Thou wilt turne againe to me,
    for of all fowles that may flye
    thou art most meke and hend.   15

Tunc emittet columbam; et erit in nave aliam columbam ferens olivam in ore, quam dimittet aliquis ex malo per funem in manibus Noe; et postea dicat Noe:

3   Ah, lord, blessed be thou aye,
    that me hast comfort thus today.
    By this sight I may well saye
    this flood beginnes to cease.
    My sweete dove to me brought hase   20
    a branch of olyve from some place.
    This betokeneth God has done us some grace,
    and is a signe of peace.

16^r   4 Ah, lord, honoured most thou be;
           all earthe dryes now I see.   25
           But yet tyll thou comaunde me,
           hence will I not hye.
           All this water is awaye.
           Therfore, as sone as I maye,
           sacryfice I shall doe in faye   30
           to thee devoutlye.

                        DEUS

       5 Noe, take thy wife anone,
           and thy children every one;
           out of the shippe thou shalt gone,
           and they all with thee.   35
           Beastes and all that can flie,
           out anone they shall hye,
           on earth to grow and multeplye.
           I will that yt be soe.

                        NOE

       6 Lord, I thanke the through thy mighte;   40
           thy bydding shall be done in height.
           And, as fast as I may dighte,
           I will doe the honoure
           and to thee offer sacrifice.
           Therfore comes in all wise,   45
           for of these beastes that bene hise,
           offer I will this stower.

Tunc egrediens archam cum tota familia sua, accipiet animalia
sua et volucres et offeret ea et mactabit.

APPENDIX Iᴮ

The Whole of Play V in MS. H

23ᵛ   Pagina Quinta: de Mose et Rege Balaak et Balaam
Propheta. The Cappers.

DEUS

1 Moyses, my servaunte life and dere,
and all the people that be here,
you wott in Egipte when you were
out of thralldome I you broughte.
I wyll you honour no God save me   5
ne mawmentrye none make yee.
My name in vayne myn not yee
for that me lykes naughte.

2 I will you hold your holy daye
and worshipp also by all waye   10
father and mother all that you maye,
and slaye no man nowhere.
Fornication you shall flee.
No mens goodes steale yee,
ne in no place abyde ne bee   15
falce wytnes for to beare.

3 Your neightboures wyves covettes noughte,
servant ne good that he hath boughte,
oxe ne asse, in deede ne thoughte,
nor anythinge that is his,   20
ne wrongefullie to have his thinge
agayne his will and his lykinge.
In all these doe my byddinge,
that you doe not amisse.

Tunc Princeps Sinagogae statuet eum in loco, et quasi pro populo
loquatur ad dominum et Moysen.

PRINCEPS SINAGOGAE

4 Ah, good lord, much of mighte,   25
thou comes with so great lighte;

we bene so afraide of this sighte,
no man dare speak ne looke.
God is so grym with us to deale;
but Moyses, master, with us thou mele; 30
els we dyen many and feele,
so afrayde bene all wee.

Tunc Moyses stans super montem loquatur ad populum.

MOYSES

5 Gods folke, drede you noughte.
To prove you with God hath this wrought,
to make you afrayd in deede and thoughte, 35
aye for to avoyde synne.
By this sight you may now see
that he is pereles of postye.
Therfore his teachinge look done yee,
thereof that you not blyn. 40

24ʳ PRINCEPS SINAGOGAE

6 Ah, highe lord God almighte,
that Moyses shynes wondrous bright.
I may no way for great lighte
now looke upon hym.
And horned he semes in our sighte. 45
Sith he came to the hyll, dight
our lawe he hase I hope aright,
for was he never so grym.

MOYSES

7 You, Gods folke of Israell,
harkens to me that loven heale. 50
God bade you sholde doe everye deale
as that I shall saye.
Six dayes boldelye worches all;
the seaventh 'sabaoth' you shall call.
That daye for ought that may befall 55
hallowed shalbe aye.

8 That doth not this deede, deade shall be;
in houses fire shall no man see.

First fruytes to God offer yee,
for so hymselfe bade. 60
Gould and silver offers also,
purple bisse and other moe,
to hym that shall save you from woe
and helpe you in your neede.

EXPOSITOR

9 Lordinges, this comaundment 65
was of the old testamente,
and yet is used with good entent
with all that good bene.
This storye all if we shold fong,
to playe this moneth it were to longe. 70
Wherfore most frutefull there amonge
we taken, as shall be sene.

10 Also, we read in this storie:
God in the mownt of Synai
toke Moises these comaundmentes verelye 75
wrytten with his owne hande
in tables of ston, as reade I.
But when men honoured mawmentry,
he brake them in anger hastelye,
for that he wold not wonde. 80

11 But afterward sone—leeve ye me—
other tables of stone made he
in which God bade wrytten shold be
his wordes that were before.
24ᵛ   The which tables shryned were 85
after as God can Moyses leare;
and that shryne to them was deare
thereafter evermore.

Tunc Moyses descendet de monte, et ex altera parte montis dicet
rex Balaac equitando.

BALAACK REX

12 I Balaack, king of Moab land,
all Israell I had it in my hand. 90

I am so wroth I wold not wond
to slaye them ech wighte.
For their God helpes them stiflye
of other landes to have mastrye
that it is bootles witterlie   95
against them for to fighte.

13 What nation soever dose them noye,
Moyses prayes anone in hye;
therefore have they sone the victorie
and other men they have the worse.   100
Therfore, how I will wroken be
I have unthought me, as mot I the:
Balaam, I will, shall come to me,
that people for to curse.

14 For sworde ne knife may not avayle   105
these ilke shroes for to assaile.
That fowndes to fight, he shall faile,
for sicker is hym no boote.
All nations they doe any,
and myselfe they can destroie,   110
as ox that gnawes biselie
the grasse right to the roote.

15 Whoso Balaam blesses, iwis,
blessed sickerlie that man is;
whoso he curses fareth amisse,   115
such loos over all hase he.
Therfore goe fetch hym, bachler,
that he may curse the people here.
For sicker on them in no manner
mon we not wroken be.   120

MILES

16 Syr, on your errand I will gone.
Yt shall be well done, and that anone,
for he shall wreak you on your fone,
the people of Israell.

BALAACK

Yea, looke thou het hym gold great wone   125
and riches for to lyve upon
to destroy them if he can,
the freakes that be so fell.

Tunc ibit ad Balaam.

25ʳ   MILES

17 Balaam, my lorde greetes well thee
and prays the right sone at hym to be,   130
to curse the people of Judy
that do hym great anoye.

BALAAM

Forsooth I tell the, bacheler,
that I may have no power
but if Gods will were;   135
that shall I witt in hye.

DEUS (in supremo loco)

18 Balaam, I comaund the
king Balaak his bydding that thou flee.
That people that is blessed of me
curse thou not by no waye.   140

BALAAM

Lord, I must doe thy byddinge
thoughe it be to me unlykeing,
for truly much wynninge
I might have had todaye.

DEUS

19 Thoughe the folke be my foe   145
thou shalt have leave thydder to goe.
But looke that thou doe right soe
as I have thee taughte.

BALAAM

Lord, it shall be done in height.
This asse shall beare me aright.   150
Goe we together anone, sir knight,
for now leave I have coughte.

Tunc equitabunt versus regem, et eundo dicat Balaam:

20 Now by the law I leve upon,
    sith I have leave for to gone,
    they shalbe cursed every one   155
    and I ought wyn maye.
    If Balaak hold that he has heighte,
    Gods hest I set at light.
    Warryed they shalbe this night
    or that I wend awaye.   160

Tunc Angelus obviabit Balaam cum gladio extracto in manu, et
stabit asina.

21 Goe forth, Burnell; goe forth, goe!
    What the dyvell? My asse will not goe.
    Served me she never soe.
    What sorrow so her dose nye?
    Rise up, Burnell, make thee bowne   165
    and helpe to beare me out the towne,
    or—as brok I my crowne—
    thou shalt full sore abye.

25ᵛ Tunc percutiet asinam, et loquetur aliquis in asina.

ASINA

22 Maister, thou dost evell witterly,
    so good an ass as me to nye.   170
    Now hast thou beaten me thry,
    that beare the thus aboute.

BALAAM

Burnell, whye begiles thou me
when I have most nede to the?

ASINA

That sight that I before me see   175
makes me downe to lowte.

23 Am I not, maister, thyne owne ass
that ever before ready was
to beare the whether thou woldest pas?
To smyte me now yt is shame.   180
Thou wottest well, master, pardy,
thou haddest never ass like to me,
ne never yet thus served I thee.
Now I am not to blame.

Tunc Balaam videns Angelum evaginatum gladium habentem
adorans dicat.

BALAAM

24 Ah, lord, to thee I make avowe   185
I had no sight of thee erre now.
Lyttle wist I it was thou
that feared my asse soe.

ANGELUS

Why hast thou beaten thy ass thry?
Now I am comen thee to nye,   190
that changes thy purpose falcelye
and woldest be my foe.

25 And the ass had not downe gone,
I wold have slayne thee here anone.

BALAAM

Lord, have pittye me upon,   195
for sinned I have sore.
Is it thy will that I forth goe?

ANGELUS

Yea, but looke thou doe this folk no woe
otherwise then God bade thee tho
and saide to thee before.   200

Tunc Balaam et Miles ibunt. Balaack venit in obviam.

BALAACK

26 Ah, welcome, Balaam my frend,
for all myne anguish thou shalt end
if that thy will be to wend
and wreake me of my foe.

BALAAM

Nought may I speake, so have I win,   205
but as God puttes me in
to forby all and my kin.
Therfore sure me is woe.

26ʳ   BALAACK

27 Come forth, Balaam; come with me.
For on this hill, so mot I thee,   210
the folke of Israell thou shalt see
and curse them, I thee praye.
Thou shalt have riches, golde and fee,
and I shall advance thy dignitye
to curse men—cursed they may be—   215
that thou shalt see today.

Tunc adducens secum Balaam in montem et ad australem partem
respiciens, dicat ut sequitur:

BALAAM

28 How may I curse them in this place,
the people that God blessed hase?
In them is both might and grace,
and that is alwayes seene.   220
Wytnes I may none beare
against God that this can were,
his people that no man may deare
ne troble with no teene.

29 I saye these folkes shall have their will,   225
that no nation shall them gryll;
the goodnes that they shall fulfill
nombred may not be.

Their God shall them kepe and save.
No other repreve may I not have; 230
but such death as they shall have
I praye God send me.

BALAACK

30 What the devilles eyles the, poplart?
Thy speach is not worth a fart!
Doted I wot well thou art, 235
for woodlie thou hast wrougt.
I bade thee curse them every one
and thou blest them blood and bone.
To this north syde thou shalt anon,
for here thy deed is nought. 240

Tunc adducet eum ad borealem partem.

BALAAM

31 Herken, Balaack, what I say:
God may not gibb by no waye;
that he saith is veray,
for he may not lye.
To bless his folk he me sent; 245
therfore I saie, as I am kent,
that in this land verament
is used no mawmentry.

32 To Jacobs blood and Israell
God shall send joy and heale; 250
and as a lyon in his weale
Christ shalbe haunsed hye,
26ᵛ and rise also in noble araye
as a prynce to wyn great paye,
overcome his enemyes, as I say, 255
and them bowndly bye.

BALAACK

33 What the devill is this? Thou cursest them naught
nor blessest them nether, as me thought.

BALAAM

Syr kinge, this I thee beheight
or that I come here. 260

BALAACK

Yet shalt thou to another place,
ther Gods power for to embrace.
The dyvell geve the hard grace
but thou doe my prayer.

Ad occidentale partem.

BALAAM

34 Ah, lord, that here is fayre wonning: 265
halls, chambers of great lyking,
valleyes, woodes, grass springing,
fayre yordes, and eke rivers.
I wot well God made all this,
his folke to lyve in joye and blisse. 270
That warryeth them, warried is;
that blessest them, to God is deare.

BALAACK

35 Popelard, thou preachest as a pie;
the devill of hell thee destroy!
I bade thee curse myne enemye; 275
therfore thou came me to.
Now hast thou blessed them here thry
for the nones me to nye.

BALAAM

So tould I the before twye
I might none other doe. 280

BALAACK

36 Out, alas, what dyvell ayles thee?
I have het thee gold and fee
to speake but wordes two or three,
and thou makes much distance.

Yet once I will assay thee, 285
if any boote of bale will be;
and if thou falcely now faile me,
Mahound geve thee mischance.

Tunc Balaam ad caelum respiciens prophetando.

BALAAM

Orietur stella ex Jacob, et exurget homo de Israell et confringet
omnes duces alieginarum, et erit omnis terra possessio eius.

37 Now one thinge I will tell you all,
hereafter what shall befall: 290
a starre of Jacob springe shall,
a man of Israell.

27^r He shall overcome and have in band
all kinges, dukes of strang land;
and all the world have in his hand 295
as lord to dight and deale.

ESAYAS

38 I saye a mayden meeke and mylde
shall conceave and beare a childe,
cleane without workes wilde,
to wyn mankinde to wayle. 300
Butter and hony shall be his meate
that he may all evill foryeat,
our soules out of hell to get—
and called Emanuell.

EXPOSITOR

39 Lordinges, these wordes are so veray 305
that exposition, in good faye,
none needes; but you know may
this word 'Emanuell.'
'Emanuell' is as much to saye
as 'God with us night and day.' 310
Therfore that name for ever and aye
to his Sonne cordes wondrous well.

Vidi portam in domo domini clausam et dixit angelus ad me:
'Porta haec non aperietur sed clausa erit' etct. Ezechiel. Capitulo 2.

EZECHIELL

40 I, Ezechiell, sothlie see
   a gate in Gods house on hye.
   Closed it was; no man came nye.   315
   Then told an angell me:
   "This gate shall no man open, iwis,
   for God will come and goe by this.
   For himself it reserved is;
   none shall come there but hee.'   320

EXPOSITOR

41 By this gate, lords, verament
   I understand in my intent
   that way the Holy Ghost in went
   when God tooke flesh and bloode
   in that sweet mayden Mary.   325
   Shee was that gate wytterly,
   for in her he light graciouslie,
   mankind to doe good.

JHEREMIA

Deducunt oculi mei lacrimas per diem et noctem, et non taceant;
contritione magna contrita est virgo filia populi mei et plaga etct.

42 My eyes must run and sorrow aye
   without ceasing night and daye,   330
   for my daughter, soth to saye,
   shall suffer great anye.
27ᵛ   And my folke shall due in faye
   thinges that they ne know may
   to that mayden by many waye   335
   and her sonne sickerlie.

EXPOSITOR

43 Lordinges, this prophesie iwis
   touches the Passion, nothing amisse.
   For the prophet see well this,
   what shall come, as I reade: 340

that a childe borne of a maye
shall suffer death, sooth to saye,
and they that mayden shall afray,
have vengeance for that deede.

JONAS

Clamam de tribulacone mea ad dominum et exaudivit; de ventre
inferi clamavi et exaudisti vocem meam et projecisti me.

44 I, Jonas, in full great any 345
to God I prayed inwardlie.
And he me hard through his mercy
and on me did his grace.
In myddes the sea cast was I
for I wrought inobedyentlie. 350
But in a whalles bellye
three dayes saved I was.

EXPOSITOR

45 Lordinges, what this may signifie
Christ expoundes apertelie,
as we reade in the Evangely 355
that Christ himself can saie.
Right as Jonas was dayes three
in wombe of whall, so shall he be
in earth lyinge—as was he—
and rise the third daye. 360

DAVID

De summo caelo egressio eius, et occisus eius ad sumum eius.
Psal.

46 I, Davyd, saie that God almighte
from the highest heaven to earth will light,
and thidder againe with full might
both God and man in feare,
and after come to deeme the righte. 365
May no man shape them of his sight,
ne deeme that to mankind is dighte;
but all then must apeare.

EXPOSITOR

47 Lordes, this speach is so veray
    that to expound it to your paye   370
    it needes nothing, in good faye;
    this speach is so expresse.
28ʳ Each man by it knowe may
    that of the Ascention, soth to saie,
    David prophesied in his daye   375
    as yt rehearsed was.

JOELL

Effundam de spiritu meo super omnem carnem, et prophetabunt
filii vestri.

48 I, Joell, saie this sickerlye,
    that my ghost send will I
    upon mankinde merciably
    from heaven, sitting in see.   380
    Then shold our childer prophesie,
    ould men meet sweens wytterly;
    yong se sightes that therby
    many wise shall be.

EXPOSITOR

49 Lordinges, this prophet speakes here   385
    in Gods person, as it were,
    and prophesies that he will apeare
    ghostlie to mankinde.
    This signes non other, in good faye,
    but of his deede on Whitsonday,   390
    sending his Ghost, that we ever may
    on hym have sadlie mynd.

MICHEAS

Tu, Bethlem, terra Juda nequaquam minima es in principibus
Juda; ex te enim exiet dux, qui reget populum meum Israell.

50 I, Micheas, through my mynde
    will saye that man shall sothlie finde:
    that a childe of kinges kinde   395
    in Bethlem shall be borne

that shall be duke to dight and deale
and rule the folke of Israell;
also wyn againe mankindes heale
that through Adam was lorne.   400

EXPOSITOR

51 Lordinges, two thinges apertlie
you may see in this prophesie:
the place certefies thee sothlie
where Christ borne will be;
and after his ending sickerlie   405
of his deedes of great mercy,
that he shold sit soveraynly
in heaven, thereas is he.

52 Moe prophetes, lordinges, we might play,
but yt wold tary much the daye.   410
Therfore six, sothe to say,
are played in this place.
Twoo speakes of his Incarnation,
another of Christes Passion;
the fourth of the Resurrection   415
in figure of Jonas.

53 The fifte speakes expreslie
how he from the highest heaven hye
light into earth us to forby,
and after thydder steigh   420
with our kinde to heaven-blisse.
More love might he not shew, iwis;
but right thereas hymselfe is
he haunshed our kinde on high.

54 The sixt shewes, you may see,   425
his Goste to man send will he,
more stidfast that they shalbe
to love God evermore.
Thus that—beleven—that leven we
of Gods deedes, that had pittye   430
one man when that he made them free,
is prophesied here before.

28ᵛ

BALAACK

55 Goe we forth; it is no boote
longer with this man to moote.
For God of Jewes is crop and roote,   435
and lord of heaven and hell.
Now see I well no man on lyve
gaynes with him for to shryve.
Therefore here, as mot I thryve,
I will no longer dwell.   440

EXPOSITOR

56 Lordinges, much more matter
is in this story then you see here.
But the substance, without were,
is played you beforne.
And by these prophesies, leav you me,   445
three kinges, as you shall played see,
presented at his Nativitye
Christ when he was borne.

Finis

APPENDIX Ic

The Final Section of Play XVIA in H

[Instead of Hm's lines 360–479, H has the following lines:]

CENTURIO

1 Lordings, I say you sickerly
that we have wrought wilfully,
for I know by the prophesy
that Gods Sonne is he.
Therfore, sirs, very ferd am I   5
to hear this noyce and this crye.
I am ashamed, verely,
this uncooth sight to see.

CAYPHAS

2 Centurio, as God me speed,
peace, and speak not of that dede, 10
for of him thou getts no meede!
What needes the so to say?
But Longeus, take this spear in hand;
to pearce his hart look thou ne wand.

LONGEUS

A, lord, I see neithe sea nor land 15
this seven year, in good fay.

90^r   FOURTH JEW

3 Take this spear and take good heede,
and do as the bishopp thee badd—
a thing that is great need.
To wonne I hould thee wood. 20

LONGEUS

I will do as you bydd me,
but on your perill it shall be.
What I doe I may not see,
wher it be ill or good.

4 High king of heaven, I call thee here. 25
What I have done well wott I near,
but on my handes and on my spear
whott water runnes ther-throe;
and on my eyes some can fall
that I may se you, some and all. 30
A, lord, wherever be the wall
that this water came froo?

Tunc sursum aspiat.

5 Alas, alas, and weale-away!
What dede have I done today?
A man I see, sooth to say, 35
I have slayne in this affray.

But this I hope very Christ be
that sick and blynd through his pitty
hath healed before in this citty
as thou has done me today.   40

6 Thee will I serve and with thee be,
for well I leeve in days three
thou wilt ryse through thy posty
and save that on thee call.

JOSEPH AB ARAMATHEA

7 A, lord God! What harts have ye   45
to slay this man that I now se?
Vengeanc uppon you, witterly
I warrand, sone shall fall.
Alas! How should I be mery
to se his body fayr and fre   50
all totorne upon a tree,
that was so principall?

90ᵛ   8 Nichodemus, sir, both you and I
have cause to worship him witterly
and his body glorifye,   55
for Gods Sonne he is.
Therfor, goe we by and hye
and worshim him devoutly,
for we may therwith, perdy,
win us heaven-blisse.   60

NICHODEMUS

9 Joseph, I leeve this sickerly,
that he is Gods Sonne almighty.
To aske of Pylate his body—
and buryed it shall be—
I shall help thee witterly   65
to take him downe devoutly,
though Cayphas goe wood therby
and eke also his meny.

JOSEPH AB ARA.

10 To Pilate, brother, will we gone,
   you and I togeather alone,   70
   to ask his body of our fone,
   if that it be thy read.
   A sepulchre, I wott, ther is one,
   well graved in a stonne.
   He shall be buryed, flesh and bone,   75
   his body that is dead.

Tunc venint simul ad Pilatum et Joseph flectando dicat:

11 Ben a voose, Sir Pilate, in hye!
   As you sitt in your sea
   a boone graunt for charity
   to my brother and me.   80
   The body of my lord, messy,
   that you neiled on a tree,
   graunt us, lord, in suffraynty,
   and buryed it shall be.

PILATUS

12 Joseph, I tell thee without nay,   85
   that body thou shalt have today;
   but let me know, I thee pray,
   whether his lyfe be gone.
   Hark, Centurio! Is Jesus dead?

CENTURIO

   Yea, sir, as ever break I bread,   90
   in him is no lyfe lead
   nor never a whole vayne.

PILATUS

13 Joseph, then take him to thee.
   Goes and let him buryed be.
   But look thou make no sigaldry   95
   to rayse him up agayne.

JOSEPH

Grauntmercy, sir of dignity.
You need not for to warn it me,
for ryse he will of his posty
and make us all full fayne.   100

Tunc ibunt pariter super montem.

14 A, swet Jesu, Jesu, swet Jesu,
that thou must dye full well thou knewe.
Lord, thou graunt us grace and vertue
to serve the in our lyfe,
that they to thy blisse renew,   105
all that ever to thee be true;
for emperour, kinge, knight ne Jew,
with thee they dare not stryve.

NICODEMUS

15 Sir Josephe, brother, as well I se,
this holy prophett is geven to thee.   110
Some worship he shall have of me,
that is of might most.
For as I leev by my luteye,
very Gods Sonne is he,
for very sightis men may se   115
when that he yeeld the ghost.

16 For the sonne lost his light;
earthquake made men afright;
the roch that never had cleft
did cleev then as men dyd know;   120
sepulchrs opened in mens sight;
dead men rysen ther by night.
I may say he is God almight,
such signes that can show.

17 Therfor brought here have I   125
an hundreth pownd of spicery.
Mirhe, aloes, and many mo therby
to honour him will I bringe,

for to balme his swete body,
in sepulchre for to lye;   130
that he may have on me mercy
when he in heaven is kinge. Amen.

Finis

APPENDIX ID

The Final Scene of Play XVIII in H and R

[After Hm 432, H and R have the following lines. H is used here as base.]

Tunc veniet Jesus alba indutus baculumque crucis manibus portans; et Maria Magdalena venienti sit obviam dicens

JHESUS

1 Why wepest thou, woman? Tell me why.
Whom seekst thou so tenderly?

MARIA MAG.

My lord, sir, was buryed hereby
and now he is away.
If thou hast done me this anye,   5
tell me, leife sir, hastely
anone this ilk day.

JHESUS

2 Woman, is not thy name Marye?

MARIA MAGDA.

A, lord, I aske the mercy.

Variants in MS. R: SD] Then cometh Jesus with a robe about hym and a crosse-staffe in his hande; and Mary Magdelena appeared unto hym in the dawninge of the day; and Jesus shall say to her   1 wepest] reamest
2 whom] and whom   seekst thou] thou seekest   5 hast] have
me] hym   9 the] om

JHESUS

Mary, touche not my body   10
for yet I have not beene
with my Father almighty;
but to my brethren goe thou in hye
and of this thing thou certify
that thou hast soothly seen.   15

3 Say to them all that I will gone
to my Father that I came from
and ther Father—he and I all one.
Hye! Looke that thou ne dwell.

MARIA MAGDA.

A! Bee thou blessed ever and oe.   20
Now wayved is all my woe.
This is joy to them and other moe.
Anone I will goe tell.

It Maria Magda. ad Mariam Jacobi et ad Mariam Solome.

MARIA MAGDA.

4 Ah, women, wayle now wonnen is.
My lord Jesu is rysen iwys.   25
With him I spake a little or this
and saw him with mync eye.
My bale is torned into blisse.
Mirth in mynd ther may none mysse,
for hee badc warne that was his   30
to heven that he would flee.

MARIA JACOBI

5 A, sister, goe we search and see
whether these wordes sooth bee.
No mirth were halfe so much to me
to see him in this place.   35

12 with] at   16 to] om   18 he and I all one] he is alsoe   20 bee
thou blessed] blessed be thou   oe] oye   SD] Here Marye Magdelen
goeth to Mary Jacobi and to Mary Salome sayinge   27 saw] see   eye]
eyes   28 blisse] bles   31 flee] stea   MARIA] MARYE   32 search]
seeke

MARIA SALOM

A, sister, I besech thee
with full mynd wynde we,
for fayne methinkes me list to fly
to see his fayre face.

Tunc ibunt mulieres et veniet obviam illis Jesus dicens.

JHESUS

6 All hayle, women, all hayle!   40

101ᵛ   MARIA JACOBI

A, lord, we leeven without fayle
that thou art rysen us to heale
and wayved us from woe.

MARIA SOLOM

A, welcome be thou, my lord sweet!
Lett us kisse thy blessed feete   45
and handle thy woundes that be so weet,
or that we hence goe.

JHESUS

7 Be not afrayd, women, of me,
but to my brethren now wend yee
and bydd them goe to Galelye;   50
ther meet with me they mon.

MARIA JACOBI

Anon, lord, done it shall be.
Well is them this sight to see,
for mankynd, lord, is bought by thee
and through thy gret Passion.   55

Tunc ibunt ad Petrum; et ait Maria Solome.

MARIA SALOM] MARYE SALOME   37 mynd] will   38 fly] flee   39 fayre]
freely   SD] Then shall the women goe, and Jesus shall meete them, sayinge
After 40] Then Marye Jacoby, makeinge curtesye, sayth   MARIA] MARYE
42 heale] wayle   SOLOM] SALOME   45 blessed] sweete   54 mankynd
lord is bought] bought be mankynde lorde   55 and] om   SD] Then
they shall goe to Peter; and Mary Salome saith

MARIA SOLOME

8 Peter, tydinges good and new!
We have seene my lord Jesu
on lyfe, clean in hyde and hew,
and handled have his feete.

PETRUS

Yea, well is yee that have bene trew,   60
for I forsware that I him knew.
Therfore shame makes me eschew
with my lord for to meet.

9 But yet I hope to se his face
though I have done so great trespas.   65
My sorrew of hart know he hase
and to yt will take heede.
Thither as he buryed was
I will hye me to rumne apace,
of my swet lord to aske grace   70
of my fowle misdeed.

Tunc veniet Jesus obvians Petro.

JHESUS

10 Peter, knows thou not me?

102^r

PETRUS

A, lord, mercy I aske thee
with full hart, knelinge on my knee.
Forgeve me my trespase.   75
My faynt flesh and my fraylty
made me, lord, falce to be,
but forgevenes with hart free
thou graunt me through thy grace.

JESUS

11 Peter, so I thee beheight   80
thou should forsake me that night,

MARIA] MARYE   58 lyfe] live   PETRUS] PETER   61 forsware] forsoke
68 thither] theire   69 rumne] runne   70 of] and of   to] om
71 of] for   SD] Here Jesus cometh in with a crosse-staffe in his hand
PETRUS] PETER   76 and] om

but of this deed thou have in sight
when thou hast soverainty.
Thinke on thyne own deed today,
that flesh is frayle and fallinge aye;   85
and mercifull be thou allway
as now I am to thee.

12 Therfore I suffered thee to fall
that to thy subjects hereafter all
that to thee shall cry and call   90
then may have minning.
Sithen thyself fallen hase,
the mere inclyne to graunt grace.
Goe forth! Forgeven is thy trespase.
And have here my blessinge.   95

Finis

86 mercifull] merciable   be thou] thou be   91 then] thou   minning]
meaninge   92 fallen] soe fallen   hase] hast   93 mere] more

APPENDIX IIa

The Manchester MS. (Play XVIII, 1–13, 21–41)

1ʳ Heare beegyneth the Pagent which mencyoneth of the Resur-
rectyon of Chryste.

PYLATE

1 Per vous, syr Cayphas,
et vous e vous, syr Annas,
et syn disciple Judas
qu'a le treason fuyt;
et graunde luyes de lucyte   5
a moy parfite delyvere,
nostre dame fuit jugge,
per lore roy escrete.

2 Yee lordes and ladyes so lufle and lere,
yee kempes, yee known knyghtes of - - nde,   10
harcken all hetharwardes my hestes to here,

for I am most fayrest and fresshest to f - nde,
and moste hyghest I am of estate;

. . . . .

1^v

3 They cryden on mee all with one voyce,
these Jewes on mee made pyteous noyse.   15
I gave leave to hange hym on croyse.
This was throwgh Jewes redd.

4 I dreade yet least hee will hus greeve,
for that I sawe I may well leeve.
I sawe the stones beegyn to cleeve   20
and dead men up ryse.
In this cytty all abowte
was none so sterne nyfe so stowte
that durst once looke up, for dowbte;
they calde so sore agryse.   25

5 And therefore, ser Cayphas, yet I dreede
least theare were perryll in that deede.
I sawe hym hange on roode and bleede
till all his blood was shed.
And when hee sholde his deathe take,   30
the weddar waxed wonderus black—
- - - - - thonder—and earth beegan to quake.
Thereof am I adred.

CAYPHAS

And this was yesterday abowt - one?

APPENDIX IIB

The Peniarth 'Antichrist'.

1^r   Incipit Pagina XX de Salla Antechristi.

Primo equitando incipiat Antechristus.

1 De celso trono poli, pollens clarior sole,
age vobis monstrare descendi, vos judicare.
Reges et principes sunt subditi sub me viventes.

Sites sapientes vos, semper in me credentes
et faciam flentes gaudere atque dolentes.   5
Sic omnes gentes gaudebunt in me sperantes.
Descendi presens rex pius et perlustrator,
princeps eternus vocor, Cristus, vester salvator.

2   All ledys in londe now bese lighte
that wyllyn be rulyde thrugheout the right.   10
Youre savyor nowe in youre sight
here may ye savely see.
Messyas, Criste, and most of might,
that in the lawe wos youe behyght,
all monkynde joy to dyght   15
ys comyn, for I am hee.

3   Off me wos spokyn in prophecye
off Moyses, Davyd, and Ysaye.
I am he they call messye,
forbyer of Israell.   20
That levyn on me stydfastly,
I shall them save frome all any,
and siche joye right as have I
with hand I thynke to dele.

De me enim dicitur Ezechiel tricesimo sexto: 'Tollam vos de
gentibus et congregabo vos de universis terris, et reducam vos in
terram vestram.'

4   But one hath laykyd hym here in londe,   25
Jhesu he hight, I understond.
To forther falsed he confounde
and ferde withe fantasye.
His wykydnes he wolde not wende
till he wos takyn and putt in bende   30
and slayne throghe vertue of my sende.
This ys sothe, sycurlye.

5   My peple of Jues he cothe twynne
1ᵛ   that theyr land come they never in.
They on theym nowe most I myn   35
and restoure theym agayn.

To bylde this temple wyll I not blyn
and as God honoryd be therin,
and endless wele I shall them wyn,
all that to me bene bayne.   40

De me enim dicitur in psalmo: 'Adorabo ad templum sanctum
tuum in timore tuo.'

6   One thing me gladys, be ye bolde.
    As Danyell the prophett fore me tolde,
    all women in worlde me love shulde
    when I were comyn rowland.
    This prophesye I shall well holde   45
    which ys most lykyng to yonge and olde.
    I thinke to faast monye folde
    and theyr fayrenesse to founde.

7   Also he tolde them, leve ye me,
    that I of giftis shulde be free,   50
    whiche prophesye don shalbe
    whan I my realme have wonen;
    and that I sholde graunte men poste,
    ryvyd riches, lond and fee—
    that shall be done, that ye shall see,   55
    whan I am hether comen.

Daniellis terciodecimo: 'Dabit eis potestatem. Mult[is] terram
dividet gratuita.'

8   What saye ye kingis that here ben lente?
    Ar not my wordys at youre assente?
    That I am Criste omnypotente,
    leve ye not thus ichon?   60

PRIMUS REX

We leven, lorde, without lett,
that Cryst, he ys not comyn yet.
Iff thowe be he, thowe sholbe sett
in temple as God alon.

9 Yff thowe be Crist callyd messye,   65
that from oure bale shall us bye,
doe byfore us some maistrye,
a signe that we may see.

2^r

TERCIUS REX

Then will I leve that hitt ys so,
yf thowe do wonders or thow goo;   70
so that thow save us of oure woo,
then honoryd shall thowe be.

QUARTUS REX

10 Fowle have we levyd mony a yer
and of oure wenyng bene in were.
And thowe be Crist now comyn here,   75
then may thowe stynt all striffe.

ANTECHRISTUS

That I am Crist and Crist wilbe
by verey signes sone shall ye see,
for dede men thrughe my poste
shall ryse from dethe to lyve.   80

11 Now wyll I turne, all thrughe my myght,
trees downe, the rote upright—
that ys marvell to youre sighte—
and frute groing upon.
So shall they growe and multiplie   85
throghe my might and my maistrey.
I putt you oute of hereysye
to leede me apon.

12 And bodyes that ben dede and slayne,
yff I may rayse theym up agayne,
then honorys me with myght and mayn.   90
Then shall no mon you gryve.
Forsothe, then after will I dee
and ryse agayn thrughe my poostye.
Yff I may do thus marvlosly,   95
I redd you on me leve.

13 Men buryed in grave as ye may see,
   what maistrye ys nowe, hope ye,
   to rayse theym up thrughe my postye
   and all thrughe my none accorde?   100
   Whyther I in my godhede be
   by every signe ye shall se.
   Ryse up, ye dede men, and honures me
   and knoys me for youre lorde.

Tunc resurgendo dicat Primus Mortuus:

14 A, lord, to the I aske mercye.   105
   I wos dede but nowe lyve I.
   Nowe wot I well and wytterly
   that Crist ys hyther comyn.

2ᵛ   SECUNDUS MORTUUS

   Hym honore we and all men,
   devotly kneling on oure knen.   110
   Wurshipte be thowe then—Amen—
   Crist that oure name has nomen.

         ANTECRISTUS

15 That I shall fulfill Holly Wrytt
   ye shall wott and knowe well hyt,
   for I am wall of welle and wytt   115
   and lord of every londe.
   And as the prophet Sophonye
   spekis of me full wytturlye
   I shall reherse here redylye
   that clerkys shall understond: 120

Sophonie tercio: 'Expecta me in die resureccionis mee in futurum
quia judicium ut congregem gentes et colligam regna.'

16 Nowe will I dye—that ye shall see—
   and ryse agayne thrughe my poostye.
   I wyll in grave that ye put me
   and wurship me alon.
   For in this temple a tombe ys made,   125
   therin my bodye shalbe leyde.

Then wyll I ryse as I have sayde—
take tente to me ychon!

17 And after my resurreccion
thenn wyll I sytt with gret renoune 130
and my gost sende to you downe
in forme of fyer full sone.

18 I dye, I dye! Nowe am I dede!

PRIMUS REX

Nowe sethe this worthy lorde ys dede
and his grace ys withe us lede, 135
to take hys bodye it ys my rede
and burye it in a grave.

SECUNDUS REX

Forsothe, and so to us he saide
in a toumbe he wolde be laide.
Nowe goo we forthe, all at a brayde; 140
frome dyssese he may us save.

Tunc transeunt ad Antechristum.

TERCIUS REX

19 Take we the bodye of this swete
and ley it loo undre the greet.
Nowe, lorde, comforde us, we the biseke,
and send us of thy grace. 145

3r
QUARTUS REX

And if he rise sone thrughe his myght
frome dethe to lyve as he hyght,
hym wyll I honor day and nyght
as God in every place.

Tunc recedent de tumulo usque ad terram, et dicat

PRIMUS REX

20 Nowe wot I well that he ys dede, 150
for now in greve we have hym layde.

Yff he ryse as he hasse sayd,
he ys of ful gret myghte.

SECUNDUS REX

I cannot leffe hym apon
but yf he ryse hymselffe alon   155
as he hass sayde to mony on,
and shoo hym here in syght.

TERCIUS REX

21 Tyll that oure savyore be ryson agayne,
in fayth my hart may not be fayne
but I hym see withe yee.   160

QUARTUS REX

I most morne withe all my mayne
tyll Crist be rison up agayn.
Off that myracle make us fayne.
Ryse up, lorde, that we may see.

Tunc Antechristus levat caput suum surgens a mortuis.

ANTECHRISTUS

22 I rise! Nowe reverence dose to me,   165
God glorifyd, grattist in degre.
Iff I be Crist, nowe levys ye
and warchis after the wyse.

PRIMUS REX

A, lord, welcome most thowe be.
That thow art God nowe leve we.   170
Therefore, go sit up in thy see
and kepe oure sacryfyse.

Tunc transient ad Antechristum.

SECUNDUS REX

23 Forsoth, in seyte thowe shalt be sett
and honoryd bothe with lambe and gete
as Moseyes lawe that lastyth yet,   175
as he as sayd beffore.

3ᵛ
TERCIUS REX
O gracius lorde, go sytt downe then,
and we shall kneling on oure knen
wurship the as thyn owne men
and worche after thy lore.   180

Tunc assendit Antechristus ad chathedr, et Tercius Rex:

24 Hethur we be comyn with good entent
    to make oure sacryfice, lord excellent,
    withe this lambe that I have here hente,
    knelyng the before.
    Thowe graunte us grace to do and saye   185
    that it be plesing to the aye,
    to thy blisse that come we may
    and never fro it be loore.

ANTECHRISTUS
25 I lord, I God, I hyght justyce,
    I Crist that made the dede to rise!   190
    Here I receyve youre sacryfyce
    and blesse you fleshe and fell.

Tunc transiunt de Antechristo.

Ye kyngis, also to you I tell
I wyll nowe send my holly goost
to knowe me lord of myghtist most   195
off hevon, yerthe, and hell.

Tunc emittit spiritum, dicens 'Dabo vobis cor novum et spritum
novum in medio vestri.'

QUARTUS REX
26 A God, a lorde, mycle of myght,
    this holye gost is in me pight.
    Methinke my hart ys verry light
    sithe it come into me.   200

PRIMUS REX
Lord, we the honor day and nyght
for thowe shewys us in sight

right as Moyses us behyght.
Honoryd most thowe bee.

ANTECHRISTUS

27 Yet worthie werkis to youre will   205
    off prophcie I will fullfill.
    As Danyell prophycied you till
    that londys I shulde devyse,
    that phrophecye it shalbe done
    that ye shall se right sone.   210
    Wurshipis me all that ye mone
    and do after the wise.

28 Ye kyngis, I shall avaunte you all
    and for youre regnis be but small,
    cities, castells shall you beffall,   215
    with townes and towres gay;
    and make yow lordis of lordishipis fere,
    and well it falles for my power.
    And loke ye do as I you lerr
    and harkens what I say.   220

29 I am verey God of myght.
    All thinge I made thrugh my myght,
    son and mone, day and nyght.
    To blisse I may you bring.
    Therfor, kyngis noble and gay,   225
    tokyn youre peple that I saye
    that I am Crist, God verey—
    and tell theym such tything.

30 My peple of Jwes were put me frome.
    Therefor gret ruthe I have theym on.   230
    Whythur they wyll leve me upon
    I wyll ful sone assaye.
    For all that wyll leve me upon,
    wordely welthe shall theym fall on
    and to my blysse shall they come   235
    to dwell withe me for aye.

31 And the giftes that I behighte
ye shall have, as ys good right.
Hens or I goo oute of youre sight
ichon shall knowe his doole.   240
Too the I gyffe Lambardye;
and to the Denmarke and Hungryo;
and take Patmouse and Italye;
and Rome hit shall be hyse.

SECUNDUS REX

32 Grauntmarsye, lorde, youre gifte today!   245
Honor the we wyll alway,
for we were nevyr so rych, in fay,
ne non of all oure kynde.

ANTECRISTS

Therefor be true and stydfast aye,
and levys trulye on my laye,   250
for I wyll harken on you today,
stydfast yf I you fynd.

Tunc sedeat Antechristus et veniant Enoke et Elysas quorum
dicat Enoke:

33 Almyghtye God in majestye,
that made the hevon and yerthe to be,
fyre, water, ston, and tree,   255
and mon als throghe thy myght—
the poyntys of thy prevytye
any erthely mon to see
is impossible, as thynkis me,
to ony worldely wighte.   260

34 Gracius lorde, that arte so gud,
that who so long in fleshe and blude
hasse grauntyd lyve and hevonly fode,
lett never oure thoughtes be fylyde;
but gyve us, lorde, might and mayn,   265
err we of this shrewe be slayne,
to convert thy peple agayne
that he hasse thus begylyd.

35 Sythe the worldis begynyng
    I have lyvyd in grett lyking   270
    thrugh helpe of highe hevon-kyng
    in paradyce without anyes,
    tyll we hard tokening
    off this theeffys comyng
    that nowe in earthe ys reynyng   275
    and Goddes folke distryes.

36 To paradyce takyn I wos that tyde,
    this theffys comyng to abyd,
    and Helye my brother, here me bysyde,
    wos after sende to me.   280
    Wythe this champion we most chyde
    that nowe in worlde walkys wyde,
    to disspreve his pompe and pryde
    and payre all his poostye.

HELYAS

37 O lorde, that maddist al thinge   285
    and long hasse lent us lyving,
    lett nevur the devyle power spryng
    this man hass hym within.
    God gyve you grace, bothe olde and yonge,
    to knowe discayte in hys doynge,   290
    that ye may come to that lykynge
    off blisse that nevere shall blyn.

38 I waarne you, all men, wytterly,
    this hys Ennoke, I am Helye,
    ben comyn thys herrors to distrye   295
    that he to you nowe shewes.
    He callis hymselffe 'Crist' and 'Messye.'
    He lyez, forsothe, appertely.
    He ys the devull, you to anye,
    and for non other hym knoys.   300

TERCIUS REX

39 A, men, what speke ye of Helye
    and Ennoke? They ben in companye.

Off oure blude they ben, wetterlye,
and we be of theyre kynde.

QUARTUS REX

We redon in bokys of oure lawe 305
that they to hevon were idrawe
and yet ben ther—ys the comyn sawe
wrytyn, as men may fynde.

ENNOKE

40 We be tho men, forsoth iwysse,
be comyn to tell ye don amysse, 310
and bring youre sowlys to hevon-blisse
yff it were ony bote.

HELYAS

This devuls lym that comyn ys,
that sayez hevon and yerthe ys hys,
nowe been we redye—leve ye this— 315
agaynst hym for to mote.

PRIMUS REX

41 Yff that we redye wytt monn
by preves off disputacion
that ye have skyll and reason,
with you we will abyde. 320

SECUNDUS REX

And if youre skyllys may do hym downe,
to dye withe you we wilbe bowne
in hope of sawle salvacon,
whatsoever betyd.

ENNOKE

42 To do hym downe we shall assay 325
thrugh myght of Jhesu, borne of a maye,
by right and reason, as ye shall say,
and that ye shall well here.

And for that cause hyther were we sent
by Jhcsu Crist omnipotente,   330
and that ye shall not all be shente.
He thought you all full dere.

43 Bese glade, therefor, and makes gud chere
and do, I redd, as I you lere,
for we ben comyn, in gud manere,   335
to save you everychon.
And drede you noght for that falsse fynde,
for ye shall se hym cast behynde
or we departe and from hym wynde,
and shame shall hym light on.   340

5ᵛ   Et sic transibunt Ennoke et Helyas ad Antechristum, quorum
dicat Ennoke:

44 Say, thowe verey devuls lyme
that sittes so grisly and grym—
from hym thowe come and shalt to hym,
for mony a sowle thowe decevys.
Thowe hasse deceyvyd men mony a day   345
and made the peple to thy pay,
and wychyd theym into a wrang wey
wykkydly with thy wylys.

ANTECHRISTUS

45 A, fals fayteors, from me ye flee!
Am I not most in majestye?   350
What men dar meyn thcym thus to me
or make such distaunce?

HELIAS

Fye on the, fayture, fye on the,
the devuls owne nurre!
Thrughe hym thowe preches and hast postye   355
a whyle thrughe sufferaunce.

ANTECHRISTUS

46 You ypocrites that so cryn!
Losells, lurdans, lowdelye you lyne!

To spyll my lawe you asspyne.
That speche ys gud to spare. 360
You that my true fayth defyne
and nedeles my folke devyen,
from hens hastely; but ye hyne,
to you comys sorowe and care.

ENNOKE

47 Thy sorowe and care cum on thy hede, 365
for falsly thrughe thy wykkyd redde
the peple ys put to pyne.
I wolde the body were from the hede,
xx mylys from hit layde,
tyll I hit broght agayn. 370

ANTECHRISTUS

48 Oute on the, wysarde, with thy wylis,
for falsly my peple thowe begylus.
I shall the hastely honge,
and that lurdayn that stondys the bye—
he puttys my folke to gret anye 375
withe his falsse flaterand tong.

49 But I shall teche you curtesye,
youre savyor to knowe anon in hye,
fals theffez with youre herysye,
and if ye darr abyde. 380

HELYAS

50 Yes, forsothe, for all thy pryde,
thrughe grace of God almyght
here we purpose for to abyde.
And all the werld, that ys so wyde,
shall wondre on the on every syde 385
sone in all mennys sight.

ANTECHRISTUS

51 Out on you, theffys bothe ii.
Iche mon may se ye be soe
all by youre araye,
muffelyd in mantyls. Non such I knowe. 390

I shall make you lowte full loo
or I departe you all froo,
to knowe me lorde for aye.

ENNOKE

52 We ben no theffys, I the tell,
thowe fals fend comyn from hell. 395
Wythe the we purpous more to mell,
my felow and I in fere,
to knowe thy power and thy myght
as we these kyngis have behight,
and thereto we ben redy dighte 400
that all men nowe may here.

ANTECHRISTUS

Stafe.

53 My myght ys most, I tell to the.
I dyed, I rose thrughe my poostye.
That all these kynges sawe with theyr ee,
and every mon and wiffe. 405
And myracles and marvels I did also.
I consell you, therfor, bothe ii,
to wurship me and no moo,
and lett us nowe no more stryve.

HELYAS

54 They were no myracles but marvells thinges 410
that thowe shewyd to these kyngis
thrughe the fendys crafte.
6ᵛ And as the floure nowe springys,
fallith, fadithe, and hyngys,
so do thy joy nowe ragnes 415
that shalbe from the rafte.

ANTECHRISTUS

55 Oute on the, theffe, that settes so styll!
Why wylte thou not one wurde speke theym tyll
that comyn me to reprove?

DOCTOR

O, lorde, maistre, what shall I say then?   420

ANTECHRISTUS

I beshrewe bothe thy kenne.
Arte thowe nowe for to kenn?
In faythe, I shall the greve.

56 Off my godhed I made the wysse
and sett the ever at micle price.   425
Nowe I wolde fele thy gud advyce
and here what thowe wolde saye.
These lowlers, they wolde full fayne me greve
and nothing on me will they leve,
but ever ben redye me to repreve   430
and all the peple of my lawe.

DOCTOR

57 O lord that art so mycle of myghte,
methynke thowe shullest not chyde nor fyghte
but curs theym, lorde, thurgh thy myght.
Then shall they fare full yll.   435
For those that thowe blesses, they shall well spede,
and those that thowe cursys, they be but dede.
This ys my concell and my rede,
yendre herytykes to spyll.

ANTECRISTUS

58 The same I purposyd, lerne thowe me.   440
All thing I knowe thurgh my postye.
But yet I thoghte thy witt to see,
what wos thyn entent.
Hit shalbe downe ful sicurlye;
the sentence gyvon full openly,   445
with my mouthe, trulye,
apon theym shalbe hente.

59 My cursse I gyve you, to mend your melys,
from youre hede unto youre helys.
Walke ye furthe youre way.   450

ENOKE

Ye, thowe shalt nevur com in celis,
for falsly with thy wylus
the peple ys put in pyne.

ANTECRISTUS

60 Out on you, thevys! Why far ye thus?
Whither hade ye lever have, payne or blisse?   455
I may you save from all amys.
I made the day and yke the nyght
and all thing that ys on yerthe groyng—
flowrez feshe that fayr can spryng;
also I made all other thing—   460
they sterrus that be so bryght.

HELYAS

61 Thowe list! Vengeance on the befall!
Oute on the, wreche! Wrothe the I shall!
Thowe callis the 'kyng' and 'lord of all';
a fynde ys the withein.   465

ANTECHRISTUS

62 Thowe liest falsly, I the tell.
Thowe wilbe dampnyd into hell.
I made the mon of fleshe and fell,
and all that ys lyvyng.
For other god have you non.   470
Therfor wurship me alon,
the wyche hasse made the water and ston,
and all at my lykyng.

ENNOKE

63 Forsothe, thowe lyes ful falsly.
Thowe art a fende comyn to any   475
Goddes peple that stondes us bye.
In hell I wolde thou were.

HELYAS

Fye on the, felon, fye on the, fye!
For all thy wychecrafte and socerye,

to mete with the I am redye, 480
thatt all the peple may here.

ANTECHRISTUS

64 Out on you, harlottys! Whens come ye?
Where have you other God then me?

ENNOKE

Yes, Crist, God in Trenyte,
thow false fayture attaynte, 485
that send his Son from hevon-see
that for monkynd dyed on rode-tree,
that shall full sone make the to flee,
thowe feayttir false and faynte.

7ᵛ

ANTECHRISTUS

65 Rybaldes, rweled out of raye! 490
What ys the Trenyte to saye?

HELYAS

Thre persons, as thowe leve may,
in on godhead in fere—
Father and Son, that ys no nay,
and the Holly Goost styrring aye. 495
That ys one God verey;
ben all thre namyd her.

ANTECHRISTUS

66 Out on you, thevys! What say ye?
Wyll ye have bothe one God and iiiᵉ?
Howe darr ye so say? 500
Maddmen, therefor levys on me
that am one God—so is not he!

Stafe

Then may ye lyve in joye and lee,
all this londe I dare lay.

ENNOKE

67 Nay, tyrand! Understond thou this: 505
but beginnyng his godhed ys

and also boute ending, ywys.
Thus fully levon we.
And thowe, that genderyd wos amys,
hasse beginnyng and nowe that blisse,   510
and ende shall have—no drede there ys—
full foule, as men shall se.

ANTECHRISTUS

68 Whrecchis! Golys! Ye ben blent.
Goddis Son I am, from hym sente.
Howe darr you maynten youre entente,   515
sithe he and I ben won?
Have I not, sithe I cam hym froo,
made the dede to speke and goo?
And tho men I sende my goste also
that levyd me apon.   520

HELYAS

69 Fye on the, felone, fye on the, fye!
For thrughe his myght and his maistrye,
by sufferaunce of God allmyghtye,
the people ys blent thrughe the.
Yff tho men be raysyd witterlye,   525
withouten the devuls fantasye,
here shall be prevyd appertely
that all men shall see.

8ʳ   #### ANTECHRISTUS

70 A, folys! I redd you, leve me apone
that myracles have shewyd many on   530
to the peple everychone,
to put theme out of doute.
Therefor I rede you hastely
convertes to me most myghty.
I shall you save from anye,   535
and that I am aboute.

ENNOKE

71 Nowe of thy myracles I wold se.

HELIAS

Therfor comyn hether be we,
to se what ys thy grate postye
and some therof to lere.   540

ANTECHRISTUS

Sone may ye se, if you will byde,
for I wyll nother fyght nor chyde.
Off all the worlde that ys so wyde,
therin ys not my pere.

ENNOKE

72 Bryng furthe those men here in oure syght   545
    that thou hase raysyd agayn the ryght.
    Yf thowe be of so mycle might
    to make theym ete and drynke,
    for verey God we wyll the knowe
    such a sygne yf thow wyll shewe,   550
    and do the reverence on a rowe
    all at thy lykyng.

ANTECHRISTUS

73 Wrecches, dampnyd all be ye!
    But noght for that! Yt fallyth me
    as gracius god abyding be,   555
    yf ye wyll mende youre liffe.
    Ye dede men, ryse thrughe my postye,
    and ete and drynke, that men may see,
    and preve me worthest in deyte;
    so shall we stynt all stryffe.   560

PRIMUS MORTUUS

74 Lorde, thy bydding I will do aye
    and for to ete I will assaye.

SECUNDUS MORTUUS

And I also, all that I maye,
wyll do thy byddyng here.

HELIAS

Have here brede bothe two. 565
But I moste blesse hyt or I goo,
that the fende, mankyndes foo,
one hit have no powere.

75 Thys brede I blesse nowe with my honde
in Jhesus name, I undarstonde, 570
the wych ys lorde of see and londe
and kyng in hevon so hye.
In nomine Patris—that all hathe wroghte—
et Filii virginis—that dere us boughte—
et Spyrytus Sancti—ys all my thoghte— 575
one God and parsons thre.

PRIMUS MORTUUS

76 Alas, put that oute of my syghte!
To loke on yt I am not light.
That pryntte that ys upon yt pight,
hit puttythe me to grett fere. 580

SECUNDUS MORTUUS

To loke on hit I am not light.
That brede to me yt ys so bryght
and ys my foo bothe day and nyght,
and puttys me to grete dere.

ENNOKE

77 Nowe, ye men that have donne mys, 585
ye seey well what his powere ys.
Convertes to hym, I rede iwysse,
that you on rode hath boughte.

TERCIUS REX

And nowe knowyn apertely
we have ben broghte in herysye. 590
With you to dethe we will forthy,
and never eft turne oure thought.

QUARTUS REX

78 Nowe, Ennoke and Helye, it ys no nay,
have tayntyd tho tyrant this same day.
Blest be Jhesu, borne of a may!   595
On hym I leve apon.

PRIMUS REX

Thowe fayture that ferde with fantesye,
with socerye, wycchcrafte, and nygrymancye,
thowe hasse us led in heresye.
Fye on thy werkys ychon.   600

9r ### SECUNDUS REX

79 Jhesu, for thy mycle grace,
forgeve us all oure tresspas
and bryng us to the hye hevynly place
as thowe art God and mon.
Nowe am I wyse made thrughe thy myght.   605
Blessyd be thowe, Jhesu, day and nyght!
This grysely grome graythes hym to fyght,
to sle us here anon.

TERCIUS REX

80 Off oure lyvys lett us not reche
thoghe we be slayne of such a wreche   610
for Jhesu sake, that may us leche
oure sowlys to bryng to blysse.

QUARTUS REX

That wos well sayde, and so I sente.
To dye, forsothe, ys myn entent
for Christes love omnipotende,   615
in cause that ys ryghtwyse.

ANTECRISTUS

81 A, falsse faytures, turne you nowe?
Ye shalbe slayne, I make a vowe;
and those traytours that turnyd you,
I shall moke theym unfayn,   620

that all other, by verey sight,
shall knowe that I am most of myght,
for with this sworde nowe wyll I fyght,
for all ye shalbe slayne.

Tunc Antechristus occidet Enoke et Eliam et omnes conversos cum gladio et redebit ad chathedram, cui dicat Michaell cum gladio in manu sua dextra.

MYCHAELL

82 Antecist, nowe ys comyn thy day.   625
   Reigne no longer thowe ne maye.
   He that hath ladd the alwey,
   nowe hym thowe most go to.
   No mo men shalbe shente by the.
   My lorde wyll dede that thou be.   630
   He that hath gyvon the this poste
   thy soule shall underfoe.

83 In syn ingendirt furst thou wos.
   In syn als lade thy lyfe thowe hasse.
9v   In syn nowe an ende thowe mas   635
   that marryd hasse mony on.
   Thowe hasse ever servyd Sathanas
   and had hys power in every place.
   Therfo thowe gayttys nowe no grace.
   With hym thowc most gon.   640

84 iii yere and an halffe on, wytterlyc,
   thowe hasse hadde leve to distrye
   Goddes people wykkydlye
   thrughe thy fowle reede.
   Nowe thowe shalt knowe and wytt in hye   645
   that more ys Goddys maystrye
   then eke the devuls and thyn therebye,
   for nowe shalt thowe be deede.

Tunc Mychaell occidet Antechristum et in occidendo dicat Antechristus 'Help, help!'

85 Help, Sathanas and Lucyfer!
   Belsabub, bolde bacheler!   650

Ragnayll, thowe art my dere!
Nowe fare I wondre evull.
Alas, alas, were is my powere?
Alas, my wytt ys in a were.
Nowe bodye and sowle bothe in fere   655
and all gose to the devyll.

Tunc morietur Antechristus et veniant duo demones quorum
dicat Primus Demon:

86 Anon, maister, anon, anon!
From hell-grounde I herde the gronne.
I thoghte I wolde not com myselff alon
for wurship of thyn astate.   660
With us to hell thowe shalt gon.
For this dethe we make gret mon.
To wyn moo sowlys into oure won—
but nowe hit ys to late!

SECUNDUS DEMON

87 With me thowe shall. Fro me thowe come.   665
Off mee shall come thy last dome,
for thowe hasse well deservyd.
And thrughe my might and my poste
thowe hasse lyvyd in dignyte
and many a sawle deceyvyd.   670

10ʳ   PRIMUS DEMON

88 This body wos getton by myn assente
in clene horedom, verament.
Off mother wombe or that he wente,
I wos hym within
and taghte hym ay with myn entente   675
syn by wyche he shalbe shente.
For he dyd my comandemente
his sowle shall never blyn.

SECUNDUS DEMON

89 Nowe, felow, in faythe gret mon we may make
for this lorde of astate that stondes in styde.   680

Mony a fatt morsell we have had for his sake
off sowlys that shulde have be savyd—in hell be
thie hyd!

Animam eius tunc capiat.

PRIMUS DEMON

90 His sawle with sorowe in honde have I hente.
He penance and payne sone shall he fele.
To Lucyffer, that lord, yt shalbe presente   685
that bren shall as a bronde; his sorow shall not kele.

SECUNDUS DEMON

91 This proctor of prophecye hasse procuryd mony on
on his lawe for to leve, and lost for his sake
theyre sowlys ben, in sorowe, and his shalbe sone.
Such maisters thrughe my myght moni on I make. 690

PRIMUS DEMON

92 With Lucyfer, that lorde, long shall he lenge;
in a sete ay with sorowe with hym shall he sytt.

SECUNDUS DEMON

Ye, by the halse in hell shall he henge
in a dungen full depe, ryght in hell-pytt!

PRIMUS DEMON

93 To hell will I hye without ony fayle,   695
with this present of pryce thedure to bryng.

SECUNDUS DEMON

Thowe take hym by the tope and I by the tayle.
An soryfull song, in faythe, shall he senge.

PRIMUS DEMON

94 A, felowe, a doule loke that thowe dele
to all this fayr compayny, hence or thou wynde. 700

SECUNDUS DEMON

Ye, sorowe and care ever shall they fele.
In hell shall they dwell at theyr last ende.

Tunc ibunt demones ad infernum cum animam Antechristi, et
sugent Ennoke e Helyas, quorum dicat Ennoke.

10ᵛ   ENNOKE

95 A, lord, that all shall lede
and bothe deme the quycke and dede!
That reverence the, thowe on theym rede   705
and theym thrughe right relevyd.
I was dede and right here slayne,
but thrughe thy myght, lord, and thy mayne
thowe hasse me raysyd up agayne.
The wyll I love and leve.   710

HELYAS

96 Ye, lorrde, blessyd most thou be.
My fleshe nowe gloryfyed I see.
Witt ne sleightte ageeynste the
conspyryd may be no way.
All that levon in the stydfastly   715
thow helpis, lorde, from all any,
for dede I wos and nowe lyve I.
Honoryd be thowe aye!

MYCHAELL

97 Ennoke and Helye, com ye anon.
My lorde wyll that ye with me gon   720
to hevens blysse, botthe blude and bon,
evermo there to be.
Ye have ben long, for ye ben wyse,
dwellyng in erthlye paradyce;
but to heven, there hymselffe ys,   725
nowe shall ye goe withe me.

Tunc ibit Angelus adducens Ennok et Helyam ad celum cantans
'Gaudete justi in domino.'

Explicit

APPENDIX IIc

The Chester 'Trial and Flagellation' (Play XVI)

1ʳ   The Fletchers, Boweyers, Cowpers, and Stringers Playe

Incipit Pagina Decima Sexta de Passione Christi.

Et primo veniente Judei adducentes Jesum ad Annam et Caypham;
et primo Judeus incipit.

PRIMUS JUDEUS

1 Sir bishoppes, heare we have broughte
a wrech that moch woo hase wrought
and woulde bringe our law to noughte—
righte soe at yt he hath spurned.

SECUNDUS JUDEUS

Yea, wydeweare we have hym soughte,   5
and dearc also we have hym boughte,
for heare many mens thought
to hym he hase torned.

Annas dicit:

2 A, jangellinge Jesu, arte thou now here?
Nowe thou maye prove thy postee power,   10
whether thy cause be cleanc and cleare;
thy Christhood wee must knowe.

1ᵛ   CAYPHAS

Methinke a masterye that yt were
other for penny or prayer
to shutt hym of his daungere   15
and such sleighte to shewe.

ANNAS

3 Sir Cayphas, I saye sykerlye,
we that bene in companye
must neede this dosyberde destroye
that wickedly hase wroughte.   20

CAYPHAS

Sir, yt is needfull—this saye I—
that one man dye witterly
all the people to forbye
that soe the perishe noughte.

TERCIUS JUDEUS

4 Sir Cayphas, harken nowe to me!   25
This babelavaunte our kinge woulde be,
whatsoever he sayes now before thee.
I harde him saye full yore
that prince he was of such postee,
destroye the temple well mighte hee   30
and buylde yt up in dayes three
righte as yt was before.

QUARTUS JUDEUS

5 Yea, sicker, that I harde hym saye,
he may not deny by noe waye;
and also, that he was God verey,   35
Emanuell and messie.
2ʳ He may not nye this ney say ney,
for more then fortye, in good faye,
that in the temple were that daye,
harden as well as I.   40

CAYPHAS

6 Saye, Jesu, to this what sayen yee?
Thou wottest now what is put one thee.
Put fourth, prince, thy postee
and perceyve what they preven.
What the devill! Not one worde speakes not
    hee!   45
Yet, Jesu, heare I conger thee;
yf thou be Godes Sonne, before me
aunswere to that the meven.

JESUS

7 As thou sayes, righte soe saye I.
I ame Godes Sonne allmightie,   50

and here I tell thee trewly
that me yet shalt thou see
sitt one Godes righte hande hym bie,
mankynde in clowdes to justiffye.

CAYPHAS

'Justifye!' Marye, fye, fye one thee, fye!   55
Wittnesse of all this companye
that falsely lyes hee!

8   Ye harken all what he sayes here.
Of wittnesse now what neede were,
for before all these folke in fere   60
lowdely thou lyes?
What saye ye men that now bene here?

PRIMUS JUDEUS

Buffittes hym that makes this beere,
for to God maye he not be deare
that our law soe destroyes.   65

2ᵛ   ### CAYPHAS

9   Destroye shall he not ytt.
Ye wretches wanten witt!
Founde that freake a fitt
and gurde hym one the face.

ANNAS

Despyse hym, spurne and spitt.   70
Lett see, or ye sitt,
who hase happ to hitt
that us this harmed hase.

Tunc Judei statuent Jesum in cathedram, et dicat torquendo
Primus Judeus:

10   For his harminge here
nighe will I neere   75
this famelande fere
that makes our law false.

SECUNDUS JUDEUS

He is, without were,
to the devill full deere.
Spytt we in fere   80
and buffytt hym else.

TERCIUS JUDEUS (exputas)

11 Yea, yea, ye harden in this place now
how he lyed hase now;
in meddest his face now
fowle will I fyle him.   85

QUARTUS JUDEUS (exputas)

Passe he shall a pase now.
For God he hym makes now,
gettes he no grace now
when I begyle hym.

3ʳ   ### PRIMUS JUDEUS (dans alapam)

12 Fye uppon thee, freike!   90
Stope now and creeke.
Thy breynes to breake
am I readie bowne.

SECUNDUS JUDEUS (dans alapam velando faciem Jesu)

His face will I steke
with a cloth, or he creke,   95
and us all wreke
for my warryson.

TERCIUS JUDEUS

13 And thou be messye
and loth for to lye,
who smott thee crye,   100
yf that thou be Christe.

QUARTUS JUDEUS

For all his prophesye
yet he failes thrye.

Though my fyst flye,
gettes he a fyst.   105

PRIMUS JUDEUS (percutiens)

14 Though he sore skricke,
    a buffytt shall byte;
    maye no man me whyte,
    though I doe hym woo.

SECUNDUS JUDEUS (percutiens)

    Hym failes to fleytt   110
    or ought to despytt.
    For he hase to lite,
    now must he have moe.

3ᵛ   TERCIUS JUDEUS (percuties)

15 And moe yet I maye.
    I shall soone assaye   115
    and shew large paye,
    thou prince, one thy pate.

QUARTUS JUDEUS

    Yff he sayes ney,
    I shall hym, faye,
    lay one. I darc lay   120
    yt is not to late.

Tunc ccssabunt ab alapis, et dicat Cayphas:

16 Lordinges, what is your best redd?
    This man hase scrved to be dead,
    and yf he lightly thus be lead,
    our law cleane will sleepc.   125

ANNAS

    Sir, yt is fully myne advise,
    leade we hym to the hie justice.
    Sir Pilate is bouth ware and wise
    and hase the lawe to keepe.

Tunc Cayphas et Annas et Judei adducant Jesum ad Pilatum.
Dicat

CAYPHAS

17 Sir Pilate, here we bringe one 130
that false is, and our elders fonne.
Tribute maye be geven non
to Ceaser for hym heare.
Wheresoever he and his fellowes gone,
they torne the folkes to them eichone. 135
Now aske we dome him upon
of thee that hase power.

4r
ANNAS

18 Sicker he is our elders foe.
Wheresoever he goeth, too or froe,
that he is Christ, and kinge alsoe, 140
he preaches apertely.
Wyst Ceaser that, he would be woo,
such a man yf we let goe.
Therfore to dampne hym we bene throo,
least hee us all destroye. 145

PILATUS

19 Per vous, sir Cayphas; die vous, sir Annas
et sum dispte Judas; vel atres in fuit.
Come up, lordinges, I you praye,
and we shall heare what he will saye
amonge this fellowshipp here. 150

20 What sayest thou, man in miscarye?
And thou be kinge of Jewes, saye!

JESUS

Soe thou sayes; men here maye
a kinge that thou me mase.

PILATUS

Noe cause fynde I, in good faye, 155
to doe this man to death today.

CAYPHAS

Sir, the people, us to misspay,
converted to him all he hase.

ANNAS

21 Yea, all the lande of Gallale
cleane torned to hym has hee.   160
Therfore dome now aske wee,
this false man to doe downe.

4ᵛ   PILATUS

Sythe he was borne ther as sayen yee,
to Herode sende sone he shalbe;
else raft I hym his royaltie   165
and blemished his renowne.

22 Goe, leade hym to Herode in hye,
and saye I sende hym to justiffye
this man of which he hath maisterye
at his owne lykeinge.   170

PRIMUS JUDEUS

Hym shall you have full hastely,
and lead hym theidder anon will I.
Come thou forth with thy ribaldric
and speake with our kinge.

Tunc ibunt duo Judei adducentes Jesum ad Herodem; et dicat

PRIMUS JUDEUS

23 Sir kinge, here Pilate hath you sente   175
a shrewe that our lawe law hase shente,
for to have his judgement
or he hense awaye weende.

HERODES

A! Welcome, Jesu, verament!
And I thanke Pilate of this presente,   180
for oftetymes I have bene in that intente
after thee to have sente.

24 Jesu, moch have I harde of thee.
Some vertue feyne now woulde I see.
Yf thou from God in majestye   185
be comen, tell us here.
I praye thee, saye now to me,
and prove some of thy postee,
and moch the gladder woulde I bee,
truely, all this yeare.   190

5ʳ Tunc nichill respondebit; et dicat Herodes:

25 What! I weene that man is wood,
or else dombe and cane no good.
Such a stalwarde before me stood,
soe stowte and sterne is hee.
Speake one, Jesus, for cockes blood,   195
for Pilate shall not, by my hood,
doe thee none amisse; but mende thy moode
and speake somewhat with me.

26 Alas, I ame nigh wood for woo.
Methinke this man is wounder throwe,   200
dome and deafe as a doted doe,
or franticke, in good faye.
Yet sithen that Pilate hath done soe,
the wrath that was betwene us too
I forgeve—noe more his foe   205
to be after this daye.

27 Cloth hym in white, for in this case
to Pilate yt maye be solace,
for Jewes custome before was
to cloth men that were wood   210
or madd, now as he him mase,
as well seemed by his face;
for hym that hase lost his grace
this garment is full good.

Tunc indeunt Judei eum veste alba ed dicat

PRIMUS JUDEUS

28 Have this, Jesus, uppon thee—   215
a worshippfull weede, as thinkes me.

of the kinges liverie
that now is one thee lighte!

SECUNDUS JUDEUS

Put thee fourth. Thou maye not fley.
Now thou arte in thy royaltie! 220
Sir Herode, kinge, beleeve well thee
and grauntmercye this guyft.

5ᵛ   Tunc exeunt Judei ad Pilatum adducentes Jesum veste alba,
et dicat Primus Judeus:

29 Sir Pilate, here the kinge hath sente
    Jesu againe, and, seyth we wente,
    he hath forgetten his male intente 225
    for thy deed today.

PILATUS

Yea, faulte in hym cane I fynde none,
ney Herode, hase seene ys heerc upon.
Therfore yt is best we let hym gone
whether he will his waye. 230

SECUNDUS JUDEUS

30 Ney, ne, all we cryen with one voyce,
   neyle hym, nayle him to the crosse.

PILATUS

Yee men, for shame! Let be your noyse!
My counsell I will saye.
Ye knowen eichone the mannere: 235
delivered must be a prisoner—
this feast that now approcheth neere—
for honour of the day.

31 Will yee Jesus delivered bee?

TERCIUS JUDEUS

Ney, suffer the death worthy is hee; 240
and therfore all cryen wee,
and Barrabam reserved.

PILATUS

What shall I doe with Jesus here
that Christ is called, and kynge in feare?

QUARTUS JUDEUS

Neyle hym one the crosse in all mannere, 245
for soe he hath deserved.

PILATUS

32 Now sythen I see you soe fervente
and shapen that he shalbe shente,
wayshe I will here in your present,
waxe ye never soe wood. 250
Ye shall all weitt verament
that I ame cleane and innocente
and for to sheede in noe intente
this righteouse mans bloude.

Tunc Pilatus lavabit manibus, et Cayphas et Annas recedent cum
Pilato; et dicat:

33 Ye prelattes here everyeichone, 255
what will you doe? Let him gone?

CAYPHAS

Nayle, nayle hym to the crosse anon
and deme him or thou leave.

PILATUS

Take ye hym, that bene so gryme,
and after your lawe deeme ye him. 260

ANNAS

Ney, that is not lawfull, leith ne lyme
for us no man to reve.

PILATUS

34 What devill of hell is this to saye?
Jesu, tell me, I thee praye,
arte thou kinge—saye yea or ney— 265
of Jewes by auncetreey?

JESUS

Whether hoopes thou yt soe be,
or other men tolde yt thee?

PILATUS

Ney, faye! Thyselfe maye knowe and see
that noe Jew ame I.   270

35 Men of thyne owne nation
suen for thy damnacion
with many accusation,
and all this day soe have.
Arte thou kynge—saye, for all there crye?   275

JESUS

My realme in this worlde, as say I,
is not; but were itt, witterly
with Jewes were I not tanc.

36 And yf my realme in this worlde were,
strive I woulde with you now here   280
and lead with me such power
shoulde pryve you of your praye.
But my mighte in this mannere
will I not prove, ne now appeare
as worldely kinge; my cause unclere   285
were then, in good faye.

PILATUS

37 Ergo, a kynge thou arte, or was.

JESUS

That thou sayes, yt is noe lesse.
That now I tell thee here exspresse
that kinge I ame and be maye.   290
In worlde I came to beare wittnesse
of southnesse, and therfore borne I was,
and all that leven sothnesse
take heede to that I saye.

PILATUS

38 What is southnes, tell thou me? 295

JESUS

Sothnes came from Godes see.

PILATUS

In earth then hath truth no postee
by thyne opinion?

JESUS

How shoulde truth in earth be
while soe deemed in earth is hee 300
of them that hath none authoritie
in earth against reason?

PILATUS

39 Lordinges, I fynde no cause, iwys,
to damne this man that here is.

CAYPHAS

Pilate, he hase done moch amisse. 305
Let hym never passe.
By Moses lawe leeven wee,
and after that law dead shall he be,
for appertlye preached hase he
Godes Sonne that he was. 310

7ᵛ

ANNAS

40 Yea, Pilate, he that makes hym a pere
eyther to kinge or kinges feere
withsayes Ceaser of his power,
and soe wee have donne with.
And whosoe calles hymselfe a kinge here 315
reeves Ceaser of his power.

PILATUS

Anon goe scowrge this losinger
and beate hym lym and lythe.

PRIMUS JUDEUS

41 Come now with care,
freake, for thy fare.   320
One thy body bare
strockes shalte thou beare.

SECUNDUS JUDEUS

Cast off thy ware,
all thy clothes, yare.
Starte now and stare.   325
This stalwarde I will steare.

Tunc spoliabunt ipsum et ligabunt ad columnam; et dicat Tercius
Judeus (Here the bynde him.):

42 Now he is bounden.
Be he never soe wonden,
sone he shalbe founden
with slappes in feare.   330

QUARTUS JUDEUS

In woe he is wounden
and his grave is grounden.
8ʳ   No ladd unto London
such law canne him leare.

Tunc postquam flagellaverent eum, postea indunt eum purpurea
ponentes in cathedram, et dicat Primus Judeus:

43 Nowe, syth he kinge is,   335
whaynte his clothinge is.
Begger, I bringe thee this,
thee for to weare.

Secundus Judeus ponnes coranam spineam super caput et dicat:

All in lythinge this is
that of olde spronge is;   340
of thornes this thinge is,
thee for to weare.

TERCIUS JUDEUS

44 Now thou hase a weed,
    have here a reed.
    A septcr I thee bed,   345
    a kinge for to bee.

QUARTUS JUDEUS

Harvye, take heede!
This must I neede,
for my fowle deed,
kneele upon my knee.   350

PRIMUS JUDEUS

45 Heale, kinge of Jewes
    that soe many men sues!
    Ribalde, now thee rewes
    with all thy reverence.

8ᵛ   ### SECUNDUS JUDEUS

With iron one him hewes   355
and his hide hewes.
Anoyntmente the newes
for thy offence.

TERCIUS JUDEUS

46 To write in his face—
    thou that thee kinge mase,   360
    now my nose hase
    good spice of the new!

QUARTUS JUDEUS

To write in his face—
thou that thee kinge mase,
with a harde grace   365
thou came to this place.
Passe thou this race,
sore shalte thou rewe.

PILATUS

47 Lordinges, here yee maye see
    your kinge all in his royaltie.   370

CAYPHAS

Nay, sir, forsoth no kinge have wee
save the emperour of Rome;
and but thou neyle him to the tree,
the emperour full wroth wilbe.

ANNAS

All we saye righte as sayth hee.   375
Deeme hym while thou hase tyme.

PILATUS

48 Whether of them will yee have,
Jesus Christ or Barrabam?

CAYPHAS

Ney, Jesus this treatour that is tane
must neyled be to the tree,   380
and let Barrabam goe his waye.

PILATUS

Take hym to you now as I saye,
for save hym I ney maye,
undone but I woulde bee.

PRIMUS JUDEUS

49 This dome is at an ende.   385
Now redd I that we wende
this shrew for to shende
a litill here besyde.

SECUNDUS JUDEUS

Here shalte thou not lende.
Come hether and behynde   390
thy backe for to bende.
Here maye thou not abide.

THE DAMSELL (to Peter)

50 Was not thou with Jesus of Nazareth?

PETER

I know hym not, nor what thou saies.

DAMSELL

Sires, I tell you plaine,   395
this man here is one of them
9v   that was with him in the gardene;
I knowe yt to be trewe.

PETER

51 It is not trewe, soe mote I thee.
I know him not by any degree.   400

THE JEWE

One of them thou arte assuredly,
and thou arte alsoe of Gallaly.
Thy speach clearely bewrayeth thee
in wittnesse of us all.

PETER

52 In fayth and truth, that is not soe.   405
Shame have I, and mickell woo,
yf ever I did him before knowe
or keepe hym companye.

Finis

TEXTUAL NOTES

MANUSCRIPT Hm

FORMS OF PLAY-ENDING

Play missing	I
Finis	II, III, IV, V, VIII, XVIII, XIX, XX, XXI
Finis + *Paginae* + Latin number in genitive	VI, IX, X, XI, XII, XIII, XIV, XV, XXIII
Finis Septimae Paginae	VII
Finis Paginae Decimae Sextae *This storye is finished in the leaves followinge*	XVI
Finis Paginae Decimae Sextae	XVIA
Finis Huius Paginae	XVII
Amen Finis	XXII

Deo gratias. This ys the laste of all the xxiiii[tie]
pageantes and playes played by the xxiiii[tes]
craftesmen of the Cyttie of Chester, wrytten in
the yeare of our lord God 1591 and in the
xxxiiii[th] *yeare of the reigne of our sovereigne*
Ladye queene Elizabeth, whom God preserve
for ever. Amen. Finis. By me Edward Gregorie,
scholler at Bunburye, the yeare of our lord God
1591.

Edwardus Gregorie   XXIV

THE NINETEENTH-CENTURY ADDITION

The sixteenth-century text of this manuscript begins with Play II on folio 6. At some time after the loss of the first five folios, twelve folios—containing the Banns and Play I—were added at the beginning. Notes on folios 1 and 5, at the opening of each segment, indicate that the material was copied from Harley 2013 (R). These notes are in the same hand as the text. This handwriting—seemingly of the nineteenth century—is neat and easily legible, except for one instance noted below.

Greg suggested (*Antichrist*, p. xv) that J. Payne Collier might have been the copyist. Collier had discussed Hm (D) in his *History of Dramatic Poetry* (1831), ii. 227–9, and, somewhat differently, in his 1879 revision of that work (ii. 150). Also, he had published the 'Play of Antichrist' from Hm in 1836, both as a separate edition and also in his *Five Miracle Plays*. The handwriting in a letter from Collier to H. H. Furness in 1831, now in the University of Pennsylvania Library, does closely resemble that of the copyist of the Banns and Play I for Hm. It is also noteworthy that the paper used here for the Banns and Play I has been dated 1829. It seems reasonable to assume that Collier was the copyist, in about 1830.

The titles of the two segments of the addition to Hm are careful imitations of the handwriting in R, but otherwise no effort was made to imitate the hand of R or that of the main body of Hm. The transcription of R's Play I differs from that printed in this edition in the following readings (the R reading is given first and that in the Hm addition last):

Play-heading angelorom] angeloram

43 onste] onsce

55 Dominationes] Dominations

71 exaltation] exaltacion

82 grante] graunte

86 nowe] now

95 tresspasse] trespasse

145+SH DOMINACIONES] DOMINATIONES

201 shoulde] shulde

201+SH DOMINACIONES] DOMINATIONES

237 maye] may

277 shoulde] should

Grace (54) and *is* (281), cancelled in R, are omitted in the Hm addition.

The following TEXTUAL NOTES relate to the addition:

To left of Running Title *Harl.* 2013

Play-heading angeloram, inferne, spiritum, creacion—cross above each and, to right, bracket; to right of bracket, (*sic*)

Guild-ascription after *playe—1600*

9 above *Trenitye*—cross and, to right of line, *MS seems to be* '*Treintye*'

15 after *in*—cross and, to right of line, [*my*]?

16 before *cum*—sign with cross above and, in margin to left, *so* with cross above

17 *viscible*—*c* inserted, with caret, above line

19 after and above *licencia*—cross and, to right of line, *MS* ll *for a*

Before 37 cross and, in left margin, *fo. 4^b*

47 above *your*—cross and, in left margin, *so*

After 49 *through* in bottom right corner as catchword

66 above *iech*—cross and, to right of line, *so for Eichone*

73 *formacion*—*i* inserted, with caret, above the line

Before 76 cross and, in left margin, *fo. 5*

77+SH *ANGELIE*—above *E*(2), cross and, to right, *so for s*

85+Latin to right of 83–5 which are bracketed
above *dignus*—cross and, in left margin, *forsan pro Agnus*

103 *be* inserted, with caret, above line

To left of 105+SH *fo. 5^b*

159 above *arte*—cross and, to right of line, (*so*)

165 *thousandfoulde*—*u*(2) inserted, with caret, above line

To left of 173+SH 6^b

174 above *wall*—cross and, to right of line, (*so*)

178 after *hense*—downstroke

After 181, 185, 189—broken rulings, each with cross above right end of ruling; to right of ruling at 181, (*so*)

192 *bouth*—*u* inserted, with caret, above line

After 193 *Lighte* in bottom right corner as catchword

After 197 to right of ruling—(*so*)

201 *fullgens*—written *full gens*; cross above and, to right of line, *so for fulgens*

To left of 209+SH *fo.* 7

After 214+Latin *Deus* in bottom right corner as catchword

220 *chaunge*—after *a*, *n* cancelled and *un* written above

To left of 237+SH *fo.* 7^b

239 *treay*—*e* inserted, with caret, above line

249 above *beanes*—cross and, to right of line, *so for beemes trumpets*

In left margin at 265+SH (*fo. 8*)

279 above *the*—cross and, in left margin, (*so*)

To right of 297 (*so*)

In left margin at 298 *fo.* 8^b

Finis *Finis Deo gracias*

CONTENT OF PAGES in the addition is as follows: Banns 1^r–4^v, (content of specific pages to be indicated in the second volume of this edition)

I 5^t, 1–21; 5^v, 22–49; 6^r, 50–71; 6^v, 72–89; 7^r, 90–109; 7^v, 110–33; 8^r, 133+SH–51; 8^v, 152–73; 9^r, 173 +SII–93; 9^v, 193+SH–213+SD; 10^r, 213+SH–33; 10^v, 233+SH–51; 11^r, 252–71; 11^v, 272–93; 12^r, 294–Finis; 12^v, blank

The page references given in the Text are to the pages in R.

What the lost folios of Hm contained cannot, of course, be known. Greg at one time assumed that they contained the Banns and Play I (*Antichrist*, p. xv). But later he decided that this material was too extensive for five folios ('Corrigendum in Introduction,' *Antichrist*) because earlier he failed to allow space for speech-headings and stage directions. The shortest version of the Banns is B's 125 lines. Play I is also shortest, among the Group MSS., in B: 320 lines, including speech-headings and stage directions. Hm's full pages vary from 41 to 57 lines to the page, depending upon the frequency of speech-headings and the frequency and extent of stage directions. Thus one may choose either of two assumptions: that Hm's missing ten pages presented the Banns and Play I, or that Play I, preceded by some other material, was contained in the lost five folios.

PLAY II

107–12 every second line indented

107 *ryse—s* written over erased *d*, in different ink

111 *thou—th* written over erasure, in different ink

119 *this* inserted, with caret, above line

124 not indented

128+SD *out* inserted, with caret, above line

140+SH *DEUS* squeezed in, in different hand and ink

146 after *of—him* cancelled

160+SH *DEMON* squeezed in

196 not indented

280+SD *minstrelles playe* below preceding SD as separate SD

344+SD *mourninglye—u* written above line

359 after *you—*letter (two letters) cancelled

377 *este—s* perhaps *f*

384+SD *minstrelles playe* in margin to left of *DEUS*

424+SD to right and below 424

477 *fayre—r* written above line

518 *to* written above line

568 not indented

614 after *to—hould*(?) cancelled

616+SD *minstrelles playe* below and to right of SD

PLAY III

13 *harmes—r* written above line

55 *sharpe—r* written above line

125 *noe* inserted, with caret, above line

189 *here* inserted, with caret, above line

230 indented

260+SD *hee—*before *h*, partially erased *s*

278 after *to—multyp* cancelled

281 *saye* written over erased word

PLAY IV

16+SD not centred but to left of page

40+SD to left of SH and 41–2

48+SD (English) to left of 49–53

88+SD *Here . . . laden—*to right of 86–8

104+SD to right of 105–7

112+SD to right of 109–12

119 after *used—*word erased and cancelled

133 *makinge—e* blotted; perhaps alteration

148+SD to left of 149–51

178 after *eyche*—two letters partially erased

236+SD (1) to left of 233–5
    SD (2) to left of SH and 237–40

249 *sonne* inserted above line

250+SD to left of 249–50

252+SD to left of 253–6

264+SD to left of 265–8

268+SD to left of 269–71

322+SD to left of 324–6

324 not indented

358+SD begins to left of 357–8 and continues below 358

364 *it*—spelt with capital *I*
    after *it—doe* cancelled

389+SD to left of 390–2

435 indented

436 *lorde—r* written above line

459+SD to left of 460–1

475+SD to left of 476–7

PLAY V

32+SD *Moyses—y* above line

64+SD to left of 65–7

80+SD after *monte*—letter erased

93 after *purpur—le*(?) erased

95 indented

108 after *therfore*—letter erased

111+SD to right of 111

115+SD to right of 115

122 *he* inserted, with caret, above line

143+SD to left of 144

160–71 in different hand, except for *eiche one* (160), *fonne* (170) and SD

163 not indented
    pryde—r written above line

167+SD to left of 168

239+SD (English) to left of 240–3

324 after *shall—have* cancelled

335+SD to left of 336–8

352 *woomen—o*(2) squeezed in; perhaps *e*

359 after *shall*—cancelled downstroke

444 *this—i* altered from *e*

PLAY VI

51 after *fruites—of* cancelled

77–82 82 only indented

83–108 different hand; no lines indented

91–6 six-line group

93 after *through—h* - - partially erased; *gave—ve* written over erasure

106 *yore—ore* not clear; *re* written over *ee*(?)

172 after *will—goe* cancelled

179 *fayre—r* written above line

Below 208 *J* and *C*(?) in lower margin

209–17 no lines indented; vertical stroke after *assembles, leez, sortes, mavolentes, sages, able, treasagyle, counsell,* and *frayle*

Below 210, 213, and 215 ruling

217 *viva—*after *a*, perhaps *x*

224 indented

328 after *in—ee* erased

356+SD to left of 357

388 *all* inserted, with caret, above line

405 after *anye—*caret erased, and, above line, *newe* erased

522 *thy—y* written over *a*?

539 indented

598 after *may—of that land* cancelled

613 *neagromancye—*downstroke below *n*(1)

643+SD *ostendet—e*(2) altered from *i*(?)

650 indented

689 after *worthye—th* cancelled

704 after *in—s* erased

Below *Finis* scratched design, scratched-over *John,* and *John Egerton esqr* appear in lower half of page

PLAY VII

44+SD to left of 44

52+SD to left of 53

56+SH in left margin with line to centre

57 *us* inserted, with caret, above line

77–196 every second line indented; rulings appear only between speeches

130 not indented

157 after *his—likinge* cancelled

165 *on* inserted, with caret, above line

170 *we* inserted, with caret, above line

197 indented

202–9 as for 77–196

225 after *any—p* cancelled

after *poore*—downstroke cancelled

234–73 as for 77–196

249 *drent—rent* inserted, with caret, above line

251 not indented

257+SH ruling after SH, not SD

274–9 every third line indented

280–99 as for 77–196

300–23 as for 274–9

323 after *will—v*(?) cancelled

328–75 as for 274–9

355 *t* erased at end of line

397+SH *GARCIUS*—squeezed in

403 not indented

404–63 as for 77–196

447+SD (English) to left of 448–50

465–71 indented, with 467, 471 more deeply indented

472–9 and 496–558 as for 77–196

549 not indented

563–74 as for 77–196

575 indented

576–95 as for 77–196

596 indented

641–96 as for 77–196

652 and 656 not indented

PLAY VIII

26 after *read—mee* erased

45 after *have—t* cancelled

60+SH in left margin with line to centre

65–72 fourth and eighth lines not indented

After 72 line-space blank

81 after *hethen—fl* cancelled

96+SD in margin to left of 97–8

120+SH after *TERTIUS—PASTOR* cancelled and *REX* written above

125+SH after *PRIMUS*—letter erased

144+SD '*Minstrells here must playe*'—to left of '*Here . . . kinge*'

145–52 every second line indented

156+SD to left of *HERODES*
196+SD to left of 197
200+SD to left of 201
204+SD to left of 205
268+Latin *auferetur*—*r*(2) altered from *s*
269–349 within each speech, every second line indented
282+SD to left of 283
326+SD to left of 325–7
341 after *misticall*—word (*p*——*s*) cancelled
349+SD to left of 350–1
357+SD to left of 358
365+SD to left of 366
379 indented
381+SD to left of 382–4
389+SD to left of 390
397+SD to left of 398

PLAY IX

29 after *here*—*or this* cancelled and *iwisse* inserted, with caret, above
47 indented

PLAY X

Play-heading above *Pagina Decima*—*Prima pagina* partially erased
88 not indented
198 indented
202 *knight*—after *g*, letter (*t*?) cancelled
203 after *dare*—*my* cancelled
205–12 every second line indented
208 *make*—after *e*, *s* erased
270 after *that*—*we*(?) cancelled
336 after *yt*—downstroke cancelled
360 after *to*—*l* cancelled
417–21 421 only indented
448 *therein*—*in* inserted, with caret, above line
To right of 454–7 bracket: 457+SD to right of bracket
472 after *hope*—*per*-abbreviation cancelled

PLAY XI

Before 1+SH *SYMEON*—after *N*, unusual decorative design
15 after *folke*—*the sooth to saye* cancelled

55 indented
81+SD to right of 81
108–10 no line indented
135 after *ryghtwise—god* cancelled
154 not indented
188 *on—o* probably altered from *i*
207–330 every second line indented
219 after *Josephe—y* cancelled
After 258+SH 263 partially erased
276 *Moyses—y* above the line
284 after *you—give* cancelled
292 not indented
324 *understand—r* written above line

PLAY XII

Play-heading desertum—s written over *c*
   Diabolus—a re-inked; perhaps alteration (from *o*?)
43 after *mans—h* cancelled
69 *through— u* written above *g*
168+SH *DOCTOUR—R* written above line
248+SH after *SECUNDUS—PASTOR* cancelled
262 after *I—chyde* cancelled
272 not indented
280+SH *DOCTOR— R* written above line

PLAY XIII

1–39 every second line in each stanza indented
18 *jeoperdye* inserted, with caret, above line
44 *instruct—r* written above line
48–51 one unit, with no line indented
70+SD *abiit—t* altered from *s*
71–6 76 only indented
77 after *I—d* cancelled
   as God—s squeezed in between *a* and *g*
113–18 118 only indented
To right of 128 scribbled *h* in margin
To right of 130+SH scribbled *r* in margin
135–40 138 only indented
150 after *parentes—p* cancelled
167 *without—*after *h*, *o* cancelled

169 *brought*—*r* written above *o*

209–14 211 and 214 indented

219–24 224 only indented

224 after *worke*—*some* cancelled

225–34 228 and 232 indented

250 *everlastinge*—*r* written above line

255–60 260 only indented

358 *freinde*—*n* written above line

365–9 one unit, with no line indented

372+SD after *versus*—*Jesus* cancelled

381–93 384, 388, 392 indented

427 after *to*—*fret* cancelled

450–7 457 only indented

464 *honour*—*r* written above line

482 *have good day*—*ave good day* written over erasure

PLAY XIV

29 *yearth*—*r* written above line: *t* squeezed in

31 *honour*—*r* written above line

79 after *say*—*I* cancelled

90 indented

112+SD to left of 113

113 after *also*—*I saye* cancelled; *to* squeezed in

116 *me* inserted, with caret, above line

152+SD *Janitro*—*t* altered from *v*

153+SH *JANITOR*—*R* written above line

176+SH *CIVIS*—*I*(2) altered from *E*

208+SD *sua*—*a* written above cancelled letter

213 *dreigh*—*i* squeezed in

262 *more*—altered from *moe*; *r* apparently written over *e* and final *e* added

289 *penyes*—*y* altered from *n*(?)

293 after *that*—*w* cancelled

332 *have*—after *a*, *d* blotted and *v* inserted, with caret, above *e*

PLAY XV

85 *to* inserted, with caret, above line

95 *on* inserted, with caret, above line

132 not indented

147 *shalt*—*t* heavily inked, with long upstroke; probably alteration

179 after *falshood*—*h* cancelled

185 *shall—l*(2) written over *t*

211 after *to—me* cancelled

275 *rowe—w* written above cancelled blotted *w*

311 after *togeather—*downstroke cancelled

313–18 318 only indented

348 *us* inserted, with caret, above line

PLAY XVI

Play-heading Annam—m followed by decorative flourish
    Caypham—m followed by decorative flourish

22 after *would—be* cancelled

49–53 53 only indented

132 *throo—r* written above cancelled letter

134–8 138 only indented

149 *nowe* inserted, with caret, above line

188 after *wonders—mad*(?) cancelled

228 after *death—he* cancelled

272 *âppere—p*(1) inserted, with caret, above line

304 *reves—v* written above blotted *v*

324 after *his—ch* cancelled

355–62 360 and 362 only indented

379–86 384 only indented

PLAY XVIA

61 *withowten—t*(2) written above line

91 after *all—three* cancelled

112+SD to right of 113

113+SD to right of 114

304+SH (English) in margin to left of Latin SH

308+SH (English) in margin to left of Latin SH

312 after *foe—*cancelled letter

345–51 351 only indented

357 indented

415 after *hee—f* cancelled

474 after *many—and* inserted, with caret, above line and partially erased

PLAY XVII

2–4 first two lines indented; 4 further indented

51 after *commen—ys* cancelled

120 after *thy—postee*(?) cancelled

138 *out* inserted, with caret, above line
After 200 *And*—most unusually as catchword at bottom right of page 107ʳ
256 not indented
258 indented
275 *singe*—*n* inserted, with caret, above line
328 *in*—after *n*, linked downstroke cancelled

PLAY XVIII

41–5 45 only indented
45 *tombe*—*m* inserted, with caret, above line
85 after *to*—*my* cancelled
102 *sooth*—downstroke below *t*; perhaps alteration from *h*
154–85 every second line indented
203 after *ys*—letter cancelled
204 before *owt*—*of* cancelled
After 221 230 cancelled
242 *sayne*—*n* written above line
298–300 no line indented
310 *wringe*—after *e*, *s* cancelled

PLAY XIX

8 *deole*—*e*(1) inserted, with caret, above line
27 *hee* inserted, with caret, above line
43 after *men*—*may* cancelled and *doe* inserted, with caret, above
57 before *yea*—*you* cancelled
71 indented
157 after *eych*—*whitt* cancelled
217+SH *THOMAS*—here and in all other instances of the name in the Play, *A* written above line

PLAY XX

38 indented
85 *in*—after *n*, cancelled downstroke
96+SH *JESUS*—squeezed in
104+Latin *vestrum*(1)—*r* written above line
144 *the*—after *e*, *e* cancelled
152+SD *psallemus*—*s*(1) altered from *h*
158 after *steede*—*ste* cancelled
183 *leevinge*—*e*(2) written above line
186 *commandement*—*n*(2) written above line

PLAY XXI

21 after *all*—*ed* partially erased

25 *wretch*—*t* altered from *c*(?)

46 *fullfill*—*ll*(1) inserted, with caret, above line

46+SD (English) to right of SD (Latin)

47 after *us*—*all un* cancelled and *there* inserted, with caret, above

76+SH *THOMAS*—here and in all other instances of the name in the Play, *A* written above line

79 *yood*—after *d, e* cancelled

92+SH *MATHIAS*—after *A*(1), *T* partially erased

96+SD after *quidem*—*baptista* cancelled

134 *put*—before *p, f* cancelled

144+SH *MATHIAS*—after *A*(1), *T* cancelled

152+SD to left of SH and 153

153-8 155 and 158 indented

190 after *bale*—*h* cancelled

209 after *in*—*this* cancelled

258 after *house*—*ys* cancelled

275 after *a*—word cancelled

286+SH to left of *MATHIAS*—*Mattheus* partially erased

342+SH to left of *MATHIAS*—*Mattheus* cancelled

346+SH *SIMON*—squeezed in above Latin

370+SH *ALIENIGENA*—*ENI* inserted, with caret, above line

PLAY XXII

Folio number *128*—after *2, 7* cancelled

8 after *flesh*—*or* cancelled

65 after *asked*—*yt* cancelled and *him* written above

107 *betoken*—after *k, g* cancelled

156+SH and 212+SH *EXPOSITOR*—*R* written above line

260+Latin *Signa 15*—in margin to left of Latin text
judicium—after *i*(2), two letters cancelled

269-332 numbers of signs in left margin

273 *as*—letter (*e*?) written above
after *read*—*I* cancelled

288 different hand

316 *the*—after *e*, two letters(?) cancelled

PLAY XXIII

1-8 every second line indented

73 *leeved*—*e*(1) written over another letter; *e*(2) written above line

133–7 137 only indented

144 *thee* inserted, with caret, above line

156 *one*—upstroke above *o*

158–60 160 indented

199 *verey*—written above cancelled *in me*

221 *God*—after *o*, *o* cancelled

269 *the*—after *e*, *s* cancelled

285 after *that*—*d* cancelled

365–76 and 381–9 every third line indented

383 *through*—*u* inserted above line

394 *no theeves*—written without word-gap and separated by horizontal stroke

401 *heare*—*a* written above line

410–12 412 indented

417–19 419 indented

431+SH *DOCTOR*—*R* written above line

444 *syckerlye*—*y*(1) altered from *e*

448–53 as for 365–76

461 after *so*—*light* cancelled

498–500 500 indented

507 after *endinge*—*hee*(?) cancelled

582 after *so*—*light* cancelled

605 *through*—after *h*(2), letter cancelled

607 *greetes*—*r* written above line

644+SD after *helpe*(2)—*p* cancelled

655 after *thought*—*was* cancelled

661–6 663 and 666 indented

678 after *should*—*have be saved* cancelled (*have* above line)
   the hydd inserted, with caret, above line

679–98 every second line indented

719 *for* inserted, with caret, above line
   after *you*—*have* cancelled

722+SD *etc*—*e* altered from *h*

PLAY XXIV

5 *three*—*r* written above blotted *r*

62 after *which*—*th* cancelled

70 after *purgatorye*—*w* cancelled

177 *noe*—*oe* written above blot

178 *face*—after *c*, *e* blotted and thus cancelled

225 after *tornes*—downstroke cancelled

231 *to* squeezed in between *mee* and *fonge*

243 *or*—above *o*, stroke cancelled

278 after *fye*—word cancelled

324+SH *MERCATOR—R*(2) written above line

After 340 four lines cancelled: 341, 346, 347, 348; with 348 *tyme*] *sythes*

364 after *I*—downstroke cancelled

425 *looke* inserted, with caret, above line, in non-scribal hand

430 *unthought—t*(2) apparently added in non-scribal hand and ink

472+SH *IMPERATOR—R*(2) written above line

481 *great*—after *t*, letter, (*e?*), cancelled

513 *yoare—o* inserted, with caret, above line

548+SH *DEMON—M* perhaps alteration; upstroke visible above letter and preceding *E* is unusually close

578 *fervent*—after *fer*, *fervent* cancelled and *vent* inserted, with caret, above

649 *death—a* written above line

MANUSCRIPT A

FOLIO-NUMBERING

Two sets of numbers, the original set to the right of the Guild-ascription as a running folio-head, and the later set near the top of the right margin. Folios 1–10 and the last two folios are unnumbered in the original set because of damage to the manuscript. The original set errs by numbering folio 89 as 90, and no correction is made from that point onward. The later set is used below.

GUILD-ASCRIPTIONS AND PLAY-HEADINGS

Throughout the manuscript the Guild-ascriptions precede the Play-headings, except for Play III which has no Play-heading.

CONTENT OF PAGES

I 1^r, 1–45; 1^v, 46–81; 2^r, 82–121; 2^v, 122–53; 3^r, 153+SH–91; 3^v, 192–229; 4^r, 229+SD–57; 4^v, 258–97; 5^r, 298–Finis

II 5^v, 1–40; 6^r, 41–82; 6^v, 83–116; 7^r, 117–40; 7^v, 140+SH–70; 8^r, 171–212; 8^v, 212+SH–48+SD; 9^r, 248+SH–74; 9^v, 275–93; 10^r, 293 +SH–334; 10^v, 335–70; 11^r, 371–404; 11^v, 405–45; 12^r, 446–92; 12^v, 493–524; 13^r, 525–60+SD; 13^v, 560+SH–96; 14^r, 596+SH–622; 14^v, 623–60; 15^r, 661–96; 15^v, 696+SH–Finis

III 16^r, 1–36; 16^v, 37–68; 17^r, 68+SH–98; 17^v, 98+SH–124; 18^r, 125–60+SD; 18^v, 160+SH–90; 19^r, 191–220; 19^v, 220+SH–48; 20^r, 249–91; 20^v, 292–Finis

IV 21ʳ, 1–22; 21ᵛ, 23–52; 22ʳ, 53–80; 22ᵛ, 80+SD–108; 23ʳ, 109–48; 23ᵛ, 148+SD–90; 24ʳ, 191–222; 24ᵛ, 223–50; 25ʳ, 250+SH–72; 25ᵛ, 272+SH–96; 26ʳ, 296+SH–326; 26ᵛ, 327–58+SD; 27ʳ, 358+SH–89; 27ᵛ, 389+SD–416; 28ʳ, 416+SH–41; 28ᵛ, 442–79; 29ʳ, 480–Finis

V 29ᵛ, 1–32; 30ʳ, 32+SD–72; 30ᵛ, 72+SH–103; 31ʳ, 104–47; 31ᵛ, 148–81; 32ʳ, 182–209; 32ᵛ, 210–33; 33ʳ, 234–59; 33ᵛ, 259+SH–95; 34ʳ, 295+SH–331; 34ᵛ, 332–71; 35ʳ, 371+SH–411; 35ᵛ, 412–51; 36ʳ, 452– Finis

VI 36ᵛ, 1–26; 37ʳ, 26+SH–64; 37ᵛ, 64+SD–108; 38ʳ, 109–46; 38ᵛ, 147– 84; 39ʳ, 184+SH–226; 39ᵛ, 227–73; 40ʳ, 273+SH–326; 40ᵛ, 327–64+2 (see VRs); 41ʳ, 364+3–402; 41ᵛ, 403–40; 42ʳ, 441–76; 42ᵛ, 476+SH–508 +SD; 43ʳ, 508+SH–43; 43ᵛ, 544–79; 44ʳ, 580–627; 44ᵛ, 626–66; 45ʳ, 666+SD–702; 45ᵛ, 703–Finis

VII 46ʳ, 1–44; 46ᵛ, 44+SD–74; 47ʳ, 75–108; 47ᵛ, 108+SH–44; 48ʳ, 144+SH–79; 48ᵛ, 180–217; 49ʳ, 218–45; 49ᵛ, 245+SH–73; 50ʳ, 274– 305; 50ᵛ, 305+SH–39; 51ʳ, 339+SH–66; 51ᵛ, 366+SH–93; 52ʳ, 393+ SH–423; 52ᵛ, 423+SH–51; 53ʳ, 451+SH–81; 53ᵛ, 482–507; 54ʳ, 507+ SH–45; 54ᵛ, 546–75; 55ʳ, 575+SH–606; 55ᵛ, 606+SH–40; 56ʳ, 640+ SH–74; 56ᵛ, 675–Finis

VIII 57ʳ, 1–32; 57ᵛ, 32+SH–64; 58ʳ, 64+SD–88; 58ᵛ, 88+SH–116; 59ʳ, 116+SH–40; 59ᵛ, 141–66; 60ʳ, 167–212; 60ᵛ, 212+SH–48; 61ʳ, 249–86; 61ᵛ, 287–324; 62ʳ, 324+SH–65; 62ᵛ, 365+SD–413; 63ʳ, 414– Finis

IX 63ᵛ, 1–24; 64ʳ, 24+SH–61; 64ᵛ, 62–97; 65ʳ, 98–135; 65ᵛ, 135+SD– 76; 66ʳ, 177–215; 66ᵛ, 216–49; 67ʳ, 250–Finis

X 67ᵛ, 1–38; 68ʳ, 39–72; 68ᵛ, 72+SH–98; 69ʳ, 99–144; 69ᵛ, 145–84; 70ʳ, 184+SH–248; 70ᵛ, 248+SH–80; 71ʳ, 280+SH–312; 71ᵛ, 312+SH– 60; 72ʳ, 360+SH–402; 72ᵛ, 403–45; 73ʳ, 446–85; 73ᵛ, 485+SH–Finis

XI 74ʳ, 1–34; 74ᵛ, 35–67; 75ʳ, 68–103; 75ᵛ, 103+SH–38; 76ʳ, 139–76; 76ᵛ, 177–220; 77ʳ, 221–54; 77ᵛ, 254+SH–84; 78ʳ, 285–318; 78ᵛ, 318+ SH–Finis

XII 79ʳ, 1–42; 79ᵛ, 43–86; 80ʳ, 87–128; 80ᵛ, 128+SD–68; 81ʳ, 168+ SH–216; 81ᵛ, 216+SD–48; 82ʳ, 248+SH–80; 82ᵛ, 280+SH–Finis

XIII 83ʳ, 1–19; 83ᵛ, 20–43; 84ʳ, 43+SH–72; 84ᵛ, 72+SD–106; 85ʳ, 107–36; 85ᵛ, 137–68; 86ʳ, 168+SH–200; 86ᵛ, 200+SH–30; 87ʳ, 230+ SH–68; 87ᵛ, 268+SH–304; 88ʳ, 304+SH–332+SD; 88ᵛ, 332+SH–62; 89ʳ, 363–90; 89ᵛ, 391–422; 90ʳ, 422+SH–50; 90ᵛ, 450+SH–Finis

XIV 91ʳ, 1–26; 91ᵛ, 27–56+SD; 92ʳ, 56+SH–90; 92ᵛ, 90+SH–134; 93ʳ, 135–60; 93ᵛ, 160+SH–92; 94ʳ, 192+SH–218; 94ᵛ, 219–48; 95ʳ, 248+SH–81; 95ᵛ, 282–322; 96ʳ, 323–60; 96ᵛ, 360+SH–92; 97ʳ, 392+ SH–420; 97ᵛ, 421–Finis

XV 98ʳ, 1–32; 98ᵛ, 32+SH–56; 99ʳ, 56+SH–88; 99ᵛ, 88+SD–116; 100ʳ, 116+SH–144+SD; 100ᵛ, 144+SH–64; 101ʳ, 165–92; 101ᵛ, 193– 224; 102ʳ, 225–68; 102ᵛ, 269–304; 103ʳ, 304+SD–22; 103ᵛ, 322+SH– 48; 104ʳ, 349–Finis

XVI 104^v, 1–20; 105^r, 20+SH–54; 105^v, 55–81; 106^r, 81+SH–105; 106^v, 105+SH–30; 107^r, 131–56; 107^v, 157–84; 108^r, 185–214; 108^v, 214 + SH–40; 109^r, 241–63; 109^v, 263 +SH–88; 110^r, 289–314+SD; 110^v, 314+ SH–40; 111^r, 341–64; 111^v, 364+SH–86; 112^r, 386+SH–Finis

XVIA 112^v, 1–28; 113^r, 28+SH–56; 113^v, 56+SH–84; 114^r, 84+SH– 114; 114^v, 115–44; 115^r, 144+SH–70; 115^v, 171–98; 116^r, 199–224; 116^v, 224+SH–59; 117^r, 260–96; 117^v, 296+SH–327; 118^r, 328–52; 118^v, 352+SH–79; 119^r, 379+SH–419; 119^v, 420–43; 120^r, 444–Finis

XVII 120^v, 1–32; 121^r, 32+Latin–72; 121^v, 72+Latin–106; 122^r, 107– 40; 122^v, 140+SH–68; 123^r, 168+SH–96; 123^v, 196+SH–228; 124^r, 228+SD–60; 124^v, 261–300; 125^r, 301–Finis

XVIII 125^v, 1–40; 126^r, 40+SH–73; 126^v, 73+SH–113; 127^r, 113+ SH–47; 127^v, 148–85; 128^r, 185+SD–215; 128^v, 216–49; 129^r, 249+ SH–85; 129^v, 285+SH–316; 130^r, 316+SH–48; 130^v, 348+SH–72; 131^r, 372+SH–98; 131^v, 399–427; 132^r, 428–Finis

XIX 132^v, 1–24; 133^r, 24+SH–54; 133^v, 55–95; 134^r, 95+Latin–119; 134^v, 119+SD–143+SD; 135^r, 143+SH–71; 135^v, 171+SH–203; 136^r, 204–39; 136^v, 239+SD–Finis

XX 137^r, 1–28; 137^v, 28+SH–62; 138^r, 63–104; 138^v, 104+SD–8; 139^r, 108+SH–46; 139^v, 147–76; 140^r, 176+SH–Finis

XXI 140^v, 1–32; 141^r, 32+Latin–64; 141^v, 64+SH–94; 142^r, 95–116; 142^v, 116+SH–42; 143^r, 143–86; 143^v, 187–238+SD; 144^r, 238+SH– 72; 144^v, 273–302; 145^r, 302+SH–326+Latin; 145^v, 326+SH–50; 146^r, 350+SH–78; 146^v, 379–Finis

XXII 147^r, 1–36; 147^v, 37–80; 148^r, 81–128; 148^v, 129–72; 149^r, 172+ SH–220; 149^v, 221–68; 150^r, 269–318; 150^v, 319–Finis

XXIII 151^r, 1–32; 151^v, 33–66; 152^r, 67–108; 152^v, 108+SH–41; 153^r, 141+SD–66; 153^v, 167–96; 154^r, 196+SD–246; 154^v, 247–84; 155^r, 284+SH–320; 155^v, 320+SH–52; 156^r, 352+SH–86; 156^v, 386+SH– 420; 157^r, 420+SH–61; 157^v, 461+SH–91; 158^r, 491+SH–528; 158^v, 528+SH–60; 159^r, 560+SH–92; 159^v, 592+SH–624+SD; 160^r, 624+ SH–56; 160^v, 657–702; 161^r, 703–Finis

XXIV 161^v, 1–32; 162^r, 32+SH–70; 162^v, 71–112; 163^r, 113–56; 163^v, 157–98; 164^r, 199–242; 164^v, 243–88; 165^r, 289–334; 165^v, 335–72; 166^r, 373–424; 166^v, 425–52; 167^r, 452+SH–92; 167^v, 493–526; 168^r, 527–68; 168^v, 569–611; last two folios lost

FORMS OF PLAY-ENDING

Finis deo gracias per me
+*Georgi Bellin*+*1592*   XIII, XVII, XIX,
                                  XXII, XXIII

+*Gorge Bellin*+*1592*   XXI
+*Geo Bellin*+*1592*   XV

+ *George Bellin*+*1592*
+ *Come lorde Jesu Come*
   Quicklye   III

+ *Georgi Bellin*+*1592*
+ *Come lorde Jesu Come*
   Quicklye   VI, VII
+ *Come lorde Jesus Come*
   Quicklye   I, II, VIII

+ *Georgi Bellin*+*1592*
+ *Come lorde Jesu Come*
   Quicklye
      +*1592*   XVIII
      +*anno 1592*   IV

+ *Georgi Bellin*+*1592*
+ *Come lorde Jesus Come*
   Quicklye
      +*1592*   XX

+ *Georgi Bellin*
+ *Come lorde Jesu Come*
   Quicklye
      +*1592*   V, X, XI, XII, XIV
      +*anno domini 1592*   IX
      +*anno 1592*+*anno*
      domini 1592 [in
      non-scribal hand]   XVIA
      +*1592 The ende of*
      this storye is
      begennan in
      the nexte leafe
      followinge   XVI
   Ending lost   XXIV

MARGINALIA

Numbers at left in this section refer to manuscript pages.

3^r written vertically downward within left marginal double-ruling, 'Thomas Lawranson is my name bee it known unto all men by this booke and legend.'

4^r several pen-scratchings in lower right

6^v ink blots in middle right

7^r three endless-knot designs in middle left

8^v pen strokes and ink blots in upper right

16^r *3*, as play-number, within diamond-shaped design, in upper left, with *1592* beneath it

21^r $S \cdot R \cdot B$ above Guild-name as running head: *Sancta Regina Beatissima* (?)

    4 as play-number in upper left

22^r *SRB* to right of running head and original folio number

23^r *SR* as in 22^r; corner of folio missing

24^r *S* as in 22^r; corner of folio missing

24^v $S \cdot R \cdot B$ to right of running head

26^r *SRB* as in 22^r

27^r $S \cdot R \cdot B$ to right of running head and original folio number

28^r pen strokes in upper left

    word, *our* (?), in lower left

28^v $S \cdot R \cdot B$ to right of running head

29^r *1592* to right of running head and original folio number

29^v *5* as play-number in upper left

30^r $S \cdot R \cdot B$, with *1592* under it, to right of running head and original folio number

31^r as for 30^r

33^r *SRB* as in 22^r

34^r written vertically upward in middle left, *John D J John Dutton is an honest man*, with *John Dutton is an honest mann* beneath first statement, and cancellation of several words to right. Another *John Dutton* is written above *John D J*, and another *D* below. *balake* is written horizontally in upper portion of each margin

35^r faint writing in upper left margin

36^r below Play-ending, in middle third of page:

    Finis de 1621

        $\underline{1592}$

        0029

    9.8.7.4.5.6.3

    4 5 6.3 9.4 2

    6.3 9.6.3.1.

    2 4 5 6 8 9

    1 4 3 2 3 9 2 5

    1 4 3 2 3 8 2 5

36^v *6* as play-number in upper left

    pen-markings and perhaps three words in lower left

37^r writing in middle left

    $S \cdot R \cdot B$ as in 27^r and in ruling at bottom

    ink blots in lower right

40^r ink-scratchings in lower left

40^v $S \cdot R \cdot B$ as in 24^v

42^r ink-scratchings in upper left

44^r ink-scratchings in middle left and blots in lower right

47^v *SRB* to right of running head

51^r pen-scratchings in lower right and low left—letters (?) *s, k, m, n, f*

53^r in middle right, written vertically downward, *Accusator debet*—(?) *omnia*. Two capital *A*'s beneath

55^r most of left margin has horizontal writing; all words are not clear: *John Holland of Brabant* and, below, *within the County* are clear
　be all (?) in middle right

57^r *8* as play-number in upper left

58^r pen-scratchings in upper left, on to text

61^r left margin has mathematics and unclear words

61^v top left, *John* vertically downward
　upper left, *Danyell full*
　a little lower, *Ed*
　a little lower, *E*
　middle left, *Edward, Ed, my*

62^r bottom left, *John*, vertically downward; *ford*(?) vertically upward

63^r below play-ending, *finis deo gratias Finis Deo Gratias Come lord Jesus*
　below, written vertically upward, *Gilbert Jre* with *b* below *r* in *Jre*

63^v *9* as play-number in upper left
　pen-scratchings in left margin

67^r below play-ending, *S⋮R⋮B⋮K* with cross below

67^v *10* as play-number in upper left

74^r *11* as play-number in upper left

75^r in upper left, *Geo, G, George, Geo* (?)

75^v in left margin, written vertically downward, *filthy thou vanity and all — serve in — — with hope — gentleman doinge in it and these occupations are little to bee prased for it*
　inside right ruling, pen-scratchings and, at lowest right, *eke* written vertically downward

76^r lower left, *noe* (?) and flourish

77^v top left, scratchings
　lower left, *Ryk* (?)

78^r *1592* to right of running head and original folio number

79^r *12* as play-number in upper left, with N-S-E-W design over it

80^v writing vertically upward in left margin: *Nihil est turpis quam assentatio inter amicos*

81^r pen-scratchings in upper left

81^v ink blots in middle left
　pen-scratchings in lower right

83^r *13* as play-number in upper left
　89 (?) cancelled as folio-number to right of *83*

86^v in middle left, *8* and *Kinge of Culanye* written vertically upward

88^r diamond-design in upper left
scratchings in middle right

89^v crosses and horizontal lines within left marginal double-ruling
Lord Lord y A and *Sr* (?) written vertically downward in middle right

91^r *14* as play-number in upper left

92^r *forthe Henery* in upper left
seventeen *y*'s, mostly vertically arranged, in upper left
thirteen *b*'s, haphazardly arranged, in lower right

93^r in upper left, written vertically upward, *David David Eduarde George Henery Francis* (?), with *Adam* beneath *David*

95^v word in middle left, *Brucker* (?)
pen marks in upper left and middle and lower right

96^r pen marks in middle and lower left

98^r *15* as play-number in upper left

104^v *16* as play-number in upper left
dog's-head design imitating finial of nearby multiple-ruling in upper right

110^r *Eloquentia* in upper left
numerous *b*'s and an *E* in right

110^v *William* written vertically upward in lower left

111^r in right, written vertically upward: *What man*
                                  can beare
                               a lofty harte
William King the Yonger his Booke 1656
John King his brother

112^r in lower left written vertically upward, *Aut quos in* [a cancelled word] with *pulsus* (?) below it and cancelled word below *pulsus* (?)
    within double-ruling in lower left, *Aut quas in sperus* (?) [a cancelled word] *in mente non a-* and beneath that *Eternuria derus meditaris inferene stellis* (?)
    in upper left, *Quo rapis Baccheane tuoinaminie plenum* (?) and beneath that, cancelled, *Aut quos in nenius a gorq que* [inserted above line] *in sperus*

119^r *lancia* in upper right, as pencilled correction

121^v in left, written vertically upward, Latin similar to that on 112^r

122^r upper two-thirds of right marginal double-ruling crosshatched

122^v pen-scratchings in middle left

123^r *Eloquentia* in upper left
crosshatching in middle of left marginal double-ruling

123^v written vertically upward in left: *Gr*, and beneath that, *George Frest* (?), and, above *Frest*, *G*; then, to right of *G*, *Gilbert Frblum*(?)

124ᵛ four lines written vertically upward in lower left [first line illegible except for final -ye: top half trimmed away]:

> when hee would hee shall have naye
> — you may affared bee
> both rich and poore of eich degrie

125ʳ four lines written vertically upward in lower left:

> [top line obscured in binding]
> though over dassed (?) now I bee
> all thinges on erth hath but a tyme
> and doth decay so well as myne

125ᵛ *18* as play-number in upper left

127ᵛ pen-scratchings in middle right

128ʳ pen-scratchings in middle left

132ᵛ *19* as play-number in upper left
two dog's-head designs in upper right imitating nearby finial of multiple-ruling

137ʳ *20* as play-number in upper left

138ᵛ Latin written vertically upward in left: *Quam loco* cancelled; then *paxis me plenum — —*; beneath that *Quam loco paxis lai* (?) cancelled; then *Non tamen I*, with *Non tamen* beneath
pen marks within left marginal rulings

140ᵛ *21* as play-number in upper left

143ʳ *my* inside right marginal ruling
filius (?) outside in middle right

145ᵛ pen-scratchings in middle left
in upper left, written horizontally leftward in vertical row, *Adam, A, Ad, A Adam, gretende, is my name*
in lower left, written vertically upward, *Bilber* (?)

147ʳ *22* as play-number in upper left

147ᵛ *my*, written horizontally rightward, in upper left
pen-scratchings in lower left

151ʳ 23 as play-number in upper left

155ᵛ in upper left, written vertically downward, *William Lenen Conne* (?)

156ʳ *Omitted 1600 and 1607* pencilled in left margin, with bracket around first six lines of Antichrist's second speech

158ᵛ written vertically upward in left:

> You that doe reed this book I do you Counsen give
> break of your sins betime If you intend to live
> or els my Counsell in your [word cancelled] face shall fly
> when you Com t hell and in the flames do ly
> Georg Renwick [see note 161ᵛ]

159ᵛ blurred pencilled note at bottom left: — *160;* — *1607*

160ᵛ written vertically upward in left: *Nicholas whimright* (?) *oeth this Buke*
near bottom left: *Not in 1600; in 1607* in pencil

161ᵛ *24* as play-number in upper left
written vertically upward in left:

> *Those tongs that have gods word abusd*
> *In profaine playes his name so used*
> *If they repent not they goe to hell*
> *and all that love them and so fare well*
> *finis per me Georg Renwick*

166ᵛ written vertically upward in left: . . . *emendatium* [two letters cancelled] *inhonestum est at vitaperandum*(?)

STARRING

Bellin's cumulative addiction to the use of small stars (*) in this manuscript is puzzling. No stars occur in the first play. In II he begins on 9ʳ putting a star before and after SHs, and using stars in the Play-ending. In III stars occur additionally in the Guild-ascription and after SDs (six on 17ᵛ, four on 18ʳ). Also in III we find the first use of a star at the end of a line of a speech (16ᵛ, last line). In IV Bellin starts putting stars within the double horizontal rulings (21ʳ) and after the running folio-heads; and the number of stars placed after SDs increases. Twenty-five times in IV (21ᵛ onward) stars in varying numbers (one to six) are placed after lines of speeches. From V through XXIV stars are regularly found before, within, and/or after Guild-ascriptions, Play-headings, running folio-heads, SHs, SDs, lines of speeches, and play-endings.

Certainly in many places, as before and after SHs, the stars serve only as decoration. Elsewhere, as after SDs, they mark the end of a unit in the text. Further, Greg suggested that Bellin intended, by putting one or more stars at ends of lines, to mark four- or eight-line stanzaic divisions and thereby to fill out the shorter lines (see *Bibliographical and Textual Problems of the English Miracle Cycles,* p. 35n). If so, no consistent usage occurs. For example, on 162ᵛ and 163ʳ, in XXIV, the speech of Rex Salvatus has two stars after the second line, making that line extend as far as the preceding line, but then only one star after the fourth line, leaving that line shorter than the preceding line. Next we find two stars after the eighth line but no more stars until the twentieth. Such inconsistency is to be found frequently from V through XXIV. It seems true, however, that in general stars follow fourth and eighth lines.

PLAY I

1–2 single line

7 *is sette* begins following line

16 inset

32–3 single line

69–77 each line as two lines—final dividing words are *begyninge, cuninge, excelente, wislye, vayne, darckenes, wroughte, donne, naughte*

85+SD in margin to left of and slightly below 85

After 153 *Cheraphin* as centred catchword
213+Latin in margin to left of SH

PLAY II

14 *nighte*—*n* alteration
101 two lines: *wroughte*/
112+SD parenthetical SD in margin to left of primary SD
After 116 *of* as catchword
After 248+SD *Eva* as centred catchword
256+SD after *shall*(2)—*f* uncancelled followed by two letters (*oe?*) blotted and cancelled
262 *forbydden*—after *for*, word-gap and *gev* cancelled, followed by further word-gap
After 293 *Eva* as centred catchword
320 *for*—after *r*, *e* cancelled
424+SD in margin to left of *ADAM*

PLAY III

13 after *sore*—*su* cancelled
129 *eaten*—*e*(1) written over cancelled letter
After 220 *Cam* as centred catchword
228 *gossippes*—*ss* altered from *od*
233 two lines: *malmsme*/
252+SD in margin to left of 250–1

PLAY IV

18–22 inset, one letter
64+SH preceded by SD
72 *hys*, with *here* written over it in seemingly later ink
72+SD *Abraham*—*a*(1) written over another letter
250+SD in margin to left of 249–50
301 in red letters
358+SD after 356
389+SD first clause follows 388 (see VRs)

PLAY V

15 after *place*—*longe* probably cancelled by two stars placed above it
64+SD to left of SH and 65
91 *firste*—after *e*, *s* cut by downstroke and blotted; perhaps cancelled

111+SD to left of 111
115+SD to left of 115
116 *anoye—y* altered from *w*(?)
143+SD to left of 144
165 *he—h* written over cancelled *y*
183+SD second sentence centred as SH
191 *todaiye—y* altered from *m*(?); first minim of *m* dotted to give *i*
241 *of thee* written above line
412 *women—wo* inserted, with caret, above line
442 *but—b* written over another letter (*w*?)

PLAY VI

54 *Marye—after e*, letter cancelled
70 after *anima—dei* cancelled
209–17 two stanzas in French set off by broken rulings
209–10 each as two lines; *asmeles*/ and *leez*/: second half of each line separated from remainder by bracket and placed in margin to right
213 two lines: *sages*/
214 *et leable* begins following line
215 *meas de tole plerunte* begins following line
216 *saen . . . pusell*—separate line
217 two lines: *un*/
468 *see—s* altered from *t*
500+SD broken ruling above
539+SD as after 500

PLAY VII

48+SD *hic—c* altered from *s*
52+SD to right of 52
136+SD broken ruling above
172 *of beastes* ends preceding line
274–5 single line
277–8 single line
279+SD broken ruling above and below
323+SD double broken ruling above
446 *all—A* altered from *f*
447+SD (English) to left of SD (Latin)
After 451 *Primus Pastor* as centred catchphrase
After 575 *Tertius Pastor* as centred catchphrase
605 two lines: *firste*/

PLAY VIII

25 after *wherfore—ye* cancelled and *we* written above
112+SD no rulings for SD
144+SD broken ruling above
153–60 all in red letters
156+SD in margin to left of 157
196+SD in margin to left of 196
200+SD in margin to left of 201
204+SD in margin to left of 205
227 after *moves—o* and part of downstroke cancelled
249 after *grace—woulde* cancelled
278 before *is—*one or more letters cancelled
282+SD to left of SH
289+SD *doctor—r* altered from *t*
326+SD in margin to left of SH
349+SD in margin to left of SH
357+SD in margin to left of 358
365+SD in margin to left of 366
381+SD in margin to left of SH and 380–2
389+SD in margin to left of 389

PLAY IX

6 *payne—a* blotted and re-written above
24+SH before *REX—*word, *PRIMUS*(?), cancelled
62 *diatie—*after *i*(1), *e* with star above apparently as cancellation
88 after *by—these,* with *h* written above line, cancelled

PLAY X

1–4 all in red letters
14 *will—l*(2) altered from *be*
37 after *knaves—*letter cancelled
63 after *bereve—me* cancelled
85 *Lansclerdepe—d* altered from *p*
124 after *be—deade* cancelled
155 *iwisse—*after *i*(1), letter cancelled, and word-gap
Below 192+SD broken ruling
289 *faste—*after *f, h* cancelled
345 *woe—*after *e, s* cancelled
389 *goe—o* blotted, and *o* written above

438 two lines: *camrocke*/
457+SD to left of 457

PLAY XI

97 *wilte*—first minim of *w* altered from *l*(?)
After 103 *Angellus* as centred catchword
168 after *thy*—*peace* cancelled
308 *facche*—*c*(1) written above *c*(2)
316 *wee*—*e*(1) with blotted upstroke; probably alteration (from *h*?)

PLAY XII

After 216 *Tunc* as centred catchword

PLAY XIII

Before 1 Latin separated from text by six-line ruling with usual finial
1–35 each line as two lines; final dividing words are *dei, walketh, life, prophettes, Jacobe, promysed, ranscome, sumus, sente, declare, hym, darlinge, againe, creatures, brethren, Bethenye, comaundments, sheapard, flocke, the, animam, brethren, worckes, sicke, me, have, flocke, flocke, hense, ofte, worde, knowe, desciples, but, doinges*
13 after *owne*—*thralle* cancelled
17 *comaundments*—abbreviated ending *mts* with no abbreviation mark, and *t* blotted and probable alteration
24 after *the*(1)—letter cancelled
50 two lines: *broughte*/
207 after *all*—*ye* cancelled
260+SD broken ruling above
356 *hym*—*ym* written over *er*(?)
406 *were*(1)—*re* inserted, with caret, above line
455 *ther*—*t* squeezed in

PLAY XIV

9 *be*—before *b, a* cancelled
20 *over*—after *er, ll* cancelled
128 after *to*—*daie* cancelled
223 after *no*—*v* cancelled
318 *avayle*—after *e*, letter cancelled

PLAY XV

9 after *thou—hie* cancelled

After 56 *Johannes* as centred catchword

61 *we—w* altered from *th*

125 *hym—y* altered from *e*

142 *wayshe—a* written above blotted *a*

150 *my—m* altered from *n*

PLAY XVI

4 *sppurned—p*(1) cancelled or blotted

132 *hym—*written over *you*?

134–5 French in red

134 two lines: *Cayphas*/

135 two lines: *vel*/

202+SD *Juddi—d*(1) altered from *e*

PLAY XVIA

112+SD to left of 113

113+SD to left of 114

131 after *thou—talk* cancelled

320 *have—h* altered from another letter

333 *will—i* blotted and probably alteration (from *e*?)
three—r written above *e*(1)

359+Latin placed as line in stanza

406 after *in—daies* cancelled
thye—y written over *r*; after *e, e* cancelled

PLAY XVII

58 *baptised—b* altered from *p*

88+SD *David* as SH

150 after *us—wh* cancelled

152+SH above ruling following SD

266 after *sayde—naye* cancelled

PLAY XVIII

14 after *am—mo* cancelled
*riches—*written on preceding line, above *man of*, preceded by symbol to
indicate insertion and further separated from end of 13 by three 'stars'

95 *understande—r* written above line

153+SDs SD(2)—continuation of SD(1)

251–2 single line

411 after *I—was* cancelled

425 before *woman—why* erased
427 *where*—first minim of *w* written over downstroke

PLAY XIX

52 *wronge*—partially blotted and rewritten above line
After 143+SD *Cleophas,* in red, as centred catchword

PLAY XX
No notes necessary

PLAY XXI

46+SD (English) below SD (Latin)
96+SH *SYMION—Y* written over another letter
158+SD *Deus dicat* centred as SH
183 *down*—after *n, de* cancelled (or perhaps only *d* cancelled)
354 after *bouth—quicke* cancelled; *good* written above line

PLAY XXII

25 after *expresslye—sh* cancelled
159 *that horne*—written without word-gap; *a* altered from *e*
260+Latin *Signa 15* in margin to left of Latin text
269–332 numbers of signs in left margin with, below each, asterisk and line to appropriate place in text
303 *whereof*—unusual initial flourish to *w*; first minim of *w* altered from *l*(?)

PLAY XXIII

214 after *your—g* cancelled
After 352 *Helias* as centred catchword
362 *devyn*—after *n,* two letters blotted
425 *and*—after *n, d* cancelled
442 after *yette—I* cancelled
512+SH *ANTECHRISTUS—A* altered from *E*
609 *reche—r* altered from *w* and blotted
693–4 three lines: *toppe/*; *songe/*

PLAY XXIV

Before 1 Latin—two lines: *oo/*
188 after *full*—letter cancelled
254 *pynchinge—y* altered from *e*
267 *ffor—f*(1) written over *m*
375 *recover—r*(2) written above blotted *r*
419 after *of*—letter cancelled
534 *hym—h* probably alteration (from *m*?)

MANUSCRIPT R
FOLIO-NUMBERING

Two sets of folio numbers. The *Proclamation* is a single folio, with writing on recto and with verso blank; unnumbered by both numerators. The Banns cover three folios with writing on both sides of each; unnumbered by the original numerator, and numbered by the later numerator. Thus Play I begins *1* (original) and *4* (later). The original numerator subsequently errs by placing *177* on two successive folios, and the error continues through to the end of the manuscript. The later numerator marks a blank page as 167; see Textual Notes, 'Contents of Pages, XX'. The later numbering is used below.

GUILD-ASCRIPTIONS AND PLAY-HEADINGS

Throughout the manuscript the Guild-ascriptions precede the Play-headings, except for Play III which has no Play-heading.

CONTENT OF PAGES

The Proclamation one folio

The Banns 1^r–3^v, content of pages will be indicated in Volume II

I 4^r–8^v, used as the Text for this edition

II 9^r, 1–24; 9^v, 25–60; 10^r, 61–92; 10^v, 93–124; 11^r, 125–52; 11^v, 153–84; 12^r, 185–216; 12^v, 217–48; 13^r, 248+SD–72; 13^v, 272+SD–92; 14^r, 292+SH–320; 14^v, 320+SH–52; 15^r, 353–84; 15^v, 384+SD–412; 16^r, 413–46; 16^v, 447–84; 17^r, 485–516+SD; 17^v, 517–48; 18^r, 549–76; 18^v, 576+SH–608; 19^r, 609–36; 19^v, 637–72; 20^r, 673–Finis

III 20^v, 1–28; 21^r, 29–60; 21^v, 60+SH–80+SD; 22^r, 80+SH–108; 22^v, 109–38; 23^r, 139–64; 23^v, 164+SH–92; 24^r, 192+SH–218; 24^v, 218+SH–44; 25^r, 244+SH–68; 25^v, 268+SH–304; 26^r, 305–Finis

IV 26^v, 1–20; 27^r, 21–48+SD(2); 27^v, 49–72; 28^r, 72+SD–96; 28^v, 96+SD–124; 29^r, 125–56; 29^v, 156+SH–92; 30^r, 192+SH–220; 30^v, 221–45; 31^r, 245+SH–64; 31^v, 264+SD–84; 32^r, 284+SH–309; 32^v, 309+SH–40; 33^r, 340+SH–64; 33^v, 365–92; 34^r, 392+SH–418; 34^v, 419–43; 35^r, 443+SD–75; 35^v, 475+SD–Finis

V 36^r, 1–24; 36^v, 24+SH–58; 37^r, 59–86; 37^v, 87–119; 38^r, 120–55; 38^v, 156–83+SD (Latin); 39^r, 183+SD (English)–209; 39^v, 210–29; 40^r, 229+SH–55; 40^v, 255+SD–79; 41^r, 279+SD–309; 41^v, 310–41; 42^r, 342–79; 42^v, 380–413; 43^r, 414–47; 43^v, 448–Finis

VI 44^r, 1–22; 44^v, 23–49; 45^r, 49+SH–82; 45^v, 83–118; 46^r, 119–52; 46^v, 153–84; 47^r, 184+SH–224; 47^v, 225–68; 48^r, 269–316; 48^v, 317–52; 49^r, 352+SH–78; 49^v, 379–414; 50^r, 415–44; 50^v, 445–72; 51^r, 473–500+SD; 51^v, 501–32; 52^r, 532+SH–59; 52^v, 560–95; 53^r, 596–637; 53^v, 638–66; 54^r, 666+SD–98; 54^v, 698+SH–Finis

VII 55^r, 1–24+1 (see VRs); 55^v, 25–60; 56^r, 60+SD–88; 56^v, 89–116; 57^r, 116+SH–44; 57^v, 144+SH–73; 58^r, 174–209; 58^v, 209+SH–39; 59^r, 239+SH–63; 59^v, 264–93; 60^r, 294–323+SD; 60^v, 324–57; 61^r, 357+SD–79; 61^v, 380–405; 62^r, 406–35; 62^v, 435+SH–61; 63^r, 462–91; 63^v, 491+SH–519; 64^r, 520–49; 64^v, 549+SH–85; 65^r, 586–610; 65^v, 611–42; 66^r, 643–75; 66^v, 676–Finis

VIII 67^r, 1–26; 67^v, 27–56; 68^r, 56+SH–80; 68^v, 80+SH–106; 69^r, 107–30; 69^v, 131–54; 70^r, 154+SH–84; 70^v, 185–218; 71^r, 219–48; 71^v, 249–75; 72^r, 276–303; 72^v, 303+SH–24; 73^r, 324+SH–53; 73^v, 354–87; 74^r, 388–Finis

IX 74^v, 1–22; 75^r, 23–53; 75^v, 54–83; 76^r, 84–117; 76^v, 118–47; 77^r, 148–83; 77^v, 183+SH+4–217; 78^r, 218–47; 78^v, 247+SH–Finis

X 79^r, 1–28; 79^v, 29–64; 80^r, 64+SH–88; 80^v, 88+SH–120; 81^r, 121–52; 81^v, 152+SH–84; 82^r, 184+SH–244; 82^v, 248+SH–76; 83^r, 276+SH–304; 83^v, 304+SH–44; 84^r, 344+SD–92; 84^v, 392+SD–421; 85^r, 422–57 +SD; 85^v, 457+SH–87; 86^r, 488–Finis

XI 86^v, 1–22; 87^r, 23–50; 87^v, 51–75; 88^r, 76–107; 88^v, 108–34; 89^r, 134+SH–66; 89^v, 166+SD–98; 90^r, 199–230; 90^v, 230+SH–58; 91^r, 258+SH–84; 91^v, 285–314; 92^r, 314+SH–Finis

XII 92^v, 1–24; 93^r, 25–60; 93^v, 60+SH–92; 94^r, 93–122; 94^v, 123–48; 95^r, 149–82; 95^v, 183–216+SD; 96^r, 216+SH–240+SD, 96^v, 241–64+ SD; 97^r, 264+SH–92; 97^v, 293–Finis

XIII 98^r, 1–21; 98^v, 22–47; 99^r, 47+SH–70+SD; 99^v, 70+SH–96; 100^r, 97–124; 100^v, 125–52; 101^r, 152+SH–76; 101^v, 176+SH–201; 102^r, 201+SH–29; 102^v, 229+SH–54; 103^r, 254+SH–84; 103^v, 284+ SD–310; 104^r, 311–32+SD; 104^v, 332+SH–58; 105^r, 359–84; 105^v, 384+SH–413; 106^r, 414–37; 106^v, 437+SH–61; 107^r, 462–Finis

XIV 107^v, 1–16 | SD; 108^r, 16+SH–40+SD; 108^v, 40 | SH 66; 109^r, 67–92; 109^v, 93–128; 110^r, 128+SH–53; 110^v, 153 | SH–80; 111^r, 180+SH–204; 111^v, 204+SH–224+SD; 112^r, 224+SH–52; 112^v, 252+ SH–78; 113^r, 279–310; 113^v, 311–40; 114^r, 341–68; 114^v, 368+SH–94; 115^r, 395–418; 115^v, 418+SH–Finis

XV 116^r, 1–20; 116^v, 21–44+SD; 117^r, 44+SH–72; 117^v, 73–96; 118^r, 96+SD–120; 118^v, 120+SD–44; 119^r, 144+SD–60 | SD; 119^v, 160+SH–85; 120^r, 185+SH–212; 120^v, 213–40; 121^r, 241–70; 121^v, 271–96+SD; 122^r, 297–318; 122^v, 318+SH–42+SD; 123^r, 342+SH– Finis

XVI 123^v, 1–16+2 (see VRs); 124^r, 16+3 (see VRs)–44; 124^v, 44+SH– 69+SD; 125^r, 69+SH–93; 125^v, 93+SH–109+SD; 126^r, 109+SH–35; 126^v, 136–60; 127^r, 161–88; 127^v, 189–214; 128^r, 214+SH–38; 128^v, 239–58; 129^r, 259–84; 129^v, 284+SH–306; 130^r, 306+SH 30; 130^v, 330+SH–56; 131^r, 356+SH–78; 131^v, 378+SH–Finis

XVIA 132^r, 1–22; 132^v, 23–52; 133^r, 52+SH–80; 133^v, 80+SH–106; 134^r, 107–36; 134^v, 136+SH–64; 135^r, 164+SH–90; 135^v, 191–216; 136^r, 216+SD–240+SD; 136^v, 240+SH–72; 137^r, 272+SH–300;

137^v, 300+SH–29; 138^r, 329+SH–59+Latin; 138^v, 359+SH–83+SD; 139^r, 383+SH–415; 139^v, 415+SH–39; 140^r, 439+SD–69; 140^v, 470–Finis

XVII 141^r, 1–24; 141^v, 24+SH–52; 142^r, 53–80; 142^v, 81–110; 143^r, 111–40; 143^v, 140+SH–62; 144^r, 163–92; 144^v, 192+Latin–212; 145^r, 212+SH–40; 145^v, 241–72; 146^r, 272+SH–304; 146^v, 305–Finis

XVIII 147^r, 1–26; 147^v, 27–57; 148^r, 57+SH–87; 148^v, 88–121; 149^r, 121+SH–51; 149^v, 153+SD–81; 150^r, 182–205; 150^v, 206–35; 151^r, 236–65; 151^v, 265+SH–93; 152^r, 293+SH–320; 152^v, 321–44+SD; 153^r, 344+SH–68+SD; 153^v, 368+SH–88; 154^r, 389–416; 154^v, 417–32+SD (see Appendix I$_D$); 155^r, 1–23+SD; 155^v, 23+SH–43; 156^r, 43+SH–67; 156^v, 68–Finis

XIX 157^r, 1–20; 157^v, 20+SH–44; 158^r, 44+SH–71; 158^v, 71+SH–99; 159^r, 99+SH–123; 159^v, 123+SD–45; 160^r, 146–69; 160^v, 170–95; 161^r, 195+SH–219; 161^v, 220–43; 162^r, 244–Finis

XX 162^v, 1–20; 163^r, 20+SH–46; 163^v, 47–76; 164^r, 77–104; 164^v, 104+SD–8; 165^r, 108+SH–36; 165^v, 137–64; 166^r, 164+SH–Finis; 166^v, blank; 167^r, blank

XXI 167^v, 1–20; 168^r, 21–48+SD; 168^v, 48+SH–74; 169^r, 75–96+Latin; 169^v, 96+SH–116; 170^r, 116+SH–40; 170^v, 140+SH–62; 171^r, 163–98; 171^v, 199–234; 172^r, 235–58; 172^v, 258+SH–82; 173^r, 282+SH–306; 173^v, 307–22+Latin; 174^r, 323–38+Latin; 174^v, 339–58; 175^r, 358+SH–82; 175^v, 382+SH–Finis

XXII 176^r, 1–24; 176^v, 24+SH–56; 177^r, 57–96; 177^v, 97–126; 178^r, 127–62; 178^v, 163–92; 179^r, 193–226; 179^v, 227–60; 180^r, 260+Latin–90; 180^v, 291–326; 181^r, 327–Finis

XXIII 181^v, 1–24; 182^r, 25–66; 182^v, 67–96; 183^r, 97–120+Latin; 183^v, 121–47; 184^r, 148–68; 184^v, 168+SH–92+SD; 185^r, 193–244; 185^v, 244+SH–72; 186^r, 273–302; 186^v, 303–26; 187^r, 327–56; 187^v, 356+SH–89; 188^r, 390–418; 188^v, 419+SH–47; 189^r, 448–73; 189^v, 473+SH–97; 190^r, 497+SH–524; 190^v, 525–52; 191^r, 552+SH–80; 191^v, 580+SH–608; 192^r, 608+SH–34; 192^v, 635–52+SD; 193^r, 652+SH–78+SD; 193^v, 698+SH–Finis

XXIV 194^r, 1–24; 194^v, 24+SH–50; 195^r, 51–96; 195^v, 97–132; 196^r, 133–68; 196^v, 169–200; 197^r, 201–32; 197^v, 233–62; 198^r, 263–96; 198^v, 297–330; 199^r, 331–64; 199^v, 365–400; 200^r, 401–32; 200^v, 433–58; 201^r, 459–88; 201^v, 489–512; 202^r, 513–44; 202^v, 545–72; 203^r, 572+SH–604; 203^v, 604+SH–36; 204^r, 636+SH–68; 204^v, 669–96; 205^r, 697–Finis

FORMS OF PLAY-ENDING

Finis deo gracias	I, V, X, XV, XVII, XX
Finis deo gracias 1600	VI, VIII, IX, XVIII, XXII
Fini deo gracias 1600	XXIII
Finis deo gracias per me Geo Bellin	XIX

Finis deo gracias per me Geo Bellin 1600   III
Finis Finis deo gracias Finis Geo Bellin
1600   XXI
Finis deo gracias per me Georgium Bellin   XIII
Finis deo gracias per me Georgium Bellin
1600   XI, XII, XIV, XVIA
Finis deo gracias per me Geo Billinges 1600
Come lorde Jesu Come Quicklye   IV
Finis deo gracias Come lorde Jesus Come
Quickely 1600   VII, XXIV
Finis deo gracias mementi mori 1600 GB   II
Finis deo gracias The End of this pagent is
fynished in the next leafes following   XVI

PLAY I

To right of *Guild-ascription 1600*
1 *alpha*—after *a*(2), *w* cancelled
1, 2, and 16 in red letters
54 after *thy*—*grace* cancelled
85+SD to right of 84, preceded by bracket for all four lines of speech
172 *brightness*—after *g*, perhaps *g* cancelled
178–93 broken rulings beneath 181, 185, and 189
281 after *yt*—*is* cancelled

PLAY II

112+SD parenthetical SD to left of primary SD
245 after *will*—*assaye* cancelled
280+SD as for 112
293 *done*—*d* altered from *w*(?)
306 *sorow*—scribe wrote *sorowowe* and cancelled *we*
355 *Maye*—*M* written over another letter
368+SD *saith*—*t* blotted and probably alteration
384+SD as for 112
424+SD to right of SH
495 *mee*—*e*(2) blottted and probably altered from *t*
688+SH squeezed in between ruling and 689

PLAY III

46 after *greeve*—*nor* cancelled
After 80+SD *Noe* centred as catchword
91 after *yarde*—*that will last* cancelled

164 *sitten—t*(1) altered from *s*
165 *Camells—C* written over *K*
180 *nighe—e* blotted and alteration (from *t*?)
After 188 usual ruling beneath fourth line omitted
209 after *is—wr*(?) cancelled
After 218 *Noe* centred; also in lower right corner as catchword
After 248 broken ruling
264 after *ame—here* cancelled
After 264 broken ruling

PLAY IV

Folio-head *The Barbers 1600*
Before 1 SD centred as SH
To right of 40+SD *1600*
After 48+SD *Messinger* centred
  mess in lower right corner as catchword
After 92 ruling omitted
148+SD to left of SH
173 after *shalte—see* cancelled
After 188 as after 92
After 212 as after 92
After 245 *Isaacke* centred
  Isaack in lower right corner as catchword
After 424 broken ruling

PLAY V

Play-heading *Moyses—s*(2) written over *n*
10 *it* inserted, with caret, above line
After 24 *Moyses* centred
  moses in lower right corner as catchword
97 after *all—ha* cancelled
111+SD to left of 108
115+SD to left of 115
136 after *true—repente* cancelled
143+SD to left of 144
153 after *or—in* cancelled
223+SD after *tunc—pertun* cancelled
After 229 *Asina/Assina* as after 24
335+SD *Balack—ck* written over *am*

After 375 usual ruling omitted
387+SD centred as SH

PLAY VI

After 48+SD usual ruling omitted
After 49 *Elizabeth* as centred catchword
After 118 *But good lorde* as catch-phrase
137 after *or—be* cancelled
After 184 *Octa* as catchword
209–13 written as six lines, inset with right-bracket and rulings; *a* . . .
    estates and *et* . . . *langoure* after *sortes*
362 after *that—man* cancelled
After 414 *by my* as catch-phrase
578 after *reade—I* cancelled
687 after *eich—maye* cancelled

PLAY VII

After 24 27 misplaced; ruling beneath meant to cancel it?
After 44+SD ruling omitted
52+SD to left of 52
After 60+SD as after 44+SD
111 *at—a* written over another letter; small *a* over capital *A*?
After 116 *Tercius pastor* centred
    Ter in lower right corner as catchword
After 164+SD as after 44+SD
165–97 usual rulings missing after each fourth line
197 two lines: *flitt/*
After 273 ruling omitted
274–5 single line
277–8 single line
After 283 ruling omitted
After 287+SD and 299+SD as after 44+SD
383 after *nor—letter* cancelled
447+SD (English) to left of 448
    SD (Latin) ruling omitted beneath SD
456 *follow—ll* written over incompleted *w*
After 463+SD as after 44+SD
464–79 rulings omitted after fourth lines within speeches
530 *her—er* written over *is*

546 before *ringe—Rig* cancelled

552–96 as for 464–79

595 *my—m* partially blotted and probably alteration

605 two lines: *will*/

609–16 and 625–84 as for 464–79

PLAY VIII

Play-heading 1600 in right margin

After 56 *Tercius Rex* centred
  Ter in lower right corner as catchword

After 64+SD ruling omitted

127 after *that—ch* cancelled

134 *so* inserted, with caret, above line

156+SD to left of 157

196+SD to left of 197

200+SD to left of 201

204+SD to left of 205

269–373 no rulings after fourth lines within speeches

282+SD to left of SH

289 two lines: *sworde*/

After 289+SD as after 64+SD

290 after *heavenly—prophesy* cancelled

294 two lines: *by*/

303 two lines: *exciled*/

304–10 each line, except 306, as two lines: final words are *such, make, godlinge, clayme, hew, borne*

326+SD to left of SH

338 two lines: *fynde*/

339 after *David—*letter (*e*?) cancelled

349+SD to left of SH

357+SD to left of 358

365+SD to left of 366

381+SD to left of 382–4

389+SD to left of 388

397+SD to left of 401

PLAY IX

15 *methinkes—k* blotted; probably alteration

47 *have—v* altered from another letter (*b*?)

After 135+SD ruling omitted
200 *all* inserted, with caret, above line

PLAY X

After 64 *Primus Miles* as centred catchphrase
119 after *knaves*—downstroke cancelled
After 152 *Primus Myles* centred; *primus* in lower right corner as catchword
242+2 catchword omitted (see VRs)
After 256+SD ruling omitted
328 after *that—I* blotted and cancelled
After 392+SD as after 256+SD
457+SD to right of 457, unruled

PLAY XI

Play-heading 1600 in right margin
19 *looke*—after *e, s* cancelled
110+SD half-ruling beneath SD
308 *us—s* blotted and probably alteration

PLAY XII

46 *Else—l* altered from *e*
After 92 *Some other sleight* as catchphrase
After 112+SD ruling omitted
Diabolus as SH
After 120+SD as after 112+3D
After 124+SD as after 112+SD
240+SD after *Jesus—dicens* cancelled
After 256+SD as after 112+SD
After 264+SD *Jesus* centred as catchword

PLAY XIII

1–35 rulings beneath 7, 14, 21, 28, 35: seven-line stanzas
22–5 each line as two lines: final words are *brethren, workes, and, me*
50 two lines: *man/*
After 70+SD *Cacus* centred
Cacus in lower right corner as catchword
218 after *is—h* cancelled

After 254 *Secundus Judeus* centred
 Secundus in lower right corner as catchword
255–6 single line
After 308+SD ruling omitted
After 332+SD *Jesus* centred as catchword
After 461 *for well* as catch-phrase

PLAY XIV

After 16+SD *Simon* centred
 Simon in lower right corner as catchword
119 *mee*—*m* blotted and alteration from *y*
After 204 *Secundus puer* as centred catchphrase
220 *commaundementes*—*m*(1) written over *g*(?)
270 after *was*—*Ro*(?) cancelled
After 368 *Secundus pharaseus* as centred catchphrase

PLAY XV

After 44+SD *peter/sir the master 114* as catchphrase
288 after *wake*—*wee* cancelled

PLAY XVI

After 69+SD *Primus Judeus* as centred catchphrase
112 *lightly*—*ly* blotted; second *ly* inserted, with caret, above line
180 after *else*—*dmb*(?) cancelled
After 214 *Pilatus* as centred catchword
After 222 ruling omitted
After 306 *Primus Judeus* as centred catchphrase

PLAY XVIA

After 120+SD ruling omitted
125–44 no rulings within speeches
264+SH *MAGDELENA*—after *N*, *A* blotted and cancelled
After 300 *Cayphas* as centred catchword
326 *there*—*t* altered from another letter and not linked to *h*
352 *sore*(2)—*r* altered from *e*
359+Latin placed as line in stanza
368–73 no ruling within speech
After 383+SD ruling omitted
 beneath SD—*Longeus* centred
 Longeus in lower right corner as catchword

After 431 ruling omitted

450 after *and*—*h* cancelled

PLAY XVII

48 *men*—*n* altered from *m* (last minim cancelled)

After 192 Latin and SD set off by right bracket; no ruling

204+SD (English) below SD (Latin)

After 212 *Mighall* as centred catchword

261 *full*—after *l*(2), *y* cancelled

PLAY XVIII

To right of Play-heading *1600*

18 after *estate*—*a* inserted, with caret, above line

After 117 ruling omitted

After 293 *Annas* as centred catchword

308+SD after *pecuniam*—*ad* cancelled

For Textual Notes on The Final Scene of Play XVIII in R, see below, heading Appendix Ⅰᴅ.

PLAY XIX

After 169 *I am* as catchphrase

After 191 ruling omitted

PLAY XX

Above first folio-heading *1600*

After 20 *Andrewas*/*160* as catchphrase

33–8 no ruling within speech

After 108 *Secundus Angellus* as centred catchphrase

After 164 *Andrewas* as centred catchword

After 188 ruling omitted

191 *wente*—first minim of *w* altered from another letter

After 192 *The fishemongers* as catchphrase

NOTE: Between the end of XX and the beginning of XXI two blank pages occur. Each of these pages is ruled for left margin and folio-heading. The last page of XX is numbered 163 (original) and 166 (later). The blank verso of this page is of course unnumbered. The blank recto of the next folio has no original numbering but it has 167 as later numbering. On the verso of this folio XXI begins. The following folio is numbered 164 (original) and 168 (later).

PLAY XXI

4 *blyse*—*l* altered from *b*; *b* squeezed in between *to* and *lyse*

46+SD rulings omitted

After 96+SD *Simeon* as centred catchword
After 116 *Andrewas* as centred catchword
134 before *put*—downstroke cancelled (*l*?)
145 *oo*—perhaps form of 'omega'
153–8 no ruling within speech
158+SD *deus dicat* as SH
241 *dread no* inserted, with caret, above line
After 258 *Andrewas* as centred catchword
After 282 *Bartholomew* as centred catchword
318 *is*—unusual ligature and unusual *s*; probably alteration (from *m*, *n*?)
After 358 *Petrus* as centred catchword
381 after *into*—*byly* cancelled
After 382 *Secundius Alienigene* as centred catchphrase

PLAY XXII

260+Latin *15 Signa* centred
269–332 numbers of signs in margin to left of corresponding lines, except that *2* is beside 273 rather than 274, and *13* is missing

PLAY XXIII

1–8 no ruling within speech
After 168 *Primus Rex* as centred catchphrase
172+SD *sacrificio*—after *o*, letter cancelled
286 *longe*—after *g*, letter (*h*?) cancelled, and between *g* and cancellation *e* squeezed in
After 326 *by righte* as catchphrase
365–70 no ruling within speech: six-line stanza
381–6 as in 365–70
421 *eyne*—before *e*(1), letter blotted and cancelled
448 two lines: *amende/*
454–61 ruling after 456
After 473 *Enocke* as centred catchword
545–52 no ruling within speech
552+SH *ANTECHRISTUS* squeezed in
553–60 and 601–8 as in 545–52
644+SD after *helpe*(4)—*ph* cancelled; *helpe* (1–4) in red, except *he* in *helpe*(1)
After 652+SD *Prinnus Demon* as centred catchphrase
661–6 as in 365–70

PLAY XXIV

After first SH Latin in two lines, *O/*; all in red ink

237 *unllykeinge—lly* blotted; *y* probably written over *l*(2) ligature

356+SD *descendit—d*(2) altered from *s*(?)

496 *blysse—l* altered from *b*

685 *saye—*after *e*, letter cancelled

After Finis etc. *To hym this booke belonges*
     I wishe contynuall health
     in daily vertues for to flow   praye ever
     with floudes of godly wealth.

in scribal hand, with *praye ever* written at a vertical angle outside the quatrain

APPENDIX ID

After first SD *Jesus* as centred catchword

10–19 no rulings within speech

48 *women—*possibly *woman*

MANUSCRIPT B

POSITION OF GUILD-ASCRIPTION

Centred before Play-heading and separated by a line-gap   I, II, III, VII, VIII, XVIA, XVII, XX, XXI, XXII

Before Play-heading which begins on the same line   XVI

Centred after Play-heading and separated by line-gap   IX, X, XI, XV

After Play-heading but following on the same line   XIII, XIV, XVIII (slightly below the line), XIX

After misplaced Play-heading   VI

To left of Play-heading   XII

Guild-ascription omitted   IV, XXIII, XXIV

Play-heading omitted   V

CONTENT OF PAGES

Banns 1ʳ–2ᵛ, content of pages will be indicated in Volume II

I 3ʳ, 1–45; 3ᵛ, 46–85; 4ʳ, 85+SD–123; 4ᵛ, 124–55; 5ʳ, 156–95; 5ᵛ, 196–229+SH; 6ʳ, 230–65; 6ᵛ, 265+SH–Finis

II 7ʳ, 1–36; 7ᵛ, 37–76; 8ʳ, 77–112; 8ᵛ, 112+SD–44; 9ʳ, 144+SD–76; 9ᵛ, 177–212; 10ʳ, 212+SH–48+SD; 10ᵛ, 248+SH–80 +SD; 11ʳ, 280+ SH–312; 11ᵛ, 312+SH–48; 12ʳ, 349–84+SD; 12ᵛ, 384+SD(2)–420; 13ʳ, 421–60; 13ᵛ, 461–88; 14ʳ–16ᵛ, blank; 17ʳ, 489–524; 17ᵛ, 525–60+SD; 18ʳ,

560+SH–96+SH; 18^v, 597–628; 19^r, 629–64; 19^v, 664+SH–80; 20^r, blank

III 20^v, 1–32; 21^r, 33–68; 21^v, 68+SH–101; 22^r, 101+SH–32; 22^v, 133–64; 23^r, 164+SH–96; 23^v, 196+SH–227; 24^r, 228–60; 24^v, 260+ SD–94; 25^r, 295–Finis; 25^v, blank

IV 26^r, 1–32; 26^v, 33–64; 27^r, 64+SH–93; 27^v, 94–130; 28^r, 131–64; 28^v, 165–200; 29^r, 201–36; 29^v, 236+SD–68; 30^r, 268+SD–300; 30^v, 300+SH–32; 31^r, 332+SH–62; 31^v, 363–96; 32^r, 396+SH–422; 32^v, 422+SH–59; 33^r, 459+SD–Finis; 33^v, blank

V 34^r, 1–36; 34^v, 37–72; 35^r, 72+SH–103; 35^v, 104–40; 36^r, 141–75+ SD; 36^v, 175+SH–205; 37^r, 206–31; 37^v, 232–63; 38^r, 263+SH–99; 38^v, 300–31; 39^r, 332–73; 39^v, 374–415; 40^r, 416–Finis; 40^v, blank

VI 41^r, 1–36; 41^v, 37–72; 42^r, 72+Latin–112; 42^v, 112+SH–48; 43^r, 149–86; 43^v, 187–226; 44^r, 227–66; 44^v, 267–304; 45^r, 304+SH–44; 45^v, 345–76; 46^r, 377–420; 46^v, 420+SH–60; 47^r, 460+SH–96; 47^v, 496+SH–532; 48^r, 532+SH–65; 48^v, 566–611; 49^r, 612–50; 49^v, 650+ SH–90; 50^r, 691–Finis; 50^v, blank

VII 51^r, 1–38; 51^v, 39–70; 52^r, 71–108; 52^v, 108+SH–34; 53^r, 135– 64+SH; 53^v, 165–201; 54^r, 201+SH–37; 54^v, 237+SH–69; 55^r, 269+ SH–305; 55^v, 305+SH–39; 56^r, 339+SH–72; 56^v, 372+SH–403; 57^r, 403+SH–35+SH; 57^v, 436–63+SD; 58^r, 464–99+SH; 58^v, 500–39; 59^r, 539+SH–75; 59^v, 575+SH–608; 60^r, blank; 60^v, 608+SH–45; 61^r, 646–84; 61^v, 684+SH–Finis

VIII 62^r, 1–36; 62^v, 37–68; 63^r, 68+SH–100; 63^v, 100+SH–32; 64^r, 132+SH–64; 64^v, 165–204; 65^r, 204+SD–40; 65^v, 241–73; 66^r, 274– 310; 66^v, 310+SH–38+Latin; 67^r, 339–79; 67^v, 379+SH–Finis

IX 68^r, 1–32; 68^v, 32+SH–67; 69^r, 68–107; 69^v, 108–45; 70^r, 146–87; 70^v, 188–227; 71^r, 228–Finis; 71^v, blank

X 72^r, 1–40; 72^v, 41–76; 73^r, 76+SH–112; 73^v, 113–52; 74^r, 152+SH– 88; 74^v, 189–224; 75^r, 225–62; 75^v, 263–96; 76^r, 296+SH–332; 76^v, 333–68; 77^r, 369–404; 77^v, 405–41; 78^r, 442–81; 78^v, 481+SH–Finis

XI 79^r, 1–36; 79^v, 37–67; 80^r, 68–105; 80^v, 106–38; 81^r, 139–74; 81^v, 175–214; 82^r, 214+SH–50+SH; 82^v, 251–90; 83^r, 291–326; 83^v, 326+ SH–Finis

XII 84^r, 1–36; 84^v, 37–72; 85^r, 73–112; 85^v, 112+SD–40; 86^r, 140+ SH–76; 86^v, 177–212; 87^r, 213–44; 87^v, 244+SH–76; 88^r, 277–Finis; 88^v, blank

XIII 89^r, 1–35; 89^v, 35+Latin–66; 90^r, 66+Latin–96; 90^v, 97–130; 91^r, 130+SH–64; 91^v, 164+SH–200; 92^r, 200+SH–34; 92^v, 234+SH– 70+2 (see VRs); 93^r, 270+3 (see VRs)–304; 93^v, 304+SH–35; 94^r, 336– 72; 94^v, 372+SD–401+SD; 95^r, 401+SH–33; 95^v, 433+SH–65; 96^r, 465+SH–Finis; 96^v, blank

XIV 97^r, 1–32; 97^v, 32+SH–68; 98^r, 69–104; 98^v, 105–44; 99^r, 144+ SH–76; 99^v, 176+SH–208; 100^r, 208+SD–32; 100^v, 232+SH–64;

101^r, 264+SH–304; 101^v, 304+SD–40; 102^r, 341–80; 102^v, 380+SH–416; 103^r, 416+SH–Finis; 103^v, blank

XV 104^r, 1–36; 104^v, 36+SD–64; 105^r, 64+SH–96+SD; 105^v, 97–133; 106^r, 133+SH–64; 106^v, 165–200; 107^r, 201–36; 107^v, 237–80+SD; 108^r, 281–312; 108^v, 312+SH–42; 109^r, 342+SD–Finis; 109^v, blank

XVI 110^r, 1–24; 110^v, 25–61; 111^r, 61+SH–93; 111^v, 93+SH–117+SD; 112^r, 117+SH–50; 112^v, 150+SH–86; 113^r, 187–220; 113^v, 220+SH–52; 114^r, 253–86; 114^v, 286+SH–318; 115^r, 318+SH–50; 115^v, 350+SH–84; 116^r, 384+SH–Finis; 116^v, blank

XVIA 117^r, 1–36; 117^v, 37–72; 118^r, 72+SH–104; 118^v, 104+SH–44; 119^r, 144+SH–80; 119^v, 180+SH–244; 120^r, 245–80; 120^v, 280+SH–316; 121^r, 317–51; 121^v, 351+SH–83; 122^r, 383+SD–419; 122^v, 420–51; 123^r, 452–Finis; 123^v, blank

XVII 124^r, 1–32+Latin; 124^v, 33–68; 125^r, 69–103; 125^v, 104–40; 126^r, 140+SH–76; 126^v, 176+SD–208; 127^r, 209–44; 127^v, 244+SH–76+SD; 128^r, 276+SH–316; 128^v, 317–Finis

XVIII 129^r, 1–36; 129^v, 37–73; 130^r, 73+SH–113; 130^v, 113+SH–53; 131^r, 153+SD–89; 131^v, 190–225; 132^r, 225+SH–61; 132^v, 262–300; 133^r, 300+SH–36; 133^v, 336+SH–68+SD; 134^r, 368+SH–400+SD; 134^v, 400+SH–Finis; 135^r, blank

XIX 135^v, 1–28; 136^r, 28+SH–60; 136^v, 61–95; 137^r, 95+Latin–123; 137^v, 123+SD–51; 138^r, 151+SH–83; 138^v, 184–215; 139^r, 215+SD–47; 139^v, 248–Finis

XX 140^r, 1–32; 140^v, 32+SH–66; 141^r, 67–100; 141^v, 101–12; 142^r, 112+SD–48; 142^v, 148+2, (see VRs)–76; 143^r, 176+SH–Finis; 143^v, blank

XXI 144^r, 1–32+Latin; 144^v, 33–68; 145^r, 68+SH–100; 145^v, 100+SH–28; 146^r, 128+SH–62; 146^v, 163–206; 147^r, 207–42; 147^v, 243–78; 148^r, 278+SH–310+SD; 148^v, 311–34 | Latin; 149^r, 335–62; 149^v, 362+SH–Finis

XXII 150^r, 1–30; 150^v, 31–68; 151^r, 69–108; 151^v, 109–44; 152^r, 145–80; 152^v, 181–220; 153^r, 221–56; 153^v, 257–92; 154^r, 293–332; 154^v, 333–Finis

XXIII 154^v (cont.), 1–24+Latin; 155^r, 25–60; 155^v, 60+SH–96; 156^r, 97–128; 156^v, 129–57; 157^r, 157+SH–88; 157^v, 188+SH–220; 158^r, 221–56; 158^v, 257–96; 159^r, 297–332; 159^v, 333–68; 160^r, 369–409; 160^v, 409+SH–45; 161^r, 446–81; 161^v, 481+SH–516; 162^r, 517–50; 162^v, 551–80; 163^r, 580+SH–612; 163^v, 612+SH–40; 164^r, 641–70; 164^v, 671–96; 165^r, 696+SH–Finis; 165^v, blank

XXIV 166^r, 1–32; 166^v, 32+SH–68; 167^r, 69–104; 167^v, 105–40; 168^r, 140+SH–76; 168^v, 177–216; 169^r, 217–52; 169^v, 253–88; 170^r, 289–324; 170^v, 324+SH–56+SD; 171^r, 356+SH–96; 171^v, 397–432; 172^r, 433–64; 172^v, 465–500; 173^r, 500+SH–32; 173^v, 533–64+Latin; 174^r, 565–96; 174^v, 597–632; 175^r, 632+SH–64; 175^v, 665–96; 176^r, 697–Finis

FORMS OF PLAY-ENDING

Finis   I, III, IV, V, VI, VII, VIII, IX, X, XI, XII, XVIA, XXI, XXII
Finis pagina+play number in Roman numerals   XIII, XXIII
+play number in Latin (genitive case)   XIV
+play number in Latin followed on the next line by the
scribe's initials, *W.B.*   XIX
+Guild-name, *de Scissoribus*   XX
Finis Deo Gracias in capitals   XXIV
Thende of this story is finished in the next leafe   XVI
Finis-form omitted   II, XV, XVII, XVIII

PLAY I

1–2 written as one line, indented and separated from 3 by a line-gap
7–8, 9–10, 11–12, 32–3 single lines
75 after *now*—*I* cancelled
77 *as* in left margin close to *I* which begins the line
85+SD in margin to left of SH
116 *beames*—*e*(1) re-inked or written over another letter
132 after *what*—hook characteristic of start of *w*, uncancelled
152 after *your*—*oss* cancelled
185 after *so*—*fes* cancelled
202 *ye*—*y* altered from *th*
213+Latin in margin to left of SH and 214
229+SD indented, beginning at centre of page

PLAY II

Play-heading creavit—scribe wrote *crait* as abbreviation
1–176 Lines are divided into quatrains with a line-space between each
group and each quatrain is numbered in the left margin beside the first
line. Numbers run from 1 to 44
28 after *sone*—*shall* cancelled
43 after *to*—*tyn* cancelled
45 after *will*—*too* cancelled
108 no line gap between 108 and 109
112+SD to left of SD—erasure (illegible)
Then indented in line with text
parenthetical SD in margin to left of SH
136+SD after *doth*—*take* cancelled
187 after *shall*—*come to* cancelled
240 after *thou*—*O* cancelled
253 after *withouten*—*feare* cancelled

261 after *I—wot*(?), with *wo* blotted, cancelled
280+SD parenthetical SD to left of 281
290 *me*—after *e*, *te* cancelled
384+SD parenthetical SD to left of 385–6
389 after *sharp—spor* cancelled
395 after *fyer—h* cancelled
404 after *must—here* cancelled
406 after *was—lyffe* cancelled
418 before *w* of *won*—downstroke cancelled
424+SD to left of 425–6
After 488 rest of page and next six pages blank
493 after *children—that* cancelled
511 after *to*—letter cancelled
569 after *how—I* cancelled
616+SD parenthetical SD to left of primary SD
670 after *that—I can flye* cancelled
674 after *howse—or* cancelled and *or* writted above
After 680 rest of page and next page blank

PLAY III

To left of *Guild-ascription Collated for Mr. Markland, who means to print it, Feb. 1818*—in pencil in a modern hand
20 before *of—thie* cancelled
69 after *good—hach*, with *h*(2) altered to *k*, cancelled
98 *ye—y* altered from another letter, perhaps *w*
217 after *goe*—start of letter cancelled
224+SH at left of text instead of in centre; only *The* has initial capital
263 after *all—b* cancelled
275 after *mon—shall yore* cancelled

PLAY IV

16+SD to left of SII and 17–20
35 *teathe* (Hm)—in B reading uncertain since word is slightly blotted, cut by downstroke, and vowels are written small; perhaps *tenth*
40+SD to left of SH and 41–2
48+SD (English) to left of 49–53
    after *of—Salem* cancelled
56+SD to left of SH and 57–62

64+SD to left of 65–8

68+SD to left of 69–70

72+SD (Latin) after *pane*—word (*S*—*per*) cancelled

72+SD to left of 73–7

76 *enemies*—*e*(3) altered from *s*

80+ *Abraham taketh the cup* written as extended SH, with *Abraham* centred

80+SD to left of 81–3

88+SD to left of 86–8 (sentence 1) and of 89–91 (sentence 2)

96+SD to left of SH and 97–9

104+SD to left of 105–6

112+SD to left of 108–10

131 after *as*—word cancelled

144+SD indented, beginning at centre of page

148+SD to left of 149–51

180 after *self*—*shall* cancelled

187 *for*—not clear; perhaps *fro*

209 after *servant*—*Ah* cancelled

228+SD to left of 229–31

245 written small and compressed into usual line-space between 244 and following SH

250+SD to left of SH and 249
   after *the*—*alter* cancelled

252+SD to left of SH and 253–6

264+SD to left of SH and 265–7; after *lest*—*I* cancelled

268 after *wee*—*ff*(?) *Not* cancelled

268+SD to left of 269–70

276 after *hart*—*in secunde*(?) cancelled

291 after *put*—*of* cancelled

322+SD to left of SH and 323–4

376 *dowmes*—*w* obscured by downstroke and reading doubtful

389+SD to left of 389, SH and 390–1

403 after *them*—start of *th* cancelled

After 411   408 repeated but cancelled and 412 written below

After 412—*ISAACK* written as SH but cancelled and, after line-space, *ABRAHAM* written

430 after *for*—*fe* cancelled

431 after *death*—*d* cancelled

443+SII *DEUS* on same line as SD

459+SD in margin to left of SH
467 *the*—*e* altered from *i* and, after *e*, *s* cancelled
after *the*—*place* cancelled
470 *that bonde* written on line below, beginning under *breake*

PLAY V

75 after *but*—*t–ll* cancelled
95+SH *BALACK*—first letter altered and partly blotted; reading doubtful
111+SD to left of 110
115+SD to left of 115
143+SD to left of 144
167 after *may*—*we* cancelled
177 after *prayes*—*they* cancelled
193 after *to*—*g* cancelled
215+SD after *cum*(1)—*lili* cancelled
238 after *so*—*serv*(?) cancelled
239+SD (English) to left of 240–2
269 after *thou*—*shath* cancelled
271 after *seest*—*de* cancelled
272 after *thou*—*dost here* cancelled
286 after *can*—*we* cancelled
319+SD after *plagam*—*montem* cancelled
335+SD to left of 336–8
After 354–351 repeated and cancelled; *lure*] *lawe*
387+SD centred
434 after *the*—*prof* cancelled

PLAY VI

Above. *Guild-ascription* —*The Painters Play* cancelled
Play-heading to left of cancelled Guild-ascription
19 *Jacobs*—*s* altered from *b*
87 after *God*—*gone*(?) cancelled
177 after *geve* —*is* cancelled
202 after *was*—*th* cancelled

209–18 a short vertical stroke divides the following lines into two parts after the words indicated:

209 assembles   215 tresagayl
210 leez   216 counsell
213 sages   218 frayl
214 alle

234 after *more*—*expresse* cancelled

236 *this*—*i* altered from *e*

243 after *and*(1)—*p* cancelled

254 after *that*—*no* cancelled

312 after *to*—*w* cancelled

After 362 359 repeated and cancelled

404 after *with*—*that* cancelled

431 *sory*—form is *sry*; *o* perhaps slight hook to *s*(?)

After 447 444 repeated and cancelled

515 after *joy*—*beging* cancelled

532+SH to left of SH in line with text—*S* erased

554 after *bringe*—*me*(?) cancelled

555 *thou me* written as one word and divided by short downstroke

After 581 586 cancelled and 582 inserted above it; this form of 586 differs from later B-form in having *was* for *wa*

After 582 587 cancelled and 583 written above

To left of *that* (579), and above *a* in *about* (588)—two asterisks

In left margin beside lines 580–96 and vertically from top to bottom of the page, lines 584–7 written as four lines, with a line-space following, and below it *This comes in at the lower starre*

600 after *and*—*tur* cancelled

647 after *heigh*—*aff* cancelled

648 after *that*(2)—*b*(?) cancelled

651 *A* written in left margin, outside line of text
     woundrous—second minim of *u*(2) altered from *s*

656 *my*—*y* blotted and obscured by downstroke; alteration

664 after *thousand*—*th* cancelled

667 after *A*—*s* (lower case) cancelled

689 *upon*—*u* written over another letter (*a*?)

692 after *wounderous*—*thin* cancelled

702 after *was*—*done* cancelled

PLAY VII

4 after *to*—*say* cancelled

36 after *them*—*date* cancelled

37 after *yf*—beginning of *th* cancelled, followed by *hit* cancelled

52+SD to right of 52

60+SD *Secundus Pastor* centred as SH with rest of SD to right

62 *thy*—*y* altered from *e*

112 after *is*—*good* cancelled

After 124 space of about 12 lines blank

128 after *from*—letter cancelled

151 before *blow*—*call* cancelled

174 after *me*—*v*(?) cancelled

After 177 176 repeated and cancelled

181 after *waye*—*b wee* cancelled

189 after *a*—*do* cancelled

229+SH *GARTIUS* centred and cancelled; *TROWLE* written to right

253 after *goe*—*all* cancelled

273 *as*—second letter blotted, perhaps altered, and doubtful

274-5 single line

277-8 single line

299+SD *pastor* written beneath *Primus* at right side of page and linked to preceding line by form of bracket

357+SD *Tunc cantat Angelus* written on line above text; Latin text indented

After 383+SH —scribe begins line *May* cancelled; then begins second line *M* cancelled; after these two lines, begins 384

394 after *was*—*a* inserted, with caret, above line

409 after *that*—*he* cancelled

423 after *hede*—*wer*(?) cancelled

432 after *word*—*tamed he* cancelled

447+SD (English) to left of 448

468 after *Bethelem*—*b* cancelled

469 before *there*—*ye* cancelled

490 after *us*—*blise* cancelled

514 after *to*—*g* cancelled

539 after *comon*—*of al* cancelled

547 after *proffer*—short downstroke marking stanza-end

559 before *loc* –letter (*l* or *b*) cancelled

605 two lines: *sirres*/

608 at page-bottom words visible (*a* — *-ke is ner* – *so*(?))

626 after *what*—*I* cancelled

PLAY VIII

38 after *sweete*—*right* cancelled

53 after *though*—*b* cancelled

59 after *not*—*consealle* cancelled

71 *desemble*—exact reading is doubtful; scribe wrote *desembler* or *desemblen* and cancelled and/or blotted last two letters

77 after *our*—*prayers*, with *er* blotted, cancelled

96+SD to left of 97-8

112+SD after *ride*—*away* cancelled and *about* squeezed in at end of line, ending being partly obscured by binding-join

144+SD sentence 2 in margin to left of sentence 1

154 before *Deu*—*die* cancelled

196+SD to left of 197

200+SD to left of 201

204+SD to left of 205

247 before *write*—*wh* cancelled

263 *Zakeny*—if *e*, unusual form, but also not usual *a* form; possibly *ar*

270 *nativite*—in abbreviated form *na^{te}*

278 after *that*—*prophecie* cancelled

282 after *our*(2)—*sess*, of which *s*(3) is incomplete, cancelled

282+SD to left of 283

286 after *which*—*is* cancelled

297 *rites*—*t* blotted and probably alteration

324+Latin *parvulum*—*p* apparently altered from *p* to *par* abbreviation after *furorem*—letter (*v*?) cancelled

336 *keene* written below *brond so* and bracketed to line above

337 after *peces*—*me* cancelled

349+SD to left of 350

357+SD to left of 358

358 *what*—unusual *w* which looks as if scribe may have written *T* and altered it; word is slightly inset, by one letter-space

365+SD to left of 366

397+SD to left of 398

410 after *one*—*every* cancelled

PLAY IX

1 after *God*—*of* cancelled
  after *of*—*might* cancelled

To left of 3-4 *ix* in margin in modern hand

15 after *but*—*by* cancelled or blotted and obscured by downstroke

27 after *ever*—*I* cancelled

30 after *is*—*this* cancelled

41 after *in*—*the land* cancelled

121 after *most*—*cle* cancelled

205 before *is*—*he* cancelled

PLAY X

To left of Play-heading Collated for Mr. Markland, who means to print it, in Feb. 1818. in pencil in modern hand

SH before 1 not centred but at left, in line with text, and on same line as *Guild-ascription*

1 after *princes—pl* cancelled

To left of 5 *X* in pencil in modern hand

23 before *and—by* cancelled

27 after *would—receave* cancelled

63 after *thus—R* cancelled

84+SH *PRIMUS MILES* written as SH, but cancelled and *HERODE* written below after line-gap

97 after *so—stowte* cancelled

101 after *yesterdaye—d* cancelled

130 after *of—c* cancelled

146 *crowne—ne* not clear; possibly *re*

158 *luddie—u* written over another letter or letters (*or?*)

185 after *in—h* cancelled

339 after *hath—be* cancelled

355 after *buffett—b* cancelled

376+SD after *Miles— tras* cancelled

378 *all* inserted, with caret, above line

394 *thou—ou* doubtful; letter visible after *th* could be almost any vowel and final letter obscured by downstroke

397 *fye*(1)—scribe seems to have written *ffyee*, but first *e* is altered or cancelled

436 after *you—sh* cancelled

439 after *and*(2)—*lowe*(?) cancelled

457+SD to right of 457

PLAY XI

To left of 6 *XI* in pencil in modern hand

17 after *I—wote* cancelled

23 after *dead—well* obscured by downstroke, blotted and cancelled
   after *were*(1)—*me* cancelled

44 before *one—downstroke* cancelled

64 after *may—w* cancelled

71+SD *altere—e*(1) not clear and *e*(2) altered from *a*

108 after *Christ—vey* cancelled

111 after *thie*(1)—*of thie* cancelled
138 indented one letter-space
163 after *have*—*tigth* cancelled
166 after *mee*—*lord* cancelled
166+SD after *demittes*—*p* cancelled
180 after *man*—*f* cancelled
197 *Christe in*—inserted, with caret, above line
      after *godhead*—*in Christe* cancelled
207 *Joseph*—*Jo* to left of text edge
244 after *age*—*thi* cancelled
246 after *clark*—*wo* cancelled
249 after *in*—*that* cancelled
257 before *me*—*b* cancelled
305 after *have*—*thought* cancelled
333 after *may*—*in* cancelled

PLAY XII

6 after *abrode*—*I* cancelled
    after *whelke*—*nere* cancelled
To left of 7 *XII* in pencil in modern hand
13 after *his*—*care* cancelled and *cane* written above
24 after *honor*—*d*(?) cancelled
42 after *finde*—*I* cancelled
44 after *craftes*—*fayles* cancelled
47 after *save*—*hongre* cancelled
    after *he*—*h wass* cancelled and *hath* written above
48 after *ellis*—*whot* cancelled
    after *what*—*him l*(?) cancelled
91 after *but*—*h*-downstroke cancelled
120+SD *Jesus* centred as SH with remainder of SD following on same line
128+SD *Diabolus* as SH, centred on line below SD
140 after *thie*—*t*(?) cancelled
After 184 *vide Genesis; Eritis sicut Dei* (*vide* written slightly above line in left margin; text inset one letter-space)
195 after *glotonie*—*lea*+minim cancelled
214 after *Jesus*—*stonde* cancelled
216+SD after *deprehensam*—*dc* cancelled
232+SD after *secoram*—*se* cancelled
265 before *woman*—*wh, h* incomplete, cancelled

4 *and* written over *pro*
  prophettes—ph cancelled between *pro* (abbreviation) and *p*
To left of 5 *XIII* in pencil in modern hand
20 *witnes—n* altered from *t* and doubtful
21 after *bonus—*letter cancelled
  after *pastor—*uncancelled downstroke and *written* cancelled
24 *sick—i* or *a*; partially obscured by downstroke
29 *har—*word cut by page-edge
30 after *in—h* cancelled
31 *my—y* obscured by downstroke; possibly scribe wrote *e*
34 after *lett—*letter cancelled
35 after *doinges—yo*(?) cancelled
  *alwayes—*trailing downstroke below *a*(2); *e* squeezed in
35+Latin after *mei—dicis*(?) cancelled
64 after *shineth—here* cancelled
82 after *which—rester*(?) cancelled (last two letters obscured by down-stroke)
89 after *men—tur* cancelled
92 after *all—my* cancelled
93 *the*(2)—*e* unusual, with downstroke; perhaps *y*
After 95 line 100 cancelled
127 after *with—clay* cancelled
137 after *it—noug* cancelled
156+SD after *tunc—s* cancelled
187 after *could—nether* cancelled
208 after *did—sh* cancelled
224+SH *PRIMUS—MU* written with six minims
229 *restored—*written below line, to right of following SH, beginning beneath *y* of *truly*
232 *calketh—*reading here is doubtful; scribe may have written *calleth—*first letter appears to be *c* and *lk* is not clear
246 *voyce—v* written on top of another letter
250 after *for—aye* cancelled
255-6 single line
260+SD after *lapides—golligust*(?) cancelled
294 after *with—my* cancelled
316+SD indented in line with text
After 333+SH scribe begins 334 *Master Juen right* (*J* blotted and altered; reading perhaps *Even*), cancelled: rest of line is blank and 334 is written on line below

356 after *him*—*h* cancelled

356+Latin *mundi*—*i* re-inked and probably alteration

370 *him*—*m* altered from *s*

408 after *in*—*bead* cancelled

417+SD no line-gap between SD and 418

419 after *Lazare*—*th* cancelled

After 449 line gap

PLAY XIV

1 after *goe*—*yee* cancelled

To left of 7 *XIV* in pencil in modern hand

15 *clensede*—*de* blotted and clearly alteration (*st*?)

25 *Jesus*—*s*(2) not clear; possibly *e*

46 *ffayle*—*f*(2) written on top of *r*

56+SD after *et*(2)—*tergeg* cancelled

89 after *these*—*p* cancelled

94 *skillfully*—after *l*(2), *full* cancelled

104 *and*—scribe began line with *weete*; *weete* cancelled and *and* written below

110 after *hath*—*ben* cancelled

112 after *her*—*b*(?) cancelled

116 after *thus*—*hase* cancelled

135 after *from*—*y* cancelled

185 *save*—*v* written over another letter

205 after *mirth*—*all* cancelled

208+SD after *benedictus*—*b* cancelled

260+SD after *ejecit*—uncancelled downstroke
after *cum*—*fug* cancelled

302 after *him*—*on* cancelled

311 *Romanes*—perhaps *Romanies*; gap between *n* and *e* is cut by downstroke and is sufficiently wide to contain *i*, and a dot is visible to left of intersecting downstroke

315 *he*—inserted, with caret, above line

321 after *saye*—*rig* cancelled

337 after *maye*—*be* cancelled

340 *fure*—reading doubtful; only absence of dot prevents reading *five*

391–2 single line

427–8 single line

PLAY XV

To left of 7 *XV* in pencil in modern hand

14 before *but*—*and* cancelled

23 *your*—*r*-superscript altered from another letter
36+SD after *vas*—*q* cancelled
39 after *must*—*ke* obscured by downstroke and probably cancelled
After 39–44 cancelled (*saye*] *saye thou*   *you* (= Hm *yee*)] *thou*), and 40
squeezed in below
80+SD *accumberit*—*eri* doubtful; perhaps *en*
144+SD *precingit*—*t* altered from *s*
150 *washe*—alteration; *a* doubtful, possibly *e*, and *s* squeezed in
190 indented one letter-space
204+SH *THOMAS*—written *THOMS*
232 after *leeve*—*a* cancelled
236 indented one letter-space
268 after *I*—*e* cancelled
280 indented one letter-space
296+SD after *tunc*—*d* cancelled
297 *you*—*y* to left of line of text
298 before *slepe*—*she*(?) cancelled; *e* obscured by downstroke and possibly
uncancelled
309 *a*—to left of line of text
331 *of*—squeezed in between *shall* and *by*
340 after *sword*—*smitheth*(?) cancelled

PLAY XVI

To left of 8 *XIX* in pencil cancelled and *XVI* written above in pencil in
same modern hand
8 after *hath*—*tur* cancelled
16+1 after *Cayphas*—*sickerley* cancelled
16+2 *in*—after *n*, minim cancelled
19 after *the*—*pe* cancelled
21 after *Caiphas*—*hang* cancelled
57 after *thou*—*l-es* cancelled
61 after *our*—*sawes* cancelled
73+SH after *SECUNDUS* *d* cancelled
126 *hye*—*y* altered from *e*
133+SH before *PILATUS*—*PIL* cancelled
138 *this*—*is* obscured by blot
141 after *men*—*maye* cancelled
187 after *I*—*ney* cancelled
201 after *for*—*them* cancelled
202+SH squeezed in between SD and 203
210 before *and*—*g* cancelled

300 *ffeare*—*f*(2) squeezed in between *f*(1) and *e*(1) and with unusual form

322+SD *flagellaverunt*—*e*(1) doubtful; perhaps *i*; *l*(2) obscured by downstroke, and another letter (*l*?) blotted and perhaps thus cancelled between *l*(2) and *l*(3)

383 after *was*—*wh* cancelled

PLAY XVIA

1 after *segger*—*b* cancelled

7 after *our*—*lyk*-, ending perhaps unfinished *es* abbreviation, cancelled

To left of 10 *XVII* in pencil in modern hand

25 *entent*—*t*(2) re-inked and probably altered from *e*

47 *of*—after *f*, *t* cancelled

75 after *seme*—*ther* cancelled

After 80+SH 85–8 cancelled

103 after *aunt*—*nere*(?) cancelled

116 after *wee*—*bu* cancelled

after *benne*—word cancelled; scribe seems to have written *f* with perhaps *ser* contraction-form, followed by *d* and possibly *y*

241 *lyffe*—*f*(2) squeezed in between *f*(1) and *e*

after *my*—*dere* cancelled

251 after *and*—*to* cancelled

283 *woundes*—*st* cancelled at end of word and *s* squeezed in

324 *blisse*—*l* blotted at base and probably alteration

330 after *keper*—uncrossed *I* cancelled with sweeping stroke

359+Latin set at text-margin as if a following verse-line; after it, short diagonal stroke indicative of line- or stanza-division. SH follows in next line

374 after *see*—*may* cancelled

423+SD after *ab*—*ama* cancelled

428 *Joseph*—in left margin

461 *Godes*—*g* apparently alteration from another letter

470 after *Sonne*—*by* cancelled

471 after *signes*—uncancelled downstroke

PLAY XVII

Play-heading hic—to left of text-line; *incipit* with initial capital

To left of 12 *XVIII* in pencil in modern hand

19 *thye*—*y* re-inked and possibly alteration from *e*

21 before *sicker*—apparently *sicker*, but all letters except *s* are heavily blotted and only top of *k* and final *r* can be distinguished; there is a cancellation-line through the form

64+Latin indented from text-line six letter-spaces

72+Latin indented from text-line ten letter-spaces
after *tollit—pect* cancelled

83 *prayer—r*(2) altered from *s*

88+SD indented from text-line six letter-spaces

89 after *heigh—of* cancelled

96+SD indented from text-line seven letter-spaces

98 *bere—b* doubtful; possibly *l*

101 after *have—monne,* with *mo* blotted and probably altered, cancelled

152+Latin below SD and indented in line with verse

176+SD one space to left of text

194 *princes—e* doubtful; form suggests scribe wrote *prince* and then added *s*

206 after *to—thie* cancelled

226 after *meyney—I maye* cancelled

244+SH before *PROPHETA*—apparently *s* at start of word

256 after *one—tree* cancelled

276+SD *Te Deum Laudamus*—centred below SD

301 *taverners—r*(2) altered from *s*

306 after *malt—bry*(?) cancelled

<h2 style="text-align:center">PLAY XVIII</h2>

To left of 15 *XIX* in pencil in modern hand

16 after *my—mam* cancelled

18 after *my*(2)—*postee* cancelled

25 after *dread—it* cancelled; exact form uncertain since scribe wrote - - *t* (*not*?) and then wrote *i* above first two letters

35 after *I—say* cancelled
after *hang—and* cancelled

51 after *after—noone* cancelled

90 after *wee—start* of *w* cancelled

123 after *geve—up* cancelled

153 after *it—were* cancelled

153+SD *Tunc* written in slightly smaller letters, slightly above line and to left of rest of SD which is aligned with the verse
cantabunt has an initial capital

153+SD(2) *Jesus Resurgens* centred, with rest of SD centred on following line

161 after *I—brought* cancelled

After 169 174 cancelled (*that I] I doe*)

184 after *fooles—read* heavily blotted and thus cancelled

212–5+SD in different script

320 after *in*—*cl* cancelled

341 after *too*—small blot resembling blotted *o*

346 after *with*—*weet* cancelled

356+SH no space left between words; perhaps *US* in *SECUNDUS* added

368+SD after *obvenient*—*s* cancelled

396+SD *sepulcrum*—diagonal stroke to right of *m*

417 after *Jesu*—*a* cancelled

PLAY XIX

To left of 5 *XX* in pencil on modern hand

46 *Nazareth*—*r* altered from *b*(?)

54 after *Israell*—*th* cancelled

58 before *sith*—*th* cancelled

At edge of page, to left of 84–5 *nite*(?)—(with *i* undotted and *t* inserted?)

167+SD after *media*—*diss* cancelled

189 before *but*—*but* cancelled; short upstroke suggests scribe may have written *w* originally as first letter and altered it to *b*

216 *A* written in left margin

244 after *and*(1)—*ss*

249+SD *manum*—line from first minim of *m* suggests possible alteration

258 after *your*—*selves shall* cancelled

264 after *whoso*—*this* cancelled

267 after *ever*—*an* cancelled

270 *heavens*—*a*, alteration from letter with upstroke; result resembles *v*

PLAY XX

To left of 11–12 *XXI* in pencil in modern hand

27 *yore*—between *o* and *r*, above line, *ur* abbreviation cancelled

32+SH *JESUS*—above *J*, *J* erased

59 after *restore*—*Is* and incompleted *s* cancelled

67 after *you*—*most* cancelled; *o* doubtful, possibly *u*

96+SD after *suos*—*et* cancelled
    after *in*(2)—*lol* cancelled

100 *for*—*or* blotted and obscured by downstroke

104+SD after *et*—*descendit* cancelled
    SD (English) below SD (Latin) and set approximately eight letter-spaces nearer left edge of page
    above—word doubtful; *b* or *l*, *v* or *n*

After 104+SD Latin indented in line with verse-edge
  Characters' names centred as SHs with SD continuing to right of SH
  Minor Angelus' words: after *sua—gradens* cancelled
137 after *these—p* cancelled
142 after *for*—letter (start of *th*?) cancelled
145 after *wicked—maye* cancelled
148+ repeated lines may be cancelled; there are four short diagonal
lines through the repeated 137, cutting *e*(2) of *these*, *p* of *dropes*, *th* of
with, and *n*(1) of *intent*. They do not reach the repeated 138
152+SD *Cantent*—centred
  Latin *psalmus—u* altered from *o*
178 after *and—by rising* cancelled
181 *upsteying—up* re-inked; *p* probably alteration
182 after *fullie—eh* cancelled
187 after *through—b* cancelled
188 *stidfastlye*—written as two words, *stid fastlye*; after *stid—as slie*(?)
cancelled
189 *with*—before *w*, *s* cancelled
190 *gost—g* re-inked and alteration
191 after *from—I s so* cancelled
192 after *this—Cny*(?) *amen* cancelled

PLAY XXI

Play-heading viz in parentheses
To left of 9–10 *XXII* in pencil in modern hand
26 after *to—pl* cancelled
32 Latin after *Episcopatum—a* cancelled
35 after *master—Is*(?) cancelled
37 after *that*(1) *—b* cancelled
  after *his—wow*(?) cancelled
39 after *dying—g* cancelled
48+SD after *omnes—populu* cancelled
56 + SD second clause half-line below first
To left of 58 *not*, perhaps *note*, at page-edge
77 no gap between *but* and *yf*
82 *what they*—written without gap but divided by vertical line
112+Latin *ad*—after *d*, letter cancelled
120+SD *Creator*—in different style; after *r*(2) letter and/or horizontal
stroke cancelled
123 after *thou—ar* cancelled
  after *mans—counsellor* cancelled

125 after *thou—t art* cancelled
151 *beloe*—upstroke, characteristic of *s*, above *o*
152 after *thie—ee*(?) cancelled
152+SD in different script
155 writing small and at times illegible
have and *will* very doubtful
158+SD *Deus dicat*—centred as SH below rest of SD
195 after *this*—loop cancelled
238+SD after *projecient—igem* cancelled
256 *feelle*—initial letter perhaps *s*
299 after *now—seigh* cancelled
312 after *made—earth* cancelled
363 *brether—e*(1) may have been altered from *o*
366+SD after *duo—ale* cancelled
366+SH *ALIENIGINA—NI* written above line, between *E* and *G*
385 before *hard—had* cancelled

PLAY XXII

Before 1 *Latin* Before *facta—factus* cancelled
To left of 10-11 *XXIII* in pencil in modern hand
18 after *rise—upe* cancelled
23 after *and*(1)—*w* downstroke and *e* cancelled
48+Latin after *et*(1)—*d* cancelled
after *et*(2)—*ex* cancelled
after *medio—tu* cancelled
54 before *silver—sis* cancelled
57 *in one*—written without word division and separated by downstroke
after *were—riding* cancelled
61 *stiffe—f*(1) altered from another letter
63 *in*—not clear; horizontal line beneath word, no dot for *i*, and form
resembling *mo* or *me*
66 after *anon—unto* squeezed up before downstroke and cancelled
67 after *said—that thou* cancelled
91 after *of*(2)—*ded* cancelled
95 after *of—f* - -(?) cancelled
100 after *and*—large, uncancelled curved downstroke
101 *mooe—o*(2) altered from *r*
124+Latin *Ego Daniell*—written without word-gap and divided by
vertical downstroke
after *et*(1)—*exce* cancelled

134 *nail*—after *l*, end of word (approximately two letters) obscured by inkblot and doubtful

141 after *that*—*mo* cancelled

187 *hundrede*—*r* blotted

After 222 219–20 repeated and cancelled

234 after *slea*—*s* cancelled

249 *toe good*—written without gap and separated by vertical stroke

260+Latin indented in line with verse-edge

300 before *and*—*glent* cancelled

303 after *no*—*mee* cancelled

After 332 333–6 cancelled (at bottom of page)

333 after *in*—*god* cancelled

334 after *to*—*y* cancelled

PLAY XXIII

24+Latin after *Ezechie*—*xx* cancelled
    reducam—after *m*, *b* cancelled

26 after *Jesu*—stroke cancelled

To left of 39–40 *XXIV* in pencil in modern hand

40 after *bene*—*bayle* cancelled, followed by uncancelled downstroke

78 after *by*—*si*(?) cancelled

104 *Amen*—letter cancelled or blotted before word; uncancelled downstroke after word

104+SH after *PRIMUS*—*REX* cancelled

108 after *Christ*—*h* cancelled

119 *rehearse*—*r*(2) written above line

124 after *and*—*worwhi* and part of another letter cancelled

133 set out as if SD, beginning five letter-spaces to left of text-edge

141+ SD *Antechristum*—as two words, divided at *e*

142 after *take*—start of *th* cancelled

162 between *Christ* and *be*—dash

180+SD *cathedram*—*d* blotted and perhaps altered; upstroke rising to right of letter characteristic of *a*

188 after *be*—*lee*, with *ee* blotted and doubtful, cancelled
    lore—before *l*, downstroke characteristic of *s*

213 after *shall*—*advaunce* cancelled

247 after *so*—*rig* cancelled

252+SD after *Enock*—*a* cancelled

257 *thy*—*y* blotted and possibly letter intended between *th* and *y* (*e*?)

266 after *this*—*th* cancelled

276 after *doth*—*do* cancelled

287 after *let—the* cancelled
420 *then—e* cancelled at end of word
530 *manie one*—as one word; separated by downstroke
549 after *thie—th* cancelled
574 after *filii*—uncancelled downstroke
605 after *made—thought* cancelled
After 644+SD *ANTE*—followed by two *xx* abbreviation-forms cancelled and SH written below
668 after *cleane—horw–h*(?) cancelled
670 after *was*—part of letter(?) cancelled
686+SD *Postquam* in left margin
    after *ab—ax* cancelled
694 after *sorrowfull—song* cancelled
After 710 line-space blank

PLAY XXIV

Before 1+Latin after *sum—alp* cancelled
To left of 9 *XXV* in pencil in modern hand
16 after *that*—letter cancelled
18 after *crowne—and* cancelled
After 28 line gap
56 after *thou—putes* cancelled
66 *both—b* doubtful; possibly *l*
130 after *hast—me* cancelled
142 after *lendeth—thie* cancelled
215 after *is—p* cancelled
245 after *in—y* cancelled
247 after I—*god*(?) cancelled
253 after *I—e* cancelled
273 after *never—wer*(?) cancelled
290 after *that—for* cancelled
316 after *ruthfullie—to* cancelled
332 *blinne—inn* one minim short
356+SD *quasi in*—one word, divided by vertical line
392 after *blode—pray* cancelled
402 after *may*—beginning of *h* cancelled
418 after *othes—fervent* cancelled
450 after *owne—sist* cancelled
457 between *one* and *earth*—curved line, resembling start of *w*, above line
513 after *hast—be* cancelled
518 after *that—for* cancelled

After 540 two-line space blank
589 after *popelard—pote* cancelled
591 after *this—I*, incomplete, uncancelled
592 *sinne*—written *sime*
611 after *therefore—for* cancelled
After 616 line gap
630 *or in*—one word, separated by vertical line
653 after *in—fier* cancelled
Below *Finis*, separated by short double line:

> This is the last of all the xxiiii^{or} pageantes
> or playes played by the xxiiii^{or} craftesmen
> of the Cittie of Chester. Written in the
> yere of our lorde God 1604, and in the
> second yere of the reigne of kinge
> James, by the grace of God of England,
> Fraunc and Ireland, Defender
> of the Faith, and of the realme of
> Scotland the xxxviith.
>   PER ME
>   GULIELMUM BEDFORD

(After *Ireland—and* cancelled
After *ME—WILL* on the same line, cancelled)

MANUSCRIPT H

POSITION OF GUILD-ASCRIPTION

After Play-heading:

and as continuation of Playheading	I, II, III, IV, V, VI, VII, VIII, IX, XIII, XIV, XVII, XVIII, XX, XXII
and centred on following line	X, XI, XII, XV, XVI–XVIA, XXIII
and in double-line space below	XXI, XXIV

Guild-ascription omitted but two lines left
blank after Play-heading for its insertion XIX

XVIA not separated from XVI: no Play-heading or Guild-ascription

CONTENT OF PAGES

I 1^r, 1–55; 1^v, 56–93; 2^r, 93+SH–129; 2^v, 130–69; 3^r, 170–213; 3^v, 213+SH–57; 4^r, 258–Finis

II 4^v, 1–36; 5^r, 37–76; 5^v, 77–116; 6^r, 117–56; 6^v, 157–96; 7^r, 197–236; 7^v, 237–76; 8^r, 276+SH–320; 8^v, 321–64; 9^r, 365–408; 9^v, 408+SH–52; 10^r, 453–96+SD; 10^v, 496+SH–544; 11^r, 545–84; 11^v, 585–624; 12^r. 625–68; 12^v, 669–Finis

III 13r, 1–40; 13v, 40+SH–80+SD; 14r, 80+SH–120; 14v, 121–60+ SD; 15r, 160+SH–204; 15v, 205–46+SD; 16r, 246+SH–Appendix IA 23; 16v, IA 24–280; 17r, 281–Finis

IV 17v, 1–36; 18r, 37–76; 18v, 77–112; 19r, 112+SH–52; 19v, 153–96; 20r, 197–236; 20v, 236+SH–76; 21r, 276+SH–316; 21v, 317–58+SD; 22r, 358+SH–400; 22v, 400+SH–39; 23r, 439+SH–Finis

V See Appendix IB

VI 29r, 1–40; 29v, 40+SH–82; 30r, 83–122; 30v, 122+SH–64; 31r, 165–204; 31v, 205–36; 32r, 237–80; 32v, 280+SH–320; 33r, 321–64; 33v, 364+4 (see VRs)–404; 34r, 405–52; 34v, 452+SH–96; 35r, 496+SH– 539+SD; 35v, 540–83; 36r, 584–627; 36v, 628–66+SD; 37r, 667–706; 37v, 707–Finis

VII 38r, 1–36; 38v, 37–76; 39r, 77–116; 39v, 116+SH–52; 40r, 152+ SH–93; 40v, 194–243; 41r, 243+SH–91; 41v, 291+SH–351; 42r, 351+ SH–99; 42v, 399+SH–443; 43r, 443+SH–91; 43v, 491+SH–551; 44r, 551+SH–650; 44v, 650+SH–Finis

VIII 45r, 1–40; 45v, 41–84; 46r, 84+SH–128; 46v, 128+SH–80; 47r, 181–228; 47v, 229–75; 48r, 276–317; 48v, 317+Latin–57; 49r, 358–401; 49v, 402–Finis

IX 50r, 1–44; 50v, 45–87; 51r, 87+SH–135; 51v, 135+SD–79; 52r, 180–223; 52v, 223+SH–Finis

X 53r, 1–40; 53v, 41–84; 54r, 84+SH–128; 54v, 129–72; 55r, 173–216; 55v, 216+SH–60; 56r, 261–304; 56v, 304+SH–48; 57r, 349–96; 57v, 396+SH–445; 58r, 446–Finis

XI 58v, 1–40+SD; 59r, 211–54; 59v, 254+SH–98; 60r, 298+SH– Finis

XII 60v, 1–40; 61r, 41–84; 61v, 85–128; 62r, 129–76; 62v, 177–216+SD; 63r, 216+SH–53; 63v, 253+SH–96; 64r, 297–Finis

XIII 64r, 1–14; 64v, 15–50+1 (see VRs); 65r, 50+1+SH–84; 65v, 84+ SH–122; 66r, 122+SH–64; 66v, 164+SH–209; 67r, 209+SH–54; 67v, 254+SH–88; 68r, 289–328; 68v, 328+SH–64; 69r, 364+SH–409; 69v, 410–50; 70r, 450+SH–Finis

XIV 70v, 1–40+SD; 71r, 40+SH–84; 71v, 85–128; 72r, 128+SH–64; 72v, 165–208; 73r, 208+SD–40; 73v, 240+SH–76; 74r, 277–312; 74v, 313–56; 75r, 357–96; 75v, 396+SH–Finis

XV 76r, 1–40; 76v, 40+SH–84; 77r, 85–124; 77v, 125–60+SD; 78r, 160+SH–96; 78v, 197–240; 79r, 241–80+SD; 79v, 281–313; 80r, 313+ SH–Finis

XVI–XVIA 80v, 1–32; 81r, 33–73; 81v, 73 + SH–109+SD; 82r, 109+ SH–58; 82v, 158+SH–98; 83r, 199–234; 8..v, 234+SH–74; 84r, 282+ SH–318; 84v, 318+SH–62; 85r, 362+SH–XVIA 28; 85v, 28+SH–72; 86r, 72+SH–116; 86v, 116+SH–56; 87r, 156+SH–92+SD; 87v, 192+ SH–233; 88r, 233+SH–60; 88v, 261–300; 89r, 300+SH–40; 89v, 341– Appendix Ic 16; 90r, 16+SH–52; 90v, 53–96; 91r, 96+SH–Finis

XVII 91^v, 1–36; 92^r, 37–80; 92^v, 81–116; 93^r, 117–56; 93^v, 156+SH–200; 94^r, 201–32; 94^v, 233–Finis

XVIII 95^r, 1–36; 95^v, 37–77; 96^r, 78–121; 96^v, 121+SH–53+SD(1); 97^r, 153+SD (2)–89; 97^v, 190–229; 98^r, 230–65; 98^v, 265+SH–304; 99^r, 305–40; 99^v, 340+SH–76; 100^r, 376+SH–412; 100^v, 412+SH–Appendix I$_D$ 11; 101^r, 12–40; 101^v, 40+SH–72; 102^r, 72+SH–Finis

XIX 102^v, 1–36; 103^r, 36+SH–75; 103^v, 76–111+SD; 104^r, 111+SH–47; 104^v, 147+SH–87; 105^r, 187+SH–223; 105^v, 223+SH–55; 106^r, 256–Finis

XX 106^v, 1–38; 107^r, 38+SH–76; 107^v, 77–104+SD; 108^r, 104+SH–28; 108^v, 129–56; 109^r, 156+SH–Finis

XXI 109^v, 1–32+Latin; 110^r, 33–64; 110^v, 64+SH–100; 111^r, 100+SH–24; 111^v, 124+SH–58+SD; 112^r, 158+SH–94; 112^r, 195–230; 113^r, 231–62; 113^v, 262+SH–98; 114^r, 298+SH–326; 114^v, 326+SH–50; 115^r, 350+SH–Finis ·

XXII 115^v, 1–28; 116^r, 29–60; 116^v, 61–96; 117^r, 97–128; 117^v, 129–64+Latin; 118^r, 165–200; 118^v, 201–40; 119^r, 241–76; 119^v, 277–316; 120^r, 317–Finis

XXIII 120^v, 1–28; 121^r, 29–60; 121^v, 60+SH–96; 122^r, 97–128; 122^v, 129–60; 123^r, 160+SH–92+SD; 123^v, 193–228; 124^r, 229–64; 124^v, 265–300; 125^r, 300+SH–40; 125^v, 340+SD–76; 126^r, 377–412; 126^v, 413–50; 127^r, 450+SH–97; 127^v, 497+SH–540; 128^r, 540+SH–76; 128^v, 576+SH–612; 129^r, 612+SH–44; 129^v, 644+SD–74; 130^r, 674+SH–98; 130^v, 698+SH–Finis

XXIV 131^r, 1–24; 131^v, 24+SH–56; 132^r, 57–92; 132^v, 93–128; 133^l, 129–56; 133^v, 157–96; 134^r, 197–228; 134^v, 229–64; 135^r, 265–300; 135^v, 301–36; 136^r, 337–68; 136^v, 369–400; 137^r, 401–32; 137^v, 433–68; 138^r, 468+SH–504; 138^v, 504+SH–36; 139^r, 537–68; 139^v, 569–604; 140^r, 604+SH–44; 140^v, 644+SH–80; 141^r, 681–Finis

FORMS OF PLAY-ENDING

Finis+genitive of Latin number+*Paginae* I, II, XIII, XIV, XXIII
Finis+genitive of Latin number+*Pagine* XVI$_A$
Finis+*Paginae*+genitive of Latin number III, IV, V, VI, VII, VIII, IX, X, XI, XII, XV, XVII, XVIII, XIX, XX, XXII

XXI is incorrectly stated: *Finis Decimae Primae Paginae*
XVI not separated from XVI$_A$: no Finis
XXIV has:

Deo Gratias
Finis Vicesimae Quartae Paginae
Anno Domini 1607 Augusti Quarto
Anno Regni Regis Jacobi Quinto
Per Jacobum Miller

The following dates and signatures are included in the Finis-formula (in chronological order):

After Finis XIV *Julii 23: 1607* (to right of Finis)
After Finis XVIA *Julii 27: 1607* (on following line)
After Finis XIX *Julii 29: Anno Domini 1607* (on following line)
(After Finis XXIV *1607 Augusti Quarto*—see above)
After Finis XI *James Miller: Augusti 6th. 1607* (on following line)

The following Table appears after XXIV. Finis in H:

fol. 141ᵛ

A Table Wherby Any of the Pageants May Easely Be Found And In What Page

			Page
The First Pageant	The Tannars	De Deo (?)	1
The Second Pageant	The Drapers	De Creatione Mundi	4
The Third Pageant	The Waterleaders and Drawers in Dee	De Deluvio Noe	13
The Fourth	The Barbars	De Abrahamo	17
The Fyfte Pageant	The Cappers	De Balaak et Balaam	23
The Syxt	The Wrightes	De Nativitate Christi	29
The Seventh	The Paynters and Glaseors	De Pastoribus	38
The Eight	The Vintners	De Tribus Regibus	45
The Neinth	The Mercers	De Oblatione Trium Regum	50
The Tenthe	The Gouldsmithes	De Occisione Innocentum	53
The Eleventh	The Blacksmithes	De Purificatione Virginis	58
The Twelft	The Butchers	De Tentatione Salvatoris	62
The Thirdtenth	The Glovers	De Ceco et de Resarrectione Lazari	66
The Fourtenthe	The Corvesars	De Jesu Intrante Domum Simonis	72
The Fiftenthe	The Bakers	De Caena Domini	78
The Sixtenthe	The Boyers, Fletchers, and Iremongers	De Passione Christi	82
The Sevententh	The Cookes and Inkepers	De Descensu Christi	93

Page

The Eightenth	The Skinners	De Resurreccione Christi	97
The Neintenth	The Sadlars	De Christo Duobus Discipulis	104
The Twenteeth	The Taylers	De Ascentione Christi	108
The One and Twenteeth	The Fishmongers	De Symbolo Apostalaram	111
The Twenteeth Two	The Shermen or Clothiars	De Antichristo	117

fol. 142r

| The XXIII | The Dyars | De Adventi Antechristi | 122 |
| The XXIIII | The Webstars | De Judicio Novissimo | 133 |

Finis

Below *Finis*] *Vive ut post vivas. Whit de sewterers.*
Rich ledsham. Other scratchings.

PLAY 1

Play-heading ffal—word cut by MS-damage

The following separate lines of God's opening speech of Hm are written as single lines in H:

1–2	26–7	36–7	46–7
18–19	28–9	38–9	48–9
20–1	30 1	40 1	50–1
22–3	32–3	42–3	
24–5	34–5	44–5	

15–19 single unit

To right of 36–7 *In principio creavit Deus coelum. Genes 1*

68–74 single unit

75–7 single unit

163–5 written in quatrain-space

189 *marked*—*r* written above line

229+SD to right of 228

To right of 230–6 *Quodquam angelos qui non servaverant suam originem sed reliquerant suum domicilium ad juditium magni diei vinculis eternis sub caligine servavit. Judae Cap 1. Esai 14. Nabuchodonozor sub figura Luciferi* (*Nabuchodonozor*—*r* perhaps alteration)

To right of 290–2 *Et dixit Deus 'Fiat lux.' Et facta est. Genes: 1.*

PLAY II

To right of 2　*Genesis Primo*

9 between *my* and *bydding*—letter(?) blotted out

To right of 15　*dies 1*

To right of 23–4　*dies 2*

37　*seede of* inserted, with caret, above line

To right of 38　*dies 3*

49　*through*—after *h*(2)—*e* cancelled

53　*planetts*—*t*(2) altered from *e*

To right of 54–5　*dies 4*

70　*fifte*—altered from *firste*

To right of 70　*dies 5*

To right of 82–3　*Faciamus hominem ad nostram similitudinem. Genes: 1*

To right of 99　*dies 6*

To right of 105–8　*Et spiritum vitae efflavit in faciem eius. Factus est Adam in animam viventem. Genes: 2*

112+SD　to right of 112

145+SD　to right of 145

To right of 157–60　*Propterea deseret homo patrem et matrem et adglutinabitur uxori suae, et erunt duo in carnem unam. Genes: 2; Math: 19; Marc: 10; Ephes: 5. 1; Cor: 6*

To right of 209–10　*Car vetuit vos Deus vesci omnibus arboribus pomarii. Genes: 3.*

214　*eat* inserted, with caret, above line

To right of 214–15　*Licet nobis vesci e fructibus arborum pomarii.*

To right of 217–18　*Tantum ea arboro quae est in medio pomarii etct.*

219　*dye* written above line in different hand

To right of 221–2　*Nequaquam moriemini propter ea sed scit etct.*

To right of 228–9　*Vos fore tanquam deos, scientes boni ac mali.*

To right of 231–2　*Sed metuo nequa fiat ut quemadmodum serpens decepit versutia sua. Evam: 2; Corr: 11.*

To right of 245–6　*Vah quam dulcis est, impertiendum est etiam marito.*

To right of 253–4　*Quando ita vis faciam*

To right of 257　*Ah flagitum fecimus*

To right of 273–5　*Texamus nobis subliquenta ex foliis quibus tegamus pudenda*

After 281 SD to right of 281, continuing below

283　*avowe*—*v* altered from *w*

294　three-letter space between *adder* and *lorde* with horizontal line from base of *r*(1)

To right of 297–8　*Quoniam istud fecisti serpens*

To right of 304　*Quin etiam conciliabo rantas inimicitias*

To right of 305–8 *Inter ce et mulierem, interque semen tuum et eius, ut id conteret tibi caput, tu autem ei calcem. Genes: 3.*

To right of 313–14 *Te quoque femina*

To right of 321–2 *Et tu, Adame, quoniam morem gerens uxori tuae, etc.*

To right of 333–4 *Tu vesceris herbis nascentibus terra, etc.* (*vesceris*— circumflex above *e*(2))

339 *againe*—*a*(1) inserted, with caret, above line

To right of 342–3 *Nam pulvis es et in pulverem redibus.*

368+SD to right of 369–70

407 *pryved*—*y* written over *o*

To right of 430 *Genes: 4*

465 *also*—*l* altered from *a*

479 *as* inserted, with caret, above line

482 *my*—*m* apparently alteration from another letter, top of which is visible and partly cancelled

After 592 *Ah well w* cancelled in gap between quatrains

To right of 617 *Cayne, ubi est Abell, frater tuus* in black ink

668 *where*—*h* altered from *e*

PLAY III

85 *boordes*—*oo* re-inked; *o*(2) squeezed in

99–100 single line

251–2 single unit

After 259 line-space blank

281 *flytte*—*t*(2) altered from *e*

308 *spill*—*s* altered from *f*

For Textual Notes on The Raven-and-Dove Scene, see below, heading Appendix IA.

PLAY IV

After 12 line-space ruled and blank

16+SD to right of 16

29 *therefore*—written in gap between quatrains with corresponding space left for word at start of 29 and two carets in left margin beside word and beside space in 29

33 after *here*—*is* cancelled

48+SD to right of 48

53 *Here*—*H* altered from *B*

56+SD to right of 56–60

After 96 quatrain-space blank and unruled

105–7 *com* in *welcome*(105), *i*(1) in *iwis*(106), *t* in *yt* partially obscured by stain

120 *Christianitye*—*i*(3) squeezed in between *n* and *t*

After 144 line-space blank

179–84 single unit, with 179–80, 181–2 each single line

211–16, 241–5 each single unit

253–7 single unit

258–62 single unit

After 260 line-gap

279 after *yt*—no word-gap

To right of 283 *J.J.*(?) in non-scribal hand

To right of and below 284 *nothing fom* in non-scribal hand

286–92, 310–14, 323–8 each single unit

343–8 single unit

351–6, 359–64 each single unit

358+SD to right of 357–8

To right of 377 *of* in non-scribal hand

To right of 379 *let mee* in non-scribal hand

423–8 single unit

To left of 440 *BRAHAM—A* in binding

443+SD to right of 442–3

443+SH *DEUS—D* in binding but partly visible

459+SH *EPOSITOR—E* in binding and partially obscured

PLAY V

For Textual Notes on Play V, see below, Appendix IB.

PLAY VI

To right of 1–3 *In mense autem sexto missus est angelus Gabriell a Deo in civitatem Galilaeae, et ct: Lucae 1. Math: 1.*

To right of 5–8 *Illa vero cum vidisset, turbata est super oracionem eius et cogitabat qualis esset illa salutatio.*

To right of 17–20 *Et dabit illi dominus Deus sestem David patris sui, et regnabit super domum Jacob in aeternum.*

To right of 21–2 *Et regni eius non erit finis.*

To right of 25–6 *Quomodo erit istud quando quidem vivum non cognosco.*

27–32 single unit

To right of 27–30 *Spiritus Sanctus superveniet in te, et virtus altissimi obumbrabit tibi. Quapropter et qui nascetur sanctus vocabitur filius Dei.* (*tibi—i*(1) altered from *e*)

To right of 33–5 *Atque ecce Elizabetha, cognata tua, et ipsa concepit filium in senectute sua.*

To right of 37–40 *Et hic mensis est sextus illi quae dicebatur sterilis; quia non erit impossibile apud Deum omne verbum.* (*pud*—d to right of magin)

To right of 45–6 *Ecce ancilla domini. Fiat mihi secundum verbum tuum.*

48+SD to right of 49

To right of 50–1 *Benedicta tu in mulieribus et benedictus fructus ventris tui.*

To right of 53–4 *Et unde hec mihi ut veniet mater domini mei ad me.*

57–60 in space ruled for three lines; 59–60 squeezed in

To right of 57–60 *Ecce enim ut facta est vox salutacionis tuae in auribus meis exultavit prae gaudio infans in utero meo.*

To right of 61–3 *Et beata quae credidit quoniam perficientur ea quae dicta sunt ei a domino.*

To right of 75–6 *Et respexit ad humilitatem ancillae suae.*

77–80 single unit

To right of 77–82 *Ecce enim ex hoc beatam me dicunt omnes generationes; quia fecit mihi magnifica qui potens est.*

To right of 83 *Et sanctum nomen eius.*

To right of 87–8 *Et misericordia eius in progeniem et progeniem timentibus ipsum.*

91–6 single unit

To right of 92–3 *Prestitit robor per brachium suum; dispersit superbos cogitatione cordis ipsorum.*

To right of 97–9 *Detraxit potentes de sedibus et evexit humiles; esurientes implevit bonis.*

To right of 101–3 *Et divites dimisit inanes. Suscepit Israell puerum suum ut memor esset misericordiae.*

To right of 104–8 *Sicut locutus est ad patres nostros. Abraham et semin eius in eterno. Gloria Patri, et Filio et Spiritu Sancto.*

To right of 109–11 *Sicut erat in principio et nunc et semper et in secula seculorum. Amen.*

To right of 113–15 *Mansit autem Maria cum illa circiter mensibus tribus, et reversa est in domum suam.*

To right of 121–2 *Math. 1.*

123–8 single unit

To right of 123–7 *Jhesu vero Christi nativitas sic habet. Cum enim mater eius Maria desponsa esset Joseph, priusque congressi fuissent deprehensa est gravida Spiritu Sancto.*

To right of 129–31 *Porro Joseph maritus eius quoniam erat justus et nolebat illam infamare.*

To right of 133–4 *Voluit clauculum ab ea depertire.*

137 *lend—d* altered from *g*

141 *to—t* altered from *f*

145–8 in space ruled for three lines; 147–8 squeezed together

To right of 149–50 *Hec autem cum is in stumio versaret, ecce angelus domini*

To right of 157–8 *in somnis visus est, illi dicens:*

To right of 161–4 '*Joseph, fili David, ne metuas adjungere Mariam, uxor tua, namquam illa conceptum est*

To right of 165–6 *a Spiritu Sancto profectum est.'*

To right of 169 *Excitatus autem Joseph a*

To right of 173–4 *somno fecit ut in minnc*(?) *erat sibi angelus domini.* (after *ut*—reading doubtful; *erat*—*e* re-inked and perhaps alteration)

To right of 185–8 *Luca. Cap. 2. Exit edictum e Cesare Augusto ut cenceretur totus orbis.*

209 two lines: *assembles/*

210 two lines: *leez/*

213 two lines: *sages/*

214 two lines: *able/*

215 two lines: *tresagail/*

216 two lines: *counsell/*

217 two lines: *frail/*

After 223 line-space blank

To left of 225 *lordes* in pencil in left margin, in non-scribal hand

252 after *begin*—*saye*(?) cancelled

272–3 single line
  bown—end of word perhaps cut off by page-edge

274–6 in quatrain-space, with line-space blank after 276

372+SD to right of 372

398 *nawger*—*n* written *m* with first minim cancelled

To right of 422–4 *Ascendit autem et Joseph a Galilea de Civitate Nazareth in Judeam in Civitatem David quae vocatur Bethlem.* (*quae* partially obscured by stain)

425–8+SD *Mariam*—*i* altered from *y*

467–8+SD to right of 468

500+SD to right of 499

To right of 501–4 *Et peperit filium suum primogenitum ac fasciis eum involvit reclinavitque eum in precepi quod non esset eis locus in divorsorio. Lucae: 2. Math: 1. John: 1.*

508+SD to right of 507

522 *swet*—after *t*, and above line, short downstroke

537–9 in two-line space with 538–9 as single line

538 after *be*—*a* inserted, with caret, above line before *cleane* in non-scribal hand

540–7 in quatrain-space with 540–1, 542–3, 544–5, 546–7 each single line

To left of 565–6 *x* in pencil

582 *has*—*h* altered from *w*

643+SD to right of 641–2

644–7 to left of each line, in margin, in non-scribal hand, letter—*a* (644), *c* (645), *d* (646), *b* (647)

646 after *of—postye* cancelled

648 after *sees—that* cancelled and *so* written above in word-gap in non-scribal hand

648–50 in quatrain-space with line-gap at end

648+ line to right of 648 in different hand (see VRs)

PLAY VII

To right of 1–3 *Et pastores erant in regione eadem vigilantes et excubantes excubias nocte super gregem suum.*

60+SD to right of 58–60

89–94 single unit

136+SD to right of 138

164+SD to right of 162–3

183 *by—y* altered from *e*

218–25 in quatrain-space with 218–19, 220–1, 222–3, 224–5 each single line

233+SD to right of 233

271 *you—y* altered from *h*

274–9 in quatrain-space with 275–6, 277–8 each single line

300–5 in quatrain-space with 300–1, 303–4 each single line

306–11 in quatrain-space with 306–7, 309–10 each single line

312–17 in quatrain-space with 312–13, 315–16 each single line

318–23 in quatrain-space with 318–19, 321–2 each single line

324–7 in two-line space with 324–5, 326–7 each single line

328–33 single unit with 328–9, 332–3 each single line

334–9 single unit with 334–5, 336–7, 338–9 each single line

340–5 in quatrain-space with 340–1, 343–4 each single line

346–51 in quatrain-space with 346–8, 349–50 each single line

352–7 in quatrain-space with 352–3, 355–6 each single line

After 357+SD

Glori   a in excel s i s deo   de o   de   o   de o

358–63 in quatrain-space with 359–60, 361–2 each single line

364–6 in two-line space with 364–5 single line

367–9 in two-line space with 367–8 single line

370–2 in two-line space with 370–1 single line

373–5 in two-line space with 373–4 single line

376–9 in two-line space with 376–7, 378–9 each single line

388–91 in two-line space with 388–9, 390–1 each single line

396 *crafte—f* altered (from *s*?)

402 *miht*—caret above line between *i* and *h*, and *g* written between them below line

464–71 in quatrain-space with 464–5, 466–7, 468–9, 470–1 each single line

480–3 in two-line space with 480–1, 482–3 each single line

484–7 in two-line space with 484–5, 486–7 each single line

488–91 in two-line space with 488–9, 490–1 each single line

492–5 in two-line space with 492–3, 494–5 each single line

496 after *that—is* cancelled

508–15 in quatrain-space with 508–9, 510–11, 512–13, 514–15 each single line

516–23 in quatrain-space with 516–17, 518–19, 520–1, 522–3 each single line

524–31 in quatrain-space with 524–5, 526–7, 528–9, 530–1 each single line

532–9 in quatrain-space with 532–3, 534–5, 536–7, 538–9 each single line

540–3 in two-line space with 540–1, 542–3 each single line

544–7 in two-line space with 544–5, 546–7 each single line

552–5 in two-line space with 552–3, 554–5 each single line

556–62 in quatrain-space with 558–9, 561–2 each single line

563–70 in quatrain-space with 563–4, 565–6, 567–8, 569–70 each single line

571–5 in quatrain-space with 571–2 single line

576–83 in quatrain-space with 576–7, 578–9, 580–1, 582–3 each single line

592–6 in quatrain-space with 592–3 single line

645–50 in quatrain-space with 645–6, 648–9 each single line

645 *saye—y* altered from *s*

661–8 in quatrain-space with 661–2, 663–4, 665–6, 667–8 each single line

669–75 single unit with 669–70 single line

676–84 single unit with 681–2, 683–4 each single line

PLAY VIII

After *Play-heading* and *Guild-ascription* ruling omitted

7 *Balaam*—hand of scribe C

To left of 41–2 *PRIMUS REX* as SH cancelled

48+SD to right of 48

64+SD to right of 64

65–72 in red ink by scribe C

69–70 and 71–2 presented as two separate two-line units

88+SD not separated from 88 by ruling
   portans—*t* altered from *e*(?)

112+SD to right of 111–12
eques—alteration from *eqes*

139–44 single unit

144+SD to right of 144

153–60 in red ink by scribe C

161–212 quatrains numbered 1–13 to left of second line of each quatrain

196+SD to right of 197

200+SD to right of 201

204+SD to right of 204

212+Latin to right of 213–15

229 after *of*—*pl* smudged

235 after *Of*—gap of about 17 spaces before *and*, evidently for insertion of missing names

265–8 set out as two lines with 265–6, 267–8 each single line

After 268 single-line gap but no ruled division

268+ here and throughout Doctor's speeches, Latin separated from text by ruling

269–345 in units of seven lines except 332–5 where ruling also after 333

298 after *Testament*—*hath* cancelled and *with* written above

346 *beforne*—*n* written over another letter (*e*?)

365+SD to right of 365

381+SD to right of 381

389+SD to right of 390

414 after *bost*—*that* cancelled

PLAY IX

To right of 1–3 *Et apertis thesauris obtulerunt munera—aurum, thus et mirrham. Mathi: 2.*

After 46 line in different hand in space between 46 and 47; perhaps scribe C

59 after *lymmes*—*also* cancelled

To right of 185–6 *I pray* in non-scribal hand

To right of 201 *dighte* in non-scribal hand

To right of 202 *I* in non-scribal hand

To right of and below 203 *as mickle* in non-scribal hand, smudged

To right of and below 207 *might*(?) in non-scribal hand

PLAY X

To right of 1–4 *Tunc Herodes ubi vidit sibi illusum fuisse a magis indignatus est vehementer et missis satellitibus interfecit omnies pueros. Math: 2.*

5 after *thinge—that* cancelled

136 before *till—tl*(?) cancelled

192+SD to right of 191–2

199 *world—l* squeezed in between *r* and *d*

After 256 no ruling

273 *Mary S*—in larger letters; *Mary* slightly above line and in red ink

After 288 no ruled division

344+SD at start of SD, beginning through bottom ruled line—*Out out a*

349–56 in quatrain-space with 351–2 to right of 349–50, 355–6 to right of 353–4

361–8 in quatrain-space with 363–4 to right of 361–2, 367–8 to right of 365–6

376+SD to right of 375–6

385–8 in two-line space with 385–6, 387–8 each single line

426–33 in quatrain-space with 426–7, 428–9, 430–1, 432–3 each single line

433+SD to right of 433

To right of 441 *Tunc faciet signum moriendi et tunc it Demon* cancelled

446–8 single unit

449 in single-line space

450–3 single unit with 452–3 single line

454–7 in three-line space with 456–7 single line

457+SD to right of 456–7

458–61 in three-line space with 460–1 single line

462–5 in three-line space with 464–5 single line

466–9 in three-line space with 468–9 single line

470–3 in three-line space with 472–3 single line

474–7 in three-line space with 476–7 single line

478–81 in three-line space with 480–1 single line

482–5 in two-line space with 482–3, 484–5 each single line

486–9 in two-line space with 486–7, 488–9 each single line

490–3 in two-line space with 490–1, 492–3 each single line

494–7 in two-line space with 494–5, 496–7 each single line

PLAY XI

232 *take*—after *a, l* cancelled

PLAY XII

48 after *what—not* cancelled

68 after *of—bll* cancelled

112+SD to right of 111–12

124+SD to right of 124

168+SD in hand of scribe C (see VRs)

173 after *gluttony*—unusually wide space

216+SD between last ruled space and bottom of page and therefore worn and faint

228 *the*—*t* heavily inked and probably alteration

232+SD to right of 232

252+SD to right of 252 with re-inking of *T* in *Tunc scripsionem*—*s-ri* in hand of scribe B

253 in single-line ruled space

269–72 no ruling for speech-division

270+SH *JHESUS*—black ink

272+SH *MULIER*—black ink

PLAY XIII

Before 1 Latin *Ego*—*E* half-line above
   after Latin—ruling dividing it from text

1–35 as seven-line units

19–20 reversed but to left of 19 § *row is misplased* in red ink

20 *scripture*—scribe wrote *scriptureth*; it is not clear if *eth* is cancelled or altered to *es*

35+Latin in two-line space

98 after *we*—*spye* cancelled

138–9 single line

148 *dowbt*—*b* altered from *y*

156+SD to right of 156

164 *poore*—above *p, o*

208–9 single line

213–14 single line

221–2 single line

223–4 single line

233 *hear*—*a* altered (from *e*?)

248 *me*—*m* altered (from *a*?)

249 *one*—*ne* re-inked and probably alteration

259–60 and SD in single quatrain space, with no ruling between text and SD

284+SD to right of 283–4

293 *dethe*—*e*(1) alteration

308+SD to right of 308

After 333 single ruled space blank
340 *not*—before *n*, letter (start of *m*?) cancelled
348 *thinkes*—*i* resembling *o*
To right of 356+Latin *Johamis Cap. 10 De Lazaro Resuscitato*
368-9 single line
370-2 to right of 365-9; both SHs in left margin
392-3 single line
401+SD *dicens*—*s* re-inked and probably alteration
408 *my*—last minim of *m* is also first minim of *y*; perhaps *ny*
417+SD to right of 416-17
423-5 and SD in quatrain space, with no division
450 in single ruled space
459-65 single unit

PLAY XIV

71 *dealt*—*d* altered from *t*
87-8 single line
89-90 single line
91-6 single unit
100 *maner*—*n* altered from *h*
112+SD to right of 112
119 after *and*—*may* cancelled
145 *shall*—*ha* probably alteration
148 *beastes*—*e*(1) re-inked and alteration
152+SD to right of 151-2
154 in one-and-a-half line space
155-6 in three-line space
164 *conninge*—*e* doubtful; perhaps cancelled or altered (from *h*?)
168+SD to right of 168
185-8 to right of 181-4; both SHs in left margin; sign in red ink before
Lazar and arrow to *day* (184)
208+SDs 1 and 2 written as one
222 *mankynds*—*k* alteration
224+SD *cum flagello*—centred and squeezed in between last line of SD
and ruling
274 *destroy*—*d* written over *s*
277 *it*—no word-gap between it and preceding and following words
357 *came*—after *e*, *s* cancelled
367 *falcly*—*l*(2) altered from *s*
387-92 single unit

411–16 single unit
419–26 quatrain-division not corresponding to stanza-form
427–32 single unit

PLAY XV

Play-heading Quinta—a blotted
44+SD to right of 44
60+SD to right of 60
104 *ghostly—h* altered from *o*
120+SD to right of 120
125 *hym—y* blotted and probably alteration (from *e*?)
203 *agayne another—*written without word-gap
233 after *ever—I* uncancelled, with *you* written above without caret
238 *gloryfied—r* altered from *f*
242 inset two letter spaces to avoid hole in page
254 *blis—*two *s* strokes, but small and close together; perhaps *ss*
281 *all—ll* alteration (from *n*?)
297 *slepen—e*(1) altered from another letter whose downstroke is visible below
343–6 in two-line space with 343–4, 345–6 each single line
347–50 in two-line space with 347–8, 349–50 each single line
351–8 in quatrain-space with 351–2, 353–4, 355–6, 357–8 each single line
359–66 in quatrain-space with 359–60, 361–2, 363–4, 365–6 each single line

PLAY XVI

12 *Christhod—d* with two upstrokes
47 *hear—*before *h*, letter cancelled
54–8 single unit
70–109 bracket to right of each quatrain
109 + bracket to right of single-line SD
111 *served—v* altered from *s*
117 + SD to right of 116–17
126 *our—u* alteration from *r*
147 *Galaly—a*(1) altered from *l*
154 *renowne—*reading doubtful; perhaps *reiowne*
178+SD to right of 178
221–7 single unit
229 *ther upon—*one word, divided by downstroke after *r*
257–63 single unit

262–3 single line

263 *cry*—*r* written above cancelled *y*

299–304 single unit

300 *kings*—*k* altered from *f*

325 *begger*—reading uncertain; *gg* or *ge*

344 *hyde*—reading uncertain; possibly *Hy* or even *Lyy*

350 after *ostern*—word erased; initial *n* visible

PLAY XVIA

2 *boots*—*oo* or *ee*

67–72 single unit

88+SD *quosque*—*o* above *q*

97 *with*—*h* written over erasure

120+SD to right of 120

120+–136+ to left of SHs—numbers: *1, 2, 3, 4*

120+SH *FYRST*—altered from *FOURTH*

130 *rowndfull*—*d* altered from *s*

131–6 single unit; 135–6 single line

143 *synes*—a *y* downstroke below *n*

152 *neyles*—*y* written over erasure

168 *play*—*l* written over *r*

208 *deserve*—*v* altered from *f* or *s*

234–6 in quatrain space

260 *say*—altered from *see*

278 *bitter*—*tt* probably alteration

After 280 Scribe has continued with 285–8 but has corrected his mistake. In quatrain-division between 280 and following 285, he has written *Come, lord* and, to left, in margin, *hic*. Below SH preceding 281 and to left of 281–3, *Thes verses must come before*

290 *his*—before *h*, *t* cancelled

292 after *to*—*skl*(?) or *slel*(?) cancelled, followed by short diagonal stroke marking line-end which is uncancelled

314 *righteously*—*e* blotted and probably alteration

321 *man*—*n* with initial downstroke; probably alteration

323–4, 325–9 each single line

344+2 after *my God*(1)—*why hast* cancelled

352 in red ink

For Textual Notes on The Final Section of Play XVIA in H, see below, heading Appendix IC.

PLAY XVII

50 *me—e* altered from *y*
87 *fyve thousand years*—red ink
88 red ink
108+Latin in red ink as fourth line of quatrain
125–8 to right of 121–4
    after *fayle* (124)—*versus 2* in red ink
137–8 in four-line space
141–4 in two-line space
141–2 single line
143–4 single line
152+SD in four-line space, set out as quatrain
153 in two-line space
154–6 in four-line space
159 *thy*(2)—*y* altered from *e*(?)
201 *him—m* altered from *s*
    lyke—e altered from *k*
223 *stry*—perhaps *striy*
255–60 single unit

PLAY XVIII

7 *nostre—r* altered from *e*(?)
9 *ladyes*—ending uncertain; *e* altered from *y* and not clear, unusual form
of *s*
40 *therof—o* probably alteration
50 *was* inserted, with caret, above line
62 after *such—s* cancelled
74–7 written in slightly smaller script in three-line space at end of page
93–4 single line
95–7 in quatrain space
Before 121+SH quatrain space blank
124–9 single unit
125 *takes—ta* blotted; loop above *t* suggests alteration (from *l*?); reading
doubtful
128 *eschew—e*(2) close to *w* and doubtful; perhaps *o*
154–85 quatrains numbered 1–8 to left of second line of each quatrain
155 *of* inserted, with caret, above line
158 *sought—g* altered from *h*
165 *they—y* added in word-gap in different ink, but scribal
194 *art—r* blotted and probably alteration
241+SD to right of 241

267 *full*—*f* altered from *s*

297 *witchcraft*—*ra* blotted and probably alteration

389 after *thou*—*may* cancelled

    after *see*—mark indicating end of line uncancelled

410 *me* altered from *wa*

413–18 single unit; line-gap between 417 and 418

420 *please*—*s* written over another letter

For Textual Notes on The Final Section of Play XVIII in H, see below, heading Appendix I<small>D</small>.

PLAY XIX

7 *day*—downstroke visible below *a*

111+SD to right of 111

119+SD to right of 119

122 *bread*—*r* altered from *l*

123+SD to right of 123

126 *he* inserted, with caret, above line

132 *masse*—altered from *made*

199+SD to right of 199

205 after *other*—*as* cancelled

213 *mymne*—no gap after preceding word

218–23 single unit

223+SH *ANDREAS*—*A*(1) altered from *T*

224 *we*—*e* added in red ink

244–9 single unit

249+SD to right of 249; *Tunc*—black ink

252–75 quatrains numbered 1–6 to left of second line of each quatrain

252 after *seest*—*in* cancelled

To right of 255 *Beati qui non viderunt et crediderunt Jho: 2.*

Before 256 two-line space blank

PLAY XX

Before 1 Latin text in larger letters with line below

12 *woundes*—*d* written over *l*

25 *on evermore*—no word-gap; *m* written over *y*(?)

33–8 single unit

52 *I* altered from *h*

61–96 quatrains numbered 1–9 to left of second line of each quatrain

63 *towcheth*—*t*(2) altered from *h*; *h* squeezed up against *t*

83 *show*—*h* alteration

104+(after *JESUS* Latin) SD *stabit*—*t*(2) altered from *s*(?)

120+SH *TERTIUS*—stroke, apparently start of *S*, before *T*(1)

125–52 quatrains numbered 1–7 to left of second line of each quatrain

152+SD(1) in two-line space, followed by canticle-lines, each in two-line space and divided after *cantabimus*

    SD(2) in double-line space with canticle as second line

To left of 161 *ANGELUS PRIMUS* cancelled and *PETRUS* written below

184 after *saved—in*, written in small letters above line, in different ink and perhaps in non-scribal hand

192 *Amen—*red ink

    to right—*1607 Julii 30.* in red ink

PLAY XXI

1–46 quatrains numbered 1–11 to left of second line of each quatrain

41–6 single unit

46+SD scribe has transposed SDs at 46+ and 56+ but has corrected error. To left of 46+SD, *hic*; to right, stylized indication-mark and *et*. To left of 56+SD, *This must come in place of 'Tunc colliget.'*; to right, stylized indication-mark

48+SD to right of 48

61 after *in—maiesty* cancelled

82 after *that—ther were* cancelled by underline

    after *were*—mark indicating end of line uncancelled

112+Latin in three-line space

115–16 single line

After 120+SD two-line ruled space blank

To right of 121 *Come holy* in non-scribal hand

129 *dayes—s* altered from *e*(?)

139 *leader—r* blotted

145 *worship—*after *p*, another *p* downstroke

153–8 single unit

159–238 quatrains numbered 1–20 to left of second line of each quatrain

193 after *me—god* (or possibly *good*) inserted with caret above line

194 *with—h* altered from another letter

210+ scribe has written two quatrains in one quatrain space, with 211–12, 213–14, 215–16, 217–18 each on single line, and to left of 213–14, *14. 15*

To left of 220 *16–6* altered from *5*(?)

220 *evar—r* altered from *s* and blotted

After 230 single-line space blank

242 *far—a* heavily blotted and altered from *o*

271 *God—*after *d, e* cancelled

278 *fulfill—l*(1) altered from *f*

283 *I am* inserted, with caret, above line

300 after *as—you* cancelled and *he* written above in different ink; perhaps non-scribal

304 *creed—*in red ink

310+SD *Duae—e* added in black ink

311–58 quatrains numbered 1–12 to left of second line of each quatrain. For speeches, Latin is to right of SH and separated from speeches by rulings

317 after *us—kent* cancelled

318 *elders—e* written over another letter

358+ two quatrains in single-quatrain space, with 359–60, 361–2, 363–4, 365–6 each single line

    Yea leif Brother underlined in red

373 *speak—e* alteration

To right of 376 *Richard Morris—*in non-scribal but contemporary hand

PLAY XXII

Before 1 here and throughout Play in Latin texts similarly quoted by characters, Latin in speeches to right of SH and separated from text by ruling

1–24 quatrains numbered 1–6 to left of first or second line of each quatrain

4 *thought—t*(2) in word-gap and perhaps added later

20 words unusually widely spaced

25–48 quatrains numbered 1–6 to left of first, second, or third line of each quatrain

32 after *and—lyfe* cancelled

33 *Therfore—The* altered from *Bel*, and *r* perhaps also alteration from *e*(?)

36 *flesh—l* altered from *k*

46 *no—o* blotted and written over erasure

49–72 quatrains numbered 1–6 to left of second line of each quatrain

To right of 51–2 *Lord have mercy on mee and grant me thy grace* (*and—*perhaps *ande*; *grace* squeezed up against page-edge) in same hand as XXI. 376 above

59 *whyte—h* inserted, with caret, above line

73–124 quatrains numbered 1–13 to left of first, second, or third line of each quatrain

111 after *as—dreden* cancelled

125–56 quatrains numbered 1–8 to left of first or second line of each quatrain

157–72 quatrains numbered 1–4 to left of first or third line of each quatrain

173–212 quatrains numbered 1–10 to left of first, second, or third line of each quatrain

To left of 186 *1260*

213–60 quatrains numbered 1–12 to left of first or second line of each quatrain

218 *thus*—*h* altered from *y*

221 *wytterly*—*y*(1) blotted and altered from *o* or *e*

260+Latin *Signa 15* in margin to left of Latin text

269–332 numbers of signs in margin to left of corresponding lines; *2* to left of 273

PLAY XXIII

1–8 no quatrain-division; lines are linked by vertical line-bracketing to right; red ink

After 8 double ruled line, upper in black ink, lower in red

9–60 quatrains numbered 1–13 to left of first or second line of each quatrain

To right of 16—*to save* in non-scribal hand

24 *deale*—*l* altered from *r*

28 *fantasy*—*t* blotted and altered from *s*

40+ scribe has transposed two Latin texts at 40+ and 56+ but has corrected error by writing *hic* to left of Latin at 40+ and *This should come in place of 'Dabit eis'* to left of Latin at 56+

77–104 quatrains numbered 1–7 to left of first or second line of each quatrain

104+SD to right of 103–4

113–33 quatrains numbered 1–5 to left of first or second line of each quatrain

120+Latin written in quatrain space

122 *posty*—*p* alteration

133 included as last line of quatrain in place of 132; in red ink

141 *disease*—*s*(2) blotted and alteration (from *c*?)

141+SD to right of 141

149+SD to right of 148–9

194 after *kinges*—*also to you* cancelled

198 after *me*—*light* cancelled

205–44 quatrains numbered 1–10 to left of first or second line of each quatrain

217 *lordships*—*s*(2) altered from *p*

241 *Lumbardy*—in different script

253–84 quatrains numbered 1–8 to left of first or second line of each quatrain

285–300 quatrains numbered 1–4 to left of first or second line of each quatrain

320+ scribe has omitted 321–4 but inserts lines after 332 and corrects error. At 320 *we will abyde* is underlined in red; to left of 320, stylized indication-mark and *hic*. To left of 321–4, SECUNDUS REX *These iiii rowes should come in after 'we will abyde.'*

321–40 quatrains numbered 1–4 to left of first or second line of each quatrain

347 *bewitched—d* alteration

358 *lyen—*after *y*, letter cancelled

361 *defyne—e*(1) written above line between *d* and *f*

371–6 presented as two three-line units

379 after *your—wyles* cancelled

381–6 single unit

387–93 single unit

401 *heare—a* written above line

478–81 to right of 474–7, with SH before 478 to left of 476 SHs in left margin
HELIAS repeated in red ink at left of 478

484–9 single unit

492–7, 498–500 each single unit

625–44 quatrains numbered 1–6 to left of first, second, or third line of each quatrain

627 *alway—a*(2) altered from *y*

661–6 two three-line units, each within a quatrain-space

After 666 671 cancelled (*taught*] *thought*)

669–70 single line

After 674 blank ruled two-line space

680 *sone shall—*written without word-division, with *s*(2) squeezed in between *e* and *h*

PLAY XXIV

Before 1 Latin—in larger letters and marked off from 1 by double-ruled line

1–24 quatrains numbered 1–6 to left of first or second line of each quatrain

41–80 quatrains numbered 1–10 to left of first or second line of each quatrain

42 *that—*written over erasure

81–108 quatrains numbered 1–7 to left of first, second, or third line of each quatrain

After 108 double-ruled line

109–40 quatrains numbered 1–8 to left of first, second, or third line of each quatrain

After 140 double ruled line

141–72 quatrains numbered 1–8 to left of first, second, or third line of each quatrain

145 *my*—apparently *r* after *y*

172+SD to right of 172

After 172 double ruled line

173–204 quatrains numbered 1–8 to left of first, second, or third line of each quatrain

After 204 double ruled line

205–36 quatrains numbered 1–8 to left of first, second, or third line of each quatrain

After 236 double ruled line

237–60 quatrains numbered 1–6 to left of first, second, or third line of each quatrain

239 *synne*—*y* written over another letter; first minim of *n*(1) doubtful
 seene—*n* with cancelled initial upstroke

247 *never*—*r* written over *e*(?)

After 260 double ruled line

261–92 quatrains numbered 1–8 to left of first, second, or third line of each quatrain

270 after *why*—*why* cancelled

After 292 double ruled line

293–324 quatrains numbered 1–8 to left of first, second, third, or fourth line of each quatrain

After 324 double ruled line

325–56 quatrains numbered 1–8 to left of first, second, or third line of each quatrain

After 356 double ruled line

357–436 quatrains numbered 1–20 to left of first, second, or third line of each quatrain

407 *iwys*—*i* undotted and with unusual ligature; alteration

433 *me*—*e* written over *y*

463 *neded*—*n* written over *dr*(?)

477–500 quatrains numbered 1–6 to left of first, second, or third line of each quatrain

509–48 quatrains numbered 1–10 to left of first, second, or third line of each quatrain

531 after *judge*—*deeme* cancelled

549–72 quatrains numbered 1–6 to left of first or second line of each quatrain

To left of 554 *2* erased before quatrain-number

To left of 564+Latin *5* partially erased

573–604 quatrains numbered *1–9* to left of first or second line of each quatrain

580+ to left of Latin—*3*, next number in quatrain-series; Latin is written as four lines but with bracket and stylized indication mark to right

581 *deliver thse*—no word division; perhaps *h* ligature to *s* intended to be abbreviation-form also

605–28 quatrains numbered *1–6* to left of first or second line of each quatrain

606 *heare*—*ear* re-inked; probably alteration

622 *naked*—*d* blotted; perhaps alteration from *s* since characteristic *s* stroke visible to right of *d*

633 *had*—written in left margin, displacing SH which is to left of 634 after *we*—*saw* cancelled

639 *them*—*e* altered from *y*

645–60 quatrains numbered *1–4* to left of first, second, or third line of each quatrain

661–76 quatrains numbered *1–4* to left of first, second, or third line of each quatrain

673 *also*—*l* altered from *s*

684 *fere*—*f* altered from *y*

To right of 708 *Laus maxima Omnipotenti*

APPENDIX IA—PLAY III

3 *where*—*h* squeezed in between *w* and *e*

13–15 single unit

APPENDIX IB—PLAY V

Guild-ascription Capp—rest obscured by binding

Play-heading Rege—*ege* visible through binding repair

32+SD to right of 30–1

37 after *by*—gap of about six spaces with decorative flourish

40+SH *PRINCEPS*—*PRI* not visible

48+SH *MOYSES*—*MO* and part of *Y* not visible

64+SH *EXPOSITOR*—*EX* and *P* downstroke not visible

66 *the*—*t* partly destroyed by damage to paper; *e* partially blotted

116 after *all*—*he* cancelled

128+SD to right of 126

160+SD *Asina* centred and squeezed into gap between SD and ruling

168+SD *Asinam*—*n* in black ink with heavy first minim; probably alteration

175–80 single unit
189–94 single unit
264+SD to right of 262
273–8 single unit
328+Latin *virgo*—*r* written above *i*
344+Latin *vocem*—*v* altered from *n*
424 after *he*—*banished* cancelled
426 *goste*—*e* altered from another form (*d*?) blotted out

APPENDIX IC—PLAY XVIA

9–14 single unit
12 *needes*—*d* altered from *s*
34+SD to right of 32
After 46 51 cancelled and 47 to right
66 *devoutly*—form of *v* indicates that scribe began to write *w*
85–9 single unit
105–6 single line
126 *spicery*—*r* altered from *l*
131 after *have*—*of* cancelled and *on* written above

APPENDIX ID—PLAY XVIII

3–7 single unit
To left of 10 *MARIA MAG* as SH cancelled and *JHESUS* written below
30 *hee*—*ee* written over *a* in different ink
37 written over ruling
39+SD *obviam*—no gap after preceding word; *o* altered from *t*, *v* not in usual form after *b* and apparently altered from *o*
65 *great*—*a* altered from *t*

MANUSCRIPT M

Play-heading Heare—top flourish of *H* smudged
  beegyneth—written on two lines, divided before *n*; *gyn* smudged and almost obscured
  after *the* and before *Pagent*—gap of about seven letters, corresponding to base of capital *B*
2 *luyes*—uncertain; perhaps *licyes*
5 *graunde*—obscured, and possibly *g^rande*
9 *e and lere*—obscured

10 after *of*—another word not clear; - - *nde* just visible

12 after *to*—*f* - - *nde* just visible

13+ at longest portion in centre of MS. some letters from following line just visible

   below *ste* of *moste*—tops of *pe* and another letter can be seen

22 MS. stained and creased across this line, making lower half of letters obscure

36 *till*—perhaps *Tyl*

38 *The*—not visible on MS.

   blacke—only tops of *b*, *l*, *k* visible on MS.

41 *abowt*—*wt* not clear, and reading might be *wte*

   -*one*—first letter not visible on MS.

MANUSCRIPT P

Play-heading after *xx*—approximately four spaces blank

   Antechristus—*An* and part of *t* only visible

1–8 lines bracketed on right as couplets

1 *trone*—*r* partially removed by hole

2 *vobis*—*s* removed by hole

After 8 line-space blank

To right of 9–33 faint red-ink line/quatrain divisions

24+Latin in gap between last line of Latin and ruled-line, below *reducam vos* and beginning below *d*—*educam* in sixteenth-century hand with a letter after *e* indistinct

25 above *laykyd*, and partially obscuring *ky*—*lyggedd* in sixteenth-century hand

31 *slayne*—*l* blotted; *sleyne* written above

39 *them*—tilde above *m*

40+Latin *templum*—written *templu* without tilde

To right of 41–60 faint red-ink line/quatrain divisions

46 *which*—*h*(1) blotted and perhaps altered from *y*

56+Latin *multis*—*is* worn away and illegible

To right of 59 *omnipotent* in sixteenth-century hand

To right of 88 (*leeve*) in sixteenth-century hand

To right of 89 (*bodyes that*) in sixteenth-century hand

95 *marvlosly*—*rvl* not clear; *v* doubtful

141+SD to right of and slightly above SH

164 *see*—*e*(2) obscured by fold-mark

166 *glorifyd grattest*—*d gra* heavily re-inked and blotted; *ra* doubtful

After 176 line erased; downstrokes visible below *b*, *f*(1) of *beffore*, and letter (*b*?) to right of *beffore*

176+SH *TERCIUS REX*—tops of *T*, *R*(2) cut by page-top

177 *go*—in modern ink and in word-gap; perhaps added

180+SD *et Tercius Rex* centred, with rest of SD to right
chathedr—rest of word lost at binding-edge

214 *regnis*—dot over second minim of *ni*; perhaps *regins*

To left of 249–51 illegible words; perhaps *here ido-offod*

To right of 250 *leves* in sixteenth-century hand

259 tops of *I* in *Is*, *ss*, *bl*, and *k* cut by page-top

279 *bysyde*—before *b*, another letter (*b*, *d* ?) visible but deleted; *y* downstroke visible in modern ink below *b*

295 *thys*—*t* in word-gap in modern ink

308 *wrytyn*—*r* blotted and doubtful

To left of 341–2 *ere ha de con s iii* (?) in sixteenth-century hand

401+SD to left of 402 in sixteenth-century hand

To right of 421 *knees* in sixteenth-century hand

To right of 458–66 ink-scratchings and illegible words in non-scribal hands

480 *mete*—in modern ink; *e*(1) doubtful, perhaps changed from *o*

486 after *his*—*his* cancelled by three dots beneath in modern ink

489 *feayttir*—re-inked; *ayt* squeezed together and doubtful; *i* doubtful

489+SH tops of letters cut by page-top

502+SD to left of 502

To left of 506 *without* in sixteenth-century hand

528+SH as 489+SH

553 after *be*—vertical stroke

554 after *that*—two vertical strokes

556 after *yf*, *ye*, *wyll*, *mende*—vertical strokes

558 after *and*—vertical stroke

564+SH as 489+SH

594 *tho*—*o* re-inked; perhaps altered from *e*

598 *wycchcrafte*—*cr* blotted and doubtful

599 *led* inserted, with caret, above line

600+SH as 489+SH

To right of 611 *leche* in sixteenth-century hand

620 *moke*—*o* doubtful; perhaps *e*

624+SH on same line as end of SD

633 *ingendirt*—*r* blotted and doubtful

635 tops of letters cut by page-top

648 *be* written above line

670+SH as 489+SH

684 *penance*—*a* written above *an*

702+SH as 489+SH

To right of 705–9 *yowrek*(?) written vertically from bottom to top of page, with tilde above *rek*

726+SD *domine*—written *dno* without abbreviation-mark

MANUSCRIPT C

In left margin, beside *Guild-ascription* and *Incipit—16 Pagent 1599* in black ink
   part of *T* cancelled in margin above

After 28 half-line space with broken black-ink line of six dashes

326+SD (English) in left margin beside SD (Latin)

Finis   Finis Deo Gracias
       per me Georgium Bellin } *1599*

EARLY ENGLISH TEXT SOCIETY

LIST OF PUBLICATIONS
1864–1974

JUNE 1974

Orders from non-members of the Society should be placed with a bookseller. Orders from booksellers for volumes in part 1 of this list should be sent to Oxford University Press, Ely House, 37 Dover Street, London W. 1. Orders from booksellers for volumes in part 2 of this list should be sent to the following addresses: orders from the United States and Canada to Kraus Reprint Co., Route 100, Millwood, N.Y. 10546, U.S.A.; orders from Germany and Japan to Kraus Reprint Co., FL 9491 Nendeln, Liechtenstein, or Oxford University Press; orders from Great Britain and all other countries to Oxford University Press, Ely House, 37 Dover Street, London W. 1.

EARLY ENGLISH TEXT SOCIETY

The Early English Text Society was founded in 1864 by Frederick James Furnivall, with the help of Richard Morris, Walter Skeat and others, to bring the mass of unprinted Early English literature within the reach of students and to provide sound texts from which the New English Dictionary could quote. In 1867 an Extra Series was started of texts already printed but not in satisfactory or readily obtainable editions. In 1921 the Extra Series was discontinued and all publications were subsequently listed and numbered as part of the Original Series. In 1970 the first of a new Supplementary Series was published; unlike the Extra Series, volumes in this series will be issued only occasionally, as funds allow and as suitable texts become available.

In the first part of this list are shown the books published by the Society since 1938, Original Series 210 onwards and the Supplementary Series. A large number of the earlier books were reprinted by the Society in the period 1950 to 1970. In order to make the rest available, the Society has come to an agreement with the Kraus Reprint Co. who reprint as necessary the volumes in the Original Series 1–209 and in the Extra Series. In this way all the volumes published by the Society are once again in print.

Membership of the Society is open to libraries and to individuals interested in the study of medieval English literature. The subscription to the Society for 1975 is £5·00 (U.S. members $14.00, Canadian members Can. $14.00), due in advance on 1 January, and should be paid by cheque, postal order or money order made out to 'The Early English Text Society', and sent to Dr. Anne Hudson, Executive Secretary, Early English Text Society, Lady Margaret Hall, Oxford. Payment of this subscription entitles the member to receive the new book(s) in the Original Series for the year. The books in the Supplementary Series do not form part of the issue sent to members in return for the payment of their annual subscription, though they are available to members at a reduced price; a notice about each volume is sent to members in advance of publication.

Private members of the Society (but not libraries) may select in place of the annual issue past volumes from the Society's list chosen from the Original Series 210 to date or from the Supplementary Series. The value of such texts allowed against one annual subscription is £6·00, and all these transactions must be made through the Executive Secretary. Members of the Society may purchase copies of books O.S. 210 to date for their own use at a discount of 25% of the listed prices; private members (but not libraries) may purchase earlier publications at a similar discount. All such orders must be sent to the Executive Secretary.

Details of books, the cost of membership and its privileges, are revised from time to time. This list is brought up to date annually, and the current edition should be consulted.

June 1974

ORIGINAL SERIES 1938–1974

O.S. 210 **Sir Gawain and the Green Knight**, re-ed. I. Gollancz, with £1·50
introductory essays by Mabel Day and M. S. Serjeantson.
1940 (*for* 1938), *reprinted* 1966.

211 **The Dicts and Sayings of the Philosophers**: translations made £4·50
by Stephen Scrope, William Worcester and anonymous
translator, ed. C. F. Bühler. 1941 (*for* 1939), *reprinted* 1961.

212 **The Book of Margery Kempe**, Vol. I, Text (*all published*), ed. £4·25
S. B. Meech, with notes and appendices by S. B. Meech and
H. E. Allen. 1940 (*for* 1939), *reprinted* 1961.

213 **Ælfric's De Temporibus Anni**, ed. H. Henel. 1942 (*for* 1940), £2·50
reprinted 1970.

214 **Forty-Six Lives translated from Boccaccio's De Claris** £3·25
Mulieribus by Henry Parker, Lord Morley, ed. H. G. Wright.
1943 (*for* 1940), *reprinted* 1970.

215, 220 **Charles of Orleans: The English Poems**, Vol. I, ed. R. £3·75
Steele (1941), Vol. II, ed. R. Steele and Mabel Day (1946 *for*
1944); *reprinted as one volume with bibliographical supplement*
1970.

216 **The Latin Text of the Ancrene Riwle**, from Merton College £2·70
MS. 44 and British Museum MS. Cotton Vitellius E. vii, ed.
C. D'Evelyn. 1944 (*for* 1941), *reprinted* 1957.

217 **The Book of Vices and Virtues**: A Fourteenth-Century English £4·50
Translation of the *Somme le Roi* of Lorens d'Orléans, ed.
W. Nelson Francis. 1942, *reprinted* 1968.

218 **The Cloud of Unknowing and The Book of Privy Counselling**; £3·00
ed. Phyllis Hodgson. 1944 (*for* 1943), *corrected reprint* 1973.

219 **The French Text of the Ancrene Riwle**, British Museum MS. £3·25
Cotton Vitellius F. vii, ed. J. A. Herbert. 1944 (*for* 1943),
reprinted 1967.

220 **Charles of Orleans: The English Poems**, Vol. II; *see above*
O.S. 215.

221 **The Romance of Sir Degrevant**, ed. L. F. Casson. 1949 (*for* £3·00
1944), *reprinted* 1970.

222 **The Lyfe of Syr Thomas More, by Ro. Ba.**, ed. E. V. Hitch- £3·75
cock and P. E. Hallett, with notes and appendices by A. W.
Reed. 1950 (*for* 1945), *reprinted* 1974.

223 **The Tretyse of Loue**, ed. J. H. Fisher. 1951 (*for* 1945), £2·50
reprinted 1970.

224 **Athelston: a Middle English Romance**, ed. A. McI. Trounce. £2·50
1951 (*for* 1946), *reprinted* 1957.

225 **The English Text of the Ancrene Riwle**, British Museum MS. £3·00
Cotton Nero A. xiv, ed. Mabel Day. 1952 (*for* 1946), *re-*
printed 1957.

226 **Respublica**: an interlude for Christmas 1553 attributed to £1·80
Nicholas Udall, re-ed. W. W. Greg. 1952 (*for* 1946),
reprinted 1969.

O.S. 227   **Kyng Alisaunder,** Vol. I, Text, ed. G. V. Smithers. 1952 (*for* £4·50
1947), *reprinted* 1961.

228   **The Metrical Life of St. Robert of Knaresborough,** together £2·50
with the other Middle English pieces in British Museum MS.
Egerton 3143, ed. Joyce Bazire. 1953 (*for* 1947), *reprinted*
1968.

229   **The English Text of the Ancrene Riwle,** Gonville and Caius £2·10
College MS. 234/120, ed. R. M. Wilson with an introduction
by N. R. Ker. 1954 (*for* 1948), *reprinted* 1957.

230   **The Life of St. George by Alexander Barclay,** ed. W. Nelson. £2·40
1955 (*for* 1948), *reprinted* 1960.

231   **Deonise Hid Diuinite** and other treatises related to *The Cloud* £3·00
of Unknowing, ed. Phyllis Hodgson. 1955 (*for* 1949), *reprinted*
with corrections 1958.

232   **The English Text of the Ancrene Riwle,** British Museum MS. £1·80
Royal 8 C. i, ed. A. C. Baugh. 1956 (*for* 1949), *reprinted*
1959.

233   **The Bibliotheca Historica of Diodorus Siculus** translated by £4·80
John Skelton, Vol. I, Text, ed. F. M. Salter and H. L. R.
Edwards. 1956 (*for* 1950), *reprinted* 1968.

234   **Paris and Vienne** translated from the French and printed by £2·50
William Caxton, ed. MacEdward Leach. 1957 (*for* 1951),
reprinted 1970.

235   **The South English Legendary,** Corpus Christi College £3·75
Cambridge MS. 145 and British Museum MS. Harley 2277,
with variants from Bodley MS. Ashmole 43 and British
Museum MS. Cotton Julius D. ix, ed. C. D'Evelyn and A. J.
Mill. Vol. I, Text, 1959 (*for* 1957), *reprinted* 1967.

236   **The South English Legendary,** Vol. II, Text, ed. C. D'Evelyn £3·75
and A. J. Mill. 1956 (*for* 1952), *reprinted* 1967.

237   **Kyng Alisaunder,** Vol. II, Introduction, commentary and £3·00
glossary, ed. G. V. Smithers. 1957 (*for* 1953), *reprinted with*
corrections 1969.

238   **The Phonetic Writings of Robert Robinson,** ed. E. J. Dobson. £1·80
1957 (*for* 1953), *reprinted* 1968.

239   **The Bibliotheca Historica of Diodorus Siculus** translated by £1·80
John Skelton, Vol. II, Introduction, notes and glossary, ed.
F. M. Salter and H. L. R. Edwards. 1957 (*for* 1954), *re-*
printed 1971.

240   **The French Text of the Ancrene Riwle,** Trinity College Cam- £3·25
bridge MS. R. 14. 7, with variants from Paris Bibliothèque
Nationale MS. fonds fr. 6276 and Bodley MS. 90, ed. W. H.
Trethewey. 1958 (*for* 1954), *reprinted* 1971.

241   **Þe Wohunge of Ure Lauerd** and other pieces, ed. W. Meredith £2·70
Thompson. 1958 (*for* 1955), *reprinted with corrections* 1970.

242   **The Salisbury Psalter,** ed. Celia Sisam and Kenneth Sisam. £5·40
1959 (*for* 1955–6), *reprinted* 1969.

243   **The Life and Death of Cardinal Wolsey by George Cavendish,** £2·70
ed. R. S. Sylvester. 1959 (*for* 1957), *reprinted* 1961.

244   **The South English Legendary,** Vol. III, Introduction and £1·80
glossary, ed. C. D'Evelyn. 1959 (*for* 1957), *reprinted* 1969.

O.S. 245 **Beowulf**: facsimile of British Museum MS. Cotton Vitellius £6·00
A. xv, with a transliteration and notes by J. Zupitza, a new
reproduction of the manuscript with an introductory note by
Norman Davis. 1959 (*for* 1958), *reprinted* 1967.

246 **The Parlement of the Thre Ages**, ed. M. Y. Offord. 1959, £2·40
reprinted 1967.

247 **Facsimile of MS. Bodley 34**: St. Katherine, St. Margaret, £3·75
St. Juliana, Hali Meiðhad, Sawles Warde, with an introduction by N. R. Ker. 1960 (*for* 1959).

248 **Þe Liflade ant te Passiun of Seinte Iuliene**, ed. S. R. T. O. £2·40
d'Ardenne. 1961 (*for* 1960).

249 **The English Text of the Ancrene Riwle: Ancrene Wisse**, £3·00
Corpus Christi College Cambridge MS. 402, ed. J. R. R.
Tolkien, with introduction by N. R. Ker. 1962 (*for* 1960).

250 **Laȝamon's Brut**, Vol. I, Text (lines 1–8020), ed. G. L. £6·00
Brook and R. F. Leslie. 1963 (*for* 1961).

251 **The Owl and the Nightingale**: facsimile of Jesus College £3·00
Oxford MS. 29 and British Museum MS. Cotton Caligula
A. ix, with an introduction by N. R. Ker. 1963 (*for* 1962).

252 **The English Text of the Ancrene Riwle**, British Museum MS. £3·00
Cotton Titus D. xviii, ed. F. M. Mack, and the Lanhydrock
Fragment, Bodleian MS. Eng. th. c. 70, ed. A. Zettersten. 1963
(*for* 1962).

253 **The Bodley Version of Mandeville's Travels**, ed. M. C. £3·00
Seymour. 1963.

254 **Ywain and Gawain**, ed. Albert B. Friedman and Norman £3·00
T. Harrington. 1964 (*for* 1963).

255 **Facsimile of British Museum MS. Harley 2253**, with an £6·00
introduction by N. R. Ker. 1965 (*for* 1964).

256 **Sir Eglamour of Artois**, ed. Frances E. Richardson. 1965. £3·00

257 **The Praise of Folie by Sir Thomas Chaloner**, ed. Clarence H. £3·00
Miller. 1965.

258 **The Orcherd of Syon**, Vol. I, Text, ed. Phyllis Hodgson and £6·00
Gabriel M. Liegey. 1966.

259 **Homilies of Ælfric, A Supplementary Collection**, Vol. I, £6·00
ed. J. C. Pope. 1967.

260 **Homilies of Ælfric, A Supplementary Collection**, Vol. II, £6·00
ed. J. C. Pope. 1968.

261 **Lybeaus Desconus**, ed. M. Mills. 1969. £3·00

262 **The Macro Plays**: The Castle of Perseverance, Wisdom, £3·00
Mankind, ed. Mark Eccles. 1969.

263 **The History of Reynard the Fox translated from the Dutch** £3·00
Original by William Caxton, ed. N. F. Blake. 1970.

264 **The Epistle of Othea translated from the French text of** £3·00
Christine de Pisan by Stephen Scrope, ed. C. F. Bühler. 1970.

265 **The Cyrurgie of Guy de Chauliac**, Vol. I, Text, ed. Margaret S. £6·00
Ogden. 1971.

266 **Wulfstan's Canons of Edgar**, ed. R. G. Fowler. 1972. £1·80

267 **The English Text of the Ancrene Riwle**, British Museum MS. £4·25
Cotton Cleopatra C. vi, ed. E. J. Dobson. 1972.

O.S. 268   **Of Arthour and of Merlin**, Vol. I, Text, ed. O. D. Macrae-   £3·00
Gibson. 1973.

    269   **The Metrical Version of Mandeville's Travels**, ed. M. C.   £3·00
Seymour. 1973.

    270   **Fifteenth Century Translations of Alain Chartier's Le Traite**   £3·00
de l'Esperance and Le Quadrilogue Invectif, Vol. I, Text, ed.
Margaret S. Blayney. (1974.)

    271   **The Minor Poems of Stephen Hawes**, ed. Florence Gluck and   £2·50
Alice B. Morgan. (1974.)

SUPPLEMENTARY SERIES

S.S. 1   **Non-Cycle Plays and Fragments**, ed. Norman Davis with an   £3·60
appendix on the Shrewsbury Music by F. Ll. Harrison. 1970.

    2   **The Book of the Knight of the Tower translated by William**   £3·25
Caxton, ed. M. Y. Offord. 1971.

    3   **The Chester Mystery Cycle**, Vol. I, Text, ed. R. M. Lumiansky   £5·50
and David Mills. (1974.)

FORTHCOMING VOLUMES

O.S. 272   **Thomas Norton's The Ordinal of Alchemy**, ed. John Reidy.   £3·00
(1975.)

    273   **The Cely Letters, 1472–1488**, ed. Alison Hanham. (1975.)   £4·50

    274   **The English Text of the Ancrene Riwle**, Magdalene College
Cambridge MS Pepys 2498, ed. A. Zettersten. (1976.)

    275   **Dives and Pauper**, Text Vol. I, ed. Priscilla H. Barnum (1976.)

LIST 2

ORIGINAL SERIES 1864–1938

O.S. 1 **Early English Alliterative Poems . . . from MS. Cotton Nero A. x,** £3·20
ed. R. Morris. 1864, *revised* 1869, *reprinted* 1965.

2 **Arthur, ed. F. J. Furnivall.** 1864, *reprinted* 1965. 60p

3 **William Lauder Ane conpendious and breue tractate concernyng ye** £1·10
Office and Dewtie of Kyngis, ed. F. Hall. 1864, *reprinted* 1965.
Also available reprinted as one volume with O.S. 41 £2·75
William Lauder The Minor Poems, ed. F. J. Furnivall. 1870, *reprinted*
Kraus 1973.

4 **Sir Gawayne and the Green Knight,** ed. R. Morris. 1864. Superseded
by O.S. 210.

5 **Alexander Hume of the Orthographie and Congruitie of the Britan** £1·10
Tongue, ed. H. B. Wheatley. 1865, *reprinted* 1965.

6 **The Romans of Lancelot of the Laik,** re-ed. W. W. Skeat. 1865, *re-* £2·50
printed 1965.

7 **The Story of Genesis and Exodus,** ed. R. Morris. 1865, *reprinted* £4·50
Kraus 1973.

8 **Morte Arthure** [alliterative version from Thornton MS.], ed. E. Brock. £1·50
1865, *reprinted* 1967.

9 **Francis Thynne Animadversions uppon Chaucer's Workes . . . 1598,** £3·25
ed. G. H. Kingsley. 1865, *revised* F. J. Furnivall 1875, *reprinted* 1965.

10, 112 **Merlin,** ed. H. B. Wheatley, Vol. I 1865, Vol. IV with essays £10·75
by J. S. S. Glennie and W. E. Mead 1899; *reprinted as one volume*
Kraus 1973. (See O.S. 21, 36 for other parts.)

11, 19, 35, 37 **The Works of Sir David Lyndesay,** Vol. I 1865; Vol. II £9·00
1866 The Monarch and other Poems, ed. J. Small; Vol. III 1868 The
Historie of . . . Squyer William Meldrum etc., ed. F. Hall; Vol. IV
Ane Satyre of the Thrie Estaits and Minor Poems, ed. F. Hall.
Reprinted as one volume Kraus 1973. (See O.S. 47 for last part.)

12 **Adam of Cobsam The Wright's Chaste Wife,** ed. F. J. Furnivall. 1865, 60p
reprinted 1965. (See also O.S. 84.)

13 **Seinte Marherete,** ed. O. Cockayne. 1866. Superseded by O.S. 193.

14 **King Horn, Floriz and Blauncheflur, The Assumption of our Lady,** £3·00
ed. J. R. Lumby. 1866, *revised* G. H. McKnight 1901, *reprinted* 1962.

15 **Political, Religious and Love Poems,** from Lambeth MS. 306 and £3·75
other sources, ed. F. J. Furnivall. 1866, *reprinted* 1962.

16 **The Book of Quinte Essence . . . Sloane MS. 73** c. 1460–70, ed. F. J. 60p
Furnivall. 1866, *reprinted* 1965.

17 **William Langland Parallel Extracts from 45 MSS. of Piers Plowman,** 55p
ed. W. W. Skeat. 1866, *reprinted* Kraus 1973.

18 **Hali Meidenhad,** ed. O. Cockayne. 1866, *revised* F. J. Furnivall 1922 £2·00
(*for* 1920), *reprinted* Kraus 1973.

19 **Sir David Lyndesay The Monarch and other Poems,** Vol. II. See
above, O.S. 11.

20 **Richard Rolle de Hampole English Prose Treatises,** ed. G. G. Perry. £1·10
1866, *reprinted* Kraus 1973.

21, 36 **Merlin,** ed. H. B. Wheatley. Vol. II 1866, Vol. III 1869; *reprinted* £10·00
as one volume Kraus 1973

22 **The Romans of Partenay or of Lusignen,** ed. W. W. Skeat. 1866, £5·50
reprinted Kraus 1973.

O.S. 23 Dan Michel Ayenbite of Inwyt, ed. R. Morris. 1866, *revised* P. Gradon, £3·20
reprinted 1965.

24 Hymns to the Virgin and Christ . . . and other religious poems, ed. F. J. £2·70
Furnivall. 1867, *reprinted* Kraus 1973.

25 The Stacions of Rome, The Pilgrims Sea-Voyage etc., ed. F. J. Furni- £1·10
vall. 1867, *reprinted* Kraus 1973.

26 Religious Pieces in Prose and Verse from R. Thornton's MS., ed. G. G. £6·75
Perry. 1867, *reprinted* Kraus 1973.

27 Peter Levins Manipulus Vocabulorum, ed. H. B. Wheatley. 1867, £6·50
reprinted Kraus 1973.

28 William Langland The Vision of Piers Plowman, ed. W. W. Skeat. £2·10
Vol. I Text A 1867, *reprinted* 1968. (See O.S. 38, 54, 67, and 81 for
other parts.)

29, 34 Old English Homilies of the 12th and 13th Centuries, ed. R. Morris. £6·00
Vol. I. i 1867, Vol. I. ii 1868; *reprinted as one volume* Kraus 1973. (See
O.S. 53 for Vol. II.)

30 Pierce the Ploughmans Crede etc., ed. W. W. Skeat. 1867, *reprinted* £1·60
Kraus 1973.

31 John Myrc Instructions for Parish Priests, ed. E. Peacock. 1868, *re-* £2·10
printed Kraus 1973.

32 Early English Meals and Manners: The Babees Book etc., ed. F. J. £8·50
Furnivall. 1868, *reprinted* Kraus 1973.

33 The Book of the Knight of La Tour-Landry (from MS. Harley 1764), £4·25
ed. T. Wright. 1868, *reprinted* Kraus 1973.

34 Old English Homilies of the 12th and 13th Centuries, Vol. I. ii. See
above, O.S. 29.

35 Sir David Lyndesay The Historie of . . . Squyer William Meldrum etc., £1·10
ed. F. Hall. 1868, *reprinted* 1965. *Also available reprinted as one*
volume with O.S. 11, 19, and 37. See above, O.S. 11.

36 Merlin, Vol. III 1869. See above, O.S. 21.

37 Sir David Lyndesay Ane Satyre . . . Vol. IV. See above, O.S. 11.

38 William Langland The Vision of Piers Plowman, ed. W. W. Skeat. £2·50
Vol. II Text B 1869, *reprinted* 1972. (See O.S. 28, 54, 67, and 81 for
other parts.)

39, 56 The Gest Hystoriale of the Destruction of Troy, ed. G. A. Panton £6·50
and D. Donaldson. Vol. I 1869, Vol. II 1874; *reprinted as one volume*
1968.

40 English Gilds etc., ed. Toulmin Smith, L. Toulmin Smith and L. £6·00
Brentano. 1870, *reprinted* 1963.

41 William Lauder The Minor Poems. See above, O.S. 3.

42 Bernardus De Cura Rei Famuliaris, with some early Scottish £1·10
Prophecies etc., ed. J. R. Lumby. 1870, *reprinted* 1965.

43 Ratis Raving, and other Moral and Religious Pieces in prose and verse, £2·60
ed. J. R. Lumby. 1870, *reprinted* Kraus 1973.

44 Joseph of Arimathie: the Romance of the Seint Graal, an alliterative £2·60
poem, ed. W. W. Skeat. 1871, *reprinted* Kraus 1973.

45 King Alfred's West-Saxon Version of Gregory's Pastoral Care, ed. H. £5·75
Sweet. Vol. I 1871, reprinted with corrections and an additional note
by N. R. Ker 1958, *reprinted* Kraus 1973. (See O.S. 50 for Vol. II.)

46 Legends of the Holy Rood, Symbols of the Passion and Cross-Poems, £4·60
ed. R. Morris. 1871, *reprinted* Kraus 1973.

47 Sir David Lyndesay The Minor Poems, ed. J. A. H. Murray. 1871 £3·60
reprinted Kraus 1973. (See O.S. 11, 19, 35, 37 for other parts.)

48 The Times' Whistle, and other poems; by R. C., ed. J. M. Cowper. £3·75
1871, *reprinted* Kraus 1973.

O.S. 49 **An Old English Miscellany**: a Bestiary, Kentish Sermons, Proverbs of £5·75 Alfred and Religious Poems of the 13th Century, ed. R. Morris. 1872, *reprinted* Kraus 1973.

50 **King Alfred's West-Saxon Version of Gregory's Pastoral Care**, ed. H. £4·00 Sweet. Vol. II 1871, reprinted with corrections by N. R. Ker 1958, *reprinted* Kraus 1973. (See O.S. 45 for Vol. I.)

51 **þe Liflade of St. Juliana**, ed. O. Cockayne and E. Brock. 1872, *re-* £2·25 *printed* 1957. (See O.S. 248 for more recent edition.)

52 **Palladius On Husbandrie**, ed. B. Lodge. Vol. I 1872, *reprinted* Kraus £3·75 1973. (See O.S. 72 for Vol. II.)

53 **Old English Homilies of the 12th Century** etc., ed. R. Morris. Vol. II £5·00 1873, *reprinted* Kraus 1973. (See O.S. 29, 34 for Vol. 1.)

54 **William Langland The Vision of Piers Plowman**, ed. W. W. Skeat. £3·25 Vol. III Text C 1873, *reprinted* 1959. (See O.S. 28, 38, 67, and 81 for other parts.)

55, 70 **Generydes**, a romance, ed. W. A. Wright. Vol. I 1873, Vol. II £4·25 1878; *reprinted as one volume* Kraus 1973.

56 **The Gest Hystoriale of the Destruction of Troy**. Vol. II. See above, O.S. 39.

57 **Cursor Mundi**, ed. R. Morris. Vol. I Text ll. 1–4954, 1874, *reprinted* £2·40 1961. (See O.S. 59, 62, 66, 68, 99, and 101 for other parts.)

58, 63, 73 **The Blickling Homilies**, ed. R. Morris. Vol. I 1874, Vol. II £4·25 1876, Vol. III 1880; *reprinted as one volume* 1967.

59 **Cursor Mundi**, ed. R. Morris. Vol. II ll. 4955–12558, 1875, *reprinted* £3·00 1966. (See O.S. 57, 62, 66, 68, 99, and 101 for other parts.)

60 **Meditations on the Supper of our Lord**, and the Hours of the Passion, £1·25 translated by Robert Manning of Brunne, ed. J. M. Cowper. 1875, *reprinted* Kraus 1973.

61 **The Romance and Prophecies of Thomas of Erceldoune**, ed. J. A. H. £2·30 Murray. 1875, *reprinted* Kraus 1973.

62 **Cursor Mundi**, ed. R. Morris. Vol. III ll. 12559–19300, 1876, *reprinted* £2·40 1966. (See O.S. 57, 59, 66, 68, 99, and 101 for other parts.)

63 **The Blickling Homilies**, Vol. II. See above, O.S. 58.

64 **Francis Thynne's Emblemes and Epigrames**, ed. F. J. Furnivall. 1876, £2·20 *reprinted* Kraus 1973.

65 **Be Domes Dæge**, De Die Judicii: an Old English version of the Latin £1·80 poem ascribed to Bede, ed. J. R. Lumby. 1876, *reprinted* 1964.

66 **Cursor Mundi**, ed. R. Morris. Vol. IV ll. 19301–23836, 1877, *reprinted* £2·40 1966. (See O.S. 57, 59, 62, 68, 99, and 101 for other parts.)

67 **William Langland The Vision of Piers Plowman**, ed. W. W. Skeat. £8·50 Vol. IV. 1 Notes, 1877, *reprinted* Kraus 1973. (See O.S. 28, 38, 54, and 81 for other parts.)

68 **Cursor Mundi**, ed. R. Morris. Vol. V ll. 23827–end, 1878, *reprinted* £2·40 1966. (See O.S. 57, 59, 62, 66, 99, and 101 for other parts.)

69 **Adam Davy's 5 Dreams about Edward II** etc. from Bodleian MS. Laud £2·20 Misc. 622, ed. F. J. Furnivall. 1878, *reprinted* Kraus 1973.

70 **Generydes**, a romance, Vol. II. See above, O.S. 55.

71 **The Lay Folks Mass Book**, ed. T. F. Simmons. 1879, *reprinted* 1968. £5·40

72 **Palladius On Husbandrie**, ed. B. Lodge and S. J. Herrtage. Vol. II £2·50 1879. (See O.S. 52 for Vol. I.)
Also available reprinted as one volume with O.S. 52.

73 **The Blickling Homilies**, Vol. III. See above, O.S. 58.

74 **The English Works of Wyclif** hitherto unprinted, ed. F. D. Matthew. £10·50 1880, *reprinted* Kraus 1973.

75 **Catholicon Anglicum**, an English–Latin Wordbook 1483, ed. S. J. H. £8·00 Herrtage and H. B. Wheatley. 1881, *reprinted* Kraus 1973.

O.S. 76, 82 **Ælfric's Lives of Saints,** ed. W. W. Skeat. Vol. I. i 1881, Vol. I. ii   £3·60
1885; *reprinted as one volume* 1966. (See O.S. 94 and 114 for other
parts.)

77 **Beowulf,** autotypes of Cotton MS. Vitellius A. xv. 1882. Superseded
by O.S. 245.

78 **The Fifty Earliest English Wills . . .** 1387–1439, ed. F. J. Furnivall.   £3·00
1882, *reprinted* 1964.

79 **King Alfred's Orosius,** ed. H. Sweet. Vol. I Old English Text and Latin
Original (*all published*) 1883, *reprinting* Kraus 1974.

80 **The Life of Saint Katherine,** from Royal MS. 17 A. xxvii etc., ed.   £4·25
E. Einenkel. 1884, *reprinted* Kraus 1973.

81 **William Langland The Vision of Piers Plowman,** ed. W. W. Skeat.   £9·50
Vol. IV. 2 General Preface and indexes. 1884, *reprinted* Kraus 1973.
(See O.S. 28, 38, 54, and 67 for other parts.)

82 **Ælfric's Lives of Saints,** Vol. I. ii. See above, O.S. 76.

83 **The Oldest English Texts,** ed. H. Sweet. 1885, *reprinted* 1966.   £6·50

84 **[Adam of Cobsam] Additional Analogs to The Wright's Chaste Wife,**   £1·00
ed. W. A. Clouston. 1886, *reprinted* Kraus 1973. (See also O.S. 12.)

85 **The Three Kings of Cologne,** ed. C. Horstmann. 1886, *reprinted* Kraus   £5·75
1973.

86 **The Lives of Women Saints** etc., ed. C. Horstmann. 1886, *reprinted*   £4·25
Kraus 1973.

87 **The Early South-English Legendary,** from Bodleian MS. Laud Misc.   £9·50
108, ed. C. Horstmann. 1887, *reprinted* Kraus 1973.

88 **Henry Bradshaw The Life of Saint Werburge of Chester,** ed. C. Horst-   £4·50
mann. 1887, *reprinted* Kraus 1973.

89 **Vices and Virtues** [from British Museum MS. Stowe 240], ed. F.   £2·40
Holthausen. Vol. I Text and translation. 1888, *reprinted* 1967. (See
O.S. 159 for Vol. II.)

90 **The Rule of S. Benet,** Latin and Anglo-Saxon interlinear version, ed.   £3·25
H. Logeman. 1888, *reprinted* Kraus 1973.

91 **Two Fifteenth-Century Cookery-Books,** ed. T. Austin. 1888, *reprinted*   £2·50
1964.

92 **Eadwine's Canterbury Psalter,** ed. F. Harsley. Vol. II Text and notes   £4·75
(*all published*) 1889, *reprinted* Kraus 1973.

93 **Defensor's Liber Scintillarum,** ed. E. W. Rhodes. 1889, *reprinted*   £4·50
Kraus 1973.

94, 114 **Ælfric's Lives of Saints,** ed. W. W. Skeat. Vol. II. i 1890, Vol. II.   £3·60
ii 1900; *reprinted as one volume* 1966. (See O.S. 76, 82 for other parts.)

95 **The Old English Version of Bede's Ecclesiastical History of the English**   £3·20
People, ed. T. Miller. Vol. I. i 1890, *reprinted* 1959.

96 **The Old English Version of Bede's Ecclesiastical History of the English**   £3·20
People, ed. T. Miller. Vol. I. ii 1891, *reprinted* 1959. (See O.S. 110,
111 for other parts.)

97 **The Earliest Complete English Prose Psalter,** ed. K. D. Bülbring.   £3·55
Vol. I (*all published*) 1891, *reprinted* Kraus 1973.

98 **The Minor Poems of the Vernon MS.,** ed. C. Horstmann. Vol. I 1892,   £7·50
reprinted Kraus 1973. (See O.S. 117 for Vol. II.)

99 **Cursor Mundi,** ed. R. Morris. Vol. VI Preface etc. 1892, *reprinted*   £2·10
1962. (See O.S. 57, 59, 62, 66, 68, and 101 for other parts.)

100 **John Capgrave The Life of St. Katharine of Alexandria,** ed. C. Horst-   £8·50
mann, forewords by F. J. Furnivall. 1893, *reprinted* Kraus 1973.

101 **Cursor Mundi,** ed. R. Morris. Vol. VII Essay on manuscripts and   £2·10
dialect by H. Hupe. 1893, *reprinted* 1962. (See O.S. 57, 59, 62, 66, 68,
and 99 for other parts.)

102 **Lanfrank's Science of Cirurgie,** ed. R. von Fleischhacker. Vol. I Text   £6·25
(*all published*) 1894, *reprinted* Kraus 1973.

O.S. 103   History of the Holy Rood-tree, with notes on the orthography of the Ormulum etc., ed. A. S. Napier. 1894, *reprinted* Kraus 1973.   £2·50

104   The Exeter Book, ed. I. Gollancz. Vol. I Poems I–VIII. 1895, *reprinted* Kraus 1973. (See O.S. 194 for Vol. II.)   £5·50

105, 109   The Prymer or Lay Folks' Prayer Book, ed. H. Littlehales. Vol. I 1895, Vol. II 1897; *reprinted as one volume* Kraus 1973.   £3·50

106   Richard Rolle The Fire of Love and The Mending of Life . . . translated by Richard Misyn, ed. R. Harvey. 1896, *reprinted* Kraus 1973.   £2·60

107   The English Conquest of Ireland, A.D. 1166–1185, ed. F. J. Furnivall. Vol. I Text (*all published*) 1896, *reprinted* Kraus 1973.   £3·20

108   Child-Marriages, Divorces and Ratifications etc. in the Diocese of Chester 1561–6 etc., ed. F. J. Furnivall. 1894 (*for* 1897), *reprinted* Kraus 1973.   £6·00

109   The Prymer or Lay Folks' Prayer Book, Vol. II. See above, O.S. 105.

110   The Old English Version of Bede's Ecclesiastical History of the English People, ed. T. Miller. Vol. II. i 1898, *reprinted* 1963.   £3·25

111   The Old English Version of Bede's Ecclesiastical History of the English People, ed. T. Miller. Vol. II. ii 1898, *reprinted* 1963. (See O.S. 95, 96 for other parts.)   £3·25

112   Merlin, Vol. IV. See above, O.S. 10.

113   Queen Elizabeth's Englishings of Boethius, Plutarch and Horace, ed. C. Pemberton. 1899, *reprinted* Kraus 1973.   £3·20

114   Ælfric's Lives of Saints, Vol. II. ii. See above, O.S. 94.

115   Jacob's Well, ed. A. Brandeis. Vol. I (*all published*) 1900, *reprinted* Kraus 1973.   £5·75

116   An Old English Martyrology, re-ed. G. Herzfeld. 1900, *reprinted* Kraus 1973.   £4·80

117   The Minor Poems of the Vernon MS., ed. F. J. Furnivall. Vol. II 1901, *reprinted* Kraus 1973. (See O.S. 98 for Vol. I.)   £5·75

118   The Lay Folks' Catechism, ed. T. F. Simmons and H. E. Nolloth. 1901, *reprinted* Kraus 1973.   £3·00

119, 123   Robert of Brunne's Handlyng Synne [and its French original], ed. F. J. Furnivall. Vol. I 1901, Vol. II 1903; *reprinted as one volume* Kraus 1973.   £6·75

120   Three Middle-English Versions of the Rule of St. Benet and two contemporary rituals for the ordination of nuns, ed. E. A. Kock. 1902, *reprinted* Kraus 1973.   £4·80

121, 122   The Laud Troy Book, Bodleian MS. Land Misc. 595, ed. J. E. Wülfing. Vol. I 1902, Vol. II 1903, *reprinted as one volume* Kraus 1973.   £9·50

123   Robert of Brunne's Handlyng Synne, Vol. II. See above, O.S. 119.

124   Twenty-Six Political and other Poems . . . from Bodleian MSS. Digby 102 and Douce 322, ed. J. Kail. Vol. I (*all published*) 1904, *reprinted* Kraus 1973.   £4·00

125, 128   The Medieval Records of a London City Church (St. Mary at Hill), 1420–1559, ed. H. Littlehales. Vol. I 1904, Vol. II 1905; *reprinted as one volume* Kraus 1973.   £9·75

126, 127   An Alphabet of Tales, an English 15th-century translation of the Alphabetum Narrationum, ed. M. M. Banks. Vol. I 1904, Vol. II 1905; *reprinted as one volume* Kraus 1973.   £9·25

128   The Medieval Records of a London City Church, Vol. II. See above, O.S. 125.

129   The English Register of Godstow Nunnery . . . c. 1450, ed. A. Clark. Vol. I 1905, *reprinted* Kraus 1971.   £6·25

130, 142   The English Register of Godstow Nunnery . . . c. 1450, ed. A. Clark. Vol. II 1906, Vol. III 1911; *reprinted as one volume* Kraus 1971.   £8·00

O.S. 131   **The Brut,** or the Chronicles of England . . . from Bodleian MS. Rawl.   £3·25
B. 171, ed. F. W. D. Brie. Vol. I 1906, *reprinted* 1960. (See O.S. 136
for Vol. II.)

132   **The Works of John Metham,** ed. H. Craig. 1916 (*for* 1906), *reprinted*   £3·60
Kraus 1973.

133, 144   **The English Register of Oseney Abbey** . . . *c.* 1460, ed. A. Clark.   £4·80
Vol. I 1907, Vol. II 1913 (*for* 1912); *reprinted as one volume* Kraus
1971.

134, 135   **The Coventry Leet Book,** ed. M. D. Harris. Vol. I 1907, Vol. II   £9·50
1908; *reprinted as one volume* Kraus 1971. (See O.S. 138, 146 for
other parts.)

136   **The Brut,** or the Chronicles of England, ed. F. W. D. Brie. Vol. II   £5·25
1908, *reprinted* Kraus 1971. (See O.S. 131 for Vol. I.)

137   **Twelfth Century Homilies in MS. Bodley 343,** ed. A. O. Belfour.   £1·65
Vol. I Text and translation (*all published*) 1909, *reprinted* 1962.

138, 146   **The Coventry Leet Book,** ed. M. D. Harris. Vol. III 1909, Vol.   £6·60
IV 1913; *reprinted as one volume* Kraus 1971. (See O.S. 134, 135 for
other parts.)

139   **John Arderne Treatises of Fistula in Ano** etc., ed. D'Arcy Power.   £2·65
1910, *reprinted* 1968.

140   **John Capgrave's Lives of St. Augustine and St. Gilbert of Sempring-**   £3·25
ham and a sermon, ed. J. J. Munro. 1910, *reprinted* Kraus 1971.

141   **The Middle English Poem Erthe upon Erthe,** printed from 24 manu-   £1·80
scripts, ed. H. M. R. Murray. 1911, *reprinted* 1964.

142   **The English Register of Godstow Nunnery,** Vol. III. See above, O.S.
130.

143   **The Prose Life of Alexander** from the Thornton MS., ed. J. S. West-   £1·85
lake. 1913 (*for* 1911), *reprinted* Kraus 1971.

144   **The English Register of Oseney Abbey,** Vol. II. See above, O.S. 133.

145   **The Northern Passion,** ed. F. A. Foster. Vol. I 1913 (*for* 1912),   £4·00
reprinted Kraus 1971. (See O.S. 147, 183 for other parts.)

146   **The Coventry Leet Book,** Vol. IV. See above, O.S. 138.

147   **The Northern Passion,** ed. F. A. Foster. Vol. II 1916 (*for* 1913),   £3·60
reprinted Kraus 1971. (See O.S. 145, 183 for other parts.)

148   **A Fifteenth-Century Courtesy Book,** ed. R. W. Chambers, and **Two**   £1·80
Fifteenth-Century Franciscan Rules, ed. W. W. Seton. 1914, *re-*
printed 1963.

149   **Lincoln Diocese Documents, 1450–1544,** ed. A. Clark. 1914, *re-*   £6·00
printed Kraus 1971.

150   **The Old English Versions of the enlarged Rule of Chrodegang,** the   £2·25
Capitula of Theodulf and the Epitome of Benedict of Aniane, ed.
A. S. Napier. 1916 (*for* 1914), *reprinted* Kraus 1971.

151   **The Lanterne of Li3t,** ed. L. M. Swinburn. 1917 (*for* 1915), *reprinted*   £3·35
Kraus 1971.

152   **Early English Homilies from the Twelfth-Century MS. Vespasian D.**   £2·50
xiv, ed. R. D.-N. Warner. 1917 (*for* 1915), *reprinted* Kraus 1971.

153   **Mandeville's Travels** . . . from MS. Cotton Titus C. xvi, ed. P.   £4·00
Hamelius. Vol. I Text 1919 (*for* 1916), *reprinted* Kraus 1973.

154   **Mandeville's Travels** . . . from MS. Cotton Titus C. xvi, ed. P.   £2·40
Hamelius. Vol. II Introduction and notes. 1923 (*for* 1916), *reprinted*
1961.

155   **The Wheatley Manuscript:** Middle English verse and prose in British   £2·50
Museum MS. Additional 39574, ed. M. Day. 1921 (*for* 1917), *re-*
printed Kraus 1971.

156   **The Donet by Reginald Pecock,** ed. E. V. Hitchcock. 1921 (*for* 1918),   £4·75
reprinted Kraus 1971.

O.S. 157 The Pepysian Gospel Harmony, ed. M. Goates. 1922 (*for* 1919), £3·00
reprinted Kraus 1971.

158 Meditations on the Life and Passion of Christ, from British Museum £2·00
MS. Additional 11307, ed. C. D'Evelyn. 1921 (*for* 1919), *reprinted*
Kraus 1971.

159 Vices and Virtues [from British Museum MS. Stowe 240], ed. F. £1·65
Holthausen. Vol. II Notes and Glossary, 1921 (*for* 1920), *reprinted*
1967. (See O.S. 89 for Vol. I.)

160 The Old English Version of the Heptateuch etc., ed. S. J. Crawford. £4·50
1922 (*for* 1921), reprinted with additional material, ed. N. R. Ker
1969.

161 Three Old English Prose Texts in MS. Cotton Vitellius A. xv, ed. S. £2·65
Rypins. 1924 (*for* 1921), *reprinted* Kraus 1971.

162 Pearl, Cleanness, Patience and Sir Gawain, facsimile of British £12·00
Museum MS. Cotton Nero A. x, with introduction by I. Gollancz.
1923 (*for* 1922), *reprinted* 1971.

163 The Book of the Foundation of St. Bartholomew's Church in London, £1·50
ed. N. Moore. 1923, *reprinted* Kraus 1971.

164 The Folewer to the Donet by Reginald Pecock, ed. E. V. Hitchcock. £4·00
1924 (*for* 1923), *reprinted* Kraus 1971.

165 The Famous Historie of Chinon of England by Christopher Middleton, £3·00
with Leland's Assertio Inclytissimi Arturii and Robinson's translation, ed. W. E. Mead. 1925 (*for* 1923), *reprinted* Kraus 1971.

166 A Stanzaic Life of Christ, from Harley MS. 3909, ed. F. A. Foster. £6·70
1926 (*for* 1924), *reprinted* Kraus 1971.

167 John Trevisa Dialogus inter Militem et Clericum, Richard Fitzralph's £4·15
'Defensio Curatorum', Methodius' 'þe Bygynnyng of þe World and
þe Ende of Worldes', ed. A. J. Perry. 1925 (*for* 1924), *reprinted* Kraus
1971.

168 The Book of the Ordre of Chyualry translated by William Caxton, ed. £3·15
A. T. P. Byles. 1926 (*for* 1925), *reprinted* Kraus 1971.

169 The Southern Passion, Pepysian MS. 2334, ed. B. D. Brown. 1927 £3·35
(*for* 1925), *reprinted* Kraus 1971.

170 Boethius De Consolatione Philosophiae, translated by John Walton, £6·00
ed. M. Science. 1927 (*for* 1925), *reprinted* Kraus 1971.

171 The Reule of Crysten Religioun by Reginald Pecock, ed. W. C. Greet. £7·50
1927 (*for* 1926), *reprinted* Kraus 1971.

172 The Seege or Batayle of Troye, ed. M. E. Barnicle. 1927 (*for* 1926), £3·35
reprinted Kraus 1971.

173 Stephen Hawes The Pastime of Pleasure, ed. W. E. Mead. 1928] (*for* £5·00
1927), *reprinted* Kraus 1971.

174 The Middle English Stanzaic Versions of the Life of St. Anne, ed. R. E. £2·75
Parker. 1928 (*for* 1927), *reprinted* Kraus 1971.

175 Alexander Barclay The Eclogues, ed. B. White. 1928 (*for* 1927), £3·25
reprinted 1961.

176 William Caxton The Prologues and Epilogues, ed. W. J. B. Crotch. £5·50
1928 (*for* 1927), *reprinted* Kraus 1973.

177 Byrhtferth's Manual, ed. S. J. Crawford. Vol. I Text, translation, £3·75
sources, and appendices (*all published*) 1929 (*for* 1928), *reprinted* 1966.

178 The Revelations of St. Birgitta, from Garrett MS. Princeton Uni- £1·75
versity, ed. W. P. Cumming. 1929 (*for* 1928), *reprinted* Kraus 1971.

179 William Nevill The Castell of Pleasure, ed. R. D. Cornelius. 1930 £2·00
(*for* 1928), *reprinted* Kraus 1971.

180 The Apologye of Syr Thomas More, knyght, ed. A. I. Taft. 1930 £6·00
(*for* 1929), *reprinted* Kraus 1971.

181 The Dance of Death, ed. F. Warren. 1931 (*for* 1929), *reprinted* Kraus £2·20
1971.

O.S. 182 **Speculum Christiani**, ed. G. Holmstedt. 1933 (*for* 1929), *reprinted* £7·50
Kraus 1971.

183 **The Northern Passion** (Supplement), ed. W. Heuser and F. A. Foster. £2·45
1930, *reprinted* Kraus 1971. (See O.S. 145, 147 for other parts.)

184 **John Audelay The Poems**, ed. E. K. Whiting. 1931 (*for* 1930), *re-* £5·00
printed Kraus 1971.

185 **Henry Lovelich's Merlin**, ed. E. A. Kock. Vol. III. 1932 (*for* 1930), £5·00
reprinted Kraus 1971. (See E.S. 93 and 112 for other parts.)

186 **Nicholas Harpsfield The Life and Death of Sr. Thomas More**, ed. £6·25
E. V. Hitchcock and R. W. Chambers. 1932 (*for* 1931), *reprinted*
1963.

187 **John Stanbridge The Vulgaria and Robert Whittinton The Vulgaria**, £3·00
ed. B. White. 1932 (*for* 1931), *reprinted* Kraus 1971.

188 **The Siege of Jerusalem**, from Bodleian MS. Laud Misc. 656, ed. E. £2·35
Kölbing and M. Day. 1932 (*for* 1931), *reprinted* Kraus 1971.

189 **Christine de Pisan The Book of Fayttes of Armes and of Chyualrye**, £5·00
translated by William Caxton, ed. A. T. P. Byles. 1932, *reprinted*
Kraus 1971.

190 **English Mediaeval Lapidaries**, ed. J. Evans and M. S. Serjeantson. £3·00
1933 (*for* 1932), *reprinted* 1960.

191 **The Seven Sages of Rome** (Southern Version), ed. K. Brunner. 1933 £3·75
(*for* 1932), *reprinted* Kraus 1971.

191A R. W. Chambers: **On the Continuity of English Prose** from Alfred to £1·50
More and his School (an extract from the introduction to O.S. 186).
1932, *reprinted* 1966.

192 **John Lydgate The Minor Poems**, ed. H. N. MacCracken. Vol. II £4·50
Secular Poems. 1934 (*for* 1933), *reprinted* 1961. (See E.S. 107 for
Vol. I.)

193 **Seinte Marherete**, from MS. Bodley 34 and British Museum MS. £3·00
Royal 17 A. xxvii, re-ed. F. M. Mack. 1934 (*for* 1933), *reprinted* 1958.

194 **The Exeter Book**, ed. W. S. Mackie. Vol. II Poems IX–XXXII. 1934 £4·50
(*for* 1933), *reprinted* Kraus 1973. (See O.S. 104 for Vol. I.) ·

195 **The Quatrefoil of Love**, ed. I. Gollancz and M. M. Weale. 1935 (*for* £1·20
1934), *reprinted* Kraus 1971.

196 **An Anonymous Short English Metrical Chronicle**, ed. E. Zettl. 1935 £4·00
(*for* 1934), *reprinted* Kraus 1971.

197 **William Roper The Lyfe of Sir Thomas Moore, knighte**, ed. E. V. £2·10
Hitchcock. 1935 (*for* 1934), *reprinted* 1958.

198 **Firumbras and Otuel and Roland**, ed. M. I. O'Sullivan. 1935 (*for* £4·05
1934), *reprinted* Kraus 1971.

199 **Mum and the Sothsegger**, ed. M. Day and R. Steele. 1936 (*for* 1934), £2·70
reprinted Kraus 1971.

200 **Speculum Sacerdotale**, ed. E. H. Weatherly. 1936 (*for* 1935), *re-* £4·70
printed Kraus 1971.

201 **Knyghthode and Bataile**, ed. R. Dyboski and Z. M. Arend. 1936 (*for* £4·00
1935), *reprinted* Kraus 1971.

202 **John Palsgrave The Comedy of Acolastus**, ed. P. L. Carver. 1937 (*for* £4·00
1935), *reprinted* Kraus 1971.

203 **Amis and Amiloun**, ed. MacEdward Leach. 1937 (*for* 1935), *reprinted* £3·00
1960.

204 **Valentine and Orson**, translated from the French by Henry Watson, £6·00
ed. A. Dickson. 1937 (*for* 1936), *reprinted* 1971.

205 **Early English Versions** of the Tales of Guiscardo and Ghismonda and £5·00
Titus and Gisippus from the Decameron, ed. H. G. Wright. 1937
(*for* 1936), *reprinted* Kraus 1971.

206 **Osbern Bokenham Legendys of Hooly Wummen**, ed. M. S. Serjeantson. £5·00
1938 (*for* 1936), *reprinted* Kraus 1971.

O.S. 207 The Liber de Diversis Medicinis in the Thornton Manuscript, ed. £2·50
M. S. Ogden. 1938 (*for* 1936), *revised reprint* 1969.

208 The Parker Chronicle and Laws (Corpus Christi College, Cambridge £9·50
MS. 173); a facsimile, ed. R. Flower and H. Smith. 1941 (*for* 1937),
reprinted 1973.

209 Middle English Sermons, from British Museum MS. Royal 18 B. £4·50
xxiii, ed. W. O. Ross. 1940 (*for* 1938), *reprinted* 1960.

EXTRA SERIES 1867–1920

E.S. 1 The Romance of William of Palerne, ed. W. W. Skeat. 1867, *reprinted* £6·50
Kraus 1973.

2 On Early English Pronunciation, by A. J. Ellis. Part I. 1867, *reprinted* £3·60
Kraus 1973. (See E.S. 7, 14, 23, and 56 for other parts.)

3 Caxton's Book of Curtesye, with two manuscript copies of the treatise, £1·30
ed. F. J. Furnivall. 1868, *reprinted* Kraus 1973.

4 The Lay of Havelok the Dane, ed. W. W. Skeat. 1868, *reprinted* Kraus £3·75
1973.

5 Chaucer's Translation of Boethius's 'De Consolatione Philosophiæ', ed. £2·40
R. Morris. 1868, *reprinted* 1969.

6 The Romance of the Cheuelere Assigne, re-ed. H. H. Gibbs. 1868, £1·10
reprinted Kraus 1973.

7 On Early English Pronunciation, by A. J. Ellis. Part II. 1869, *reprinted* £3·60
Kraus 1973. (See E.S. 2, 14, 23, and 56 for other parts.)

8 Queene Elizabethes Achademy etc., ed. F. J. Furnivall, with essays on £3·25
early Italian and German Books of Courtesy by W. M. Rossetti and
E. Oswald. 1869, *reprinted* Kraus 1973.

9 The Fraternitye of Vacabondes by John Awdeley, Harman's Caveat, £2·40
Haben's Sermon etc., ed. E. Viles and F. J. Furnivall. 1869, *reprinted*
Kraus 1973.

10 Andrew Borde's Introduction of Knowledge and Dyetary of Helth, with £6·50
Barnes's Defence of the Berde, ed. F. J. Furnivall. 1870, *reprinted*
Kraus 1973.

11, 55 The Bruce by John Barbour, ed. W. W. Skeat. Vol. I 1870, Vol. IV £3·75
1889; *reprinted as one volume* 1968. (See E.S. 21, 29, for other parts.)

12, 32 England in the Reign of King Henry VIII, Vol. I Dialogue between £7·00
Cardinal Pole and Thomas Lupset, ed. J. M. Cowper (1871), Vol. II
Starkey's Life and Letters, ed. S. J. Herrtage (1878); *reprinted as one
volume* Kraus 1973.

13 Simon Fish A Supplicacyon for the Beggers, re-ed. F. J. Furnivall, £2·20
A Supplycacion to . . . Henry VIII, A Supplication of the Poore
Commons and The Decaye of England by the great multitude of shepe,
ed. J. M. Cowper. 1871, *reprinted* Kraus 1973.

14 On Early English Pronunciation, by A. J. Ellis. Part III. 1871, *re-* £6·50
printed Kraus 1973. (See E.S. 2, 7, 23, and 56 for other parts.)

15 The Select Works of Robert Crowley, ed. J. M. Cowper. 1872, *re-* £3·75
printed Kraus 1973.

16 Geoffrey Chaucer A Treatise on the Astrolabe, ed. W. W. Skeat. 1872, £2·40
reprinted 1968.

17, 18 The Complaynt of Scotlande, re-ed. J. A. H. Murray. Vol. I 1872, £5·50
Vol. II 1873; *reprinted as one volume* Kraus 1973.

19 The Myroure of oure Ladye, ed. J. H. Blunt. 1873, *reprinted* Kraus £7·50
1973.

20, 24 The History of the Holy Grail by Henry Lovelich, ed. F. J. Furnivall. £8·00
Vol. I 1874, Vol. II 1875; *reprinted as one volume* Kraus 1973. (See
E.S. 28, 30, and 95 for other parts.)

E.S. 21, 29   **The Bruce by John Barbour**, ed. W. W. Skeat. Vol. II 1874, Vol.   £5·40
III 1877; *reprinted as one volume* 1968. (See E.S. 11, 55 for other part.)

22   **Henry Brinklow's Complaynt of Roderyck Mors**, The Lamentacyon of a   £2·75
Christen agaynst the Cytye of London by Roderigo Mors, ed. J. M.
Cowper. 1874, *reprinted* Kraus 1973.

23   **On Early English Pronunciation**, by A. J. Ellis. Part IV. 1874, *re-*   £7·75
printed Kraus 1973. (See E.S. 2, 7, 14, and 56 for other parts.)

24   **The History of the Holy Grail** by Henry Lovelich, Vol. II. See above,
E.S. 20.

25, 26   **The Romance of Guy of Warwick**, the second or 15th-century   £4·50
version, ed. J. Zupitza. Vol. I 1875, Vol. II 1876; reprinted as one
volume 1966.

27   **John Fisher The English Works**, ed. J. E. B. Mayor. Vol. I (*all pub-*   £7·75
lished) 1876, *reprinted* Kraus 1973.

28, 30, 95   **The History of the Holy Grail** by Henry Lovelich, ed. F. J.   £6·75
Furnivall. Vol. III 1877; Vol. IV 1878; Vol. V The Legend of the Holy
Grail, its Sources, Character and Development by D. Kempe 1905;
reprinted as one volume Kraus 1973. (See E.S. 20, 24 for other parts.)

29   **The Bruce by John Barbour**, Vol. III. See above, E.S. 21.

30   **The History of the Holy Grail** by Henry Lovelich, Vol. IV. See above,
E.S. 28.

31   **The Alliterative Romance of Alexander and Dindimus**, re-ed. W. W.   £2·20
Skeat. 1878, *reprinted* Kraus 1973.

32   **England in the Reign of King Henry VIII**, Vol. II. See above, E.S. 12.

33   **The Early English Versions of the Gesta Romanorum**, ed. S. J. H.   £6·00
Herrtage. 1879, *reprinted* 1962.

34   The English Charlemagne Romances I: **Sir Ferumbras**, ed. S. J. H.   £3·20
Herrtage. 1879, *reprinted* 1966.

35   The English Charlemagne Romances II: **The Sege of Melayne, The**   £3·60
Romance of Duke Rowland and Sir Otuell of Spayne, ed. S. J. H.
Herrtage. 1880, *reprinted* Kraus 1973.

36, 37   The English Charlemagne Romances III and IV: **The Lyf of**   £3·20
Charles the Grete, translated by William Caxton, ed. S. J. H. Herrtage.
Vol. I 1880, Vol. II 1881; *reprinted as one volume* 1967.

38   The English Charlemagne Romances V: **The Romance of the Sowdone**   £3·00
of Babylone, re-ed. E. Hausknecht. 1881, *reprinted* 1969.

39   The English Charlemagne Romances VI: **The Taill of Rauf Coilyear,**   £2·50
with the fragments of Roland and Vernagu and Otuel, re-ed. S. J. H.
Herrtage. 1882, *reprinted* 1969.

40, 41   The English Charlemagne Romances VII and VIII: **The Boke of**   £10·75
Duke Huon of Burdeux translated by Lord Berners, ed. S. L. Lee. Vol. I
1882, Vol. II 1883; *reprinted as one volume* Kraus 1973. (See E.S. 43,
50 for other parts.)

42, 49, 59   **The Romance of Guy of Warwick**, from the Auchinleck MS.   £6·50
and the Caius MS., ed. J. Zupitza. Vol. I 1883, Vol. II 1887, Vol. III
1891; *reprinted as one volume* 1966.

43, 50   The English Charlemagne Romances IX and XII: **The Boke of**   £4·25
Duke Huon of Burdeux translated by Lord Berners, ed. S. L. Lee.
Vol. III 1884, Vol. IV 1887; *reprinted as one volume* Kraus 1973.

44   The English Charlemagne Romances X: **The Foure Sonnes of Aymon**,   £5·50
translated by William Caxton, ed. O. Richardson. Vol. I 1884, *re-*
printed Kraus 1973.

45   The English Charlemagne Romances XI: **The Foure Sonnes of Aymon**,   £6·50
translated by William Caxton, ed. O. Richardson. Vol. II 1885, *re-*
printed Kraus 1973.

46, 48, 65   **The Romance of Sir Beues of Hamtoun**, ed. E. Kölbing. Vol. I   £8·00
1885, Vol. II 1886, Vol. III 1894; *reprinted as one volume* Kraus 1973.

E.S. 47 The Wars of Alexander, an Alliterative Romance, re-ed. W. W. Skeat. £8·50
1886, *reprinted* Kraus 1973.
48 The Romance of Sir Beues of Hamtoun, Vol. II. See above, E.S. 46.
49 The Romance of Guy of Warwick, Vol. II. See above, E.S. 42.
50 The English Charlemagne Romances XII: The Boke of Duke Huon of
Burdeux, Vol. IV. See above, E.S. 43.
51 Torrent of Portyngale, re-ed. E. Adam. 1887, *reprinted* Kraus 1973. £2·70
52 A Dialogue against the Feuer Pestilence by William Bullein, ed. M. W. £2·70
and A. H. Bullen. 1888, *reprinted* Kraus 1973.
53 The Anatomie of the Bodie of Man by Thomas Vicary, ed. F. J. and £5·75
P. Furnivall. 1888, *reprinted* Kraus 1973.
54 The Curial made by maystere Alain Charretier, translated by Caxton, 75p
ed. P. Meyer and F. J. Furnivall. 1888, *reprinted* 1965.
55 The Bruce by John Barbour, Vol. IV. See above, E.S. 11.
56 On Early English Pronunciation, by A. J. Ellis. Part V. 1889, *reprinted* £15·75
Kraus 1973. (See E.S. 2, 7, 14, and 23 for other parts.)
57 Caxton's Eneydos, ed. W. T. Culley and F. J. Furnivall. 1890, *reprinted* £3·00
1962.
58 Caxton's Blanchardyn and Eglantine, ed. L. Kellner. 1890, *reprinted* £3·75
1962.
59 The Romance of Guy of Warwick, Vol. III. See above E.S. 42.
60 Lydgate's Temple of Glas, ed. J. Schick. 1891, *reprinted* Kraus 1973. £5·00
61, 73 Hoccleve's Works: The Minor Poems, Vol. I ed. F. J. Furnivall £3·75
(1892), Vol. II ed. I. Gollancz (1925 *for* 1897); reprinted as one volume
and revised by Jerome Mitchell and A. I. Doyle 1970.
62 The Chester Plays, ed. H. Deimling. Vol. I 1892, *reprinted* 1967. (See £2·20
E.S. 115 for Part II.)
63 The Earliest English Translations of the De Imitatione Christi, ed. J. K. £5·50
Ingram. 1893, *reprinted* Kraus 1973.
64 Godeffroy of Boloyne, or the Siege and Conqueste of Jerusalem by £6·75
William, archbishop of Tyre, translated by William Caxton, ed. M. N.
Colvin. 1893, *reprinted* Kraus 1973.
65 The Romance of Sir Beues of Hamtoun, Vol. III. See above, E.S. 46.
66 Lydgate and Burgh's Secrees of old Philisoffres: a version of the £2·75
Secreta Secretaorum, ed. R. Steele. 1894, *reprinted* Kraus 1973.
67 The Three Kings' Sons, ed. F. J. Furnivall. Vol. I Text (*all published*) £3·75
1895, *reprinted* Kraus 1973.
68 Melusine, ed. A. K. Donald. Vol. I (*all published*) 1895, *reprinted* £7·00
Kraus 1973.
69 John Lydgate The Assembly of Gods, ed. O. L. Triggs. 1896, *reprinted* £2·50
1957.
70 The Digby Plays, ed. F. J. Furnivall. 1896, *reprinted* 1967. £1·80
71 The Towneley Plays, re-ed. G. England and A. W. Pollard. 1897, £7·50
reprinted Kraus 1973.
72 Hoccleve's Works: The Regement of Princes and fourteen minor poems, £4·75
ed. F. J. Furnivall. 1897, *reprinted* Kraus 1973.
73 Hoccleve's Works: The Minor Poems, Vol. II. See above, E.S. 61.
74 Three Prose Versions of the Secreta Secretorum, ed. R. Steele and £5·00
T. Henderson. Vol. I (*all published*) 1898, *reprinted* Kraus 1973.
75 Speculum Gy de Warewyke, ed. G. L. Morrill. 1898, *reprinted* Kraus £5·25
1973.
76 George Ashby's Poems, ed. M. Bateson. 1899, *reprinted* 1965. £1·80
77, 83, 92 The Pilgrimage of the Life of Man, translated by John Lydgate £13·75
from the French by Guillaume de Deguileville, Vol. I ed. F. J.

Furnivall (1899), Vol. II ed. F. J. Furnivall (1901), Vol. III introduction, notes, glossary, etc. by K. B. Locock (1904); *reprinted as one volume* Kraus 1973.

E.S. 78 Thomas Robinson The Life and Death of Mary Magdalene, ed. H. O. Sommer. 1899. £1·80

79 Dialogues in French and English by William Caxton, ed. H. Bradley. 1900, *reprinted* Kraus 1973. £1·60

80 Lydgate's Two Nightingale Poems, ed. O. Glauning. 1900, *reprinted* Kraus 1973. £2·20

80A Selections from Barbour's Bruce (Books I–X), ed. W. W. Skeat, 1900, *reprinted* Kraus 1973. £9·00

81 The English Works of John Gower, ed. G. C. Macaulay. Vol. I *Confessio Amantis* Prologue–Bk. V. 1970. 1900, *reprinted* 1969. £3·60

82 The English Works of John Gower, ed. G. C. Macaulay. Vol. II *Confessio Amantis* V. 1971–VIII, *In Praise of Peace.* 1901, *reprinted* 1969. £3·60

83 The Pilgrimage of the Life of Man, Vol. II. See above, E.S. 77.

84 Lydgate's Reson and Sensuallyte, ed. E. Sieper. Vol. I Manuscripts, Text, and Glossary. 1901, *reprinted* 1965. (See E.S. 89 for Part II.) £3·00

85 The Poems of Alexander Scott, ed. A. K. Donald. 1902, *reprinted* Kraus 1973. £2·10

86 The Poems of William of Shoreham, ed. M. Konrath. Vol. I (*all published*) 1902, *reprinted* Kraus 1973. £4·40

87 Two Coventry Corpus Christi Plays, re-ed. H. Craig. 1902; *second edition* 1957, *reprinted* 1967. £1·80

88 Le Morte Arthur, a romance in stanzas, re-ed. J. D. Bruce. 1903, *reprinted* Kraus 1973. £3·00

89 Lydgate's Reson and Sensuallyte, ed. E. Sieper. Vol. II Studies and Notes. 1903, *reprinted* 1965. (See E.S. 84 for Part I.) £2·10

90 English Fragments from Latin Medieval Service-Books, ed. H. Littlehales. 1903, *reprinted* Kraus 1973. 55p

91 The Macro Plays, ed. F. J. Furnivall and A. W. Pollard. 1904. Superseded by O.S. 262.

92 The Pilgrimage of the Life of Man, Vol. III. See above, E.S. 77.

93 Henry Lovelich's Merlin, ed. E. A. Kock. Vol. I 1904, *reprinted* Kraus 1973. (See E.S. 112 and O.S. 185 for other parts.) £7·25

94 Respublica, ed. L. A. Magnus. 1905. Superseded by O.S. 226.

95 The History of the Holy Grail by Henry Lovelich, Vol. V. See above, E.S. 28.

96 Mirk's Festial, ed. T. Erbe. Vol. I (*all published*) 1905, *reprinted* Kraus 1973. £6·50

97 Lydgate's Troy Book, ed. H. Bergen. Vol. I Prologue, Books I and II, 1906, *reprinted* Kraus 1973. (See E.S. 103, 106, and 126 for other parts.) £7·00

98 John Skelton Magnyfycence, ed. R. L. Ramsay. 1908 (*for* 1906), *reprinted* 1958. £3·25

99 The Romance of Emaré, ed. E. Rickert. 1908 (*for* 1906), *reprinted* 1958. £1·80

100 The Middle English Harrowing of Hell and Gospel of Nicodemus, ed. W. H. Hulme. 1908 (*for* 1907), *reprinted* 1961. £3·00

101 Songs, Carols and other Miscellaneous Poems from Balliol MS. 354, Richard Hill's Commonplace-book, ed. R. Dyboski. 1908 (*for* 1907), *reprinted* Kraus 1973. £4·25

102 The Promptorium Parvulorum : the First English–Latin Dictionary, ed. A. L. Mayhew. 1908, *reprinted* Kraus 1973. £9·50

E.S. 103, 106　**Lydgate's Troy Book,** ed. H. Bergen. Vol. II, Book III, 1908;　£8·00
　　　　　 Vol. III, Books IV and V, 1910; *reprinted as one volume* Kraus 1973.
　　　　　 (See E.S. 97, 126 for other parts.)

　　 104　**The Non-Cycle Mystery Plays,** ed. O. Waterhouse. 1909. Super-
　　　　　 seded by S.S. 1.

　　 105　**The Tale of Beryn,** with a Prologue of the Merry Adventure of the　£4·25
　　　　　 Pardoner with a Tapster at Canterbury, ed. F. J. Furnivall and W. G.
　　　　　 Stone. 1909, *reprinted* Kraus 1973.

　　 106　**Lydgate's Troy Book,** Vol. III. See above, E.S. 103.

　　 107　**John Lydgate The Minor Poems,** ed. H. N. MacCracken. Vol. I　£4·25
　　　　　 Religious Poems. 1911 (*for* 1910), *reprinted* 1961. (See O.S. 192 for
　　　　　 Vol. II.)

　　 108　**Lydgate's Siege of Thebes,** ed. A. Erdmann. Vol. I Text. 1911.　£3·00
　　　　　 reprinted 1960. (See E.S. 125 for Vol. II.)

　　 109　**The Middle English Versions of Partonope of Blois,** ed. A. T. Bödtker.　£8·25
　　　　　 1912 (*for* 1911), *reprinted* Kraus 1973.

　　 110　**Caxton's Mirrour of the World,** ed. O. H. Prior. 1913 (*for* 1912),　£3·00
　　　　　 reprinted 1966.

　　 111　**Raoul Le Fevre The History of Jason,** translated by William Caxton,　£3·60
　　　　　 ed. J. Munro. 1913 (*for* 1912), *reprinted* Kraus 1973.

　　 112　**Henry Lovelich's Merlin,** ed. E. A. Kock. Vol. II 1913, *reprinted*　£2·60
　　　　　 1961. (See E.S. 93 and O.S. 185 for other parts.)

　　 113　**Poems by Sir John Salusbury and Robert Chester,** ed. Carleton Brown.　£2·80
　　　　　 1914 (*for* 1913), *reprinted* Kraus 1973.

　　 114　**The Gild of St. Mary, Lichfield:** Ordinances and other documents,　£1·50
　　　　　 ed. F. J. Furnivall. 1920 (*for* 1914), *reprinted* Kraus 1973.

　　 115　**The Chester Plays,** ed. Dr. Matthews. Vol. II 1916 (*for* 1914), *re-*　£2·20
　　　　　 printed 1967.

　　 116　**The Pauline Epistles in MS.** Parker 32, Corpus Christi College,　£6·50
　　　　　 Cambridge, ed. M. J. Powell. 1916 (*for* 1915), *reprinted* Kraus 1973.

　　 117　**The Life of Fisher,** ed. R. Bayne. 1921 (*for* 1915), *reprinted* Kraus　£2·60
　　　　　 1973.

　　 118　**The Earliest Arithmetics in English,** ed. R. Steele. 1922 (*for* 1916),　£1·90
　　　　　 reprinted Kraus 1973.

　　 119　**The Owl and the Nightingale,** ed. J. H. G. Grattan and G. F. H.　£2·20
　　　　　 Sykes. 1935 (*for* 1915), *reprinted* Kraus 1973.

　　 120　**Ludus Coventriæ,** or The Plaie called Corpus Christi, Cotton MS.　£3·60
　　　　　 Vespasian D. viii, ed. K. S. Block. 1922 (*for* 1917), *reprinted* 1961.

　　 121　**Lydgate's Fall of Princes,** ed. H. Bergen. Vol. I 1924 (*for* 1918),　£3·75
　　　　　 reprinted 1967.

　　 122　**Lydgate's Fall of Princes,** ed. H. Bergen. Vol. II 1924 (*for* 1918),　£3·75
　　　　　 reprinted 1967.

　　 123　**Lydgate's Fall of Princes,** ed. H. Bergen. Vol. III 1924 (*for* 1919),　£3·75
　　　　　 reprinted 1967.

　　 124　**Lydgate's Fall of Princes,** ed. H. Bergen. Vol. IV 1927 (*for* 1919),　£5·40
　　　　　 reprinted 1967.

　　 125　**Lydgate's Siege of Thebes,** ed. A. Erdmann and E. Ekwall. Vol. II　£4·00
　　　　　 Introduction, Notes, Glossary etc. 1930 (*for* 1920), *reprinted* Kraus
　　　　　 1973.

　　 126　**Lydgate's Troy Book,** ed. H. Bergen. Vol. IV 1935 (*for* 1920), *re-*　£9·75
　　　　　 printed Kraus 1973. (See E.S. 97, 103, and 106 for other parts.)

University Press, Oxford, England